W9-CQI-284

Bankruptcy and Debtor/Creditor

EXAMPLES&EXPLANATIONS

Bankruptcy and Debtor/Creditor

Sixth Edition

Brian A. Blum
Professor of Law
Lewis & Clark Law School

Wolters Kluwer
Law & Business

Published by Wolters Kluwer Law & Business in New York.

Wolters Kluwer Law & Business serves customers worldwide with CCH, Aspen Publishers, and Kluwer Law International products. (www.wolterskluwerlb.com)

To contact Customer Service, e-mail customer.service@wolterskluwer.com, call 1-800-234-1660, fax 1-800-901-9075, or mail correspondence to:

> Wolters Kluwer Law & Business
> Attn: Order Department
> PO Box 990
> Frederick, MD 21705

Printed in the United States of America.

1 2 3 4 5 6 7 8 9 0

ISBN 978-1-4548-3391-8

Library of Congress Cataloging-in-Publication Data

Blum, Brian A., author.
 Bankruptcy and debtor/creditor : examples & explanations / Brian A. Blum, Professor of Law, Lewis & Clark Law School. — Sixth edition.
  p. cm. — (Examples & explanations)
 Includes bibliographical references and index.
 ISBN-13: 978-1-4548-3391-8 (alk. paper)
 ISBN-10: 1-4548-3391-2 (alk. paper)
 1. Bankruptcy–United States. 2. Debtor and creditor–United States. I. Title.

KF1524.85.B58 2014
346.7307'8–dc23

                                                          2013045074

About Wolters Kluwer Law & Business

Wolters Kluwer Law & Business is a leading global provider of intelligent information and digital solutions for legal and business professionals in key specialty areas, and respected educational resources for professors and law students. Wolters Kluwer Law & Business connects legal and business professionals as well as those in the education market with timely, specialized authoritative content and information-enabled solutions to support success through productivity, accuracy and mobility.

Serving customers worldwide, Wolters Kluwer Law & Business products include those under the Aspen Publishers, CCH, Kluwer Law International, Loislaw, ftwilliam.com and MediRegs family of products.

CCH products have been a trusted resource since 1913, and are highly regarded resources for legal, securities, antitrust and trade regulation, government contracting, banking, pension, payroll, employment and labor, and healthcare reimbursement and compliance professionals.

Aspen Publishers products provide essential information to attorneys, business professionals and law students. Written by preeminent authorities, the product line offers analytical and practical information in a range of specialty practice areas from securities law and intellectual property to mergers and acquisitions and pension/benefits. Aspen's trusted legal education resources provide professors and students with high-quality, up-to-date and effective resources for successful instruction and study in all areas of the law.

Kluwer Law International products provide the global business community with reliable international legal information in English. Legal practitioners, corporate counsel and business executives around the world rely on Kluwer Law journals, looseleafs, books, and electronic products for comprehensive information in many areas of international legal practice.

Loislaw is a comprehensive online legal research product providing legal content to law firm practitioners of various specializations. Loislaw provides attorneys with the ability to quickly and efficiently find the necessary legal information they need, when and where they need it, by facilitating access to primary law as well as state-specific law, records, forms and treatises.

ftwilliam.com offers employee benefits professionals the highest quality plan documents (retirement, welfare and non-qualified) and government forms (5500/PBGC, 1099 and IRS) software at highly competitive prices.

MediRegs products provide integrated health care compliance content and software solutions for professionals in healthcare, higher education and life sciences, including professionals in accounting, law and consulting.

Wolters Kluwer Law & Business, a division of Wolters Kluwer, is headquartered in New York. Wolters Kluwer is a market-leading global information services company focused on professionals.

To Helen, Trevor, and Shelley

Summary of Contents

Contents   *xi*

Preface   *xxvii*

Acknowledgments   *xxxi*

Chapter 1   The Formation and Framework of the Debtor/
Creditor Relationship and an Introduction to
Unsecured Debt   1

Chapter 2   Secured Debt and Priorities   7

Chapter 3   Debt Collection under State Law   33

Chapter 4   Fraudulent Transfers   71

Chapter 5   The Nature, Source, and Policies of Bankruptcy Law   85

Chapter 6   Participants in the Bankruptcy Case   103

Chapter 7   Bankruptcy Jurisdiction, the Powers of the
Bankruptcy Court, and Sovereign Immunity   125

Chapter 8   Debtor Eligibility and the Different Forms of
Bankruptcy Relief   167

Chapter 9   The Commencement and Dismissal of the
Bankruptcy Case   201

Chapter 10   The Automatic Stay   243

Chapter 11   Relief from Stay and Adequate Protection   267

Chapter 12   Property of the Estate   291

Chapter 13   Exemptions, Redemption, and Reaffirmation   305

Chapter 14   The Trustee's Avoidance Powers: General Principles
and Policies   339

Chapter 15   The Trustee's Avoidance Powers: Unperfected
Interests and Statutory Liens   349

Chapter 16   The Avoidance of Preferences, Setoff, Fraudulent
Transfers, and Postpetition Transfers   363

Chapter 17   The Trustee's Power to Deal with Estate Property
and to Obtain Credit   405

Chapter 18   Executory Contracts and Unexpired Leases   423

Chapter 19   Claims against the Estate   441

Summary of Contents

Chapter 20   The Chapter 13 Plan   477
Chapter 21   The Chapter 11 Plan   523
Chapter 22   The Debtor's Discharge   563

Glossary   607
Table of Cases   631
Table of Statutes   641
Index   649

Contents

Preface   *xxvii*

Acknowledgments   *xxxi*

Chapter 1   The Formation and Framework of the Debtor/ Creditor Relationship and an Introduction to Unsecured Debt   **1**

§1.1   Debtors and Creditors   1
§1.2   State Law and Federal Law: An Introductory Note   2
§1.3   Formation and Planning Concerns   2
§1.4   The Enforcement of Unsecured Debt—An Overview   4

Chapter 2   Secured Debt and Priorities   **7**

§2.1   Definition and Terminology   7
    §2.1.1   Definition   7
    §2.1.2   Terminology   8
§2.2   The Relationship between the Debt and the Collateral   8
    §2.2.1   The Link between the Debt and the Collateral   8
    §2.2.2   The Distinction between Personal Liability and the Charge on the Property   9
    §2.2.3   Noncontemporaneous Creation of the Debt and the Lien   10
    §2.2.4   After-Acquired Collateral   11
    §2.2.5   Purchase Money Security Interests   11
§2.3   The Creation of a Lien   11
    §2.3.1   Attachment   12
    §2.3.2   Perfection   12
    §2.3.3   Summary   13
§2.4   The Different Categories of Lien   13
    §2.4.1   Consensual Liens   13
    §2.4.2   Judicial Liens   14
    §2.4.3   Statutory Liens   15
    §2.4.4   Common Law Liens   17
    §2.4.5   Equitable Liens   17

§2.5		The Effect of a Valid Lien	18
	§2.5.1	Against the Debtor and Subsequent Transferees	18
	§2.5.2	On Preexisting Third-Party Interests in the Property	19
	§2.5.3	Oversecured and Undersecured Debt	19
§2.6		Enforcement of the Lien	20
	§2.6.1	Seizure of the Property	20
	§2.6.2	Application of the Property in Satisfaction of the Debt	21
§2.7		Priorities among Liens and Other Interests	22
	§2.7.1	The Function of Priority Rules	22
	§2.7.2	The General Rule of Priority	23
	§2.7.3	Departures from the First-in-Time Rule for the Protection of Certain Subsequent Lienholders	24
	§2.7.4	Priorities between Liens and Other Interests in the Property	24
	§2.7.5	A Summary of the Issues to Be Considered in Dealing with Priorities	25

Chapter 3		**Debt Collection under State Law**	**33**
§3.1		Preliminary Observations on Debt Collection by Judicial Process at State Law	33
§3.2		Executable Property and Levy	34
	§3.2.1	Executable Property	34
	§3.2.2	Levy	37
§3.3		Judicial Prejudgment Remedies	38
	§3.3.1	General Principles Applicable to All Prejudgment Remedies	38
	§3.3.2	Due Process in Prejudgment Remedies	39
	§3.3.3	Attachment	40
	§3.3.4	Prejudgment Garnishment	44
	§3.3.5	Prejudgment Replevin or Claim and Delivery	46
	§3.3.6	Receivership	47
	§3.3.7	Injunctions	48
	§3.3.8	Lis Pendens	49
§3.4		The Judgment and Its Enforcement	49
	§3.4.1	Judgment by Default or Consent (Confession)	49
	§3.4.2	The Duration of the Judgment	51
	§3.4.3	The Judgment Lien	51

		§3.4.4	The Enforcement of Judgments in Other States	53
	§3.5	Execution		54
	§3.6	Garnishment		57
	§3.7	Proceedings in Aid of Execution		58
	§3.8	Bankruptcy and the State Law Collection Process		59
	§3.9	State Law Insolvency Proceedings		59
		§3.9.1	Introduction to State Law Insolvency Proceedings	59
		§3.9.2	Compositions and Extensions	61
		§3.9.3	Assignments for the Benefit of Creditors	62

Chapter 4 Fraudulent Transfers — **71**

	§4.1	Background — The Basis and Purpose of Fraudulent Transfer Law		71
		§4.1.1	State Fraudulent Transfer Law	71
		§4.1.2	The Avoidance of Fraudulent Transfers in Bankruptcy	72
	§4.2	An Overview of the Avoidance Suit		72
	§4.3	Actual Fraud		73
		§4.3.1	Dishonest Intent	73
		§4.3.2	Proof of Fraud — Badges of Fraud	74
	§4.4	Constructive Fraud		74
		§4.4.1	General Principles	74
		§4.4.2	Reasonable Equivalence in Value	75
		§4.4.3	Financial Condition	76
	§4.5	The Relationship between the Grounds of Constructive Fraud and Actual Fraud		77
	§4.6	The Remedy of Avoidance and the Rights of the Transferee		78
	§4.7	Fraudulent Transfer Law and Leveraged Buyouts		80
		§4.7.1	What Is a Leveraged Buyout?	80
		§4.7.2	The Application of Fraudulent Transfer Law to LBOs	81

Chapter 5 The Nature, Source, and Policies of Bankruptcy Law — **85**

	§5.1	What Is Bankruptcy?		85
	§5.2	The Federal Nature of Bankruptcy Law		86
		§5.2.1	The Federal Power over Bankruptcy	86
		§5.2.2	Bankruptcy Law and Nonbankruptcy Law	86
	§5.3	Uniformity in Bankruptcy Law		87

§5.4   The Statutory Source of Bankruptcy Law   89
     §5.4.1   Federal Bankruptcy Legislation   89
     §5.4.2   The Structure and Organization of
         the Code and Ancillary Statutes   90
     §5.4.3   Dollar Amounts in the Code   92
     §5.4.4   The Bankruptcy Rules   92
§5.5   The Policies and Goals of Bankruptcy Law   93
     §5.5.1   Introduction   93
     §5.5.2   The Fundamental Goals and Policies of
         Bankruptcy   94

Chapter 6   Participants in the Bankruptcy Case   103

§6.1   The Bankruptcy Court   103
§6.2   The Trustee   104
     §6.2.1   Appointment and Qualification, Generally   104
     §6.2.2   Ch. 7 Cases   104
     §6.2.3   Ch. 12 and 13 Cases   105
     §6.2.4   Ch. 11 Cases   106
     §6.2.5   Trustee's Fees   107
§6.3   The U.S. Trustee   107
§6.4   The Debtor   108
     §6.4.1   The Debtor's Role in the Case   108
     §6.4.2   Equity Security Holders   109
§6.5   Creditors and Creditors' Committees   109
§6.6   Attorneys and Other Professional Consultants   111
     §6.6.1   The Employment of Professionals by the
         Estate, the Debtor, and Creditors   111
     §6.6.2   Conflicts of Interest, Client Confidentiality,
         and Loyalty   112
§6.7   Debt Relief Agencies   115
     §6.7.1   The Meaning of "Debt Relief Agency":
         Persons, Including Attorneys, Who Provide
         Assistance or Representation in Connection
         with a Modest-value Consumer Bankruptcy
         Case   115
     §6.7.2   The Regulation of Debt Relief Agencies   116
     §6.7.3   The Constitutionality of §§526 and 528
         as Applied to Attorneys   117
§6.8   Other Participants   118

Chapter 7   Bankruptcy Jurisdiction, the Powers of the Bankruptcy Court, and Sovereign Immunity   125

§7.1	Introduction	125
§7.2	District Court Jurisdiction over Bankruptcy	125
	§7.2.1 Personal Jurisdiction	126
	§7.2.2 Subject Matter Jurisdiction	126
	§7.2.3 The Purpose of §1334	130
§7.3	The Exercise of Bankruptcy Jurisdiction by Bankruptcy Courts	130
	§7.3.1 Jurisdiction Prior to 1978	131
	§7.3.2 The Bankruptcy Reform Act of 1978	132
	§7.3.3 1984 Reforms	133
	§7.3.4 Proposals for Change by the 1994 National Bankruptcy Review Commission	134
	§7.3.5 An Overview of the Current System	134
	§7.3.6 A Summary of the Operation of §157 and Its Constitutionality	141
§7.4	The Jury Trial in Bankruptcy	141
§7.5	The Injunctive, Contempt, and Sanctioning Powers of the Bankruptcy Court	143
	§7.5.1 Injunctions	143
	§7.5.2 Contempt of Court	144
	§7.5.3 Sanctions for Improper Conduct	145
§7.6	Appeals from the Bankruptcy Court	145
	§7.6.1 The Appellate Structure in General	145
	§7.6.2 Bankruptcy Appellate Panels	146
§7.7	Abstention	147
	§7.7.1 Introduction	147
	§7.7.2 Abstention under §305 of the Code	147
	§7.7.3 Abstention under 28 U.S.C. §1334(c)	148
§7.8	Removal and Remand under 28 U.S.C. §1452	150
§7.9	Sovereign Immunity	150
	§7.9.1 Background and the General Principle of Sovereign Immunity	150
	§7.9.2 The Statutory Abrogation of Sovereign Immunity under §106(a)	152
	§7.9.3 Waiver of Sovereign Immunity by Consent and by the Filing of a Proof of Claim under §106(b)	153
	§7.9.4 Setoff of Claims by and against a Governmental Unit under §106(c)	154

**Chapter 8   Debtor Eligibility and the Different Forms
of Bankruptcy Relief   167**

§8.1   Introduction   167
§8.2   An Overview of the Distinction between Liquidation
        and Rehabilitation   167
        §8.2.1   Liquidation   167
        §8.2.2   Rehabilitation Bankruptcy   168
        §8.2.3   A Practical Perspective on the Distinction
                  between Liquidation and Rehabilitation   169
§8.3   Different Types of Debtor   170
        §8.3.1   Individuals, Partnerships, and
                  Corporations   170
        §8.3.2   Consumer and Business Debtors   171
        §8.3.3   Family Farmers and Fishermen   173
§8.4   Debtor Eligibility   173
        §8.4.1   The General Qualifications and
                  Limitations   174
        §8.4.2   Eligibility for Relief under Each of the
                  Separate Chapters   181
§8.5   Conversion from One Chapter to Another   184
§8.6   Choice of Relief   187
        §8.6.1   The Debtor's Choice of Relief   187
        §8.6.2   A Summary of the Significant Differences
                  between Chs. 7, 11, 12, and 13 That May
                  Influence the Choice of Relief   189

**Chapter 9   The Commencement and Dismissal of
the Bankruptcy Case   201**

§9.1   Introduction   201
§9.2   Venue   202
§9.3   The Voluntary Case   203
§9.4   The Voluntary Petition as an Order for Relief   204
§9.5   Joint Cases, Jointly Administered Cases, and
        Consolidation   205
        §9.5.1   Joint Cases   205
        §9.5.2   Joint Administration   206
        §9.5.3   Consolidation of Cases   206
§9.6   Involuntary Cases   207
        §9.6.1   Introduction   207
        §9.6.2   Qualifications for Filing under
                  §303(a), (b), and (c)   208

	§9.6.3	Procedures from the Filing of the Petition to the Order for Relief	212
	§9.6.4	The Grounds for Relief	213
	§9.6.5	The Effect and Consequences of the Order for Relief in an Involuntary Case	215
	§9.6.6	Petitioner Liability for Dismissal of the Petition	216
§9.7		General Grounds for Dismissal of a Bankruptcy Case — Voluntary Dismissal, Cause, and Improper Debtor Conduct	217
§9.8		Dismissal of a Ch. 7 Consumer Case on Grounds of Abuse	221
	§9.8.1	The Application of §707(b) to "Individuals Whose Debts Are Primarily Consumer Debts"	221
	§9.8.2	The Background to BAPCPA's Amendment of §707(b): "Substantial Abuse" and the 1994 National Bankruptcy Review Commission	223
	§9.8.3	Overview of the BAPCPA Amendments	224
	§9.8.4	Distinguishing Debtors Who Earn Above and Below the Median Family Income and the Protections of §707(b)(6) and (7) to Below-Median Debtors	225
	§9.8.5	The Finding of Abuse Where the Presumption of Abuse Does Not Apply	227
	§9.8.6	The Formula in §707(b)(2) to Determine if the Presumption of Abuse Applies	228
	§9.8.7	Rebuttal of the Presumption of Abuse	233
	§9.8.8	Sanctions	234
§9.9		The Creditors' Meeting	234

Chapter 10 The Automatic Stay 243

§10.1	Introduction	243
§10.2	The Purpose of the Automatic Stay	243
§10.3	The Nature and Scope of the Stay	244
§10.4	The Range of the Stay: §362(a) and (b)	246
	§10.4.1 Activity Included in the Stay — §362(a)	247
	§10.4.2 The Impact of the Stay on Setoff Rights	249
	§10.4.3 Activity Excluded from the Stay — §362(b)	250

§10.5   Termination of the Stay   253

     §10.5.1   Termination of the Stay of Acts against Estate Property   253

     §10.5.2   Termination of the Stay of Other Acts   254

     §10.5.3   Termination of the Stay following Serial Filings   254

§10.6   The Effect of the Stay on Limitation Periods — §108   256

§10.7   The Effect of Violating the Stay   257

     §10.7.1   The Nullification of Advantages Gained by the Violation   257

     §10.7.2   Willful Violations: Compensatory Damages, Including Costs and Attorneys' Fees   258

     §10.7.3   Emotional Distress Damages   259

     §10.7.4   Punitive Damages   260

     §10.7.5   Sanctions for Contempt of Court   260

Chapter 11   Relief from Stay and Adequate Protection   267

§11.1   Introduction   267

§11.2   The Procedure for Relief from Stay   267

§11.3   Forms of Relief   268

§11.4   Grounds for Relief   270

     §11.4.1   Relief from Stay for Cause (§362(d)(1))   270

     §11.4.2   Relief from Stay of Acts against Property on the Ground That the Debtor Has No Equity in the Property and the Property Is Not Necessary to an Effective Reorganization (§362(d)(2))   271

     §11.4.3   Single Asset Real Estate Cases   273

     §11.4.4   In Rem Relief Relating to Real Property Collateral   274

§11.5   Lack of Adequate Protection as Cause for Relief from Stay under §362(d)(1)   275

     §11.5.1   The Interests Entitled to Adequate Protection   275

     §11.5.2   The Circumstances under Which the Need for Adequate Protection Arises   276

     §11.5.3   Factors to Be Considered in Determining the Need for Adequate Protection   277

     §11.5.4   The Means and Method of Furnishing Adequate Protection   279

     §11.5.5   The Failure of Adequate Protection: Superpriority under §507(b)   280

Chapter 12   Property of the Estate   291

§12.1   The Creation of the Bankruptcy Estate and
Debtor's New Estate   291

§12.2   The Composition of the Estate   293

§12.2.1   Legal and Equitable Interests of the
Debtor at the Time of the Petition   293

§12.2.2   Restrictions on the Transfer of Property
Rights under Nonbankruptcy Law or
Contract   295

§12.2.3   Property Acquired after the Filing of the
Petition   296

§12.3   The Trustee's Power to Compel Delivery of
Property of the Estate ("Turnover")   298

§12.4   Abandonment of Property by the Trustee   299

Chapter 13   Exemptions, Redemption, and Reaffirmation   305

§13.1   The Concept of Exemptions   305

§13.2   Exemptions Applicable in Bankruptcy Cases   306

§13.2.1   Uniformity of Exemptions — State
Opt-Out   306

§13.2.2   Determining Which State's Law Governs
Exemptions — the Debtor's Domicile   308

§13.2.3   Exemption Planning and Controls on
Abuse of the Homestead Exemption   309

§13.3   The Nature of Exempt Property   313

§13.4   The Procedure for Claiming Exemptions   314

§13.5   The Debtor's Power to Avoid Certain Interests
That Impair Exemptions   316

§13.5.1   General Scope and Purpose of the
Debtor's Avoidance Power   316

§13.5.2   Judicial Liens   316

§13.5.3   Avoidable Nonpossessory, Nonpurchase-
Money Security Interests   317

§13.5.4   Avoidance "to the Extent" of Impairment   318

§13.5.5   A State Cannot Override the Avoidance
Power in Its Opt-Out Statute   318

§13.5.6   How Impairment Is Measured   319

§13.6   The Individual Debtor's Redemption Right in
Ch. 7 Cases   322

§13.7   Reaffirmation   323

§13.7.1   The General Principles of Reaffirmation   323

§13.7.2 The Reaffirmation of Secured Debt as an
Alternative to Redemption 327
§13.7.3 The Reaffirmation of Unsecured Debt 327
§13.8 The Ch. 7 Debtor's Retention of the Collateral
under the Original Contract — the
"Ride-Through" 328

Chapter 14   The Trustee's Avoidance Powers: General Principles and Policies   339

§14.1 Introduction 339
§14.2 The Structure of the Avoidance Provisions 340
§14.3 Applicability of the Avoidance Powers in
Liquidation and Rehabilitation Cases 341
§14.4 Exercise of the Avoidance Power by a Debtor
in Possession or Other Parties 342
§14.5 The Avoidance Suit and the Enforcement of a
Judgment of Avoidance 342
§14.6 Preservation of the Transfer for the Benefit of
the Estate 344
§14.7 The Statute of Limitations and "Reach-Back"
Provisions 344
§14.8 The General Purpose and Goals of the Avoidance
Powers 345

Chapter 15   The Trustee's Avoidance Powers: Unperfected Interests and Statutory Liens   349

§15.1 The Avoidance of Unperfected Interests under
§544 349
    §15.1.1 Introduction 349
    §15.1.2 The Trustee's Status as a Hypothetical Lien
Creditor, Execution Creditor, or Bona Fide
Purchaser of Real Property under
§544(a) 349
    §15.1.3 The Trustee's Status as Successor to an
Actual Unsecured Creditor under §544(b) 352
§15.2 The Avoidance of Statutory Liens under §545 354
§15.3 The Effect of §546 on the Trustee's Avoidance
Rights under §§544 and 545 356
    §15.3.1 The Preservation of Nonbankruptcy
Backdating Rules by §546(b) 356
    §15.3.2 The Preservation of the Seller's
Reclamation Rights by §546(c) 356

Chapter 16 The Avoidance of Preferences, Setoff, Fraudulent Transfers, and Postpetition Transfers 363

§16.1   Preferential Transfers under §547   363
    §16.1.1   Introduction   363
    §16.1.2   The Elements of §547(b)   365
    §16.1.3   The Timing of the Transfer   369
    §16.1.4   Exceptions to Avoidance under §547(c)   372
§16.2   Setoff under §553   381
    §16.2.1   Setoff in Nonbankruptcy Law   381
    §16.2.2   The Effect of Setoff Rights in Bankruptcy   381
    §16.2.3   Limitations on the Right of Setoff   383
§16.3   Fraudulent Transfers under §548   385
    §16.3.1   Avoidance under §548 as an Alternative
         to §544 and State Law   385
    §16.3.2   Actual Fraud   386
    §16.3.3   Constructive Fraud   386
    §16.3.4   Reach-back and the Effect of Avoidance   388
    §16.3.5   The Fraudulent Transfer of Exempt
         Property   389
    §16.3.6   Charitable Contributions by an
         Individual Debtor   389
§16.4   Postpetition Transfers under §549   390

Chapter 17 The Trustee's Power to Deal with Estate Property and to Obtain Credit 405

§17.1   Introduction   405
§17.2   The Use, Sale, or Lease of Estate Property under
    §363   406
    §17.2.1   The Distinction between Ordinary and
         Extraordinary Transactions   406
    §17.2.2   The Approval of Transactions outside the
         Ordinary Course of Business under
         §363(b)(1)   408
    §17.2.3   The Protection of Interests in Property
         That Is to Be Used, Sold, or Leased   408
    §17.2.4   Insolvency or Bankruptcy Clauses in
         Prepetition Contracts or Nonbankruptcy
         Law   409
    §17.2.5   Restrictions on Dealing with Cash
         Collateral   410

§17.3 Postpetition Credit under §364   411
       §17.3.1   The Rationale of §364   411
       §17.3.2   The Credit Arrangements Permitted
                 by §364   412
       §17.3.3   Cross-Collateralization   414
       §17.3.4   Protection on Appeal   415

Chapter 18   Executory Contracts and Unexpired Leases   423

§18.1   Introduction   423
§18.2   The Meaning of "Executory Contract" and
        "Unexpired Lease"   424
§18.3   The Special Treatment of Selected Transactions   425
§18.4   The Estate's Right to Assume or Reject Executory
        Contracts   426
§18.5   The Procedure and Standards for Assumption or
        Rejection   427
§18.6   Interim Performance   428
§18.7   The Assumption of Contracts in Default   429
§18.8   Nonassumable Contracts   430
        §18.8.1   Contracts That Are Not Assignable in
                  Nonbankruptcy Law   430
        §18.8.2   Loan and Financing Transactions   431
§18.9   Bankruptcy Termination or Ipso Facto Clauses   432
§18.10 Postpetition Termination by the Other Party on
        Grounds Other Than an Ipso Facto Clause   433
§18.11 Problems of Rejection in Partially Executed
        Contracts   433
§18.12 Assignment   434

Chapter 19   Claims against the Estate   441

§19.1   Introduction   441
§19.2   What is a Claim?   441
        §19.2.1   The Definition of "Claim"   441
        §19.2.2   Unliquidated, Contingent, Unmatured,
                  and Disputed Claims   443
        §19.2.3   Prepetition and Postpetition Debts   444
        §19.2.4   Claims against the Debtor's Property   445
        §19.2.5   Determining When a Claim Arises   445
§19.3   Determining and Estimating Contingent and
        Unliquidated Claims   447
§19.4   The Proof and Allowance of Claims   449
§19.5   Interest on Claims   451
§19.6   Claim Classification and Priorities   452

§19.6.1   General Principles   452
§19.6.2   The Order of Distribution   453
§19.6.3   Secured Claims   454
§19.6.4   Priority Claims   460
§19.6.5   General Unsecured Claims and Lower
           Classes   467
§19.7   Subordination and Recharacterization of Claims   467
§19.7.1   Consensual Subordination   467
§19.7.2   Equitable Subordination   467
§19.7.3   Recharacterization   468

Chapter 20   The Chapter 13 Plan   477

§20.1   Introduction and Review   477
§20.2   Outline of the Ch. 13 Proceedings   479
§20.3   Overview of the Plan and the Prerequisites for
       Confirmation   481
§20.4   The Funding of the Plan and the Debtor's
       Obligation to Make Payments   484
§20.5   The Length of the Plan   484
§20.6   Good Faith   485
§20.7   The Classification of Claims and the Standards
       Applicable to Each Class   487
§20.7.1   Secured Claims   487
§20.7.2   Priority Claims   490
§20.7.3   Unsecured Claims   491
§20.8   The Modification of a Claimant's Rights and the
       Cure of Default   502
§20.8.1   Introduction and General Note on Cure   502
§20.8.2   The Modification and Cure of Claims
           Other Than Specially Protected Home
           Mortgages   503
§20.8.3   The Special Treatment of Claims Secured
           Only by a Security Interest in Real
           Property That Is the Debtor's Principal
           Residence   504
§20.9   Long-Term Debt   506
§20.10   Modification of a Confirmed Plan   507
§20.11   Successive Filings under Chs. 7 and 13: the
       "Chapter 20" Tactic   509

Chapter 21   The Chapter 11 Plan   523

§21.1   Introduction to Ch. 11 and Its Debtors   523
§21.1.1   General Introduction   523

§21.1.2 Eligibility for Ch. 11 and Distinctions between Ch. 11 Debtors, Particularly Individuals and Small Businesses 524

§21.2 The Purpose of a Ch. 11 Case 528

§21.3 The Importance of Negotiation and Business Judgment in a Ch. 11 Case 529

§21.4 Outline of the Ch. 11 Case 530

§21.4.1 Commencement of the Case 530

§21.4.2 The Roles of the Debtor in Possession, Creditors, and Interest Holders 530

§21.4.3 The Formulation of the Plan by the Debtor or Other Parties in Interest 533

§21.4.4 Disclosure 534

§21.4.5 Voting on the Plan 536

§21.4.6 Confirmation 537

§21.4.7 Modification of the Plan 537

§21.4.8 The Effect of Confirmation 538

§21.4.9 Consummation of the Plan 539

§21.5 Prepackaged Plans 540

§21.6 The Content of the Plan 540

§21.6.1 Overview 540

§21.6.2 The Mandatory Provisions under §1123(a) 541

§21.6.3 Permissive Provisions under §1123(b) 545

§21.7 Confirmation Requirements 546

§21.7.1 Overview 546

§21.7.2 Confirmation under §1129(a) 547

§21.7.3 Confirmation under §1129(b) 550

§21.7.4 Undersecured Creditors and §1111(b) 556

Chapter 22 The Debtor's Discharge 563

§22.1 Introduction 563

§22.2 The Scope of the Discharge 565

§22.3 The Effect of the Discharge 566

§22.4 Waiver of the Discharge and Reaffirmation of the Debt 568

§22.5 The Ch. 7 Discharge 568

§22.5.1 Procedure and Scope 568

§22.5.2 Denial of the Discharge under §727 569

§22.5.3 Revocation of the Discharge 572

§22.5.4 Exclusions from the Ch. 7 Discharge by §523 572

§22.5.5 The Discharge of Nondischargeable Debts in a Subsequent Case 589

Contents

§22.6 The Ch. 11 Discharge 590
§22.7 The Ch. 13 Discharge 591
  §22.7.1 Procedure and Scope 591
  §22.7.2 Preconditions to the Grant of the Ch. 13
          Discharge 592
  §22.7.3 Exclusions from the Ch. 13 Discharge 592
  §22.7.4 Discharge in Successive Cases 595
  §22.7.5 Waiver of Revocation of the Ch. 13
          Discharge 596
  §22.7.6 The Hardship Discharge 596
§22.8 The Ch. 12 Discharge 597

Glossary 607
Table of Cases 631
Table of Statutes 641
Index 649

Preface

BANKRUPTCY AND DEBTOR/CREDITOR, SIXTH EDITION

This book begins with a basic overview of debt collection under state law and an introduction to concepts and principles that underlie both state debtor/creditor law and bankruptcy. It then undertakes a systematic coverage of bankruptcy law and principles, dealt with at a level of depth and complexity appropriate to a basic bankruptcy and debtor/creditor course. In deciding on the most suitable scope and depth of coverage, I have been guided by my own experience in teaching this course over many years and by the content of published casebooks and other course materials.

In this edition, I have made some refinements to the text and to the Examples and Explanations, I have updated the case law throughout the book, and I have added discussion on issues that have become prominent since the last edition. I have not made significant changes to the organization, approach, coverage, and structure of the book. However, I have made organizational changes in some chapters to improve coherence and readability. The most significant of these is a tighter discussion of jurisdiction and sovereign immunity in Chapter 7 and an expansion of the treatment of the Ch. 11 plan in Chapter 21, including a set of new Examples and Explanations. I have also made some changes to the endmatter. I have eliminated the appendix summarizing the differences between Chs. 7, 11, 12, and 13, and have integrated this material into the body of Chapter 8. I have added tables of statutes and cases.

STATE LAW AND FEDERAL BANKRUPTCY LAW

Debtor/creditor law encompasses both state debt collection law and federal bankruptcy law. Some law school courses omit the state law component in favor of more extensive bankruptcy coverage, while others cover debt collection under state law as well. Some exposure to state collection law is helpful, not only because knowledge of general principles of state debtor/creditor law is useful in itself, but also because it contains fundamental concepts and principles that play an important role in bankruptcy. For this reason, the first three chapters of this book cover general principles of state debtor/creditor law. The treatment is broad and condensed. It emphasizes general themes and key concepts, and it sets the stage for the later discussion of the connections and distinctions between state law and bankruptcy law. This level of detail should be sufficient for most courses that include a component on state debtor/creditor law. It should also make the concepts and procedures of state law accessible to students whose course omits state law but who would like to do some background reading on the subject. Chapter 4 also deals with state law. It covers the avoidance of fraudulent transfers under state law, and ties in with the trustee's power to avoid such transfers in bankruptcy, which is discussed in Chapter 16.

THE ORGANIZATION AND APPROACH OF THIS BOOK

Although legal rules are important, a full appreciation of the subject requires an understanding of the policy behind the rules, their efficacy, and their transactional impact. *Bankruptcy and Debtor/Creditor: Examples & Explanations* is not simply an outline of legal rules. It discusses the reasons behind the rules and the impact of their operation.

This book combines expository text with Examples and Explanations. The textual portion provides a clear and readable exposition of the topic, beginning with the basics and moving to more intricate and advanced issues. It focuses on material that is likely to be covered in a bankruptcy or debtor/creditor course. I have tried to ensure that basic assumptions are clearly articulated, that the transactional context is clear, and that technical language is explained. To assist you in remembering terminology, I have included a lengthy glossary at the end of the book that provides ready definitions of technical terms and terms of art that are commonly encountered in the bankruptcy context.

The Examples and Explanations are based on the textual discussion. Their purpose is to provide concrete illustrations of how the principles discussed in the text apply. They are also intended to allow you to test your knowledge and understanding of the topic. If you try to resolve the questions asked in the Examples before reading the Explanations you will derive the greatest benefit from this feature of the book.

CITATIONS IN THIS BOOK

Sections of the Bankruptcy Code, Title 11 U.S.C., are simply cited by a section symbol (§) followed by the section number. Code chapters are cited by the abbreviation "Ch." followed by the chapter number.

Preface

Bankruptcy law generates a large volume of reported cases. Decisions of courts at all levels, from the bankruptcy courts to the U.S. Supreme Court, are reported, and one can find contrary decisions on almost every issue that arises under the Bankruptcy Code. This book cites and discusses many cases, but case citations are necessarily selective. In choosing cases, I look for those that contain helpful discussion and good illustrative facts. I keep the citations simple, and do not use extended captions or citations to multiple sets of law reports. I do not cite secondary sources.

Acknowledgments

I owe thanks to many people who have helped me over the years with successive editions of this book. My work on the original edition and on several of the revisions has been supported by summer research grants from Lewis & Clark Law School. I have had able research assistance from a number of Lewis & Clark students who have helped me to find and update material. In every edition of this book, I have benefited from the guidance and thorough editorial work of many members of the staff of Wolters Kluwer Law and Business. Finally, I am grateful to the many students and professors who have used this book and who have offered suggestions for changes or corrections.

Bankruptcy and
Debtor/Creditor

The Formation and Framework of the Debtor/Creditor Relationship and an Introduction to Unsecured Debt

§1.1 DEBTORS AND CREDITORS

In the broadest terms, a debtor is a person who owes money, and a creditor is a person to whom it is owed. Of course, most people and corporate entities fill both roles in their financial relationships — they have debts due to them by some persons and owe debts to others. In most transactions, debtors pay their debts. However, where a debtor defaults on a debt, the law must provide mechanisms for the creditor to enforce the debtor's legal obligation to pay it. In establishing these mechanisms, the law must balance the creditor's right to enforce payment against the need to protect the debtor from unduly harsh or aggressive creditor conduct.

The first four chapters of this book provide an overview of the rules of state law governing the creation and collection of debt and introduce some basic concepts about different kinds of debt that are crucial to an understanding of both state law and federal bankruptcy law. The remainder of the book focuses on bankruptcy law. Even if your course on bankruptcy law does not cover state law on debt collection, I recommend that you read these first four chapters to gain some basic information about debt that you will need to understand bankruptcy law.

§1.2 STATE LAW AND FEDERAL LAW: AN INTRODUCTORY NOTE

The principal federal law in the area of debtor/creditor relations is the Bankruptcy Code.[1] However, the Bankruptcy Code is not applicable unless the debtor has become bankrupt. In the absence of bankruptcy, the rights of debtors and creditors are governed by the law prevailing in the state that has jurisdiction over the transaction. This law consists of state law and any federal statutes (other than the Bankruptcy Code) that are applicable to the enforcement of debt. For example, federal statutes restrict the garnishment of wages, regulate debt collection practices, protect entitlements under federal benefits programs, and confer special rights on the federal government to collect taxes or other revenues.

Discussion of bankruptcy law is deferred until Chapter 5. In these first four chapters, the focus is on state debtor/creditor law. (The federal statutes regulating the enforcement of debt, just referred to, are not covered in this book.) This treatment of state law is condensed and presented in generalized form, using commonly accepted principles. Obviously, this overview cannot take into account all the variations in the laws of different states. Its purpose is to introduce and explain central principles and concepts of state law and to build a foundation for the later discussion of bankruptcy law.

§1.3 FORMATION AND PLANNING CONCERNS

Debtor/creditor law is essentially remedial in nature; it is concerned with the enforcement of debts rather than with their creation. However, the creditor's ability to enforce the debt and the debtor's power to resist payment are influenced by the circumstances and the terms under which the debt was created.

Where a debt is created contractually, the parties have some opportunity to plan the transaction. The party who anticipates being a creditor under the contract will try to minimize the risk of loss if the debtor fails to perform as promised. The debtor party will be concerned about protection against harsh enforcement action or intrusive creditor behavior. Where debts arise other than contractually, especially if they are created by an unexpected event, such as negligent injury giving rise to a tort claim, there may be no opportunity for planning. Even here, however, some general planning may

---

1. See section 5.2.1 for an explanation of why bankruptcy law is federal and a discussion of the role of state law in a bankruptcy case.

have occurred. For example, one or both parties may have bought liability insurance.

When a contractual debt is created, the creditor's dominant concern is probably that the debt will be repaid with interest on the due date. Although the creditor realizes that it may have to resort to collection procedures, its principal goal is to get the benefit of its bargain with the least amount of cost and aggravation. To best achieve this goal, a careful creditor will do two things. First, it will investigate the debtor's creditworthiness, and second, it will try to structure the transaction by including contract terms that put it in the best position to collect the debt if the debtor should default. There are many terms of this kind: For example, an acceleration clause enables the creditor to sue on the entire debt if the debtor fails to pay the installment currently due. Provisions entitling the creditor to receive financial statements and to conduct inspections at periodic intervals allow the creditor to monitor the debtor's business affairs and to anticipate unstable or deteriorating conditions. A clause that defines "default" broadly gives the creditor the power to commence collection activity in response to specified acts or circumstances, short of nonpayment of the debt. Provision for collection costs, late payment charges, and attorneys' fees gives the creditor the right to reimbursement for expenses that are otherwise not normally recoverable. This is not an exhaustive list, but these examples show that the contract terms can be helpful to a creditor in policing the transaction or pursuing the debt.

Of course, contract rights against the debtor may not ultimately help the creditor if the debtor is in such severe financial trouble that she has no capacity to pay the debt. To gain fuller protection in such a situation, the creditor needs protection that is not totally dependent on the debtor's ability to pay. This protection takes the form of security. The two forms of contractual security in common use are suretyship or guarantee, and the security interest. Under a suretyship, a third party acceptable to the creditor undertakes to pay the debt if the debtor defaults. Obviously the security afforded by this arrangement is only as good as the financial health of the surety. Security interests are introduced in Chapter 2. The powerful rights that a security interest gives the creditor feature prominently in the remainder of this book.

Every right or power given to the creditor to facilitate the collection of the debt comes at some cost or detriment to the debtor. For example, a creditor's right to financial reports or to inspections may be disruptive and detracts from the debtor's business autonomy; the grant of a security interest hampers free use of the debtor's property and prevents use of the property to raise funds from other sources; strict default provisions may place the debtor in breach too easily and may result in harsh forfeiture.

In deciding whether to agree to terms favorable to the creditor, the informed and rational debtor evaluates the risks and burdens imposed and decides whether the benefits of the transaction outweigh its burdens. If the debtor's decision to sacrifice rights or to curtail freedom of action is an exercise of the debtor's contractual autonomy, the agreement is usually binding. However, pressures from a variety of sources may affect the debtor's ability to resist harsh terms. When apparent assent to such terms is exacted by illegitimate means, the law of contract has doctrines, such as unconscionability or duress (to name two), under which rights of enforcement can be cut down to reasonable proportions.

In addition, many statutes, on both the state and federal level, regulate contract terms and curtail abusive practices in consumer credit transactions. For example, the Consumer Credit Protection Act, Title XV of the U.S. Code deals with such matters as discrimination in the grant of credit, credit reporting, disclosure of information in credit agreements, the issuance of credit cards, and the advertising of credit. The CCPA and other such statutes are not discussed in this book.

§1.4 THE ENFORCEMENT OF UNSECURED DEBT — AN OVERVIEW

The difference between unsecured and secured debt surely ranks among the most fundamental and far-reaching dichotomies in debtor/creditor law. Secured debt is discussed in Chapter 2. To fully appreciate the potency of security, one needs to have some idea of the difficulties that an unsecured creditor could face in trying to collect an unpaid debt.

Suppose a seller sold goods on credit to a buyer. The sales contract obliged the buyer to pay a specified price 30 days after delivery. The debt is unsecured because no contractual provision or rule of law provides for security. The goods were delivered and accepted without objection. Thirty days have passed and the debt is due, but no payment has been made by the buyer. The buyer has no complaint about the goods or grounds for withholding payment, but has simply defaulted. To be paid, the seller must take the initiative and pursue the debt.

The seller will probably begin by asking for payment. If this does not work, the seller may decide to hand the matter over to a collection agency or an attorney who will make further efforts at recovery by contacting the debtor. State and federal statutes and the common law of torts place limits on the tactics that may be used by a creditor or its collection agent or attorney in the collection of debt — particularly consumer debt. As a general principle, collection efforts must be kept within reasonable bounds and may not harass, abuse, or coerce the debtor into paying the debt. Overzealous collection activity could give rise to liability for actual and punitive damages.

If approaches to the buyer do not result in payment of the debt, the seller may decide to resort to suit on the debt. The seller's attorney files and serves a complaint and, unless the buyer decides at this stage to dispute the debt, the case proceeds to judgment by default. Following judgment, the creditor is able to use the court's authority and public officers to enforce payment of the debt by the process of execution described in Chapter 3.

However, this enforcement procedure is subject to a significant practical limitation: Its success is dependent upon assets of the debtor being found. If the debtor has no funds, income, or other assets to seize, there is no source from which to derive money to pay the debt. As discussed in the following chapters, even if the debtor does have some property, the creditor may not be able to seize it because it may be immune from execution or subject to the superior claims of others. In addition, a debtor who is trying to evade payment of debts may have concealed assets, so that they are hard to find or identify. Furthermore, a debtor who has failed to pay one creditor has possibly defaulted on other debts too. Several creditors may be involved in enforcement proceedings, and some may have begun the process of debt collection earlier or moved more quickly than the seller. As a result, the debtor's available property may have been seized before the seller has had the chance to execute. (Because the seller did not retain a security interest in the goods as explained in Chapter 2, full unencumbered ownership passed to the buyer upon sale, and the seller has no special claim to them — they are fair game for any creditor who levies on them first.)

If the seller is unsuccessful in finding property upon which to execute, it has various investigatory procedures at its disposal to assist in trying to locate and execute upon property. (These are discussed in Chapter 3.) However, these procedures are only helpful if there are assets to uncover and if the buyer has not been dishonest and wily enough to secrete them thoroughly. If nothing is brought to light, the seller has to wait vigilantly in the hope that the buyer will eventually acquire property, whereupon further writs of execution can be issued. If not, the judgment eventually reaches the end of its term and expires unrequited.[2]

The seller's right to pursue collection efforts under state law could also come to an end if the buyer becomes bankrupt. As we shall see later, the seller becomes an unsecured creditor of the estate and typically will receive only a partial payment — or in some cases, no payment at all — and the unpaid balance of the debt will be discharged.

In short, the unsecured creditor extends credit on the faith of the debtor's willingness and ability to pay. If that faith was misplaced, the creditor has legal means to extract payment from the debtor, but employment of

---

2. *See* Chapter 3 for more detail. Also, the subject of judicial liens is omitted from this discussion for the sake of simplicity but is discussed in Chapters 2 and 3.

those means may not be successful. If the debtor does not pay voluntarily, compulsion of payment is only possible to the extent that the debtor has economic resources. An unsuccessful judgment creditor is worse off at the end of the frustrated enforcement process because the size of the unpaid debt has been swollen by unrecovered collection expenses and legal fees.

Secured Debt and Priorities

§2.1 DEFINITION AND TERMINOLOGY

§2.1.1 Definition

A secured debt differs from an unsecured debt in one important respect: The personal obligation of the debtor to pay the debt is reinforced by a right *in rem* acquired by the creditor in certain property of the debtor. This means that if the debtor fails to pay, the secured creditor may have recourse to the property to satisfy the debt. Most commonly, the debt is satisfied by the sale of the property and the application of its proceeds to the debt. In certain cases, however, the law permits the creditor to take over the property and to keep it in full settlement of the debt. A secured creditor is therefore in a much stronger position than an unsecured creditor: Not only does it have a right of action against the debtor on the debt, but it also has a claim to property of the debtor to back up that right.

This interest in property does not typically give the creditor title to the property but is characterized as a charge against it. In other words, the creditor does not acquire an ownership right in the property when the security interest is created. Rather, ownership remains with the debtor, encumbered by the creditor's interest. It is only when the debtor defaults on the debt that the creditor becomes entitled to take action to terminate the debtor's ownership and to sell the property or take transfer of it.

§2.1.2 Terminology

The Latin verb "to bind" is *ligare*, from which (via French) we derive our word "lien." "Lien" is frequently used as a generic term to describe all kinds of security interests. Other common terms that are often used synonymously with lien are "security interest" and "encumbrance." (Sometimes "lien" is used more restrictively to describe only nonconsensual interests, while "security interest" is used to refer to interests created by contract—*e.g.*, interests under UCC Article 9 or mortgages. The context should make it clear whether the term is used in a generic or specific sense.) The holder of a lien is a lienor or lienholder, the holder of a security interest is a secured party, the holder of a mortgage is a mortgagee (as distinct from the mortgagor, who is the debtor whose property is mortgaged), and the holder of an encumbrance is an encumbrancer.

In addition to these general terms, different categories of lien have their own names (*e.g.*, statutory lien, judicial lien, and so on), and each specific type of lien in those categories has its own label. For example, mechanics liens and tax liens are both forms of statutory lien, and judgment liens and execution liens are both forms of judicial lien. In section 2.4 the different categories of lien are classified and illustrated.

The property subject to the lien is usually called the security or collateral. The Latin roots of the latter word also reflect the concept that it represents. It combines *com* ("together with") and *latus* ("a side"), suggesting that the interest in property parallels the debt.

§2.2 THE RELATIONSHIP BETWEEN THE DEBT AND THE COLLATERAL

§2.2.1 The Link between the Debt and the Collateral

For a lien or security interest to exist there must be both a debt and property of the debtor securing that debt. Without property, the debt cannot be secured; similarly, the interest in the property must secure some obligation. It has no meaning as a right in the abstract.

How is property linked to the debt? Most liens are created in a specific piece, class, or collection of the debtor's property.[1] Where the lien is created

---

1. There are such things as general liens that encumber all the debtor's property. The federal tax lien is one example. However, general liens are not very common. Usually, the property to be subjected to the lien must be specifically described in the instrument that creates the lien.

by contract, the parties agree on the collateral. Where a lien is created by operation of law or by judicial process, legal rules determine what property is subjected to the lien.

As a general rule, lien rights can be created in almost every kind of property — real or personal, tangible or intangible. However, different types of liens may be confined to particular types of property. For example, an Article 9 interest can relate only to personal property or intangibles, and a judgment lien is usually confined to real property.

Although the lien and the debt are inextricably linked, they are distinguishable as two separate components of the creditor's parcel of rights: The debt is a personal claim against the debtor, while the lien is a right in the property. The relationship between these connected but distinct rights gives rise to the following consequences and attributes.

§2.2.2 The Distinction between Personal Liability and the Charge on the Property

In many cases, the distinction between the debt as a personal obligation and the lien as a charge on the property is not practically significant. The debtor is usually the owner of the property, and a judgment foreclosing the lien is also a judgment on the debt. However, it sometimes happens that the right to foreclose the lien on the property is separated from the right to pursue the debtor for payment of the debt.

This occurs, for example, where state law requires the creditor to make an election of remedies (*i.e.*, to choose between suing on the lien or on the debt). It could also happen where the debtor has transferred the encumbered property, so that the creditor has to sue the new owner to foreclose the lien,[2] but must sue the debtor to recover on the debt. (Normally, the creditor would only be interested in suit on the debt if the property cannot be traced or its value is insufficient to satisfy the debt.) A third situation in which the debt and lien are separate occurs under certain statutes that allow a person to acquire a lien on property even without a contractual relationship between the lienholder and the owner. For example, if a subcontractor works on the improvement of real property under a contract with a prime contractor, the prime contractor is the person liable to the subcontractor on the debt. Unless the prime contractor is an actual agent of the owner, no contractual privity exists between the owner and the subcontractor. Nevertheless, if the subcontractor is not paid by the prime contractor, it is entitled by statute to file a construction lien (also called a mechanic's lien) on the property. This lien

---

2. As explained in sections 2.5 and 2.7, the transferee takes the property subject to the lien.

can be foreclosed to satisfy the debt, even though the owner cannot be sued personally on the debt.

§2.2.3 Noncontemporaneous Creation of the Debt and the Lien

Although the ultimate enforcement of the lien is predicated on the existence of a debt at the time of enforcement, it is possible that the lien and the debt could arise at different times and could be created by separate agreements or legal events. The fact that these rights can be created separately or successively can be very useful in some types of transactions. It can also present some interesting legal problems, which will be considered later. The present purpose is to introduce this concept and to describe situations to look out for.

(1) An unsecured debt can be subsequently secured. When it is originally created, a debt may be unsecured. At some later time, before the debt is paid, it could be changed into a secured debt. This could happen, for example, if the parties make a later contract under which the debtor grants a security interest to the creditor to secure the preexisting debt. It could also occur by nonconsensual means through the operation of a statute or the judicial process.

As long as the security is created before the time for enforcement has arrived, the debt will be enforceable as a secured debt. However, if some third party acquired rights in the property during the gap period between the creation and securing of the debt, those rights could be superior to the security interest. In addition, the delay in securing the debt could have consequences if the debtor later becomes bankrupt.

(2) A lien can be created in property in anticipation of future indebtedness. A prospective borrower and lender may plan a relationship under which funds or credit is to be provided by the lender in the future. Particularly when a long-term relationship is contemplated and a line of credit is to be advanced as the debtor needs it, it may be convenient for the parties to create a lien in property at the beginning of the transaction. Of course, the lien is not enforceable until advances are actually made by the creditor, but as soon as the debt arises, it will be secured by the preexisting lien. If a line of credit is provided, then each future advance will be secured by the lien. This arrangement protects the creditor to the fullest extent possible and avoids the inconvenience of creating a new security interest every time an advance is made. This type of transaction is illustrated in Example 3.

§2.2.4 After-Acquired Collateral

As was stated in section 2.2.1, a lien must attach to particular property; a lien in the abstract is meaningless. However, a lien can be created in a piece or class of property before that property has come into existence or before the debtor has acquired rights in it.

To create such a lien, the creditor completes the legal procedure to establish the lien before the debtor acquires the property, or all of the property, that will ultimately be subject to the lien. Prior to the debtor's acquisition of the property, the lien does not extend to it, of course, but as soon as it comes into the debtor's estate, the lien latches onto it. The property that will fall within the lien must be clearly identified when the lien is created. The utility of liens on after-acquired collateral is illustrated in Example 3.

§2.2.5 Purchase Money Security Interests

It is common for people to borrow money or to obtain credit for the purpose of acquiring specific property. For example, the buyer of a home or a car usually pays only a portion of the price in cash and covers the balance by a bank loan or credit from the seller. When a loan or credit is given to the debtor for the express purpose of enabling the debtor to acquire particular property and the property is itself used as collateral to secure the debt, the lien is called a "purchase money security interest" (PMSI).

The link between collateral and debt is particularly striking when the debtor's acquisition of the collateral was made possible by the value given by the creditor. For this reason, strong equities favor the holder of a purchase money interest, who is sometimes given special concessions in law. For example, UCC Article 9 allows greater flexibility in the perfection of purchase money interests and enhances their priority under some circumstances. (For the most part, these rules are beyond the scope of this book.) In some situations the Bankruptcy Code treats a purchase money interest more generously. (*See, e.g.,* section 16.1.4.) Although it is important to recognize that purchase money interests sometimes receive more favorable treatment than other liens, this difference should not be exaggerated. For many purposes, they are merely one type of consensual lien, subject to the same rules that govern other liens of that kind.

§2.3 THE CREATION OF A LIEN

A lien must be created by following procedures prescribed by law. Different liens are established in different ways under a wide variety of statutes, common law rules, and equitable principles. These different types of lien are identified and explained in the next section. Although each has its own set of rules and precepts governing its creation, operation, and effect, some common principles can be stated in broad terms.

To be fully effectual, a lien must be valid not only against the debtor but against third parties as well. The process of creating a lien valid against the debtor is known as "attachment." Expansion of that interest to make the lien binding on third parties is called "perfection." Sometimes a single procedure is followed to achieve both attachment and perfection, but some liens require two separate legal acts to be accomplished.

The importance of a lien's validity against third parties cannot be too strongly emphasized. If the creditor's right to the property is enforceable only against the debtor, the creditor has no protection against the claims of third parties who subsequently acquire rights in the property. Such a transferee of the property will be able to acquire it free of the lien, and the creditor will be left with a suit on the debt against the defaulting debtor. However, if the right to the property is perfected, the property will remain subject to the creditor's claim, which cannot usually be extinguished by the subsequent transfer of the property or rights in it.

§2.3.1 Attachment

For a creditor to acquire a lien in the debtor's property that is valid against the debtor, some transaction or relationship must exist from which such an interest arises. A creditor does not, merely by virtue of being owed money, receive rights in the debtor's property. The lien may attach because of the terms of a contract, because a statute or common law grants it to secure payment for services performed on the property, because equity recognizes the lien, or because the use of a particular judicial process gives rise to a lien. This is discussed more fully in section 2.4. For now, it may be observed that the law that provides for the creation of each type of lien will prescribe the requirements for attachment, such as the execution of a contract in proper form, the giving of a notice following the rendition of some service, or the completion of some other act or process.

§2.3.2 Perfection

The rules governing perfection vary depending upon the type of lien in question. For some liens, the very act of attachment required to create a lien valid against the debtor will simultaneously perfect the lien and make the interest effective against third parties, making any additional procedure unnecessary. However, many liens do not fall under this rule and do require some additional step to be taken before the lienholder's rights will avail against third parties. This usually involves either possession and control of the property by the lienholder, or some form of recording designed to publicize the interest.

§2.3.3 Summary

The attachment date is the date on which the lien becomes enforceable against the debtor, but the perfection date is the date on which it becomes effective against third parties. This means that until the acts required for perfection have been completed, the lienholder is not fully protected. Although an enforceable lien exists against the debtor, it has not yet been turned into a right of universal effect. It could therefore be defeated if some third party acquires rights in the property, whether voluntarily or under compulsion of law. (This does not mean that every subsequent third party will necessarily take precedence over the unperfected lien. Some later transferees will not prevail over a prior unperfected lienholder. This is discussed in section 2.7.)

§2.4 THE DIFFERENT CATEGORIES OF LIEN

Lien classification is not simply a technical or formal exercise. It has significant substantive implications. The different categories of lien are each subject to distinct rules and produce different consequences for their holders, the debtor, and third parties. Each category of liens is made up of a number of specific liens. The liens in each category can be quite diverse in the needs they are designed to meet, the circumstances under which they arise, their procedural prerequisites and the level of protection that they bestow on the lienholder.

What follows below is not a comprehensive treatment of all the liens that may be found in each category. However, some of the more common liens are described and used as illustrations.

§2.4.1 Consensual Liens

A consensual lien is created by contract between the debtor and the creditor. The two most common forms of consensual lien are a security interest in personal property, created under UCC Article 9, and a mortgage on real property. The contract must be valid and enforceable under the common law of contracts, and it must also comply with the specific rules of statute or common law that govern the creation of the particular security interest. At a minimum, the contract must describe the property and contain a grant of the interest to secure the debt. Other terms may be required for validity. Apart from that, the arrangement is consensual, so the parties have discretion in formulating the detailed terms and conditions under which the lien is granted and may be enforced.

The grant of the lien is usually part of the consideration demanded by the creditor for the extension of credit. It is often found in the contract that governs the underlying debt, or is executed simultaneously with it. However, as mentioned in section 2.2.3, these two elements do not have to be contemporaneous. (Examples 1, 2, and 3 illustrate consensual liens.)

§2.4.2 Judicial Liens

Judicial liens arise out of the court proceedings initiated by the creditor for recovery of the debt. They are not dependent on a contract with the debtor but are imposed on the debtor's property as a consequence of a particular legal procedure followed in the suit. The distinction between attachment and perfection is not relevant to most judicial liens because a single act or event both creates and perfects the lien.

Some judicial liens may come into existence prior to judgment. For example, under some circumstances the plaintiff-creditor, through the process of prejudgment attachment, may be entitled to seize property of the debtor and to have the property held as security for the prospective judgment. This seizure creates an attachment lien. Other judicial liens arise only upon or after judgment. For example, the judgment itself, when properly recorded or docketed in the prescribed recording office, creates a lien on real property in the county of recording or docketing. The levy of execution on property following judgment gives rise to an execution lien on the property.

Judicial liens are essentially last-ditch affairs. They are neither planned for nor obtained at the inception of the debt. A judicial lienholder is, in fact, nothing more than a formerly unsecured creditor who has been able to exercise the right to levy on property or to docket a judgment as part of the process of enforcing the debt by judicial action. As noted in section 1.4, there is an element of luck in acquiring the status of judicial lienholder. If the debtor is in some financial trouble, competition for assets may be fierce and a creditor may find that the debtor has no lienable property left. Even if a creditor is able to obtain a judicial lien, it is not assured that the advantage of security will not be lost. If the debtor should become bankrupt shortly after the lien is obtained, the bankruptcy trustee may be able to avoid the lien as a preference. This is discussed in Chapter 16. Judicial liens are discussed further in sections 3.3 and 3.4 and are illustrated by Examples 2, 3, and 4 in Chapter 3.

§2.4.3 Statutory Liens

Many consensual and judicial liens are governed by statute. For example, UCC Article 9 applies to security interests in personal property, and the state's civil procedure code typically provides for judicial liens. However, even though these liens may be controlled or permitted by statute, they are not statutory liens. True statutory liens are not created by contract or judicial process but arise under the terms of a statute because the legislature has determined that a creditor of that class or a debt of that type is worthy of the protection of security, even in the absence of an agreement to create the lien. Some statutory liens have antecedents in common law and are merely legislative codifications or modifications of preexisting common law liens while others are legislative innovations.

There are many different types of statutory liens. Three of the most common are the landlord's lien, the repairer's lien (also known as the artisan's lien), and the construction lien (also known as the mechanic's or materialman's lien.) These liens are described briefly as examples and are followed by a survey of some of the common features of statutory liens.

A landlord's lien is granted to a lessor of premises. (Although this lien was originally a common law lien, it is now typically codified by statute. It was originally available to all landlords, but is now usually not permitted in residential leases and is confined to commercial premises.) Because the lien arises by operation of law, the tenant need not agree to it. It comes into effect if the tenant defaults on rent payments. It extends to all the tenant's personal property brought onto the premises. The lien attaches at a specified date after the rent becomes due. To perfect the lien and maintain perfection, the landlord must take and retain physical possession of the tenant's personal property.

The repairer's lien was created by common law but is now commonly codified. It grants a lien to the repairer of personal property to secure the price or value of the repairs. Customarily, the lien is possessory — that is, possession is the act of publicity and control that creates and perfects the lien against the owner and third parties. Where possession is the required means of perfection, the repairer must keep the repaired property until he has been paid. If he relinquishes the property, the lien lapses. Many contemporary statutes provide for filing as an alternative means of perfection. Where filing is a permitted means of perfection, a lienholder who complies with the filing requirements can return the property without losing the lien. (*See* Example 4.)

The construction lien is purely statutory in derivation and has no common law antecedent. It is available to any person who, at the request of the owner of real property or his actual or constructive agent, supplies labor, services, or material in connection with the repair or improvement of the real property. Because prime contractors on construction projects usually subcontract work, hire laborers, and buy materials to perform the construction, these subcontractors, laborers, and material suppliers are commonly protected by the construction lien statute, even though they never contracted directly with the owner of the property. The rules governing construction liens are particularly intricate, but their essential purpose and effect is quite straightforward: If the contractor, subcontractor, or material supplier is not paid for its work or services, it is entitled to assert a lien on the real property within a specific time after the completion of its performance. The right to the lien arises in inchoate form as soon as the value is furnished by the claimant, and it must be fully perfected by notice, filing, and suit within a period prescribed by the statute. (*See* Example 4.)

Apart from these three, there are many other examples of statutory liens, such as the lien on crops or harvests in favor of agricultural workers to secure the value of their labor; the attorney's lien on a documentary work product, to secure professional fees; and liens in favor of the state and federal governments to secure unpaid assessed taxes. Some of these liens were originally recognized by common law, and others were created by statute.

While statutory liens all have particular features set out in the statute that creates the lien, they do typically have a number of features in common:

(1) *A statutory basis.* The lien is, of course, provided for by statute (either state or federal). The statutes are very specific about the type of debt and the class of creditor that may benefit from the lien and about the identity of the property that is subject to the lien. The transaction and the creditor must fall within the protected category for the lien to be claimed and the property must be lienable under the statute.

(2) *Strict procedural requirements.* Lien statutes prescribe the procedures that must be followed for creation of the lien and usually require the creditor to take certain steps to claim it. These requirements can be very exacting, and the courts normally demand careful compliance as a prerequisite to lien validity.

(3) *Attachment and perfection.* Most statutory liens are subject to the general principle that some form of notice or possession is required to effectuate the lien against the debtor, and some form of control or publicity is necessary to make the lien viable against third parties who claim rights in the property. Sometimes a single act will accomplish both ends.

2. Secured Debt and Priorities

(4) An underlying relationship. Even though statutory liens are not consensual, they are obviously founded in some underlying relationship between the lienholder and the person whose property is subject to the lien. In some cases this relationship may itself be contractual in nature, but contractual privity in the underlying relationship is not always a prerequisite. The lien may be based on other grounds, such as an implied agency, the breach of a statutory duty, or unjust enrichment. When conferring a statutory lien on a particular class of creditor, the legislature has made the determination that there is some equity in favor of the creditor or some special merit to its claim, so that the law should afford the protection of security, notwithstanding that such security was never bargained for with the debtor.

§2.4.4 Common Law Liens

Common law liens are quite similar to statutory liens in their underlying purpose and effect. They arise by operation of law, without the agreement of the debtor, to secure an otherwise unsecured obligation incurred in a particular transaction recognized at common law as worthy of protection. The difference between them is that common law liens have not been created or codified by statute but are recognized under principles of common law applied by the courts. The most familiar common law liens are very old. They apply only to personal property, and they require possession for their creation and continued validity. They arise only when possession of the personal property is obtained and expire as soon as it is lost.

Many liens that originally arose from common law have been codified and have thereby been converted to statutory form. In the process of codification, legislatures have often restricted or expanded the scope of the lien, imposed new regulations on it, or provided for perfection by filing as an alternative to the traditional possessory form. Because of this legislative activity, common law liens are less frequently encountered today than they used to be.

As noted in section 2.4.3, several of the statutory liens used as examples there originated at common law (and in some states may still be uncodified and based in common law), such as the artisan's lien, the landlord's lien, and the attorney's lien.

§2.4.5 Equitable Liens

Like judicial liens, equitable liens derive from the judicial process, though the circumstances and the purposes of their creation are quite different.

Equitable liens do not arise as an incident of collection procedures at law, but are a remedy granted by the court in the exercise of its equitable jurisdiction.

The role of the equitable lien can be illustrated by an example: An employee embezzles money from an employer and uses it as part of the purchase price of a new car. The employer sues the employee for recovery of the embezzled funds. In awarding restitution, the court may impress an equitable lien on the car to ensure that the employer will be able to recover the stolen money by seizing and selling the very item that was bought with it.

The traditional role of equity is to provide relief where available legal remedies are inadequate. Therefore, a creditor who claims equitable relief must usually show that legal remedies cannot place it in its rightful position. However, the mere fact that legal remedies are inadequate or unavailable is not necessarily enough to make a case for equitable relief. The court will balance all the equities in exercising its discretion to grant a remedy in equity. For example, say that a subcontractor was hired by a prime contractor to perform work on a construction project. After it did the work, but before it was paid, both the prime contractor and the property owner became bankrupt, and the subcontractor had no prospect of recovering the price of its work from them as an unsecured creditor. The subcontractor would have been entitled to a construction lien on the owner's property to secure the value of the unpaid work, but the subcontractor failed to file the lien claim within the period required by statute. Because of this failure, the subcontractor has lost the legal protection of the statutory lien. Even though the subcontractor has no adequate legal remedy, the court would not be likely to award it an equitable lien on the property. To do so would undermine the procedural requirements of the statute and condone the subcontractor's negligent failure to protect its own interests.

§2.5 THE EFFECT OF A VALID LIEN

§2.5.1 The Lien's Effect Against the Debtor and Subsequent Transferees

A transfer of property conveys only those rights that the transferor has in the property. Therefore, a transferee acquires the debtor's property subject to any encumbrances on the debtor's ownership. This means that once the creditor has properly complied with the rules governing attachment and perfection of the lien, an interest is created in the property that is effective not only against the debtor but also against any third party who thereafter acquires an interest in the property, whether by voluntary transfer (*e.g.*, purchase) or involuntary transfer (*e.g.*, execution).

If the debtor defaults on the secured debt, the lienholder is entitled to foreclose on the lien, and the interest of any subsequent transferee is confined to whatever surplus may be left after the lien has been fully satisfied. There are exceptions to this general rule, which are dealt with in section 2.7 and in later chapters. However, the rule is widely applicable, and in most cases the perfected lienholder is fully protected from the claims of persons whose interests arose after the lien.

§2.5.2 The Lien's Effect On Preexisting Third-Party Interests in the Property

The same rule that protects the lienholder against subsequent transferees makes the lien subservient to third-party interests in the property that were perfected before the lien. These preexisting interests may be earlier perfected liens or other recorded (and sometimes unrecorded) rights that have been conveyed by the debtor or imposed on the property by law. (Section 2.7 has a more detailed discussion of the ranking of rights in property.)

Because the lien is subject to valid preexisting third-party rights in the property, a prospective lienholder should check filing records and make other appropriate inquiries before agreeing to give credit to the debtor on the strength of a security interest in property. If the lender does not investigate, it may later find that superior interests encumber all or a substantial portion of the property's value. (Of course, a nonconsensual lienholder, such as a judicial lienholder, does not have the same opportunities for planning as a person who acquires a lien by contract.)

§2.5.3 Oversecured and Undersecured Debt

The security afforded by collateral is only as valuable as the property itself. If the value of the property (or, the remaining value, if there are already senior claims of record) is less than the amount of the debt, a portion of the debt will be unsecured. When the property is liquidated, this unsecured balance — the deficiency — will be left unsatisfied. To collect it, the lienholder must undertake the uncertain collection process outlined in section 1.4.

To avoid or at least to minimize the risk of a deficiency, a prospective lienor must satisfy itself that the debtor's equity (i.e., the debtor's unencumbered economic interest) in the property is worth enough to cover the debt. If the value of the debtor's equity just barely covers the debt, the lienholder has no margin of safety to accommodate possible depreciation of the property or to cover accumulation of interest or any legal fees that may be incurred in trying to collect the debt. For this reason, a careful prospective lienholder tries to ensure that the value of the collateral exceeds the debt (as well as any senior claims) by a comfortable margin. This excess of collateral value over the debt is known as an "equity cushion": It is the debtor's surplus equity that can absorb any adverse change in the ratio of collateral to debt.

Thus, in addition to checking for preexisting interests in the proposed collateral, a careful prospective lienholder must also attempt to make a realistic appraisal of the property and an accurate prediction of likely decreases in its value. The lienholder should also take precautions to ensure that the property is protected from damage or destruction during the period of the lien. These precautions could include contract provisions that regulate the use of the property and require the debtor to keep it insured, as well as periodic monitoring of the collateral. As stated before, these opportunities for planning are more likely to be available where the lien arises out of a contractual relationship. A nonconsensual lien-holder must usually settle for whatever property is available.

§2.6 ENFORCEMENT OF THE LIEN

The procedure for enforcing liens varies considerably depending on the type of lien involved. This description is therefore just a generalized overview of basic principles. A comparison of the enforcement process sketched here to that for unsecured debt (described in section 1.4) shows why security is a potent right. *See* Example 1.

Liens are enforced by the process of foreclosure. Some liens require judicial foreclosure — the lienholder must obtain a judgment of foreclosure before proceeding with enforcement. Other liens can be enforced by creditor action immediately upon default, and the foreclosure does not come before a court unless it is challenged by the debtor or some other interested party. The realization of the collateral involves two steps. The first is the seizure of the property, and the second is its application to satisfaction of the debt.

§2.6.1 Seizure of the Property

As mentioned in sections 2.3.2 and 2.4, some liens are perfected by the creditor taking possession of the property. (For example, possession is the means of perfecting a possessory security interest under UCC Article 9 and some statutory or common law liens.) Because the lienholder is already in possession of the property at the time of default, no act of seizure is needed, although some form of notice may be required.

If the lienholder does not already have possession at the time of default, it must seize the collateral as a prelude to foreclosure sale. With some liens, this seizure of the property can be accomplished by the lienholder on its own, without the assistance of the court. This is known as "self-help." In other cases (or if the debtor resists the lienholder's attempt at seizure), a court order and the employment of court officials is necessary. If litigation concerning the foreclosure is likely to take some time, the lienholder may be able to replevy the collateral pending final determination of the suit. *See* section 3.3.5.

§2.6.2 Application of the Property in Satisfaction of the Debt

Once the property is placed under the lienholder's control, the process of realizing it takes place. There are two methods of applying the property to satisfaction of the debt: foreclosure by sale and strict foreclosure. Strict foreclosure is not universally available and can only be used with regard to certain types of liens, so foreclosure by sale is more typical.

a. Foreclosure by Sale

The most common method of applying the collateral to the payment of the debt is by foreclosure sale. In the case of some liens (an Article 9 security interest, for example), the sale may be conducted by the lienholder itself, and in others the sale is handled by the sheriff or a similar court official. Normally, the sale is by public auction, but private sales by the lienholder are authorized for some liens (Article 9, for example). Foreclosure sales are regulated by statute to ensure that they are honest, properly conducted, and offer the best chance possible of maximizing the proceeds of the sale. However, the reality is that these distress sales often do not realize as much value as the property would have attracted had it been sold in the normal course on the market. Therefore, unless the statute provides otherwise, foreclosure sales are not usually overturned in the absence of improper sale procedures merely because the price was not equivalent to the normal market value. With regard to some liens on some property, the debtor may have an equity of redemption, which allows the debtor to avert the foreclosure sale by paying the debt and costs in full before the sale.

Once the property has been sold in accordance with the prescribed procedure, the proceeds are applied to the payment of the debt, including the costs and charges of the sale. If the price realized is insufficient to cover the debt in full, a deficiency is due to the creditor by the debtor. With some liens, foreclosure operates as a waiver of the action on the debt, so that the deficiency cannot be recovered. In many cases this is not so, however, and the creditor can proceed to recover the deficiency from the debtor as an unsecured debt, following the procedure outlined in section 1.4. If the price paid at the sale exceeds the amount of the debt and foreclosure costs, the surplus is applied to payment of the claims of any junior lienholders who are parties to the foreclosure. *See* section 2.7. If no such claimants exist, or if there is a surplus remaining after they have been paid, the balance is paid to the debtor.

The lienholder is usually allowed to bid and buy at its own public foreclosure sale. This benefits the lienholder where the distress price is lower than the market price, because the lienholder acquires the property at an advantageous price and credits the deflated sale price against the debt. Where the law does not bar the foreclosing lienholder from claiming the deficiency from the debtor, the lienholder has a claim against the debtor for the deficiency.

b. Strict Foreclosure

For some liens, strict foreclosure is available to lienholders as an alternative to foreclosure by sale. In strict foreclosure, the lienholder does not sell the property but takes transfer of it from the debtor in full satisfaction of the debt. This means that the lienholder has no right to claim a deficiency and no obligation to pay any surplus to the debtor.

Although strict foreclosure may sometimes be the same in effect as the lienholder's purchase of the property at the foreclosure sale — especially where a deficiency action is barred after sale — the two remedies are distinct. At a foreclosure sale there is always a possibility of competing bids, and a chance that a surplus may be realized. If the lien is strictly foreclosed, no bidding takes place and there is no recoverable deficiency or accounting for surplus value. Therefore, a lienholder will only elect strict foreclosure if the value of the property equals or exceeds the debt. Because the debtor loses the surplus equity in strict foreclosure, this process is not allowed for many types of lien. Even where it is permitted (for example, in UCC Article 9), it is subject to limitations, controls, and a right of objection.

Foreclosure issues are illustrated in Examples 1 and 2.

---

§2.7 PRIORITIES AMONG LIENS AND OTHER INTERESTS

§2.7.1 The Function of Priority Rules

It often happens that more than one lien is created in a single piece of property. For example, a homeowner whose home is already subject to a first mortgage may borrow money on the security of a second mortgage, or a car repairer may acquire a repairer's lien in a car that is already subject to a security interest, or a judgment creditor may acquire a judicial lien on property that is already encumbered by someone else.

When the property is valuable enough to accommodate all the liens against it as well as all legal costs and fees, ranking of the liens is not practically important. If foreclosure occurs, enough proceeds will be realized to satisfy all the liens. However, when the property is worth less than the total amount of liens, there must be rules to determine how the fund should be distributed between them. The law does not usually treat all liens as equal so that they share in the proceeds of the collateral pro rata. Rather, it ranks the liens, and the proceeds are applied to the full satisfaction of each lien in order of priority until the fund is exhausted.

For example, suppose collateral worth $900 has three liens on it, each securing a debt of $500. The senior lien is paid in full. The second-ranking lien receives the remaining proceeds of $400, leaving an unsecured deficiency of $100. The junior lien receives nothing and becomes an unsecured claim.

This section introduces the concept of priority and surveys the general principles applicable to the ranking of liens and interests in property. Priority is a pervasive issue in debtor/creditor law, and the themes discussed here will be raised and built upon in many later chapters on both state law and bankruptcy.

§2.7.2 The General Rule of Priority

The most common method of ranking is based on the chronological sequence in which the liens arose. That is, the earliest lien has first claim to the proceeds, followed by subsequent liens, in the order that they arose. The "first-in-time" rule derives from the general principle, introduced in section 2.5, that rights conveyed in property cannot exceed those held by the transferee. Therefore, if a debtor's property is already encumbered by a valid lien, a second and subsequent lien can only extend to the debtor's unencumbered equity in the property.

The effective date of a lien for priority purposes is usually its perfection date. This stands to reason, because it is perfection that makes the lien viable against persons other than the debtor. See section 2.3.2. Sometimes a statute or the common law recognizes an exception to this general rule and allows the lien's priority to date from attachment or to backdate to the date of attachment once it is perfected. See Examples 6 and 7.

§2.7.3 Departures from the First-in-Time Rule for the Protection of Certain Subsequent Lienholders

Although the earlier lien is generally given priority, in a number of situations a statute or a court decision creates an exception to this rule. Therefore, while one can usually assume that liens rank in order of seniority, it is important to consult the law applicable to the competing interests to make sure that no exception applies. The repairer's (or artisan's) lien illustrates one situation in which the first-in-time rule does not apply. As noted in sections 2.4.3 and 2.4.4, a repairer of goods is entitled to a statutory or common law lien to secure the price or value of the repairs. This lien usually takes priority over an existing security interest in the goods because the repair has maintained or enhanced the value of the property. If the preexisting lien took priority over the repairer's lien, the senior lienholder would be unfairly benefited by the repair at the expense of the unpaid repairer.

§2.7.4 Priorities between Liens and Other Interests in the Property

Priority disputes are not confined to competing lienholders. A co-owner or purchaser of the property, or some other person or entity that has legal or equitable rights in it, may be in competition with the holder of a lien. These priority disputes are governed by the same general rules as apply to competing liens: The interest that first took effect usually prevails. If a valid co-ownership interest existed when the lien was created, or the debtor had validly transferred the property or rights in the property prior to the effective date of the lien, the lien only extends to any interest that the debtor may have retained. Similarly, if the debtor conveys rights in the property after the effective date of the lien, the transferee takes subject to the lien.

As in the case of competing liens, exceptions to this general rule are intended to protect certain parties who acquire rights in the property in good faith and in circumstances under which they are not expected to be concerned about other interests or to check public filing records. For example, a department store may have borrowed money to purchase inventory and may have secured the loan by giving the lender a security interest in the inventory. If the first-in-time rule was to be rigidly applied, a customer who buys goods from the department store would take the goods subject to the financier's priority security interest in the inventory. Even if the customer paid the store for the goods, the financier could assert its interest in them if the store defaulted on its loan. Because such a rule would make consumer transactions very risky and would inhibit retail trading, the first-in-time rule is not applied in this case. Title to the goods passes to the customer free of the financier's security interest, provided that the purchase was an honest, routine transaction.

§2.7.5 A Summary of the Issues to Be Considered in Dealing with Priorities

The ranking of liens and interests becomes important when the property is not valuable enough to satisfy all the claims against it. Use a three-step process to determine priorities:

Step 1: Determine if all the competing liens and interests are valid and effective. An invalid or unenforceable claim to the property cannot have priority, even if it was purportedly created before its competitors. To decide this question, one must identify the liens or interests and the nature of the property in which they are asserted. Then, the applicable statute or common law rule must be consulted to determine whether each lien or interest has been properly created and effected.

Step 2: Consult the applicable statute or common law rule to determine the effective date of each lien or interest. Usually, the effective date for priority purposes is the perfection date, but there are exceptions to this rule.

Step 3: Identify and apply the rules of ranking. The first-in-time rule commonly applies, but a statute or rule of common law may provide for a different treatment between these competing liens or interests.

Examples

1. Grim Repo, Inc. sold a video security system to Minnie Mart on credit for use in her convenience store. At the time of sale, Grim Repo had Minnie sign a security agreement that granted it a security interest in the security system to secure its purchase price. The security system qualifies as goods, and Grim Repo's interest is governed by UCC Article 9. The security agreement complies with Article 9 and is valid. Grim Repo immediately filed a copy of the agreement with the Secretary of State, which is the appropriate state recording office for Article 9 security interests.

    A few weeks later, Minnie failed to pay an installment due under the contract. She has persisted in her default despite a demand for payment by Grim Repo.

    What course of action can Grim Repo take? How do its rights differ from those of a seller who sold goods on unsecured credit?

2. How would you answer Example 1 if, just before Minnie stopped paying her installments, she sold the security system for cash to a used electronics store?

3. Pawnporker Industries, Inc. manufactures bacon and sausages, which it sells to grocery chains and wholesalers. It typically sells to its customers on credit, and it always has a large volume of outstanding accounts receivable. Pawnporker's receipts from customers trickle in too slowly to meet its demands for cash. To assure the liquidity needed to pay its expenses without having to wait for payments from its customers, Pawnporker entered into a loan agreement with Couchon Equity, Inc. The loan is secured by its customers' accounts. The security agreement provides that Couchon Equity will advance funds to Pawnporker in an amount equal to 75 percent of its current accounts receivable. As customers pay, Pawnporker is obliged to remit a percentage of its receipts to Couchon Equity to reduce the loan balance. All new accounts that are created by future sales will automatically be included in Couchon Equity's security interest. Provided that Pawnporker complies fully with the terms of the security agreement, Couchon Equity will make additional advances to Pawnporker in the future. These advances will fall within the existing security interest and will be secured by Pawnporker's accounts.
   a. Can something as nebulous as accounts serve as collateral?
   b. Is a transaction like this valid? More specifically, can parties create a security interest that covers not only existing collateral and advances, but also collateral that comes into being and advances that are made in the future?

4. One evening, as Alec Smart was returning home from work, he swung his car into his driveway. As was his habit, he jabbed at the button on his garage door opener as he entered the driveway at excessive speed, intending to zoom into the garage just under the rising door. Alec had executed this maneuver successfully in the past, and he enjoyed the sensation of split-second timing as the car barely cleared the moving door. On this occasion, he was not as agile as usual. His finger missed the button, and the door did not open.
   a. The next day he took his crumpled car to Arty Zan, a specialist in restoring auto bodies. Arty quoted a price of $1,000 to repair the damage, and Alec accepted. Arty set to work immediately and completed the repair two days later. When Alec arrived to collect his car, Arty presented his account. Alec told Arty that he had left his checkbook at home and promised to mail a check to Arty as soon as he returned home. Arty refused to release the car to Alec until he received payment of the repair charges. Is Arty justified in holding on to the car?

b. On the same day that he took his car to Arty, Alec employed Mac & Nick's Construction Co. to remove his mangled garage door, repair the door frame, and install a new door. The contract price for this work was $5,000. Mac & Nick's completed the repair, and Alec gave it a check for $5,000. The check was subsequently dishonored. Does Mac & Nick's have any security to protect it as it seeks to recover the money from Alec?

5. Buddy Beautiful bought a bodybuilding machine from Señor Lean Sweatshop on credit. He signed a contract that obliged him to pay the price of $3,000 in monthly installments over one year. This was a simple sale on credit. The contract did not grant a security interest to Señor Lean to secure the price. Two weeks after Buddy took delivery of the machine, one of his creditors obtained a judgment against him and obtained a writ of execution. The sheriff levied on the machine pursuant to the writ. Señor Lean found out about this before the sale in execution took place. Is Señor Lean entitled to demand release of the machine from the sheriff?

6. Crash Land Investments, Inc. owns a plot of land, which is its only asset. Although the land was worth about $500,000 a couple of years ago, there has been a downturn in the real estate market, and it is now reliably appraised at $250,000. Over the last five years, the following interests have been created in the property:

a. Five years ago Crash Land borrowed money from Foremost Finance, Inc. and granted a mortgage in the property to Foremost to secure the loan. The mortgage was properly executed and recorded at the time that the loan was advanced. The current balance on the mortgage is $200,000.

b. Two years ago, Crash Land borrowed money from Sequacious Security, Inc. and granted a second mortgage on the property to Sequacious to secure that loan. The mortgage was properly executed and recorded at the time that the loan was advanced. The current balance on the second mortgage is $80,000.

c. Last year, Crash Land failed to pay taxes due on the property and the county recorded a tax lien on the property. The arrear taxes secured by the lien are $3,000.

d. A few weeks before the county filed the tax lien, Sally Fourth obtained a judgment against Crash Land for $20,000. Sally docketed the judgment in the real property records of the county in which the property is situated a week after the tax lien was filed.

Crash Land is insolvent and cannot pay its debts. If the property is foreclosed upon and realizes its value of $250,000. how should the proceeds be distributed? (Disregard foreclosure costs and assume that the full $250,000 is available to pay the claims against the property.)

7. Given your answer to Example 6, could any one of the parties have done anything earlier in its transaction to improve the priority of its claim to the proceeds of the property?

Explanations

1. Grim Repo has a consensual security interest in the security system, governed by UCC Article 9. Because the credit was given to Minnie to enable her to acquire the goods, the security interest in the goods is a purchase money security interest. Because the agreement was properly executed, the security interest attached at that time. Upon recording the interest in compliance with Article 9, Grim Repo perfected it.

   Following Minnie's default, UCC Article 9 permits Grim Repo to repossess the goods. It may do so on its own, without a court order, provided that it can effect the repossession without a breach of the peace. After taking possession of the goods, Grim Repo has the right to sell them either at auction or by way of private sale. Article 9 also permits the alternative of strict foreclosure if specified conditions are satisfied. No court is involved in this stage of the procedure either, unless Minnie files a suit challenging some aspect of it. Even if Minnie is able to delay the sale by instituting court proceedings, Grim Repo will probably be able to obtain possession of the goods pending final determination of the action by applying for prejudgment replevin.

   If you compare Grim Repo's enforcement rights as described here with the enforcement rights of an unsecured seller, described in section 1.4, you will see that the secured creditor's priority right to seize and sell specified collateral gives it a significant advantage. It does not have to engage in the chancy and often futile and expensive process of trying to find assets to satisfy its judgment.

2. A third party has purchased the goods and taken transfer of them. As a general matter, Grim Repo, as a prior perfected secured party, will take precedence over the rights of a subsequent buyer of the goods under the first-in-time principle. There are some exceptions to this rule, but they do not apply in this case. (Note also that the cash received by Minnie from the sale qualifies as proceeds of Grim Repo's collateral and the security interest extends to the cash as well, provided that it can be identified as proceeds and Minnie still has it.)

3. a. Accounts can serve as collateral. Unlike the goods in Examples 1 and 2, the accounts have no physical existence. They are intangible claims that Pawnporker has against its customers. Nevertheless, they have economic value to the extent that they represent collectible funds due to the debtor in the future, and they are an asset that can be used as

collateral to secure a loan to the debtor. Their intangible nature necessitates some variation in the rules governing the creation and enforcement of a consensual lien in them. These details are beyond our scope, but it is enough to note that as with goods, the interest must attach. This occurs when the agreement is executed, value is given by the secured party, and the accounts come into existence. In addition, the interest must be perfected by filing. A security interest in accounts, as well as in many other intangible assets, is subject to UCC Article 9.

b. As stated in sections 2.2.3 and 2.2.4, a security interest can be structured to cover after-acquired collateral and future advances. The interest is effective immediately with regard to the first advance and the current accounts. As new accounts arise, it will attach to them, and when further advances are made, they will be added to the debt secured by the collateral.

The facts of this Example illustrate why parties may wish to enter into a transaction of this type. They contemplate a continuing relationship that is much more complex than the single secured sale in Example 1. The collateral is not constant or fixed but will change over time as current accounts are paid by customers and new ones are generated by future sales. The debt will also fluctuate as payments are made, and new amounts are advanced.

Because it is inefficient for the parties to create a new security interest each time Pawnporker needs money and to file new financing statements each time new accounts are created, they have set up what is known as a floating lien at the beginning of the relationship. A security interest is created immediately in all the accounts of Pawnporker, both current and future, to secure both present and future advances. The description of the collateral in the agreement and the financing statement (i.e., the document filed to record the interest) expressly covers after-acquired accounts.

A transaction of this kind requires careful monitoring by Couchon Equity. It must keep track of payments by Pawnporker's customers to make sure that the loan is being repaid as accounts are settled. It will not make new advances until a sufficient volume of new accounts have been generated to cover the existing loan balance plus the new advance. It will also ensure that the ratio of equity to debt stays within an acceptable margin of safety, so that there is an equity cushion to buffer its interest against reductions in collateral value resulting from uncollectable accounts or other contingencies.

This transaction is represented diagrammatically in Diagram 2a.

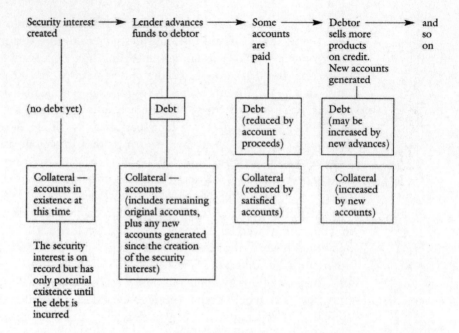

4. Arty and Mac & Nick's have both entered into contracts with Alec under which they have provided labor and materials for the repair of his property. However, neither of the repairers has been granted a consensual lien by Alec to secure the contract price.

    It is common for states to afford such people special protection by granting them liens on the repaired property to secure the agreed price (or, in some cases, the reasonable value) of their services and supplies. The rationale for conferring lien rights on these claimants is that they have furnished performance at the request of the debtor that has conserved or enhanced his property and that it would be unfair to allow the debtor to keep that benefit without paying for it.

    a. Arty Zan is justified in holding on to the car. He has a repairer's lien (or artisan's lien), as described in section 2.4.3, which secures his claim for payment for the repairs to the car. Arty has retained possession of the car, so the lien is perfected. (Traditionally, possession is the only means of perfection, but some states now allow perfection by recording.) The lien is provided for by statute (or common law) so Arty acquires it by virtue of performing the repairs, and it is not necessary that Alec agree to grant the lien to Arty.

    b. Mac & Nick's is entitled to a construction lien, as described in section 2.4.3. To acquire the lien, Mac & Nick's must follow the procedures set out in the statute to perfect it. Typically, the claimant is given a period of time after completion of the work to file a lien claim against the real estate records and must then commence suit on the claim within a specified time. The statute may contain additional procedures to give the owner notice of the lien, especially where the lien is asserted against residential property.

5. Señor Lean is an unsecured seller who retained no interest in or ownership of the machine sold to Buddy. Title to the machine passed upon the sale, and Señor Lean was left with an unsecured debt for its price. (*See* section 1.4.) The judgment creditor obtained a judicial lien when the sheriff levied on the machine and Señor Lean has no basis to assert prior rights in the machine. As an unsecured creditor, Señor Lean's only remedy is to insist on payment under the contract and if Buddy defaults, to commence collection proceedings against him in the hope that he has other assets that can be levied upon to satisfy the judgment.

6. Each of the four interests asserted here must be capable of attaching to real property and must be perfected in the manner required for real property:

   a.-b. The mortgages are consensual liens. The facts state that both have been executed and recorded in accordance with the state's law governing mortgages on real property. Mortgages are normally effective upon perfection, that is, when they are recorded.

   c. The county's tax lien is a statutory lien. Unless the statute provides otherwise, it attaches and becomes effective only upon its recordation.

   d. The docketing of a judgment created a judgment lien (a judicial lien) that takes effect on recording in the county real estate records and extends to all real property that the debtor owns in the county. The recording of the judgment, rather than its grant by the court, is normally the effective date of the lien for priority purposes. (Judgment liens are discussed further in section 3.4.)

Based on these principles, Foremost's mortgage was effective first, then Sequacious's mortgage, then the county's tax lien, and, finally, Sally's judgment. Having fixed the effective dates of the interests, we can determine the distribution of the proceeds of the property by applying the first-in-time rule. (This rule applies unless the governing statute or common law doctrine provides otherwise.) This means that Foremost's mortgage of $200,000 is fully satisfied out of the fund of $250,000, leaving a balance of $50,000. This balance is applied to the payment of the mortgage debt of Sequacious. That debt is $80,000, so it is not fully covered by the remaining value in the collateral, leaving a deficiency of $30,000. The county would have been third in line, and Sally would have been fourth, but the fund has run out, and they receive nothing.

7. Only Foremost, the senior secured party, recovered its claim in full. Sequacious received only partial satisfaction of its second mortgage, and the property did not have enough value to cover the two most junior liens. Sequacious, a consensual lienholder, must have known about Foremost's first mortgage when it agreed to lend money to Crash Land, secured by a second mortgage. Presumably, it realized that its interest would be junior to Foremost, but must have decided that the property was valuable enough to cover both claims. It may have been at the time of the transaction, but the value of the property at the time of default is what counts. The downturn in the property market so significantly reduced the property's value that Sequacious was left only partially secured.

   The county and Sally were both unsecured creditors who acquired their liens only after Crash Land defaulted in its payment of the unsecured debts. The county's ability to claim a lien is circumscribed by statute. Property tax liens can usually be filed only after the tax becomes delinquent. The statute could grant special priority to tax liens, but in the absence of a legislative decision to do that, they take effect only upon recording and do not supersede prior interests in the property. Sally extended unsecured credit to Crash Land. She did not protect herself by requiring security when entering the transaction. When she obtained and recorded her judgment, her judgment lien attached to whatever real property the debtor owned in the county. That property was already so heavily encumbered that it had no value left. This illustrates the point made in section 2.4.2 that judicial liens are essentially last-minute rights that may arise too late to be helpful.

Debt Collection under State Law

§3.1 PRELIMINARY OBSERVATIONS ON DEBT COLLECTION BY JUDICIAL PROCESS AT STATE LAW

Section 1.4 contained an overview of debt collection by court proceedings. This chapter deals more fully with state law procedures available to a creditor for the enforcement of a money obligation. Sections 3.1 through 3.8 cover state law judicial proceedings for the collection of debt. A creditor usually resorts to these collection procedures only after the debtor has not paid in response to requests or demands for payment. Section 3.9 introduces nonjudicial insolvency proceedings under state law.

The treatment of state law judicial proceedings is chronological, moving from prejudgment process to the judgment itself and then to postjudgment enforcement methods. The focus here is on enforcement issues, both in the prejudgment stage of the case and after judgment. This activity takes place within a civil suit, which may or may not be defended. If the debtor does not defend the suit, the creditor may obtain judgment by default. If the debtor does defend, judgment will be granted only after the creditor succeeds in the litigation. Whether or not the debtor contests liability, the creditor may be able to seek prejudgment remedies as the case proceeds. Once the creditor has obtained judgment, it must follow postjudgment collection procedures if the debtor fails to satisfy the debt voluntarily. At some point in the process of judicial enforcement, the creditor with a formerly unsecured claim may be able to obtain a judicial lien that secures the claim.

As was discussed in section 1.4, because the debtor's failure to pay may be symptomatic of more extensive financial difficulties, there is often some urgency in the pursuit of collection remedies. Other creditors may be engaged in collection proceedings and competing for the debtor's assets. In addition, the collection efforts may be stayed or reversed by a bankruptcy filing.

This treatment of state law is generalized. Notable and sometimes dramatic variations occur from one state to another. Also, judicial procedures for debt collection may be used in federal courts outside of the bankruptcy context, and these procedures may differ from those in state courts. Where appropriate, alternative approaches are indicated, but no attempt is made to account for all the differences between jurisdictions. Diagram 3a roughly traces the chronology of a debt collection case and identifies the principal issues that are discussed below.

§3.2 EXECUTABLE PROPERTY AND LEVY

When secured claims are involved, the link between the debt and the encumbered property is crucial. *See* Chapter 2. Unsecured claims are not identified with any particular property, but their enforcement is dependent on property of the debtor being found and realized. Unless the debtor pays voluntarily, payment can only be extracted by the seizure and sale of the debtor's property to generate funds to satisfy the judgment. For this reason, the seizure and realization of the debtor's property is a recurring theme in debt collection by judicial process. Two concepts are central to this pervasive theme: executable property and levy.

§3.2.1 Executable Property

Even where the creditor's claim is undisputable and has been reduced to judgment, no enforcement can take place unless the debtor has property that can be applied to payment of the debt. Gone are the happy times when the debtor could be thrown into prison, sold into slavery, or carved up into little bits for failure to pay creditors.[1]

---

1. Imprisonment for debt was recognized by the common law both in England and America until fairly recent times. The Romans were even nastier. They allowed execution on the person of the debtor, so that he could be seized and sold *trans tiberium* (across the Tiber) into slavery. Another possibility in Roman law was for creditors to divide up the body of the debtor and distribute it among themselves. The idea here was to terrorize the debtor's kin and friends into paying his debts.

Although imprisonment for debt has generally been abolished in the United States, some states still allow a creditor to obtain a writ of *capias ad satisfaciendum* (body execution) under certain restricted circumstances. The right to body execution may, for example, be confined to cases where the debt arose out of willful or malicious conduct, or where the debtor is able to pay but deliberately evades payment of the judgment.

3. Debt Collection under State Law

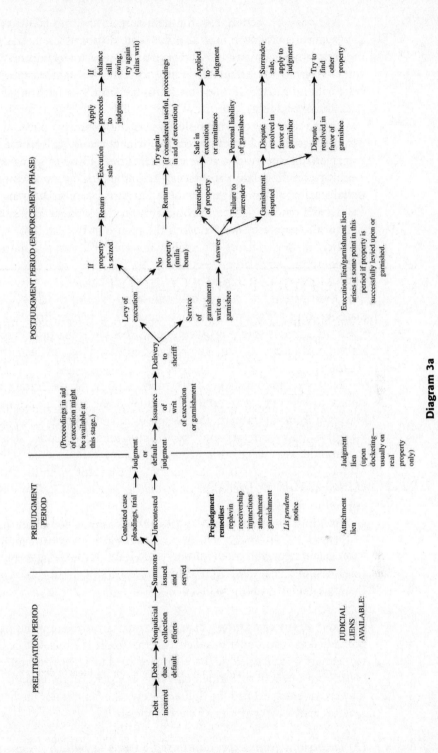

Diagram 3a

As noted in section 1.4, the debtor may have no property available for seizure, because it has already been disposed of, seized by other creditors, or encumbered by prior liens. Even if unencumbered property can be found, the creditor's ability to seize the debtor's property may be further limited: It may be immune from the claims of creditors (*i.e.*, nonexecutable).

In the absence of a specific rule to the contrary, one can generally assume that all the debtor's property, whether tangible or intangible, real or personal, is subject to the claims of creditors. However, some statutes and rules of common law provide exceptions to the general rule and make certain property nonexecutable. The reasons for protecting the property from creditors vary. They may arise from the identity and status of the debtor, the nature of the property, the nature of the claim, or some combination of these factors. The following are the most common bases for excluding property from execution:

(1) Exemptions in favor of individual debtors. By statute, most states exempt certain property of an individual debtor from the claims of creditors. Broadly speaking, exemptions are intended to protect some of the debtor's property so that seizure by creditors does not leave the debtor destitute.

State exemption statutes vary considerably. Some simply allow the debtor to select property up to a particular value; some specifically identify classes or items of property that are protected; some prescribe both categories of exempt property and value limitations. When the worth of the exemptible asset exceeds a value limitation, the asset is only partially exempt: It is subject to execution, but the debtor is entitled to be paid the amount of the exemption out of the proceeds. The surplus is then applied to the debt.

Exemptions are discussed in greater detail in the context of bankruptcy in Chapter 13. However, it is important to note here that exemptions are claimable by the debtor in collection proceedings under state law as well as in bankruptcy. The scope of the exemptions and the procedure for claiming them are dictated by the state exemption statute.

(2) Exemptions of statutory benefits. Apart from exemptions provided to individual debtors under the state's exemption law, other statutes may protect certain property from the claims of creditors. For example, a statute conferring a benefit or entitlement, such as a pension or disability benefits, may provide that neither the right to receive the benefit nor the benefit itself may be seized by creditors of the beneficiary.

(3) Exclusions from execution based on public policy. Some assets are not executable because of various different public policies that are

recognized by statute or common law. For example, if the state wishes to maintain control over the qualifications and character of those who are permitted to sell liquor, it may prohibit the assignment or transfer of liquor licenses whether by voluntary or involuntary means. Another example reflects a different public policy: Because public property serves the interest of the community, the legislature may protect it from seizure by creditors of public authorities. Therefore, the assets of a state, a local authority, or a government agency may be nonexecutable. Another common exclusion from execution protects speculative claims in property. Uncertain interests such as equitable interests in property or contingent or unliquidated claims of the debtor are often not executable. The policy behind this is the protection of the debtor's rights in inherently valuable property that is probably of little worth to the creditor. Because the rights have an uncertain value, they are likely to realize very little in an execution sale in relation to their potential worth to the debtor. Although this is not an exhaustive list, these examples show that when property of the debtor is spoken of in the context of debt enforcement, there is always an implicit qualification that the property must be executable.

§3.2.2 Levy

The law's act of asserting control over the debtor's property on the creditor's behalf is known as levy. The procedures leading up to the act of levy are discussed in sections 3.4 to 3.6. The point to be made at this stage is that until the levy occurs, the debtor's property has not been subjected to the power of the law and the creditor acquires no rights in it by judicial process. The act of levy differs depending on the type of property involved. Levy on tangible personal property is usually the sheriff's act of physically seizing the property, removing it from the debtor, and taking it into custody. In some states, the sheriff may levy on tangible personal property (goods) by taking constructive possession of them by, for example, posting a notice on the goods. (In some states, constructive possession is permitted only where the goods are not readily removable.) Real property is levied upon not by physical seizure but by filing the writ in the real estate records. Intangible rights identified in an indispensable document (e.g., a negotiable instrument or a share certificate) are levied on as if they were tangible goods — the sheriff takes custody of the document. Other intangible rights are levied upon by serving notice on the obligor through the process of garnishment.

Sometimes a writ will specify that the sheriff must levy on specific, identified property. It is quite usual, however, for the writ to simply indicate the amount of the debtor's claim and to call upon the sheriff to find and levy upon sufficient property of the debtor to satisfy it. After completion of the levy, the sheriff submits a return to the court, which reports the action taken and describes the property levied upon.

In summary, levy consists of the actual realization of the court's order or judgment by finding property, placing it in *custodia legis*, and removing it from the debtor's legal (and often physical) control. For many purposes, the act of levy is the legally and practically crucial event in the enforcement process, because it identifies and binds particular property of the debtor to the creditor's claim. In many instances, the levy is the act that gives rise to a judicial lien in the property, thereby affording the creditor some protection against subsequent third parties.

§3.3 JUDICIAL PREJUDGMENT REMEDIES

§3.3.1 General Principles Applicable to All Prejudgment Remedies

Prejudgment remedies (also known as provisional remedies or provisional process) are forms of relief available to an eligible litigant during the period between the commencement of suit and the final judgment in the case. Each prejudgment remedy has its particular purpose, but as a general matter they all serve the same basic goal: to permit the plaintiff to take steps early in the case to ensure that the ultimate judgment will not be a hollow victory. When a creditor initiates suit to recover an overdue debt, it may not know whether there will be any funds or assets to satisfy the debt by the time judgment is obtained. Prejudgment remedies take some of the risk out of the collection suit by allowing an eligible plaintiff[2] to secure executable property in anticipation of a successful judgment.

The most common of these remedies — attachment, prejudgment garnishment, prejudgment replevin, receivership, and injunctions are discussed in sections 3.3.3 to 3.3.7. Section 3.3.8 covers *lis pendens*, which, while not a prejudgment remedy in the usual sense, provides prejudgment protection to the plaintiff in certain cases. Each of the remedies has its own characteristics, purpose, and rules; each is available on specific grounds and may be sought only by a party who qualifies for it. However, because

---

2. Although under appropriate circumstances certain prejudgment remedies are available to defendants (*e.g.*, a defendant may seek an injunction to restrain some act of the plaintiff), these are primarily plaintiff's remedies. They are designed to enhance the plaintiff-creditor's chances of collecting on the ultimate judgment.

prejudgment remedies are available in the phase of the case preceding the final adjudication on the merits, they share three important characteristics:

(1) Prejudgment remedies are ancillary in nature. They are related to and are inextricably tied to an underlying suit initiated by the plaintiff against the defendant. This means that the remedy cannot be sought or granted until the underlying suit has been commenced (or, in some states, is about to be commenced) and that the relief cannot survive if the underlying suit has been dismissed or terminated.

(2) Prejudgment remedies are necessarily provisional and temporary in nature. They are designed to last only until the disposition of the underlying case on its merits. Upon judgment, if the plaintiff succeeds in the action, the relief is incorporated into or superseded by the judgment and its enforcement remedies. If the plaintiff loses, the relief comes to an end. In addition, the defendant is likely to be entitled to an award of damages to compensate for loss caused by the provisional remedy, which, as it turned out, was not justified.

(3) Prejudgment remedies are awarded before the plaintiff has finally established its underlying case on the merits. The grant of the remedy deprives the defendant of property or restrains the defendant from acting before an adjudication of liability on the debt. Because the plaintiff has not yet obtained judgment on the debt when the prejudgment remedy is granted, the interim deprivation of property or the temporary restraint on the defendant's action could cause unjustified harm to the defendant if it later turns out that the plaintiff did not have a valid and enforceable claim against the defendant.

For this reason, prejudgment remedies are carefully controlled. The statutes under which they are granted usually reflect a cautious approach to provisional relief. They require the plaintiff to make a substantive application showing reasonable prospects of success on the merits, and they impose eligibility standards, procedural safeguards, bonding requirements, and plaintiff liability for misuse of the process. Courts typically construe these statutory controls strictly and do not grant relief unless there has been proper compliance with them.

§3.3.2 Due Process in Prejudgment Remedies

The federal constitution and state constitutions protect the defendant's due process rights in the context of prejudgment remedies. In particular, the Fourteenth Amendment requires that a defendant receive proper notice and a meaningful hearing before being deprived of property through the grant of a prejudgment remedy. (Although the creditor seeking the remedy may be a private person, the judicial grant and enforcement of the remedy involve state action, to which the Fourteenth Amendment applies.) The basic protection accorded by the Fourteenth Amendment in the prejudgment context was addressed by the U.S. Supreme Court in the late 1960s and early 1970s,[3] and the requirements laid out by the Court have been incorporated into state prejudgment procedures by statute or judicial decision.

In essence, to satisfy due process standards, in the absence of demonstrated grounds of urgency, the debtor must be given adequate notice of the application for prejudgment relief and be afforded a meaningful opportunity to be heard by a judge before the relief is granted. Where the creditor can show that forewarning the debtor of the application will likely damage the creditor's vital interest or the public interest, an ex parte procedure is permissible. However, this must be regarded as an exceptional case and confined to situations of demonstrated urgency in which compelling reasons exist for dispensing with prior notice and hearing. As a broad principle, a court, when deciding whether to grant ex parte relief, must try to balance the debtor's right to preseizure notice and hearing against the creditor's need for immediate relief. To support an application for ex parte relief, the creditor must file an affidavit containing substantive, nonconclusory factual allegations that demonstrate grounds for relief. In addition, the judge must properly evaluate the application, the debtor must be given the opportunity for a prompt postseizure hearing, and the debtor must be entitled to compensation if the seizure turns out to have been wrongful.

The prejudgment seizure of some types of property is either forbidden or controlled very tightly. For example, the prejudgment garnishment of the wages of an individual debtor is heavily restricted or altogether prohibited.

§3.3.3 Attachment

Attachment is an old remedy. Its original purpose was to compel the appearance in court of a nonresident defendant who had property within the court's jurisdiction. By taking custody of the defendant's property, the court forced him or her to submit to its power. (This is known as "quasi in rem jurisdiction.") As the remedy developed, it acquired a second purpose: The defendant's property was seized early in the case and kept

---

3. See *Sniadach v. Family Finance Corp.*, 395 U.S. 337 (1969); *Fuentes v. Shevin*, 407 U.S. 67 (1972); *Mitchell v. W.T. Grant Co.*, 416 U.S. 600 (1974); and *North Georgia Finishing, Inc. v. Di-Chem, Inc.*, 419 U.S. 601 (1975). The Court revisited these standards in *Connecticut v. Doehr*, 501 U.S. 1 (1991).

in the custody of the law so that when the plaintiff finally obtained judgment, the property was available to be executed upon. The use of attachment to acquire quasi in rem jurisdiction fell away in 1977, upon being declared unconstitutional by the U.S. Supreme Court. Therefore, the only contemporary purpose of attachment is prejudgment seizure of property to secure the plaintiff's claim. Diagram 3b sketches the steps that are likely to be followed in an attachment procedure. It shows both the normal procedure, in which seizure is preceded by notice to the debtor and a hearing, and the emergency ex parte procedure.

Like other prejudgment remedies, attachment is ancillary to a suit on a substantive claim and cannot be sought unless such a suit is in progress. The plaintiff can only apply for it after the issue of summons or, in some states, at least simultaneously with or in immediate anticipation of the commencement of suit. It is not available to all plaintiffs nor in all types of cases. For example, it is commonly confined to money claims or to certain types of money claims, such as claims arising out of an express or implied contract. Attachment may be unavailable for consumer debts, secured debts, or unliquidated debts. In some states, the plaintiff can only obtain attachment by showing special circumstances, such as evasive behavior by the debtor. Traditionally, attachment is available only in legal actions and not in equitable suits. However, equity has a procedure (sequestration) that serves a similar purpose.

The attachment remedy presupposes that the creditor has a simple money claim against the debtor that is unsecured by and unrelated to any specific item of the debtor's property.[4] Therefore, the applicant for attachment does not need to allege a right to any particular asset, but simply asks the court to authorize the attachment of unspecified property of the debtor that is sufficient in value to cover the amount of the debt. Only executable property can be attached. Indeed, in some states attachable property is even more restricted than executable property, so that certain types of property cannot be attached even though they may be executed upon after judgment.

Because attachment deprives the debtor of the possession and use of her property before the creditor has obtained judgment, courts construe attachment statutes strictly and insist that the plaintiff demonstrate eligibility for the remedy and comply exactly with the procedural requirements. An eligible creditor applies for attachment by filing a notice of motion supported by an affidavit that establishes grounds for attachment and shows a prima facie underlying claim on the merits. The creditor must also post a bond indemnifying the debtor for damages for wrongful attachment. The bond guarantees the payment of compensation if the attachment is

---

4. When the creditor does allege a right to or interest in a particular item of property and requires its delivery, other prejudgment remedies, such as replevin (discussed in section 3.3.5) are appropriate.

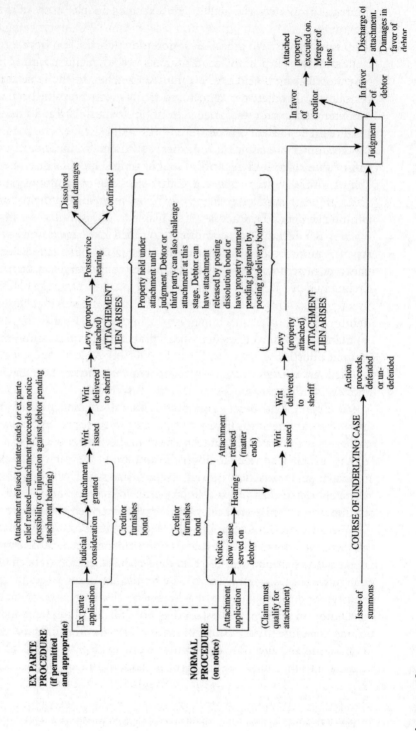

Diagram 3b

42

overturned or the plaintiff fails to obtain judgment in the suit. These requirements protect the debtor as fully as possible from unjustifiable attachment.

Where there are no grounds for ex parte relief, the application is served on the debtor with a notice to show cause why attachment should not be granted. A hearing is held on the appointed date, at which the debtor has an opportunity to contest the application. If the creditor establishes a right to attachment, the court authorizes a writ. It is issued and delivered to the sheriff or an equivalent official, who levies on the debtor's executable property as outlined in section 3.2.2. After levy, the sheriff submits a return to the clerk of the court. If the sheriff is unable to find executable property, she submits a nulla bona return and the plaintiff's attempt at attachment has failed. (If the plaintiff subsequently discovers executable property, a further attempt at levy can be made.)

Only the debtor's property can be attached. If the creditor causes property of a third party to be levied upon, the third party can challenge the attachment and obtain damages for conversion. Because the sheriff is also potentially liable for damages for wrongful attachment, the plaintiff is usually required to provide an indemnity bond to the sheriff before levy is attempted.

Once levy is accomplished, an attachment lien arises in the property. This judicial lien secures the formerly unsecured debt until judgment is obtained and execution can be effected on the property. (Example 2 illustrates the attachment lien.)

Normally, attachment remains in effect until judgment is obtained. However, the debtor is usually able to have the property returned or the attachment released by posting a bond supported by a qualified surety. Two types of bond are commonly recognized. A redelivery bond is an undertaking by the debtor to redeliver the property or its value if the creditor ultimately obtains judgment. The bond releases the property to the debtor but does not terminate the attachment or the creditor's attachment lien.

The other type of bond, a dissolution or discharging bond, also undertakes to pay if the creditor obtains judgment. It differs from the redelivery bond in that it completely releases the property from the attachment and extinguishes the attachment lien. The bond substitutes for the property as security.

Quite apart from the debtor's ability to reacquire the property by posting an appropriate bond, the debtor also has the right to move for discharge of the attachment for cause — for example, if the creditor fails to prosecute the suit to judgment. Discharge of the attachment for cause entitles the debtor to damages for wrongful attachment.

Once the creditor obtains judgment, the undischarged attachment converts into an execution. This means that a new writ is issued and delivered to the sheriff, who formally levies again on the attached property, conducts an execution sale, and applies the proceeds to satisfaction of the judgment debt. Execution procedure is described more fully in section 3.5.

§3.3.4 Prejudgment Garnishment

The essential similarity between prejudgment garnishment and attachment is that they serve the same basic goal of enabling the creditor to secure the ultimate judgment by seizing property of the debtor early in the case. The fundamental difference between them is that attachment is used to seize property in the control of the debtor or to levy on real property by an act of recording, while garnishment is used to levy on the debtor's tangible personal property in the possession of a third party or to levy on an intangible obligation owed to the debtor. In other words, prejudgment garnishment is the proper remedy when levy involves a third party, either as possessor of the debtor's personal property or as obligor on an intangible right of the debtor's. Garnishment has procedures designed to protect the rights of this third party, to compel the third party's compliance with the writ, and to ensure that the debtor is given notice of the levy and an opportunity to oppose it.

In many states, prejudgment garnishment is just a variation of the attachment procedure, adjusted to accommodate the presence of the third party. Where this is so, the two remedies have the same rules and procedures except for those relating to the levy and response to the writ. In other states, the remedies are more distinct. In some jurisdictions garnishment is treated as a separate action, with the garnishing creditor as plaintiff and the third party as defendant.

Where garnishment is just a variation of the attachment procedure, once the court has authorized the writ, the creditor (the garnishor) has a writ of garnishment issued and delivered to the sheriff. The writ is served on the garnishee, and a copy of it is served on the debtor. It calls on the garnishee to file an answer within a prescribed time and describes any obligation owed to the debtor or any of the debtor's property in the garnishee's possession. This notice of garnishment, in addition to the earlier notice of application, gives the debtor the opportunity to claim any available exemptions or make any appropriate challenges.

Upon receipt of the writ, the garnishee must answer it. He may simply acknowledge owing a mature obligation to the debtor or having possession of property of the debtor and turn over the property or make payment to the sheriff. However, he may decline to pay or surrender anything to the sheriff, either because he has no debt to, or property of, the debtor, or because he has the right, as against the debtor, to withhold the property or payment. As the garnishee is only obliged to surrender or pay what is due to the debtor at the time of the writ, any rights good against the debtor may be asserted as an

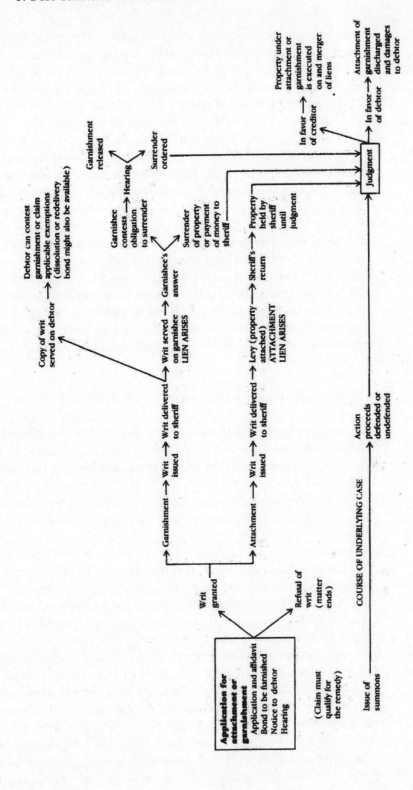

Diagram 3c

excuse to payment or delivery under the writ. If the creditor disputes the answer, the garnishee's rights are adjudicated by a summary procedure.

Whatever the basis of the answer, the garnishee is obliged to respond to the writ and answer it truthfully. Failure to do so or to surrender the garnishable asset to the sheriff renders the garnishee personally liable to the garnishor for any loss suffered. Furthermore, willful disregard of the writ may result in sanctions for contempt of court.

In most jurisdictions the levy of a writ of garnishment creates a lien in the garnished property equivalent to the attachment lien discussed in section 3.3.3. Once the property is taken into the custody of the law, it is retained, as in the case of attachment, until the final judgment in the underlying action. The rules governing the postseizure stage of the proceedings are usually the same as those for attachment. Diagram 3c sketches the sequence of prejudgment garnishment procedure and compares it to attachment.

As noted in section 3.3.2, because an individual debtor's salary, wages, or other earnings are so central to the debtor's survival, their prejudgment garnishment is barred completely or tightly restricted. (Although the postjudgment garnishment of wages is more commonly allowed, it is also restricted and confined to a prescribed percentage of the wages.)

§3.3.5 Prejudgment Replevin or Claim and Delivery

Prejudgment replevin (also called "claim and delivery") is somewhat similar to attachment. Both remedies allow the creditor to seize the debtor's property prior to judgment so that it can be held secure pending the final resolution of the case. The essential difference between them is that attachment is available in an action on an unsecured money claim, while prejudgment replevin is available to a creditor who sues for possession of specific property.

Prejudgment replevin is a provisional remedy derived from the common law action of replevin. Replevin is a possessory action at law for the recovery of specific tangible personal property that has been wrongfully taken and detained or lawfully taken but thereafter wrongfully detained by the defendant. In its prejudgment version, it is only available to a plaintiff who has a right to immediate possession of specific property, and it can only be sought when the principal action includes a claim of possession of the property in question. The principal suit may be the action of replevin itself or some other possessory action. For example, a secured party under UCC Article 9 must sue to recover possession of the collateral if it cannot be obtained from the defaulting debtor by self-help. (See section 2.5.) This suit qualifies as a possessory action, which entitles the secured party to seek prejudgment replevin. If the remedy is granted, the secured party is given possession of the collateral immediately, and holds it pending the final determination of the case. In this way, the secured party is assured that the debtor cannot harm or dispose of the collateral while the case is proceeding.

The procedure for obtaining prejudgment replevin is similar to that for attachment. The creditor makes an application after initiating the underlying suit. The application is supported by an affidavit that demonstrates, among other things, that the debtor is entitled to immediate possession of the specific personal property. Notice of the application is served on the debtor, and a hearing is held unless the state has a procedure for emergency ex parte relief. Any ex parte procedure must comply with the due process safeguards discussed in section 3.3.2. If the court authorizes a writ of replevin, it is issued and delivered to the sheriff who levies on the property. Unlike attachment, the sheriff does not retain the property while the case is pending, but delivers it to the creditor. As custodian of the property, the creditor is obliged to protect and preserve it. This duty is guaranteed by a surety bond.

Apart from the fact that the creditor, and not the sheriff, keeps the property during the course of the case, the postseizure rights and obligations of the parties are much like those in attachment proceedings. Also, like attachment, prejudgment replevin is provisional: The creditor must ultimately obtain judgment in the underlying possessory action. If the creditor fails to do so, the property is restored to the debtor who is entitled to damages for the wrongful seizure and retention of the property.

§3.3.6 Receivership

Although it has been codified in many states, receivership is an equitable remedy. When a party with an interest in an asset or estate demonstrates that the property is in need of protection, preservation, or orderly liquidation, a court of equity has the discretion to appoint a receiver to take control of the property, to administer it, and to deal with it as the court directs.

As a prejudgment remedy,[5] receivership is used to preserve property pending litigation. Like attachment, it removes property from the clutches of the defendant. However, receivership allows the property to be actively administered or conserved to prevent its deterioration or to maintain its value. It is therefore more appropriate than attachment where the property requires administration or maintenance while it is in legal custody.

Like other prejudgment remedies, receivership is ancillary to a principal action. Because receivership dispossesses the debtor of property pending resolution of the case on its merits, the procedural rules and safeguards are similar to those for attachment. Grounds for the appointment of a

---

5. Receivership is not necessarily confined to the prejudgment phase of a case. A receiver may be appointed after judgment to realize specific property, to protect it, or to prepare it for execution. Also, receivership still serves a limited role as a liquidation procedure at state law.

receiver must be shown, including a probability of success on the underlying action and a likelihood that the property will suffer harm if it is not placed under the control of an impartial administrator.

Once seizure has been effected, the property is entrusted to the receiver, who is also required to post a bond guaranteeing the proper administration of the property. The powers and duties of the receiver are defined in the court order. The receiver is an officer of the court and must report and account to it.

§3.3.7 Injunctions

Courts of equity have the discretion to issue injunctions to restrain or compel action that is likely to cause irreparable harm to the applicant. The injunction is a widely used remedy that is not confined to debt collection or to the prejudgment period. When used in a pending suit, the injunction's role is to forestall conduct of the debtor that threatens to undermine the creditor's ability to enforce the ultimate judgment. For example, a creditor who has reasonable grounds to believe that the debtor is about to conceal or dispose of executable assets can seek to enjoin that prejudicial activity.

Because an injunction does not result in removal of property from the debtor, its protective power is weaker than the other prejudgment remedies. Its effectiveness depends on the debtor's obedience to the court order. A debtor who disregards the injunction is subject to civil or criminal sanctions for contempt of court. However, if the debtor violates the injunction, a contempt sanction (such as the punishment of the debtor or a monetary award to compensate for disobedience) may not help the creditor if the debtor's conduct cannot be reversed and the debtor has no means of satisfying the judgment.

To obtain an injunction, the creditor makes an application on notice. An ex parte temporary restraining order may be available if the creditor can demonstrate urgency and can show that the injunction will be ineffectual if it is not issued immediately. An ex parte restraint is effective for only a brief period and must be followed shortly by an application, with notice and hearing, for a provisional injunction.

As in the case of other prejudgment remedies, the application for an injunction must be supported by an affidavit that demonstrates grounds for relief. The affidavit must establish a probability of success in the underlying action and a likelihood of irreparable harm if the injunction is not granted. The debtor may oppose the creditor's application. If the injunction is issued and later turns out to have been unjustified, the debtor has a claim for damages for wrongful enjoinder.

§3.3.8 *Lis Pendens*

The doctrine of lis *pendens* is not a prejudgment remedy, properly speaking, but it does provide some protection to a creditor in the prejudgment phase of litigation concerning rights to real property.

When a suit is in progress in which title, possession, or other rights in real property are at issue, the creditor may file a notice of pendency in the appropriate recording office (usually the deeds registry). The notice sets out the names of the parties, the description of the property, and the nature of the suit. Once the notice is filed, any person who acquires rights in the property from the debtor takes subject to the court's final disposition of the case. If the court ultimately grants judgment against the debtor, that judgment binds the transferee as well. The filing operates as constructive notice of the pending litigation and is effective even if the transferee did not check the filing records and had no actual knowledge of the pending suit.

Unlike an injunction, lis *pendens* does not prohibit the debtor from disposing of the property. It is also unlike attachment: Although the filing of the notice may seem the same as filing an attachment lien on real property, the notice does not create a lien. Rather, its effect is to warn third parties at large that the debtor's rights in the property are in dispute and that any interest transferred by the debtor is an uncertain one.

Another distinction between lis *pendens* and the prejudgment remedies discussed above is that the creditor does not need court authorization to file the notice. Provided that the doctrine applies to the case, the notice may be filed without application to court.

§3.4 THE JUDGMENT AND ITS ENFORCEMENT

§3.4.1 Judgment by Default or Consent (Confession)

The judgment is the court's determination that the debt is due. It is the authorization needed for enforcement of the debt, whether or not provisional relief was obtained by a prejudgment remedy. This section does not deal comprehensively with judgment issues but is concerned only with the creditor's ability to obtain judgment in the absence of a defense on the merits.

(1) Default judgment. When the debtor's failure to pay is the result of a lack of funds rather than a dispute over the debt, the debtor may not defend the action or, having begun to do so, may fail to prosecute the defense.

In such a case, the creditor is entitled to apply for judgment by default. If the debt is a liquidated contract claim and personal service has been affected, some states follow the traditional practice of allowing the clerk of the court to grant the judgment. Otherwise, judgment must be granted by the court. Normally the procedure is summary. Provided that the uncontested allegations in the summons state a cause of action, the judgment is granted for the relief requested in the summons. Evidence is not normally required unless some matter has to be resolved by testimony, such as evidence to fix unliquidated damages. After the judgment has been granted, it is entered by the clerk of the court in the appropriate record. The judgment becomes effective upon entry.

A debtor who permits a judgment to be obtained by default is deemed to have acquiesced in it and cannot normally appeal it. However, under some circumstances, a debtor is able to apply for reversal of the judgment on the basis of excusable neglect or the creditor's fraud or misconduct.

(2) Consent or confession to judgment. The debtor's failure to defend the suit amounts to a tacit consent to judgment. However, a debtor may explicitly admit liability for the debt and consent in writing to the entry of judgment. This formal waiver of the right to defend the suit is "consent" or "confession" to judgment. When this concession is made after default, courts usually accept it provided that it was voluntarily and knowledgeably made. However, if the debtor consents to judgment before default, this waiver of the right to defend the suit is treated as suspect and is likely to be disregarded. This is particularly true if the confession was executed when the debt was incurred and is contained in the instrument of debt or the contract.

A confession to judgment executed at the inception of the debt is also called a "cognovit" or a "warrant of attorney." It has been known in the common law for centuries, but over the years its original purpose has become obsolete, and its modern function is simply as a device to enable the creditor to act as the debtor's agent in acquiescing in a judgment upon the debtor's default on the debt.

Because of its potential for abuse and its harsh effect on the debtor's due process rights, the confession to judgment is heavily regulated by courts and legislatures. Federal Trade Commission rules make the confession to judgment an unfair trade practice in various kinds of consumer transactions, and many states forbid it entirely in consumer credit transactions. In other situations, even where a confession is permitted, the court scrutinizes it to determine whether it has been voluntarily and knowledgeably given under fair circumstances. In addition, the confession may have to comply with specific and strictly enforced formal prerequisites to be valid.

§3.4.2 The Duration of the Judgment

After obtaining judgment, the creditor usually takes steps to enforce it as soon as possible. However, it sometimes happens that immediate execution is not possible or desirable: The debtor may have no executable assets or may persuade the creditor to defer execution pending promised voluntary payment of the judgment debt. Where enforcement of the judgment is delayed for any reason, the issue of its duration becomes relevant.

All judgments have a finite lifespan; they expire or become unenforceable after a period of years. The period varies from state to state and the rules concerning the continuing vitality of a judgment are not uniform. For example, the state's statute governing judgments may provide that a judgment lasts for a fixed period (say ten years) after which it expires and becomes unenforceable. The statute may allow an application to be made during the period for a renewal of the judgment to extend its effectiveness for a further span. Some statutes require periodic attempts at execution on the judgment during its lifetime, failing which the judgment becomes dormant and must be revived by motion before enforcement can be attempted. A creditor who does not obtain immediate satisfaction of the judgment must take care to follow whatever procedures are necessary to keep it alive and enforceable for its full term.

§3.4.3 The Judgment Lien

A creditor who obtains a final, liquidated money judgment in a court of general jurisdiction[6] is able to obtain a judgment lien, which is one of the judicial liens discussed in section 2.4.2. To create and perfect the lien, the creditor records the judgment in a docket maintained by the clerk of the court or in some other filing system (often, the county deeds registry) designated by state law.

Upon being docketed, the judgment creates a lien on all of the debtor's real property within the county of docketing. The lien can be extended to property situated in other counties by filing the judgment in the recording offices for real estate in those counties. In most states the lien is confined to realty, but some permit it to cover personal property as well if a filing is made in the registry where security interests in personal property are recorded. Although personal property may be subjected to the lien in some states, the remaining discussion here assumes that it applies only to real property.

---

6. The judgment of a court of limited jurisdiction may not be capable of creating a lien or may have to be recorded in a more senior court to establish a lien.

Remember that the basis for the lien is simply that the creditor has obtained a money judgment against the debtor. It is not necessary that the property had any connection to the creditor's claim. It is subjected to the lien purely because it is owned by the debtor and located in the county in which the creditor docketed the judgment. The judgment lien statute and state property law determine what interests in property are lienable. Property of which the debtor is legal owner of record surely will be subject to the lien, but lesser interests (*e.g.*, equitable interests or joint ownership rights) may not be.

The lien is subject to any preexisting third-party interests recorded in the property, such as prior recorded mortgages and liens. The judgment lien may also be junior to an earlier, unrecorded interest in the property granted by the debtor to a good faith transferee for value. This is because the judgment lienholder is not a consensual lienholder who has extended credit to the debtor in reliance on real estate records and so the equities may dictate that the rights of the prior unrecorded interest-holder should be protected. As a general rule, the judgment lien is superior to any interest acquired in the property after the recording of the judgment lien. This rule is also subject to some exceptions where policy dictates that a subsequent bona fide transferee should be protected from the lien.

A judgment lien does not take precedence over any exemption to which the debtor is entitled. State statutes generally give an individual debtor an exemption in the home in which the debtor resides (called the homestead exemption). This exemption protects the debtor's homestead, fully or partially, from execution by a creditor, even where the creditor has obtained a judgment lien. If the property is fully exempt, the lien cannot affect it at all. Partially exempt property is lienable only to the extent of the debtor's non-exempt equity. Examples 3 and 4 deal with priority of judgment liens.

Once the judgment lien is recorded, it attaches not only to the real property held by the debtor at the time of filing but to any property in the county acquired by the debtor in the future, as long as the lien remains in effect. The lien will similarly encompass any improvements on the debtor's property and any increases in its value or augmentation of the debtor's rights in it. The judgment lien's attachment to after-acquired property rights of the debtor is an important advantage to the creditor. If the debtor owns no executable realty at the time of judgment or has only a small equity in existing property, the creditor can wait in the hope that new property will be acquired or the value of the debtor's interest will increase. Unless the statute provides a separate period of effectiveness for the lien, it lasts as long as the judgment. A judgment lienor therefore needs to be particularly sensitive to the question of duration of the judgment discussed in section 3.4.2. (Example 4 deals with the judgment lien on after-acquired property.)

When the lien is to be enforced, the lienholder follows a foreclosure procedure to sell the property and realize its proceeds. In some states the foreclosure of a judicial lien follows a public sale procedure such as that described in section 3.5. In others, special rules are prescribed for the fore-closure of a judgment lien.

§3.4.4 The Enforcement of Judgments in Other States

After a court has granted judgment, it is enforced by the means described in the following sections. However, enforcement activity is only permissible within the territorial boundaries of the court's state. The court of one state cannot simply send forth its minions to seize property located in another. To enforce a judgment in another state, the creditor must have the judgment recognized by a court in that state, whose own officials will enforce it. Under Article IV, section 1 of the Constitution, a state must give full faith and credit to a valid final judgment of another, provided that the judgment complies with the jurisdictional requirements of the Constitution and the law of the state in which it was granted.

State law prescribes the procedure to be followed by a creditor to have the judgment of another state recognized and enforced. There is some uni-formity in this procedure because many states have adopted the Uniform Enforcement of Foreign Judgments Act. (The word "foreign" in the title of the Act refers to judgments of other states or to federal courts, not to judg-ments of the courts of foreign nations. A separate uniform act, mentioned briefly below, deals with judgments from other nations.)

The Uniform Act provides for a straightforward method of registering a foreign judgment by a clerical act, with recourse to the court of the record-ing state only if a dispute arises concerning the registration. This is a simpler process than the traditional means of enforcement, which requires the plain-tiff to commence suit on the judgment in the second jurisdiction. This method remains an alternative even in states that have adopted the Uniform Act. (If the judgment is enforced by suit, the defendant is confined to defenses based on the validity of the judgment, and may not raise defenses on the merits.)

Judgments of the courts of foreign nations are not entitled to full faith and credit under the Constitution, and they are not subject to the same procedures or laws that govern the judgments of sister states. However, principles of international comity do favor the recognition of such judg-ments when the judicial process of the foreign nation satisfies standards of fairness and due process. At common law, courts in the United States have recognized and enforced the judgments of foreign courts where principles of comity and due process so dictate. This common law basis for recognition has been codified in the Uniform Foreign Money-Judgments Recognition Act. The courts of a state that has enacted it have discretion to recognize and enforce judgments of the courts of foreign nations if the judgment satisfies the standards mentioned above and recognition does not offend the state's public policy.

§3.5 EXECUTION

If the debtor does not pay the judgment voluntarily, the creditor must resort to execution to enforce it. Execution is the process whereby the sheriff or an equivalent official is directed by a writ to find property of the debtor, seize it, and sell it to realize proceeds with which to pay the judgment debt. Execution is regulated by statute. Courts tend to insist upon strict compliance with the statutory requirements and to invalidate deficient executions.

(1) Writ of execution. Execution begins with the issuance of a writ by the clerk of the court, directing the sheriff to find and levy on property of the debtor and to report back to the clerk by a specific date (called the return date). In some states the creditor cannot begin execution until the expiration of a waiting period after entry of the judgment. In other states, execution can proceed immediately following entry of the judgment. The debtor can apply for a stay of execution pending appeal, but the stay is usually conditioned on the debtor furnishing a bond, which can be costly.

There is also usually an outer time limit for issuing a writ. If it is not issued within a certain time of the judgment, the judgment becomes dormant and has to be revived by motion or action.

(2) Levy. After issuance, the writ is delivered to the sheriff, who tries to levy on property of the debtor, often with the creditor's active guidance. The procedure for the levy of a writ of execution is basically the same as that for a writ of attachment. (*See* sections 3.2.2 and 3.3.3.) Personal property in the debtor's possession and documents that reify intangible rights are levied upon by seizure. The sheriff normally takes the property into custody pending the sale in execution, but some states permit cumbersome property to be left in the debtor's possession and posted with a notice of execution. Real property is levied upon by recording the writ in the real estate records. Other intangibles and personal property in the possession of a third party cannot be reached by a writ of execution but must be garnished.

After levy, the sheriff files a return reporting on the action taken and describing the property that has been levied upon. If the sheriff found no property, he so certifies by submitting a nulla bona ("no goods") return by the date specified in the writ.

As in the case of attachment, if the sheriff seizes property that belongs to a third party, the true owner is able to challenge the levy and claim damages for trespass or conversion. Some execution statutes provide an expedited procedure for adjudicating the adverse claim and having the property released from execution. Because the sheriff could be liable for any tort damages, the plaintiff must provide an indemnity when delivering the writ.

Even though real and personal property are both subject to execution, the seizure and ultimate sale of real property is often subject to special restrictions, which have developed as a result of the historical importance of real property[7] and remain because real property is often the debtor's most valuable asset. For example, it is common for execution statutes to require the creditor to attempt levy on personal property first and to have recourse to real property only if insufficient personal property can be seized to satisfy the judgment. Also, the sale in execution of real property is usually subject to precautionary rules.

(3) Execution sale.   As soon as possible after completion of the levy, the process of realization takes place. After advertising and notice to the debtor, the sheriff conducts a sale of the property by public auction. The sale procedures prescribed by execution statutes attempt to ensure that the fairest price possible will be obtained. Notwithstanding, it is generally accepted that the value of property is depressed at forced sales of this nature, and prices seldom approximate true market value.

The proceeds realized, less costs of execution, are remitted to the creditor in satisfaction of the judgment. If insufficient funds are generated to pay the judgment in full, the creditor may begin the process of execution again by issuing a further writ and attempting another levy and sale. If the sale proceeds exceed the debt and costs, the surplus goes in order of priority to any junior judgment creditors who participated in the sale. Any remaining surplus is paid to the debtor.

As mentioned earlier, if real property is sold in execution, the statute may afford special protection to the debtor. These protective mechanisms may be available only when the debtor's residence is being sold and may not apply to other real property. For example, the statute may require an appraisal of the property before sale and will not permit the sale at a price that is less than a defined percentage of the appraised value. Some states provide for an automatic confirmation hearing at which the court must review and confirm

---

7. In early common law the writ of execution, known as *fieri facias*, was confined to chattels. Real property could not be executed upon at all. If the debtor owned land, the creditor could obtain a writ of *elegit* that could reach a limited portion of the revenues from the land over a defined period of time.

the sale before it is final. If there has been some irregularity in the proceedings, or if the price is unconscionably low, the court can refuse confirmation.

(4) Redemption. Even after the sale, the property is not necessarily lost to the debtor. It is common for execution statutes to allow the debtor[8] to redeem real property sold in execution. The redemption must be effected within a fixed period after the sale by the payment of the redemption value of the property to the purchaser.[9] The redemption price is the price paid by the purchaser at the sale; it is adjusted upward to include interest and to reimburse the purchaser for any costs and expenditures on the property, and adjusted downward to give the debtor credit for the economic value of fruits and revenues received by the purchaser.

The right of redemption enables the debtor to reacquire the property at the approximate distress price, so it helps a debtor who is able to raise the necessary funds before the redemption period expires. Of course, it is not of great practical value to many debtors who have no hope of finding the cash needed for redemption. The disadvantage of statutory redemption is that the purchaser acquires uncertain title at the time of the sale. This makes purchase at execution unattractive to some potential buyers, and it further depresses the prices at such sales. As a result, some states have abolished or curtailed the right of post-sale redemption.

(5) Execution lien. An execution lien attaches by operation of law to any property levied upon. Like the other liens discussed in this chapter and the last, it falls within the general category of judicial liens. The effective date of the lien differs from one state to another. The date of levy seems to be the most prevalent alternative, but some states have selected the date of delivery of the writ to the sheriff or some other point in the process.

The purpose of the lien is to protect the creditor while the sale is pending. Because the sale is supposed to proceed expeditiously after levy, the lien is intended to be of fairly short duration and to last only as long as necessary to cover the property until realization by sale. It is not a long-term security interest, and it expires if the sale is not held within the period

---

8. The right of statutory redemption may also be given to lienholders whose liens are junior to that of the execution creditor. It is therefore possible that there are two or more persons who are entitled to redeem. Multiple redemptions are not dealt with here. Even if a lienholder does redeem, the debtor has the ultimate redemption right and can redeem from the lienholder.

9. This statutory right to redeem property sold in execution should not be confused with the debtor's equity of redemption in the foreclosure of some security interests, alluded to in section 2.6.2. Where a security interest is foreclosed upon, the equity of redemption gives the debtor the right to avert the sale of the collateral by paying the debt before the sale takes place, but does not allow the debtor to redeem the property after sale.

prescribed by the statute or, if no period is provided, within a reasonable time.

When several creditors have executed on the same property, or when there are competing interests in the property, the liens and interests must be ranked in accordance with rules of priority. The first-in-time rule applies unless there is specific provision to the contrary. If an execution creditor has a preexisting lien (*e.g.*, an attachment lien, judgment lien, or consensual lien), the execution lien merges with the earlier one and backdates for priority purposes.

§3.6 GARNISHMENT

Postjudgment garnishment is an execution procedure used to levy on personal property of the debtor in the possession of someone else, or on an intangible obligation due to the debtor. Although in some states post-judgment garnishment is a separate suit against the garnishee, it is more commonly just a variety of execution procedure with some variations to account for the protection of the garnishee's rights and to ensure that the debtor is notified of the garnishment so that he can assert any exemptions in the property. It is, therefore, very much like the prejudgment remedy described in section 3.3.4.

The debtor's rights of due process require that he is given notice of the garnishment that sets out his exemption rights, and must also have an opportunity to challenge the garnishment. A statute that does not provide for such notice and a hearing either before or promptly after the garnishment does not meet constitutional standards. The fact that the debtor received notice of the suit itself does not satisfy this notice requirement.

Upon delivery of the writ of garnishment to the sheriff, the levy follows the same course as the prejudgment procedure. The garnishee is obliged to answer the writ and must surrender the property or state grounds for not doing so. If the creditor does not accept those grounds, a hearing is held. If the debt is not due or the property is not returnable at the time of the writ, it must be paid or surrendered to the appropriate court official on the date that it becomes due. In many states a garnishment lien arises on levy. A garnishee who disposes of garnished property in violation of the writ becomes personally liable to the creditor for the loss suffered as a result of the disposition.

Upon payment of a garnished debt to the clerk of the court or the sheriff, the funds are remitted to the creditor to the extent necessary to satisfy the judgment. Property surrendered by the garnishee to the sheriff (whether voluntarily or after the court has conducted the hearing and ordered surrender) is sold in execution in the same way as property levied on by a writ of execution.

§3.7 PROCEEDINGS IN AID OF EXECUTION

A creditor whose attempt at execution ended with a nulla bona return may be unconvinced that the debtor truly has no executable property. The creditor may try to conduct some investigations by checking real estate records or pursuing other sources of information. In addition, two generally recognized types of judicial proceeding may be used by a disappointed execution creditor to gain information from the debtor about the existence and whereabouts of executable assets.

(1) The creditors' bill in equity. This is the older, more cumbersome procedure under which the creditor must commence a separate ancillary action grounded (as are all equitable suits) on the creditor's allegation that its remedies at law for the enforcement of the debt are exhausted or inadequate. This means that the creditor must either have received a nulla bona return or must be able to show that it would be fruitless to attempt levy.

The creditors' bill can be used to achieve a number of different goals. For example, the creditor may ask for an order compelling the debtor or other persons with knowledge of the debtor's affairs to submit to an examination by the creditor in court. If assets are revealed, the bill can be used to recover them from one who acquired them in fraud of creditors,[10] to enjoin their disposition, or to appoint a receiver to administer them pending execution. A creditors' bill can also be used to execute on equitable assets that cannot be reached by a writ of execution at law.

(2) Statutory proceedings in aid of execution. This more modern and streamlined procedure serves some or all of the ends accomplished by a creditors' bill. It is part of the original suit, rather than a separate action. Statutory procedures provide at least for an examination or discovery, but some go beyond this and authorize the court to order payments by installments, to enjoin the disposition of property, to appoint a receiver, or to take other steps to apply the property to the satisfaction of the debt. In some jurisdictions the statutory inquiry proceedings, like the creditors' bill, can only be used after a nulla bona return unless execution is shown to be futile. In others, the examination can take place before any writ has been issued.

---

10. Chapter 4 deals with fraudulent transfers. Most states also have a statutory procedure for avoiding fraudulent transfers which is designed to be more efficient than the creditors' bill.

§3.8 BANKRUPTCY AND THE STATE LAW COLLECTION PROCESS

The possibility of the debtor's bankruptcy is one of the hazards that creditors face in pursuing collection efforts at state law. There is always a danger that the debtor or a group of qualified creditors will file a petiton for the debtor's bankryotcy while other creditors are in the process of attempting to enforce their claims through the state courts. If that should happen, the collection under state law is disrupted. All action is stayed, and advantages obtained by a creditor through attachment, judgment, or execution may be avoided. The possibility of bankruptcy could influence decisions and strategies in the collection process: It may spur a creditor into speedy action, or it may have the opposite effect of encouraging a circumspect approach, so as not to precipitate a petition.

§3.9 STATE LAW INSOLVENCY PROCEEDINGS

§3.9.1 Introduction to State Law Insolvency Proceedings

There are two commonly recognized processes available to a debtor under state law for the restructuring and compromise of debts: compositions (including extensions) and assignments for the benefit of creditors. This section outlines some general principles applicable to both.

The collection processes described in the preceding sections involve individual action by each creditor. Creditors act on their own and are concerned with the enforcement of their own claims. Although creditor activity may be individual, it is often not isolated — a debtor in financial difficulty is likely to have defaulted on several debts. When a number of creditors are attempting to enforce their claims, those furthest ahead in the collection process have the best chance of finding executable property.

Competition for the debtor's resources can be handled more fairly and efficiently through an arrangement for the collective management of claims. By such a collective proceeding (so called to distinguish it from creditors' individual pursuits of their claims), the debtor may be able to deal with creditors in an orderly way and to preserve assets that would otherwise be seized and disposed of at distress prices in an execution sale. Bankruptcy is the predominant and most powerful collective proceeding, but the composition and extension and the assignment for the benefit of creditors, provided for by state law, also facilitate the collective treatment of claims. These procedures are also sometimes called insolvency proceedings.

Although the debtor need not be insolvent to be eligible to use these proceedings, a solvent debtor is less likely to resort to them. Insolvency is determined by one of two well-established alternative tests. Under the balance sheet or bankruptcy test, insolvency is an excess of liabilities over assets. Under the equity test, insolvency is the inability to pay debts as they become due.

State law insolvency proceedings have one attribute in common with bankruptcy: They are designed to enable the debtor to deal with creditors as a group to achieve an overall settlement of their claims. However, the analogy should not be exaggerated. Bankruptcy is a much more powerful and pervasive remedy. Among other things, the Bankruptcy Code confers extraordinary rights on the trustee to collect and administer the estate, and it has unique provisions for the protection of creditor interests, the control of creditor activity, and the discharge of debts. State law proceedings do not have the same compulsive strength. They fall far short of being equivalents of bankruptcy and are constitutionally barred from providing equivalent relief.[11] As a result, the proceedings under state law are less formal, simpler, and more dependent on cooperation between the debtor and creditors.

Because these state law proceedings do not give the debtor the same protection as bankruptcy, they are often a less desirable remedy. In some cases, however, bankruptcy is either not attractive to the debtor or is not feasible. There are many reasons why this may be. For example, the debtor may want to avoid the expense and formality of bankruptcy administration, or may not want the stigma of bankruptcy, or may not be eligible for bankruptcy relief.[12] Where bankruptcy is not a suitable option for the debtor, the state law procedures do at least provide some of the advantages that arise from the orderly management of debt. By surrendering assets for liquidation and distribution among creditors or by making a commitment to payment by future installments, the debtor may be able to persuade creditors that their interests are better served by cooperating in a collective proceeding rather than by attempting collection individually.

The two insolvency proceedings discussed here are voluntary: Only the debtor may bring them into effect. Although creditors may exert pressure on the debtor to make an assignment or a composition, they cannot initiate suit to force them on the debtor.

Under the common law, these insolvency proceedings are not judicial remedies. Unless a state has provided otherwise by statute, the debtor does not apply to court to sanction the proceeding, and the court does not supervise its performance. The court only becomes involved in the matter if a challenge or dispute arises.

---

11. The federal bankruptcy power is discussed in section 5.2.

12. For a fuller discussion of eligibility for bankruptcy and some of the considerations that may motivate the filing of a bankruptcy petition, *see* Chapter 8.

§3.9.2 Compositions and Extensions

On hearing the word "composition," a normal person might think of Beethoven or Mozart scribbling down musical notes by the flickering light of a candle, or of Raphael or Tiepolo plotting out the spatial relationships between hordes of saints and seraphim. To a lawyer, the word simply means a contract. More specifically, in modern usage a composition is a contract between the debtor and two or more creditors under which a partial payment of claims is promised and accepted in full settlement.

An extension is a contract between the debtor and two or more creditors under which the debtor is allowed an extension of time within which to pay the debts. A single contract can include both a composition and an extension, providing for a reduction in the debt as well as an extension of the payment period.[13] From now on, the word "composition" is used to refer to a contract with both these elements.

Although compositions have been codified by some states (sometimes with additional statutory requirements), they are generally subject to the rules and principles of contract law. Thus, doctrines governing formation, performance, and breach all apply. Because compositions are contractual in nature, the specific structure of each one can be molded by the parties to meet the needs of their situation. As a contract, a composition needs consideration, which courts hold to be present by virtue of the creditors' mutual forbearance and the debtor's undertaking to procure assent from other creditors. It is not necessary that all participating creditors sign the same contract. They may each make a separate contract with the debtor, as long as the contracts are interdependent and entered into in reliance on others being executed.

Because a composition is a contract, it is only binding on creditors who assent to it. They are not likely to agree to reduction or extension of their claims unless the debtor can persuade them that it serves their best interests to do so. This means, at a minimum, the debtor must demonstrate genuine financial distress and a good faith effort to deal with it. The distribution offered to creditors (which may be committed from future earnings or the liquidation of selected assets or both) must be enough to make it worthwhile for creditors to accept the settlement, rather than to press ahead with collection efforts. A debtor is held to a high standard of good faith in entering into a composition and must disclose financial information honestly and accurately. If creditors are misled, they have grounds for avoiding the composition.

---

13. Because the purpose of a composition and extension is to resolve the debtor's financial problems by consent–by working out the debtor's financial problems–these agreements are sometimes called "workouts."

As long as two or more creditors accept the composition, consideration problems are overcome. A debtor is therefore able to make a legally valid composition with fewer than all of the creditors. However, if acceptance of the composition is not widespread, it cannot achieve its desired end. Nonconsenting creditors can be expected to proceed with individual collection activity, thereby preventing preservation of the debtor's estate and discouraging more cooperative creditors from exercising forbearance. A debtor may have some flexibility in offering preferred treatment to a creditor who holds out — as long as this is fully disclosed to other creditors. However, the other creditors may not be willing to enter the composition if one of them is treated more generously.

If the composition is executed, its terms supersede the debtor's former obligations toward participating creditors. If the debtor consummates it as promised, the debtor's performance satisfies not only the composition but also the original obligations that were subsumed in it. The consensual forgiveness of the unpaid balance of the original debt is an important advantage of a composition, because a state cannot grant a discharge to a debtor in the absence of creditor assent — the discharge is an incident of the bankruptcy power conferred on Congress by the Constitution. If the debtor breaches the composition, creditors are entitled to disregard it and to sue for the full outstanding balance of the original debt.

§3.9.3 Assignments for the Benefit of Creditors

An assignment for the benefit of creditors (sometimes abbreviated to ABC), is a voluntary transfer of property in trust by the debtor to another person (the assignee) with instructions to liquidate the property and to distribute its proceeds to those creditors who have elected to participate. The purpose of the assignment is to place the debtor's executable property in the hands of an impartial custodian so that individual creditors cannot levy on it, permitting its orderly liquidation and distribution for the benefit of the creditor body as a whole. The debtor transfers the property in trust to the custodian, specifying the terms on which it is to be realized and its proceeds distributed.

Each creditor may choose whether or not to participate in an ABC. However, unlike a composition, the ABC is not contractual in nature. The debtor's power to make the assignment is an incident of rights of ownership, deriving from the law of property. The ABC is a common law device, but it has been codified and regulated by statute in some states.

As you will see when liquidation bankruptcy (under Ch. 7 of the Code) is introduced in Chapters 5 and 8, the ABC has some similarity to liquidation in bankruptcy. However, the ABC is a weaker and less comprehensive remedy, and it affords considerably less protection to the debtor and creditors. For example, it does not stay the creditors' pursuit of any unassigned assets or shield the debtor from other collection pressure; and it does not confer on the assignee the extensive powers wielded by a bankruptcy trustee. Probably even more important, the ABC cannot, by statute, operate as a discharge because a state statute conferring a discharge of unpaid debt is an unconstitutional encroachment on the federal bankruptcy power. The constitutional problem does not arise if creditors themselves grant the discharge by agreement, but courts are wary of coerced consent. They generally demand that the assent be truly voluntary, and not simply imposed by a condition of participation in the ABC. In fact, many courts consider that the inclusion of such a condition is prima facie bad faith, and some states forbid it altogether.

An ABC is less formal than bankruptcy. In some states it requires no judicial approval or supervision at all and only comes before a court if someone challenges or disputes some aspect of it. In other states, judicial participation has been imposed by statute, but even there the procedure is much less involved than bankruptcy. Because an ABC lacks the force of bankruptcy, it is often not a workable alternative for the debtor. However, for the reasons mentioned in section 3.9.1, the ABC may suit some debtors more than bankruptcy.

An ABC is meant to benefit creditors, as its name suggests. If creditors derive no advantage from it, it is simply a conveyance of property by the debtor without return consideration, having the effect of removing the property from the reach of execution. As such, it is a fraud on creditors (a fraudulent transfer) and avoidable. (*See* Chapter 4.) The debtor's discretion in deciding on the terms of the assignment is limited by this consideration and is subject to an overriding duty of good faith. An ABC that has the effect of frustrating and obstructing creditors rather than facilitating the evenhanded distribution of funds may be invalidated in its entirety or modified by the court.

There are a number of terms that are considered improper or, at best, questionable in an ABC. For example, ABCs usually cannot allow the debtor to retain the use or control of the property or to reserve some interest in it apart from the right to have any surplus proceeds returned; provide for the administration of the assets for an extended period; grant preferential treatment to a particular creditor;[14] stipulate that participating creditors must discharge the unpaid balance of their claims; or include less than all the debtor's executable property. In some states, these principles are based in common law. In others, statutes have been passed that codify them and may impose further restrictions.

After the instrument of assignment has been executed and the assignee has accepted the appointment, the debtor must deliver the property to the

---

14. Preferences are not generally forbidden under common law. Therefore, a fully disclosed preference may be permitted in some states. However, other states have changed this rule by judicial decision or statute and forbid preferences in ABCs.

assignee. Ownership of the property passes to the assignee, who holds it in trust for the benefit of the creditors. The assignee acquires no greater rights in the property than the debtor had. Therefore, the assignee's interest in the property is subject to any valid preexisting third party rights.

On the effective date of the assignment, the property is treated as being in *custodia legis* and cannot be levied upon. The effective date of the assignment varies from one state to another: It may be the date of the instrument's delivery to the assignee, the date of the property's delivery, or the date the assignee accepted the transfer. In some states, the assignment must be recorded to become effective.

The assignee's essential task is to notify creditors, to call for claims, to realize the property, and to distribute the proceeds to those creditors who have proved claims. In addition to complying with the law governing the administration of assigned property, the assignee is bound by the terms of the assignment. The proper performance of the assignee's duties is secured by a surety bond. In some states the assignee is obliged to file an inventory, appraisals, and accounts.

On being notified of the assignment, a creditor may decide to participate in the ABC, file a claim, and receive whatever distribution is made. The creditor's participation is treated as tacit consent to any lawful conditions expressed in the deed of assignment. Alternatively, the creditor may refuse to participate. Unlike bankruptcy, an ABC does not stay collection activity, so the creditor is free to pursue efforts to recover the debt. As noted before, the creditor cannot execute on the property assigned under a valid ABC, so the creditor's prospects or immediate satisfaction of its claim outside of the ABC are poor. However, if there is some flaw or fraudulent design in the ABC, the creditor may be able to avoid it, unless the flaw is one that can be corrected.

Even if the ABC is valid, the creditor may be able to use it as the basis of an involuntary bankruptcy petition, provided that the requirements of §303(b)(2) of the Bankruptcy Code are satisfied. (*See* Chapter 9.) Stated broadly, the Code gives creditors the power, under some circumstances, to override the ABC and force the debtor into bankruptcy. If the petition is granted, the assignment is terminated and the assignee must surrender the property to the trustee.

Examples

1. Some months ago, Abe Scond borrowed money from Surge & Caesar, Inc. Abe undertook to repay the unsecured loan in installments over a two-year period. Abe paid conscientiously at first, but his payments stopped at the beginning of last month. After Abe ignored demands for payment, Surge & Caesar commenced suit to recover the debt. Shortly after summons was issued, and before default judgment could be applied for, Surge & Caesar discovered that Abe had recently lost his job. His wife

and children have just left the state for an unknown destination, taking the family car and a fully-loaded trailer. Surge and Caesar has reason to believe that Abe's furniture, appliances, and some personal property are still in his rented apartment, but he has advertised an "everything-must-go" moving sale for next weekend, four days hence.

Surge & Caesar would like to seize Abe's remaining property before he sells it and disappears. Can this be done?

2. Eartha Plott owns a piece of land. Two of Eartha's creditors claim interests in the land based on the following sequence of events:
   a. On January 15, Victor Pyrrhic, one of Eartha's creditors, commenced suit against her to recover a debt.
   b. On February 20, Lien & Hungry Loan Co., another of Eartha's creditors, commenced suit against her to recover a debt. Shortly after issuing summons, Lien & Hungry filed and served an application for attachment. Eartha failed to appear at the attachment hearing, and the court authorized a writ that was delivered to the sheriff. On March 10 the sheriff levied on Eartha's land by properly filing the writ in the real estate records.
   c. On March 20, Victor obtained default judgment in his suit against Eartha. On March 25, Victor docketed the judgment in the county in which the land is situated.
   d. On April 1, Lien & Hungry obtained default judgment in its action against Eartha. Its judgment was properly docketed on April 3.

   The land is worth $25,000. Victor's judgment is for $15,000, and Lien & Hungry's judgment is for $20,000.

   What are the creditors' interests in Eartha's land? How should they be ranked?

3. On January 15, Lienora obtained a money judgment against Homer LeBrave, which she properly docketed in the county on January 30.

   On January 20, Lienardo obtained a money judgment against Homer. He properly docketed the judgment in the county on January 25.

   At this time, Homer owned no real property in the county. However, on February 28 he acquired title to a piece of land that he inherited from his late father.

   Assume both judgments are still current and enforceable. How should they be ranked?

4. Homer owns a commercial building in another county. Lienardo discovered this property by searching the real estate records. He recorded his judgment in the second county on March 1. On April 30, Homer sold the property to Emptor B. Ware. Emptor did not check the real estate records before he bought the property, and did not know about Lienardo's recording. He discovered it only when he attempted to take transfer of

the title at the closing of the transaction. Is Lienardo's lien superior to Emptor's rights as purchaser of the property?

5. Penny Foolish owns and operates a small retail store from which she derives a modest but steady income. Although she runs her business carefully, she is undisciplined and irresponsible as a consumer. Through her abuse of credit cards she has accumulated an unmanageable amount of debt. She has tried to juggle her affairs and to make some payment to everyone, but she has fallen into arrears on most of her debts. Some creditors have threatened collection action. Because Penny's inventory and business assets are her only valuable executable property, she fears that she will lose her business if she cannot settle her debts.

    Penny has shredded her credit cards and wishes to try to make an arrangement with her creditors. What options are open to her?

6. Abraham ("Abie") Cede has made an ABC. Included in his assigned assets is a truck worth $10,000. The truck is subject to a valid, perfected security interest, securing a debt of $8,000.

    What happens to the rights of the secured party when Abie transfers the truck to his assignee?

Explanations

1. Surge & Caesar has initiated suit but has not yet obtained judgment. To seize Abe's property immediately, it must apply for attachment. Because Abe's planned sale and departure will be over before the usual notice period has expired, Surge & Caesar's only chance to prevent the sale is to apply for an ex parte attachment order.

    If state law permits emergency ex parte attachment, Surge & Caesar must make a convincing case that the remedy will be ineffective if it is delayed by notice and a hearing and that failure to take immediate action will cause it irreparable prejudice. The ex parte application must also satisfy the other due process standards set out in section 3.3.2: The application must be evaluated by a judge, Surge & Caesar must furnish a bond, and a meaningful postseizure hearing must be held.

    On the facts of this case, Surge & Caesar appears to qualify for ex parte attachment. The debt is a noncontingent, liquidated, unsecured monetary obligation arising out of contract. There is no indication that Abe has a defense to the claim on the merits. If Surge & Caesar's information is reliable, Abe is planning to liquidate his assets immediately and to disappear with the proceeds. Delay will leave Surge & Caesar with the expensive and possibly futile task of trying to find him and enforce its claim in another jurisdiction.

If Abe is likely to obey a court order, a temporary restraining order is an alternative to an ex parte attachment. It would enjoin Abe from disposing of the assets or leaving the jurisdiction pending an attachment hearing on notice. If a temporary injunction is likely to be effective, courts prefer it to an ex parte attachment because it is not as drastic. The debtor is not deprived of possession of the property without notice and a hearing.

Even if Surge & Caesar obtains an ex parte attachment order, this will not guarantee a successful conclusion to this process. The property in Abe's apartment may be protected fully or in part by exemptions provided by state statute, and his executable property may be relatively valueless.

2. This question involves a priority contest between two judicial liens on Eartha's land. The sequence of events is as follows:

Jan. 15	Feb. 20	Mar. 10	Mar. 20	Mar. 25	Apr. 1	Apr. 3
Victor commenced suit	Lien & Hungry commenced suit	Lien & Hungry levied attachment	Victor obtained judgment	Victor docketed judgment	Lien & Hungry obtained judgment	Lien & Hungry docketed judgment

Victor's judgment lien became effective when his judgment was docketed in the county on March 25. Lien & Hungry's judgment lien was docketed on April 3. However, Lien & Hungry had attached the land on March 10. An attachment lien was created upon levy, which was accomplished by recording the attachment in the real estate records. When Lien & Hungry obtained its judgment lien on April 3, that lien merged with the attachment lien, so that Lien & Hungry's priority backdated to March 10.

On the basis of the first-in-time rule, Lien & Hungry's lien has priority over Victor's lien. It is a first charge against the property for the full amount of $20,000 plus costs. Victor's lien extends only to the surplus of approximately $5,000. Victor will have to seek other assets to cover his deficiency.

This Example illustrates the value of attachment. By attaching the property at the commencement of its suit, Lien & Hungry was able to secure its ultimate judgment and to take priority over Victor. By failing to attach the property, Victor lost the advantage even though he commenced suit and obtained judgment first.

Eartha is an individual, so she is entitled to any exemptions provided by state law. Because the property is unimproved land rather than Eartha's home, she has no homestead exemption in it. However, the statute must be consulted to determine whether it provides a general exemption or some other exemption category that could include the land. If it does, Eartha's exemption would protect her interest in the property to the extent of the dollar limit of the exemption.

3. The sequence of events is as follows:

Jan. 15	Jan. 20	Jan. 25	Jan. 30	Feb. 28
Lienora obtains judgment	Lienardo obtains judgment	Lienardo's judgment docketed	Lienora's judgment docketed	Homer acquires property

Although Homer is an individual, entitled to exemptions, the property is not his home, so as in the case of Eartha in Example 2, he has no homestead exemption in the property. Let us assume that the state exemption statute does not give him some other basis for asserting an exemption in the land. The question states that both judgment liens were properly recorded. Irrespective of when the judgment was obtained, a judgment lien becomes effective only upon docketing. It does not backdate to the time of judgment.

If Homer had owned real property in the county when the judgments were docketed, each would have attached to the property upon docketing. Because the first-in-time rule governs priority, Lienardo's lien, effective on January 25, would have had priority over Lienora's lien, which became effective on January 30. However, this property was only acquired by Homer on February 28. As explained in section 3.4.3, both liens automatically attached to the after-acquired property on February 28.

In some states, preexisting judgment liens are treated as effective on attachment to the after-acquired property. Even though they were docketed at different times, they attach simultaneously and rank equally. In other states, judgment liens or after-acquired property backdate to the time of docketing. Under such a rule, Lienardo's lien has priority.

4. Lienardo's judgment lien took effect before the property was sold to Emptor. Even if Emptor bought in good faith and without actual knowledge of the lien, the valid filing gave him constructive notice of the lien. The first-in-time rule applies and Emptor cannot acquire the property free of Lienardo's lien. (In some situations, the first-in-time rule is varied to protect a bona fide purchaser. However, Emptor's constructive notice disqualifies him from that status.)

5. Penny has a number of alternative means of trying to resolve her debt problems. She could select state law remedies such as those discussed in this chapter, or she could choose one of the forms of relief provided by the Bankruptcy Code. The advantages and drawbacks of bankruptcy will be discussed later. For the present, merely note that it is one of her options. Much more information is needed about Penny's affairs for a judgment to be made on her most appropriate course of action. The present facts do allow the following tentative observations to be made:

First, an ABC will not fit Penny's needs. It requires the assignment and liquidation of all her executable property. Because she needs this property for her livelihood, an ABC defeats the purpose for which she seeks to approach creditors.

Second, a composition may be possible provided that Penny's creditors are amenable to it and her financial affairs are such that she can make a proposal that will satisfy them. If she can negotiate a composition she will be able to avoid the loss of her business and will be able to settle her debts by proportional payment over time without the need for the expense and trauma of a bankruptcy case.

Creditors of a business are often suppliers or others who have a stake in the survival of the business, so they may be amenable to a workout. However, Penny's creditors are not creditors of the business, so they may have less incentive to preserve it, especially if Penny's business assets are valuable enough to cover all her debts. However, if Penny is insolvent and she proposes a reasonable plan of payment from future income, creditors may be persuaded that acceptance of her offer is more advantageous than an uncertain race for her assets. The percentage of payment on claims and the period of payment must be realistic and attractive in light of the creditors' prospects of immediate satisfaction. As noted before, the cooperation of creditors is essential to an effective composition.

Finally, if significant creditors are hostile to the idea of a composition, Penny will have to consider filing a bankruptcy petition to force them into a collective proceeding. The choice of bankruptcy relief is discussed further in Chapter 8.

6. Abie can transfer to the assignee only those rights that he himself has in the property. The truck therefore passes to the assignee subject to the security interest, which was properly perfected prior to the effective date of the assignment.[15] The secured party can assert its right to the collateral notwithstanding the assignment.

---

15. An assignee for the benefit of creditors is included in the definition of "lien creditor" in UCC 9-102(52). Under UCC 9-317(a)(2), a lien creditor takes priority over a secured party who has not perfected its security interest at the effective date of the assignment, but is junior to a secured party who has perfected by that date.

3. Debt Collection under State Law

Even if Abie is not behind in his payments on the truck, the assignment of the collateral is likely to constitute a default under the security agreement. This entitles the secured party to foreclose on the truck. It may either recover the truck from the assignee or it may allow the assignee to sell the truck and to pay its secured claim as a priority charge on the proceeds. The assignee is entitled to any surplus that remains after the secured claim has been satisfied.

Fraudulent Transfers

§4.1 BACKGROUND — THE BASIS AND PURPOSE OF FRAUDULENT TRANSFER LAW

§4.1.1 State Fraudulent Transfer Law

As noted before, an unsecured creditor takes the risk that the debtor will have no executable property to satisfy a delinquent claim. If the absence of assets is the natural result of economic adversity, the creditor can do little about it. However, if a creditor can show that the debtor has disposed of assets under circumstances that improperly place them beyond the reach of execution, the creditor may be able to avoid the transfer and recover the property or its value. A debtor's concealment or disposition of assets to evade creditors is an old problem, and the law allowing a creditor to over-turn such actions goes back many centuries. It was codified during the Elizabethan period, and the Elizabethan statute forms the basis of modern fraudulent transfer law. The avoidance of fraudulent transfers in state collection proceedings is governed today by state statutes. Most states have adopted a uniform model act on fraudulent transfers, the *Uniform Fraudulent Transfer Act* (UFTA), which was drafted by the National Conference of Commissioners on Uniform State Laws in 1984. (This model statute is an update of an earlier uniform model law, the *Uniform Fraudulent Conveyance Act* (UFCA), which had been drafted in 1918.) The widespread enactment of the UFTA has resulted in a relatively uniform state fraudulent transfer law.

The discussion in this chapter is based on the UFTA, and the citations are to sections of that Act.

The action under state law to avoid a fraudulent transfer is available to unsecured creditors and is not used by a creditor who has a perfected lien or other interest in the transferred property, valid against third parties. Such perfected liens and interests are usually superior to the rights of a transferee, so the holder of the lien or interest does not need fraudulent transfer law to assert its interest or recover the property. By contrast, as explained in section 1.4 and Chapter 3, an unsecured creditor has no rights in the debtor's property and is vulnerable to the debtor's attempt to place executable property beyond its reach. Although an unsecured creditor normally has no power to interfere with the debtor's use or disposition of property, fraudulent transfer law qualifies this general rule to the extent that the debtor's transfer of property constitutes an abuse of the debtor's ownership rights, having the effect of defeating the justifiable recourse to that property by the unsecured creditor.

§4.1.2 The Avoidance of Fraudulent Transfers in Bankruptcy

Although fraudulent transfer law is discussed here as a creditor's remedy in the context of debt collection under state law, the avoidance of fraudulent transfers is very important in bankruptcy cases as well. Trustees in bankruptcy examine the debtor's prepetition conduct and frequently bring actions to avoid fraudulent transfers made by the debtor within a quite lengthy period preceding the bankruptcy petition. In a bankruptcy case, the trustee has the power to avoid prepetition fraudulent transfers either under the provisions of applicable state law (which is most commonly the UFTA) or under a provision of the Bankruptcy Code that is worded very much the same as the UFTA. Therefore, the general principles set out in this chapter are applicable in bankruptcy as well as under state collection law. The trustee's power to avoid fraudulent transfers in bankruptcy is discussed in section 16.3. That section builds on what is said here and explains variations between avoidance by a creditor in the state law collection process and avoidance in bankruptcy. Section 16.3 contains references to this chapter and you will find it worthwhile to refer back to this chapter when dealing with the avoidance of fraudulent transfers in bankruptcy.

§4.2 AN OVERVIEW OF THE AVOIDANCE SUIT

This overview sets the stage for consideration of the detailed rules of the UFTA by illustrating the circumstances that could give rise to an avoidance suit and sketching the broad outlines of the action. For example, after attempting execution and receiving a nulla bona return, the creditor discovers that the debtor recently transferred property to a relative for apparently inadequate consideration, under circumstances that establish grounds for avoidance. The creditor commences suit against the transferee. The debtor may be joined in the suit, but the transferee is the essential party. The relief sought by the creditor is a judgment ordering restoration of the property to the debtor so that it can be levied upon to satisfy the judgment. As an alternative, the creditor is able to claim damages from the transferee based on the value of the asset.

Because the transferee is a stranger to the debtor/creditor relationship, the UFTA provides protection for his or her legitimate interests. Therefore, the grounds for avoidance require examination not only of the debtor's conduct and motives but also of the role played by the transferee in the transaction. If the transferee behaved honestly and gave value to the debtor, the transfer may not be avoidable despite the debtor's ill motives in making it, or the transferee may at least be compensated for the value given.

The UFTA is available to creditors of the transferee. Section 1(4) read with §1(3) defines "creditor" to include persons with a wide variety of claims against the debtor. The UFTA distinguishes between creditors whose claims existed at the time of transfer, who are given broader rights of avoidance, and those whose claims arose afterward, whose avoidance rights are more limited. The UFTA is aimed at avoiding "transfers," defined in §1(12) read with §1(2) to include all dispositions of an interest in assets. "Assets" include only property to the extent that it is nonexempt and not subject to a security interest.

The UFTA provides two different grounds for avoidance. The first is actual fraud, §4(a)(1), and the other is constructive fraud, which can take one of three different forms, §§4(a)(2) and 5(a). The grounds of avoidance are alternative, which means a creditor need only establish one of them.

§4.3 ACTUAL FRAUD

§4.3.1 Dishonest Intent

A creditor can avoid a transfer made by the debtor with actual intent to hinder, delay, or defraud any creditor. §4(a)(i). This ground of avoidance is available both to creditors whose claims existed at the time of transfer and to those whose claims arose afterward, because all creditors should be able to respond to actual fraud. To avoid the transfer on the basis of actual fraud, the creditor must prove that the debtor made the transfer with the deliberate motive of removing the property from the reach of creditors.

§4.3.2 Proof of Fraud — Badges of Fraud

Unless a debtor has admitted dishonest intent, a creditor cannot prove fraud by direct evidence of the debtor's state of mind. Therefore, fraudulent intent is usually shown by proof of the debtor's conduct in circumstances that reveal a dishonest motive. Over the centuries, courts have identified typical patterns of behavior that create suspicion of fraud — these are called badges of fraud.

Badges of fraud are not presumptions. Nor do they relieve the creditor of the burden of proving actual fraud. They are simply inferences that help to establish the creditor's case. If the creditor can show that suspicious circumstances attended the disposition of property, the factfinder may draw an inference of fraud unless the debtor offers a plausible explanation to the contrary.

The term "badges of fraud" is traditional. It is not used in the UFTA. However, §4(b) recognizes the evidentiary value of inferences. It lists examples of suspicious behavior and states that such factors may be considered, together with any other circumstances, in deciding the question of fraudulent intent. The list in §4(b) is drawn from badges of fraud that have been recognized by courts. It is not intended to be definitive. The determination of fraud is a factual matter, and the conduct of the debtor must be evaluated in each case. Also, some indicia of fraud are more compelling than others, and a combination of several suspicious factors strengthens the inference.

Some of the examples selected from the list illustrate the kinds of activity or circumstances that may give rise to an inference of fraud: The transfer was to an insider or someone with close family or other connections with the debtor; the debtor sought to conceal the transfer; the transfer occurred just before litigation or in the face of other impending collection activity; the transfer was made just before a significant debt was incurred. (The use of inferences is illustrated by Examples 1 and 2.)

It is the debtor's state of mind, rather than the transferee's, that is relevant. However, as discussed in section 4.6, the absence or presence of good faith on the transferee's part has an impact on the creditor's avoidance rights.

§4.4 CONSTRUCTIVE FRAUD

§4.4.1 General Principles

Constructive fraud is very different from actual fraud established by inference. If the facts constituting constructive fraud are established, a conclusive presumption of fraud is created, and inquiry into the debtor's state of mind is irrelevant. The word "constructive" indicates that fraud is construed as a matter of law rather than established by evidence of a guilty mind. The policy basis for recognizing this type of presumptive fraud is that a disposition under the defined circumstances unfairly diminishes the debtor's executable estate and should not be allowed, even if it was not deliberately dishonest. Constructive fraud was recognized by courts long before the drafting of the UFCA in 1918. The UFCA, and its successor, the UFTA, incorporate the concept of constructive fraud, even though the term "constructive fraud" is not used in the UFTA.

Constructive fraud has two basic elements: (1) the debtor did not receive reasonably equivalent value in exchange for the transfer, and (2) the debtor was in a shaky financial condition at the time of the transfer. This second element is only satisfied if the creditor can establish one of three specific factual situations at the time of transfer:

1. The debtor was involved in or was about to engage in a business venture, and the transfer left the debtor with insufficient capital for the project (§4(a)(2)(i)); or
2. the debtor was about to incur debts with the actual or imputed intention of not paying them when due (§4(a)(2)(ii)); or
3. the debtor was insolvent (§5(a)).

A creditor whose claim existed at the time of the transfer may use any one of the three forms of constructive fraud as grounds to avoid a transfer. (Section 5(b) provides an additional basis for avoidance on grounds of constructive fraud if the transfer was made to an insider. This section is not discussed further.) A creditor whose claim arose after the transfer may not rely on insolvency, but may use either of the other two. This is because undercapitalization and intent not to pay future debts are both concerned with prospective financial difficulties arising from the transfer.

§4.4.2 Reasonable Equivalence in Value

Under §3(a), value is given by the transferee if the debtor receives property in exchange for the transfer or a prior debt of the debtor is satisfied or secured. The UFTA itself does not provide a formula for determining whether value is reasonably equivalent. This is left to the courts.

The test of reasonable equivalence would be easy if courts simply used a mechanical formula in which economic values were compared and the quid pro quo received by the debtor was required to be worth at least a fixed percentage of the property transferred by the debtor. However, this approach is too rigid. After all, the test requires not simply equivalent value but reasonably equivalent value.

Therefore, it is not enough that the transaction was somewhat disadvantageous to the debtor. The values exchanged are highly relevant, of course (the less that the debtor received for the transfer the greater the likelihood of avoidance), but the entire context must be examined. The court will usually take into account the relationship of the parties, the market environment, and the apparent motive for the transfer. Even though constructive fraud is not premised on actual fraudulent intent, this does not mean that suspicious or unusual circumstances in the transfer are completely disregarded. The context may justify the lower value of the exchange, based on legitimate market considerations, or it may suggest that the return value was not reasonably equivalent. (*See also* section 4.5.)

It should also be noted that the value of property may be uncertain. Valuation is a factual issue on which there could be conflicting evidence. Where value is subject to doubt, it may be more difficult to be sure that the consideration received by the debtor was deficient.

§4.4.3 Financial Condition

a. Insolvency

There are two alternative tests for determining insolvency under the UFTA. The primary test, articulated in §2(a), is the balance sheet or bankruptcy test. Under this test, a debtor is insolvent when the sum of the debtor's debts exceeds the fair value of its assets. As mentioned before, the term "assets" is defined in §1(2) to exclude property to the extent of any exemption or encumbrance. It can be difficult for a creditor to prove insolvency under the balance sheet test, especially if it does not have access to the debtor's financial data. Therefore, §2(b) provides an alternative means of establishing insolvency, known as the equity test: A presumption of insolvency is created if the creditor can prove that the debtor is not paying its debts as they become due. That is, if the creditor cannot establish insolvency on the balance sheet test, a showing that the debtor is not generally paying debts when due creates a presumption of insolvency under the equity test, which shifts the burden to the debtor to show that it is in fact solvent under the balance sheet test. To show the general non-payment of due debts, the creditor must establish that there is a general pattern of nonpayment of a significant portion of the debtor's undisputed debt.[1]

Insolvency is measured at the time of the transfer. This means that the debtor may already have been insolvent when the transfer was made or may

---

1. As discussed in section 9.6.4, the debtor's general nonpayment of due debts is also grounds for the filing of an involuntary bankruptcy petition. Section 9.6.4 discusses the standards used for determining if the debtor is not generally paying due debts in that context.

have been rendered insolvent as a result of the disposition of the transferred property.

Proof of insolvency under either test may involve difficult issues. The balance sheet test requires assets to be given fair value, and the appraisal of assets can be a contentious matter. A creditor may similarly have difficulties in trying to establish insolvency on the equity test to take advantage of the presumption in §2(b). To determine whether a debtor is not generally paying debts as they become due, the court must consider the proportion of debts that are not being paid on time, the patterns of payment or nonpayment, and the reasons for nonpayment.

b. Undercapitalization or Intent to Incur Debts That Will Not Be Paid

As an alternative to showing insolvency, a creditor can rely on one of two other forms of financial instability. These two alternative tests move the focus from the traditional measure of financial precariousness — liabilities in excess of assets — to the relationship between the debtor's financial condition and intended future business activity. In broad terms, they allow the creditor to impugn a transfer for inadequate value if it was reckless or irresponsible in light of the debtor's prospective commercial dealings or if it would likely doom the debtor's planned venture to fairly certain failure. In some cases, the debtor's transfer under such circumstances may be tantamount to deliberate fraud, but this is a variety of constructive fraud; no deliberate intent to cheat creditors need be shown. Because these tests involve debtor action subsequent to the transfer, they may be relied on by future creditors as well as existing ones.

The factual issues presented by these alternative tests can be even more daunting than those involved in establishing insolvency. In an obvious case, it may be easy to show that a debtor was undercapitalized or was incurring debts without the justifiable expectation of repaying them. However, in many situations there could be quite divergent opinions about the level of assets needed for a venture or the debtor's prospects of generating future earnings sufficient to support new debt.

§4.5 THE RELATIONSHIP BETWEEN THE GROUNDS OF CONSTRUCTIVE FRAUD AND ACTUAL FRAUD

Actual fraud and constructive fraud are doctrinally distinct, as the last two sections have shown. However, in some cases the conduct of the debtor may furnish grounds for avoidance under both of them. Where this happens, the creditor has to decide which ground is more likely to succeed and provide the best relief.

For example, in addition to being the elements of constructive fraud, insolvency and lack of reasonable return consideration are suspicious circumstances that can be used by a creditor to build a case of actual fraud. (They are included in the list of relevant considerations in §4(b).) In deciding whether to proceed under actual or constructive fraud when these factors are present, the creditor will evaluate the degree to which they are clearly demonstrable and the existence of other indicia of fraud. Sometimes other tactical considerations may influence the creditor's choice when the facts support either ground. For example, a post-transfer creditor who cannot avoid the transfer on the basis of constructive fraud under §5(a) can use the facts of insolvency and inadequate consideration as part of the case for actual fraud.

The intersection of actual and constructive fraud is also illustrated by the contextual approach taken in determining reasonably equivalent value. As noted in section 4.4.2, courts look at factors beyond the arithmetical comparison of values when deciding the issue of reasonable equivalence. Underhanded behavior by the debtor could influence the court to find that the quid pro quo received by the debtor was not reasonably adequate, and conversely, honest motives could justify a low price.

In short, there is a clear doctrinal distinction between actual and constructive fraud. The former is concerned with the state of the debtor's mind, while the latter relies on specific objective criteria. However, in some cases the distinction may be blurred. The grounds have some components in common, and sometimes even objective criteria must be interpreted in context.

---

§4.6 THE REMEDY OF AVOIDANCE AND THE RIGHTS OF THE TRANSFEREE

Traditionally, the creditors' bill in equity had to be used to avoid a fraudulent transfer.[2] This cumbersome equitable suit[3] was replaced by a more efficient statutory cause of action under the UFCA. The statutory remedy has been further refined in §§7 and 8 of the UFTA. The creditor has a choice of two remedies:

---

2. The creditor's bill was introduced in section 3.7 in connection with proceedings in aid of execution.

3. Although the creditors' bill was an equitable remedy, the creditor's power of avoidance is legal in derivation. Therefore, prior to the creation of the statutory remedy, a suit to avoid the transfer was equitable, but a suit to recover damages from the transferee was legal. This classification may sound esoteric, but as you will see in section 7.4.2, it can have practical significance. In *Granfinanciera, S.A. v. Nordberg*, 492 U.S. 33 (1989), the U.S. Supreme Court held that the legal nature of a monetary claim against the transferee entitled the parties to a jury trial.

1. recovery of the property from the transferee so that it can be subjected to levy and sold in execution, or
2. a money judgment against the transferee for the lesser of either the value of the property measured at the time of transfer or the amount of the debt due by the debtor.

Whichever course is selected, the court has the discretion to order prejudgment remedies or other appropriate ancillary relief.

Suit may be brought against the person who acquired the property from the debtor or against a subsequent transferee. However, the UFTA protects the rights of persons who acquired the property in good faith. Therefore, even though the debtor's conduct provides grounds for avoidance, the creditor's power to recover the property or to obtain damages from the transferee is subject to a number of limitations. The rules can be summarized as follows:

(1) A good faith transferee from the debtor who gave reasonably equivalent value for the property is fully protected. No matter how guilty the debtor's motives were in conveying the property, the creditor cannot recover the property or damages from a transferee who gave the debtor fair equivalent value for it and acted honestly and without knowledge or reason to know of the debtor's fraudulent purpose.

(2) A transferee who acquired the property from the debtor in good faith, but for a value that was less than reasonably equivalent, receives partial protection. Where the transferee from the debtor acted in good faith, but the value for the transfer is not reasonably equivalent, the transfer is avoidable. The creditor can recover the property or obtain a money judgment. However, the transferee is entitled to offset against that recovery the value that had been given to the debtor for the property. If the property is returned for execution, this offset is secured by a lien and must be paid to the transferee from the proceeds of the execution sale. If the creditor receives a money judgment, the transferee's liability under the judgment is reduced by the offset.

(3) A bad faith transferee from the debtor is given no protection against the creditor. A transferee who acted in bad faith by actively or passively colluding with the debtor receives no protection from avoidance. Even if the transferee gave value to the debtor for the property, that value is not deductible from the creditor's recovery. The transferee may try to obtain restitution from the debtor, but that is not likely to be a promising enterprise. Not only is the debtor in financial difficulty, but also the court may not be inclined to award restitution to one who participated in the debtor's fraud.

(4) A subsequent transferee (i.e., one who did not take directly from the debtor) who acquired the property in good faith and for value is fully protected. Because the subsequent transferee did not deal with the debtor, the qualifications for immunity are somewhat lower than those for a transferee from the debtor. As long as the transferee acted in good faith and gave some value for the transfer, the equivalence of the value given for the property is not inquired into.

(5) A subsequent transferee, whether or not in good faith, shelters under the rights of a prior good faith transferee. A transferee who qualifies for protection from avoidance cuts off any rights that the creditor may have to recover the property. For that reason, the creditor has no right of avoidance against any person who acquired the property from the protected transferee, or later transferees.

(6) A subsequent transferee who did not act in good faith and did not derive rights through a good faith transferee has no protection. Like a bad faith transferee from the debtor, this transferee is subject to avoidance or a money judgment and has no offset for any value given for the property.

---

§4.7 FRAUDULENT TRANSFER LAW AND LEVERAGED BUYOUTS

§4.7.1 What Is a Leveraged Buyout?

A leveraged buyout (often referred to in abbreviated form as an LBO) is a transaction in which the purchase of shares in a corporation is financed by the corporation itself or secured by the assets of the corporation. In essence, the corporation makes available its own funds or other assets to enable the buyer to finance the purchase of its shares. This is in the nature of a loan by the corporation, and the expectation is that the corporate assets will be restored over time from future profits that the buyer will make from the operation of the corporation's business.

LBOs are structured in many different ways. One method is for the corporation to allow the buyer to use its unencumbered assets to secure the purchase price of the shares. The seller may give the buyer credit for the price of the shares and secures this credit by having the corporation grant a security interest in its assets; or the corporation may borrow money secured by its assets, and then it may lend this money to the buyer as an unsecured loan; or the buyer may borrow money from a financial institution, and the corporation guarantees this debt, using its assets to secure its guarantee.

A transaction like this is intended to enable the buyer to purchase the shares by using the resources of the corporation to acquire funding that would otherwise not be accessible to the buyer. Its effect is to encumber the assets of the corporation for a debt that benefits not the corporation itself, but its buyer. If the corporation is successfully managed, this prejudice to the corporation will eventually be reversed as the buyer's profits generate funds to settle the debt and release the corporate assets from the encumbrance. However, if the business does not produce large enough profits, the debt will not be repaid, and the assets will be foreclosed upon. The risk of failure is borne not only by the corporation, but also by its unsecured creditors who have lost the protection of recourse to unencumbered assets. Stated differently, before the LBO, the prior owner of the corporation had an equity interest that was junior to the claims of unsecured creditors. Following the LBO, this equity has been paid out and replaced by senior secured debt.

Some people view LBOs as serving useful purposes, such as the facilitation of changes in corporate management, the promotion of efficiency, and the enhancement of investment opportunities. Those who feel this way are likely to be persuaded by the argument that fraudulent transfer law should not be applied to LBOs unless they are actually fraudulent. The contrary view is that LBOs are manipulative devices that result in the appropriation of corporate assets and the imposition of crippling debt on a formerly viable corporation. From this perspective, fraudulent transfer law serves the useful purpose of shifting risk of the corporation's failure from the creditors to the parties who were responsible for the arrangements.

§4.7.2 The Application of Fraudulent Transfer Law to LBOs

LBOs are not per se fraudulent. However, when a corporation fails to pay its debts after an LBO, its creditors may look to fraudulent transfer law to avoid the transfer made by the corporation in connection with the LBO. In the type of transaction described above, this transfer is the grant of a security interest by the corporation. (The grant of a security interest is a disposition of rights in property that meets the definition of transfer under the UFTA.) To avoid the transfer, the creditor must establish either actual or constructive fraud in accordance with the general principles discussed above.

Sometimes actual fraud is present (that is, the LBO is dishonestly used as a pretext to plunder the corporation's assets). However, in most cases, the LBO is not a sham or fraud, but a good faith attempt to finance the sale of ownership in the corporation, undertaken in the expectation that the debt assumed by the corporation will ultimately be satisfied from future profits. In such cases, the basis for attacking the LBO is constructive fraud: The grant of a security interest in the corporate assets increased its debt over its assets, rendering it insolvent. It is not relevant that the owner may have received equivalent value for the transfer. The corporation, which is the debtor, did not.

Examples

1. Some years ago, when Awful Artful was a successful entrepreneur, he bought a painting by Claude Monet. Awful's business collapsed, and he is deeply in debt. He owes more than $25 million to his creditors. The Monet, worth $10 million, is his only remaining valuable asset. To ensure that his creditors could not get their hands on the painting, Awful sold it to his friend Hyde Hastily for $500 on the understanding that Hyde would not dispose of the painting to anyone else and that Awful had the right to buy it back whenever he wished for $600.

   Six months after the sale, one of Awful's unsecured creditors obtained judgment against him for $12 million. The creditor tried to levy on Awful's property, but the sheriff could find no property of value at Awful's home and rendered a nulla bona return. The creditor investigated and found out about the painting. Does the creditor have grounds to avoid the transfer from Awful to Hyde?

2. Assume that Awful did not sell the painting to Hyde as described in Example 1. Instead, he decided to sell the painting on the market and to use the proceeds to maintain the lavish lifestyle to which he had become accustomed. He therefore hired an art dealer and instructed him to find a buyer. Awful told the dealer to act quickly and discreetly and to insist on a cash sale. The dealer did find a buyer, Rob Grave, who offered to buy the painting for $8 million. Awful accepted, and the painting was exchanged for the cash. It did not take long for Awful to fritter away every cent of the $8 million on ludicrous extravagances. He is now destitute and has no executable assets. One of his unsecured creditors has found out about the sale of the painting. Does the creditor have grounds to recover the painting from Rob?

Explanations

1. This question is meant to illustrate a clear case of actual fraud. The creditor (defined in §1(4)) should succeed in avoiding the transfer under UFTA §4(a)(i). The sale of the painting is a transfer as defined in §1(12). The painting is an asset of Awful's under §1(2).[4] The grounds of

---

4. Assume, for the sake of simplicity, that Awful has no claim to an exemption in the painting under the state exemption statute. If he did have an exemption that covered the painting, it would likely be subject to a value limitation that would make the exemption minuscule in relation to the worth of the Monet. Where fraudulently transferred property is only partially exempt, the creditor may still recover and execute on it, but the debtor may be able to claim the amount of the exemption from the proceeds of the execution sale. Note, however, that a court may hold that the debtor waived any exemption in the property by fraudulenty transferring it.

actual fraud are satisfied because Awful made the transfer with the intent of hindering, delaying, or defrauding creditors. The creditor must prove fraudulent intent, but can do so by offering circumstantial evidence of intent — badges of fraud. The transaction exhibits several badges of fraud: It occurred while Awful was besieged by creditors, and shortly before this creditor's unsuccessful levy, Awful was insolvent on the balance sheet test, the painting was his last remaining asset, he received laughably inadequate consideration for it, Hyde is a close friend, and Awful had an understanding with Hyde for the return of the painting for a nominal sum in the future.

Because the creditor can likely prove actual fraud, it does not have to rely on grounds of constructive fraud, but under the circumstances of the case, the elements of constructive fraud are present — Awful was insolvent at the time of the transfer, and the painting was disposed of for an amount that does not even come close to reasonably equivalent value. (Note that the two grounds for constructive fraud also count as badges of fraud for the purposes of proving actual intent to defraud.) The creditor can therefore rely on constructive fraud as an alternative ground of avoidance. Note that only a creditor whose claim was in existence at the time of the transfer can use constructive fraud as a basis of avoidance. The facts indicate that this claim was in existence at the time of the transfer.

Even where a debtor has acted with fraudulent intent, the transferee is protected from avoidance if he is a good faith transferee for reasonably equivalent value. If he acted in good faith, but the value was not reasonably equivalent, he may be entitled to a lien for the value that he gave the debtor. In this case, Hyde appears to have knowingly collaborated with Awful in attempting to hide the painting, and therefore does not qualify for any protection.

2. Analysis of this problem can be broken up as follows:

(a) **Actual fraud.** Awful's disposition is motivated here, as it was in Example 1, by the desire to keep the Monet from his creditors. This case has several indicia of fraud in common with Example 1, but there are a few differences: Awful does not have a close relationship with the transferee, and the value received for the painting is much closer to being equivalent. On the other hand, Awful speedily dissipated the proceeds of the painting. There are surely enough suspicious circumstances to provide a solid case for actual fraud.

(b) **Constructive fraud.** The facts make it clear that Awful was already insolvent before the transfer, which aggravated this condition. However, the question of whether he received reasonably equivalent value is less clear. The consideration for the painting is much closer to its true value. (Although the value of the transferred property is stated in the Example, remember that value can be a difficult factual issue, often requiring expert testimony.) Eighty percent of the painting's value may or may not be a reasonably equivalent value in exchange for the painting. This decision should not be made solely on an arithmetical comparison, but should be determined in light of all the circumstances of the transaction. If the disposition was a fairly bargained, regular market transaction, there may be a justification for the buyer's offering and the seller accepting less than the market price. However, where the price is depressed as a result of a hasty clandestine disposition and is paid in cash, a good case can be made that 80 percent of the market value was not a reasonably equivalent exchange.

(c) **The transferee's defense or offset.** To be completely protected from avoidance of the transfer, Rob must qualify as a good faith purchaser for reasonably equivalent value. To receive the lesser protection of a lien or offset for the consideration paid, Rob must at least have acted in good faith. It has already been suggested that the price may not be reasonably equivalent. If this is so, the transfer will be avoided and the issue of the lien or offset arises.

There is a good argument that Rob did not act in good faith. Although there was no express collusion and the parties did not know each other, the transaction is unsavory. Rob may not have known the specifics of Awful's situation, but the suspicious circumstances of the sale should have put Rob on inquiry. Courts often attribute knowledge to one who avoids inquiry under circumstances that strongly suggest fraud. If Rob is found to have lacked good faith, he receives no offset or lien. His restitution claim against Awful is valueless because Awful has no assets.

The Nature, Source, and Policies of Bankruptcy Law

§5.1 WHAT IS BANKRUPTCY?

When a debtor becomes bankrupt, the debt collection procedures that are otherwise applicable in the jurisdiction are replaced by a powerful and wide-ranging system of laws and procedures. Bankruptcy has a profound impact on the debtor, creditors, and most other parties that have an interest in the debtor's affairs.

Bankruptcy takes different forms and is flexible enough to provide different goals. It is therefore difficult to devise a general definition of bankruptcy that is both precise and meaningful. However, one can begin to define bankruptcy by identifying some of the distinctive characteristics (expanded upon in the rest of this chapter) that make it so different from collection remedies under state law:

1. Bankruptcy is a remedial system provided for by federal law — more specifically, by Title 11 of the U.S. Code. (From now on, Title 11 is referred to as "the Code." When a Code section is cited, only the section symbol and number are used.)
2. It is a collective proceeding that draws in all the debtor's creditors and, with a few exceptions, encompasses all of the debtor's assets.
3. It is designed to fulfill two functions that are often in tension with each other: It affords relief to the debtor by resolving and settling current debts, while at the same time protecting creditors and

guarding their interests. As part of this function, it is aimed at pre-serving and maximizing the value of the debtor's estate.

4. It is administered by a "system" consisting of specialized courts, government officials, and private persons.

§5.2 THE FEDERAL NATURE OF BANKRUPTCY LAW

§5.2.1 The Federal Power over Bankruptcy

Outside of bankruptcy, the creation, performance, and enforcement of obli-gations is governed by state law, or in the case of some obligations, by generally applicable federal nonbankruptcy law.[1] (For example, an obliga-tion arising out of contract or tort is enforced in a state court under state law, while an obligation, say, to pay federal tax is enforced in a federal court under the Internal Revenue Code.). However, as soon as bankruptcy relief is sought, federal bankruptcy law is brought into effect. A new regime is established over the debtor's affairs that largely displaces the enforcement mechanisms that would normally be used outside of bankruptcy.

Bankruptcy law is federal because the Constitution grants to Congress the power "[t]o establish . . . uniform laws on the subject of bankruptcies throughout the United States." Art. I, §8. In addition, the supremacy clause states that the laws of the United States made pursuant to the Constitution shall be the supreme law of the land and take precedence over state laws. Art. VI, cl. 2.

Although the records of the Constitutional Convention say very little about the bankruptcy power, contemporaneous writings indicate that a centralized bankruptcy law was regarded as one of the economic reforms essential to a viable union. The frustrating diversity of the debtor/creditor laws of the Confederated States was a barrier to interstate commerce. By establishing a uniform bankruptcy law, the Drafters hoped to promote commercial order and efficiency and to lessen the disruptive influence of local interests and rivalries. The need for uniformity and the nationwide enforcement of the bankruptcy remedy remain an important justification of federal bankruptcy power.

§5.2.2 Bankruptcy Law and Nonbankruptcy Law

The Code uses the rather inelegant term "nonbankruptcy law" to describe the generally prevailing law of the jurisdiction in which a bankruptcy case is

---

1. The term "nonbankruptcy law" is explained in section 5.2.2.

filed. This includes the law of the state as well as all federal laws other than the Code.

In the absence of bankruptcy, nonbankruptcy law is the only law applicable to the debtor/creditor relationship. When bankruptcy occurs, bankruptcy law interacts with this body of prevailing nonbankruptcy law in a complex and multifaceted way. Under the Supremacy Clause, bankruptcy law preempts state law to the extent that they are inconsistent. However, because bankruptcy law is primarily focused on the treatment of rights that arise under state law, the field of federal preemption is quite narrow: It relates to the way in which rights are handled and enforced, and is not usually concerned with their creation and validity. These questions are generally still resolved under state law, even in the context of bankruptcy. You will therefore see that many matters in a bankruptcy case are resolved by a complex interaction between bankruptcy law and state law. In addition to preempting inconsistent state law, bankruptcy law may alter the effect of otherwise applicable federal nonbankruptcy law. This is not a matter of preemption. Rather, when provisions of bankruptcy law cannot be reconciled with other federal statutes, the court must interpret congressional intent to decide which is to prevail. (*See* Example 2.)

In the discussion of bankruptcy in the following chapters, there will be many examples of the interaction between nonbankruptcy and bankruptcy law. For the present, simply note that bankruptcy brings into effect a whole legal structure that may alter or affirm rights and procedures provided by the underlying network of state common and statute law and federal law. The extent to which nonbankruptcy law is overridden is usually expressed in the particular provisions of the Code. Sometimes, where congressional intent is less clear, questions of statutory interpretation may be presented.

§5.3 UNIFORMITY IN BANKRUPTCY LAW

Because rights in bankruptcy are frequently determined with reference to nonbankruptcy law (consisting largely of applicable state law), there can never be absolute and literal uniformity in the application of bankruptcy law. Diversity in local law inevitably produces non-uniform resolution of many identical issues in bankruptcy cases in different states. The question of whether this contravenes the constitutional requirement that there must be a uniform bankruptcy law throughout the United States was settled by the U.S. Supreme Court over a century ago. The Bankruptcy Act of 1898 deferred completely to state exemption laws so that the exemptions available to an individual debtor in bankruptcy varied from state to state.[2] In *Hanover National Bank v. Moyses*, 186 U.S. 181 (1902), the Court upheld the Act's incorporation of state exemption laws and laid down what has remained a fundamental principle governing uniformity: Absolute uniformity is not required. Uniformity is "geographical and not personal," and the requirement of uniformity is met when "the trustee takes in each state whatever would have been awardable to the creditors if the bankrupt law had not been passed." Therefore, the requirement of uniformity should not be viewed too literally or absolutely. While a uniform bankruptcy law is required, in the sense that the same rules of bankruptcy law must apply nationwide, the impact of applicable local laws on those uniform rules of bankruptcy law does not render the law nonuniform. Although *Hanover National Bank* concerned uniformity in exemption laws, this is just one area in which one should expect to find diversity in the application of bankruptcy law. There are many other variations in prevailing nonbankruptcy law that affect the outcome of important issues to be settled in the bankruptcy case, including the extent and validity of liens, the legitimacy of creditors' claims, and the estate's right to property.[3]

Quite apart from variations in nonbankruptcy law, the requirement of uniformity in bankruptcy law must be understood in light of the structure of the federal court system and the operation of judicial precedent. There are many diverse (and sometimes dramatically diverse) judicial interpretations of provisions of the Code. Because the decisions of bankruptcy and district courts do not create binding precedent, and because the courts of one circuit are not bound by decisions in another, it is common to find that sections of the Code are applied differently by different courts. The U.S. Supreme Court occasionally resolves divergent interpretations of bankruptcy law, but for the most part, we have to live with fact that there cannot be true and literal nationwide uniformity in the judicial interpretation and application of the rules that Congress enacted in the Code.

---

2. As explained in section 3.2, and more fully discussed in section 13.2, an exemption is a right granted to an individual debtor in both state law and bankruptcy law to immunize certain types or items of property from the claims of creditors. Under state law, a creditor may not levy on exempt property to satisfy a debt, and in bankruptcy, the individual debtor may exclude exempt property from assets available for the payment of creditors, As discussed in section 13.2, the Code still allows state exemptions to apply in bankruptcy if the state so elects. so that state law exemptions are still applicable in most bankruptcy cases.

3. The issue of whether a Code provision violated the constitutional requirement of uniformity came up again in relation to the enactment in 2005 of a means test for Ch. 7 eligibility, provided for in §707(b). The means test was held not to violate the constitutional requirement of uniformity. See section 9.8.4.

§5.4 THE STATUTORY SOURCE OF BANKRUPTCY LAW

§5.4.1 Federal Bankruptcy Legislation

The current code, 11 U.S.C. §§101 *et seq.*, was enacted as the Bankruptcy Reform Act in 1978, and has been amended several times since then, as detailed below. It is the fifth bankruptcy statute enacted by Congress. The first three were passed at various times in the nineteenth century, but none of them lasted very long, and for much of that century there was no federal bankruptcy law, leaving debtor/creditor relations to be governed only by state law. In 1898, Congress passed the Bankruptcy Act, which turned out to be the first durable bankruptcy statute. It lasted, with much amendment and judicial embellishments, until it was replaced in 1978 by the current Code. By the end of the 1960s, it had become clear that the old Act was outdated and had been patched up too much by amendments, judicial decisions, and procedural rules promulgated by the courts. Congress, therefore, appointed a commission in 1970 to study the bankruptcy law and to recommend a new comprehensive statute. The commission's report and proposed statute, released in 1973, drew on the traditions established under the old Act, and preserved many of its rules and principles. However, it also made many significant changes to substantive law and procedure. The report was controversial, leading to much debate and the passage of different bills in each house of Congress. Ultimately, differences were resolved in compromise, and the 1978 Code was enacted. Some of the compromises were uneasy, and never finally settled the differences that underlay them. As a result, some of these questions continue to generate debate and calls for reform.

Since its enactment in 1978, the Code has been amended several times. In addition to occasional piecemeal changes to individual sections, it has been subjected to four wide-ranging amending statutes. The first, passed in 1984, was principally concerned with trying to overcome constitutional problems relating to bankruptcy court jurisdiction. (*See* section 7.3.) The second, passed in 1986, made a number of small amendments, introduced a new form of debt adjustment for family farmers, and established a nationwide U.S. Trustee system.

The third, the Bankruptcy Reform Act of 1994, began its progress through Congress in 1992. It originated as a fairly comprehensive and extensive revision of the Code, but it was pared down to a less ambitious undertaking when it became apparent that its more controversial aspects would not pass. A compromise bill was drafted too late in the session to be acted upon, but it was revived the following year and enacted. With its controversial elements abandoned, the 1994 statute is quite tame. It deals with a variety of discrete problems that had arisen in the application and interpretation of the Code. These various changes affect both consumer and business bankruptcies, and they are noted in later chapters where pertinent to the topic under discussion.

The more complex and contentious issues were left for further consideration by a National Bankruptcy Review Commission established under the 1994 Act, whose charge was to evaluate and propose reforms to the Code. After extensive hearings and study, the Commission submitted its report in 1997. The Commission's report and recommendations are noted in connection with the relevant topics in the rest of this book. In some areas, the commissioners made unanimous recommendations for reform. However, they disagreed on others, on which they submitted a majority and dissenting report. The most explosive issue that divided the commissioners related to the problem of dealing with the high rate of individual bankruptcies in the United States. Some of the commissioners believed that this problem is best addressed by imposing greater demands on debtors to pay more to creditors in a bankruptcy case. Others believed that the problem is systemic and caused by factors beyond the control of most debtors, such as job loss, the lack of medical insurance, and an inadequate social safety net. On this view, imposing more rigorous standards on debtors just increases hardship without addressing the root problem.

The report engendered fierce reaction from the public and in Congress, and formed the backdrop to the fourth significant amendment to the Code, the Bankruptcy Abuse Prevention and Consumer Protection Act of 2005 (BAPCPA). Congress was very selective in picking which of the Commission's recommendations to adopt. It disregarded some of them and even passed some provisions that conflicted with what was recommended. Because some aspects of the statute were so controversial, it took Congress several attempts between 1998 and 2005 to pass it. The various amendments to the Code enacted in BAPCPA are discussed in the appropriate places throughout this book. For now it is enough to make two general observations about BAPCPA. First, it adopted a more rigorous approach to individual debtors, imposing tougher demands on debtors who are deemed to be capable of making greater payments to creditors in a bankruptcy case. Second, many provisions of BAPCPA were poorly drafted, leading to interpretational puzzles and divergent judicial resolutions of unclear language.

§5.4.2 The Structure and Organization of the Code and Ancillary Statutes

It is useful to take note of the structure of the Code and other laws pertaining to bankruptcy. An understanding of this structure can help you to find Code provisions and to recognize the scope of their application.

a. The Code Itself

In its current form (which has been somewhat changed since its original enactment in 1978) the Code consists of nine chapters: 1, 3, 5, 7, 9, 11, 12, 13, and 15. This book does not cover Ch. 9, which governs municipal bankruptcies, or Ch. 15, which was enacted by BAPCPA to deal with cross-border (international) insolvency cases. The remaining seven chapters fall into two broad categories. The first three (Chs. 1, 3, and 5) contain general provisions that are meant to apply to all bankruptcy cases under consideration unless they are irrelevant on the facts or some overriding provision in the specific governing chapter applies instead. Each of the other chapters (Chs. 7, 11, 12, and 13) is devoted to a separate and different form of bankruptcy. When a bankruptcy petition is filed, one of these chapters must be selected, and the specific provisions of that chapter will govern the case, together with general Chs. 1, 3, and 5. The provisions of the other specific chapters are not of force unless they are expressly incorporated by the governing chapter. It is important to remember this because the temptation to generalize some of the sections in a specific chapter can be strong.

The four different types of bankruptcy covered by Chs. 7, 11, 12, and 13 are explained more fully in Chapter 8. In short, Ch. 7 covers liquidation and may be used by both individuals and corporate entities where the goal is to liquidate the estate — that is, to realize its assets and distribute the proceeds to creditors. The remaining three chapters provide for various form of rehabilitation, under which the debtor proposes a plan that devotes income or property to making a distribution to creditors over time. Each of these three rehabilitation chapters is designed for different types of debtor. Ch. 11 is the most widely applicable and is available both to individual debtors and to corporate entities. Ch. 12 is confined to debtors who qualify as "family farmers" or "family fishermen," and Ch. 13 is confined to individual debtors with relatively small levels of debt.

b. Other Statutes Related to Bankruptcy Cases

Section 5.2.2 noted that various federal statutes might apply in a bankruptcy case by virtue of being part of the nonbankruptcy law that is pertinent to transactions, rights, or obligations involved in the case. This note does not refer to federal laws that make up part of nonbankruptcy law. Rather, it identifies federal statutes, in addition to the Code, that have a direct bearing on bankruptcy. Title 28 of the U.S. Code has a number of important provisions relating to the bankruptcy system: Ch. 6 (§§151-158) deals with the appointment, duties, and functions of bankruptcy judges; Ch. 39 (§§581-589a) provides for the U.S. Trustee system; Ch. 85 (§1334) governs bankruptcy jurisdiction; and Ch. 87 (§§1408-1412) deals with matters of venue.

These provisions of title 28 are considered in Chapter 7. Title 18 (not discussed further in this book) also has direct relevance to bankruptcy: 18 U.S.C. §§151-155 deals with crimes of dishonesty and embezzlement committed during the course of a bankruptcy case.

§5.4.3 Dollar Amounts in the Code

Many sections of the Code specify dollar amounts for a variety of different purposes, such as prescribing debt ceilings for eligibility for certain forms of relief, limiting the debtor's exemptions in property, limiting the amount of a qualifying claim that may be accorded priority status, or determining if a debtor's income is sufficient to support a payment plan. As originally enacted in 1978, the Code had no mechanism for the adjustment of these dollar amounts for inflation. As a result they shrank in value as the years passed. This problem was rectified by the Bankruptcy Reform Act of 1994, which increased the dollar amounts to account for inflation over the preceding 16 years and provided for the administrative adjustment of dollar amounts every three years thereafter. The adjustments, based on changes in the Consumer Price Index, are made by the Judicial Conference of the United States at three-year intervals and apply to cases filed after the effective date of the adjustment, which is April 1.

The most recent adjustment took effect on April 1, 2013, and the next will be made on April 1, 2016. Because the 2013 dollar amounts are in effect at the time of writing this edition of the book, they are used in this edition. Note, however, that the adjusted dollar amounts apply only to cases commenced after their effective date. Therefore, the amounts used in this book apply only to cases commenced after April 1, 2013, and before the next adjustment on April 1, 2016. Cases commenced before April 1, 2013, are subject to whatever lower amount was in effect at the date of commencement, and cases commenced after April 1, 2016, will be subject to the new amounts applicable after that date. Although it is necessary to know the applicable amount in an actual bankruptcy case, for purposes of studying and understanding the law, you can simply rely on the amounts stated in this book and should not be confused if you see different amounts reflected in cases or in the version of the Code that you are using.

§5.4.4 The Bankruptcy Rules

The Code deals with the substantive law of bankruptcy. While it prescribes procedures in broad terms, it does not set out rules of procedure in detailed form. These rules have been promulgated by the Supreme Court in the exercise of its power under 28 U.S.C. §2075. They are intended to effectuate the provisions of the Code and are meant to supplement rather than contradict it. The rules may not alter substantive rights under the Code, and in the case of conflict the Code prevails.

In addition to the bankruptcy rules, the Federal Rules of Civil Procedure are relevant to bankruptcy practice to the extent that the rules incorporate them or do not provide for a contrary procedure. Of importance to local practitioners is Bankruptcy Rule 9029, which allows each district court to make its own local rules provided that they are not inconsistent with the Bankruptcy Rules.

§5.5 THE POLICIES AND GOALS OF BANKRUPTCY LAW

§5.5.1 Introduction

The policies and goals of bankruptcy law are raised frequently in the discussion of the substantive rules and principles of bankruptcy law in the rest of this book. It is important to identify and understand the reasons for the substantive rules and the ends that they are intended to achieve. This section is just an overview of these themes, which will recur in the remainder of the book. It introduces and alerts you to the fundamental goals that underlie bankruptcy law. As you read through this overview of bankruptcy policy, bear in mind:

1. Bankruptcy relief is usually sought only after the debtor's economic difficulties have become serious enough to merit the drastic step of a bankruptcy filing. Therefore, the principal goal of bankruptcy is to manage financial distress and to do the best job possible of preserving what can be saved for the benefit of the debtor, creditors, and others whose interests are impacted by the debtor's financial circumstances.
2. Bankruptcy law is sensitive to the rights that creditors and other parties have under nonbankruptcy law. Although bankruptcy will have an adverse effect on many of these rights, the goal is to affect them only to the extent necessary to further the aims of the Code.
3. Bankruptcy policy cannot be considered in a vacuum. There are many other public policies, reflected in other state and federal laws, which may be implicated in a bankruptcy case. Where other public policies have to be taken into account, these policies may not be congruent with policies of bankruptcy law, so it may be necessary to reconcile or prioritize countervailing policy goals. For example, the bankruptcy goal of providing relief to the debtor from prepetition obligations may not be in accord with the policies and the goals of criminal

law, tort law, environmental law, or family law, which may be obstructed by releasing the debtor from those obligations. Sometimes the Code itself indicates how bankruptcy policy should be accommodated to other public policies, but in other cases courts are left with the task of deciding how to accommodate bankruptcy policy to other public interests.

§5.5.2 The Fundamental Goals and Policies of Bankruptcy

a. The Protection of Both Debtor and Creditor Interests

In its original conception, bankruptcy was purely a creditor's remedy. It allowed creditors to place a delinquent debtor in bankruptcy for the purpose of liquidating his assets for the payment of his debts. To the extent that the bankruptcy distribution was not enough to pay the debts in full, the debtor could be imprisoned until friends or family could raise the money to settle what he owed. As the law developed, it gradually became more sympathetic to the protection of an honest debtor who suffered financial adversity and could not pay his creditors in full. In modern law, it is well established that bankruptcy serves not only the interests of creditors, but also aims at providing relief from overwhelming debt to an honest debtor. It helps creditors by providing an evenhanded and controlled environment for the settlement of the debtor's affairs and the distribution of available assets. It helps the debtor by providing relief from the pressures of financial failure and making available the means of settling otherwise unmanageable debt.

Of course, the interests of the creditors and the debtor are often in conflict, so one of the difficult tasks of bankruptcy law is to strike an appropriate balance between them. The best way to balance these competing interests is subject to ongoing debate. Some commentators emphasize creditor protection and advocate for bankruptcy laws that will maximize creditor returns. Others take a broader view of the social costs and consequences of bankruptcy, and argue for rules that will best protect vulnerable debtors and place the least amount of stress on the social fabric. You will find the tension between these goals at the base of many discussions in later chapters of this book.

b. The Collective and Evenhanded Treatment of Creditors

The mandatory collective nature of the bankruptcy remedy is often identified as one of its most important hallmarks. Upon the filing of a bankruptcy petition, creditors are stayed from pursuing individual debt collection efforts and, whether they like it or not, are compelled to have their claims handled in the bankruptcy case. The debtor's assets at the time of the petition are placed under the control of the bankruptcy court and cannot be disposed of except in accordance with bankruptcy law. It is a fundamental principle of bankruptcy that creditors must be treated evenhandedly so that claims of equal legal rank must be treated the same. This does not mean that all creditors are paid the same. Secured claims are entitled to payment to the extent of their security interests, and the Code gives certain unsecured claims priority. However, differentiation between creditors is based on the strength of their legal rights, rather than on their speed in initiating collection procedures.

c. The Preservation of the Estate

One of the crucial goals of bankruptcy is the preservation of the debtor's assets. This both protects the debtor from creditor collection activity and protects creditors by preserving property so that it can ultimately be made available for distribution to pay their claims. Estate preservation is not simply a passive handover of the debtor's existing property. The Code provides several means by which the bankruptcy trustee can enhance the value of the estate, for example, by recovering dispositions, challenging claims to property, and dealing with unperformed contracts. In addition to protecting the debtor and creditors, the preservation of the estate of a business debtor can achieve wider social goals where the aim of bankruptcy is the debtor's rehabilitation. Successful rehabilitation can benefit employees of the debtor, the community in which the business operates, and customers or suppliers reliant on the business.

d. The Debtor's "Fresh Start"

Provided that the debtor has complied with the Code's requirements and has surrendered executable assets or sufficient property and future income for distribution to creditors, the debtor is entitled to a new financial beginning, unburdened by the unpaid balance of prebankruptcy debts. This is commonly referred to as the debtor's "fresh start," and it is a firmly established goal of modern bankruptcy law. There are several Code provisions that aim at the debtor's fresh start: for example, the individual debtor's exemptions, the limitations on property to be included in the estate, and the discharge. Of these, the discharge is the most central. It releases the debtor from the balance of prepetition debts that were not fully paid in the case. The fresh start has an obvious and important benefit to the debtor, but it is also intended to benefit society as a whole by giving the debtor the opportunity of becoming self-sufficient and productive. Of course, the discharge comes at the expense of creditors, who lose the unpaid balance of their claims. Therefore, the Code seeks to balance the debtor's fresh start against the protection of creditor rights, and has a number of provisions that allow courts to restrict or refuse the discharge where the debtor has engaged in dishonest, improper, or abusive conduct.

e. Efficient Administration

The Code and related statutes create a system to handle bankruptcy cases, so it is worth adding efficient administration to the goals of bankruptcy law, none of which could be properly achieved if the system for administering the law is inadequate. Many provisions of the Code and related statutes deal with the structure and operation of the bankruptcy system, the efficient implementation of the law, and the prevention of abuse. The question of whether current statutory provisions succeed in making the system as efficient as it could be is the subject of ongoing debate.

f. The Preference for Reorganization and Debt Adjustment

As introduced in section 5.4.2 and explained more fully in section 8.2, the Code provides for two forms of bankruptcy — liquidation and rehabilitation. In essence, in a liquidation (provided for in Ch. 7), all the debtor's prepetition property is taken over by the bankruptcy trustee who realizes it and uses the proceeds to pay creditors. Where the proceeds are insufficient to pay creditors in full, they receive payment only to the extent of available proceeds. Where the debtor is an individual, the balance of the debts is discharged provided that the debtor is in compliance with the requirements of the Code. In a rehabilitation case (provided for in Chs. 11, 12, and 13),[4] the debtor is able to retain prepetition property and provides for the payment of debts through a payment plan over a number of years. As a general principle, the expectation in these chapters is that payments to creditors under the plan must at least equal but should ideally exceed what creditors would obtain in a liquidation. The Code has a preference for rehabilitation over liquidation. It could be argued that this is not really a goal in itself, but rather a mechanism through which bankruptcy may achieve its fundamental goals of creditor protection and the debtor's fresh start. Nevertheless, the Code's emphasis on rehabilitation as the preferred form of bankruptcy is strong, and therefore worth including in this overview of bankruptcy policies.

The benefits of rehabilitating a corporation are easy to see. If the corporation is liquidated, it dies. Its business comes to an end, its owners (shareholders) lose their investment, its employees lose their jobs, and its creditors recover no more than the liquidation value of its assets. Therefore,

---

4. As noted in section 5.4.2, Ch. 9 also provides for rehabilitation, but Ch. 9 is confined to municipalities and is not covered in this book.

if it is possible to reorganize the corporation so that it emerges from bankruptcy as a viable business, creditors have a prospect of greater recovery and the enterprise can continue to provide jobs and to participate in the marketplace. (This does not mean that the corporation's employees and owners emerge unscathed. Reorganization often results in a reduction in the corporation's workforce and in employee benefits. Also, reorganization may wipe out the equity of prepetition shareholders and pass ownership to creditors or new investors.)

Where the debtor is an individual, liquidation under Ch. 7 is the debtor's only choice where he does not have enough income to support a payment plan that will give creditors at least as much as they would have gained from the liquidation. However, where a debtor does expect a good future income and has executable property of relatively low value, liquidation may be an attractive option to the debtor but a bad deal for creditors. By sacrificing his prepetition property to creditors, the debtor settles his debt at a fraction of its amount, obtains a discharge of the balance, and can keep his future income for himself. Although this promotes the fresh start policy, it has been a concern ever since the enactment of the Code in 1978 that liquidation can provide an easy way out for a debtor who has the financial ability to pay a greater percentage of his debts through rehabilitation under Ch. 13 or Ch. 11. Prior to the passage of BAPCPA, the Code provided some incentives to encourage an individual debtor to pursue rehabilitation rather than liquidation. However, the incentives were quite weak, which led to the argument that a firmer approach was needed to press individual debtors into making a greater effort to commit to a payment plan. Congress was persuaded by this argument, and it did include provisions in BAPCPA that make it more difficult for an individual debtor to seek liquidation bankruptcy under Ch. 7 where he has the apparent means to support a payment plan that would result in a greater return to creditors.

Those who favor the BAPCPA amendments believe that they strike the proper balance between debtor and creditor interests. Those who criticize the amendments say they have created undue complexity, cause hardship to many debtors, and hamper courts in the use of discretion to achieve fair and workable results in bankruptcy cases. (This is discussed in Chapter 8 and in section 9.8.)

Examples

1. The debtor sold a house some years before he filed a Ch. 7 petition. Although the buyer paid the full price of the house to the debtor, the parties never got around to executing and filing the documents that would transfer title to the buyer. Section 541(a) includes in property of the estate "all legal or equitable interests of the debtor in property as of the commencement of the case." Although the section does not state so

expressly, it is well established that the question of whether a debtor has a legal or equitable interest in property must be determined under non-bankruptcy law.[5] Under the law of the state in which the debtor is domiciled, he still has a legal interest in the property because he is still the owner of record. However, in the law of some other states, the sale of the house to the buyer and full payment of the price would extinguish the debtor's rights in the property, so he would not be treated as having a legal interest in the house, despite the fact that the title is still registered in his name. The effect of this is that in the debtor's state, the house will be property of the estate, but in other states it would not be. Can an argument be made that different treatment of the debtor's interest in the house, dependent merely on the debtor's state of domicile, offends the constitutional requirement that Congress enacts a uniform law of bankruptcy?

2. A (hypothetical) federal statute enacted in 1975 provides for the issuance of a trading license to enable the license holder to import certain types of goods. The statute clearly states that the bankruptcy of the license holder results in automatic revocation of the license. As we will discuss more fully in Chapter 12, upon filing a bankruptcy petition, all the legal and equitable interests that a debtor holds as at the petition date become property of the bankruptcy estate under §541. The more inclusive the bankruptcy estate, the better creditors will fare in recovering their claims from the estate, so the policy of maximizing creditor returns is strongly implicated in ensuring that the estate does receive all the debtor's property. For this reason, §541(c) invalidates any provision in an agreement or applicable nonbankruptcy law that restricts the transfer of the debtor's property to the estate or that effects a forfeiture of it on bankruptcy. Does §541 preempt the provisions of the 1975 federal statute?

3. In college, Bratford Binge was described as a boy wonder. He was the youngest summa cum laude to graduate from a prestigious business school. As a result, he had no trouble landing a glorious job at an impressive salary. Although immensely talented at his work, Bratford is spoiled, and he denies himself nothing. As a result, he has accumulated massive credit card debt by taking expensive vacations and eating at the finest restaurants. He has now accumulated so much debt that, even on his generous salary, he cannot cope with the payments due his creditors. Because his expenditures are related to travel and entertainment, he has not acquired assets of any value. Bratford would like to eliminate this crushing debt and start over. Should he be able to file a bankruptcy

---

5. The issue of deciding what property of the debtor becomes property of the estate is discussed in section 12.2.

petition so that he can enjoy the advantages of the Code's fresh start policy?

4. Precious Little, Inc. has filed a petition for liquidation under Ch. 7. It is badly insolvent. Its debts amount to $750,000 and the total value of its assets is $20,000. Its business has declined badly in the last couple of years, and its revenue is insufficient to cover its operating expenses. How does this significant disproportion between its assets and liabilities and its inadequate revenue affect the achievement of the goals of bankruptcy law in this case?

Explanations

1. As explained in section 5.3, this issue has been long settled. The constitutional requirement of uniformity means that the provisions of bankruptcy law enacted by Congress must apply nationwide. Congress cannot enact provisions that apply only to select states. Uniformity does not require that the rules in the Code apply with the same effect in each state. Section 541(a) does apply throughout the United States even though its interaction with the law of particular states may lead to different results. Section 541(a) is one of many provisions that require recourse to nonbankruptcy law for the determination of rights that will be impacted by the bankruptcy case. This should not be surprising because it is one of the goals of bankruptcy law to try to mesh as closely as possible with rights held by parties under nonbankruptcy law.

2. Although federal bankruptcy law preempts conflicting state law, it is not appropriate to talk of preemption where the conflicting nonbankruptcy law is federal. Rather, the contradictory statutes must be reconciled by the process of statutory interpretation. The court must decide which provision was intended by Congress to be controlling. Congressional intent is clearest where one or the other statute expressly states that it overrides the other. In the absence of such a clear indication, a court will have to glean legislative intent by interpretation of the language of the statute, any legislative history, and enunciated or apparent policy goals. One of the canons of interpretation that may help in close cases is that Congress is supposed to remember what its earlier legislation said, so that a provision in a later statute is assumed to take precedence over an earlier conflicting statute. On the basis of this rule, the argument could be made that the Code, enacted three years after the other statute, was intended to override it. It must be stressed, however, that this canon of interpretation is just one factor to be considered, and it is not appropriately used where there are more reliable indications of congressional intent.

3. Bratford is a reckless spendthrift. He used credit irresponsibly and now wishes to discharge that debt and get a fresh start. Bankruptcy relief is intended to help the honest debtor who has encountered financial difficulty. A debtor whose financial troubles were caused by circumstances beyond his control, such as the loss of his job, unmanageable uninsured medical expenses, or the failure of his business, is a more sympathetic figure than a debtor who brought his problems upon himself by the irresponsible use of credit. Nevertheless, unless it can be shown that Bratford acted fraudulently or in bad faith in incurring the debt or in relation to the bankruptcy filing, his self-indulgent behavior is not likely to be grounds for refusing him bankruptcy relief. However, Bratford will be disappointed if he hopes to file a petition under Ch. 7 so that he can discharge most of his debt by sacrificing his few nonexempt assets. Because he has assets of little value and a significant income, provisions of Chs. 7 and 13 will preclude him from taking the easy way out under Ch. 7 and will require him to propose a plan under Ch. 11 or 13. To get the plan confirmed, he will have to commit his disposable income (his salary less his expenses as calculated under the Code) over some years to the payment of his debts. This is discussed in detail in Chapters 9 and 20. For now, this broad description of the obligation of higher payment, imposed on an individual consumer debtor with a good income, is used merely to highlight the balance between the policies of debtor relief and creditor protection.

4. The goals and policies of bankruptcy law can only be fully satisfied where the estate is at least large enough to achieve all its purposes. Financial resources are needed to rehabilitate a business, and where, as here, the debtor has insufficient assets and no source of adequate future income, the Code's policy of providing a fresh start to the corporation and favoring its rehabilitation cannot be achieved. Where there is no means of funding a rehabilitation, it is simply not an option. This leaves the alternative of liquidation, but even here the paucity of assets means that the bankruptcy cannot fully satisfy all its desired ends. It can ensure that creditors are treated evenhandedly (so that the race for remaining assets can be stopped and any preferential payments made shortly before the filing can be recovered for the benefit of the estate as a whole), but the small pool of assets is likely to be expended fully or in substantial part on the costs of liquidating the bankrupt estate. This means that unsecured creditors will either receive no distribution at all or will receive a minimal payment on their claims.

   It is one of the sad realities of bankruptcy that many estates are just too poor to afford any significant distribution to unsecured creditors. The costs of administering an estate are paid as high priority before general unsecured creditors can receive anything, and these costs can be large. They include not only the trustee's compensation, but also any fees that must be paid to professionals (such as attorneys or accountants) engaged by the estate, and the costs of caring for and disposing of the estate's property. It does not take much to eat up a small estate, leaving it devoid of assets for funding a distribution. Of course, the policy of efficient and cost-effective administration dictates that the trustee's management of the estate should not be disproportionately expensive or wasteful, and the trustee has a duty to try to keep costs down as much as possible.

6

Participants in the Bankruptcy Case

§6.1 THE BANKRUPTCY COURT

The bankruptcy court, presided over by a bankruptcy judge, is the court most directly and intimately involved with the bankruptcy case from its inception to its final closing. Routinely, it deals as court of first instance with all matters that require judicial supervision, determination, or approval during the course of the case.

However, as explained in Chapter 7, the constitutional stature of the bankruptcy court is awkward. Bankruptcy judges are not appointed with life tenure under Article III of the U.S. Constitution, but are appointed for a fourteen-years term under Article I. Because they are not appointed under Article III, their jurisdiction is limited and many issues in a bankruptcy case have to be decided finally by district courts. The bankruptcy court is statutorily described as a "unit" of the U.S. district court. The complexities of bankruptcy court jurisdiction and the impact of limitations on that jurisdiction is left for discussion in chapter 7. Notwithstanding these limits on its jurisdiction, the bankruptcy court is the judicial forum at the very center of the bankruptcy case.

§6.2 THE TRUSTEE

§6.2.1 Appointment and Qualification, Generally

The trustee is a private person (not a public official) who represents and administers the bankruptcy estate. The trustee's duties vary, depending on chapter under which the case is filed, as explained below. In broad terms, she is responsible for all aspects of estate administration, she litigates on behalf of the estate, processes and makes distributions on claims, controls estate property, investigates the debtor's affairs, and, in general, acts to further the interests of the estate and the collective interests of creditors. A trustee is required in cases under Chs. 7, 12, and 13. A trustee is not usually appointed in a Ch. 11 case, in which the debtor assumes the trustee's functions as a debtor in possession, as explained in section 6.2.4. The Code authorizes the election of a trustee by creditors in cases under Chs. 7 and 11. In other cases, or where creditors do not exercise the right of election in a Ch. 7 or 11 case, the trustee is appointed by the U.S. Trustee (a public official) who is introduced in section 6.3. The trustee is appointed from a panel established by the U.S. Trustee, consisting of qualified persons who have applied to serve.

The Code does not have any detailed provisions relating to the qualifications of a trustee. Section 321 states general requirements of residency and competence. Sections 701, 1104(b), and 1302(a) require the trustee to be a "disinterested person," which is defined in §101(14) to exclude a wide variety of persons such as creditors, owners, insiders, officers, employees, and others whose interests are materially adverse to those of the estate. 28 U.S.C. §586(d) requires the Attorney General to prescribe more detailed and specific qualifications for membership on the trustee panels. The qualifications so promulgated include honesty, impartiality, professional qualifications (such as a law degree or a CPA), and requirements of general competence and experience. In addition to these qualifications, a trustee is required by §322 to post a bond guaranteeing the faithful performance of her duties. A trustee may be removed under §324(a) for cause, which includes incompetence, violation of fiduciary duty, misconduct, or conflict of interest.

§6.2.2 Ch. 7 Cases

The duties of a trustee in a Ch. 7 case are set out in general terms in §704. In essence, the trustee's principal function is to liquidate and distribute the bankrupt estate. This primarily involves the collection of property of the estate, its realization, and its distribution to creditors. While this process may involve some interim administration of property to preserve its value, the trustee is not normally involved in the long-term management of the assets or operation of a business. The goal is to liquidate the estate as expeditiously as possible.

In pursuing this general goal, the trustee performs a number of specific duties discussed in succeeding chapters, such as investigating the debtor's affairs, employing professionals, recovering voidable dispositions, examining and contesting claims, litigating over estate interests, and making recommendations to the court on questions such as the debtor's discharge.

The permanent trustee only takes office at the meeting of creditors. Therefore, §701 provides for the appointment of an interim trustee by the U.S. Trustee. In voluntary cases, the interim trustee is appointed promptly after the filing of the petition, while in involuntary cases, the interim trustee is appointed only after the court has granted the involuntary petition. However, the court is empowered by §303(g) to order the earlier appointment if it is shown that the estate needs immediate protection. Unless creditors choose to elect a trustee at the creditors' meeting, the interim trustee becomes the permanent trustee.

§6.2.3 Ch. 12 and 13 Cases

A trustee is also required in debt adjustment cases under Chs. 12 and 13. Her powers and duties are set out generally in §§1202 and 1302. As explained more fully in section 8.2, these cases differ from a liquidation case under Ch. 7 because their goal is not to liquidate the debtor's estate, but to revest all or part of the estate in the debtor upon confirmation of a plan of payment. Thus, the central role of the trustee is not the realization of property of the estate. The trustee is more concerned with other functions such as investigating the debtor's affairs, examining and contesting claims, recovering voidable dispositions, making recommendations on the debtor's plan, and ensuring its implementation. If the Ch. 13 debtor has a business at the time of bankruptcy, the debtor continues to operate it under the supervision of the trustee. A Ch. 12 debtor continues to conduct farming operations as a debtor in possession under the trustee's supervision. (The term "debtor in possession" is explained in relation to Ch. 11 in section 6.2.4. As stated there, in a Ch. 11 case, the debtor in possession conducts the debtor's business and essentially assumes the trustee's functions in the case. By contrast, the role of the Ch. 12 debtor in possession is narrower. The Ch. 12 debtor in possession does not assume all the functions of the trustee, but operates under the trustee's supervision.)

The process of trustee selection is also different in debt adjustment cases. Unlike Ch. 7, Chs. 12 and 13 provide for the immediate appointment of a permanent trustee by the U.S. Trustee. There is no interim appointment and no provision for creditor election. In some regions, a trustee is appointed for each case, but in others, where the volume of cases warrants it, the U.S. Trustee is empowered by 28 U.S.C. §586(b) to appoint one or more standing trustees who serve as trustees for all Ch. 12 and Ch. 13 cases in the region. As in the case of persons appointed to the panel of trustees, the standing trustees must meet qualifications prescribed by the Attorney General.

§6.2.4 Ch. 11 Cases

a. The Debtor in Possession

In a reorganization case under Ch. 11, the usual practice is not to appoint a trustee. Instead, the debtor exercises the trustee's function as debtor in possession, subject to the oversight of the court and creditors' committees. Unless the context indicates otherwise, the word "trustee" includes the debtor in possession whenever it is used in Code provisions relating to a Ch. 11 case. Because a reorganization, like a debt adjustment, is designed not to liquidate but to restructure and rehabilitate the debtor, the duties of the debtor in possession focus on the operation of the business of the estate and the creation and consummation of the Ch. 11 plan. In addition, the debtor in possession performs many other trustee functions, such as collecting estate property, challenging claims, and employing professionals. Some of the trustee's duties, such as investigation of the debtor's affairs and supervision of the debtor's activities, cannot be exercised by a debtor in possession. In a Ch. 11 case those functions are exercised by the creditors' committee.

b. The Appointment of a Trustee

Although the appointment of a trustee is not the norm in a Ch. 11 case, the court does have the authority to appoint a trustee for cause, or where necessary to protect the rights of creditors or other interest holders. This appointment is made under §1104 upon application of a party in interest or the U.S. Trustee, and follows notice and a hearing. Cause for the appointment includes dishonesty or incompetence by the debtor in possession. Prior to 1994, there was no provision for electing a trustee in Ch. 11 cases. This was changed by the Bankruptcy Reform Act of 1994. Section 1104(b) permits a party in interest (which includes a creditor, equity interest holder, the debtor in possession, and the U.S. Trustee) to request the election of a trustee within 30 days of the court ordering the appointment of a trustee. If a timely request is made, the U.S. Trustee must convene a meeting of creditors at which the election takes place under the same procedure as in a Ch. 7 case.

In the absence of a timely request, the U.S. Trustee makes the appointment in consultation with creditors and interest holders, and subject to the court's approval. Whether elected or appointed by the U.S. Trustee, the trustee must be a disinterested person and must be eligible under §321. The appointment can be terminated and the debtor returned to possession, on the application of a party in interest. §1105.

c. The Appointment of an Examiner

The appointment of a trustee displaces the debtor in possession as manager of the estate. If there are not grounds for such severe action, but some investigation of the debtor's management or conduct is appropriate, the court may appoint an examiner under §1104(b). This appointment also requires an application by the U.S. Trustee or a party in interest, followed by notice and a hearing. In estates of a specified size, the examiner must be appointed if the application is made. Otherwise, appointment is ordered only if the court finds this to be in the best interests of creditors and interest holders.

§6.2.5 Trustee's Fees

Trustee's fees are governed by §§326 and 330. The general rule is that a trustee is entitled to reasonable compensation for services, based on the nature of the services, the time spent, and the market rate for those services. The reasonable fee is determined by the court, and must fall within the range set by §§330 and 326. Section 330 provides for a minimum fee for trustees, and §326 prescribes maximum limits on the fee, based on the value of the distribution from the estate. The minimum payment to and limitations on the fees of standing trustees are set by 28 U.S.C. §586(e). The trustee's fee is an expense of administering the estate, which is given second priority for payment out of the funds of the estate. (Priorities are discussed in Chapter 19.)

§6.3 THE U.S. TRUSTEE

Prior to the enactment of the Code in 1978, the bankruptcy court exercised wide administrative and supervisory functions in relation to the bankruptcy case, as well as judicial functions. For example, the court appointed trustees, participated in the debtor's examination, and closely watched the administration of the case. The court's involvement in these administrative functions created problems because its administrative duties intruded on its judicial role, and its close supervisory relationship with the trustee compromised its impartiality. Congress therefore decided to create the office of U.S. Trustee to take over the court's former administrative and supervisory functions. The office of U.S. Trustee was initially established as a pilot program. It worked well and was made permanent in 1986. The entire country is divided into regions, and a U.S. Trustee is appointed to each region by the Attorney General. The powers and duties of the U.S. Trustee are set out in 28 U.S.C. §§581-589a, as well as in various provisions of the Code itself.

The U.S. Trustee is a public official whose general responsibility is to ensure that the public interest is being properly served in the administration of bankruptcy cases. In addition to appointing trustees, the U.S. Trustee is responsible for supervising their work to ensure that estates are being competently and honestly administered. The U.S. Trustee also has extensive duties, enumerated in 28 U.S.C. §586, concerning other aspects of the bankruptcy case: monitoring plans under Chs. 11, 12, and 13; ensuring that debtors are properly filing fees, schedules, and reports; watching for debtor abuse and other illicit behavior; and assisting the U.S. Attorney in prosecuting crimes committed in the course of a bankruptcy case. The U.S. Trustee is also empowered in a number of Code sections to participate in litigation and other proceedings arising in the bankruptcy case, and may, for example, examine the debtor (§343), recommend dismissal of a case (§707), or object to a discharge (§727(c)). The Bankruptcy Abuse Prevention and Consumer Protection Act of 2005 (BAPCPA) expanded the statutory duties of the U.S. Trustee in evaluating whether an individual Ch. 7 debtor's filing is abusive under §707, and in arranging for and supervising credit counseling for the debtor. (This is discussed in sections 8.4.1 and 9.8.) BAPCPA also increased the U.S. Trustee's statutory supervisory responsibility in small business cases. (See Chapter 21.)

While the bankruptcy court is responsible for the judicial supervision of the case, the U.S. Trustee's concern is administrative oversight. The U.S. Trustee is not an official of the bankruptcy court, but an independent officer who exercises those supervisory and administrative functions that cannot and should not be performed by the bankruptcy court itself. Also, as noted above, the U.S. Trustee can appear before the court as a party in various proceedings in the case.

§6.4 THE DEBTOR

§6.4.1 The Debtor's Role in the Case

The debtor is the person whose estate is administered in bankruptcy. With some restrictions discussed in Chapter 8, most persons, whether individuals or incorporated entities, are eligible to be debtors under one or more chapters of the Code. The debtor's role in the bankruptcy case is relatively passive in a Ch. 7 liquidation, where the trustee is responsible for administering the estate, liquidating assets, and making distributions to creditors. The debtor is typically more involved in the estate in rehabilitation cases. Where the debtor seeks to rehabilitate a business under Ch. 12 or Ch. 13, the debtor normally operates the business under the trustee's supervision. As explained in section 6.2.3, unless there are grounds to appoint a trustee in a Ch. 11 cases, the debtor becomes a debtor in possession who not only operates the business, but generally exercises the functions that a trustee would perform under other chapters. (Ch. 12 also confers the status of debtor in possession on the debtor but without the trustee functions, which are exercised by an independent trustee.)

§6.4.2 Equity Security Holders

If the debtor is a corporate entity, it has shareholders or other holders of ownership interests. The Code uses the term "equity security holder," defined in §101(16) to refer to persons who hold an ownership interest in a corporation or limited partnership. "Corporation" is defined in §101(9) to include a variety of incorporated entities. It is a fundamental principle that the interests of owners of a debtor are subservient to the claims of creditors. Therefore, if the debtor's assets are insufficient to settle its debts, the holders of ownership interests are unlikely to recover anything from the debtor on account of their interests. This is invariably true in the Ch. 7 liquidation of an insolvent debtor. However, in rehabilitation bankruptcy, there is a chance that the investment may be salvaged if a plan of reorganization can be devised under which the equity security holders are able to retain all or part of their interest in the corporation. They therefore have a stake in the debtor's reorganization effort under Ch. 11 and have the right to participate in the case. They may be represented by a committee similar in structure to a creditors' committee.

§6.5 CREDITORS AND CREDITORS' COMMITTEES

"Creditor" is defined in §101(10) to include any entity who has a provable claim against the estate. "Entity" is defined in §101(15) to include almost every kind of legal person, including both individuals and corporate entities. "Claim" is defined very broadly in §101(5) to cover all legal or equitable rights to payment, even if they are unliquidated, unmatured, contingent, or disputed. It is clear from these definitions that although creditors are brought together in bankruptcy's collective proceeding, they are a very diverse group with claims of different levels of certainty arising from a wide variety of transactions or relationships with the debtor or the estate. Furthermore, claims do not all have the same rank. With some exceptions, secured claims have the same status in bankruptcy as they have in nonbankruptcy law and are entitled to full payment from the proceeds of the collateral. In addition, the Code provides an order of priority for unsecured claims so that certain categories of claims are given preference over others.

As the representative of the estate, the trustee commonly acts in the collective interest of creditors through her efforts to enhance and preserve the value of the estate. However, although the trustee acts in the best interests of the creditor body as a whole, the trustee is not the representative of individual creditors. Frequently, the interests of the estate are opposed to those of an individual creditor or group of creditors, who are adversaries of the trustee. Litigation between the trustee and specific creditors is common.

When the debtor in possession acts as trustee in a Ch. 11 case, the debtor assumes fiduciary responsibilities. However, it requires an unusually charitable view of human nature to believe that a debtor in possession is likely to be as solicitous of creditor interests as an independent trustee would be. To ensure that creditor interests are properly safeguarded in a Ch. 11 case, the Code provides for the appointment of creditor committees.[1] Under §1102, the U.S. Trustee must appoint at least one committee of creditors holding unsecured claims. More than one committee can be appointed either if the U.S. Trustee deems it appropriate for the adequate representation of creditors or if a party in interest so requests.

The general duties of the committees are set out in §1103. They may employ legal counsel or other consultants, confer with the debtor in possession in the administration of the estate, conduct investigations into the debtor's financial affairs, participate in plan formation, and generally represent the interests of their constituent creditors. Ch. 11 usually involves negotiation between the debtor and creditors and between different creditor groups. The committees play a significant role in this respect as well. In short, the idea behind the creditors' committees is that they are representative bodies that safeguard the interests of the class of creditors they represent, not only in general oversight of the debtor but also in the negotiations that lead to the formulation of a plan.

The value of a creditors' committee is dependent on the committee taking an active role in the case. Studies have shown that in smaller Ch. 11 bankruptcies, creditors often do not have a large enough stake in the outcome of the case to participate vigorously or at all in the committee. As a result, creditors' committees often do not serve the vital monitoring and

---

1. Creditor committees can also be appointed in Ch. 7 cases, but they are not very common.

adversarial function they were intended to have. Therefore, if the debtor qualifies as a "small business debtor" (defined in §101(51D) to mean, essentially, a debtor in business with total debts of under $2,490,925[2]), the court may dispense with a creditors' committee if a party in interest so requests. If no committee is appointed, the U.S. Trustee must fulfill the monitoring function that would have been exercised by the committee.

§6.6 ATTORNEYS AND OTHER PROFESSIONAL CONSULTANTS

§6.6.1 The Employment of Professionals by the Estate, the Debtor, and Creditors

The trustee, the debtor, and creditors are commonly represented by attorneys. In addition, they may require the services of other professionals (*e.g.*, an accountant) for advice on the complexities of the case. These professional relationships are mostly governed by generally applicable rules of law and of professional responsibilty. However, some provisions in the Code affect attorneys for the debtor, creditor, and trustee. For example, §329 gives the court policing power over certain fees of the debtor's attorney, §327(c) allows the debtor's attorney to be appointed to represent the estate in certain matters, §503(b)(3) and (4) allow creditors to claim their legal fees for an involuntary petition and certain other matters from the estate as an administrative expense, and §1107(b) allows a creditor's attorney to act for the creditors' committee under certain circumstances.

If the estate requires the services of an attorney or other professionals, the trustee is authorized by §327(a) to engage such services with court approval. The reasonable fee due for the services rendered, if approved by the court, is treated as an administrative expense of the estate. Sections 327 to 330 and §503 govern the appointment and fees of attorneys and other professionals used by the estate. Trustees are often accountants or lawyers, and under §327(d) the court may authorize the trustee to perform professional services for the estate in that capacity. If the professional work is distinct from and in excess of the normal functions of a trustee, §328(b) allows the court to authorize additional compensation for it.

Although §330(a) makes it clear that the fees of the estate's attorney may be approved as an administrative expense of the estate, it had not been

---

2. This is the dollar amount as adjusted with effect from April 1, 2013. It will be adjusted again with effect from April 1, 2016. *See* section 5.4.3 for an explanation of the periodic adjustment of dollar amounts in the Code.

clear whether the same treatment could be given to the fees of the attorney representing the debtor. Of course, in a Ch. 11 case, where the debtor in possession acts for the estate, the debtor's attorney is the attorney for the estate. However, in other cases, the debtor's attorney represents the interests of the debtor, while the trustee's attorney acts for the estate. Prior to 1994, §330(a)(1) expressly included the debtor's attorney as one of the professional persons to whom fees could be awarded as an administrative expense. This language was removed from the subsection by the 1994 amendments. It was unclear whether this omission was deliberate or an oversight, so some lower courts held that the debtor's attorney's fees could still be claimed as an administrative expense, while others held that it they could not be. The U.S. Supreme Court settled this uncertainty in *Lamie v. U.S. Trustee*, 540 U.S. 526 (2004). The Court adopted a plain-meaning approach to the language of §330(a) as amended and held that the section no longer authorizes the payment of the debtor's attorney's fees as an administrative expense of the estate.

§6.6.2 Conflicts of Interest, Client Confidentiality, and Loyalty

a. Rules of Professional Responsibility

An attorney (or other professional) who is appointed trustee in a bankruptcy case, or one who represents the estate, the debtor, or some other party in interest, must be careful to comply with both the rules of professional responsibility and the provisions of the Code concerning the representation of parties. An ethical question that often arises in bankruptcy representation involves the avoidance of actual or apparent conflicts of interest. For example, Rule 1.7 of the ABA Model Rules of Professional Conduct prohibits an attorney from representing a client if the representation would cause a conflict of interest, and Rule 1.6 forbids an attorney from divulging client confidences. These rules of professional conduct require the attorney to make sure that her work in relation to the bankruptcy case is not affected by other relationships or interests, and that it does not compromise her duty to keep confidential information acquired in the representation of other clients.

b. Code Provisions Relating to an Interest Adverse to the Estate

In addition to these general rules of professional conduct, the Bankruptcy Code itself addresses the question of conflicts of interest, confidentiality and the duty of loyalty to a client. Section 327(a) requires that an attorney (or other professional) employed by the estate does not hold or represent an interest adverse to the estate, and is a "disinterested person." An attorney holds an interest adverse to the estate if she has some personal interest (such as a prepetition claim against the debtor) that may undermine her duty of loyalty and independence. She represents an interest adverse to the estate if she acts for a client (such as a creditor of the estate or a stockholder of the debtor) whose interests actually or potentially conflict with those of the estate. "Disinterested person" is defined in §101(14) to exclude creditors, various persons with ownership interests in or close connections to the debtor, and persons who "have an interest materially adverse to the interests of the estate. . . ." A similar requirement of disinterest can be found in §327(e), governing the use by the estate of the debtor's attorney, and §1103(b), concerning representation of a creditors' committee. An attorney who acts as trustee is bound by fiduciary responsibilities to be impartial and independent (*see* section 6.2).

The degree to which an adverse interest disqualifies an attorney from representing the estate is not clear. The definition of "disinterested person" in §101(14) talks of an interest "materially adverse" to that of the estate, but §327(a) does not include a requirement of materiality. Some courts have allowed an attorney to represent the estate if she has a minor adverse interest that is not material (such as a small unsecured claim), but others have disqualified an attorney from representing the estate if she has any adverse interest, no matter how small.[3]

c. Disclosure to the Court

Since the court must approve the appointment of an attorney under §327(a), it is the court, not the attorney herself, who must make the ultimate decision on whether a disqualifying conflict of interest exists. To enable the court to make a proper determination, the attorney seeking appointment has the duty to disclose all relevant information. Failure to make disclosure of pertinent information is a serious breach of good faith that could subject the attorney to disciplinary proceedings and also result in forfeiture of fees under §328(c). The same is true of an attorney appointed to represent a creditors' committee under §1103. (Rule 2014 requires the application for authorization to disclose all the attorney's connections with interested parties so that the court is informed at the time of application of any possible conflicts.)

---

3. The 1994 National Bankruptcy Review Commission recommended that §327(a) be amended to clarify that an insubstantial adverse claim should not disqualify an attorney, but BAPCPA did not make this change. This question therefore remains unresolved.

d. Conflict of Interest Arising out of an Installment Arrangement for the Payment of Fees

An awkward conflict of interest situation can arise where an attorney agrees to take on the bankruptcy representation of a client who does not have the means to pay the attorney in full in advance of the filing of the petition. For example, an individual debtor who seeks Ch. 7 bankruptcy relief engages an attorney to file the petition and represent him during the case. Ideally, the attorney should determine a flat fee (a retainer) to cover both the prepetition and postpetition representation of the debtor, and should ensure that the fee is paid in full in advance of the petition. Provided that the fee is fair and legitimate, it will not be overturned in the bankruptcy case, and because the debtor has paid in full, the attorney will not be a creditor in the bankruptcy. However, if the debtor cannot afford to pay the full fee in advance, the attorney must make other arrangements. The obvious solution may seem to be to allow the debtor to pay the fee in installments. However, it is not usually practical to delay filing the petition while the debtor pays the fee, and if the petition is filed immediately so that the installments extend into the period after the petition, the unpaid balance of the fee will be classified as a general unsecured debt. This is because the contract under which the debtor agreed to pay the retainer was entered into before the petition was filed.[4] As a result, the attorney will be stayed from taking any action to collect the debt, which will eventually be paid only to the extent of the Ch. 7 distribution and discharged.

In addition to the problem of collecting the fee, the attorney's status as an unsecured creditor creates a conflict of interest that could result in the attorney's disqualification from representing the debtor. For example, in In re Martin, 197 B.R. 120 (Bankr. D. Colo. 1996), the court upheld the trustee's objection to such a fee arrangement on the grounds that it created a conflict of interest. Because the attorney's claim for his fee is unsecured and dischargeable, the attorney has a disincentive to advise the debtor frankly that his own claim is uncollectible. See also In re Waldo, 417 B.R. 854 (Bankr. E.D. Tenn. 2009), in which the court held that by taking postdated checks in payment of the fee and not informing the debtor that they would likely not be payable, the attorney created a conflict of interest. Some courts, recognizing the need to make it easier for indigent debtors to secure representation, have been less inclined to disqualify an attorney on grounds of conflict where installments were still due on the fee after the petition was filed. See In re Hines, 147 F.3d 1185 (9th Cir. 1998).

---

4. It becomes a general unsecured "Claim" because, as noted in section 6.6, the U.S. Supreme Court made it clear in Lamie v. U.S. Trustee, 540 U.S. 526 (2004), that the debtor's attorney's fee is not covered by §330(a)(1). It therefore cannot be approved as an expense of the estate and does not qualify for priority as an administrative expense.

One way to avoid this problem is to structure the representation arrangement differently: Instead of entering into a contract for a flat fee in advance of filing, the attorney should segregate the fees for prepetition and postpetition services. The fee for prepetition services must be paid before the filing, and the fee arrangement should specify that the fees for postpetition services only become due and payable once the services are performed. Because fees for postpetition services are not prepetition debts, they are not subject to the stay or the discharge, and there is no unsecured debt that could create a conflict of interest. See In re Mansfield, 394 B.R. 783 (Bankr. E.D. Pa. 2008).

§6.7 DEBT RELIEF AGENCIES

§6.7.1 The Meaning of "Debt Relief Agency": Persons, Including Attorneys, Who Provide Assistance or Representation in Connection with a Modest-value Consumer Bankruptcy Case

BAPCPA added §§526 through 528 to the Code with the goal of strengthening the professional standards applicable to a "debt relief agency" that assists or represents a person in connection with a consumer bankruptcy case involving nonexempt assets of relatively small value. "Debt relief agency" is defined in §101(12A) to include "any person who provides any bankruptcy assistance to an assisted person in return for the payment of money or other valuable consideration . . ." as well as petition preparers. The definition excludes various persons such as nonprofit organizations, creditors of the debtor who assist in debt restructuring, and authors of books. "Bankruptcy assistance" is broadly defined in §101(4A) to cover a variety of goods and services provided to an "assisted person," such as advice, document preparation, or representation in connection with a bankruptcy case. "Assisted person" is defined in §101(3) to mean any person whose debts consist primarily of consumer debts and whose nonexempt property has a value of less than $186,825.[5]

Although these provisions do not expressly mention attorneys, the definitions are broad enough to include an attorney who represents a debtor with regard to any aspect of the bankruptcy case. The question of whether attorneys are debt relief agencies had engendered much uncertainty. Most

---

5. This is the amount as adjusted under §104 with effect from April 1, 2013. See section 5.4.3.

bankruptcy courts held that they were included, but some held otherwise. This question was settled by the U.S. Supreme Court in *Milavetz, Gallop & Milavetz, P.A. v. U.S.*, 559 U.S. 229 (2010). The court held that the plain language of §101(12A), bolstered by its legislative history, makes it clear that Congress did intend to include attorneys in the definition. Although attorneys do fall within the definition of "debt relief agency," that definition is qualified by the requirement that the person must provide the bankruptcy assistance "in return for the payment of money or other valuable consideration." Therefore, an attorney who acts for an assisted person pro bono should not be classified as a debt relief agency. See *In re Reyes*, 361 B.R. 276 (Bankr. D. Fla. 2007) aff'd 2007 WL 6082567 (S.D. Fla 2007).

An "assisted person" is commonly a debtor. However, the language of §101(3) uses the word "person" rather than "debtor," and "bankruptcy assistance" is therefore not clearly confined to services provided to the debtor. An attorney who provides assistance in a bankruptcy case to a creditor or other party in interest may fit the definition of a debt relief agency if that client's debts consist primarily of consumer debts and his nonexempt property is worth less than $186,825. An attorney's representation of a person other than the debtor does not constitute services relating to the relief of that person's client. Therfore, it may that Congress did not actually intend the definition to apply to non-debtors even though the plain language appears to include them. In any event, the practical effect of including non-debtors in the definition of "assisted person" may not be significant because a debt relief agency that represents someone other than the debtor does not appear to be subject to the regulation and restrictions set out in §§526 to 528. In *Milavetz* the U.S. Supreme Court read those sections as governing only those who offer bankruptcy-related services to consumer debtors.

§6.7.2 The Regulation of Debt Relief Agencies

Sections 526 to 528 set out the rules that apply to debt relief agencies. Section 526 imposes restrictions on their conduct, §527 sets out the disclosures that they are required to make to an assisted person, and §528 specifies the content of the agency's required written contract with an assisted person and prescribes required content in advertisements. These sections are quite detailed and are full of vague, ambiguous, and obscure language. Their gist is as follows.

Section 526(a) contains prohibitions on deceptive or improper conduct. Section 526(a)(1) prohibits a debt relief agency from failing to perform a service that was undertaken. Sections 526(a)(2) and (3) forbid the agency from making misleading statements or misrepresentations itself and from advising an assisted person to do so. Section 526(a)(4) forbids the agency from advising an assisted person to incur more debt "in contemplation of" filing a bankruptcy case. Section 526(b) makes any waiver of protections or rights under the section unenforceable against the assisted person. Section 526(c) provides for remedies and penalties against a debt relief agency that violates §§526 to 528, in addition to any remedies that are otherwise available under state law. The section states that a contract in material violation of the provisions is void and cannot be enforced by any person other than the assisted person. The debt relief agency is liable to the assisted person for actual damages, reimbursement of fees, and attorney's fees and costs for any intentional or negligent failure to comply with these provisions or with other material requirements of the Code, or where the case is dismissed for failure to file documents. In addition to suit by the assisted person, an action to enjoin a violation or for damages may be brought by the state in either state or federal court. Finally, the district court, either on its own motion or on motion of the U.S. Trustee or the assisted person, may enjoin intentional or persistent violations of the provisions or impose civil penalties on the agency. Section 526(d) makes it clear that §§526 to 528 do not curtail the ability of the state to regulate the practice of law. Nor do they affect or exempt compliance with any state law, except to the extent that the state law is inconsistent with the provisions of those sections.

Section 527 requires debt relief agencies to make extensive written disclosures to an assisted person, to explain the need for accurate information in the petition and supporting documents, to alert the assisted person to the availability of legal assistance, and to caution the assisted person about various aspects of bankruptcy, including eligibility for and choice of relief. The agency must also provide the assisted person with necessary information on how to assemble the content of and complete the lists of creditors, the schedule of assets and liabilities, and other documentation required to be filed by the assisted person under §521.

Section 528(a) requires the agency to enter into a written contract with the assisted person before the bankruptcy petition is filed, conspicuously setting out the services to be provided and the fees to be charged. An executed copy of the contract must be given to the assisted person. Section 528(b) requires specific disclosures in advertising that identify the advertiser as a debt relief agency and clearly describe the nature of the bankruptcy assistance being offered.

§6.7.3 The Constitutionality of §§526 and 528 as Applied to Attorneys

In *Milavetz*, the U.S. Supreme Court considered the constitutionality of §§526 and 528, as applied to attorneys, and concluded that the provisions did not violate the U.S. Constitution. The court of appeals had held that the prohibition in §526(a)(4) on advising an assisted person to incur more debt in contemplation of filing bankruptcy violated the attorney's First Amendment rights. The court of appeals found this prohibition to be overbroad because it covered not only improper advice, but also appropriate and lawful advice that constitutes prudent bankruptcy planning. It thereby chilled speech that is fundamental to the attorney-client relationship. The Supreme Court[6] held that the court of appeals had interpreted the words "in contemplation of" bankruptcy too broadly to refer to all advice to incur any additional debt when contemplating bankruptcy. However, on a proper and commonsense reading of the phrase, taken in the context of the section and in light of the use of that phrase in bankruptcy law generally, the prohibition focuses on advice to engage in abusive or manipulative conduct such as the loading up on debt with the expectation of discharging it. Section 526(a)(4) does not preclude an attorney from counseling the client about incurring new debt in contemplation of filing a bankruptcy case or in recommending that the debtor take on new debt for legitimate, non-abusive purposes.

The disclosure requirements relating to advertising, prescribed by §528, were also challenged in *Milavetz* as a violation of the First Amendment. The Court rejected this argument, holding that the disclosure requirement is not an impermissible limitation on commercial speech, but merely a requirement to provide information, which is constitutionally permissible provided that it is rationally related to the government's interest in safeguarding consumer debtors from deceptive advertising. The court found that the section's disclosure requirements satisfy this standard: They are intended to combat the problem of misleading advertisements, and they require only the divulgence of the advertiser's legal status as a debt relief agency and the type of assistance to be provided.

§6.8 OTHER PARTICIPANTS

In the preceding sections, the principal participants in a bankruptcy case have been introduced. However, every debtor is different; depending on the debtor's activities, interests, and affairs, there may be a variety of other persons who are not necessarily creditors, but whose rights are at stake in the case. For example, the debtor may be a party to unperformed (i.e., executory) contracts that may be assumed or rejected by the estate; most debtors have debtors of their own who become debtors of the estate; some

---

6. The court's judgment was unanimous. However, Justices Scalia and Thomas delivered concurring opinions in which they concurred in the judgment and in most of the majority's reasoning, but disagreed with the majority on narrow questions that are not detailed here.

debtors have dependents; some have sureties or other co-obligors. Also, bankruptcy may attract the interest of a public agency. For example, the Securities and Exchange Commission may be concerned with, and is entitled to be heard in, a Ch. 11 case.

Examples

1. Luce Canons, an attorney, performed some legal work for Down & Out Enterprises, Inc., for which a fee of $5,000 was charged. Down & Out has not paid the fee, and it has now filed a Ch. 11 petition. Down & Out, as debtor in possession, has asked Luce Canons to represent it in a lawsuit to recover a debt due to the estate. Should Luce Canons accept the case?

2. Hiram Gunn used to be the attorney for Erstwhile Enterprises, Inc. Hiram represented Erstwhile for many years and had handled all its legal work, so he is thoroughly familiar with its affairs. A few years ago, Hiram and Erstwhile became embroiled in a fee dispute that led to the termination of their relationship. Erstwhile recently filed a Ch. 11 petition. May Hiram represent a creditors' committee in the bankruptcy case?

3. Bill A. Billhours had long been the attorney for Adverse Investments, Inc., a corporation of which his friend Able Skimmer was president and principal stockholder. When Adverse Investments filed a Ch. 11 petition, it applied under §327(a) for the court to approve Bill as its attorney. Bill disclosed that he had been Adverse Investments' legal advisor prior to its bankruptcy, but failed to mention that he had also legally represented Able in his personal affairs for many years. The court approved Bill's appointment, and he set to work conscientiously and vigorously representing the estate in negotiations aimed at developing a plan of reorganization. The negotiations broke down when creditors discovered that Able had made several transfers of funds from Adverse Investments to himself and family members shortly before the petition was filed. The creditors' committee successfully applied to oust the debtor in possession from control of the estate and to replace it with a trustee. The trustee terminated Bill's employment and hired her own counsel. She is now investigating whether Able's transfers of corporate assets were fraudulent.

   a. Bill has applied to court for compensation for the services that he rendered to the estate from the time of his appointment until his dismissal. It is conceded that he performed good-quality legal work for the estate during his tenure as its counsel, and no one contends that he participated in or even knew about Able's transfers of corporate property. Notwithstanding, the trustee objects to Bill receiving any payment of his fees. Is this a sound objection?

b. Quite apart from the issue of whether Bill is entitled to his fees, consider his responsibilities with regard to the trustee's investigation of the improper conduct of Able and Adverse Investments. Is the information obtained by Bill during his representation of Adverse protected by the attorney-client privilege?

4. The law firm of Filenow & Palater handles a large volume of consumer bankruptcies. When it is engaged by a prospective debtor, the firm charges a retainer (a flat fee) to cover the fees for the prepetition work, the filing of the petition, and basic postpetition representation. Where a client cannot afford to pay the flat fee in advance of the bankruptcy, the firm accepts a down payment on its fee and permits its client to pay the balance in monthly installments in the period following the petition. The firm has the client sign postdated checks, which are then banked as they become due. Is this a good practice?

5. Fido Fidelio is an attorney and a member of the panel of trustees established by the U.S. Trustee. He was appointed as the trustee of a corporation in liquidation under Ch. 7. At the time of his appointment he filed the required declaration of disinterestedness, but did not mention in the declaration that he had represented a former employee of the debtor some time ago. During the course of that representation, Fido learned of financial improprieties committed by the debtor. Should Fido have disclosed the former relationship with the debtor's ex-employee? Does this representation render Fido unqualified to act as trustee for the debtor?

Explanations

1. Luce Canons must obtain court approval of his appointment as attorney for the estate under §327(a). In the application for approval, he must disclose to the court the fact that he is an unsecured creditor of the estate. The court will not approve his appointment unless he qualifies as a disinterested person who does not hold an interest adverse to the estate. One of the requirements to qualify as a disinterested person, as defined in §101(14), is that the person is not a creditor. (See §101(14)(A).) This would seem to settle the matter, because Luce is owed $5,000 by the estate for unpaid prepetition services. Several courts have disposed of this issue in those simple terms. However, other courts have been less wedded to the literal language of §101(14)(A), and have held that the mere fact that the attorney has a claim against the estate should not automatically disqualify him. The case must be examined to decide if there is an actual conflict between the attorney's interest as a creditor, and the estate's interests that he will represent in the task to be accomplished

on behalf of the estate. For example, if the attorney is retained to represent the estate in recovering a voidable preference paid to another creditor, it would seem that the attorney's interest is congruent with rather than opposed to that of the estate. By contrast, the potential for adverse interests is strong if the attorney's role is to represent the estate in negotiating a plan of reorganization with creditors.

Note that this is a Ch. 11 case, so the estate is administered by the debtor in possession. The basis for disqualifying Luce is that he is a creditor, and not because he represented the debtor prior to bankruptcy. In a Ch. 11 case, §1107(b) makes it clear that an attorney is not disqualified merely because he represented the debtor before bankruptcy. However, the circumstances of that prior representation could give rise to an actual or potential conflict, so it must be disclosed to the court and evaluated. Some courts have held that in a Ch. 11 case, the fact that fees are still owed from that prior representation of the debtor is not in itself enough to preclude representation of the estate. See, for example, In re Talsma, 436 B.R. 908 (Bankr. N.D. Tex. 2010), which concerned the estate's employment of the debtor's pre-petition accountant who was still owed fees for the prepetition work.

2. The ethical barrier to Hiram's representation of the creditors' committee is not really a conflict of interest. After all, Hiram has not been Erstwhile's attorney for years. Rather, Rule 1.6 of the ABA Model code of professional conduct precludes Hiram from accepting this appointment.

Rule 1.6 forbids an attorney from divulging the confidences of a client. During the course of their attorney-client relationship, Hiram was privy to details of Erstwhile's affairs. Hiram cannot represent Erstwhile's creditors without violating the trust and confidence inherent in the former relationship. In re Kujawa, 112 B.R. 968 (Bankr. E.D. Mo. 1990), is a particularly startling example of an attorney's violation of confidence. The law firm represented the debtor for about two years. It represented him in several lawsuits, counseled him on bankruptcy issues, and had intimate knowledge of his affairs. A few months after doing legal work for the debtor, the law firm represented some of his creditors in a petition to place him into involuntary bankruptcy. When those creditors retained other counsel, the firm represented another group of creditors who sought to intervene in the case. The firm also filed as an intervening creditor on its own behalf for unpaid fees owed by the debtor. The court granted the debtor's motion to disqualify the firm and ordered the firm to pay the debtor's costs and attorney's fees relating to the motion. The bankruptcy court's disposition was upheld on appeal, subject to a reduction in the amount of the award (see In re Kujawa, 270 F.3d 578 (8th Cir. 2001)).

Even if Hiram argues that he has no information about Erstwhile's affairs that can be used to its detriment, an attorney should not act in a way that creates the appearance of impropriety. Hiram's efforts on the part of the creditors would surely create a sense of suspicion and would justify Erstwhile in feeling wronged. See, for example, In re Global Video Communications Corp., 19 Bankr. Ct. Dec. (CCR) 1311 (Bankr. M.D. Fla. 1989); In re Davenport Communications Ltd., 19 Bankr. Ct. Dec. (CCR) 1980 (Bankr. S.D. Iowa 1990).

3. a. The facts of this example are loosely based on Rome v. Braunstein, 19 F.3d 54 (1st Cir. 1994), in which the court refused to award the attorney compensation for his services even though he performed valuable work, he did not act contrary to the interests of the estate, and there was no indication that he had collaborated in or knew of the owner's dishonesty. The court said it is not necessary to identify a negative impact on the estate. It is enough that the attorney put himself in the position in which his loyalty was weakened and he might be tempted to give tainted advice. It is the court's role, not the attorney's, to decide if the attorney is disqualified from representing the estate. The attorney's failure to make immediate and candid disclosure to the court precluded the court from exercising this function. (Quite apart from the sanction under §328, an attorney who fails to avoid a conflict of interest is subject to disciplinary action by the bar.) The objection in Bill's case is therefore sound and the court may deny all compensation to him under §328(c).

   b. This question raises an ancillary issue: When a trustee is appointed and proceeds to investigate possible improprieties by the debtor's management, is the debtor's attorney precluded by attorney-client privilege from furnishing information that he obtained during the course of representing the debtor? In In re Blinder, Robinson & Co., Inc., 123 B.R. 900 (Bankr. D. Colo. 1991), the court resolved this question by finding that the trustee succeeded to the debtor's right to waive the attorney-client privilege. The court reasoned that if this were not so, the management of the debtor would control the privilege and could frustrate the trustee's investigation and shield itself from the trustee's efforts to find misappropriated assets.

4. The safest practice would be to require payment of the full fee before the petition is filed. However, because the debtor does not have the means to pay the full retainer in advance, Filenow & Palater has entered into an installment plan with him. There are two problems with the installment plan. First, because the contract under which payments are to be made was entered into before the petition was filed, the balance due on the fee will be classified as a general unsecured claim, and most, if not all of it, will be unpaid and discharged. Second, because it has made itself a

creditor of the debtor, the firm has created a conflict of interest that may preclude it from representing the debtor. Where a debtor cannot afford to pay the retainer in advance, it would be better to structure the representation arrangement by separating the fees for prepetition and postpetition services. The fee for prepetition services must be paid before the filing, and the fees for postpetition services should be made due and payable only upon performance of the postpetition services. Because these fee claims will now arise only after the petition, they will be postpetition debts of the debtor, rather than claims against the estate.

5. A trustee must qualify as a "disinterested person" as defined in §101(14). In *In re AFI Holdings, Inc.*, 530 F.3d 832 (9th Cir. 2008), the court found, using a "totality of the circumstances" test, that a similar former relationship precluded the trustee from qualifying as a disinterested person. His knowledge of prior improprieties committed by the debtor could affect the independence and impartiality required of a trustee. In his declaration of disinterestedness filed with the court, a trustee must fully set out all interactions and past connections with the debtor, a creditor, or any other party in interest so that the court has full information on which to make its decision on disinterestedness. The trustee's failure to disclose the relationship to the court constituted cause for his removal under §324.

Bankruptcy Jurisdiction, the Powers of the Bankruptcy Court, and Sovereign Immunity

§7.1 INTRODUCTION

Section 5.2 explained why Congress, rather than the states, is responsible for enacting bankruptcy law. It follows that bankruptcy matters fall within the realm of the federal courts. For reasons discussed in section 7.3, Congress has not conferred jurisdiction over bankruptcy cases directly on bankruptcy courts. Instead, jurisdiction over bankruptcy is conferred on the federal district courts by 28 U.S.C. §1334, while 28 U.S.C. §157 provides for the referral of bankruptcy matters from district courts to bankruptcy courts. This has led to a complex and sometimes confusing jurisdictional structure that has generated much litigation. Section 7.2 deals with §1344 and its grant of jurisdiction to district courts. This describes the overall range of federal bankruptcy jurisdiction. Section 7.3 then discusses the way in which the district courts' bankruptcy jurisdiction is passed on to bankruptcy courts.

§7.2 DISTRICT COURT JURISDICTION OVER BANKRUPTCY

A court is competent to adjudicate a case only if it has both personal and subject matter jurisdiction. In other words, the parties must be legitimately within the court's power and the case must concern a controversy that is justiciable by the court.

§7.2.1 Personal Jurisdiction

Personal jurisdiction in bankruptcy cases is not expressly addressed by 28 U.S.C. §1334. However, it is well established that the reach of the Code is nationwide, and the bankruptcy jurisdiction of the federal district courts extends to all persons who are present within the territorial boundaries of the United States. Therefore, the usual jurisdictional concept of minimum contacts does not apply in a bankruptcy case. As long as the court has subject matter jurisdiction, a party to a proceeding or suit in a bankruptcy court cannot challenge jurisdiction on the basis that minimum contacts are lacking between the transaction or property in issue and the forum. For example, In re Tribune Co., 418 B.R. 116 (Bankr. D. Del. 2009) involved a dispute between the actor Warren Beatty and the debtor over rights to the cartoon character, Dick Tracy. Beatty challenged the Delaware bankruptcy court's jurisdiction to deal with the dispute on the grounds that he had no minimum contacts with the state or the court. The court observed that in bankruptcy, the defendant's minimum contacts with the forum is determined nationally and not on the basis of the locale of the court within the United States.

It should be noted that even though the court has personal jurisdiction over the defendant, it may not be the most appropriate venue for the case. If that is so, the defendant may move to have the case transferred to a different court. The question of venue is discussed in section 9.2.

§7.2.2 Subject Matter Jurisdiction

The federal district courts are granted jurisdiction over five categories of proceeding by 28 U.S.C. §1334. In the first two, the jurisdiction is exclusive — that is, no other court may entertain proceedings in these categories. The second three confer nonexclusive jurisdiction on the district courts, so that some other court also has the power to adjudicate these matters. Diagram 7a sketches the five categories, which are explained below.

a. Exclusive Jurisdiction

The district court has original and exclusive jurisdiction over the actual bankruptcy case itself under §1334(a). This is a narrow category, interpreted to include only the petition and its adjudication. No other court may hear and determine a bankruptcy petition.

Under §1334(e)(1), once a bankruptcy case has been filed, the district court has exclusive jurisdiction over the debtor's property as at the commencement of the case, wherever situated, and also over property of the estate. This provision brings the property under the control of the court upon commencement of the case, even though some other court previously had jurisdiction over it. The Bankruptcy Abuse Prevention and

Bankruptcy Jurisdiction under 28 U.S.C. §1334

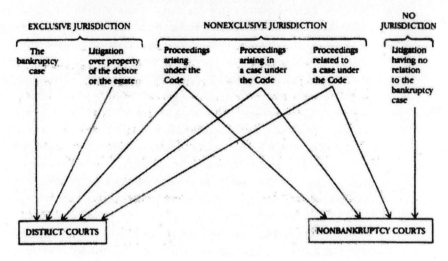

Diagram 7a

Consumer Protection Act of 2005 (BAPCPA) added §1334(e)(2), which also grants to the district court in which the case is pending exclusive jurisdiction over any disputes that arise from the estate's employment of professionals under §327.

In *Tennessee Student Assistance Corp. v. Hood*, 541 U.S. 440 (2004), and *Central Virginia Community College v. Katz*, 126 S. Ct. 990 (2006), the U.S. Supreme Court described bankruptcy jurisdiction as principally in *rem* — it is premised on the court's power over the estate, a *res*, and the adjudication of rights concerning the assets of the estate. Most proceedings in the bankruptcy case either stem directly from this in *rem* jurisdiction or are closely related to and ancillary to it.

b. Nonexclusive Jurisdiction

Section 1334(b) grants the district court original but nonexclusive jurisdiction over three types of civil proceeding. (Civil proceedings include all litigated civil matters, whether suits or motions.) Because the three categories of litigation in §1334(b) all fall within the original nonexclusive jurisdiction of the district court, the distinctions between them are not significant for the purpose of determining district court jurisdiction. Provided that the case does fall within one of the three categories, the District Court has jurisdiction over it. However, as explained in section 7.3, the distinction is important to bankruptcy court jurisdiction. The three categories of proceeding covered by §1334 are set out below and Example 1 is an exercise in distinguishing them.

(1) Civil proceedings "arising under title 11."   This category covers bankruptcy litigation other than the actual case itself. For a proceeding to arise under the Code, it must involve the adjudication of rights and obligations provided in the Code. In essence, the cause of action must be created by the Code, or it must involve an issue that is so linked to the Code that the issue either would not have arisen or it would have been decided differently in the absence of the Code.

(2) Civil proceedings "arising in" a case under title 11.   This is an intermediate classification that contemplates proceedings that, while not necessarily dependent on provisions of the Code for their existence, are more connected to it than related proceedings. In essence, this category covers proceedings that are likely to arise only in a bankruptcy case so that the litigation would not exist had the bankruptcy case not been filed. Some types of "arising in" litigation are obvious and straightforward. Disputes that are intimately involved with the administration of the estate, such as those concerning the allowance of claims, or the approval of a loan to the estate, would not come about outside of bankruptcy. In *In re Mullarkey*, 536 F.3d 215 (3d Cir. 2008), the court found that a Ch. 13 debtor's suit alleging that creditors had presented false claims and concealed money from the estate was a civil proceeding arising in the case, because all the alleged events occurred in the course of administering the estate and implicated the integrity of the bankruptcy process. In *Baker v. Simpson*, 613 F.3d 346 (2d Cir. 2010) the court held that the Ch. 11 debtor's malpractice claim against an attorney, relating to services rendered in the bankruptcy case, arose in the case. It did not matter that the malpractice claim was governed by state law because the claim would have no existence outside of the bankruptcy. Sometimes a dispute arises in the case, even though it is tangential and does not really have an impact on the estate. For example, in *In re A.H. Robbins Co.*, 86 F.3d 364 (4th Cir. 1996), *cert. denied*, 519 U.S. 993 (1996), the court held that a dispute between attorneys over the distribution of fees from a trust created under a Ch. 11 plan did arise in the bankruptcy case because the trust would never have existed in the absence of bankruptcy. This conclusion was reached even though the dispute between the attorneys really had no conceivable impact on the estate.

(3) Civil proceedings "related to" a case under title 11.   Although these proceedings have a relationship to the bankruptcy case, they are furthest from its central core. They involve litigation that has some relationship to the bankruptcy case but that arises out of rights and issues of nonbankruptcy law. In the absence of bankruptcy, these disputes would be heard by another court. However, because bankruptcy has occurred, the dispute affects the estate and the district court acquires nonexclusive jurisdiction to deal with it.

Related litigation falls into one of two categories. The first, and least problematical, type of related matter is one that involves a cause of action that could have been brought by or against the debtor under nonbankruptcy law but that has passed to the estate from the debtor to become a claim of or against the estate. In this type of controversy, the estate is actually a party to the litigation, so there is little trouble in identifying the matter as related to the bankruptcy case. The second category of related proceeding has generated much more difficulty. Cases in this category concern litigation in which the estate is not involved — it is between other parties — but the outcome of the litigation could have some impact on the estate. In these types of cases a broad view of relationship would enable one to trace some connection to the bankruptcy case, even where the litigation's actual impact on or importance to the estate is marginal. Because the scope of related litigation would be too broad if the test were simply to find some point of relationship between the third-party litigation and the case, most courts require something more. They have struggled to devise a test that distinguishes truly related litigation — over which the assertion of related-to jurisdiction is proper — from that which is tangential and of little actual or potential significance to the estate — which does not give rise to bankruptcy jurisdiction.

The most influential formulation of the test is that enunciated in *Pacor, Inc. v. Higgins*, 743 F.2d 984, 994 (3d Cir. 1984): A civil proceeding is related to the bankruptcy case only if its outcome could conceivably have any effect on the estate — if its disposition could alter the rights, liability, freedom of action or options of, or have an impact on the handling or administration of the estate. This test has been adopted by several other courts of appeal and was referred to with approval by the Supreme Court in *Celotex Corp. v. Edwards*, 514 U.S. 300 (1995). However, although the test is widely followed, there is still some uncertainty as to its application. The test refers to conceivable impact, which suggests a very broad scope of related jurisdiction. However, courts tend not take the concept of conceivable impact too literally, out of concern that an overbroad conception of relatedness would expand the jurisdiction of the bankruptcy forum beyond proper limits. Therefore, a matter should not be found to be related merely because it might have some speculative or remote possible consequence to the bankruptcy case. The appropriate scope of related jurisdiction, where the case does not involve the estate as a party, should be confined to litigation that has a direct and demonstrable legal or economic impact on the estate, so that it affects the debtor's or estate's freedom of action, the administration of the estate, or the distribution to creditors. See, for example, In re *Fed-pak Systems*, 80 F.3d 207 (7th Cir. 1995); In re *Ray*, 624 F.3d 1124 (9th Cir. 2010). In each of these cases, the court found no related-to jurisdiction over a dispute between third parties relating to an asset sold by the estate — there was insufficient nexus between the litigation and the bankruptcy cases.

By contrast, in In re Farmland Industries, Inc., 567 F.3d 1010 (8th Cir. 2009), the court found that third-party litigation relating to the implementation of a confirmed Ch. 11 plan did fall within the court's related-to jurisdiction because there was a definite and non-speculative prospect that the estate could be liable to indemnify the losing party.

§7.2.3 The Purpose of §1334

By conferring exclusive jurisdiction on the district court over the case and over the debtor's and estate's property, §1334(a) and (e) ensure that the bankruptcy remedy may be granted only by federal courts, which are also given control over the economic resources of the estate. The court's non-exclusive jurisdiction is more complicated. There had been uncertainty and much litigation over the scope of bankruptcy jurisdiction prior to the enactment of the Code in 1978. It was unclear whether it covered only the actual bankruptcy case itself or extended to issues of nonbankruptcy law that were in some way related to the bankruptcy case. Congress decided to resolve this question in favor of a broad grant of bankruptcy jurisdiction over proceedings arising in and related to the case. This was designed to allow the bankruptcy forum to deal not only with the central bankruptcy case but with all litigation pertaining to the case. The advantage of this broader bankruptcy jurisdiction is the convenience and efficiency of having the bankruptcy forum dispose of all controversies that are intertwined with the bankruptcy case or affect the rights and obligations of the estate. The disadvantage is that in some cases, state courts are the better forum for resolving issues that are governed by state law. This broad grant of jurisdiction detracts from the jurisdiction of those state courts that are the usual arbiters of nonbankruptcy law and are best qualified to pronounce on it. Recognition of this may persuade a bankruptcy forum to exercise restraint in finding that litigation is related to the case, or it may be the basis of a decision to abstain (explained in section 7.7) or to lift the automatic stay so that litigation can proceed in state court.[1]

§7.3 THE EXERCISE OF BANKRUPTCY JURISDICTION BY BANKRUPTCY COURTS

As stated earlier, although §1334 grants jurisdiction to district courts, this jurisdiction is actually exercised by bankruptcy courts, in which the

---

1. The automatic stay is discussed in Chapter 10, and relief from stay in Chapter 11.

bankruptcy case is commenced and issues relating to the case are disposed of, either finally or in the form of proposed findings of fact and conclusions of law (recommendations) to the district court. If bankruptcy judges were appointed in the same way as district court judges, with life tenure under Article III of the Constitution, they would simply be able to exercise the jurisdiction conferred by §1334. This would clearly be the most efficient way in which to establish the bankruptcy system. This was recognized both by the commission whose work led to enactment of the 1978 Code and by the 1994 National Bankruptcy Review Commission. However, the political obstacles to granting this status to bankruptcy judges have been insuperable. Instead, bankruptcy judges are appointed for fixed terms under Article 1 of the Constitution, without life tenure and protection from salary reduction. As a result they do not have the full constitutional status and authority of an Article III federal judge. This restricts the scope of their jurisdiction, which is channeled to them through the district courts. The result is a complex jurisdictional system in which bankruptcy courts can make final determinations in some matters but must make a recommendation to the district court for its disposition in others. The present state of bankruptcy court jurisdiction can only be understood in light of historical developments. This section therefore begins with a brief historical introduction.

§7.3.1 Jurisdiction Prior to 1978

The Bankruptcy Act of 1898 vested jurisdiction over bankruptcy in the federal district courts. The district courts did not hear the bankruptcy cases themselves but appointed referees for set terms to deal with them. These referees were the predecessors of the contemporary bankruptcy courts. Because referees were not Article III federal judges, their power to dispose of issues in bankruptcy cases was limited. They exercised what was known as "summary jurisdiction," which covered questions relating to the administration of the estate and estate property. They could decide little else without the consent of the non-debtor party — and the question of what constituted consent was murky. All other matters had to be decided by a court that had "plenary jurisdiction," such as a federal district court or a state court. This jurisdictional system was a mess. It led to much litigation on jurisdictional issues and was inefficient because litigation relating to matters in the case was dispersed among different courts. The confusion and expense generated by the distinction between summary and plenary jurisdiction was regarded as a serious flaw in the bankruptcy system, and reform of the jurisdictional scheme was identified as an important goal of the 1978 Act.

§7.3.2 The Bankruptcy Reform Act of 1978

One of the goals of the 1978 Act was to reform the law relating to bankruptcy court jurisdiction so that the bankruptcy court could deal with and make final determinations on all matters involved in the case — in essence to exercise jurisdiction as described in section 7.2.2 over all matters arising in or under the Code and proceedings related to the case. The problem was that there was considerable resistance to appointing bankruptcy judges under Article III, so Congress decided to appoint them for a set term under Article I, without life tenure and salary protection. In an attempt to avoid the constitutional problems of conferring extensive jurisdiction on nontenured judges, Congress granted bankruptcy jurisdiction to the district courts and, in the same statutory provision, legislatively delegated this jurisdiction to the bankruptcy courts. In other words, the district courts were used as a conduit for empowering bankruptcy courts to exercise expanded jurisdiction.

The expedient did not work. A relatively short time after passage of the 1978 Act, the Supreme Court toppled the statute's jurisdictional structure. In *Northern Pipeline Constr. Co. v. Marathon Pipe Line Co.*, 458 U.S. 50 (1982) the party who had been sued by the estate in bankruptcy court on a contract claim related to the bankruptcy case challenged the bankruptcy court's jurisdiction over the case. A plurality of the Supreme Court held that the bankruptcy court had no jurisdiction to adjudicate the contract suit. The essence of the plurality opinion is that Congress violated the separation of powers doctrine and the principle of judicial independence by conferring extended jurisdiction on a judge who did not have security of tenure and salary protection under Article III of the Constitution. The Court held that the channeling of jurisdiction through the district court by legislative delegation did not overcome the constitutional objection.

In expounding on the permissible range of adjudication that Congress may constitutionally confer on a non-Article III judge, the court distinguished between public rights — those that arise between the government and others — and private rights — those that involve the liability of one private party to another. In enacting the Code, Congress created a regulatory scheme for the restructuring of debtor/creditor relations, and thereby brought into existence rights that would not exist in the absence of bankruptcy law. Such rights, which owe their existence purely to congressional action, fall into the classification of public rights and, because Congress created them, Congress may assign power to a nontenured judge to adjudicate them. However, rights that exist outside of the Code, and are not solely created by Congress, are private rights and Congress has no constitutional authority to assign their adjudication to a non-Article III judge.

The court returned to this public rights doctrine in *Granfinanciera, S.A. v. Nordberg*, 492 U.S. 33 (1989). It stated that Congress only has the constitutional power to allocate adjudication of a right to a non-Article III judge where the issue to be resolved either involves a public right between the government and others or involves private rights inextricably tied up with a federal regulatory program that virtually occupies the field. That is, the doctrine permits a non-Article III judge to adjudicate private rights provided that the private rights are so intertwined with the program that they take on the character of a public right. The public rights doctrine exhibits some considerable degree of mushiness, and *Northern Pipeline* and subsequent cases show that the justices are not in agreement on its scope. However, its basic point is that a nontenured bankruptcy judge does have power to adjudicate bankruptcy rights purely created by the Code, and has some limited power beyond that to dispose of non-bankruptcy rights that are inextricably linked to bankruptcy's overall federal regulatory scheme of restructuring debtor-creditor relations. Beyond this, matters falling within the bankruptcy jurisdiction of federal courts must be decided finally by district courts.

§7.3.3 1984 Reforms

The effect of the *Northern Pipeline* decision was stayed for a time to enable Congress to resolve the problem. The controversy about whether bankruptcy judges should be appointed under Article III arose again, and while it raged, the stay expired. For a time the bankruptcy system operated under emergency rules promulgated by each circuit, under which the district court maintained jurisdiction over bankruptcy cases and the bankruptcy court operated under referrals from the district court. With regard to those matters that arose directly from the Code itself, the bankruptcy court could render judgments and orders, but with regard to related matters, the bankruptcy court would make recommendations to the district court, which would itself make the final determination.

The emergency rules were controversial, and their constitutionality was challenged. However, the rules were upheld by various Courts of Appeal, and remained in effect until 1984, when Congress finally passed the Bankruptcy Amendments and Federal Judgeship Act. This statute created the current jurisdictional system found in Title 28 U.S.C.

Congress decided against the option of giving bankruptcy judges Article III status. Instead, the 1984 amendment continues to provide for their appointment for fixed terms (14 years), subject to termination for cause such as incompetence or misconduct. The constitutional problem is dealt with by limiting the bankruptcy judges' power to decide matters and making them subject to the control and supervision of the district court. In many respects, the 1984 amendment is based on the system set up under the Emergency Rules, and it has affinities to the old referee system. It does make improvements over the referee system, however, because it consolidates jurisdiction and reduces the scattered litigation that plagued bankruptcy cases under the 1898 Act. However, because the bankruptcy court cannot constitutionally exercise this consolidated jurisdiction, the district court must play a broader role than was intended when the 1978 reforms were devised.

§7.3.4 Proposals for Change by the 1994 National Bankruptcy Review Commission

The 1994 National Bankruptcy Review Commission studied the jurisdictional scheme established in 1984 and recommended that bankruptcy judges be given Article III status to avoid the constitutional issues generated by the present system and to eliminate the complexity, litigation, and delay resulting from them. The Commission report contemplated a transitional period during which current judges would serve out their 14-year terms (with the right to apply for appointment under Article III if they chose), and new appointments would be under Article III.. Congress did not adopt the Commission's recommendation in BAPCPA, so the system set up in 1984 is still in place.

§7.3.5 An Overview of the Current System

Diagram 7b represents the way in which bankruptcy jurisdiction is channeled to the bankruptcy court through the district court.

The system works as follows:

1. *The grant of jurisdiction to the district court.* Jurisdiction over bankruptcy is conferred on the district court by §1334, as discussed in section 7.2. This jurisdiction covers the bankruptcy case itself as well as matters arising under the Code and relating to the case.

2. *District court referral to the bankruptcy court.* The district court refers these matters to the bankruptcy court, which is described in 28 U.S.C. §151 as a "unit" of the district court. The process of referral, the relationship between the district court and its bankruptcy "unit," and the exercise of power by the bankruptcy court is dealt with in 28 U.S.C. §157. Section 157(a) allows each district court to make a blanket referral of all bankruptcy matters to the bankruptcy court. Thus, the district court does not make case-by-case referrals; all bankruptcy litigation commences as a matter of course in the bankruptcy court.

3. *District court control.* Under §157(d), the district court retains ultimate control over all bankruptcy cases. If cause is shown it may, either on

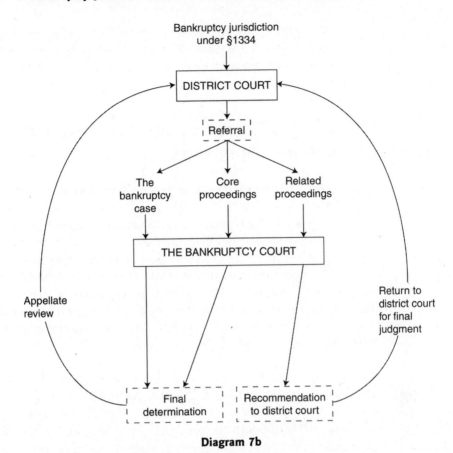

Diagram 7b

its own motion or on the motion of a party, withdraw any case or portion of a case from the bankruptcy court. Withdrawal of reference is not granted lightly and is confined to situations in which it is justified by exceptional circumstances. For example, cause for withdrawal is established where a party has the right to a jury trial and does not consent to the trial being conducted in the bankruptcy court. (*See* section 7.4.2.) If a case involves both issues of bankruptcy law and some other federal law regulating interstate commerce (*e.g.*, an antitrust issue), the district court must withdraw the proceeding on the timely motion of a party.

4. *Final adjudication.* The final disposition of bankruptcy litigation depends on the nature of the rights in issue. Because bankruptcy judges do not have Article III status, the bankruptcy court cannot finally adjudicate all matters brought before it. It is empowered to make a final judgment or order in matters called "core proceedings," which concern rights that arise out of the Code itself or are inextricably linked to the administration of the bankruptcy case. Under *Northern Pipeline*, Congress may provide for the determination of

these rights by a nontenured judge, because the rights were created by Congress or are inextricably linked to the regulatory scheme (that is, the restructuring of debtor-creditor relations through bankruptcy) set up by Congress. However, the bankruptcy court may not render a final judgment in matters that are merely related to the bankruptcy case but require the resolution of nonbankruptcy rights. Congress cannot entrust the disposition of these cases to a nontenured judge. Therefore, where a bankruptcy court deals with a related matter, it must submit its findings of fact and conclusion of law to the district court, which the district court must review de novo and dispose of finally.

To accommodate this distinction, §157(b) differentiates the bankruptcy case and core proceedings, which may be finally adjudicated by the bankruptcy court, and noncore proceedings, in which the bankruptcy court's resolution takes the form of findings of fact and conclusion of law, submitted to the district court, that is then responsible for rendering final judgment. In some situations, it is relatively easy to categorize a proceeding as core or noncore. In others, the distinction is elusive and has generated much litigation. It is important to note that this goes beyond being a matter of statutory interpretation, and the fact that Congress has denoted a particular proceeding as core in §157 is not dispositive. The U.S. Supreme Court has held that the statutory classification is subject to scrutiny under constitutional principles.

(1) The scope of the case and core proceedings "arising under" the Code or "arising in a case" under the Code.

Section 157(b) allows the bankruptcy court to hear, determine, and enter orders in "all cases under title 11 and all core proceedings arising under title 11, or arising in a case under title 11." This means that the general referral by the district court enables the bankruptcy court to hear and decide the bankruptcy case as well as core bankruptcy proceedings. The role of the district court in these matters is generally limited to appellate review. §§157(b)(1) and 158.

A core proceeding under §157 corresponds to proceedings "arising under" or "arising in a case under" the Code, over which bankruptcy jurisdiction is conferred on the district court by §1334(b). In *Stern v. Marshall*, 131 S.Ct. 2594 (2011), the Supreme Court made it clear that core proceedings encompass only proceedings "arising under" the Code or "in a case under" the Code. If a proceeding does not fit within one of these two categories, it is noncore, and hence related to the case. (That is, "noncore" and "related" are synonymous.) A core proceeding has been defined as one that "invokes a substantive right provided by title 11 or . . . that, by its nature, could arise only in the context of a bankruptcy case." This test was enunciated in *In re Wood*, 825 F.2d 90, 97 (5th Cir. 1987) and has been widely followed in later cases. See, for example, In re Wolverine Radio Co., 930 F.2d 1132, 1144 (6th Cir. 1991); In re Exide Technologies, 544 F.3d 196 (3d Cir. 2008). If the right in issue owes its existence to the Code, the litigation over it is a core proceeding "arising under" the Code. However, even if the right in issue does not owe its existence to (that is, is not created by) the Code, the proceedings involving it could qualify as core proceedings "arising in" the case if they concern an essential part of the administration of the estate.

The question of whether a proceeding qualifies as core is muddled and difficult to decide. A reasonably clear example of a core proceeding seems to be the allowance or disallowance of a claim proved against the estate: The bankruptcy court has jurisdiction to determine the validity and extent of a creditor's claim against the estate. Although the claim may be based on state law, the process of allowing or disallowing claims against the estate is a central component of the bankruptcy process. (In addition, by filing the claim, the creditor effectively consents to the bankruptcy court's jurisdiction to determine it.) However, to the extent that the proceeding goes beyond this central function of claim determination, it likely loses its status as a core proceeding and is better characterized as related to the case. As discussed below, the U.S. Supreme Court so decided in Stern v. Marshall. Although the Court held that the bankruptcy court did have jurisdiction to make a final determination of the creditor's claim, the resolution of a tangentially related counterclaim by the estate was beyond its jurisdiction. In Waldman v. Stone, 698 F.3d 910 (6th Cir. 2012), the debtor in possession disputed a creditor's claim on the grounds that the claim was based on fraud. The bankruptcy court found that the creditor had committed an egregious fraud on the debtor prior to the bankruptcy. It therefore disallowed the claim. In addition, it awarded compensatory and punitive damages to the debtor. The court of appeals held that the bankruptcy court had jurisdiction to disallow the claim. Although the fraud defense to the claim was based on state law, it arose under the bankruptcy statute because it was inextricably linked to the claims allowance process. However, even though the award of damages was based on the same facts as the claim disallowance, the damages award was not part of this process. It would require the proof of additional facts beyond that process. It was therefore not core, but related, and required final determination by the district court.

One might think that a judgment avoiding a preferential transfer would also be a good example of a core proceeding. Under §547 the trustee has the power to avoid a transfer made by the debtor to the creditor before bankruptcy if that transfer satisfies all the elements of the section, and results in the creditor receiving more than it would have been entitled to receive in a distribution from the estate.[2] This right of avoidance is

---

2. Voidable preferences are discussed in Chapter 16.

created by the Code and does not exist outside of bankruptcy. Although the U.S. Supreme Court recognized in *Langenkamp v. Culp*, 498 U.S. 42 (1990) that the bankruptcy court has jurisdiction to decide a preference action against a creditor who filed a proof of claim (so that the avoidance issue is part of the process of allowing or disallowing the claim), it is not clear if the preference action qualifies as core on its own merits where the creditor has not filed a claim. See *In re Oldco M Corpn.*, 484 B.R. 598 (Bankr. S.D. N.Y. 2012).

A few further illustrations indicate the scope of core jurisdiction: in *In re Ben Cooper, Inc.*, 896 F.2d 1394 (2d Cir. 1990), *reinstated on remand*, 924 F.2d 36 (2d Cir. 1991), the court found that litigation between the estate and an insurer to determine the validity of an insurance policy taken out by the estate was a core proceeding "arising in" the case. Even though nonbank-ruptcy law governed the dispute, the insurance contract was entered into postpetition for the purpose of protecting estate property, and was therefore essentially tied up with the administration of the estate. By contrast, in *In re Electric Machinery Enterprises, Inc.*, 479 F.3d 791 (11th Cir. 2007), the dispute related to the amount of money owed by the nondebtor to the estate, arising from a constructive trust in favor of the debtor. Although the dispute was related to the bankruptcy case, it was not a core proceeding because it neither involved a right created by the Code nor could it arise only in bankruptcy. Because the proceeding was noncore, the estate was bound to have the dispute arbitrated under an arbitration agreement entered into by the debtor.

(2) The power of Congress to prescribe what qualifies as a core proceeding.

Section 157(b)(2) sets out a nondefinitive list of core proceedings. This list is a guide, but it is not entirely reliable. Litigation is only a core proceeding if it satisfies the test stated above. Congress cannot simply declare something to be a core proceeding and confer jurisdiction on the bankruptcy court over it: If a matter does not legitimately qualify as a core proceeding, its designation as such in §157(b)(2) is wrong and the provision can be struck down as unconstitutional. In *Granfinanciera, S.A. v. Nordberg*, 492 U.S. 33 (1989), the Supreme Court went behind Congress's categorizations in §157(b)(2) and determined, based on the substance of the proceeding, that a suit against a non-creditor to avoid a fraudulent transfer, although included in §157(b)(2) as a core proceeding, did not in fact so qualify.[3]

---

3. As noted above, it is also not clear if a suit to recover a preferential transfer qualifies constitutionally as a core proceeding, even though it too is included in the list of core proceedings in §157(b)(2).

In *Stern v. Marshall* the Supreme Court again evaluated a proceeding identified as core in §157(b)(2). A five-justice majority concluded that the statutory classification was unconstitutional. The case involved litigation between the estates of the debtor, Vickie Lynn Marshall (better known as Anna Nicole Smith), and Pierce Marshall, the son of her late husband, over the debtor's rights to the late husband's multimillion dollar estate. Pierce had filed a claim in Vickie's bankruptcy case, contending that Vickie had defamed him. Vickie counterclaimed, alleging that Pierce had tortiously interfered with her rights to acquire half of her late husband's property. The issue before the Supreme Court was whether the counterclaim was a core proceeding. The counterclaim clearly involved a matter of state tort law, but §157(b)(2)(C) includes as core proceedings "counterclaims by the estate against persons filing claims against the state." Although the majority recognized that the counterclaim in this case fell within the statutory definition of a core proceeding, it could not be so treated under the constitution. The counterclaim was unquestionably a suit at common law. It did not involve a claim that was created by the Code, and it did not involve adjudication of the same issues that had to be resolved in deciding whether or not to allow Pierce's claim. It was therefore not a matter of public right, closely intertwined with a federal regulatory scheme. Rather, it was a related matter over which the bankruptcy court did not have the power to make a final determination. The majority intimated that the result might be different if the counterclaim was either based on a right conferred by the Code (for example, if it was for the avoidance of a preference that is avoidable only in bankruptcy) or if the counterclaim was directly related to the claim, so that they would both be determined by the same factual and legal questions. The dissenting justices expressed the view that the majority had overemphasized the precedential effect of *Northern Pipeline*, adopted too formalistic an approach to bankruptcy court jurisdiction, and reversed a more pragmatic trend found in recent cases involving administrative adjudication in areas other than bankruptcy. The question should not simply be whether private rights are involved, but whether, in light of all the circumstances, adjudication by a non-Article III court enhances the efficiency of the process and does not really undermine judicial independence and the separation of powers. The dissent concluded that the majority's holding would have a significant impact on the adjudication of bankruptcy cases by requiring district courts to resolve questions that are best left to the bankruptcy courts.

(3) Noncore (related) proceedings. If a matter is not a core proceeding but is related to the bankruptcy case, the bankruptcy judge may hear it but cannot enter an order. The judge must make a finding and submit a recommendation to the district court, which must enter the final judgment after considering the bankruptcy court's recommendation and reviewing de novo any matters to which a party has objected. §157(c)(1). This process allows the related litigation to be conducted before the bankruptcy court, but preserves a level of district court control intended to be sufficient to satisfy the constitutional limits on bankruptcy court jurisdiction. Under §157(c)(2), the district court may refer a related proceeding to the bankruptcy court for final disposition provided that all parties to the proceeding consent.

(4) Consent to bankruptcy court jurisdiction in noncore proceedings. The question of consent to bankruptcy court jurisdiction is difficult. To begin with, a non-Article III court cannot acquire jurisdiction by consent of the parties where the right to trial by an Article III judge is a structural constitutional right deriving from the separation of powers. That is, individual consent to jurisdiction is not effective if the determination of a matter by a non-Article III judge would violate core separation of power principles and would be an encroachment on the judicial function. However, if the right does not qualify as structural, a party can consent to jurisdiction by a non-Article III court. The U.S. Supreme Court indicated in *Stern* that pierce's consert to the bankruptcy court's jurisdiction over his defornation claim was effective because structural constitutional principles were not implicated.

Nevertheless, the question of whether a party did consent to bankruptcy court jurisdiction can be unclear where the consent is not express. *Stern* shows just how tricky the consent issue can be. The court recognized that by filing a claim in the estate for damages for defamation, Pierce had consented to the jurisdiction of the bankruptcy court over his defamation claim. Even though defamation is a matter of state tort law, once a claim is filed, the determination of whether and in what amount it should be allowed is a core proceeding. However, that consent only covered the adjudication of the claim itself and did not constitute implicit consent to the bankruptcy court's jurisdiction over the counterclaim. The majority reasoned that the act of filing a claim could not be treated as assent to jurisdiction over the counterclaim because the apparent assent was not truly voluntary. Once bankruptcy had been filed, Pierce could not bring the claim in another forum and had little choice but to file a claim if he wanted any remedy. The dissent disagreed, arguing that prior cases had regarded this as sufficient consent.

In *In re Bellingham Insurance Agency, Inc.*, 702 F.3d 553 (9th Cir. 2012), the court held that in light of *Stern*, a defendant in a suit to avoid a fraudulent conveyance consented to the jurisdiction of the bankruptcy court by failing to object. Similarly, in *Oldco M Corpn.*, the bankruptcy court, following long-standing practice, inferred consent to jurisdiction where a party failed to respond to a complaint by the trustee claiming avoidance of a preferential transfer.

§7.3.6 A Summary of the Operation of §157 and Its Constitutionality

In summary, §1334 confers bankruptcy jurisdiction on the district court and §157 empowers that court to refer its bankruptcy powers to the bankruptcy court. Although the district court makes a general referral of all bankruptcy matters to the bankruptcy court, it retains final say over all proceedings beyond the bankruptcy case and its core. The bankruptcy court can only make a final adjudication outside the core with the specific referral from the district court and the consent of the parties. The district court is able to withdraw its reference in any matter.

Notwithstanding the restriction on their power, bankruptcy courts do deal with most aspects of the bankruptcy case and do make final determinations on a wide range of issues that arise in the case. Even where the court cannot make a final determination of an issue, the findings of fact and conclusions of law by an expert specialist bankruptcy judge are given great weight by the district court. Nevertheless, it is unfortunate that the system selected by Congress continues to lead to uncertainty and litigation over the extent of bankruptcy court power, and imposes an additional workload on district courts.

§7.4 THE JURY TRIAL IN BANKRUPTCY

The Seventh Amendment preserves the right to trial by jury in suits at common law. It is well accepted that the words "suits at common law" refer only to actions in law that would have been tried by jury at the time of the enactment of the Seventh Amendment. It does not include proceedings in equity, which had never been tried by jury. Where the cause of action in issue did not exist at the time that the Seventh Amendment was enacted, but was created afterward, the right to a jury trial is determined by examining its inherent nature and its analogy to forms of relief that did exist at that time. Bankruptcy relief originates in equity, not law, so the Constitution does not guarantee a jury trial for the bankruptcy case itself, or for those core proceedings that are purely an aspect of the equitable remedy of bankruptcy. It also does not guarantee a jury trial for proceedings involving nonbankruptcy rights or remedies, whether core or related to the case, that are equitable in nature. However, where a proceeding arising in or related to the case involves a legal right or remedy, the parties are entitled to a jury trial. The interaction of the Seventh Amendment with bankruptcy jurisdiction has given rise to two questions: First, in which kinds of proceedings is a party entitled to a jury trial? Second, where the right to a jury trial exists, does the bankruptcy court have the power to conduct it?

(1) The type of proceeding in which a jury trial is available. This issue was addressed by the Supreme Court in *Granfinanciera*, in which the trustee had sued to avoid a prepetition transfer of property by the debtor as fraudulent. The Supreme Court held that it was not dispositive that §157(b)(2)(H) included suits to avoid fraudulent transfers in its list of core proceedings. Congress cannot turn a private right into a public right just by so classifying it. The Court found that a suit to avoid a fraudulent transfer is long-established as a creditor's suit in state law. The suit therefore involved private rights, and that it qualified as a legal suit at common law for which the Seventh Amendment guarantees a jury trial.[4]

A party can waive the right to a jury trial in much the same way as he can consent to the jurisdiction of the bankruptcy court. In *Granfinanciera* the court indicated in dictum that such a waiver could occur merely if the party filed a claim against the estate, thereby submitting to the bankruptcy court's jurisdiction to restructure the debtor/creditor relationship. The Court decided this question directly about a year later in *Langenkamp v. Culp*, 498 U.S. 42 (1990). The trustee sought to avoid a preferential transfer given by the debtor to a creditor before bankruptcy. The creditor had proved a claim against the estate. The court characterized the avoidance suit as legal in nature so that the creditor would have been entitled to a jury trial had it not proved a claim. However, the creditor lost this right by filing a claim, making the avoidance suit part of the claim allowance process, integral to the courts equitable jurisdiction to restructure the debtor/creditor relationship.

(2) The bankruptcy court's power to conduct a jury trial. In *Granfinanciera*, the Supreme Court left open the issue of whether a bankruptcy judge may conduct a jury trial. Neither the Code nor Title 28 contains any guidance on this issue in general. The only reference to the jury trial is in 28 U.S.C. 157(e), which empowers the bankruptcy judge to conduct a jury trial provided that the district court specifically designates the bankruptcy judge to conduct that trial, and all the parties consent. This is, of course, the easiest case for arguing that the court's exercise of power is constitutional, and §157(e) does not venture beyond it.

In cases where there is no district court designation and party consent under §157(e), the question of whether the proceeding is core or noncore

---

4. The trustee sought money damages for the value of the property, and did not claim return of the property itself. Because the claim was monetary in nature, and not an action for the turnover of property, the Court's characterization of the avoidance suit as legal should be confined to monetary claims. Therefore, there may be no right to a jury trial where the avoidance suit aims at recovering the actual property that was fraudulently transferred. See *In re Pasquariello*, 16 F.3d 525 (3d Cir 1994); *In re Prosser*, 2008 WL 3892147 (D.V.I. 2008). Note, also, that the transferee had not proved a claim in the estate. Had it done so, the trustee's suit to avoid the transfer could be part of the claim allowance process, and therefore part of a core proceeding.

has a bearing on the bankruptcy court's ability to conduct a jury trial. If the legal matter is not a core proceeding, there is general agreement that a bankruptcy court may not conduct a jury trial because the finding of the bankruptcy court is a mere recommendation to the district court. The district court's de novo review of the bankruptcy court's disposition would implicate review of the jury's verdict as well, which would violate the Seventh Amendment's bar on re-examination of the jury's verdict. If the legal matter is a core proceeding, some courts have held that a bankruptcy court is empowered to hold a jury trial because the bankruptcy court can render a final disposition in such a case, and the jury verdict would therefore not fall within any de novo review by the district court. Other courts have held that notwithstanding this, jury trials are not within the power of a bankruptcy court, even in core proceedings, because bankruptcy courts have not been expressly granted the power to conduct jury trials.

§7.5 THE INJUNCTIVE, CONTEMPT, AND SANCTIONING POWERS OF THE BANKRUPTCY COURT

Section 105(a) confers general authority on the court to "issue any order, process, or judgment that is necessary or appropriate to carry out the provisions of this title," and to act *sua sponte*, where necessary, to take action to enforce its orders or to prevent abuse of process. Three of the significant powers encompassed by this general provision are the court's power to issue injunctions, to deal with contempt of court, and to sanction improper conduct in relation to the case.

§7.5.1 Injunctions

The two most important forms of injunction in a bankruptcy case are routine, self-executing bars to action that are not expressly ordered by the court, but arise as a matter of law — that is, automatically — at certain stages of the proceedings. The first is the automatic stay under §362, which takes effect immediately upon the filing of the bankruptcy petition and enjoins all action to collect debts due by the debtor or to seize or dispose of the debtor's property. (*See* Chapters 10 and 11.) The second is the injunction on actions to collect a discharged debt, which goes into effect under §524(a)(2) as an incident of the discharge. (*See* Chapter 22.) As important as these two injunctions are, they are of limited scope: They are concerned only with action to collect property or money from the estate or the debtor through legal proceedings or other means. It frequently happens that other conduct must be restrained to ensure that the case proceeds as desired or the estate is not harmed. For example, it may be necessary to forbid creditor action against a third party guarantor, or to prevent obstructive or harassing action against a person associated with the debtor. The court's general equitable power under §105(a) gives it authority to issue injunctions of this type. The injunction can only be issued if the court has jurisdiction generally over the matter in issue, which means that the proceedings in which the injunction is issued must arise under the Code, or in a case arising in or related to a case under the Code. The Supreme Court recognized the bankruptcy courts' general injunctive power in *Celotex Corp. v. Edwards*, 514 U.S. 300 (1995), in which it upheld an injunction issued by a bankruptcy court in a suit that was related to the bankruptcy case.

§7.5.2 Contempt of Court

A court enforces obedience to its orders and respect for its processes by the power to sanction disrespectful conduct on violations of its orders. Contempt sanctions fall into two principal categories: civil and criminal. Civil contempt itself is divided into two types. Compensatory civil contempt is simply a money judgment to compensate the plaintiff for loss caused by the defendant's disobedience to the order. Coercive civil contempt takes the form of a fine or imprisonment imposed for the purpose of persuading the party to comply with an order. Its coercive purpose means that the sanction is imposed only as long as the disobedience continues. Once the party stops resisting the order, the fine ceases to accrue, or the imprisonment ends. (For example, the court may fine the violator $100 per day until the violation ceases, or may order the violator imprisoned until he comes into compliance.)

Criminal contempt is, like other criminal sanctions, a punishment for wrongful conduct. Its goal is not to amend the violator's conduct, but to impose a penalty on him for having committed the violation. For this reason it normally takes the form of a set fine or prison term, without the option of bringing the punishment to an end by ceasing the improper behavior.

Because of the jurisdictional limitations on bankruptcy courts, the extent of their power to deal with contempt is unclear. The 1978 Code did not impose any limits on the bankruptcy court's civil contempt powers. However, 28 U.S.C. 1481 did place limits on its power to punish for criminal contempt. Section 1481 was repealed in 1984, removing all statutory reference to the bankruptcy court's contempt power.

In the absence of statutory authority, courts generally find the power to sanction civil contempt to be inherent in the powers conferred on the court in §105(a). The bankruptcy court's power to impose penalties for criminal contempt is less clear. Some courts have found a criminal contempt power, but others have not, based on the reasoning that the imposition of criminal sanctions implicates the right to a jury trial and other procedural safeguards that are not adequately assured by an Article I court. (For example, see In re Dyer, 322 F.3d 1178 (9th Cir. 2003).) Dyer shows that the distinction between civil and criminal contempt is not always obvious. The bankruptcy court had made an award for compensatory civil contempt that included substantial punitive damages. The court of appeals held that a civil contempt order that imposes a significant penalty takes on the nature of criminal contempt and exceeds the court's power under §105(a).

§7.5.3 Sanctions for Improper Conduct

Under Bankruptcy Rule 9011, a bankruptcy court has the power to impose monetary sanctions on an attorney or party who, in pleadings or other documents submitted to the court, has made a representation that is frivolous or otherwise for an improper purpose, or has made unwarranted legal claims or factual allegations that have no evidentiary support. In re Rainbow Magazine, 77 F.3d 278 (9th Cir. 1996), held that even if the improper conduct is not covered by Rule 9011 (say, for example, it does not involve the submission of a document to the court), the bankruptcy court has the inherent power under §105(a) to sanction conduct that is vexatious or disobedient. The court's power to deal with matters of decorum and respect are part of the power granted by Congress in §105(a) to carry out the provisions of the Code.

§7.6 APPEALS FROM THE BANKRUPTCY COURT

§7.6.1 The Appellate Structure in General

In related proceedings, where the bankruptcy court's determination is merely a proposed finding of fact and conclusion of law, the district court makes the final order or judgment. Under 28 U.S.C. §157(c)(1). This is not an appeal, of course, but just the district court's determination of the issue, which may or may not follow the bankruptcy court's recommendation. The decision of the district court is subject to appeal to the court of appeals and then to the Supreme Court in the usual way. In core proceedings (or in related proceedings where the district court, with the consent of the parties, has referred the matter to the bankruptcy court for final determination under §157(c)(2)), the decision of the bankruptcy court is appealable under §158 to the district court or, if the circuit has established a bankruptcy appellate panel, as described in section 7.6.2, to the panel. (The bankruptcy appellate panel, consisting of three bankruptcy judges, substitutes for the district court as the court of first review.[5]) From there it is appealable in the usual way.

§7.6.2 Bankruptcy Appellate Panels

One of the innovations of the 1978 reforms (enacted in 28 U.S.C. §158) was to authorize the judicial council of each circuit to establish a bankruptcy appellate panel (abbreviated as BAP), consisting of three bankruptcy judges, to substitute for the district court as an appellate tribunal of first instance. The idea was to lift some of the workload from the district courts and to create a specialist appellate panel that would have great expertise in bankruptcy matters. The Code made it voluntary for the circuits to establish these courts, and only two — the First and Ninth Circuits — initially took advantage of this power. The First Circuit abolished its BAP after Northern Pipeline cast uncertainty over the extent of bankruptcy judges' jurisdiction, so only the Ninth Circuit BAP remained.

Because the Ninth Circuit BAP was generally regarded as a successful and valuable court, Congress decided in 1994 to press the other circuits into using such panels. It therefore amended §158(b) to require the establishment of a BAP in every circuit unless the circuit's judicial council finds that there are insufficient judicial resources available in the circuit, or the establishment of the panel would result in undue delay or in increased cost to the parties in bankruptcy cases. The determination to have or not to have a BAP is capable of reconsideration by the judicial council at periodic intervals. It is also possible for two or more circuits to establish joint BAPs. At present five circuits have created BAPs.

Even where a circuit has a BAP, §158 imposes two restrictions on the panel's power to hear appeals. If either precondition is not satisfied, the appeal must go to the district court instead: First, under §158(b)(1) and (c)(1) all the parties to the suit must consent to the submission of the appeal to the BAP. Second under §158(b)(6) the majority of district judges in the district must have voted to authorize the BAP to hear appeals from that district. That is, the district court judges, by declining to vote to authorize appeals to the BAP in their district, can in effect veto the establishment of a BAP insofar as their district is concerned.

As noted earlier, the BAP is composed of bankruptcy judges from within the circuit. It would not be appropriate for a member of the panel to participate in deciding an appeal from the district in which she normally sits as a

---

5. The 1994 National Bankruptcy Review Commission recommended eliminating this initial level of appeal, so that appeals from a bankruptcy court decision would go immediately to the court of appeals. Congress did not follow this recommendation.

trial judge. Therefore, §158(b)(5) forbids any member of the panel from hearing an appeal originating from a case in her own district.

Because BAPs are made up of panels of bankruptcy judges, the constitutional infirmities of bankruptcy courts must inevitably raise questions about the powers of the BAPs. However, as a BAP hears appeals only when the judges of the district court have authorized them and the parties have consented, constitutional issues generally do not arise. The precedential weight of decisions of the BAPs has been controversial. It is not clear if their decisions have any precedential value at all or, if they do, whether they bind all bankruptcy courts in the circuit or only those in the district from which the appeal originated. Some bankruptcy courts within a BAP's circuit have considered themselves bound by all BAP decisions, but others have not. The precedential weight of BAP decisions on district courts or courts of appeal is even more dubious. It seems inconceivable that an Article III judge, who reviews and hears appeals from the very judges on the BAP panel, could be bound by their decision. The 1994 National Bankruptcy Review Commission noted the unsatisfactory consequences of appellate courts whose precedential value is unclear.[6]

§7.7 ABSTENTION

§7.7.1 Introduction

Where a court does have jurisdiction over a matter, it may decide to forgo that jurisdiction by abstaining from hearing the matter. The nature and effect of the court's abstention depends on whether the court's jurisdiction is exclusive or nonexclusive. If it has exclusive jurisdiction, no other court can hear the matter, so abstention is equivalent to dismissal (or if a temporary abstention, suspension) of the case. This form of abstention is governed by §305 of the Code. If the court has nonexclusive jurisdiction, abstention leaves it open for another court to hear the case. The purpose of this kind of abstention, governed by 28 U.S.C. §1334(c), is to defer to that other court.

§7.7.2 Abstention under §305 of the Code

Section 305 concerns the bankruptcy court's abstention from the bankruptcy case. Because the bankruptcy court has exclusive jurisdiction over

---

6. As noted earlier, the Commission made two recommendations, either of which would have avoided these consequences: appointing bankruptcy judges under Article III, or abolishing the initial level of appeal from bankruptcy courts. Congress did not adopt either of these recommendations.

the case, abstention under §305 does not result in the case being taken up by another court: There is no other court in the United States with jurisdiction to hear a bankruptcy petition. Thus, the effect of abstention under §305 is the dismissal of the case or, if the court abstains temporarily, its suspension. Notice and a hearing must precede the court's decision to abstain.

There are two bases for the court's abstention under §305. The first is a general equitable ground — dismissal or suspension of the case would better serve the interests of creditors and the debtor. (For example, the court may dismiss or suspend an involuntary case initiated by uncooperative creditors because the debtor and other creditors are working together to achieve a composition.)

The second is more specific. The court may dismiss or suspend the case in deference to bankruptcy or equivalent insolvency proceedings pending in a court of a foreign country, provided that the foreign law has safeguards and protections for all parties reasonably equivalent to those provided by the Code, and reasons of efficiency and international comity favor abstention in favor of the foreign court.

§7.7.3 Abstention under 28 U.S.C. §1334(c)

As discussed in section 7.2, 28 U.S.C. §1334(b) gives the district court wide nonexclusive jurisdiction over proceedings arising under the Code or arising in or related to the bankruptcy case. This jurisdiction is then referred by the district court to the bankruptcy court. Although the court possesses this broad jurisdiction, it is not always appropriate to exercise it. Sometimes the best interests of justice dictate that related proceedings be dealt with by the state court that has concurrent jurisdiction over them. This is particularly true where the proceedings had already begun in state court before the bankruptcy was filed. Abstention under §1334(c) permits, and in some cases requires, the district court to defer to the state court where it is the most appropriate forum. Although §1334(c) mentions only the district court, motions to abstain are dealt with by the bankruptcy court under the general referral from the district court.

Section 1334(c) provides for two forms of abstention: permissive abstention under §1334(c)(1) and mandatory abstention under §1334(c)(2). Each has its own grounds:

(1) Permissive abstention. In a core proceeding, a court is permitted to abstain in favor of a state court where it considers that abstention is in the interest of justice, or in the interest of comity with state courts or respect for state law. In some core proceedings, the issue of abstention does not arise because the right adjudicated is provided by the Code and no state court has jurisdiction to deal with it. However, recall that core proceedings include matters that could only arise in the context of a bankruptcy case. These proceedings can involve issues of state law. In deciding whether to abstain in core proceedings of this kind, the bankruptcy court weighs several factors, including the effect on the efficient administration of justice, the extent to which state law issues predominate, the degree to which the applicable state law is settled, the relationship of the proceeding to the bankruptcy case, and the prejudice to the party who desires resolution by the bankruptcy court. See, for example, In re National Eastern Corp., 391 B.R. 663 (Bankr. D. Conn. 2008).

At the edges, core proceedings involving state law can be difficult to distinguish from related proceedings. For example, in In re Southmark Corp., 163 F.3d 925 (5th Cir. 1999), the proceeding in issue involved adjudication of a malpractice claim made by the debtor in possession against accountants hired by the estate to investigate prepetition investment transactions. Although state law governed the malpractice claim, the court held it to be a core proceeding because it was generated in the course of administering the estate and could therefore, by its very nature, arise only in the context of bankruptcy. The state law basis of the claim was not dispositive, and the bankruptcy court's control over professionals hired by the estate is a crucial aspect of bankruptcy administration, having a direct bearing on the distribution of the estate. In addition, the accountants' advice directly affected the assets of the estate because it influenced the estate's decision on asset recovery. See also In re Seven Fields Development Corp., 505 F.3d 237 (3d Cir. 2007).

(2) Mandatory abstention. The court is obliged to abstain when the following requirements are satisfied:

- A timely motion for abstention is made by a party to the proceeding in question.
- The proceeding is based on a state law claim or cause of action.
- The proceeding is related to the bankruptcy case, but does not arise under the Code or in the bankruptcy case. (In other words, mandatory abstention is only required in related matters. The distinction between these categories is set out in section 7.2.)
- The jurisdiction of the district court is based solely on §1334. That is, there are no grounds for federal jurisdiction independent of bankruptcy (e.g., diversity jurisdiction).
- The dominant view is that action must already have commenced in the appropriate state court. However, some courts interpret §1334(c)(2) to apply, even if action has not yet commenced, provided that it clearly will be instituted.
- The action can be timely adjudicated in the state court.

If the court determines that all these requirements are met, it must abstain from the matter. If all the requirements are not satisfied, abstention is not mandatory, but the court may nevertheless exercise its discretion to abstain under §1334(c)(1).

§7.8 REMOVAL AND REMAND UNDER 28 U.S.C. §1452

Removal may be thought of as the opposite of abstention. When a court abstains, it forgoes its jurisdiction in favor of another court. When a matter is removed, it is transferred from another court and taken up in the bankruptcy forum.

After a bankruptcy petition has been filed, a party to a related civil proceeding that is pending in another court may remove that proceeding to the bankruptcy court under §1452(a). (Again, the section refers only to the district court, but removal is to the bankruptcy court under the general referral.) A matter cannot be removed to the bankruptcy court unless it falls within the court's jurisdiction under §1334. Section 1452(a) expressly confines removal to civil matters and forbids removal of cases before the U.S. Tax Court and cases by a governmental unit to enforce its police or regulatory power.

Upon removal, the bankruptcy court is seized of the matter and can deal with it in the same way as it deals with other cases. However, the court may not necessarily keep the case after removal. Section 1452(b) allows the court to remand it back to the original court on any equitable ground. Also, the grounds for abstention in §1334(c) are applicable, so the court can abstain from a matter that is removed to it, thereby returning it to the original court. Remand may be requested by a party who objects to the removal, or may be decided upon by the court *sua sponte*.

§7.9 SOVEREIGN IMMUNITY

§7.9.1 Background and the General Principle of Sovereign Immunity

Issues of sovereign immunity can arise in a bankruptcy case where the estate has a claim against a governmental unit and seeks to recover that claim by suit. Sovereign immunity is a complex subject, and a full discussion of its impact in a bankruptcy case is beyond the scope of this introductory text.

However, this explanatory note will give you some idea of the role that the doctrine might play in the bankruptcy context.

The doctrine of sovereign immunity entered American law as a basic principle of common law — the sovereign cannot be sued without consent in its own courts by its own subjects. The doctrine precludes a suit by a citizen against either state or federal government in state or federal court unless the government in question has consented to the suit, has waived the immunity, or has abrogated it by statute. With regard to federal courts, the principle of sovereign immunity is embodied in the Eleventh Amendment to the U.S. Constitution, which provides that "[t]he judicial power of the United States shall not be construed to extend to any suit in law or equity, commenced or prosecuted against one of the United States, by citizens of another state, or by citizens or subjects of a foreign state." Although the express language of the Eleventh Amendment mentions only suits in federal court against states by noncitizens of that state, it is well established that the doctrine applies more broadly to cover suits by any private party against both state and federal governments in both state and federal court.

The Eleventh Amendment refers only to "suits in law and equity," so it does not apply to orders or judgments of a court that are not specifically directed against the government as a consequence of a suit against the government. Therefore, for the doctrine of sovereign immunity to apply, the plaintiff (in the bankruptcy context, the estate or sometimes the debtor) must commence litigation against the government as a defendant. A proceeding does not qualify as a suit (and is therefore not barred by sovereign immunity) if it is not directed specifically against the government, even if it may implicate the government's rights. For example, the bankruptcy petition itself is not a suit against the government, even if the government is a creditor of the debtor. Although the petition will impact the government's right to recover the debt, it is not directed against the government, which is not obliged to appear in court and defend against the petition.

The Bankruptcy Act of 1898 had no provision relating to the sovereign immunity of state or federal governments. This meant that bankruptcy courts were hampered in their ability to dispose of claims that the estate had against government agencies, or to render orders binding on those agencies, because the agencies could not be subjected to suit without their consent. This was inefficient and contrary to the bankruptcy goals of collective and evenhanded treatment of creditors and the debtor's fresh start. Congress therefore attempted to remedy the problem by enacting §106 in the 1978 Code.

Section 106 applies to a "governmental unit," which is widely defined in §101(27) to include a variety of foreign and domestic governmental entities. It encompasses both the federal and state governments, including their agencies and departments, and may also include Indian tribal governments.[7] Section 106 covers three distinct situations. First, §106(a) seeks to abrogate the sovereign immunity of governmental units, making them subject to the bankruptcy process where they have claims against the debtor or the estate has claims against them. The essential purpose of §106(a) is to get rid of the sovereign immunity doctrine by abolishing it legislatively with regard to most central aspects of the bankruptcy case. Second, §106(b) codifies a principle, long recognized by judicial precedent prior to its enactment, that a governmental unit, by proving a claim against the estate, waives sovereign immunity in relation to matters arising out of that claim. This principle arises from the well-established rule that a governmental unit may waive sovereign immunity by consenting to suit, either expressly or by implication, or by initiating action in a court, thereby subjecting itself to the court's jurisdiction. Third, §106(c) provides for the setoff of claims by and against a governmental unit.

§7.9.2 The Statutory Abrogation of Sovereign Immunity under §106(a)

Section 106(a) only applies where the governmental unit has not waived sovereign immunity as discussed in sections 7.9.3 and 7.9.4. The purpose of §106(a) is to abrogate the sovereign immunity of state and federal governmental units in bankruptcy cases, so that they would be treated no differently from other parties against whom the estate has a claim.[8] It may be that Congress did not need to enact §106(a) with regard to states, because they may have consented not to assert sovereign immunity in bankruptcy cases when they ratified the Constitution.[9] However, the statutory abrogation is clearly necessary with regard to suits against the federal government. At least, with regard to the federal government, it is clear that sovereign

---

7. It is not entirely clear that Indian tribes are covered by the definition of "governmental unit." They are not expressly mentioned in the definition but could constitute "domestic governments," which are listed in the definition. Some courts have relied on this language to find that tribes are governmental units. See, for example, *Krystal Energy Co. v. Navajo Nation*, 357 F.3d 1055 (9th Cir. 2004). Other courts have questioned whether this inference can be drawn in the absence of clearer language of inclusion. See, for example, *In re Mayes*, 294 B.R. 145 (B.A.P. 10th Cir. 2003).

8. As originally enacted in 1978, the section (then numbered §106(c)) did not adequately express the intent to abrogate sovereign immunity, but Congress amended the section (and renumbered it 106(a)) in 1994 to make this clear.

9. In *Central Virginia Community College v. Katz*, 546 U.S. 356 (2006), the court confronted the question of whether Congress had exceeded its powers under Article I in seeking to abrogate the sovereign immunity of the states. The Court suggested that by ratifying the Constitution, states may have already acquiesced in forgoing their sovereign immunity in bankruptcy cases, making the statutory abrogation of state immunity unnecessary.

immunity may not be asserted in bankruptcy proceedings. With regard to states, it is not clear exactly how far the abrogation of sovereign immunity extends.[10]

§7.9.3 Waiver of Sovereign Immunity by Consent and by the Filing of a Proof of Claim under §106(b)

A general abrogation of immunity, whether by ratification of the Constitution (in the case of states), or under §106(a) (in the case of the federal government), must be distinguished from waiver of immunity by a governmental unit that is party to the proceedings. It is a well-established principle that even where sovereign immunity has not been abrogated, a governmental unit can waive its immunity by consenting to suit. Prior to *Central Virginia Community College*, there was doubt over whether Congress could validly abrogate state sovereign immunity under §106(a), so the question of whether there had been a waiver under §106(b) was crucial. However, since *Central Virginia Community College* found a basis in the Constitution for abrogation of state immunity, the need to establish a waiver is important only in those cases that do not fit within the bankruptcy court's *in rem* jurisdiction.

A waiver must be voluntary,[11] but it can be express or implied. Where the waiver is expressed unequivocally, there is no difficulty in finding that the governmental unit is subject to the suit and cannot invoke the Eleventh Amendment. However, if there is no express waiver, the court must examine the circumstances to determine if the governmental unit has acted in a way that gives rise to an implication of waiver. The most common form of implied waiver arises out of a governmental unit's voluntary invocation of the jurisdiction of the federal court. Therefore, if a governmental unit

---

10. The opinion in *Central Virginia Community College* is murky on the scope of the abrogation of state sovereign immunity, and it does not articulate the extent to which states have subordinated their sovereign immunity to the bankruptcy power. The court did indicate that this subordination is not absolute, and relates only to the bankruptcy court's *in rem* jurisdiction and to ancillary litigation necessary to effectuate that *in rem* jurisdiction. The Court found that the suit in issue — to avoid a preferential transfer — fell within the bankruptcy court's *in rem* jurisdiction and indicated that this *in rem* jurisdiction extends to other matters central to or ancillary to the court's jurisdiction over the *res* of the debtor and the estate. However, the Court did not define the contours of *in rem* jurisdiction, and cautioned that it did not cover every possible proceeding arising in the bankruptcy case.

11. In *College Savings Bank v. Florida Prepaid Postsecondary Education Expense Board*, 527 U.S. 666 (1999) (a case involving trademark legislation, not bankruptcy law), the Court made it clear that the waiver must be voluntary. Congress cannot create a constructive waiver merely by deeming that a state governmental unit waives immunity by participating in a federal program or federally regulated activity.

institutes suit in federal court, or if it files a proof of claim[12] in the estate, it implicitly waives sovereign immunity with regard to any compulsory counterclaim that the estate may have against it. To qualify as compulsory, the counterclaim must involve the same general subject matter as the claim, must arise out of the same occurrence or transaction, and must have been in existence at the time the government asserted its claim. (See In re Pegasus Gold Corp., 394 F.3d 1189 (9th Cir. 2005).) It is not clear if the filing of a claim constitutes the waiver of immunity in relation to a counterclaim that does not qualify as compulsory. Some courts have held that the waiver must be confined to compulsory counterclaims. (See, for example, In re Jackson, 184 F.3d. 1046 (9th Cir. 1999); Arecibo Community Health Care v. Commonwealth of Puerto Rico, 270 F.3d 17 (1st Cir. 2001).) In short, §106(b) ameliorates the sovereign immunity doctrine by subjecting a governmental creditor to the power of the bankruptcy court, but only where that creditor chooses to institute suit against or prove a claim in the estate. Even if it does so, the waiver likely relates only to counterclaims that qualify as compulsory. (See Example 3(c).)

§7.9.4 Setoff of Claims by and against a Governmental Unit under §106(c)

Section 106(c) provides that any claim that the estate may have against a governmental unit may be offset against a claim that the governmental unit has against the estate. Under general principles of law, where two parties are mutually indebted, the debts may be set off against each other so that no payment exchanges hands except to the extent that one of the debts is larger than the other. Setoff rights arise in bankruptcy where a creditor of the estate is also a debtor of the estate. As a general rule, provided that the creation of the mutual debts is legitimate, the Code recognizes setoff rights under state law and permits a creditor to deduct the full amount of his debt to the estate from his claim. The setoff rights of creditors are dealt with in §553, which is discussed in section 16.2.

Where a government is the creditor, the setoff right is complicated by the state's sovereign immunity. If the estate is barred from enforcing its

---

12. Proof of claim is discussed in section 19.4. In essence, it is the submission of a claim in the estate by a creditor that will allow that creditor to participate in any distribution from the estate. There are a number of reasons why a governmental unit may not prove a claim in the estate. For example, the government may not be a creditor of the estate, but may instead owe the estate money or some obligation. Even if the government is a creditor, there are a number of reasons why it may not file a claim. For example, in a Ch. 11 case it is not usually required to file a claim to be included as a creditor in the estate. In a Ch. 7 or 13 case, where it must file a claim to participate in the distribution from the estate, it may choose not to file a claim because there is no prospect of distribution or because the government does not wish to compromise its immunity.

claim against the government, this could mean that the government could assert its claim against the estate, but cannot be made to pay its debt to the estate. The simple purpose of §106(c) is to overcome this obstacle to setoff by providing that an assertion of sovereign immunity does not preclude the setoff between the government's claim and a claim that is property of the estate. Although §106(c) does not express the prerequisite that the government prove a claim against the estate, courts have held that this is a condition of the setoff. In In re Charter Oaks Associates, 361 F.3d 760 (2d Cir. 2004), the Court explained why the state must have proved a claim. Because Congress cannot constitutionally abrogate the states' sovereign immunity, §106(c) would not be constitutional unless it is based on the state's voluntary waiver by proving a claim. In light of Central Virginia Community College, this reasoning may not apply where the matter falls within or is ancillary to the in rem jurisdiction of a bankruptcy court.

Setoff under §106(c) does not contemplate affirmative recovery by the estate. If the government's claim exceeds the claim against it by the estate, setoff merely reduces the government's claim. Even if the estate's claim against the government is larger than the government's claim against the estate, the setoff is confined to elimination of the government's claim and does not permit the estate to recover the balance of the debt. For this reason, setoff is not confined to compulsory counterclaims. For example, in In re Microage Corp., 288 B.R. 842 (Bankr. D. Ariz. 2003), the court allowed the setoff of the state's claim for taxes against the estate's claim for a tax refund under a different and unrelated program. (See Example 3(c).) It is also not necessary that the estate's claim must be against the government agency that has a claim against the estate as long as both agencies are part of the same government and funded from the same treasury. For example, in Charter Oaks Associates the court allowed a setoff of the estate's claim of reimbursement from the state department of social services against a claim for taxes by the state department of revenue.

Examples

1. Julie Dixon resides in State A, where she owns and operates a retail store. Her business has done poorly over the last couple of years, and she has fallen behind on her payments to creditors. Her credit has been cut off, and she does not have the cash to buy any more inventory. A number of Julie's creditors have decided to file a petition to place her in involuntary Ch. 7 bankruptcy.

   Each of the controversies described below has arisen or will arise either in connection with the bankruptcy case itself or in relation to Julie's affairs. Consider whether or not the federal district court in State A (referred to in this Example as "the court") has jurisdiction over each of them in terms of 28 U.S.C. §1334(a), (b), or (d). (Focus on §1334 in this Example. The question of whether the bankruptcy court has jurisdiction to dispose of these controversies under §157 is covered in Example 2.)

a. Does the court have jurisdiction to hear the petition and to grant an order adjudicating Julie bankrupt?

b. About a year before her bankruptcy, Julie purchased some new display cases on credit for her store and gave the seller a security interest in the display cases to secure their price. Because she defaulted on the installments, the seller repossessed the display cases a few weeks prior to the filing of the petition. The seller scheduled a foreclosure sale, but was prevented from proceeding with it because the filing of the bankruptcy petition automatically stays all actions by creditors to enforce a lien against property of the estate or the debtor. Under §362, the creditor may apply to court for relief from this stay if grounds for relief are present. (*See* Chapters 10 and 11.) Does the court have jurisdiction to hear and determine the application for relief from stay?

c. A few weeks before the petition was filed, Julie, realizing that she was insolvent and that creditors would soon take action to collect their debts, repaid to her brother an unsecured loan of $5,000. Although the loan was not yet repayable, Julie was concerned that if she did not repay it immediately, her other creditors would pounce on her assets and leave her insufficient funds to settle her brother's loan. This preferential transfer is avoidable by Julie's trustee under §547. (*See* Chapter 16.) Does the court have jurisdiction over the trustee's avoidance suit against Julie's brother?

d. Prior to bankruptcy, Julie bought some inventory from one of her suppliers. When the inventory was delivered, Julie protested that it was defective and demanded a price reduction. The supplier refused. At the time of Julie's bankruptcy, this dispute has still not been resolved. The supplier has proved a claim for the sale price of the goods, and the trustee has objected to it. Does the court have jurisdiction to resolve this dispute?

e. A few months before bankruptcy, Julie obtained a loan from a finance company. Because the finance company was concerned about her credit, it insisted that she find a surety to guarantee her debt. Julie's sister undertook the suretyship obligation. When Julie became bankrupt, the finance company decided to sue the surety for payment of the debt. Does the court have jurisdiction to deal with the suit between the finance company and the surety?

f. About three months before Julie's bankruptcy, she hired a contractor to perform some repairs to her shop. Julie paid the contractor in full for the work. After the project was completed, a subcontractor who worked on the project sued the contractor for the price of its work. The contractor is defending the suit on the grounds that the subcontractor's performance was unsatisfactory and had to be redone. Does the court have jurisdiction over this suit?

g. Shortly before bankruptcy, Julie had sold goods to a buyer who resides in State X, located some 2,000 miles from State A. The transaction was conducted through the mail, and the buyer has never set foot in State A. Although payment for the goods was due on receipt, the buyer has not paid for the goods. Does the court have jurisdiction to deal with the trustee's suit against the buyer for payment?

h. A year or so before her bankruptcy, Julie bought a computer on credit. The seller retained a security interest in it to secure the unpaid balance of the price. The security interest is valid and unavoidable, and the debt to the seller exceeds the value of the computer. The trustee therefore abandoned it under §554 so that the seller could foreclose on it. (As discussed in section 12.4, §554 permits the trustee to abandon estate property if the debtor has no equity in it and the property is of no value to the estate.)

After recovering the computer, the seller refurbished it and fraudulently sold it as new. Upon discovering this, the buyer demanded cancellation of the sale and return of the price. Does the court have jurisdiction over the suit between the buyer and seller?

2. Decide whether the controversies described in Example 1 are core or noncore proceedings. In answering the question, consider the general guidelines identified in section 7.3.5 as well as the nonexhaustive list provided by 28 U.S.C. §157(b)(2). For convenience, the proceedings referred to in Example 1 are summarized here:

a. The bankruptcy petition.

b. The secured party's application for relief from stay.

c. The trustee's suit to avoid a preferential transfer.

d. A seller's claim for sale price of goods, challenged by the trustee on the grounds that the goods were defective.

e. A creditor's suit against a debtor's surety.

f. The suit between the subcontractor and the contractor relating to work on Julie's shop.

g. The trustee's suit against the buyer of goods from the debtor who has not paid for the goods..

h. A suit between the buyer and seller of the computer abandoned by the estate.

3. Sophie Wren filed a Ch. 7 bankruptcy petition. In her schedule of liabilities, she listed back taxes due to the federal government. Although (as you will see in sections 19.6.4 and 22.5.4) certain tax debts are given priority and are nondischargeable, these back taxes were owed for a period for some years before bankruptcy, and they were too old to qualify for priority or for exclusion from the discharge. Another debt

listed in Sophie's schedule was a debt of $10,000 owing to the state Department of Economic Development for license and permit fees, incurred in connection with a failed land development project in which Sophie had been engaged. Both these claims were general unsecured claims. There were no funds in Sophie's Ch. 7 estate to pay general unsecured claims. During the course of the Ch. 7 case, the court granted Sophie a discharge.

   a. The I.R.S., realizing that the estate would make no distribution to general unsecured creditors, did not prove a claim in Sophie's Ch. 7 case. Shortly after the case was closed, the I.R.S. wrote a letter to Sophie demanding payment of the back taxes. Sophie moved to reopen the bankruptcy case and filed suit against the I.R.S., seeking an order enjoining the I.R.S. from seeking to collect them. May the I.R.S. resist the suit on the grounds of sovereign immunity?

   b. Like the I.R.S., the state Department of Economic Development did not prove a claim in Sophie's Ch. 7 case. After the case was closed, it wrote to her, demanding payment of the license and permit fees. May Sophie obtain an injunction from the bankruptcy court, prohibiting the state Department of Economic Development from attempting to collect the debt?

4. This question also concerns Sophie Wren's Ch. 7 bankruptcy. A month before her bankruptcy, Sophie's car was involved in a collision with a van owned by the state Department of Forestry. The van was driven by an employee of the forestry department on official business, and it is clear that the accident was caused by his negligence. The cost of repairing Sophie's car is $4,000. At the time of her bankruptcy, she had claimed the cost of repair from the state, but the state had not yet responded to her claim.

   The state Department of Economic Development proved a claim in the estate for $10,000 in respect of the license and permit fees. The trustee would like to recover the tort claim of $4,000 from the state. If the state refuses to pay the tort claim, will the trustee's enforcement rights be affected by sovereign immunity?

Explanations

1. a. The petition, the consequent hearing, and the order for relief are the "case under Title 11" (i.e., the bankruptcy case) over which the court has exclusive jurisdiction under §1334(a).

   b. Even though this application for relief from stay is intimately connected with the bankruptcy case, it is not the "case under Title 11" referred to in §1334(a). However, it is a "civil proceeding arising under Title 11" over which the court has jurisdiction in terms of §1334(b).

In the clearest case, a matter arises under Title 11 when the proceeding in question arises from the provisions of the Code itself and the right asserted owes its existence to the Code. In other words, if the proceedings would not exist under nonbankruptcy law and there would be no cause of action in the absence of the Code, they arise under it. A proceeding may arguably also arise under the Code and qualify as a core proceeding if it involves an issue so linked to the Code that the provisions of the Code are determinative of it, and the issue would not have arisen or would have been decided on a different basis under nonbankruptcy law. Matters arising under Title II are core proceedings. *See* section 7.3.5.

Note that §1334(b) gives the court original but not exclusive jurisdiction over these matters arising under the Code, so it contemplates that some of them might be entertained by other courts. Nevertheless, it is hard to imagine that matters so intimately connected with the bankruptcy case could or should be dealt with in other courts. This issue is not likely to come up very often, because other courts would not normally be motivated to adjudicate such matters.

c. The trustee's right to avoid the transfer owes its existence to §547. However, the avoidance suit will likely implicate rights created by nonbankruptcy law. Therefore, even though the suit does arise under the Code, the presence of nonbankruptcy issues may place it in the category of related proceedings. This makes no difference to the applicability of §1334(b), which covers both categories. However, it does have an impact on bankruptcy court jurisdiction under §157, as discussed in section 7.3 and Explanation 2c.

d. The dispute in this question involves issues of state law: the rights of a seller and buyer under UCC Article 2. Had Julie not become bankrupt, the case would have been resolved in a state court. However, as she is bankrupt, the seller must claim against her estate, and the trustee succeeds to her defense. The outcome of the case will have an impact on the estate, because it will affect the size of the seller's claim against the estate.

Although the claim and objection procedure are provided for by the Code, the substantive rights do not arise under the Code. Rather, they are related to the bankruptcy case. Such related proceedings also fall within the court's jurisdiction under §1334(b). As in question (c), it makes no difference for the purpose of district court jurisdiction whether the litigation arises under the Code or is related to the case because both categories are covered by §1334(b). However, this difference is significant with regard to the bankruptcy court's jurisdiction over them, as discussed in section 7.3 and Explanation 2d.

Where the impact on the estate is as clear as this — the related litigation actually involves the estate and the outcome binds it and affects the distribution to creditors — there is no difficulty in seeing that the litigation is related to the bankruptcy case. However, matters are considerably more difficult where the impact of the proceeding is less direct and obvious — as discussed in questions (e) and (f).

e. Like the sales dispute in question (d), the suit between the finance company and the surety involves issues of state law that exist in the absence of bankruptcy and would normally be resolved by a state court. Therefore the suit against the surety certainly does not arise under the Code. The question is whether the suit is related to the bankruptcy case so that the court has jurisdiction over it. The fact that the estate is not a party to the suit is a strong indicator that the suit is not related to the bankruptcy case. However, this is not conclusive. Even though the estate is not a party, a suit between outsiders can have enough connection with and impact on the estate to be related to the bankruptcy case.

Where the litigation does not involve the estate directly, the widely accepted test, enunciated in *Pacor, Inc.* and approved in general terms by the Supreme Court in *Celotex Corp.* (both cases are cited in section 7.2.2), is that the outcome of the proceeding must have some conceivable effect on the bankruptcy case, altering the rights, liabilities, freedom of action, or options of the debtor, or affecting the handling or administration of the estate. Although some courts have been willing to think of conceivable impact in broad terms, the prevailing view is to require a convincing demonstration that the litigation will likely have a direct, nonspeculative, and measurable legal or economic consequence on the estate. This impact is a factual question to be determined by analyzing the effect of the litigation.

If the finance company wins the suit and is paid by the surety, the impact on the estate is a substitution of creditors. The finance company falls away as a creditor, and the surety, who has a right of recourse against the debtor, becomes a creditor in the estate. If this is all that happens, there is no real impact on the estate. Its liabilities are unaltered. However, the litigation between the surety and finance company could do more than simply determine the identity of the creditor. The case could determine the validity of the debt or could fix the amount of the claim. If so, the impact on the estate could be significant.

Therefore, if the extent and validity of the debt is in issue in the case, the litigation would surely satisfy the test of relatedness — its outcome would have a measurable and preclusive effect on the estate's liability to the surety. In *In re Brentano's*, 27 B.R. 90 (Bankr. S.D.N.Y. 1983), the court found that an action between a creditor and surety had enough of a relationship to the bankruptcy case to fall within the court's jurisdiction. This view was cited with approval in *Pacor, Inc.*

   f. Like question (e), this situation involves litigation between third
      parties. Julie has no liability to the contractor, whom she has paid
      in full, and has no contractual relationship with the subcontractor.
      The only conceivable impact on the estate of this litigation between
      the contractor and subcontractor is that if the contractor is held liable
      to pay the subcontractor and does not pay, the subcontractor may be
      entitled to file a construction lien on the property. However, it is not
      clear that the subcontractor has complied with statutory requirements
      to obtain the lien. Even if he has, it is also not clear from the facts that Julie
      is the owner of the property. Therefore, the gives facts do not provide
      enough information to determine whether this third-party dispute is
      sufficiently connected to the case to qualify as a related proceeding.
   g. The buyer is the debtor's debtor. He resides in State X, remote from
      State A in which the court sits. In addition, many essential elements of
      the transaction occurred in State X. Nevertheless, the court's jurisdic-
      tion to hear the action for the price of the goods is not dependent upon
      the defendant's presence in State A nor on any concept of minimum
      contacts. Instead, it arises out of §1334(b), and the court has juris-
      diction over this action for payment because it arises in or is related to
      the bankruptcy case.
   h. This controversy is very remote from the bankruptcy case.
      The computer has been abandoned, and the dispute between the seller
      and the new buyer has no relevance to the estate. The matter is not
      related to the bankruptcy case as required by §1334(b). The court has
      no jurisdiction over it.

2. a. The bankruptcy petition is the case under title 11. It may be heard and
      finally disposed of by the bankruptcy court under §157(b)(1).
   b. The application for relief from stay is specifically identified in
      §157(b)(2)(G) as a core proceeding. It is correctly so listed. Because
      the stay is created by the Code and the proceedings would not exist in
      the absence of the Code, Congress has the power to permit them to be
      finally adjudicated by a nontenured judge. The bankruptcy court can
      make a final order reviewable by the district court only on appeal.
   c. The trustee's suit to avoid the transfer is also specifically listed as a core
      proceeding in §157(b)(2)(F). However, this is one of the areas in
      which Congress may have overstepped its authority in identifying core
      proceedings in §157(b)(2). If a matter is not directly related to the
      adjudication of rights granted by the Code, Congress cannot, simply
      by listing it, make it a core proceeding.

      The avoidance of preferential transfers is dealt with in Chapter 16.
      As explained there, the power to avoid preferences is conferred on the
      trustee by the Code and does not exist outside of bankruptcy. On this
      basis, there is some argument for treating it as a core proceeding.

However, the avoidance power is also tied up with the rights of the transferee under nonbankruptcy law, and litigation concerning the avoidance of a preferential transfer involves adjudication of these private rights. This may take the avoidance suit out of the core.

This issue was raised by the Supreme Court in relation to a fraudulent transfer in *Granfinanciera, S.A. v. Nordberg*, 492 U.S. 33 (1989). The Court was not directly concerned with the legitimacy of the listings in §157(2). The focus of the case was whether the defendant was entitled to a jury trial in a trustee's suit to avoid a fraudulent transfer. Although §157(b)(2)(h) treats the avoidance of a fraudulent transfer as a core proceeding, and although the trustee was asserting the avoidance power provided by §548, the court characterized the avoidance suit as a matter of private right — a quintessentially common law suit clearly within the protection of Article III.

Should the same analysis apply to a suit to avoid a preferential transfer? There is an important difference between suits to avoid fraudulent transfers, which have been available to creditors outside of bankruptcy for centuries, and suits to avoid preferential transfers, which are inherently a bankruptcy remedy, and could therefore be treated as solely a creature of the Code. (Even prior to the enactment of a uniform bankruptcy law, preference suits were always connected to some sort of bankruptcy process, and, unlike fraudulent transfer suits, were never available as a general creditors' suit. They serve the bankruptcy goal of evenhanded treatment of creditors, which is not an aim of nonbankruptcy law.) This would suggest that although Congress erred in including suits to avoid fraudulent transfers in §157(b)(2), it was correct in characterizing preference avoidance suits as within the core — after all, such suits could not exist outside of bankruptcy.

Granfinanciera and *Langenkamp v. Culp*, 498 U.S. 42 (1990), make it clear that a suit to avoid a preference is a legal claim, which would give rise to a right to a jury trial. However, characterizing it as legal, rather than equitable, is not tantamount to saying that it is thereby necessarily noncore. Although many core proceedings are equitable, it is possible to have a core proceeding that is legal in nature. Therefore, the determination of whether the suit falls within the core of bankruptcy has to be decided on the "public rights" analysis expounded by the Supreme Court. It is not clear how a preference suit should be classified. As intimated earlier, the trustee's right to avoid a preference is based on a combination of Code and nonbankruptcy principles, and the adjudication of the latter are an integral part of the avoidance suit. However, this, of itself, does not conclusively mean that the matter is noncore. If the source of the right is the Code, it seems appropriate to treat the matter as a core proceeding, even though nonbankruptcy law is implicated in its resolution. Nevertheless, there is some doubt about the correct characterization of an avoidance suit. Note that under *Stern v. Marshall* the answer would be clearer if the creditor had proved a claim in the estate for any balance due on the debt and the trustee had asserted the avoidance power in response. This would make the determination of avoidability part of the claim allowance process, which is within the bankruptcy court's core jurisdiction. (Further examples of suits involving a combination of bankruptcy and nonbankruptcy rights are discussed in question (d).)

d. The seller's claim for the price of the goods is a claim against the estate. Clearly, the resolution of the dispute relating to the sale of goods must be resolved under state law, which, under some circumstances, would make this a contract of the kind held to be outside bankruptcy court jurisdiction in *Northern Pipeline*. However, the seller has proved a claim in the estate, and the trustee's assertion that the goods were defective is raised in the course of the claim allowance process. The allowance or disallowance of claims is part of the bankruptcy process and listed as a core proceeding in §157(b)(2)(B). Of course, as stated before, the mere fact that §157 lists a matter as a core proceeding does not make it so if Congress did not have the power under the Constitution to confer jurisdiction over that matter on the bankruptcy court. However, in *Stern v. Marshall* the Supreme Court indicated that Congress did not mischaracterize the claim allowance or disallowance process as a core proceeding. Therefore, provided that (as in this case) resolution of the trustee's dispute is part of the process of claim allowance or disallowance, and it involves the same transaction and factual issues as the claim, the trustee's claim becomes integral to the restructuring of the debtor/creditor relationship and fits within the bankruptcy court's core jurisdiction.

e. In Explanation 1(e), the suit against the surety was treated as falling within the district court's jurisdiction over related proceedings. This is not a core proceeding because it does not involve the enforcement of any right conferred by the Code. Even though the bankruptcy court may hear the action and make a determination, the bankruptcy court's findings of fact and conclusions of law must be submitted to the district court under §157(c)(1), and the district court will enter judgment after considering the bankruptcy court's proposed disposition.

f. At best, this would be no more than a related proceeding. However, as Explanation 1(f) indicates, the connection to the bankruptcy case may be too remote for the suit to be treated as related at all.

g. In this case the trustee is a party to the suit and is acting pursuant to the duty to collect estate property. Nevertheless, the trustee's suit for the price of the goods is not a core proceeding. The substantive and central right that is being enforced here is the debtor's right to payment under a contract for the sale of goods. This right is not conferred by the Code but by state law, even if its enforcement is undertaken for the benefit of the estate. It is thus a related noncore proceeding. In *Northern Pipeline*, the court found a contract suit to be beyond the bankruptcy court's core jurisdiction.

h. In Explanation 1(h), the suit between the seller and buyer of the computer did not qualify as a related matter for jurisdictional purposes. Obviously, if it does not fall within the district court's bankruptcy jurisdiction under §1334, the question of whether or not it is a core proceeding cannot even arise.

3. a. Congress clearly does have the power to abrogate the sovereign immunity of the federal government. One of the sections included in the list in §106(a) is §524, which provides that the discharge operates as an injunction against any further efforts to collect the debt. As an agency of the federal government, the I.R.S. is subject to the abrogation of sovereign immunity in §106(a), and cannot raise immunity to resist Sophie's suit to declare the debt discharged and to restrain collection efforts.

b. *Central Virginia Community College* found that by ratifying the constitution, states had consented to abrogate immunity with regard to matters within or ancillary to the court's *in rem* jurisdiction. Because the matter in question was within the court's *in rem* jurisdiction, the court did not have to decide if the statutory abrogation of state sovereign immunity in §106(a) is valid with regard to matters outside of the *in rem* jurisdiction. The discharge itself falls within the *in rem* jurisdiction of the bankruptcy court, and a proceeding to enforce it should be treated as ancillary and encompassed by the states' subordination of their sovereign immunity to the bankruptcy power at the time of ratifying the Constitution.

4. The claim arising out of Sophie's collision belongs to the trustee. It was a legal interest of the debtor at the time of the petition, and therefore (as you will see in section 12.2.1) it became property of the estate upon commencement of the case. It is not clear if the estate could sue the state on the claim under the general abrogation of sovereign immunity in §106(a). It seems unlikely that the claim would be within the court's *in rem* jurisdiction, and it is doubtful whether the statutory abrogation is effective for matters outside of that range. However, because the state Department of Economic Development has proved a claim in the estate for Sophie's unpaid taxes, §106(b) or (c) might apply.

Once the state has proved a claim in the estate, §106(b) deems the state to have waived sovereign immunity with respect to any claim against it by the estate that is property of the estate and that arises out of the same transaction or occurrence as the state's claim. Courts have confined §106(b) to compulsory counterclaims — those that arise out of the same transaction or occurrence and have a logical connection to the claim. Sophie's counterclaim is not compulsory. It arises out of the collision, which is not in any way related to the state's claim for license and permit fees. The decisions that confine the estate to compulsory counterclaims are based on an understanding that, despite the use of the word "deemed" in §106(b), Congress did not have the power to subject the state to any claim beyond the narrow range of compulsory counterclaims. Although the state's proof of claim does not result in a waiver under §106(b), the estate's tort claim can be asserted as a setoff under §106(c), which is not confined to compulsory counterclaims against the same state agency.[13] The setoff can only be used defensively and cannot result in affirmative recovery from the state. Because the estate's claim is $4,000 and the state's claim is $10,000, this problem does not arise because the setoff will merely reduce the state's claim to $6,000.

---

13. The claim against the estate is by the state Department of Economic Development, and the estate's claim is against the state Department of Forestry. However, this should not preclude the setoff provided that both agencies are within the same governmental entity.

CHAPTER 8

Debtor Eligibility and the Different Forms of Bankruptcy Relief

§8.1 INTRODUCTION

The distinction between liquidation under Ch. 7 and rehabilitation under Chs. 11, 12, or 13[1] was introduced in section 5.5.2 and is taken up again here and examined from the perspective of a debtor who is about to file a bankruptcy petition. This chapter is concerned with the eligibility of different debtors for the alternative forms of bankruptcy relief provided in Chs. 7, 11, 12, and 13, the factors that may influence a debtor in selecting between those alternatives, and the possibility of postpetition conversion from one form of relief to another.

§8.2 AN OVERVIEW OF THE DISTINCTION BETWEEN LIQUIDATION AND REHABILITATION

§8.2.1 Liquidation

Liquidation under Ch. 7 is bankruptcy in its oldest traditional sense. Its aim is the surrender and dissolution of the debtor's executable estate for the

---

1. As mentioned in section 8.4.2, Ch. 9 is also concerned with rehabilitation, but it is confined to municipalities and is not discussed in this book.

purpose of generating a fund to be applied to the payment of creditors. After the debtor has become bankrupt, a trustee is appointed who has responsibility for collecting the debtor's nonexempt unencumbered assets, turning them into liquid form by converting them to cash, and making a distribution to creditors who have proved claims in the estate. The fund is paid out to creditors in the Code's order of priority. Because it is common for Ch. 7 debtors to be insolvent, most creditors, particularly those who hold nonpriority unsecured claims, receive only a pro rata payment of their claims. Often, the pro rata distribution is no more than a small fraction of the claim, and in quite a high percentage of cases, the estate has so few assets that after the costs of administration are paid, there are no funds left to pay unsecured creditors any distribution at all. The unpaid balance is usually discharged when the debtor is an individual. A corporate debtor does not receive a discharge under Ch. 7. As a result, it becomes a shell with no assets, no business, and an accumulated unpaid debt. The defunct corporation is usually deregistered under state corporation law. If not, the existence of the undischarged debt creates a strong disincentive to anyone who might wish to revitalize the shell.

§8.2.2 Rehabilitation Bankruptcy

Chs. 11, 12, and 13 each have their own rules and principles, which are discussed more fully in Chapters 20 and 21. However, they share a common purpose that distinguishes them from Ch. 7. Their general goal is not to liquidate the debtor's assets[2] but to provide the debtor the opportunity of preserving all or part of the prepetition estate in return for a commitment (formulated in a plan of rehabilitation) to make specified payments or other distributions of value to creditors over a period of time. The level of payment required by the Code is too complex for discussion at this point and is left for Chapters 20 and 21. As a general yardstick, one can say that the premise of the Code is that the value received by creditors under the plan must at least be equal to the present value of what creditors would have received if the debtor had been liquidated under Ch. 7. Of course, this is regarded as the minimum. The goal is that creditors will, in fact, do better than they would have in a liquidation. The Bankruptcy Abuse Prevention and Consumer Protection Act of 2005 (BAPCPA) added provisions to the Code that emphasize this goal. Amendments to Ch. 7 make it much more difficult for an individual consumer debtor to choose liquidation over rehabilitation where

---

2. Some or all of the debtor's assets might be liquidated as part of a rehabilitation plan, and Ch. 11 recognizes the possibility of a liquidation plan that fully liquidates a corporate debtor. Nevertheless, the principal goal of rehabilitation bankruptcy is to preserve the assets of the estate.

the debtor has the means, calculated under a complex formula, to make payments under a plan of rehabilitation. (*See* section 9.8.) Amendments to Ch. 13 (and to Ch. 11 cases involving individual debtors) impose a more stringent standard on the debtor in determining how much the debtor can afford to pay in the Ch. 13 or 11 case. (*See* sections 20.7 and 21.1.)

Rehabilitation under Chs. 11, 12, or 13 is only a viable alternative to liquidation if the debtor has some reasonable prospect of honoring the commitments made in the plan. As a requirement of having the plan confirmed by the court, the debtor must be able to show that it is feasible and that there is likely to be a stream of income or other sources of funding or property to support the plan. Once the plan has been confirmed by the court, it becomes the blueprint for the debtor's rehabilitation. During the period that the debtor is in bankruptcy, that is, from the filing of the petition until the ultimate consummation of the plan, creditors are not permitted to pursue any collection activity outside the bankruptcy process, and the debtor has the opportunity to restructure business operations or to reorder financial affairs with the goal of achieving financial health. If the debtor fails to consummate the plan, the debtor might end up in liquidation. Alternatively, the case might be dismissed so that the creditors' collection rights under state law are restored.

The discharge of prepetition debts is an important element of bankruptcy. Both individuals and corporations can receive a discharge in rehabilitation bankruptcy. The discharge rules vary. *See* Chapter 22. For the present, the following general principle can be stated: Discharge is intended to be the reward of a successful plan of rehabilitation. It was noted in section 5.5.2 that the Code has a general preference for rehabilitation bankruptcy. Prior to 2005, the Code largely used incentives to encourage individual debtors to choose rehabilitation over liquidation. BAPCPA toughens the Code's preference for rehabilitation by making it more difficult for an individual consumer debtor to obtain Ch. 7 relief. This is discussed generally in section 8.5 and in Examples 1 and 2, and in more depth in section 9.8.

§8.2.3 A Practical Perspective on the Distinction between Liquidation and Rehabilitation

Although it is possible to draw a fairly clear line between liquidation and rehabilitation based on the premises and the provisions of the Code, it is important to remember that matters become much muddier as the Code is applied in actual cases. Some of this lack of precision will become apparent later, as we take a closer look at the various specific aspects of the different types of bankruptcy, but a general observation may be helpful at the start. Although some cases do proceed exactly along the lines of a pure liquidation (that is, all the estate's assets are realized and the proceeds distributed) or a full rehabilitation (that is, the plan is completely and successfully consummated, leaving the debtor rehabilitated and creditors better off than they would have been had liquidation occurred), things are often not that tidy. For example, an individual Ch. 7 debtor has various means of avoiding the liquidation of all her property, primarily because of exemptions, but also because when the property is subject to a security interest, it may be possible for the debtor to make an arrangement with the secured creditor to keep the property in exchange for a commitment to keep paying installments due on the contract. Likewise, a rehabilitation plan under Ch. 11 or 13 may provide for the partial liquidation of assets as a means of deriving the resources needed to fund the plan. Furthermore, rehabilitation is usually a long-term process, dependent on predictions of future economic conditions, the debtor's abilities, and the cooperation of creditors or other persons (such as an employer, a lender, or investor) whose help is needed in the debtor's revival. Even if the plan is not unrealistically optimistic to begin with, economic conditions may be less than desired, the debtor may just not have the ability to do what is needed, or the anticipated cooperation may not be forthcoming. This may lead to the failure of the rehabilitation attempt and ultimate liquidation. In the end, creditors may be worse off than they would have been had liquidation taken place immediately.

§8.3 DIFFERENT TYPES OF DEBTOR

Before discussing eligibility for relief, it is useful to identify the different types of natural or legal persons that may become debtors under the Code and to draw some distinctions between them.

§8.3.1 Individuals, Partnerships, and Corporations

A debtor is a "person or municipality concerning which a case under this title has been commenced."§101(13). "Person" includes an individual, partnership, and corporation, but not a governmental unit. §101(41). "Corporation" includes a variety of juristic persons, both incorporated and unincorporated. §101(9). "Individual" is not statutorily defined. It means a real, honest to goodness, living, breathing, warm-blooded mammal of the species homo sapiens. "Partnership" is also not defined in the Code and must be determined with reference to state law. (The Code recognizes a partnership as an entity distinct from the individual partners and contemplates the possibility that a partnership may be a debtor even if the partners are not.)

The Code therefore recognizes four general categories of debtor: individuals, partnerships, corporations, and municipalities. The distinction between the groups is often important because many provisions of the Code, and indeed some chapters of the Code in their entirety, exclude one or more of them. It is useful to remember this, and to be attentive to whether a particular Code section speaks generally of "the debtor" or is restricted to a more narrow category, such as "individual debtor."

This book does not deal with municipal bankruptcy nor with the specific rules applicable to partnership bankruptcy; the two principal types of debtors discussed here are individuals and corporations. The distinction between them is pervasive, because the impact of bankruptcy on a corporation is bound to differ in many respects from that on an individual. Sometimes these differences are purely factual, reflecting the different scope and nature of corporate and individual economic operations. However, they sometimes arise from Code provisions that reflect a policy of conferring rights or imposing duties on one type of debtor but not on the other. For example, exemptions are intended to save the individual debtor from penury, so they are made available to individuals but not corporations.

§8.3.2 Consumer and Business Debtors

It is easy to draw the distinction between individual and corporate debtors, because corporations are distinct legal entities in nonbankruptcy law and the Code itself recognizes this. It expressly provides for different treatment of individuals and corporations in several respects. By contrast, the Code itself does not as clearly articulate the difference between consumer and business debtors. The only definition pertinent to the distinction is §101(8), which describes a "consumer debt" as one "incurred by an individual primarily for a personal, family or household purpose." From this it is clear that one should not simply equate individual and consumer debtors: An individual is not a consumer debtor unless the bulk of his or her debt is incurred in the course of domestic consumption. Where an individual debtor owns a business as a sole proprietorship or otherwise incurs debts in the course of commercial or other activity unrelated to household or personal purposes, some of his debts are likely to be consumer debts and some, business debts.

For many purposes, it is not legally significant to differentiate between consumer or business debtors because most provisions of the Code apply equally in the bankruptcy of each. When the Code intends to provide a special rule for one or the other, it does so expressly. An important example is §707(b), which provides for the dismissal of a Ch. 7 case on grounds of abuse where the debtor is an individual whose debts are primarily consumer debts. (*See* section 9.8.)

Notwithstanding, the distinction between consumer and business debtors is functionally significant and pervasive because the property, obligations, and affairs of a consumer are likely to be quite different from those of a business. This creates factual differences between these two types of bankruptcy so that provisions of the Code relevant to the one often just do not come into issue in the other. The importance of this factual difference is accentuated by the distinct policy concerns that dominate each type. Business bankruptcies tend to implicate larger concerns of economic welfare, such as productivity, market stability, and employee protection. Consumer bankruptcies often highlight social policies such as the prevention of homelessness and the protection of the common person and her dependents, the social ills of the abuse of credit, and (because uninsured medical expenses precipitate many bankruptcies) the shortcomings in the health care system. It should be stressed, however, that this distinction is likely to be more obvious where the business is a legal entity distinct from its owners (such as a corporation), and has operations of some size. At the margins, the difference between business and consumer bankruptcies is less functionally significant. For example, the stereotypical consumer debtor is a person who earns his income from employment and spends most of it on living expenses or on buying goods and services for personal use. However, if the same debtor is self-employed or engages in business activity, his purchases, loans, and credit card debt may commingle household and business transactions.

Because of these very different factual contexts and policy concerns, it is common for consumer and business bankruptcy to be seen as quite distinct legal regimes. This dichotomy is reflected not only in specialization by practitioners, but also in the way that some books, articles, and law school courses are organized. Although it is important to keep this in mind, it is also necessary to recognize that many provisions of the Code do not differentiate between consumers and businesses, and are potentially applicable to both.

Within the field of business bankruptcy, there is a practical distinction between small and large businesses. As noted already, different practical considerations and some different legal rules apply to those businesses that are incorporated and those that are conducted by the individual owner in unincorporated form. Even among incorporated businesses, there are significant distinctions between the scope of operations and needs of small and large enterprises. In particular, many complex procedures in Ch. 11 were drafted with large corporations in mind, and they have proved to be cumbersome and unduly burdensome and complicated in the rehabilitation of smaller businesses. There has been growing recognition of this since the Code was enacted in 1978. Congress began to make changes to the Code to simplify the rules relating to small businesses when it enacted Ch. 12 in 1986. To ease the bankruptcy process for smaller family-owned farming operations (whether or not in corporate form), Ch. 12 combined

the principles in Chs. 11 and 13 to create a simplified and expedited rehabilitation process for these farming enterprises. (ch.12 was later extended to
family fishing operations as well.) Ch.12 has proved to be successful and
effective. However, it is confined to businesses that qualify as family farming
operations, and there has never been an equivalent of Ch. 12 for other
businesses. Some years ago, a bill was proposed to create a new Ch. 10
for other small businesses, but it was never enacted. The 1994 amendments
added some provisions to Ch. 11 that allowed a small business to elect
expedited procedures in a Ch. 11 case. BAPCPA has taken a bolder step in
this direction by enhancing these provisions and making them mandatory
for debtors that fall within the statutory definition of "small business
debtor." These expedited procedures are discussed in Chapter 21.

While this book does often point to the difference between consumers,
small businesses, and large corporations, it is not so organized as to treat
each category as a self-contained subject. Rather, because they do have so
many rules and principles in common, the preferred approach here is to
focus on substantive topics, and to point out, where appropriate, that certain
rules and procedures are applicable to or are likely to be more relevant to
some types of debtors than to others.

§8.3.3 Family Farmers and Fishermen

Ch. 12 of the Code is exclusively devoted to family farmers. (As noted in
section 8.4.2, BAPCPA extended it to include family fishermen.) The term
"family farmer" (defined in §101(18) describes a farming operation conducted by a family, either in their capacity as natural persons or in the form
of a family-held corporation.

Ch. 12 was enacted in 1986, following a period of great economic
hardship suffered by farmers. Ch. 12 is largely based on Ch. 13, but it
includes some elements of Ch. 11 and some special provisions designed
to make it suitable for smaller, family-owned operations. Only a debtor who
qualifies as a family farmer may choose to file for relief under Ch. 12, but a
family farmer is not confined to Ch. 12 and may seek relief under any other
applicable chapter. Ch. 12 was originally enacted with a sunset clause that
provided for its automatic repeal if not re-enacted. Congress did re-enact it
for successive short periods several times, but BAPCPA finally made it a
permanent chapter of the Code.

§8.4 DEBTOR ELIGIBILITY

Section 109 states who may be a debtor under the Code. The section has a
broad rule dealing with eligibility for bankruptcy generally and a set of more

specific rules that govern eligibility for each type of bankruptcy relief under Chs. 7 through 13. A debtor must meet both the general prerequisites and those for the specific chapter under which relief is sought. Section 109 is sometimes described as providing threshold qualifications: Qualification under §109 is necessary for the debtor to be entitled to relief. However, even if the debtor is eligible, other provisions in the Code may preclude relief. For example, a debtor may be eligible for Ch. 13 but may not be able to satisfy the further requirements for plan confirmation. Also, for example, the debtor may be eligible for some forms of relief under a voluntary petition but may not be compelled into that chapter by an involuntary petition.

§8.4.1 The General Qualifications and Limitations

a. General Qualifications under §109(a)

Section 109(a) sets out the general qualification for bankruptcy relief. It covers almost everyone who is resident, domiciled, conducts business, or owns property in the United States: individuals, partnerships, corporations, and municipalities. There are no other general qualifications. The debtor does not have to show grounds for seeking relief such as insolvency or creditor pressure. (Note, however, that creditors who file a petition for involuntary bankruptcy do have to establish grounds for relief, as discussed in section 9.6.)

b. Limitation on Successive Filings under §109(g)

Section 109(g) imposes a temporary (180 day) limitation on general eligibility to prevent abusive successive filings by individuals and family farmers.[3] Section 109(g)(1) precludes the individual debtor or family farmer from becoming a debtor if, within the preceding 180 days, he was a debtor in a case that was dismissed because of willful uncooperative or disobedient behavior. Willfulness requires more than inadvertence. The party moving to dismiss the case must show deliberate conduct.

Section 109(g)(2) precludes eligibility if, within the preceding 180 days, the debtor requested and obtained the voluntary dismissal of a prior case following a creditor's application for relief from stay. Section 109(g)(2) is intended to make it difficult for a debtor to file consecutive

---

3. Apart from §109(g) which makes a debtor ineligible for relief for the 180-day period, §§727(a)(8) and (9) (discussed in section 22.5.2) place a restriction on the debtor's ability to get a discharge in a Ch. 7 case for a number of years after obtaining a discharge in an earlier case. Although both §109(g) and §727 aim at the problem of successive bankruptcies, they are distinct and should not be confused.

petitions for the purpose of obstructing creditors' collection efforts at state law by interrupting them with the automatic stay. Courts differ on the exact scope of this subsection. Many courts take the §109(g)(2) at its face meaning, interpret the word "following" to mean "after," and apply it mechanically, so that the debtor is barred from filing for bankruptcy simply if voluntary dismissal occurred subsequent to the filing of a motion for relief from stay. For example, in In re Richardson, 217 B.R. 479 (Bankr. M.D. La. 1998), the court concluded that the clear language of §109(g) indicates that Congress intended to impose a simple standard for barring serial filings, and that the test is simply one of sequence — the section comes into effect whenever a motion for voluntary dismissal is made after a motion for relief from stay. The court declined to adopt a more flexible reading of the section because it felt that this would weaken its effectiveness in curbing abusive serial filings. Other courts have adopted a more flexible approach. Some have interpreted the word "following" to mean "as a result of" so that there must be some causal link between the request for relief from stay and the voluntary dismissal. These courts consider that such an interpretation is more in accord with the purpose of §109(g)(2), which is aimed at curbing abuse and therefore should only apply where the voluntary dismissal was in response to the request for relief from stay. See, for example, In re Payton, 481 B.R. 460 (Bankr. N.D. Ill. 2012). Others have recognized that, notwithstanding the literal language of §109(g)(2), courts have the discretion to permit the debtor to file for relief where a strict application of the section would lead to an absurd or unjust result. See, for example, in In re Beal, 347 B.R. 87 (E.D. Wis. 2006). In addition to the question of the proper meaning of §109(g) in relation to the debtor's successive filings, there is an apparent absurdity that arises out of the literal language of the section. By providing that no individual or family farmer "may be a debtor" under the Code, §109(g) suggests that they are impervious to involuntary petitions during that 180-day period as well. This cannot be the intended result, considering that the rule is aimed at debtor abuse and should not deprive creditors of their involuntary bankruptcy remedy.

c. Limitation Requiring Credit Counseling under §109(h)

i. The Purpose of §109(h)

When Congress enacted BAPCPA, it had been persuaded that many individual bankruptcies result from financial incompetence, ignorance, and mismanagement, as well as the abuse of credit. In an attempt to address this problem, and to ensure that individual debtors understand the impact of a bankruptcy filing, BAPCPA added a new subsection (h) to §109. Section 109(h) requires individual debtors to receive credit counseling as a prerequisite to eligibility for bankruptcy relief. The principal purpose of prepetition counseling is to give the debtor the opportunity, before filing the petition, to have assistance in evaluating her financial position and to become informed about the consequences of bankruptcy, the different choices of bankruptcy relief, and alternatives to filing for bankruptcy. Although §109(h) seeks to further the laudable goal of educating debtors in financial management, it was controversial when enacted and it has proved to be troublesome. It is criticized as not being particularly effective in achieving its goal, while creating a procedural and administrative barrier to prompt debtor relief. In In re Elmendorf, 345 B.R. 486 (Bankr. S.D.N.Y. 2006), the court summed up the section's shortcomings by noting that this "facially well-intentioned" provision "has evolved into an expensive, draconian gatekeeping requirement" that has not achieved its purpose, while making it more difficult for deserving debtors to obtain timely relief. In In re Enloe, 373 B.R. 123 (Bankr. D. Colo. 2007), the court noted that there is a "developing consensus . . . that the credit counseling requirement is largely a procedural hurdle without value or consequence." Not surprisingly, courts have struggled to develop a rational and coherent application of §109(h), given its dubious value, its negative impact on debtors, and its poor drafting.

ii. The Requirement of Counseling under §109(h)(1)

Subsection 109(h)(1) provides that an individual may not be a debtor under any chapter of the Code unless he has received a briefing from an approved nonprofit budget and credit counseling agency during the 180 days preceding the date of filing the petition. The briefing may be given to the debtor individually or in a group, and it may be in person, by phone, or via the Internet. The provision gives rise to administrative and practical questions, such as the determination of reliable standards for approving an agency and the development of Internet- or phone-based programs that provide meaningful education. It has also raised a number of interpretational issues. One of these is whether the debtor may receive the counseling on the same day that she files the petition. Section 109(h)(1) requires the debtor to have received the counseling "during the 180-day period preceding the date of filing of the petition." Some courts have interpreted this language literally to mean that the counseling must have been completed by not later than the day before the petition is filed, while others have held that because the filing of the petition is generally the legally significant point for many purposes in bankruptcy, counseling may occur on the same day as the petition, as long as it precedes the petition. In re Francisco, 390 B.R. 700 (B.A.P. 10th Cir. 2008), discussed this debate and sided with the courts that have taken the latter approach. Another interpretational issue is whether §109(h) applies to involuntary petitions. Taken literally, the language "an individual may not be a debtor" suggests that §109(h) applies whether the petition is voluntary or involuntary. However, the court pointed out the absurdity of such an interpretation in In re Oberle, 2006 WL 3949174 (Bankr. N.D. Cal. 2006), and refused to allow a debtor to dismiss an involuntary petition on the grounds that he had not received the mandatory credit counseling under §109(h). The court pointed out that such a literal reading of §109(h) would obliterate creditors' ability to seek involuntary relief.

The most profound interpretational difficulty relates to the impact on the court's discretion of the language in §109(g) that "an individual may not be a debtor" under the Code if he has not received the required counseling. Some courts have concluded that the section is jurisdictional in nature so that a court may not entertain a petition by a debtor who has not complied with or demonstrated statutory grounds for dispensing with credit counseling. Other courts, such as in In re Zarnel, 619 F.3d 156 (2d Cir. 2010), have held that the section is not jurisdictional, but rather sets forth elements that must be established to sustain the voluntary bankruptcy proceeding. On this interpretation, the petition brings a bankruptcy case into existence, even if the failure to comply with §109(h) may ultimately lead to dismissal of the case for cause under §707(a).[4] The practical significance of this conclusion is that some of the incidents of filing the petition, such as the automatic stay, will come into effect immediately. The question of whether §109(h) is jurisdictional and mandatory also affects the court's discretion to waive or loosen the counseling requirement where the debtor has not complied with it at all or has not fully complied with it. If §109(h) is mandatory, a court has no equitable power to waive its requirements, which are prerequisites to filing. See In re Gee, 332 B.R. 602 (Bankr. W.D. Mo. 2005); In re Giles, 361 B.R. 212 (Bankr. D. Ut. 2007).[5] However, if §109(h) is not jurisdictional and mandatory, a court does have the discretion to provide relief from its provisions where requiring strict compliance would cause manifest injustice to the debtor. For example, in In re Hess, 347 B.R. 489 (Bankr. D. Vt. 2006), debtors in two separate cases had failed to obtain counseling before filing the petition. Although neither debtor qualified under any of the exceptions in §109(h) (to follow), the court allowed them to obtain the counseling after filing. The court reasoned that although §109(h) did not itself give the court discretion to forgive noncompliance and allow postpetition counseling, that discretion can be found in §707(a), under which the court has the power to dismiss a case for cause. In deciding to exercise its discretion, the court examined all the equities of the case,

---

4. Section §707(a) gives the judge discretion to decide whether to dismiss a case for cause. It is discussed in section 9.7.

5. Giles based its conclusion not only on the clear language of §109(h) that requires absolute compliance, but also on the principle that courts should not develop new exceptions because Congress has already provided specific, narrow exceptions in subsections 109(h)(2), (3), and (4), discussed later in this section.

including the debtors' good faith and reasonable efforts to comply with §109(h) and the lack of prejudice to other parties. Although the question of whether §109(h) is jurisdictional and mandatory usually arises where the debtor is seeking to avoid dismissal of the case, it has sometimes arisen where the debtor has sought to dismiss the case voluntarily. This has happened, for example, where the debtor filed a voluntary petition without undergoing the required counseling. Thereafter, the debtor had second thoughts about being in bankruptcy and sought to dismiss the case on the grounds that he never received the required counseling. (Under §707(a) even a voluntary dismissal by the debtor requires court approval for cause.) Courts have generally not allowed a debtor to rely on his own failure to follow the requirements of §109(h) as a basis for voluntary dismissal. See, for example, In re Mendez, 367 B.R. 109 (B.A.P. 9th Cir. 2007); In re Timmerman, 379 B.R. 838 (Bankr. N.D. Iowa 2007). Both courts rejected the argument that §109(h) was jurisdictional. Timmerman noted that although lack of eligibility is cause for dismissal under §707(a), the court has the discretion under that section to refuse to dismiss a case on motion of the debtor where the debtor had not acted in good faith.

iii. Circumstances under Which Prepetition Counseling May Be Excused: §109(h)(2), (3), and (4)

To provide some flexibility to debtors who cannot comply with the credit counseling requirement before filing the petition, Congress made provision in §109(h)(2), (3), and (4) for a softening of the requirement in limited, narrow circumstances. In some situations, the court may dispense with the counseling. In others, the court may merely allow it to be deferred for a short period after the petition. These subsections are clearly intended to be limited in scope, and courts have generally interpreted them in that spirit.

Section 109(h)(2): Lack of Available Counseling Services

Section 109(h)(2) dispenses with the counseling if the U.S. Trustee for the debtor's district of residence determines that the approved nonprofit counseling agencies in the debtor's place of residence are not able to cope with the demand for services created by §109(h)(1) and cannot reasonably provide the additional services. The U.S. Trustee must reassess this situation at least annually.

Section 109(h)(3): Exigent Circumstances

Section 109(h)(3) permits the court to grant the debtor a temporary "exemption" from counseling under "exigent circumstances" so that the debtor may file the petition before receiving the counseling and obtain the counseling shortly afterward. (Therefore, although §109(h)(3) uses the words "exemption" and "waiver," it does not forgive compliance completely, but just allows for an extension of time.) This subsection is designed to deal with situations in which the debtor has an urgent need to file and cannot obtain the counseling expeditiously enough. The requirements of §109(h)(3) are strict, and the grounds for getting an extension are limited. To obtain the extension, the debtor must submit a satisfactory certification to the court describing exigent circumstances that justify the filing of the petition despite the absence of prepetition counseling, and establishing that the debtor sought but could not obtain requested counseling during the seven-day period[6] beginning on the date the debtor made the request.

"Exigent circumstances" are not defined in the Code. Courts have held that circumstances are exigent where the immediate need for action renders counseling infeasible. The question of what constitute "exigent circumstances" can be difficult. In In re Romero, 349 B.R. 616 (Bankr. N.D. Cal. 2006), the court described exigent circumstances as a threat of serious and immediate creditor action that would render it infeasible to obtain counseling before filing the petition. In Romero the creditor action in question was the impending garnishment of the debtor's wages. In In re Cleaver, 333 B.R. 430 (Bankr. S.D. Ohio 2005), the court found that the impending loss of the debtor's home through a sheriff's sale was an exigent circumstance. In In re Henderson, 364 B.R. 906 (Bankr. N.D. Tex. 2007), the court found that the debtor had demonstrated exigent circumstances because he urgently needed to file the petition to stay foreclosure on his home. Many courts have addressed the question of whether a debtor can claim exigent circumstances where the urgency has come about because he failed to take timely action to avert the crisis. Both Romero and Cleaver did not find that the debtor's delay in dealing with the foreseeable creditor action precluded relief. By contrast, in In re Dixon, 338 B.R. 383 (B.A.P. 8th Cir. 2006), the court refused to find impending foreclosure to be an exigent circumstance where the urgency was self-inflicted by the debtor through failure to act promptly on receiving the notice of foreclosure. (See also Example 4.)

In addition to showing exigent circumstances, the debtor must satisfy the court that he requested but was unable to obtain credit counseling services from an approved agency during the seven-day period beginning on the date that he made the request. It is not clear if the statute means that the debtor cannot file at all until the expiry of the seven-day period or if the debtor can file immediately, provided that he can show that the counseling services will not be available for seven days after they were requested. In In re Otero, 2010 WL 580033 (2010) (not reported in B.R.), the court held that the request must be made at least five days[7] before the bankruptcy filing. The debtor had filed his bankruptcy petition on the day that the foreclosure sale of his home was to take place. He contacted the credit counseling agency

---

6. The section originally provided for a five-day period, which was increased to seven days in 2009.
7. As indicated in footnote 6, the period has now been increased from five to seven days.

on the same day but was not able to get the counseling before the time scheduled for the sale, so he filed the petition with a request for temporary waiver under §109(h)(3). The court found that the debtor had demonstrated exigent circumstances but did not qualify for the waiver because the agency would have been able to provide the counseling within five days of the request, even if it could not have done so before the foreclosure sale. In *Romero* and *Henderson*, the courts read the section more sympathetically and held that the debtor could file before the expiry of the five-day period, provided that he could show that the agency's services would not be available within that period. (In *Henderson* the debtor had consulted with his attorney on a Saturday and the attorney determined that the petition must be filed by the following Tuesday to forestall the foreclosure sale. On the advice of his attorney, the debtor tried many times on the weekend and Monday to obtain Internet counseling, but he could not get a connection to the site until the day after the petition was filed.) *See also* Example 4.

If the court is satisfied with the debtor's certification of exigent circumstances, it may authorize the deferral of the counseling for a period of up to 30 days after the petition. The court can extend this period to a maximum of 45 days for cause. Many courts have indicated that all the requirements of §109(h)(3) — the debtor's certification of exigent circumstances, the showing of an unsatisfied request for counseling, and the court's finding that the certification is satisfactory — must be strictly complied with before the court can permit the debtor to file a petition in advance of obtaining the counseling. For example, in In re *Hubbard*, 332 B.R. 285 (Bankr. S.D. Tex. 2005), the court refused a Ch. 13 debtor's motion to extend the time for credit counseling for 45 days because the debtor's unverified motion contained no affidavit or other declaration as to its accuracy and therefore did not qualify as a certification. In addition, the debtor had not demonstrated exigent circumstances and did not show that she had requested but could not obtain counseling within five days of the request. The court also noted that if the debtor wanted an extension beyond the 30-day period to 45 days, she must separately show cause and explain why she needs the extra time. In In re *Cleaver* the court found exigent circumstances, but nevertheless refused to find that §109(h)(3) was satisfied. The court dismissed the case because the debtor's motion did not contain a written affirmation of the truth of its contents, so it did not constitute a certification, and the debtor made no attempt to obtain counseling. In In re *Mingueta*, 338 B.R. 833 (Bankr. C.D. Cal. 2006), the court, while noting that the requirements of §109(h) were among the most absurd provisions of BAPCPA, held that the mandate of §109(h)(3) is unambiguous and must be strictly enforced. It therefore refused to accept an unsubstantiated request to extend the time for filing the certification and dismissed the case.

Most courts require that the certification be an attestation, sworn to by the debtor under penalty of perjury. See In re *Cobb*, 343 B.R. 204 (Bankr. C.D.

Ark. 2006). However, some courts have been less exacting, and have allowed the debtor to make an unsworn written and signed certification that the facts asserted are true.

Section 109(h)(4): Incapacity

Section 109(h)(4) authorizes the court, after notice and a hearing, to dispense with counseling if the debtor establishes an inability to comply because of incapacity, disability, or active military duty in a combat zone. This is sometimes called the "permanent exemption" from credit counseling because it completely excuses compliance, rather than just allowing an extension of time to comply. Section 109(h)(4) makes it clear that these excuses are confined to narrow and severe circumstances. The military duty must be in a combat zone; the subsection defines incapacity narrowly to mean mental impairment of such severity that the debtor is incapable of making rational decisions about his financial responsibilities; and disability is defined to mean that the debtor is so physically impaired as to be unable, after reasonable effort, to participate in the briefing. In *In re Anderson*, 397 B.R. 363 (B.A.P. 6th Cir 2008), the debtor, incarcerated in state prison, filed a motion to be excused from counseling on grounds of disability. The court dismissed the case, holding that incarceration was not a disability as contemplated by §109(h)(4), and that the debtor could have received phone counseling.

§8.4.2 Eligibility for Relief under Each of the Separate Chapters

In addition to the general qualifications, each chapter has its own eligibility requirements, set out in §109(b) through (f). These qualifications are summarized below, and some of them are considered in Examples 1 and 2.

(1) Ch. 7 (§109(b)). Ch. 7 relief is widely available. Anyone who may be a debtor under the Code may be a debtor under Ch. 7 except for railroads, insurance companies, and various kinds of banking and investment institutions. (The financial failure of these types of businesses is dealt with by other statutes.) A debtor may be placed in Ch. 7 bankruptcy voluntarily or involuntarily.

Although §109(b) provides for wide Ch. 7 eligibility, it is subject to an important qualification that is expressed not in that section but in §707(b). Where the debtor is an individual whose debts are primarily consumer debts, §707(b), as amended by BAPCPA, requires the court to dismiss the Ch. 7 case if it finds that the granting of relief would be an abuse of Ch. 7. Abuse is presumed under §707(b) if an individual consumer debtor has disposable income deemed sufficient to make payments under a Ch. 13 plan. (This has come to be known as the "means test" and is fully discussed in section 9.8.) Section 707(b) does not, strictly speaking, impose an eligibility requirement. Grounds for dismissing a case must be distinguished from threshold eligibility requirements of the kind set out in §109. However, the effect of §707(b) is to create a significant barrier to Ch. 7 relief for individual consumer debtors whose disposable income is not low enough or whose circumstances are not desperate enough to allow them to pursue Ch. 7 relief.

(2) Ch. 9 (§109(c)). Ch. 9 relief is confined to municipalities. It is not dealt with in this book.

(3) Ch. 11 (§109(d)). In essence, §109(d) makes Ch. 11 relief available to any person who is eligible to be a debtor under Ch. 7. (Section 109(d) sets out some specified exceptions to this general rule for various kinds of brokers and financial institutions, which need not concern us.) A debtor may be placed in Ch. 11 voluntarily or involuntarily.

Because the means test in §707(b) (mentioned above in section 8.4.2(1)) applies only in a Ch. 7 case, it presents no barrier to an individual consumer debtor's filing under Ch. 11. However, a debtor may not avoid the means test by filing under (or converting the case to) Ch. 11 and then proposing a plan that is equivalent to liquidation under Ch. 7. Although Ch. 11 does contemplate the possibility of a liquidating plan for other debtors, an individual consumer debtor is required to propose a rehabilitation plan in Ch. 11, under which the debtor commits future earnings or income to the payment of creditors. BAPCPA added subsection (8) to the mandatory plan requirements in §1123(a), which makes it clear that the plan proposed by an individual consumer debtor must provide for payments to creditors from the debtor's future earnings or income.

(4) Ch. 12 (§109(f)). Only a family farmer or family fisherman with regular annual income may file a Ch. 12 petition. A debtor may not be placed in Ch. 12 involuntarily. The meaning of "family farmer with regular annual income" is defined in §101(18) and (19). The definition of "family farmer" in §101(18) is complex. In essence it covers an individual or individual and spouse who conduct a farming operation, or a family farming operation organized as a privately held corporation or partnership. In addition to qualifications concerning source of income for an individual (and shareholding and assets for a corporation), the debtor must meet debt limits both with regard to the total indebtedness and its source. BAPCPA raised the debt limits substantially and added §101(18) to the list of sections in §104 that have their dollar amounts adjusted for inflation every three years. Under the most recent adjustment, which became effective on April 1, 2013, and will continue in effect until adjusted again on April 1, 2016, the amount is $4,031,575. (The process of dollar adjustment in the Code is explained in section 5.4.3.)

BAPCPA also changed the rule relating to the source of debts. Now only half the debt (as opposed to the 80 percent formerly required) must arise from farming operations. The general purpose of the qualifications is to confine Ch. 12 to relatively small individual or family-owned farming operations having debts and income substantially related to the farming activity. Section 101(19) defines "family farmer with regular annual income" to mean that the farmer's annual income is sufficiently stable and regular to enable payments to be made under a Ch. 12 plan. Income is measured on an annual basis because farming is cyclical and may not generate regular income for shorter periods. *See also* §101(20) (the definition of "farmer") and §101(21) ("farming operation").

Family fishermen were added to Ch. 12 by BAPCPA. "Family fisherman" is defined in §101(19) in terms similar to, but not the same as, those used in the definition of "family farmer." In essence, the definition includes not only an individual (or individual and spouse), but also a corporation or partnership in which the family has a stated minimum ownership interest. The debtor must be engaged in a "commercial fishing operation" as defined in §101(7A) and must derive a stated percentage of its debt and income from these operations. Section 101(19) has an aggregate debt limit of $1,868,200 (to be next adjusted with effect from April 1, 2016, under §104), which is lower than the limit applicable to family farmers.

(5) Ch. 13 (§109(e)).   Only an individual with regular income whose debt falls within the limits of §109(e) may be a debtor under Ch. 13. A debtor may not be placed in Ch. 13 involuntarily. Section 109(e) sets out three distinct requirements for eligibility. First, the debtor must be an individual; second, he must have regular income; and third, his total debt at the time of filing must not exceed the prescribed limit.

An "individual with regular income" is defined in §101(30) to mean an "individual whose income is sufficiently stable and regular to enable such individual to make payments under a plan under chapter 13. . . ." Section 109(e) does not state the date on which the regular income requirement must be measured. The date of filing is pertinent, but the court may consider this issue prospectively, so that even if the debtor does not have regular income at the time of filing, he will be eligible if he has a good prospect of regular income when the time for payments under the plan arrives. If the debtor has a job and earns a periodic wage or salary, there is little difficulty in establishing that he has a stable and regular income. This is true even if he is an at-will employee who could be fired at any time. However, where the debtor's earnings come from a less conventional or predictable source, there could be a dispute over his eligibility for Ch. 13. For example, in In re Baird,

228 B.R. 324 (Bankr. M.D. Fla. 1999), the debtor lost his job and suffered a stroke after filing the Ch. 13 petition but before the plan was confirmed. The court found that regular voluntary payments under the plan[8] by the debtor's son qualified as regular income. The court noted that it did not matter that the payments were voluntary and that the debtor's son could cease making them at any time, because the same might be said of a debtor's salary under an at-will employment contract.

Section 109(e) imposes debt limits that confine Ch. 13 to debtors with relatively small estates, as measured by the extent of indebtedness. Under the dollar amounts currently in effect, a debtor is not eligible for Ch. 13 relief unless her noncontingent, liquidated[9] unsecured debts are less than $383,175, and her noncontingent, liquidated secured debts are less than $1,149,525. (As with other dollar amounts, these debt limits will be next adjusted under §104 with effect from April 1, 2016.) If the debtor's secured or unsecured debts exceed the limit, she may not obtain Ch. 13 relief; she must file for rehabilitation under Ch. 11. (Liquidation under Ch. 7 may also be an alternative for some debtors but will not be available to a consumer debtor whose income exceeds the means test discussed in section 9.8.)

A debtor and spouse may file a joint Ch. 13 petition, but their combined debts must be within the limits set for an individual. An individual who is otherwise qualified for Ch. 13 but is a stockbroker or commodity broker cannot file under Ch. 13.

§8.5 CONVERSION FROM ONE CHAPTER TO ANOTHER

The selection of relief under a particular chapter is not irreversible. The debtor and other parties in interest are able, subject to certain restrictions, to apply to court to convert a case under one chapter into a case under another. For example, a debtor may have filed a petition for relief under Ch. 13. During the course of the case, it may become apparent to the debtor that the choice was not the best one, or circumstances may have changed to alter the prospects of successful debt adjustment. The debtor is able to

---

8. The challenge to the debtor's eligibility was made some time after the petition had been filed but before plan confirmation. Under §1326 a debtor is required to begin making payments under the proposed plan 30 days after filing the petition. Therefore, payments under the proposed plan must begin before confirmation.
9. A debt is contingent if the debt has been created (for example, by contract or tort) but the debtor's obligation to pay it will only arise upon the occurrence of an uncertain future event. A debt is therefore noncontingent if the debtor's payment obligation is not subject to any such future contingency. A liquidated debt is one that is capable of being calculated by arithmetical means from established information. The meaning of contingent and liquidated debts is discussed more fully in section 19.2.2.

convert the case into a case under another chapter, such as a liquidation under Ch. 7. Similarly, the creditors may be able to show that the debtor's Ch. 13 case is abusive or has little chance of successful consummation. Instead of applying for dismissal of the case, they may decide to seek conversion of the case into a Ch. 7 liquidation. A debtor also has the right to convert a case initiated by an involuntary petition. For example, if creditors have filed a petition for involuntary relief under Ch. 7, the debtor may convert the case to Ch. 13, thereby avoiding liquidation in favor of debt adjustment. Each chapter of the Code has its own rules and limitations relating to conversion. Sections 706, 1112, 1208, and 1307 govern conversion from Chs. 7, 11, 12, and 13, respectively. The rules relating to conversion are rather intricate; the general principles are as follows.

A case cannot be converted to a particular chapter unless the debtor is eligible for relief under that chapter. Therefore, the eligibility requirements (discussed in section 8.4.2) apply to conversions as they do to the original petition.

As noted in section 8.4.2(1), the grounds for dismissal of a Ch. 7 case for abuse in §707(b) must be distinguished from threshold eligibility for Ch. 7. Nevertheless, some courts have interpreted §707(b) as creating a barrier to an individual debtor converting a Ch. 13 case to Ch. 7. Section 707(b) requires the dismissal of a Ch. 7 case filed by an individual debtor whose debts are primarily consumer debts if the granting of relief would be an abuse of Ch. 7. Abuse is presumed if the debtor's income exceeds the means test set out in the section.[10] By its terms, §707(b) applies to a case "filed" by a debtor under Ch. 7. It is not clear if the subsection is applicable where a debtor first files under Ch. 13 and then converts the case to Ch. 7. Courts have differed in answering this question. Some courts adopt a plain meaning approach and hold that the use of the word "filed" and the omission of any reference to conversion in §707(b) makes the means test inapplicable where the original case is filed under Ch. 13 and later converted to Ch.7. See, for example, In re Fox, 370 B.R. 639 (Bankr. N.J. 2007); In re Layton, 480 B.R. 392 (Bankr. M.D. Fla. 2012). Other courts have rejected the plain meaning approach on the grounds that the purpose of §707(b) is to preclude Ch. 7 relief to a debtor who does not qualify for it under the means test. To allow a debtor to evade the means test by first filing under Ch. 13 and then converting to Ch. 7 undermines the intent of the section. See, for example, In re Kellett, 379 B.R. 332 (Bankr. D. Or. 2007). The court in Layton responded to this concern by observing that if a debtor deliberately uses this strategy to evade §707(b), the court has the means, either under §707(a) (dismissal for cause) or §105 (the court's general power to issue appropriate orders), to dismiss the case.

---

10. *See* section 9.8 for a full discussion of §707(b).

Conversion may occur in both voluntary and involuntary cases and at the behest of the debtor, a creditor, the trustee, or another party in interest. The debtor is treated more liberally than other parties in converting from one chapter to another. In some situations, the debtor's ability to convert is specifically restricted by qualifications expressed in the Code. *See, e.g.,* §706(a) and §1112(a). However, for the most part, the debtor has a broad and largely unrestricted right to convert to any chapter under which he is eligible. For example, §706(a) provides that the debtor "may" convert the case from Ch. 7 to a case under Ch. 11, 12, or 13 "at any time." Similarly, §§1208(a) and 1307(a) say that the debtor "may" convert to Ch. 7 "at any time."

Although the right to convert under these sections is broad, it is not absolute. In *In re Marrama*, 549 U.S. 365 (U.S. 2007), the majority of the U.S. Supreme Court held that although §706(a) is written in broad permissive terms, the bankruptcy court has the discretion to forbid the conversion if it is motivated by bad faith or is an abuse or manipulation of the Code. In *Marrama* the debtor filed misleading schedules and made a transfer of valuable property for the purpose of insulating it from creditors' claims. When the trustee sought to recover and liquidate the property, the debtor moved to convert the case to Ch.13. The majority of the Supreme Court affirmed all the lower courts in holding that the debtor had forfeited the right to convert. The court found the basis for the bankruptcy court's discretion to refuse conversion in §706(d), which allows conversion only if a debtor "may be a debtor under such chapter," read with §1307(c), which allows a case to be dismissed for cause. The court reasoned that because there was cause to dismiss the Ch. 13 case for bad faith, it cannot be said that the debtor may be a debtor under that chapter. The court also found that the bankruptcy court had discretion to refuse conversion under the general power conferred in §105(a) to issue orders to accomplish the aims of the Code. *Marrama* was concerned with a motion to convert a Ch. 7 case to Ch. 13. It is not clear what impact the decision has on conversions to other Chapters. In *In re Euro-American Lodging*, 365 B.R. 421 (Bankr. S.D. N.Y. 2007), the court held that the decision did apply to a conversion to Ch. 11. However, in *In re DeFrantz*, 454 B.R. 108 (B.A.P. 9th Cir. 2011), the court held that differences in procedural rules justified not applying *Marrama* to a conversion from Ch. 13 to Ch. 7, which the debtor could accomplish as a matter of right.

If the conversion is sought by a party other than the debtor, the court can only order the conversion after notice and a hearing and upon a showing of cause. The restrictions applicable to an involuntary petition, discussed in Chapter 9, apply to conversion as well: If a creditor could not have filed an involuntary petition to place the debtor in bankruptcy under a particular chapter, the case cannot be converted to that chapter without the debtor's consent. (For example, a creditor cannot file an involuntary petition under Ch. 12 or 13, and cannot move for conversion to those chapters either.)

As explained in sections 9.4 and 9.6, the dates of the filing of the petition and the order for relief are significant for many purposes. When a case is converted, the date of conversion is treated like the filing of a new case for some purposes but not for others. Section 348 sets out the rules concerning the impact of conversion and indicates which incidents of bankruptcy are treated as arising on the conversion date and which of them continue to be measured from the original petition or order for relief.

With some limitations, a case can be converted from one chapter to another at any time during the course of the bankruptcy proceeding. Conversion is not confined to the initial stages of the case.

---

§8.6 CHOICE OF RELIEF

§8.6.1 The Debtor's Choice of Relief

When a debtor is eligible for relief under more than one chapter of the Code, the debtor must decide which form of relief is most appropriate. In most cases, the choice is between liquidation or some form of rehabilitation. However, some debtors may qualify for more than one of the rehabilitation chapters and must decide not only between liquidation or rehabilitation but also between the advantages and drawbacks of the different applicable types of rehabilitation. A full understanding of the factors that influence choice of relief can only come after a thorough study of bankruptcy law, so a detailed discussion of this issue is premature at this stage. However, section 8.6.2 provides some guidance on these factors by summarizing the significant differences between the different forms of bankruptcy relief. Some of the issues that influence the choice of relief are introduced in Examples 1, 2, and 3.

a. Corporate Debtors

For a corporate debtor in financial difficulty, the choice between liquidation (whether under Ch. 7 or Ch. 11) and rehabilitation is stark. Liquidation means the end of the debtor. Its business closes down, its assets are sold off, its employees lose their jobs, and the ownership interests of its stockholders are wiped out. It is only by seeking reorganization that the corporation has any prospect of overcoming its financial problems and surviving as a viable business. As explained in section 8.4.2, a corporation can reorganize only under Ch. 11 unless it qualifies for Ch. 12 as a family farmer or fisherman.

b. Individual Debtors

The individual debtor's choice between liquidation under Ch.7 or rehabilitation under Ch. 13 or Ch. 11 (or in the case of a family farmer or fisherman under Ch. 12) is not as dramatic. In either event, the individual will be able to handle her financial difficulties, and may hope to emerge from bankruptcy with a discharge and a fresh start. Therefore, the debtor's choice of relief will be heavily influenced by the determination of which form of bankruptcy best serves her interests. However, the debtor is not given untrammeled discretion in making this decision. Congress has believed ever since the Code was enacted in 1978 that a payment plan under Ch. 13 would usually pay a higher percentage of creditor claims than liquidation under Ch. 7. This is because the liquidation value of the debtor's nonexempt assets is commonly not nearly as much as the amount of disposable income that a debtor could commit to payments under a Ch. 13 plan. Notwithstanding this Congressional preference for rehabilitation, the Code, as enacted in 1978, gave debtors wide discretion to choose between Chs. 7 and 13 but included incentives that were intended to encourage debtors to choose Ch. 13. (Ch. 13 is usually the most appropriate alternative to Ch. 7 for an individual debtor, but bear in mind that Ch. 11 may also be an alternative. BAPCPA made several changes to Ch. 11 to bring it more closely into alignment with Ch.13 where the debtor is an individual.)

The original decision to give the individual debtor free choice between liquidation and rehabilitation has always been controversial. This controversy flared up during the deliberations of the 1994 National Bankruptcy Review Commission. Advocates for limiting debtor choice argued that the incentives in favor of Ch. 13 had little effect on most individual debtors and were usually far outweighed by the advantages of liquidation under Ch. 7. They believed that a significant number of Ch. 7 debtors had good incomes and could afford to pay more of their debt under a Ch. 13 plan. Their choice of Ch. 7 was an easy way out that allowed them to give up relatively low-value nonexempt assets to discharge their debts, thereby shielding their future income. The opposing view was that the perceived abuse of Ch. 7 was greatly exaggerated and that many Ch. 7 consumer debtors were in genuine financial distress and in need of Ch. 7 relief. The Commission was divided on this issue, but Congress accepted the position that individual consumer debtors were abusing the free choice of Ch. 7 and that controls on choice were needed. This lead (after several years of unsuccessful attempts to pass it) to the enactment of the means test in BAPCPA in 2005. The details of the means test and its impact on an individual consumer debtor's choice of relief are discussed in section 9.8.

§8.6.2 A Summary of the Significant Differences between Chs. 7, 11, 12, and 13 That May Influence the Choice of Relief

As noted in sections 8.2 and 8.5, the principal choice to be made in selecting bankruptcy relief is that between liquidation and rehabilitation. However, even if rehabilitation is selected, there are differences between the rehabilitation chapters that will make one of them more appropriate than the others. This is a brief overview of the significant differences between the forms of bankruptcy relief under Chs. 7, 11, 12, and 13 that may have a bearing decision of which form of bankruptcy should be selected. Of course, as explained in section 8.4.2, the debtor's choice between chapters is confined to those chapters for which the debtor is eligible. This summary of the important differences in the various forms of bankruptcy is intended to give you a broad perspective. It is necessarily simplified and lacks the detail and qualifications that will become apparent in the treatment of these topics in the following chapters of the book. (Examples 1, 2, and 3 illustrate how some of these differences between the Code chapters may be relevant to a debtor's choice of relief.)

(1) Involuntary petition. An involuntary petition can be filed only in a Ch. 7 or 11 case.

(2) The automatic stay. The stay applies under all chapters, but it protects certain co-debtors only in Chs. 12 (§1201) and Ch. 13 (§1301). However, in Chs. 7 and 11, the court has the discretion within its general equitable powers under §105 to enjoin action against a co-debtor where appropriate.

(3) Property of the estate. In a Ch. 7 case and a Ch. 11 case involving a corporation, property of the estate consists of the debtor's property at the time of the petition. Postpetition property is generally not part of the estate. In a Ch. 12 or 13 case, or a Ch. 11 case involving an individual debtor, the estate consists of both property of the debtor at the time of the petition and postpetition property (§§541, 1115, 1207, and 1306).

(4) The disposition of estate property. In a Ch. 7 case, estate property is liquidated and the proceeds distributed to creditors. It may be possible for the debtor to reacquire estate property by redemption under §722 or reaffirmation under §524. In cases under Chs. 11, 12 and 13, estate property is

revested in the debtor upon confirmation of the plan (§1141, 1227, and 1327).

(5) The debtor's postpetition income. A Ch. 7 case does not affect the debtor's postpetition income, which is part of his fresh start estate. In cases under Chs. 12, and 13, the debtor's disposable postpetition income must be applied to payments under the plan (§§1225(b), 1222(a), 1322(a) and 1325(b)). There is no set rule on postpetition income in a corporate Ch. 11 case. Its allocation to the plan depends on the terms of the plan. However, an individual Ch. 11 debtor must commit disposable postpetition income to the plan (§§1123 and 1129).

(6) Sources of funding payments to creditors. In a Ch. 7 case, the funding of payments comes primarily from the proceeds of nonexempt estate property (§§704 and 726). In a Ch. 11 case, the debtor has flexibility in devising sources of funding, such as the sale of assets, future income, investments, or loans. Payment may be in money, property, or securities (§1123). In a Ch. 12 or 13 case, plan payments are funded by disposable future income, but property of the estate may be sold to generate funds, or may be surrendered to satisfy creditor claims (§§1222 and 1322).

(7) The administrator of the estate and operator of the debtor's business. In a Ch. 7 case, the trustee administers the estate and, if the debtor has a business, conducts short-term business operations. The business is liquidated as soon as possible (§§701 to 703 and 721). In a Ch. 11 case, the debtor in possession assumes the functions of the trustee and operates the business, unless there is cause to appoint a trustee (§§1104 and 1108). In a Ch. 12 case a trustee is appointed, but the debtor continues to operate the farm as a debtor in possession, under the trustee's supervision (§§1202 and 1203). In a Ch. 13 case, a trustee is appointed and performs investigative and supervisory functions. If the debtor has a business, he continues to operate it under the trustee's supervision but does not have the status of a debtor in possession (§§1302 and 1304).

(8) Conversion of the case to another chapter. In cases under Chs. 7, 12 and 13, the debtor has a broad but not absolute right to convert the case to another chapter for which the debtor is eligible (§§707, 1208, and 1307). A creditor can convert a Ch. 7 case to Ch. 11 for cause (§706). A creditor can convert a Ch. 12 or 13 case to Ch. 7 for cause (§§1208 and 1307). In a Ch. 11 case, the debtor has a right to convert with some limitations (§1112). A creditor can convert the case to Ch. 7 for cause (§1112).

(9) Dismissal of the case. A Ch. 7 case may be dismissed by the debtor or other party in interest only for cause. In the case of an individual consumer

debtor, cause for dismissal by a creditor or other party in interest abuse of the Code (§707). A Ch. 11 case may be dismissed by the debtor or another party in interest for cause (§1112). In a Ch. 12 or 13 case, the debtor has a broad but not absolute right to dismiss. Other parties in interest can dismiss for cause (§§1208 and 1307).

(10) The duration of the case. In a Ch. 7 case, property is realized and the proceeds distributed as expeditiously as possible (§704). There is no statutory limit to the duration of a Ch. 11 plan, but an individual Ch. 11 debtor must commit disposable income to the plan for five years (§1129(a)(15)). In a Ch. 12 case, payments under the plan must be made over a period of not more than three years or, with court approval, five years (§1222). In a Ch. 13 case, the maximum payment period for a debtor who earns below the median family income is three years or, with court approval, five years. The maximum (and possibly also the minimum) payment period for an above-median debtor is five years (§1322).

(11) Standards fixing the minimum level of payment to creditors. There is no minimum level of payment prescribed in a Ch. 7 case because creditors cannot get more than the proceeds of the liquidation of the estate. These proceeds are distributed in the order of priority prescribed by the Code. Secured claims are paid to the full value of their collateral. Unsecured claims are ranked in priority order. Where the estate is badly insolvent, claims with lower priority (in particular, general unsecured claims) may get no payment at all (§§506, 507 and 726). The standards for minimum payment in a Ch. 11 case are complex. Their applicability is dependent on whether the debtor has been able to negotiate creditor assent to the plan, or must force it on unwilling classes of creditor in a cramdown. The complexity of these rules defies encapsulation here. They are governed by §1129 and are explained in Chapter 21. In cases under Ch. 12 or 13, secured claims are entitled to payment in full to the value of the collateral. The debtor may surrender the property to the creditor. However, if the debtor chooses to keep the collateral, the creditor retains its lien, and the payments made on the secured claim under the plan must equal the present value of the claim — that is, its face value plus interest. Priority claims must be paid in full, and payments to general unsecured claims must at least equal the present value of what they would have received in a liquidation. In addition, the debtor is required to commit all disposable income to the plan for a prescribed period (§§1222, 1225, 1322, and 1325).

(12) Claim classification. Apart from the statutory classifications of claims into secured, priority, and general claims, alluded to in item (11), there is no claim classification in a Ch. 7 case. However, in Chs. 11, 12, and 13, the debtor does have some ability to designate classes of creditor in the

plan and to treat those classes differently, provided that there is a rational basis for the classification and the discrimination is fair (§§1122, 1123, 1129, 1222, and 1322).

(13) The cure of default and restructuring or modification of secured obligations. In a Ch. 7 case, the debtor cannot usually keep encumbered property by restructuring the obligation, unless the debtor enters into a reaffirmation agreement with the creditor under §524. One of the benefits of rehabilitation under Chs, 11, 12, or 13 is that the debtor is able (with some limitations) to cure default and restructure secured obligations (§§1123, 1222, and 1322).

(14) Creditor participation in formulating and voting on a plan. There is no plan in a Ch. 7 case, so this is inapplicable. Creditor consent does not feature in a Ch. 7 distribution. In a Ch. 11 case, creditors are involved in plan formulation and under some circumstances may even propose a plan in competition with the debtor's plan. Creditors vote on the plan, and the debtor needs a prescribed level of creditor approval to get the plan confirmed (§§1103, 1121, 1125, 1126, and 1129). In Ch. 12 or13 cases, only the debtor may propose a plan, and creditors do not vote on it. The plan is confirmed if it complies with the Code requirements (§§1221, 1225, 1227, 1321, 1325, and 1327).

(15) Discharge. A corporation cannot receive a discharge under Ch.7 (§727) but can receive a discharge under Ch. 11 (§1141). A corporation that qualifies as a family farmer or fisherman can receive a discharge under Ch. 12 (§1228). An individual may receive a discharge under all chapters of the code. There are differences in the debts encompassed by the discharge under the different Code chapters, and there is also some variation among chapters on the time that the discharge is granted and the basis for denying the discharge or excluding debts from it (§§523, 727, 1141, 1228, and 1328).

Examples

1. Yokel Yummy Family Farm Foods, Inc. processes dairy products and vegetables into frozen microwaveable meals that it sells at wholesale to supermarkets. Yokel Yummy had done well until it suffered a series of calamities last year. Expensive equipment broke down and had to be replaced; its workers went on strike, shutting down its operations for three months; and bacteria in its packaged food made consumers seriously ill, resulting in lawsuits claiming millions of dollars in damages.

   These crises have drained Yokel Yummy resources and have left it exposed to extensive potential liability to its poisoned customers.

In addition, adverse publicity has badly damaged sales of its products. Yokel Yummy has not been able to keep current on repayment of its debts, and many of its loans are in default.

Yokel Yummy has decided to seek bankruptcy relief. Under which chapters is it eligible for relief? What factors should it take into account in choosing between the chapters for which it is eligible?

2. What impact would it have on your answers to Example 1 if the debtor was not Yokel Yummy Family Farm Foods, Inc., but rather Mr. Yokel Yummy, doing business as a sole proprietor under the trade name "Yokel Yummy's Family Farm Foods"?

3. Viva Voce is a soprano who has gained international renown for her large voice and awesome temper. She used to be a great prima donna, but now, in her twilight years, she earns her living by making guest appearances, usually for one or two performances, at various provincial opera productions. In a typical season, she may sing in as many as 20 cities. The season usually lasts from September to May. During the rest of the year, she does some teaching and a few concerts. This year, her earnings were $90,000. Last year, her income was $110,000, and the year before $75,000.

Viva does not have many assets. She owns a house, valued at $250,000, subject to a mortgage of $120,000; a car worth $15,000, subject to a security interest of $10,000; and an assortment of household goods and other personal property worth approximately $80,000. In addition to the two above-mentioned secured debts, Viva owes unsecured debts in a total amount of $45,000.

A few months ago, Viva was rehearsing for a performance in a small city, quite remote from the cultural mainstream. The conductor of the orchestra was a nervous, plodding man of limited musical insight. When he spoiled Viva's famous mad scene by employing the wrong tempo, Viva lost her temper: She grabbed his baton and chased him around the concert hall, beating him on the head with it while heaping the vilest and most slanderous abuse upon him.

The conductor sued Viva for $1 million in damages. The trial of the tort action has just begun, and Viva can feel the hostility of the jury as the story of her excessive rage unfolds. Sure that the conductor will win the case, she decides to seek refuge under the Bankruptcy Code. For which chapters is Viva eligible? What factors should she take into account in choosing between those chapters?

4. Bud Getary has been in financial difficulty for some time. On February 1, he consulted with a commercial (for profit) credit counseling agency and received advice on how to manage his debt and negotiate with creditors for payment extensions. He followed the advice and managed to make agreements with his creditors for the time extensions. However, he could

not cope with the payment schedule and soon fell behind. Several creditors initiated collection proceedings. On August 5 the finance company that held a security interest in his car repossessed it. On August 6, he received notice that his bank account had been garnished by another creditor. On August 7, he consulted an attorney who recommended immediate bankruptcy filing to stay the foreclosure on the car and the garnishment. The Ch. 13 petition was filed on August 7. On August 8, Bud's attorney realized that Bud's consultation with the credit counseling agency had occurred more than 180 days prior to the petition. He therefore advised Bud to make a telephone call immediately to a specified agency, approved by the U.S. Trustee, and to receive counseling by phone. Bud did this on August 9. Bud satisfies the eligibility requirements for Ch. 13 as set out in §109(e).

Is there any other barrier to his eligibility for relief? If so, is there anything that he can do to overcome that barrier?

Explanations

1. Yokel Yummy is clearly eligible for relief under Chs. 7 and 11 because none of the exclusions in §109(b) or (d) are applicable. As noted before, these two chapters of the Code are the most universally available. Yokel Yummy, a corporation, may not be a debtor under Ch. 13, which is confined to individuals. §109(e). (Although §109(f) makes Ch. 12 available to corporations that qualify as family farmers with regular annual income, there are no facts to suggest that Yokel Yummy, despite its name, qualifies as a family farmer under the definitions in §101(18), (19), and (21).) In deciding whether to liquidate its business or attempt to rehabilitate it, a corporate debtor must determine, in essence, whether its financial difficulties are such that it is feasible to restructure the business operation and deal with its liabilities. If there is no prospect of reorganization, liquidation is the appropriate choice, which can be accomplished either under Ch.7 or Ch.11.[11] It will result in cessation of the corporation's business, the realization of its assets, and the distribution of the proceeds to creditors. The corporation will not be rehabilitated and it will become defunct, and the shareholders will lose their equity in the corporation.

On the other hand, if there is a prospect that the corporation's business can become viable again after reorganization, Ch. 11 is an attractive alternative. It gives the debtor a great deal of flexibility in reordering its

---

11. As mentioned in footnote 2, it is possible to liquidate a corporation under Ch. 11. The ultimate impact of liquidation will be the same as in Ch. 7, but the debtor retains greater control of the liquidation process.

affairs. The filing of the Ch. 11 petition gives the debtor the ability to negotiate with creditors under the protection of the Code in an attempt to formulate a plan of reorganization that will allow it to continue in business while compromising its debts and restructuring its operations. Among other things, it may sell off unprofitable or unwanted assets or operations; reject or restructure its contractual relationships; resolve unliquidated, contingent, and disputed claims; and alter the terms of its secured obligations. The debtor usually remains in control of its business as a debtor in possession and is entrusted with administration of the estate. If the debtor is able to have a plan confirmed and can consummate it, it will ultimately emerge from bankruptcy in a more efficient and viable form. Although existing shareholders are not assured of retaining any equity in the reorganized corporation, they do at least have a shot at doing so.

The facts of this question are not detailed enough for a full analysis of Yokel Yummy's prospects of effective reorganization. However, there are some hints that Ch. 11 may be feasible. The corporation's financial problems have been caused by a series of setbacks, rather than by marketing or management difficulties (although the calamities may, of course, be attributable to lapses in management). Some ugly product liability claims have to be disposed of, but if the corporation is able to deal with this issue and restore consumer trust, its business could revive and become profitable again.

2. On this variation of the facts, the business is not a corporation, legally distinct from its owners (shareholders), but simply the individual debtor himself, Yokel Yummy, doing business in his individual capacity under a trade name. Therefore, if the debtor elects to rehabilitate instead of liquidate, he may not be confined to a choice between Chs. 7 and 11, but may be able to choose Ch. 13 instead of Ch. 11. Although Ch. 13 is commonly associated with consumer bankruptcies, it is not confined to consumer cases and is available to any individual debtor who satisfies its other eligibility requirements. In fact, many small businesses are conducted as sole proprietorships, and it is quite common to find Ch. 13 debtors who aim not only to deal with household and personal debt, but also handle business debt and attempt to save a business.

The question does not give us enough information to determine if Yokel's income from the business is likely to be stable and regular. We are also not told how much debt he has. Apparently his potential tort liability is huge and would surely put him over the limitation on unsecured debt. However, until the tort claimants have obtained judgment against him, the tort debts are not liquidated and would not be counted for eligibility purposes under §109(e). If Yokel does not qualify for Ch. 13 relief, either because he cannot show stable and regular income or because his debt is too high, he would be confined to Ch. 11 for rehabilitation relief. If he is eligible for Ch. 13 relief, he would have to decide whether Ch. 13 or 11 is more suitable to his circumstances. Section 8.6 gives you some broad idea of the differences between Chs. 11 and 13 that may influence a debtor in choosing between those chapters. As a general matter, Ch. 13 is much simpler and more streamlined, so it is often the best choice for a small business debtor who is eligible for it. However, Ch. 11 gives the debtor more control over the estate and allows greater flexibility.

As regards the choice between rehabilitation (under either Ch. 11 or 13) and Ch. 7 liquidation, many of the same considerations apply as those outlined in Explanation 1. An individual debtor also has to be concerned about the potential that he will not be allowed to obtain Ch. 7 relief under §707(b), but this section will not apply to an individual in business whose debts are not primarily consumer debts. Unlike a corporation, Yokel Yummy will survive Ch. 7. (As regards an individual debtor, "liquidation" is not really used in the same sense as, say, Joseph Stalin may have used it.) Nevertheless, Ch. 7 will result in the liquidation of Yokel's nonexempt assets (both business and personal) and the termination of his business, so if he believes that there is a chance of rehabilitating the business, Ch. 13 is the better alternative.

3. As an individual debtor, Viva is eligible for relief under both Chs. 7 and 11, and could also be eligible for relief under Ch. 13. However, as noted in section 8.4.2(1), while Viva may be eligible for Ch. 7 relief under §109(b), she may face a motion to dismiss the case on grounds of abuse if her debts are primarily consumer debts[12] and her disposable income exceeds the means test in §707(b). For the present, just note that possibility, which is fully discussed in section 9.8.

To be eligible for Ch. 13 relief, Viva must meet its prerequisites: She must be an individual with regular income, having noncontingent liquidated unsecured debts of less than $383,175 and noncontingent liquidated secured debts of less than $1,149,525, based on the 2013 adjustment under §104. (After April 1, 2016, these figures will increase based on increases in the Consumer Price Index.)

Section 101(30) defines an "individual with regular income " as one whose income is sufficiently stable and regular to enable payments to be made under the Ch. 13 plan. Over a three-year period, Viva's income ranged from a low of $75,000 to a high of $110,000. She does not have a steady job, but enters into short-term employment contracts each year. Although the Code does not require a person to be a regular wage earner

---

12. The facts suggest that the conductor's tort claim is likely to be Viva's biggest debt by far, and it is not a consumer debt. The relative value of consumer and nonconsumer debt is highly relevant to the determination of whether an individual's indebtedness is primarily consumer debt. If Viva's debt is not primarily consumer debt, §707(b) does not apply.

to qualify for Ch. 13, it does require some predictability in income so that performance under the plan is reasonably assured. When a debtor is in Viva's position, the court must assess the likelihood of a reliable source of income, based on all of her circumstances: for example, her ability to budget irregular earnings, the likelihood of her being able to secure future performance engagements, and the amount she needs to maintain herself. In short, while the stability of Viva's income is an issue, she is not necessarily disqualified because of its irregularity as long as the facts show sufficient reliability to support a plan.

Viva satisfies the debt limitations. Her secured debt (the mortgage and the security interest in the car) totals $130,000, which is well within the $1,149,525 limit. Her unsecured debt is $45,000 plus a potential liability to the conductor of $1 million. The debt to the conductor is not counted in determining Viva's eligibility for Ch. 13 relief because it is unliquidated. (Note: Do not confuse the issue of excluding a debt for eligibility purposes from the issue of allowing the debt as a claim against the estate. Once Viva has filed her Ch. 13 petition, the conductor will prove a claim that will either be admitted or objected to and resolved by negotiation or litigation.) The debt is unliquidated because its amount cannot be computed arithmetically from settled facts, such as a contract term or other known figures. The conductor's claim can only be determined following a trial and judgment or a settlement agreement. The conductor's claim is disputed, but that would not have excluded it from the debt calculation. Also, even though the debt is dependent on a jury finding that Viva is liable to the conductor in tort, that does not make the debt contingent. A contingent debt is one that is conditional upon a future uncertain event occurring. The tortious conduct creating the debt has already occurred. The jury determination is a process of factfinding, not a legal contingency in the sense that the term is used in law. (Some courts have taken a different view and have treated disputed debts as unliquidated or contingent.)

The fact that the conductor's claim is unliquidated explains why it may be advantageous to Viva to file now, rather than to wait until the tort action is over. Once judgment is handed down in favor of the conductor, the debt becomes liquidated and is included in Viva's unsecured debt for eligibility purposes. Because the judgment may be quite large, it likely would increase her unsecured debt from $45,000 to an amount over the limit.

There are a number of factors that a debtor must take into account in deciding whether to file under Ch. 7, 11, or 13. These considerations are identified in general terms here. They will be discussed in greater detail in later chapters.

(1) Chs. 11 and 13 will allow Viva to keep her assets and to formulate a plan providing for the payment of claims from future income. In a Ch. 7

case, Viva's assets will be liquidated. Although she is entitled to exemptions, the exemptions may not be large enough to cover her full equity in the assets, in which case she will lose the property and will be paid the amount of her exemption from the proceeds of the sale of the property. Ch. 7 allows Viva to retain property through redemption or a reaffirmation agreement, but debtors are often not able to take advantage of these procedures because of lack of funds or creditor resistance.

With regard to the secured debts, Chs. 11 and 13 give the debtor the opportunity to maintain payments to the secured party and to cure defaults in prebankruptcy installments. The debtor is even able to modify the terms of some contracts to provide for an extended payment period. (However, the right to modify does not extend to the home mortgage.)

(2) The extent of the discharge may vary depending on the chapter chosen. For some debts, Ch. 13 offers the debtor a more generous discharge than Chs. 7 and 11. However, Congress has whittled away at this distinction over the years since it was first established in 1978. At present, the Ch. 13 discharge covers only a few types of debt that would not be dischargeable under the other chapters. The particular large debt in this case — the conductor's tort suit — would not be dischargeable under Chs. 7 or 11 because it likely qualifies as a debt for willful and malicious injury. Some debts for willful and malicious injury are dischargeable in Ch. 13 but not to the extent that they are for damages for personal injury awarded in a civil action against the debtor. Some but not all of the conductor's claim may relate to personal injury.

(3) In a Ch. 7 case, the distribution to creditors is made from the proceeds of the debtor's nonexempt assets. She does not have to pay anything further into the estate. Under Chs. 11 and 13 the debtor may keep her nonexempt assets, but must commit to a plan under which she will make payment for distribution to creditors over a period of years. The required level of payment is fixed at certain minimum levels by Chs. 11 and 13. Various factors go into the determination of the total amount that the debtor must pay under the plan. These are discussed in detail in Chapters 20 and 21. The two most important basic principles are that payments under the plan must be at least as much as what creditors would have received in Ch. 7, plus interest, and the debtor must commit all her disposable income to the plan.

(4) Because Ch. 7 involves liquidation and distribution as soon as possible, the bankruptcy administration usually comes to an end much earlier than a case under Ch. 11 or 13, which involves a payout period that extends over some years.

(5) The above distinctions focus primarily on the choice between Ch. 7, on the one hand, and Chs. 11 and 13, on the other. As between Chs. 11 and 13 themselves, the choice is usually dictated by the extent and complexity of the debtor's estate. As the eligibility discussion

indicates, some debtors are obliged to use Ch. 11 for rehabilitation simply because Ch. 13 is not available. In Viva's case, for example, this would occur if the conductor's suit reaches the stage of judgment before she files, and his damages award increases her liquidated unsecured debt above the limit.

Ch. 13 is usually more appropriate than Ch. 11 for an eligible debtor with straightforward financial affairs. It is simpler and has fewer procedures and safeguards that have to be complied with. A trustee is appointed, so the debtor plays a less active role in administering the estate. Creditors, too, have lesser rights of involvement. In addition, Ch. 13 has some advantages over Ch. 11. As mentioned above, its discharge is somewhat broader, and it protects cosigners on any consumer debts incurred by the debtor. Notwithstanding this, in some cases a debtor who is eligible for Ch. 13 may nevertheless decide to file under Ch. 11 because it provides more flexibility and allows the debtor more control over the estate.

(6) A debtor who is eligible for relief under more than one chapter has the discretion to select the most advantageous relief. However, this discretion is not unbridled. When a debtor's choice of relief is motivated by bad faith or an intent to abuse the spirit of the Code, the court may refuse the relief and dismiss the case. The issue of the debtor's good faith in choosing between alternative types of relief is raised in several contexts later. It is merely noted here as a qualification to the discussion on Viva's rights. Quite apart from the possibility of dismissal under §707(b), mentioned before, the debtor's good faith is one of the prerequisites for plan confirmation under Chs. 11 and 13.

4. Bud was not eligible for relief at the time that he filed the petition because he did not satisfy the requirements of §109(h)(1). Although he did receive credit counseling from a credit counseling agency before the petition, the counseling occurred too long ago—more than 180 days before the petition was filed. (Even had the counseling been within the 180-day period, it would still not have satisfied §109(h) because it was not by a nonprofit agency approved by the U.S. Trustee.) Some (but not all) courts are willing to exercise discretion in allowing something short of strict compliance with the requirements of §109(h). However, it is likely a rare case in which the court would consider the requirements of §109(h) to have been satisfied by counseling received prior to the statutory 180-day period. This did happen in In re Enloe (cited in Section 8.4.1(c)(i)). The court found that it had discretion to depart from the strict language of §109(h)(3). It held, under all the circumstances of the case, that counseling received by the debtor 189 days before the petition was sufficient to satisfy §109(h)(3). The court felt that this was justified because the debtors delayed filing while they attempted to sell their

home to avoid foreclosure and bankruptcy; the debtors' failure to receive counseling again before they filed was due to their attorney's oversight; the debtors' financial circumstances had not changed since the counseling; and the debtors did undergo further counseling after filing the petition. Given the plain language of §109(h)(3), and its purpose of requiring the counseling to be relatively fresh, one should not expect this kind of leeway in most cases. (As noted above, even if Bud satisfies the other factors set out in *Enloe*, the early counseling could not be deemed compliant because it was not by an approved nonprofit agency.)

Bud could try to invoke one of the three exemptions from prepetition counseling set out in §109(h)(2), (3), and (4). He clearly does not qualify for the exemptions in subsections (2) and (4), so his only chance to avoid dismissal of his case is to ask the court to validate his postpetition counseling under subsection (3). The requirements for the court's approval of postpetition counseling under §109(h)(3) are stringent. The counseling must occur within the short time limit specified — 30 days from the petition, or for cause, not more than 45 days. Bud's counseling did occur within this period — he received it the day after filing the petition.

The debtor must file a motion with the court to approve the post-petition counseling. The motion must include a certification, satisfactory to the court, asserting specific facts that describe and explain the exigent circumstances that merit deferral. The certification must state that the debtor requested the services of an approved agency, but was unable to obtain them during the seven-day period after he requested them. Many (but not all) courts require the certification to be attested to under oath.

"Exigent circumstances" are not defined in the Code, but, as, noted in section 8.4.1(c)(iii), impending creditor action, such as foreclosure on or seizure of important property, could qualify as exigent circumstances. However, some courts are less sympathetic to a claim of urgency where the debtor has failed to take earlier steps that may have prevented matters reaching a crisis point. Bud is confronted with a crisis that could qualify as exigent circumstances, and some courts may so find. However, a court that adopts a more rigorous standard for exigent circumstances may regard him as the author of his own misfortune because he stopped paying creditors and then waited for the inevitable creditor response before consulting an attorney.

In addition, Bud's complete failure to seek counseling immediately before filing the petition prevents him from being able to certify that he requested and was unable to obtain the services during the seven-day period after requesting them, even on a sympathetic reading of §109(h)(3), such as that adopted by *In re Henderson* and *In re Romero*, cited in section 8.4.1(c)(iii).

The Commencement and Dismissal of the Bankruptcy Case

§9.1 INTRODUCTION

The commencement of the bankruptcy case is governed by §§301 to 303. The cardinal distinction made in those sections is between voluntary and involuntary petitions. As was noted in section 5.5.2, although bankruptcy originated purely as a creditor's remedy against a debtor, in its modern form it is well established as a remedy available to a debtor as well. Today, voluntary petitions make up the vast bulk of bankruptcy filings.

Sections 9.1 to 9.6 and 9.9 cover voluntary and involuntary petitions and proceedings associated with the initial phase of the bankruptcy case. For the sake of simplicity, the Ch. 7 case involving an individual debtor is used as the model for this discussion. With some variations, bankruptcy under the other chapters follows a similar path in the initial stages. Diagram 9a traces the sequence of routine core proceedings in a Ch. 7 case. The time periods are as stated in the Rules, but most can be extended by the court.

Rough Skeleton Showing the Sequence of a Ch. 7 Case

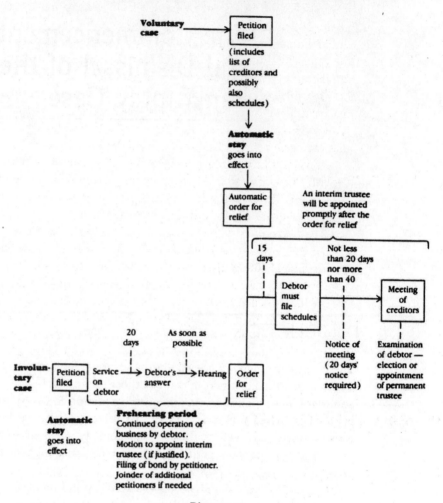

Diagram 9a

Sections 9.7 and 9.8 cover dismissal of the case. Although dismissal is not confined to the early stages of the case, motions to dismiss the case are often filed soon after the case is filed, so this is a convenient place to discuss them. Section 9.7 covers dismissal generally under all chapters of the Code. Section 9.8 deals with dismissal of a Ch. 7 case on the grounds of abuse under §707(b).

§9.2 VENUE

Section 7.2 explained that 28 U.S.C. §1334 grants jurisdiction over bankruptcy to district courts generally. 28 U.S.C. §§1408, 1409, and 1412 deal with the question of which federal district is the most appropriate geographical locale for the disposition of the proceedings. As with other sections of title 28, these provisions refer only to the district court. Once venue is determined, the bankruptcy courts in that federal district deal with the proceedings under the general referral from the district court. Venue rules curtail the petitioner's or plaintiff's freedom to choose a geographic location for the bankruptcy case or other proceedings. They are intended to prevent forum shopping and to make it difficult for a person to initiate proceedings in an unsuitable place that is awkward or inconvenient for other parties in interest. This does not mean that the correct venue is always convenient for everyone. The appropriate location could be distant from the situs of a transaction or property or from the home base of a party. However, restrictions on venue give the courts some control over the choice of federal district by the debtor, petitioning creditors in an involuntary case or plaintiffs in related cases.

The venue rules are not discussed here in detail. As a general matter, the proper venue of the bankruptcy case is determined by the debtor's location (defined in §1408 by alternative tests) for the 180 days before the petition. Under §1409, the venue of the case itself is also usually the proper venue for proceedings ancillary to the case, but the section recognizes exceptions to this rule in defined circumstances under which another venue is more appropriate. Section 1412 empowers a court to transfer of a case to another district in the interest of justice or for the convenience of the parties.

§9.3 THE VOLUNTARY CASE

When an attorney is consulted by a client who needs bankruptcy relief, the first task is to obtain information about the client's affairs. Detailed knowledge is required for the accurate completion of the schedules that must be filed with, or shortly after, the petition. In addition, the attorney needs a comprehensive understanding of the debtor's economic history and current financial position to fulfill the role of counseling the debtor on choice of relief, identifying potential problems, and planning the appropriate course of action to be taken in the case. For example (without attempting to be definitive), the attorney needs to have information about the debtor's location to determine venue, and to have full details about the debtor's financial history, assets and liabilities, business affairs, pending lawsuits, disposition of assets, income, and future plans and desires.

Once all this information is gathered, the case is commenced by filing a petition. (Ideally, an attorney should not file a petition until she has all the pertinent information and can assess the impact of filing and anticipate potential problems. However, reliable information is not always available. In addition, sometimes the need to file immediately means having to proceed without complete information.) In a voluntary case, the filing of the petition operates automatically as an order for relief—that is, as an order placing the debtor in bankruptcy. The form of the petition set out in the Bankruptcy Rules (Form 1) is simple. It does not even look like a pleading, because it has been designed so it can easily be completed by checking boxes, and can be computer-generated. In essence, it provides information about the debtor, contains minimal assertions establishing venue and eligibility for relief and identifies the chapter under which relief is sought. A consumer debtor must acknowledge understanding the choice of relief, and this acknowledgment must be certified by the debtor's attorney. The debtor's signature of the petition certifies the accuracy of the allegations in the petition and constitutes an assertion, under Rule 9011, that the petition is filed in good faith and not for abusive purposes.

The supporting documents required by §521 and the Bankruptcy Rules are filed with, or shortly after, the petition. They include a list or schedule of liabilities, with the identity of creditors so that the clerk can notify them of the filing; a schedule of property; a schedule of claims, properly categorized into secured and unsecured classes, and identified as to whether they are contingent, liquidated or disputed; a claim of exemptions; a schedule of income and expenses; a schedule of executory contracts; a summary of the debtor's financial history and current financial position; and a statement of intent by the debtor with regard to the proposed surrender of encumbered property, or its retention by reaffirmation or redemption, or the avoidance of any liens on it. The Bankruptcy Abuse Prevention and Consumer Protection Act of 2005 (BAPCPA) significantly increased the debtor's duty to provide information and disclosures under §521. Section 521(a) requires the debtor to file copies of payment advices and other evidence of payments received from an employer in the 60 days before the petition, an itemized calculation of net monthly income, and a statement of reasonably anticipated increases in income or expenses over the next 12 months. Section 521(e) requires the debtor to file a copy of the debtor's federal income tax return for the most recent tax year prior to the petition. Section 521(b) requires the debtor to file a certificate from the nonprofit credit counseling agency consulted by the debtor under §109(h) (*see* section 8.4.1(c)), showing what services were rendered to the debtor.

§9.4 THE VOLUNTARY PETITION AS AN ORDER FOR RELIEF

In an involuntary case, the debtor does not become bankrupt until a hearing is held and the court gives judgment granting the creditors' petition. *See* section 9.6. This judgment is referred to in the Code as the order for relief.

In a voluntary case, there is no formal adjudication of bankruptcy. In terms of §301(b), the filing of the petition automatically places the debtor in bankruptcy. In other words, in a voluntary case, the filing of the petition itself constitutes the order for relief.

Many provisions in the Code specify that certain consequences come into effect on the filing of the petition. Others specify that the date of the order for relief is the relevant date for particular purposes. It is important to remember that in voluntary cases, the filing and the order for relief are the same date, while in involuntary cases they are different. For example, §701 requires an interim trustee to be appointed after the order for relief. This means that the trustee is appointed immediately after the petition in a voluntary case but is only appointed after the hearing and adjudication of bankruptcy in an involuntary case. (Even in an involuntary case, a creditor can apply to court for the appointment of a trustee before the order for relief. The creditor must show cause, such as grounds to believe that the debtor will mismanage the estate in the interim period.) By contrast, §362 provides that the automatic stay comes into effect upon filing of the petition. Therefore, in both voluntary and involuntary cases, the stay takes effect at the commencement of the case.

§9.5 JOINT CASES, JOINTLY ADMINISTERED CASES, AND CONSOLIDATION

§9.5.1 Joint Cases

If spouses own assets and owe obligations jointly, the bankruptcy of only one of the spouses does not provide full relief to the family as an economic unit: The nonbankrupt spouse remains liable on joint debts. Therefore, both spouses may need to file for bankruptcy. They may file separate petitions but are permitted by §302 to file a joint case. This saves costs, because the joint debtors pay a single filing fee and a single set of administrative costs. Joint filing does not mean that the estates of the spouses are combined. The court has the discretion under §302 to allow them to be consolidated or to require them to be kept separate. The considerations that affect the decision to consolidate or separate the estates are noted below. A joint petition can only be filed voluntarily. Creditors cannot file an involuntary petition against spouses jointly. In an involuntary case, the creditors of each spouse must file a petition against the spouse that is their debtor. Often spouses are joint debtors, so the separate petitions could be filed by the same creditors.

Section 302 is applicable only to spouses. (The Code does not define "spouses," but the plain meaning of §302 is to confine the availability of joint petitions to those who are legally married under state law.) There is no provision in the Code for a joint case to be filed by debtors other than spouses (for example, affiliated corporations or a corporation and its owner), no matter how closely connected or related they may be. (A partnership is treated as a separate entity under the Code, so a partnership petition is not a joint petition.) Although the bankruptcy of a corporation may result in its owner's bankruptcy as well, these two separate legal entities must file separate petitions.

§9.5.2 Joint Administration

Even though closely related debtors other than spouses cannot file a joint petition, the court is able to order the joint administration of their cases. Joint administration keeps the estates separate so that each has its own assets and liabilities but places the estates under the administration of the same trustee, thereby cutting down administrative costs and allowing for the more convenient disposition of the cases. Joint administration is therefore an administrative device to save costs and allow for the more efficient handling of the separate estates. It is provided for in Rule 1015(b).

§9.5.3 Consolidation of Cases

a. Procedural Consolidation

Rule 1015(a) provides for the procedural consolidation of cases where two petitions have been filed in the same court involving the same debtor. This might occur, for example, where two sets of creditors have both filed involuntary petitions against the same debtor. The rule permits the court to combine the cases. As only one debtor is involved, procedural consolidation is distinct from the other situations described here.

b. Substantive Consolidation

In addition to the above type of procedural consolidation, the court also has the power as a court of equity to order the substantive consolidation of cases against separate debtors. Substantive consolidation is not provided for in the Code, but is a judicially devised remedy based on the court's equitable discretion. Where spouses (whether they have filed jointly or separately) or other closely related debtors, such as an individual and his corporation or a parent corporation and its subsidiaries, are in bankruptcy, the court can combine their estates so that assets are pooled and creditors of each become creditors in the consolidated estate.

Substantive consolidation is different from joint administration because it combines the two separate estates into a single bankruptcy estate. This could prejudice creditors of the debtor with the higher asset-to-debt ratio. Substantive consolidation is therefore not routinely permitted even if the debtors are closely affiliated, and a court will not likely use its equitable consolidation power unless the party seeking consolidation can prove that the overall equities favor consolidation. This may happen where creditors have dealt with the debtors as a single economic unit, without relying on their separate identities, or where it is apparent that the affairs of the debtors are so entangled that it is very difficult to separate their assets and liabilities. For example, in In re Owens Corning, 419 F.3d 195 (3d Cir. 2005), the court refused to permit the consolidation of the estates of the parent corporation and its 17 subsidiaries because it would have had a negative impact on the rights of creditors of the parent by eliminating guarantees from the subsidiaries, the affairs of the debtors were not so entangled that they could not be separated, and consolidating the estate would not result in significant cost savings to the benefit of all creditors. In In re Amco Insurance, 444 F.3d 690 (5th Cir. 2006), the court held that the bankruptcy court had abused its discretion in allowing the substantive consolidation of the estates of a corporation and its principal shareholder where the equities did not favor it. In addition, the bankruptcy court had ordered the consolidation nunc pro tunc, so that it took effect at a time before the shareholder had filed his bankruptcy petition. The court held that it is not permissible to consolidate estates with effect from a date prior to the bankruptcy of both debtors.

There is a link between substantive consolidation and the equitable remedy of piercing the corporate veil, in which a court disregards the separate identity of the corporate entity and its shareholder. While the doctrines are conceptually related, they are distinct. For additional discussion of the factors to be taken into account and the considerations to be weighed in deciding whether the estates of debtors should be substantively consolidated, see In re Augie/Restivo Baking Co., Ltd., 860 F.2d 515 (2d Cir. 1988); In re Giller, 962 F.2d 796 (8th Cir. 1992); In re Reider, 31 F.3d 1102 (11th Cir. 1994).

§9.6 INVOLUNTARY CASES

§9.6.1 Introduction

Involuntary cases make up quite a small percentage of the bankruptcy filings each year. Section 303, which governs involuntary cases, has many restrictions and limitations, making involuntary relief available only in a narrow range of circumstances. To obtain an involuntary order for relief, petitioners must satisfy two distinct sets of requirements. First, the qualifications for filing prescribed by §303(a), (b), and (c) must be met. Thereafter, at the hearing of a controverted involuntary case, the petitioners must establish grounds for relief under §303(h). Congress deliberately set these exacting requirements for an involuntary petition to deter a creditor from using the remedy of involuntary bankruptcy as a tool for collecting an isolated debt and to ensure that placing the debtor into involuntary bankruptcy serves the interests of the creditor body as a whole. See In re Murrin, 477 B.R. 99 (D. Minn. 2012). As an additional disincentive to inappropriate use of an involuntary petition, if the petition is not successful, the petitioners could be liable to the debtor for attorney's fees, costs, and damages. This is discussed in section 9.6.3.

§9.6.2 Qualifications for Filing under §303(a), (b), and (c)

An involuntary petition is permitted only if all the qualifications set out in §303(a), (b), and (c) are satisfied.

a. Section 303(a): The Nature of the Debtor and the Relief

The debtor must be subject to involuntary bankruptcy. Most debtors can be subjected to an involuntary petition, with a few exclusions set out in §303(a). An involuntary case may not be filed against a noncommercial (essentially, charitable) corporation or a farmer. ("Farmer," defined in §101(20), is a broader category than "family farmer.") Section 303(a) confines involuntary petitions to cases under Chs. 7 and 11. A debtor cannot be placed involuntarily into bankruptcy under Chs. 12 or 13.

b. Section 303(b): The Number and Qualification of Creditors

Section 303(b)(1) requires that the aggregate amount of claims held by all the petitioners be at least $15,325,[1] excluding claims that are contingent as to liability, the subject of a bona fide dispute as to liability or amount, or secured by a lien. (As discussed below, there must be at least three petitioning creditors unless §303(b)(2) applies.) That is, to determine if the monetary qualification for the petition is satisfied, any contingent claim, bona fide disputed claim, or secured claim held by the petitioners is excluded.

---

1. This is the current amount under the 2013 administrative adjustment to dollar amounts under §104. The amount will be adjusted again with effect from April 1, 2016. See section 5.4.3 for an explanation of these dollar adjustments.

Having excluded these claims, the total balance of the amounts due to the petitioners must be at least $15,325.

(1) Secured claims. Section 303(b)(1) does not completely exclude secured creditors from participating in the petition. Section 303(b)(1) uses the language "more than the value of any lien on property of the debtor securing such claims. . . ." If a creditor is fully secured (that is, the collateral is worth at least as much as the debt), none of its claim can be counted. However, if a creditor is only partially secured, the debt can be counted to the extent that it exceeds the value of the collateral.

Section 303(b) relates only to whether the claim qualifies the creditor to be a petitioner in an involuntary case. The subsection has no impact on the manner in which the claim will be treated in the estate if the court grants the petition and places the debtor in bankruptcy.

(2) Contingent claims. The meaning of contingent is discussed in section 19.2.2. A broad definition is enough for present purposes: A contingent claim is one that is conditional on a future uncertain event. The debtor's potential liability has already been created by contract or by wrongful act (so the legal basis for the debt has already been created), but the debtor will only become liable to pay the debt if a future uncertain event occurs.

(3) Claims subject to bona fide dispute. Subsection §303(b)(1) states that a debt cannot be counted for purposes of qualifying the petition if it is "the subject of a bona fide dispute as to liability or amount." The words "as to liability or amount" were added to §303(b)(1) by BAPCPA. Prior to the amendment, some courts had held that a dispute that related only to the amount of the claim did not render the whole claim subject to a dispute, so the undisputed portion could be counted for qualification purposes. The addition of this language suggests that a good faith dispute as to amount should be treated the same as one as to liability: Provided that the dispute arises out of the same transaction as the claim and is directly related to the claim, the dispute disqualifies the entire claim for purposes of §303(b)(1). See In re Regional Anesthesia Associates, 360 B.R. 466 (Bankr. W.D. Pa. 2007). Although "bona fide" may suggest a subjective test of honest belief in the merits of the claim, courts generally adopt a stricter objective standard and require that there is either a genuine dispute of material fact or a meritorious legal argument against the claim. See, for example, In re Byrd, 357 F.3d 433 (4th Cir. 2004), In re Dilley, 339 B.R. 1 (B.A.P. 1st Cir. 2006). The dispute must be specific and articulated, not merely a general denial or challenge. In In re Dilley the court said that once the petitioner establishes the existence of a claim, it creates a prima facie case that it is undisputed, and the debtor must then show that there is a bona fide dispute. To do this, the debtor cannot simply deny the claim, but must present facts that demonstrate, by a preponderance of the evidence, the existence of a bona fide dispute.[2] The court does not adjudicate the dispute at this stage. It merely determines if there is a genuine dispute. The dispute must relate to the debt itself, so the debtor cannot claim that a debt is disputed merely because she has a counterclaim against the creditor arising out of a different transaction or event. See In re Regional Anesthesia Associates.

(4) The number of creditors. The number of petitioners required for an involuntary petition depends on the size of the creditor body. In simple terms, if the debtor has 12 or more creditors, at least three must join in the petition. If the debtor has 11 or fewer creditors, only one petitioner is needed. The petitioners must, of course, satisfy the claim requirements described in paragraph (3) above. The qualification of a party as a creditor is measured as at the date of the petition. In In re Faberge Restaurant of Florida, 222 B.R. 385 (Bankr. E.D. Fla. 1997), the court held that a debtor could not defeat an involuntary petition by paying a petitioner after the petition had been filed.

(i) The three-creditor rule where the debtor has 12 or more creditors. The purpose of the three-creditor rule is to protect a debtor from an involuntary petition by a single creditor who cannot muster support for the petition from any other creditors. To prevent evasion of the rule, courts require the petitioning creditors to be separate legal entities independent of each other. The creditors may be related (such as a parent corporation and its subsidiary or a shareholder and his corporation) provided that they each have genuinely separate claims against the debtor, and neither controls the other. Therefore, a creditor cannot artificially create another creditor by, say, assigning part of its claim to the other entity.

Courts look at all the circumstances of the relationship between related petitioners to decide if each of them has independent decision-making capacity. For example, in In re Sims, 994 F.2d 210 (5th Cir. 1993), the three petitioners were affiliated corporations that had the same officers. Notwithstanding that relationship, the court found them to be separate entities for purposes of §303(b). Each petitioner's claim arose out of a

---

2. In In re Dilley the debtor had been indicted for killing his estranged wife and his mother. His two children witnessed the alleged murders. The debtor had pleaded not guilty to the charges, and the criminal case was pending when the estate of the debtor's deceased ex-wife and the guardians of his two children filed an involuntary petition against him. The claim of the ex-wife's estate was for wrongful death and for maintenance, and the children's claims were for the intentional infliction of emotional distress and for support. Although the debtor had not presented any facts to demonstrate a bona fide dispute, the bankruptcy court held that the debtor's not-guilty plea in the criminal case was sufficient to establish a bona fide dispute as to liability. The B.A.P. reversed, holding that a not-guilty plea was no better than a bare denial of liability. It did not demonstrate a bona fide dispute because it did not present substantial factual or legal questions bearing on liability.

different transaction entered into by the debtor and that petitioner. The petitioners operated in different regions as distinct businesses, had separate bank accounts, and had strictly honored corporate formalities in their ownership of assets, the payment of taxes, and their dealings with each other. (The analysis used to decide if a corporate entity is a truly independent petitioner is analogous to that conducted by courts under the equitable doctrine of piercing the corporate veil, which is used to hold a shareholder liable for corporate debts where he has employed the corporation manipulatively and inequitably.)

(ii) *Filing by a single creditor where the debtor has fewer than 12 creditors.* Not all creditors are counted in deciding if the debtor has fewer than 12 creditors. Section 303(b)(2) sets out a formula that excludes five categories of creditors from the count. The subsection expressly excludes employees of the debtor, insiders of the debtor, and recipients of avoidable transfers. In addition, the subsection, by using the language "12 *such* holders" refers back to the "holders" described in §303(b)(1), which excludes another two classes — holders of contingent claims and holders of claims subject to a bona fide dispute.

The reason for requiring only one petitioner where the debtor has fewer than 12 creditors is that it would be very difficult to find three petitioners in such a small creditor pool. Holders of contingent and disputed claims are excluded from the count because they are not qualified to be petitioners. Employees, insiders, and recipients of avoidable transfers are excluded because they have a stake in preventing the debtor's involuntary bankruptcy and are not likely to join an involuntary petition.

A couple of cases illustrate how creditors are counted for the purpose of §303(b)(2). In *In re Skye Marketing Corp.*, 11 B.R. 891 (Bankr. E.D.N.Y. 1981), the court reduced the debtor's list of 24 creditors to fewer than 12 by excluding an insider, voidable claims, and contingent claims. By contrast, in *Atlas Machine and Iron Works v. Bethlehem Steel Corp.*, 986 F.2d 709 (4th Cir. 1993), the petitioning creditor argued that about 60 of the debtor's 66 creditors should be excluded from the count because the debts owing to them were not overdue and should therefore be regarded as disputed. The argument was that because the debts were not due yet, the debtor would have disputed the obligation to pay if the creditors sued on them at the time of the petition. The court rejected this argument on the basis that a debt is not to be treated as disputed unless it involves a meritorious existing conflict.

(5) The nature of §303(b): jurisdictional or substantive. If the requirements of §303(b) are jurisdictional, they must be satisfied as a prerequisite for bringing an involuntary petition. If the requirements are not satisfied, the bankruptcy court has no subject matter jurisdiction to entertain the petition. However, if the requirements are not jurisdictional, but are merely substantive elements to be established for relief, the petition is effective to commence the bankruptcy case, and the court can grant relief if the debtor waives objection by failure to challenge the petition. Although some courts have held §303(b) to be jurisdictional, this conclusion no longer seems tenable. In *Arbaugh v. Y&H Corp.*, 546 U.S. 500 (2006), the Supreme Court articulated the general principle that a court should not interpret statutory requirements as being jurisdictional unless Congress has made it clear in the language of the statute that it intends them to be. The court again enunciated this principle in *Stern v. Marshall*, 131 S. Ct. 2594 (2011) in relation to consent to bankruptcy court jurisdiction.[3] There is no language in §303 to suggest Congressional intent to make it jurisdictional. Subject matter jurisdiction over claims arising under the Code is conferred by 28 U.S.C. §1334,[4] and the requirements of §303 are more properly treated as elements to be proved to obtain relief. See *In re Trusted Net Media Holdings, LLC*, 550 F.3d 1035 (11th Cir. 2008); *In re Zarnel*, 619 F.3d 156 (2d Cir. 2010).

c. Section 303(c): Subsequent Joinder of a Petitioner

If a single creditor files the petition genuinely believing that the debtor has fewer than 12 creditors, and it later appears that there are more, the petitioner may solicit additional petitioners. Section 303(c) permits a qualified creditor to join the petition at any time before the case is dismissed or relief is ordered. Although §303(c) does not expressly allow the court to cut short the period in which additional petitioners must be found, *In re DSC, Ltd.*, 486 F.3d 940 (6th Cir. 2007), held that the court has the discretion to curtail the time for joinder by setting a bar date. In *In re Bock Transportation, Inc.*, 327 B.R. 378 (B.A.P. 8th Cir. 2005), the court stressed that a single petitioner must have a genuine and reasonable belief that the debtor has fewer than 12 creditors. If the petitioner does not have this reasonable belief but files in the hope that she will later find two more creditors to join the petition, the court may refuse to allow the joinder and dismiss the case.

§9.6.3 Procedures from the Filing of the Petition to the Order for Relief

An involuntary petition is served on the debtor. If the debtor does not controvert the petition, §303(h) requires the court to order relief by granting the petition. If the debtor wishes to controvert the petition, he must file an answer within the period prescribed by the rules. The answer may raise

---

3. See section 7.3.5(4).
4. See section 7.2.2.

defenses available to the debtor under nonbankruptcy law (a substantive defense to the claim of a petitioner) or under the Code (such as failure to satisfy §303), or may move to dismiss the case on grounds such as improper venue. If the debtor challenges the petition, he may demand a bond under §303(e) to secure any costs or damages that may be awarded if the petition is dismissed. If the debtor controverts the petition, there must be a trial on the issues raised by the pleadings, and the petitioners must establish one of the two grounds for relief set out in §303(h). It must be stressed that the petitioners are not required to establish grounds for relief under §303(h) if the debtor does not defend the involuntary case.

Because there is some period of delay between the filing of the petition and the grant of the order for relief, §303(f) permits the debtor to continue the operation of a business and to deal with property during the period between the petition and the order for relief. However, if a creditor is able to show that the debtor is likely to mismanage property or harm the estate by this activity, the creditor is entitled to apply to the court under §303(g) for the appointment of an interim trustee to take over the debtor's affairs. The order can only be granted following notice to the debtor and a hearing.

§9.6.4 The Grounds for Relief

If the debtor controverts the petition, §303(h) permits an order for relief to be granted only if the petitioners are able to establish one of two alternative grounds for relief:

1. The debtor is generally not paying debts as they become due, unless such debts are the subject of a bona fide dispute as to liability or amount; or
2. Within 120 days before the filing of the petition, a custodian was appointed or took possession of the debtor's property. This requirement is not satisfied if the custodian was appointed to take possession of less than substantially all the debtor's property for the purpose of lien enforcement.

The grounds for relief serve an important function in contested involuntary cases: They constitute a justification for forcing an unwilling debtor into bankruptcy and limit the power of creditors to obtain bankruptcy relief. It is not enough for creditors to show merely that the debtor owes them money and has not paid. By demonstrating one of the two grounds of relief, they also show that the debtor's financial problems are more general. The two situations that constitute grounds of relief are indicative of broad financial instability in the debtor's affairs.

The requirement that creditors establish grounds for relief has a long tradition in bankruptcy law. Prior to 1978, the petitioners had to establish that the debtor had committed one of several "acts of bankruptcy" that included making fraudulent or preferential transfers, admitting inability to pay, or making an assignment for the benefit of creditors. The grounds in §303(h) replace these acts of bankruptcy by substituting circumstances regarded as directly relevant to the debtor's financial condition. The two grounds are alternative. Only one need be established by the petitioners.

a. General Nonpayment of Due Debts (§303(h)(1))

Section 303(h)(1) requires a general pattern of nonpayment of undisputed mature debts during the period immediately preceding the petition. The general failure to pay due debts is known as equity insolvency. (*See* sections 3.9.1 and 4.4.3.) Insolvency on the equity test is a good barometer of the debtor's financial difficulty, and easier for creditors to prove than insolvency on the balance sheet test (an excess of liabilities over assets). Because wide default on debts is a manifestation of financial distress, concerned creditors are given the ability to place the debtor in involuntary bankruptcy so that they can prevent deterioration of the estate and a race for assets by creditors.

In deciding whether a debtor is generally not paying due debts, courts are obviously influenced by the percentage of debts in default, both in number and value. The more widespread the default and the larger the proportionate value of overdue debt, the more likely that general nonpayment will be found. However, courts also look beyond the bare figures and take into account such factors as the relative importance of the unpaid debts, the length of time that they are overdue, the extent to which the size of overdue payments has increased over a period of time, the degree of irresponsibility shown by the debtor, and other factors that tend to demonstrate that the debtor's position is precarious enough to justify involuntary relief. See, for example, In re *Westside Community Hospital Inc.*, 112 B.R. 243 (Bankr. N.D. Ill. 1990); In re *Murrin* (cited in section 9.6.1). Examples 3 and 4 deal with the test of general nonpayment of debts.

The requirement that unpaid debts not be subject to a bona fide dispute means that if the debtor's reason for not paying the debt is a legitimate factual or legal dispute with the creditor, the debt may not be taken into account in deciding whether the debtor is generally not paying debts when due. Courts generally apply the same objective test here as they do when considering whether a petitioner's claim is the subject of a bona fide dispute for purposes of qualifying the petitioners: There must be a *prima facie* meritorious defense. Thus, "bona fide" is not wide enough to cover an honest but misguided dispute by the debtor. See, for example, In re *Rimell*, 946 F.2d 1363 (8th Cir. 1991).

Where a debtor has only one creditor, default on that debt inevitably constitutes universal default. Nevertheless, some courts have refused to grant involuntary relief where the debtor has only one creditor on the basis that the nonpayment of a single debt is contrary to the concept of general nonpayment. An exception is made to this rule where there is evidence of fraud by the debtor. In In re Concrete Pumping Service, Inc., 943 F.2d 627 (6th Cir. 1991), the court questioned the propriety of precluding the use of §303(h)(1) in a single-creditor case. It considered that general nonpayment should be found where there is default on the debtor's only debt, and the totality of the circumstances justifies relief.

b. The Appointment of a Custodian within 120 Days Prior to the Petition (§303(h)(2))

Section 101(11) defines "custodian" to mean a receiver or trustee appointed under nonbankruptcy law or an assignee for the benefit of creditors. The appointment could result from a voluntary arrangement initiated by the debtor or from a court order in a nonbankruptcy case. Custodial proceedings are usually used by or against insolvent debtors. Therefore this ground, like the first one, is premised on a manifestation of the debtor's insolvency. By filing an involuntary petition, concerned creditors are able to take the debtor's estate out of the state law trusteeship and bring it under the aegis of the Code. However, they must act within 120 days of the appointment or taking of possession. Section 303(h)(2) is expressly not available when the appointment of the custodian is for the purpose of enforcing a lien against less than substantially all of the debtor's property.

§9.6.5 The Effect and Consequences of the Order for Relief in an Involuntary Case

If the petitioners are able to establish grounds for relief at the hearing, or if the case is uncontroverted and the petition shows grounds for relief, the court grants the order for relief under Ch. 7 or Ch. 11. The order for relief is the judgment placing the debtor in bankruptcy. Its effect is explained in section 9.4. Following the order for relief, the debtor must file the schedules discussed in section 9.3. The time period for filing them is the same as in a voluntary case but is measured from the order for relief rather than the petition date. Unless an interim trustee was appointed for cause earlier in the proceedings, the interim trustee is appointed after the order for relief.

§9.6.6 Petitioner Liability for Dismissal of the Petition

Creditors who petition for involuntary bankruptcy take a risk. Section 303(i)(1) authorizes the court to award costs and a reasonable attorney's fee to the debtor if the petition is dismissed, unless the dismissal is by consent of all parties and the debtor waives the right to the award. Section 303(i)(2) authorizes the court to award compensatory or punitive damages against a petitioner that filed the petition in bad faith. Section 303(i) states that the court "may" grant judgment for costs, attorney's fees, or damages, so the decision to make any such award is within the discretion of the court.

(1) Attorney's fees and costs under §303(i)(1).   To obtain an award of attorney's fees and costs, the debtor need not show that the petition was filed vexatiously or in bad faith. Bad faith is a requirement for an award of damages under §301(i)(2), but it is absent from §301(i)(1). This does not mean that bad faith is irrelevant to a determination to award costs and attorney's fees because the presence or absence of bad faith is one of the factors the court takes into account in exercising its discretion. See, for example, In re Hentges, 351 B.R. 758 (Bankr. N.D. Okla. 2006). Some courts adopt a very loose standard for awarding costs and attorney's fees and make the award as a matter of course where the petition fails. Others hold that the dismissal of the petition creates a presumption in favor of the award unless the creditor can show circumstances that overcome the presumption. See, for example, Higgins v. Vortex Fishing Systems, Inc., 379 F.3d 701 (9th Cir. 2004); In re Maple-Whitworth, Inc., 556 F.3d 742 (9th Cir. 2009). Still others adopt an even more stringert standard for making an award. For example, in In re Starlite Houseboats, Inc., 470 B.R. 191 (Bankr. D. Kan. 2012), the court found that a true exercise of discretion based on the totality of the circumstances is most consistent with the plain language of the section and with the usual rule that each party bears its own litigation expenses. In evaluating the totality of the circumstances, the court takes into account factors such as the merits of the petition, the motivations and reasonableness of the creditors in filing it, and any improper conduct on the part of the debtor. (In In re Starlite Houseboats the petition was dismissed because the claim of one of the three creditors was disqualified as being subject to a bona fide dispute. The court refused to award costs and attorney's fees to the debtor because the petitioners had legitimate motives for seeking bankruptcy protection and reasonably believed that the claim was valid and undisputable.)

Where three creditors have joined to file the petition, each of the petitioners is liable for costs and fees. Maple-Whitworth held that the debtor may proceed against all of the petitioners, or against only some of them. It is within the bankruptcy court's discretion to determine how the liability for the fees and costs should be apportioned. It could hold the petitioners jointly and severally liable, or it could hold only some of them liable, and may apportion liability among them depending on their culpability.

(2) Damages for bad faith filing.   If any petitioner has filed in bad faith, §303(i)(2) authorizes the court to award against that petitioner not only fees and costs but also compensatory or punitive damages. (If only one of the petitioners has acted in bad faith, the other petitioners are not liable for the judgment under §303(i)(2).) Courts have used various tests in deciding whether a petitioner has filed in bad faith. Generally, they include the use of the petition vexatiously, frivolously, or for an ulterior motive or improper purpose. For example, a creditor acts in bad faith where it files to obtain a disproportionate advantage, or it uses bankruptcy where state collection remedies are more appropriate, or it is motivated by spite, ill will, or malice. See, for example, In re John Richards Home Building Co., LLC, 312 B.R. 849 (E.D. Mich. 2004), in which a homeowner who had a dispute with the builder of his $3 million home filed an involuntary petition against the builder on the basis of that disputed claim. The bankruptcy court found that the petition was a vindictive attempt to intimidate the builder and harm his business reputation. The district court affirmed the bankruptcy court's award to the builder of $4.1 million in compensatory damages, $2 million in punitive damages, and costs and attorney's fees.

In In re Miles, 430 F.3d 1083 (9th Cir. 2005), the court held that by vesting exclusive bankruptcy jurisdiction in federal district courts and providing a comprehensive remedial scheme in §301(i), Congress intended the remedies provided for in §301(i) to be the exclusive remedies available for the improper filing of a bankruptcy petition. They completely preempt state law causes of action such as malicious prosecution, abuse of process, defamation, and intentional infliction of emotional distress. The court reasoned that it would undermine the uniformity of bankruptcy law and federal control of the bankruptcy system to permit state law or state courts to decide on the propriety of a petition and the consequences of wrongful filing. The court also held that the remedies under §301(i) are available only to the debtor and may not be sought by third parties, such as the debtor's spouse or other entities related to the debtor.

§9.7 GENERAL GROUNDS FOR DISMISSAL OF A BANKRUPTCY CASE — VOLUNTARY DISMISSAL, CAUSE, AND IMPROPER DEBTOR CONDUCT

The debtor's right to dismiss an involuntary case was mentioned in section 9.6.3. This note more generally surveys the possibility of dismissal of the case by the debtor, a creditor, or another party in interest. This section deals with general grounds of dismissal. The more specific form of dismissal for abuse in a Ch. 7 consumer case is discussed separately in section 9.8. Dismissal may not always be the best form of relief for a party that wishes to stop or change the course of a bankruptcy case. An application for abstention or conversion may sometimes be a more desirable alternative. (Abstention and conversion are discussed in sections 7.7.2 and 8.6.) The issues involved in dismissal can be intricate. This survey deals only with a broad description of its scope and purpose.

Each chapter of the Code has its own section governing dismissal: §§707, 1112, 1208, and 1307. Dismissal terminates the bankruptcy case: The debtor and the estate are released from bankruptcy and the creditors' collection rights at state law are no longer stayed. Section 349 lists the effects of dismissal. There are myriad reasons why a debtor, creditor, or other party in interest may seek dismissal of a case, and depending on the circumstances, dismissal may serve or run counter to the interests of different parties. There are three different situations in which the case may be dismissed:

(1) Voluntary dismissal by the petitioner. A debtor who has filed a voluntary case may, in effect, seek to "withdraw" the petition by requesting dismissal. In a Ch. 7 or 11 case the debtor must show cause for dismissal, and the case can be dismissed only after notice and a hearing. *See* §§707(a) and 1112(b). In Chs. 12 and 13, the debtor has a broad right to dismiss unless the case has previously been converted from Ch. 7, 11, or (in a Ch. 13 case) from Ch. 12. Both §1208(b) and §1307(b) state that the court "shall" dismiss the case on request of the debtor unless it had been converted from one of the chapters mentioned above. The clear statutory language indicates that the debtor's right to dismiss an unconverted Ch. 12 or 13 case is absolute, and many courts have so interpreted it. See, for example, In re *Williams*, 435 B.R. 552 (Bankr. N.D. Ill. 2010). However, other courts have read into these sections a discretion to deny the debtor's motion to dismiss if the debtor has acted in bad faith or has abused the bankruptcy process. This qualification of the debtor's absolute right to dismiss is based on the U.S. Supreme Court's opinion in *Marrama v. Citizen's Bank of Massachusetts,* 549 U.S. 365 (U.S. 2007). *Marrama* did not involve a debtor's motion to dismiss, but was concerned with the debtor's attempt to convert a Ch. 7 case to Ch. 13. The court held that the debtor could not convert the case to Ch. 13 because he had forfeited the right to proceed under Ch. 13 as a result of his bad faith conduct. (*Marrama* is discussed in section 8.5). Although voluntary dismissal was not involved in the case, some courts have read the opinion as indicating that the same principle would apply to dismissal. For example, in In re *Rosson,* 545 F.3d 764 (9th Cir. 2008), the court rejected the debtor's argument that he had an absolute right to dismiss his Ch. 13 case, and upheld the bankruptcy court's discretion to deny his motion to dismiss on grounds of bad faith. However, this approach was criticized in In re Williams on the basis that the debtor's absolute right to dismiss is unequivocally provided for in §1307(b), and Marrama was concerned with the different statutory provisions governing conversion from Ch. 7 to Ch. 13.

Petitioners in an involuntary case may also decide to withdraw their case. Section 303(j) requires that such a voluntary dismissal be preceded by notice to all creditors and a hearing. If the debtor does not consent to the dismissal, the petitioners could be liable for costs or damages under §303(i). As noted in section 9.6.1, costs and fees may be awarded even if the petition was filed in good faith. If the petition was filed in bad faith, the court may also award compensatory, and even punitive, damages to the debtor.

(2) Dismissal for cause by a party other than the petitioner. Dismissal for cause is available under all chapters of the Code. The motion to dismiss must be heard by the court after notice. As discussed in section 9.6.3, the debtor may move to dismiss an involuntary petition on the grounds that there is a defect in the case or that it has not been properly prosecuted. Also, a creditor or other party in interest may move to dismiss the debtor's voluntary case for cause. Cause may consist of any one of a variety of reasons. Each of the sections dealing with dismissal sets out a nonexclusive list of some of these reasons, which, in the case of a voluntary petition, include various types of dilatory or uncooperative behavior by the debtor.

(3) Dismissal by the court on grounds of lack of cooperation, abuse of process, or bad faith. Various provisions of the Code empower the court or the U.S. Trustee to dismiss the case on specific or general grounds of improper conduct by the debtor. For example, §§707(a)(3), 1112(e), and 1307(c)(9) allow the U.S. Trustee to move for dismissal if the debtor in a voluntary case fails timely to file the information and schedules required under §521. In addition to these specific provisions, the court's equitable power under §105(a) allows it, on the motion of a party in interest or sua sponte, to dismiss a case in appropriate circumstances.

A common basis for dismissing a case on the motion of a party in interest or by the court is that the debtor filed the petition in bad faith. Bad faith is well established as cause for dismissal under Chs. 11, 12, and 13 because each of those chapters requires the debtor's plan to be proposed in good faith. As discussed in section 9.8.5, bad faith is also a cause for the dismissal of a consumer debtor's Ch. 7 case under the express terms of §707(b). However, the general grounds of dismissal in §707(a) make no express reference to bad faith as a cause for dismissal, and there is no provision in Ch. 7 that expressly imposes an obligation of good faith on a

Ch. 7 debtor. The nonexclusive list of grounds for dismissal set out in §707(a) includes only various forms of procedural noncompliance such as unreasonable delay by the debtor and failure to pay fees or to file required schedules. Although the list in §707(a) is nonexclusive and can therefore include cause beyond that specified, courts are divided on whether bad faith may be one of those causes. Some courts have concluded that §707(a) does not allow for dismissal on grounds of bad faith. They reason that the nonexclusive list of grounds for dismissal includes only forms of procedural noncompliance and that any additional unspecified basis for dismissal must likewise be based on technical or procedural violations of the Code. In addition, had Congress intended to include bad faith as a ground of dismissal under §707(a), it would have included it, as it did in §707(b), when it extensively amended §707 in BAPCPA. See, for example, In re Padilla, 222 F.3d 1184 (9th Cir. 2000); In re Adolph, 441 B.R. 909 (Bankr. N.D. Ill. 2011). Other courts have disagreed with this approach and have held that there is nothing in §707(a) that indicates congressional intent to restrict courts to dismissal for procedural noncompliance. Good faith and candor are prerequisites to the bankruptcy relief of a deserving debtor, and the court always has the discretion to dismiss a case on grounds of the debtor's lack of honesty or abusive motives. See, for example, Perlin v. Hitachi Capital America Corp., 497 F.3d 364 (3d Cir. 2007); In re Lombardo, 370 B.R. 506 (Bankr. E.D.N.Y. 2007). Quite apart from the basis of dismissal under 707(a), some courts have found the authority to dismiss a Ch. 7 case for bad faith in §105(a), which grants courts the general power to make orders necessary or appropriate to carry out the provisions of the Code. See In re Kestell, 99 F.3d 146 (4th Cir. 1996).

Courts that treat bad faith as grounds for dismissal evaluate many factors and look at all the circumstances of the case in deciding whether a debtor has filed a petition in bad faith. The factors that may indicate bad faith include the absence of attempts to pay creditors, the failure to reduce living expenses to a reasonable level, manipulation of assets and finances, a lack of candor in dealing with creditors or the court, and the ability to make substantial payments to creditors under a Ch. 11 or 13 plan. There is some controversy over the appropriateness of considering the debtor's ability to pay creditors under a plan. Some courts consider that any such means test should be confined to §707(b), and is not authorized in §707(a). Others, such as Perrin, hold that the fact that §707(b) specifically requires the court to consider the consumer debtor's ability to support a Ch. 13 plan does not lead to the negative implication that consideration of the debtor's ability to pay is excluded from the general grounds of dismissal in §707(a).

§9.8 DISMISSAL OF A CH. 7 CONSUMER CASE ON GROUNDS OF ABUSE

§9.8.1 The Application of §707(b) to "Individuals Whose Debts Are Primarily Consumer Debts"

Section 707(b) was originally enacted in 1984 and was significantly amended by BAPCPA. Its purpose, both in its earlier form and as amended by BAPCPA, is to attempt to control abusive Ch. 7 filings by consumer debtors. The entire discussion in this section applies only to consumer debtors, referred to in §707(b) as "individual debtors whose debts are primarily consumer debts." The Code does not define "individual, " but it means a human, as opposed to an incorporated entity.

The term "consumer debt" is defined in §101(8) to mean "debt incurred by an individual primarily for a personal, family, or household purpose." Although consumer debts are often thought of as being incurred in relation to consumable goods and services, courts generally read the definition in §101(8) more broadly to include debt used to acquire or maintain capital assets, provided that these assets are used for personal or household purposes. In In re Price, 280 B.R. 499 (9th Cir. B.A.P. 2002), the court, following In re Kelley, 841 F.2d 908 (9th Cir. 1988), held that a debt incurred to buy a home and secured by a home mortgage is a consumer debt.

As a general guideline, if the motive of a transaction was the generation of income, the indebtedness arising from it is not a consumer debt. If the individual debtor is engaged in business, any debts that she incurs in relation to that business will not be consumer debts. However, even a debtor who does not operate her own business may have debts that were not incurred for "personal, family, or household purposes." Courts evaluate the nature, source, and purpose of the debt in deciding whether an individual's debt, not directly related to the operation of a business, should be classified as a consumer debt. For example, income tax debts are generally held not to be consumer debts for various reasons: Income tax liability is incurred in the production of income — an economic pursuit. Even if a debtor uses this income for personal, household, or domestic purposes, it is the generation of income (a commercial activity), not its expenditure, that creates the tax liability. In addition, the involuntary nature of tax debt makes it awkward to assert that the debtor had the required household or personal purpose (or any purpose at all, for that matter) in incurring it. A tax debt does not arise from the extension of credit, and its purpose is public, not personal. See In re Brashers, 216 B.R. 59

(Bankr. N.D. Okla. 1998); In re Rucker, 454 B.R. 554 (Bankr. M.D. Ga. 2011). A debt for unpaid property or sales taxes is likewise generally not treated as a consumer debt. At first sight, a property tax on a debtor's home or a sales tax on consumer goods or services seems to be incurred for domestic and household purposes and seems, like a mortgage or car loan, to be a debt relating to the acquisition or upkeep of the debtor's household or personal property. However, courts apply the reasoning that the debt is involuntary and incurred for public purposes, rather than for household or personal purposes. Therefore, even if the debt is not a business debt, this does not mean that it is a consumer debt. This was the reasoning applied in relation to a debt for personal property taxes (a sales tax on a car that the debtor had bought) in In re Stovall, 209 B.R. 849 (Bankr. E.D. Va. 1997). See also In re Westberry, 215 F.3d 589 (6th Cir. 2000).

Courts have had difficulty in characterizing student loan debts. Some courts have held that education is an inherently personal benefit because knowledge is instilled in the student's mind. On this theory, it is a consumer debt. Other courts have held that education enhances a student's ability to earn, so educational debt is better characterized as incurred for a profit motive, and hence not a consumer debt. The situation is complicated further by the fact that many students use a portion of their loans for tuition and a portion for living expenses. In In Re Rucker, the court grappled with these questions and concluded that it is not possible to apply a per se rule to categorize a student loan debt. Instead, the court must examine the debt to determine whether and to what extent it was incurred for personal or profit purposes.

Note that both §707(b) and §101(8) use the word "primarily." Both sections contemplate that the individual may have some debt that is not consumer debt but that when the debtor's total indebtedness is analyzed, consumer debt predominates. In deciding whether an individual's debts are primarily consumer debts, courts tend to focus on the value but also take number into account. See, for example, In re Booth, 858 F.2d 1051 (5th Cir. 1988); In re Kelley, Where a debtor has both consumer and nonconsumer debts and the consumer debts are significantly greater in both number and amount, it is relatively easy to conclude that the debtor primarily owes consumer debts. However, this question is harder where there is a close equivalence between the consumer and nonconsumer debts, or where one category predominates in amount and the other in number. Courts tend to avoid any mechanical formula and try to glean the underlying nature and pattern of the debtor's affairs by looking at a combination of factors, including the number, amount, and nature of the debts as well as any other relevant circumstances. (See Examples 4 and 5.)

§9.8.2 The Background to BAPCPA's Amendment of §707(b): "Substantial Abuse" and the 1994 National Bankruptcy Review Commission

Section 8.6 briefly described the longstanding debate over the question of whether access to Ch. 7 liquidation should be easily available to all consumer debtors, or tightly restricted, so that it is reserved for those consumer debtors who really cannot afford to support a Ch. 13 plan. It is helpful to recount the background to the current version of §707(b) more fully before analyzing it.

Prior to 1984, the Code had no specific provision that allowed a court to dismiss a case on the grounds of abuse. Therefore, where a court felt that a debtor was taking the easy way out by filing under Ch. 7 instead of under Ch. 13 or Ch. 11, the basis for dismissing the case was the general ground of cause in §707(a). In 1984, Congress added §707(b), which provided simply that a court could dismiss a Ch. 7 case filed by an individual whose debts were primarily consumer debts if the court found that granting relief would be a "substantial abuse" of Ch. 7. Although §707(b) did not expressly mention that a consumer debtor's Ch. 7 filing would be abusive if the debtor could afford to support a Ch. 13 plan, this was the intended focus of the subsection. In 1984 Congress did consider, but rejected, a clearer and more absolute provision that would have required courts to take into account the debtor's ability to perform a Ch. 13 plan. Instead, Congress chose a provision that was relatively modest in its reach. The provision applied only to individuals whose debts were primarily consumer debts, could only be invoked by the court on its own motion or on the motion of the U.S. Trustee, required the abuse to be "substantial," and contained a presumption in favor of granting relief. "Substantial abuse" was not defined in the Code, and courts exercised discretion in deciding whether a Ch. 7 filing was substantially abusive. Some courts did treat the debtor's ability to pay more under Ch. 13 as a ground for dismissal on its own. Others took this into account but looked at the totality of the circumstances to decide if there had been substantial abuse. Many courts observed that Congress had given debtors the right to choose Ch. 7 relief, and that the presumption in favor of the debtor in §707(b) discouraged dismissal except in egregious cases.

The question of whether §707(b) should be amended to make it more restrictive divided the 1994 National Bankruptcy Review Commission. The majority did not recommend imposing any further restrictions on Ch. 7 relief, while dissenting Commissioners recommended that Congress impose a means test that would exclude consumer debtors from Ch. 7 if they had the means to pay their debts from future income under a Ch. 13 plan. Many members of Congress shared the view of the dissenting Commissioners, and a reform bill that included a means test was proposed in 1998, shortly after the Commission had submitted its report in 1997.

After several unsuccessful attempts to pass the reform bill, Congress did eventually enact BAPCPA in 2005, which amends §707(b) by including the means test. The amendment of §707(b) is probably the most controversial change that was made by BAPCPA. At the time of its enactment many critics predicted that it would be unworkable, would not achieve its desired ends, and would cause hardship to debtors who were not trying to abuse the Code but needed relief from genuine financial adversity. Quite apart from these policy concerns, the section presents great interpretational challenges because it is lengthy and is written in convoluted language that is difficult to read. Since its enactment, courts have done what they can to apply it in a coherent and rational manner, but it remains a troublesome provision.

§9.8.3 Overview of the BAPCPA Amendments

BAPCPA made no amendments to §707(a) relating to dismissal for cause. That section continues to operate as explained in section 9.7. BAPCPA did extensively amend §707(b), adding numerous tortuous (and torturous) subsections to it as well as a new subsection (c). The principal difference between the current §707(b) and its predecessor is the addition of the means test, explained below. The different spirit and tone of the amendment is suggested by three other changes: First, §707(b) no longer uses the term "substantial abuse," but merely speaks of "abuse." While this may not make a substantive difference, it does suggest an orientation away from the debtor. This shift away from the debtor is reinforced by the elimination of the presumption in the former version of §707(b) in favor of granting bankruptcy relief. BAPCPA also removed another barrier to dismissal. In its earlier form, a dismissal under §707(b) could be initiated only by the U.S Trustee or by the court on its own motion. The current §707(b) also gives standing to bring the motion to dismiss to the trustee and other parties in interest unless the debtor's annual income is below the median family income (as explained in section 9.8.4.)

Before tackling the provisions of §707(b), it is helpful to emphasize its basic purpose and to chart the relationship between its subsections. Its purpose is to act as a gatekeeper to Ch. 7 relief by allowing for the dismissal of abusive Ch. 7 petitions filed by individual consumer debtors. If the debtor's financial resources exceed the statutory means test, §707(b) creates a presumption of abuse, which the debtor must rebut to remain in Ch. 7. The section makes it clear that the debtor must make a compelling case, showing special circumstances, to rebut the presumption. If the debtor's financial resources are small enough to be below the level prescribed by the means test, the presumption does not arise. The case will only be dismissed if the party seeking dismissal can establish grounds based on the debtor's bad faith or the totality of the circumstances. The following analysis of §707 begins (in section 9.8.4) with subsections (b)(6) and (7). If a debtor meets the income qualifications of subsections (b)(6) and (7), there are restrictions on who may apply to dismiss the case, and the presumption of abuse is not to be applied. In that situation, the case is only to be dismissed where there are grounds to conclude, under §b(3), that the Ch. 7 filing is in fact an abuse of the Code. (*See* section 9.8.5.) Subsection (b)(2), discussed in sections 9.8.6 to 9.8.8, creates the means test that gives rise to the presumption of abuse and also provides for the grounds of its possible rebuttal. Subsection (b)(4) imposes sanctions on a debtor's attorney who acted unjustifiably or vexatiously in representing the debtor in filing an abusive Ch. 7 petition. Subsection (b)(5) permits the award of costs and attorney's fees to a debtor who successfully challenges a motion to dismiss that was filed unjustifiably.

§9.8.4 Distinguishing Debtors Who Earn Above and Below the Median Family Income and the Protections of §707(b)(6) and (7) to Below-Median Debtors

a. The Purpose of the Inquiry into the Relationship between the Debtor's Income and the Median Family Income

The first basic inquiry to be conducted under §707(b) is to determine if the debtor's income exceeds or is below the median family income for the "applicable state," that is, the debtor's state of residence. No presumption of abuse applies to a debtor whose income is below the median, and his case will not be dismissed unless actual abuse is established. A debtor whose income is above the median is subjected to the means test, and if he does not qualify under it, a presumption of abuse arises. The median family income therefore plays a crucial role in calculations under §707(b)(6) and (7). (As discussed in section 9.8.6, it is also significant in relation to the presumption in §707(b)(2).)

By using the median income of the debtor's state as a yardstick, §707(b) inevitably treats debtors from different states differently because median state incomes vary. It is therefore possible that a debtor's income may exceed the median in one state, but fall below it in another. In *Schulte v. United States*, 529 F.3d 343 (6th Cir. 2008), the debtor challenged the constitutionality of §707(b) on the grounds that its use of the median state income violated the constitutional requirement that Congress enact a uniform law of bankruptcy. The debtor's income exceeded the median for his home state, but would have been below the median in several other states. The court, applying the test of uniformity enunciated by the U.S. Supreme Court in *Hanover National Bank v. Moyses*, 186 U.S. 181 (1902) (discussed in section 5.3), rejected the debtor's argument. As long as the law is uniform in its general operation, the constitutional requirement of uniformity is not violated merely because the law operates differently as a result of the laws or circumstances applicable in different states.

b. The Determination of the Debtor's "Current Monthly Income"

The debtor's "current monthly income" is defined in §101(10A) to mean the average monthly income from all sources that the debtor receives during the six-month period ending on the last day of the calendar month preceding the filing. (The definition has some qualifications about the ending date of the time period, which we will not explore.) The definition specifies that it does not matter whether or not the income is taxable, and it includes regular payments made by another entity to the debtor for household expenses. These regular payments could be contributions to living expenses made by a relative or friend, or from any other source. For example, in *Blausey v. U.S. Trustee*, 552 F.3d 1124 (9th Cir. 2009), the court held that disability insurance benefits received regularly by the debtor should be included in the debtor's current monthly income. The definition expressly excludes Social Security benefits and certain payments made to victims of war crimes and terrorism.

The essential point about this definition is that it requires the debtor's income for a very short period—six months before the petition—to be averaged. It makes no allowance for longer-term income patterns, future changes in income, or temporary increases or decreases in income within the six-month period (such as the debtor being unemployed during any period, or working unusual amounts of overtime). The income calculation was described in *In re Littman*, 370 B.R. 820 (Bankr. D. Idaho 2007), as a snapshot of the debtor's income at the time of filing, intended as an immediate screening device. It is a bright-line cutoff that does not take into account whether the prefiling income is an accurate reflection of the debtor's actual prospective income during the course of the bankruptcy.[5] However, where the debtor's prefiling income is unusually inflated in the six-month period, this could form the basis of a showing of special circumstances to rebut the presumption of abuse. (*See* section 9.8.7.) Conversely, if the six-month income is unusually deflated, the debtor's actual prospective income could be the basis of dismissal for actual abuse. (*See* section 9.8.5.)

Because the median family income is an annual average, the debtor's current monthly income must be multiplied by 12 to get the debtor's annual income for comparison purposes. (Example 6 contains an exercise in comparing the debtor's current monthly income with the median family income.)

---

5. As you will see in section 20.7.3, if the debtor files under Ch. 13 (either because his Ch. 7 case is dismissed for abuse under §707(b) or because he chooses to file under Ch. 13) the debtor's current monthly income features in the calculation of the debtor's projected disposable income for purposes of determining the minimum amount that the debtor must pay to general unsecured creditors under the plan. As explained in section 20.7.3.b, in calculating projected disposable income, the court will take into account whether the debtor's current monthly income, as calculated under the statutory formula, is a reasonable representation of the income that the debtor will be likely to earn over the period of the plan.

c. The Meaning of "Median Family Income"

"Median family income" is defined in §101(39A) to mean the median family income as calculated and reported by the Bureau of the Census for the most recent year. If the Bureau has not reported the median income in the current year, the figure for the most recent year must be adjusted to reflect changes in the Consumer Price Index. The Census Bureau calculates and publishes median family income figures for each state. (These figures are available on the Bureau's website, *http://www.census.gov.*) The median income statistics show what the annual median income is in each state for households of various sizes.

d. The Different Treatment of Above- and Below-Median Debtors

If the debtor's income is greater than the median, any party in interest can move for dismissal of the case, and the formula set out in subsection (b)(2) must be used to decide if the presumption applies. However, the presumption does not apply to a below-median debtor. (*See* Example 6 for an illustration of this point.) This is because Congress accepted that debtors who earn less than the median family income do not earn enough to make any appreciable payment to creditors under a Ch. 13 plan and that such debtors should be allowed to obtain Ch. 7 relief unless abuse is clearly apparent as a ground for dismissal. Subsections (b)(6) and (7) therefore place two restrictions on the dismissal of a below-median debtor's Ch. 7 case for abuse. First, under subsection (b)(6), only the court on its own motion or the U.S. Trustee can initiate a dismissal under §707(b). The motion to dismiss may not be made by the other parties in interest who would otherwise have standing to move for dismissal. Second, subsection (b)(7) creates what is called a "safe harbor." It precludes application of the presumption of abuse where the debtor's current monthly income (for this purpose, combined with that of his spouse, even if the petition is not a joint petition) is less than the applicable median family income. (Note that the calculation of the debtor's current monthly income is different for purposes of subsections (b)(6) and (7).)

§9.8.5 The Finding of Abuse Where the Presumption of Abuse Does Not Apply

In cases where the presumption of abuse does not arise or is rebutted, the court may nevertheless dismiss the Ch. 7 case for abuse under §707(b)(1) if the applicant for dismissal establishes, or the court on its own motion determines, that the filing is abusive. BAPCPA added subsection (b)(3) to provide guidelines on what the court should consider in deciding if there has been abuse in the absence of the presumption: Whether the debtor has filed the petition in bad faith or the totality of the circumstances of the debtor's financial situation demonstrates abuse. The grounds of bad faith and totality of the circumstances are derived from pre-BAPCPA case law, and are separate and distinct grounds for dismissal. The ground of bad faith covers situations in which the debtor's conduct shows improper motives for filing the petition.[6] The totality of the circumstances test allows the court to consider a variety of factors to decide if, on balance, the filing constitutes an abuse of the Code. Courts take a number of considerations into account, including, for example, whether the petition was a response to sudden illness or calamity, whether the debtor had made excessive consumer purchases or racked up debt before filing, whether the debtor's budget is reasonable, whether the debtor had made attempts to deal with his creditors through negotiation or state law remedies, and whether the debtor's schedules are accurate. Courts are divided on the question of whether the debtor's ability to support a Ch. 13 plan should be taken into account in deciding abuse under the totality of the circumstances. Some courts consider this a proper consideration, while others hold that the means test calculation covers this issue, which should not be raised again in determining abuse on the totality of the circumstances. For an example of a case that deals with this issue and the other considerations to be taken into account in deciding abuse on the totality of the circumstances, see In re Walker, 381 B.R. 620 (Bankr. M.D. Pa. 2008).

In its reference to the totality of the circumstances test, subsection (b)(3) refers specifically to the filing of a Ch. 7 petition for the purposes of rejecting a personal services contract. This is a response to a number of cases where a well-paid debtor — typically a recording artist — sought to use bankruptcy as a means of getting out of a contract so that she could make a more lucrative contract with someone else. That motivation would be taken into account in determining abuse based on the totality of the circumstances.

§9.8.6 The Formula in §707(b)(2) to Determine if the Presumption of Abuse Applies

As noted before, §707(b)(1) contains the basic rule that the court, on its own motion or on the motion of the U.S. Trustee, the trustee, or any party in interest, may dismiss a case filed by an individual whose debts are primarily consumer debts if the court finds that the granting of relief would be an abuse of Ch. 7. Section 707(b)(2) makes it easier to establish abuse by creating a

---

6. As discussed in section 9.7, the grounds for dismissal for bad faith are expressly mentioned only in §707(b), so there is some difference of opinion on whether they might also be a basis for dismissal under §707(a). This is also discussed in Example 5.

presumption of abuse under prescribed circumstances. The presumption arises if, based on the formula set out in §707(b)(2), the debtor's disposable income would be sufficient to support a payment plan under Ch. 13. This is the means test that has often been mentioned previously in this book and has been the subject of so much debate and disagreement. It is important to understand the mechanics of the means test: If the debtor is shown to have disposable income in excess of that prescribed by the formula, a presumption arises that the debtor is abusing the provisions of Ch. 7. Unless the debtor can rebut this presumption, grounds for dismissal under §707(b)(1) are established. Section 707(b)(2)(C) requires the debtor's schedule of income and expenditures, filed under §521, to provide information on current monthly income as well as a calculation showing whether the presumption applies. Under the former version of §707(b), courts had considerable discretion in deciding whether substantial abuse existed. Section 707(b)(2) is deliberately intended to reduce that discretion and to impose a less flexible test under which the court "shall" presume abuse if the calculation of the debtor's income and expenses under the prescribed formula shows that the debtor will have disposable income deemed sufficient to support a five-year Ch. 13 plan.

The formula for determining the presumption of abuse is set out in §707(b)(2)(A)(i):

---

1. Calculate the debtor's **current monthly income** as defined in §101(10)(A).
2. Deduct from this monthly income **the debtor's monthly expenses**, which are determined by adding together the amounts allowed under subsections (b)(2)(A)(ii), (iii), and (iv).
3. This will provide a figure for the debtor's **net monthly income** (that is, his disposable income).
4. This disposable income is then multiplied by 60 to provide a **five-year total figure** for the debtor's **net disposable income.**
5. This 60-month disposable income figure is then compared to the prescribed standards. Abuse is presumed if the figure is **not less than the lesser of:**
   (a) the greater of 25% of the debtor's nonpriority unsecured claims in the case, or $7,475,
   or
   (b) $12,475.[7]

---

7. The dollar amounts in §707(b)(2)(A)(i) are adjusted every three years under §104. The amounts here are those in effect from April 1, 2013. They will be adjusted again with effect from April 1, 2016.

That is, if the debtor's disposable income in item 4 of the formula equals or exceeds the amount calculated under item 5, the debtor fails the means test and the presumption of abuse arises. The debtor must then try to rebut the presumption to avoid dismissal of the Ch. 7 case. The components of this formula need further explanation:[8]

(1) The debtor's current monthly income. The meaning of "current monthly income" has already been explained in section 9.8.4. It is essentially the average of the monthly income that the debtor derived from all sources within the six months before filing the petition. As noted before, this six-month snapshot of the debtor's earnings may or may not accurately represent his real historic earnings over a longer term or his likely prospective earnings.

(2) The debtor's monthly expenses. Subsections (b)(2)(A)(ii), (iii), and (iv) set out the permissible monthly expenses that the debtor may deduct from her current monthly income to arrive at the net disposable income. These provisions are very restrictive: Their purpose is to control very tightly what a debtor may claim as living expenses. The expense allowances are complex and raise many interpretational questions. They fall into three broad categories: living expenses, secured debt payments, and priority debt payments.

With a few adjustments, mentioned below, the maximum living expenses that the debtor may claim are fixed by the National Standards and Local Standards issued by the I.R.S. and in effect for the debtor's place of residence at the time of the order for relief. (These standards may be found on the websites of the I.R.S. and the U.S. Trustee.) Some of the standardized expenses are applicable nationwide, and some take local conditions into account. The I.R.S. promulgated these standardized expense allowances for its own purposes. They are guidelines to provide a consistent approach in determining how much a delinquent taxpayer should be required to pay each month under a payment plan to satisfy a tax debt. Congress decided to use these same standards for the purpose of controlling a debtor's claim of living expenses for purposes of §707(b). The standards include amounts for housing, utilities, transport, food, clothing, and other necessary expenses for the support and welfare of the debtor. In calculating expenses for the purposes of the formula, the debtor may use the amounts specified in the standards even if they are higher than the debtor's actual expenses. However, the debtor is confined to the amount specified in the standards, even if his own actual expenses are higher. Courts had been split on whether a debtor was allowed to claim a listed expense irrespective of

---

8. *See* Example 6 for an exercise in applying the formula.

whether he actually incurred any expense in that category. For example, the standards allow the debtor to include a set amount for vehicle ownership expenses. Some courts only permitted a debtor to include this amount in his expenses if he actually had payments on a car loan or lease. Other courts held that because the expenses were standard, the debtor could deduct an expense item irrespective of his personal circumstances. This question was settled by the U.S. Supreme Court in *Ransom v. FIA Card Services, N.A.*, 131 S. Ct. 716 (2011),[9] which held that a debtor who owns his car free of debt and has no actual loan or lease expenses cannot claim the car ownership expense. The court reached this conclusion on a plain meaning interpretation of §707(b)(2)(A)(ii)(1), which allows the debtor to claim "applicable" expense amounts under the National and Local Standards. In its ordinary meaning, "applicable" connotes appropriate and relevant expenses that correspond to the debtor's actual financial circumstances. The court found this reading of the section to be reinforced by the Code's purpose of maximizing payment to creditors. (Although the debtor could not claim car ownership expenses, he was entitled to claim the allowance for car operating costs, which is included as a separate item in the Standards.)

In addition to the expenses allowed by the I.R.S. standards, §707(b)(2) recognizes a limited and carefully circumscribed group of additional expenses that a debtor can include as expenses in his budget. Some are generally available, and some apply only to debtors in special circumstances. For example, all debtors may claim reasonably necessary health and disability insurance; a debtor can claim an increase of up to 5 percent in the I.R.S. standards for food and clothing if the debtor demonstrates this as reasonable and necessary; a debtor may claim a housing and utility allowance above the I.R.S. standards if these are his actual costs and if he can demonstrate why the expense is reasonable and necessary; a debtor who has been supporting an elderly, chronically ill, or disabled household member or family member may include those payments provided that they are a continuation of payments made before bankruptcy, they are actual, reasonable, and necessary expenses, and the dependent is not able to pay these expenses himself; some allowance is made for additional educational expenses for a dependent child, subject to a maximum amount and to proper explanation and justification.

Because the goal of the budget is to determine how much disposable income a debtor would have in a Ch. 13 case, the debtor's monthly expenses also take into account some of the payments and expenses that the debtor would incur in a Ch. 13 case in relation to secured and priority debts.

---

9. *Ransom* involved a Ch.13 case, so the calculation of the debtor's disposable income was for the purpose of determining the amount the debtor was required by §1325(b)(2) to pay under the plan, not for the purpose of deciding if a Ch. 7 petition should be dismissed. However, §1325(b)(2) uses the Local and National Standards adopted by §707(b)(2) in calculating disposable income for Ch. 13 purposes.

Therefore, a debtor who is eligible for Ch. 13 may include in her monthly expenses the actual expenses of administering a Ch. 13 plan in the district in which the debtor resides, up to 10 percent of projected plan payments. The debtor may also include as expenses her average monthly payments on secured debts. These payments are calculated by using the total of all amounts due on secured debt in each month over the 60-month postpetition period, plus any additional amounts that the debtor would have to pay a secured claimant to keep possession of her primary residence, motor vehicle, or other property reasonably necessary for the support of the debtor or her dependents. The debtor's allowable expenses also include the amount that would be payable on priority claims in a Ch. 13 case, calculated by adding all the priority claims in the estate and dividing them by 60 to get the monthly payment amount. Although a debtor can include secured and priority claims in her budget, the subsection makes it clear that payments due on unsecured debt are not to be included. The obvious reason for this is that the formula seeks to establish the debtor's disposable income available to pay these very claims.

The provision for including secured and priority debts in the expense calculation is expressed here in simplified terms that mask its many interpretational difficulties. One of these is whether some degree of double-counting results from allowing the debtor both a standard I.R.S. living expense deduction and a secured claim deduction for an automobile and a home.

(3) The final calculation.   After the debtor's current monthly income and allowable monthly expenses have been determined, the expenses are deducted from income to give a net monthly surplus, which is the amount that the debtor is deemed to have available to pay to the trustee each month under a Ch. 13 plan. The final calculation (in point 5 of the formula set out in the box above) is intended to determine if this disposable income is sufficient to support a viable Ch. 13 plan. The calculation sounds really confusing because of its horrible combination of "less," "lesser," and "greater." It boils down to this: If, after the debtor's allowable monthly expenses are deducted from her current monthly income —

1. There is $124.58 or less left over per month as disposable income, the debtor's 60-month disposable income is $7,475 or less. The debtor therefore satisfies the means test (more accurately described as a "lack of means" test), and the presumption of abuse does not apply.
2. There is $207.91 or more left over per month as disposable income, the debtor's 60-month disposable income exceeds $12,475. The debtor therefore fails the means test, and the presumption of abuse applies.
3. There is between $124.58 and $207.91 left over per month as disposable income, the presumption applies if the debtor's 60-month disposable income exceeds 25 percent of her nonpriority unsecured debt.

Stated slightly differently, if the debtor's monthly repayment capacity under the formula is less than $124.58, no presumption arises. If it is more than $207.91, the presumption takes effect. If it is between these two amounts, the presumption only arises if the debtor's 60-month payment capacity exceeds 25 percent of her nonpriority unsecured debt. Say, for example, that the debtor's monthly repayment capacity is $150, making a 60-month capacity $9,000. His nonpriority unsecured debt is $34,000, 25 percent of which is $8,500. Abuse is presumed. However, if his nonpriority unsecured debt is $37,000, no presumption arises because 25 percent of the debt is $9,250, which exceeds his 60-month capacity.

§9.8.7 Rebuttal of the Presumption of Abuse

If the presumption of abuse arises because the debtor's 60-month disposable income exceeds the limits set by §707(b)(2), the debtor has an opportunity to rebut the presumption. (As mentioned in section 9.8.5 above, if the presumption is rebutted, the court must decide whether or not to dismiss the case under the considerations set out in subsection (b)(3).)

Subsection (b)(2)(B) sets out what a debtor must show to rebut the presumption. The basis for rebuttal is written in narrow and stringent terms. Subsection (b)(2)(B)(i) provides that the presumption of abuse may only be rebutted by demonstrating special circumstances, such as a serious medical condition or a call to active military duty, and only to the extent that the special circumstances justify an increase in expenses or an adjustment to current monthly income for which there is no reasonable alternative. The two examples of special circumstances set out in the subsection suggest that Congress has quite desperate circumstances in mind to justify a departure from the standardized expenses or the statutorily determined current monthly income. Therefore, although courts are given some flexibility in subsection (b)(2)(B) to take the debtor's personal circumstances into account and to mitigate any harsh or unrealistic results of the standardized means test, this discretion seems quite circumscribed. Courts have differed on how stringent a test to employ in deciding whether the debtor has shown circumstances sufficiently exigent to rebut the presumption. Some courts have refused to find the debtor's circumstances compelling enough to overcome the presumption unless they are equivalent in severity to the two examples set out in the section, and are beyond the debtor's control. Others have adopted a more flexible approach, and have been willing to overturn the presumption on a showing by the debtor of a reasonable basis for finding that the disposable income projected by the formula is unrealistic. For an example of a case that adopts the more flexible approach, see In re Littman, 370 B.R. 820 (Bankr. D. Idaho 2007).

Subsection (b)(2)(B)(ii) places the burden on the debtor to provide full itemization, documentation, and an explanation of any claim of adjustment. Subsection (b)(2)(B)(iii) requires the debtor to attest under oath to the accuracy of the information. Subsection (b)(2)(B)(iv) provides that the presumption of abuse may only be rebutted if the adjustments established by the debtor have the effect of reducing the debtor's disposable income to a level below that which gave rise to the presumption in the first place. That is, if the court accepts the debtor's claim of special circumstances, the adjustments to expenses or income are made, and the end result of the formula (the final step of item 5 of the formula in section 9.8.7) must be recalculated. The presumption is only rebutted if the ultimate figure, as adjusted, shows a low enough 60-month disposable income to pass the means test.

§9.8.8 Sanctions

Subsections 707(b)(4) and (5) are intended to sanction improper or vexatious conduct, either by the attorney representing a debtor or by a party in interest who files a motion to dismiss. Subsection (b)(4)(C) provides that an attorney's signature on a petition or other pleading or motion constitutes a certification that the attorney has reasonably investigated the circumstances; has determined that the petition, pleading, or motion is well grounded in fact and warranted in law; and has no knowledge, after inquiry, that any information in the document is incorrect. Subsection (b)(4)(B) authorizes the court, on its own motion or on motion of a party in interest, to award the trustee's costs and attorney's fees against the debtor's attorney where the court grants the trustee's motion to dismiss for abuse and the court finds that the debtor's attorney has acted wrongfully in filing the case by violating the provisions of Bankruptcy Rule 9011. Subsection (b)(4)(C) also allows for the award of a civil penalty against a debtor's attorney for a violation of Rule 9011.

Subsection (b)(5) allows for an award of attorney's fees and costs to the debtor where the debtor successfully contests a motion to dismiss and the party in interest (other than the trustee or the U.S. Trustee) acted unjustifiably in moving to dismiss the Ch. 7 case.

§9.9 THE CREDITORS' MEETING

After the order for relief, the U.S. Trustee must convene a meeting of creditors under §341. The meeting is held in all cases, whether under Ch. 7, 11, 12, or 13. Rule 2003 requires the meeting to take place between 21 and 40 days after the order for relief in a Ch. 7 or 11 case (the periods are slightly different in Ch. 12 and 13 cases), subject to some leeway for the court to set a different time. Under Rule 2002, the clerk of the court must give creditors at least 21 days' notice of the meeting.

Section 341 requires the U.S. Trustee to preside at the creditors' meeting. The bankruptcy judge is not involved and is in fact barred from attending by §341(c).[10] The principal purpose of the meeting is the examination of the debtor under §343 by creditors, the trustee, or the U.S. Trustee. A debtor who fails to appear or to answer truthfully can be penalized by dismissal of the voluntary petition, denial of the discharge, or even criminal charges if perjury or fraud are involved. Rule 2004 governs the content and scope of the examination, which may range over the debtor's financial affairs, conduct, and other matters relevant to the administration of the estate or the discharge. In addition to examining the debtor, creditors in a Ch. 7 case may elect a trustee or a creditors' committee at the meeting. As noted in sections 6.2 and 6.5, this power is not frequently exercised.

Examples

1. Cookie Crumbles owns and operates a bakery. She has the following creditors:

   Seven trade creditors to which she owes a total of $100,000 for goods supplied on unsecured credit.

   Her dough supplier, U.O. Dough Co., to which she owes $20,000 for goods supplied. This debt is secured by a perfected security interest in accounts receivable valued at $3,000.

   A finance company, to which she owes $15,000 on a loan, secured by a perfected security interest in equipment worth $20,000.

   A bank, to which Cookie is obligated under a suretyship agreement. She executed the suretyship to guarantee a loan of $50,000 made by the bank to her son. The bank's loan to Cookie's son is not yet payable, and therefore not in default.

   Two employees, to whom she owes $5,000 in arrear wages.

   An advertising agency, which claims $8,000 for advertising services. Cookie has refused to pay the agency because she says it failed to properly perform services under their contract.

   Cookie's mother, who lent her $12,000 to pay operating expenses.

   Cookie's bakery business has been struggling over the last several months, and she has had trouble paying her debts. She has missed payments to five of her seven trade creditors, as well as to U.O. Dough Co., the finance company, and her employees. She has managed to make arrangements for extensions with two trade creditors, the finance

---

10. Prior to 1978, the judge did preside at the meeting. This function was terminated and placed in the hands of the U.S. Trustee as part of the reforms designed to eliminate the court's administrative functions. *See* section 6.3.

company, and her employees, but the other three trade creditors have commenced collection proceedings against her. Cookie's mother has not yet asked for payment of her loan. Cookie is litigating with the advertising agency over its claim. U.O. Dough Co. has just filed an involuntary Ch. 7 petition against her. Is U.O. Dough Co. qualified to file the petition?

2. Assuming that U.O. Dough Co. is qualified, may it file the petition on its own, or must it find two other creditors to join as petitioners?

3. Irrespective of your answers to Examples 1 and 2, assume that U.O. Dough Co. is qualified and may file the petition on its own. Cookie controverts the petition. Does it seem, on the facts given, that U.O. Dough Co. will be able to establish grounds for relief?

4. An individual debtor has just filed a Ch. 7 petition. Her schedule of assets and liabilities shows that she has three secured debts totaling $300,000 and 15 unsecured debts totaling $90,000. Her largest secured debt, constituting 60 percent of her total secured indebtedness, is a loan for the purchase of investment property, secured by the property itself. The other two secured debts, making up the remaining 40 percent, are a home mortgage and a purchase money interest on an expensive luxury car. Of her unsecured debts, 14 are for credit purchases of consumer goods and services. These make up 50 percent of her total unsecured debt. The other half of her unsecured debt consists of a single debt for attorney's fees incurred in litigation concerning her investment activities. Is the debtor's case subject to dismissal under §707(b)?

5. Tex E. Vader has just filed a Ch. 7 petition. His largest debts are owed to the federal and state governments for arrear income taxes and overdue property taxes on his home. Although part of this indebtedness is a nondischargeable priority claim (as will be discussed in Ch. 22), the greater portion of it does not qualify for priority treatment and will be discharged in the Ch. 7 case. These tax debts constitute about 70 percent of the claims against the estate. The rest are for consumer loans and credit cards. Tex earns a good income and could afford to pay a significant part of his dischargeable debt under a Ch. 13 plan. He has filed a Ch. 7 petition because, as he has told many people, "I worked hard for that money and need it more than the government does."

   Should Tex's petition be dismissed for abuse?

6. Lois Incum is unmarried and lives alone in a rented apartment. She is employed as a bartender. Her gross monthly salary before taxes is $2,000, and she also receives income from tips that varies from month to month. Her total tip income for the last six months was $3,000. Her kindly grandmother sends her a check of $100 every

month "to help her out," and has been doing so regularly for some years. Three months ago, Lois took unpaid leave for two months to travel. Lois has been living above her means and has accumulated debt of $75,000, all incurred in purchases of consumer goods and services. Lois finds it impossible to pay off this indebtedness, and her creditors are losing patience. Lois's only assets are a retirement account, an old car, a small bank account, and miscellaneous clothing, furniture, and household goods.

Lois wishes to file a Ch. 7 petition because she does not like the idea of committing herself to sacrificing any of her future income to the payment of her creditors under a Ch. 13 plan. It is clear that if Lois enters Ch. 7 bankruptcy, her creditors will receive little or no payment because her assets are either exempt or of low value.

Assume that the median family income for a single person in Lois's state of residence is $40,000 per annum. Assume also that Lois's allowable monthly expenses, based on the I.R.S. National and Local Standards plus the additional expenses permitted by §707(b)(2), amount to $4,000 per month.

a. If Lois files a Ch. 7 petition, is it likely that her case will be dismissed for abuse?

b. In addition to her salary, tips, and the payment from her grandmother, Lois receives $2,500 a month from a trust fund established by her father for her benefit. Does this additional fact make it likely that her case will be dismissed for abuse?

c. How does the answer to question (b) change if Lois's allowable expenses under §707(b)(2) are $4,400 per month?

d. Assume that Lois's unsecured nonpriority debt is $75,000. Her current monthly income is as in questions (b) and (c), but her allowable monthly expenses are $4,300. How does this change the answer?

Explanations

1. U.O. Dough Co. is qualified to be a petitioner. Although it has some security for its claim, the value of the collateral is only $3,000. U.O. Dough Co. therefore has an unsecured deficiency of $17,000. Its unsecured claim exceeds the $15,325 required by §303(b)(1). (As noted in section 9.6.2, the qualifying amounts in §303(b) are adjusted periodically under §104.) The facts do not suggest that there is any problem in satisfying the other qualifying requirements of §303(b): The claim is not contingent or subject to a bona fide dispute.

2. Even though U.O. Dough Co. qualifies as a petitioner, it cannot proceed on its own unless Cookie has 11 or fewer creditors. Section 303(b) requires 3 creditors to file the petition if the debtor has 12 or more

creditors. Cookie has 14 creditors — 7 unsecured trade creditors, U.O. Dough Co., the finance company, the bank, 2 employees, her mother, and the advertising agency. However, not all of these creditors are counted for the purpose of §303(b). In counting the number of claim holders for the purpose of determining whether there are fewer than 12, employees, insiders, and transferees of avoidable transfers are excluded by the express terms of §303(b)(2). In addition, §303(b)(2) says that there must be fewer than 12 "such holders." The "such" refers to the claimants described in §303(b)(1), whose claims must be noncontingent and undisputed. Thus, in addition to the three express exclusions, §303(b)(2) also excludes from the count all holders of contingent or bona fide disputed claims. The bank's claim on the suretyship is contingent because a surety's obligation is contingent on a future uncertain event — the default of the principal debtor. Cookie's son has not yet defaulted on the debt. The advertising agency's claim is subject to a dispute that is apparently bona fide — there seems to be a legitimate dispute that is currently under litigation. In addition, the claims of the two employees and Cookie's mother are excluded because they are insiders as defined in §101(31). Although a secured claim cannot be counted for the purpose of determining the aggregate amount of debt for the creditor qualifications under §303(b)(1), secured creditors are not excluded from the creditor count under §303(b)(2). The reference to "such holders" in §303(b)(2) relates only to the requirements of non-contingency and lack of bona fide dispute in §303(b)(1). Therefore, neither U.O. Dough Co. nor the finance company is excluded from the creditor count.

Once the five creditors listed above are excluded, Cookie is left with nine creditors for the purpose of §303(b), and U.O. Dough Co. may petition on its own.

3. If the debtor controverts the petition, §303(h) requires the petitioner to establish one of two grounds for relief. The second ground in §303(h) does not apply. No custodian had been appointed or took possession of Cookie's property. Relief must therefore be based on the fact that Cookie is not paying her debts as they become due. The express language of §303(h)(1) excludes bona fide disputed debts from the determination of general nonpayment. Therefore, provided that Cookie's dispute over the advertising agency's debt has genuine merit, it must not be treated as an unpaid debt. If that debt is excluded, Cookie is in default on eight of her 14 debts. However, she has made extension agreements with all but three of these creditors. In determining whether a debtor is generally not paying debts as they become due, the court takes into account not only the number, value, and importance of overdue debts but also the debtor's overall financial situation, including the period and circumstances of

default, arrangements made with creditors to cure defaults, and the debtor's general financial viability. A court will not likely place a debtor in involuntary liquidation if it appears that the debtor may overcome her financial adversity and that the overall interests of the debtor and her creditors are best served by allowing the debtor to try to cope with her financial difficulties under state law. Although we do not have enough facts for a final determination, it appears that U.O. Dough Co. will not likely be able to establish grounds for relief.

4. Section 707(b) is only applicable to an individual whose debts are primarily consumer debts. Section 101(8) defines "consumer debts" as those incurred primarily for personal, family, or household purposes. A debt incurred to acquire a capital asset (such as a home or a car) is properly characterized as a consumer debt if the asset is to be used for personal or household purposes. Conversely, if the motive of a transaction was the generation of income, the indebtedness arising from it is not a consumer debt. Only two of the debtor's debts have a business purpose — the secured claim for the purchase of the investment property and the attorney's fee. This means that two out of three secured debts, constituting 40 percent in value of total secured debt, and 14 out of 15 unsecured debts, constituting 50 percent in value of the total unsecured debt, are consumer debts. If the secured and unsecured debts are looked at in combination, 16 of 18 of her debts, constituting 42 percent of her total debt in value are consumer debts: They are a majority of her debts in number, but a minority in amount.

In deciding whether an individual's debts are primarily consumer debts, courts tend to look at both the number and value of the debts. In this case, these factors pull in opposite directions. The relative amounts of consumer and nonconsumer debt may be decisive, but it is difficult to predict this with certainty. If the court finds that the nonconsumer debt predominates, the only basis for dismissal is for cause under §707(a). If it finds that the debts are primarily consumer debts, the debtor will be subject to dismissal for abuse under §707(b).

5. If the tax debts are consumer debts, Tex's debts would clearly be primarily consumer debts, and the issue would be whether the petition should be dismissed for abuse under §707(b). However, as explained in section 9.8.1, tax debts (whether for income tax or property tax) are generally held not to be consumer debts. Income tax liability is incurred in the production of income — an economic pursuit, and liability for both income and property taxes is imposed by law and therefore cannot be said to be incurred by the debtor for personal, family, or household purposes.

Although Tex's filing seems to be abusive — he is trying to use Ch. 7 to discharge debt that he could afford to pay under a Ch. 13 plan — Tex's debts are not primarily consumer debts in nature, so the case cannot be dismissed for abuse under §707(b). Therefore, if the court considers it proper to dismiss Tex's case, it has to do so on grounds other than abuse under §707(b). There are two other possible bases of dismissal.

The court has the power to dismiss a case on the general ground of cause under §707(a). As discussed in section 9.7, it is not clear if "cause" under §707(a) includes bad faith or abuse of the provisions of Ch. 7. Some courts have confined §707(a) to procedural noncompliance and have declined to extend it to bad faith and abuse. Other courts have disagreed, and have held that the court does have discretion to dismiss for bad faith under §707(a). Given the Code's goal of affording relief to an honest and deserving debtor, the latter approach seems more appropriate. Apart from dismissal under §707(a), the court should be able to order dismissal of the case by using its general power under §105(a) to make any order necessary or appropriate to carry out the provisions of the Code.

6. a. Lois is an individual, and the facts state that her debt is all consumer debt, so §707(b) is clearly applicable. To determine how it will operate in Lois's situation, we divide the inquiry into logically successive steps.

   Step 1. Determine Lois's current monthly income as defined by §101(10A). This includes all the actual income that Lois receives from all sources over the six-month period ending on the calendar month prior to filing the petition, added up and divided by six to get a monthly average. Section 101(10A) does not expressly say whether or not this is pretax income, but gross income is used. (*See* Official Form 22.) The definition makes it clear that income includes income from all sources, not just salary, irrespective of whether the income is taxable, and including regular contributions to the debtor's living expenses from other people. (The definition excludes Social Security payments or payments to the debtor on account of her status as a war or terrorist victim.)

   Therefore, the fact that Lois only earned a salary for four of the last six months reduces her current monthly income for the purpose of §707(b), even though the trip may be a one-time event, and Lois normally works full-time and plans to continue to do so. Her total income from all sources in the last six months is $11,600 ($8,000 in salary, $3,000 in tips, and $600 from her grandmother). By dividing this figure by six, we get a current monthly income of $1,933.

   Step 2. Compare the debtor's income to the median income for the debtor's state. If the debtor's current monthly income multiplied by 12 (to get the debtor's annual income) is less than the median annual income for a household of the debtor's size in the debtor's state of residence, the presumption of abuse does not apply, so the petition can be dismissed only if abuse is established on other grounds. In addition, only the court on its own motion or the U.S. Trustee may raise the issue of abuse. Lois's annual income is $23,196 ($1,933 multiplied by 12). Because Lois lives alone, this must be compared to the median family income for a single-person household in Lois's state, as published by the Census Bureau. The facts state that this is $40,000. Lois's annual income is lower than the median, so the presumption is inapplicable. Lois's Ch. 7 case can only be dismissed on other grounds, at the instance of the court or the U.S. Trustee. We do not get beyond step 2 on these facts, but question (b) allows us to proceed to step 3.

b. The additional income changes matters considerably.

Steps 1 and 2. Lois's current monthly income is now increased by the trust fund payments, which come to $15,000 for the six months prior to the petition. Her total income for the six-month period is therefore $26,600 ($11,600 plus $15,000). By dividing this figure by six, we arrive at a current monthly income of $4,433. This figure multiplied by 12 gives us an annual income of $53,196, which exceeds the applicable median family income. Because Lois's income is higher than the median, the formula in §707(b)(2) must be applied to decide if there is a presumption of abuse.

Step 3. Apply the formula to determine Lois's disposable monthly income. To perform this step, we must deduct Lois's monthly expenses from her current monthly income to determine if the income she has available each month after paying her expenses is deemed enough to support a Ch. 13 plan. For the income figure, we use her current monthly income of $4,433, as calculated in step 1. For her expenses, we do not use her own budget and are not concerned with what she actually spends or what she says she needs. Rather, we use the standardized expenses promulgated by the I.R.S. in its National Standards and Local Standards, together with those additional expenses authorized by §707(b)(2). The nature of these expenses is explained in section 9.8.6(b). The facts state that her allowable monthly expenses are $4,000. After her allowable expenses are deducted from her current monthly income, she is left with a surplus of $433 per month, which is the disposable income that she is deemed to have each month after paying her necessary living expenses.

Step 4. Determine if Lois's disposable income is high enough to trigger the presumption of abuse. Lois's monthly disposable income must be multiplied by 60 to give her total expected disposable income over the period of a five-year repayment plan. If this figure is under $7,475, the presumption does not apply. If it is over $12,475, the presumption does apply. If it is between these two figures, the presumption applies if the five-year disposable income exceeds 25 percent of Lois's general unsecured debt. Lois's five-year disposable income is $25,980 ($433 multiplied by 60), so she is well over the $12,475 ceiling and her filing is presumed abusive. Her Ch. 7 petition will be dismissed unless she can rebut the presumption by showing special circumstances as explained in section 9.8.7.

c. Steps 3 and 4 need to be recalculated if we increase Lois's allowed monthly expenses to $4,400. She now has monthly disposable income of $33 ($4,433 minus $4,400). Her five-year disposable income ($33 multiplied by 60) is $1,980, which is below the $7,475 minimum. Although Lois's income is high enough to call for application of the formula, once her expenses are taken into account, her five-year disposable income turns out to be too low to give rise to the presumption of abuse.

d. Again, we must recalculate steps 3 and 4. Lois's monthly expenses are now $4,300, which, deducted from her income of $4,433, leaves her with a monthly disposable income of $133. Multiply this by 60 to get a five-year disposable income of $7,980. This is between the minimum cutoff of $7,475 and the maximum of $12,475, so the presumption only applies if $7,980 exceeds 25 percent of Lois's general unsecured debt. Twenty five percent of $75,000 is $18,750, which is more than Lois's 60-month disposable income. The presumption does not arise.

The Automatic Stay

§10.1 INTRODUCTION

In simple terms, the automatic stay is an injunction that arises by operation of law immediately upon the commencement of the bankruptcy case. The act of filing the bankruptcy petition is all that is required to bring it into effect. No application for the injunction is made, and no court order is needed.

The stay is provided for in §362. Its effect is to impose a wide-ranging prohibition on all activity outside the bankruptcy forum to collect prepetition debts from the debtor or to assert or enforce claims against the debtor's prepetition property or estate property. The range of the stay, delineated by §362(a) and (b), is examined in section 10.4. Before studying the details of those provisions, it is helpful to outline the purpose, nature, and scope of the stay.

§10.2 THE PURPOSE OF THE AUTOMATIC STAY

The automatic stay is a very important incident of bankruptcy. It is essential to the accomplishment of its two central goals: the debtor's fresh start and the evenhanded treatment of creditors. By halting individual creditor action to enforce or collect debts due by the debtor, the stay prevents depletion of the debtor's assets and preserves them for surrender to the trustee or retention by the debtor in possession. Creditors can no longer seek advantage by pressing on with nonbankruptcy enforcement measures; they are compelled to channel their claims through the bankruptcy process. In addition to preserving the estate, the stay gives the debtor sanctuary from creditor pressure so that orderly liquidation can be arranged or a plan formulated for the debtor's rehabilitation.

The stay is also vital to the bankruptcy court's power to deal effectively with the case and related litigation. By stopping enforcement proceedings in other courts, it allows the bankruptcy court to exercise its jurisdiction and to assume the central role described in Chapter 7. Henceforth, all litigation relating to the case must be brought before the bankruptcy court and will be resolved there, unless the court itself permits continuation of the proceedings elsewhere by abstaining or granting relief from the stay.

The freezing of all debt collection activity benefits the creditor body as a whole by preserving the estate for evenhanded distribution. However, the interests of creditors in general often run counter to the interests of a particular creditor whose enforcement or collection efforts are halted by the stay. Usually the creditor can do no more than accept the inevitability of the stay, prove a claim in the estate, and await whatever distribution it will receive from the estate. However, in some situations a creditor whose enforcement efforts are impeded by the stay may be able to demonstrate grounds for lifting it so that the bankruptcy court authorizes the continuation of the enforcement process. The circumstances under which relief from stay may be granted are discussed in Chapter 11.

§10.3 THE NATURE AND SCOPE OF THE STAY

As stated before, the stay is an automatic injunction that bars a broad range of action against the debtor, the property of the debtor, and property of the estate. The nature and scope of the stay can be best understood if the following general principles are kept in mind.

(1) The stay is binding on all entities.   "Entities" is defined in §101(15) to include individuals, corporate entities of all kinds, and governmental units.

(2) The stay comes into effect upon the filing of the petition.   This holds true for both voluntary and involuntary cases. In an involuntary case, therefore, the stay precedes the order for relief and operates much like a preliminary injunction prior to the adjudication of bankruptcy.

(3) The stay generally remains in effect until the case is closed or dismissed.   (*See* section 10.5 for details.) Therefore, if an involuntary

petition is denied, the stay ends. However, it was fully effective pending the order for relief, so any act in violation of the stay prior to dismissal of the case is ineffective and could result in sanctions. The same is generally true in a voluntary case: Although dismissal ends the stay, the termination of the stay is prospective, not retrospective, so the dismissal does not validate or excuse violations that occurred before dismissal. Courts are not in agreement on the effect of the stay where a voluntary case is dismissed because the debtor is ineligible for relief under §109. Some courts have interpreted the requirements of §109 as jurisdictional because the section talks of who may or may not be a debtor under the Code. On this view, the filing is a nullity where the debtor is ineligible for relief, so that no stay arises at all. The more prevalent view, however, is that §109 is not jurisdictional, but merely sets out qualifications to be satisfied to avoid dismissal of the case. On this approach, even if the case is dismissed, the stay was effective between the time of filing and dismissal, and creditor action in violation of the stay can be sanctioned. See, for example, In re Brown, 342 B.R. 248 (Bankr. D. Md. 2006); In re Zarnel, 619 F.3d 156 (2d Cir. 2010), in which the courts held that the stay was effective until dismissal, even though the debtor was ineligible for relief for failure to undergo the credit counseling required by §109(h). (See also section 8.4.1(c).)

(4) Upon the debtor's discharge, the stay is succeeded by a discharge injunction. The discharge injunction permanently enjoins efforts to collect the discharged debt. Therefore, for many creditors the advent of the stay forever ends collection efforts under nonbankruptcy law. (Qualifications to this broad observation are discussed in section 10.5 and Chapter 11.)

(5) The stay applies in all forms of bankruptcy. However, because there are significant differences between liquidation and the different forms of rehabilitation, the impact of the stay is likely to vary depending on the type of relief sought. For example, because Ch. 7 is intended to provide for the expeditious liquidation of the estate, the stay is likely to focus on preservation of property and the protection of the debtor for the relatively short period during which the estate is collected, realized, and distributed. By contrast, a debtor under Ch. 11 is engaged in plan formulation, negotiations, the operation of a business, and the use of estate assets. The debtor's ability to restrain creditor action during this process of restructuring is vital to the success of the effort at rehabilitation, but creditors assume a greater risk of loss while the debtor uses estate property and works on reorganization. If the attempt at rehabilitation fails, the delay in enforcement of rights caused by the stay could have resulted in irreparable damage to a creditor. The means of ameliorating this problem is discussed in Chapter 11.

(6) The effectiveness of the stay does not depend on creditors' notice of the filing.   The stay binds them as soon as the petition is filed, even if they only find out about it later. Therefore, a creditor cannot seek to retain an advantage gained by violating the stay on the grounds that it had no knowledge of the bankruptcy when it took the action barred by the stay. Some courts have characterized acts in violation of the stay as voidable, so that the trustee or the debtor must apply to court to have the act set aside. Other courts — the majority, it seems — treat acts in violation of the stay as null and void, so that no affirmative steps need be taken to avoid them. *See* section 10.7 and Example 1.

Although innocent violations of the stay are ineffective, deliberate violations can have even more serious consequences. In addition to losing any advantage gained by the violation, a willful transgressor is liable to the debtor for any actual damages suffered and, if the disobedience is egregious, for punitive damages too. The violator may also be held in contempt of court. *See* section 10.7 and Example 1.

(7) The stay does not preclude action in the bankruptcy court.   Creditors and other parties in interest may institute proceedings in the bankruptcy court itself concerning matters that are otherwise subject to the stay.

(8) The stay is not an end in itself.   It does not determine the validity of claims or dispose of them. It simply suspends action on the claim outside of the bankruptcy process. In due course the claim will be asserted against the estate and will be dealt with in the claim procedure. Any issues concerning the claim will be adjudicated by the bankruptcy court itself or will be resolved in another forum following relief from stay.

(9) Although the stay is comprehensive, it does not cover every conceivable activity.   When the stay does not apply to a particular action but it is in the best interests of the estate to restrain that action, §105 gives the court the power to issue an injunction. The injunction under §105 is not automatic and must be issued by the court following an application on notice and a hearing. The applicant for the injunction must demonstrate good cause for the grant of relief.

§10.4 THE RANGE OF THE STAY: §362(a) AND (b)

Section 362(a) and (b) set out what activity is stayed and what is not. Section 362(a) prescribes eight different categories of activity that must stop when the petition is filed, and §362(b) lists a number of specific types of activity that are not stayed. If a particular act is not mentioned in either subsection, and §362(a) cannot be interpreted to encompass it, the act is not subject to the stay. To prevent it from occurring, the debtor or trustee must convince the court to use its injunctive powers under §105.

§10.4.1 Activity Included in the Stay — §362(a)

The different types of activity stayed by §362(a) can be classified into three broad categories:

(1) Activity against the debtor. The stay prohibits all activity against the debtor relating to the collection of claims that arose before the commencement of the bankruptcy case. This includes the commencement or continuation of judicial or administrative proceedings to adjudicate or enforce the claim as well as private nonjudicial action (such as correspondence, personal contact, or exercise of a right of set off) aimed at recovering the debt. This activity against the debtor is forbidden by §362(a)(1), (2), (6), (7), and (8). In most cases, a creditor's attempt to collect a debt by nonjudicial means takes the obvious and unsubtle form of an oral or written communication to the debtor demanding or cajoling payment or threatening consequences of nonpayment. However, sometimes collection activity can be surprisingly innovative. For example, in In re Hampton, 319 B.R. 163 (Bankr. E.D. Ark. 2005), a car dealer installed a "PayTek" device on cars sold on credit to debtors with poor credit ratings. The device disabled the car unless the driver entered a valid code number before starting the car. The code was valid for only one month, so that each month the buyer had to get a new code from the dealer, which she received only upon making her monthly payment. After the buyer filed for bankruptcy, the dealer became very uncooperative about giving her new monthly codes. The court held that this was a violation of the stay.

Most of the provisions in §362(a) are aimed at staying action relating to the enforcement of prepetition debts due by the debtor or actions relating to property of the estate. However, §362(a)(1) is broad enough to extend beyond attempts to pursue debts. It states, in general terms, that the filing of the petition stays "the commencement or continuation . . . of a judicial, administrative, or other action or proceeding against the debtor that was or could have been commenced before the commencement of the case . . . ." This broad language could include, for example, a suit for an injunction, even though it may not be for the purpose of debt collection and merely seeks to restrain the debtor from acting in a way that harms the plaintiff's rights. However, a court may recognize a "judicial exception" to the stay where the injunction aims to restrain the debtor's tortious or illegal conduct. For example, in Dominic's Restaurant of Dayton, Inc. v. Mantia, 683 F.3d 757

(6th Cir. 2012), the court found that the stay did not apply to contempt proceedings in state court to enforce an injunction against the debtor's infringement of the plaintiffs' trademark. The court reasoned that if the stay was to be applied to these proceedings, the debtor would be able to continue to violate the plaintiff's rights with impunity. Notwithstanding cases like this, a party who continues any kind of proceeding against the debtor after the petition is filed takes the risk that the action will violate the stay, so the safest course of action is to seek relief from stay before continuing the proceedings.

The stay of actions against the debtor applies only to prepetition claims. Postpetition transactions by the debtor do not give rise to claims against the estate but are the debtor's own responsibility. They can be enforced against the debtor through the normal collection methods of nonbankruptcy law.

(2) Activity against property of the debtor. Section 362(a)(5) prohibits any steps to create, perfect, or enforce a lien against property of the debtor to secure a prepetition claim. As explained in Chapter 12, the debtor's prepetition property becomes property of the estate. However, it commonly happens that while the bankruptcy case is pending the debtor begins to acquire a new estate, which consists of prepetition property that may have been returned to the debtor and postpetition property acquired by the debtor. Section 362(a)(5) protects the debtor's postpetition property by forbidding prepetition creditors from seeking to satisfy their claims by attempting to establish or enforce liens against the debtor's postfiling property. The stay covers only prepetition debts. A postpetition creditor has full rights of enforcement against the debtor's property.

(3) Activity against property of the estate. A bankruptcy estate is created upon the filing of the petition. (*See* Chapter 12.) The preservation of estate property and the evenhanded treatment of creditors call for a wide-ranging stay on all postpetition activity to remove property from the estate or to establish or enforce an interest in it. The stay of action against estate property is wider than the stay protecting the debtor and property of the debtor, in that it applies to both prepetition and postpetition claims. A postpetition creditor of the debtor has no claim to property of the estate and has no right to try to reach estate property. However, the estate itself may incur obligations. The stay prevents creditors of the estate from taking action to assert their claims against estate property outside of the normal claim procedures.

The stay of activity against property of the estate is provided for in §362(a)(2), (3), and (4). These provisions cover the enforcement of prepetition judgments as well as acts to obtain possession of property of or from the estate, to exercise control over estate property, or to establish or enforce a lien against estate property.

§10.4.2 The Impact of the Stay on Setoff Rights

Under nonbankruptcy law, where two persons are mutually indebted, the debts may be set off against each other. That is, either party may deduct the amount due to him from what he owes the other. An account in a bank or other depository institution is a debt due by the bank to its customer. Therefore, if the customer also owes money to the bank, it can refuse to permit withdrawal from the customer's account, and can set off the monies in the account against what the customer owes. Section 553 gives full effect to nonbankruptcy setoff rights in bankruptcy, and treats the creditor with a right of setoff as a secured claimant to the extent of the setoff. For example, if the debtor has borrowed $10,000 from a bank and has $4,000 in an account at the bank, upon the debtor's bankruptcy the bank has a secured claim of $4,000 and an unsecured claim of $6,000. (Setoff is discussed in section 16.2.)

However, the bank is stayed by §362(a)(7) from exercising its right of setoff. That is, although it will ultimately have the right to claim the setoff, it cannot simply effect the right of setoff upon the filing of the petition by taking the funds in the account. It must seek the permission of the court to do so by applying for relief from stay. This creates a problem for the bank because the customer can destroy the bank's setoff right by withdrawing the funds from the account before the bank is able to get relief from stay. In *Citizens Bank of Maryland v. Strumpf*, 516 U.S. 16 (1995), the U.S. Supreme Court protected creditors from this vulnerability by allowing the creditor to freeze the account pending relief from stay. It held that the placing of a temporary administrative hold on a bank account while the bank applies for relief from stay is not, in itself, a violation of §362(a)(7). The court reasoned that a temporary freeze merely suspends payment from the account and does not constitute an exercise of the right of setoff by permanently removing the funds from the account. To refuse to recognize the creditor's power to do this would eviscerate its right to claim a setoff, which is preserved in bankruptcy by §553. It is also inconsistent with §542(b), which requires a party to pay a debt due to the estate only when it is due and payable. The court also rejected the debtor's argument that the hold violated two other provisions of §362(a). It did not violate §362(a)(3) because the hold was not an act to obtain possession of or control over estate property. From the bank's perspective, the account was not property, but merely a debt to the estate. Nor did it violate §362(a)(6), which precludes the creditor from attempting to recover a claim from the debtor.

Strumpf makes it clear that it applies only where the hold is temporary, so the creditor must move diligently to obtain relief from stay. The consequence of delay is illustrated by In re *Wicks*, 215 B.R. 316 (E.D.N.Y. 1997). The debtor's credit union placed a hold on the account upon learning of the bankruptcy and did nothing about applying for relief from stay until the debtor initiated proceedings, four months later, to obtain damages for violation of the stay. The court said that because the credit union had shown no intent to move diligently for relief from stay, the hold could not be regarded as temporary, within the contemplation of *Strumpf*, and it must therefore be taken to be an actual attempt to exercise the right of setoff in violation of §362(a)(7). See also *In re Schafer*, 315 B.R. 765 (Bankr. D. Colo. 2004).

§10.4.3 Activity Excluded from the Stay — §362(b)

This note does not summarize all the exclusions from the stay in §362(b). Some of them are very specific and technical and relate to particular types of debtors or narrow classes of regulated transactions. Section 362(b) sets out a long list of actions that are excluded from the stay (several of which were added by the Bankruptcy Abuse Prevention and Consumer Protection Act of 2005 (BAPCPA).) This section addresses only the four most widely applicable exclusions, and does not discuss the many narrow ones that apply to very specific and limited types of claim. As a general matter, the exclusions from the stay reflect a decision by Congress that in some situations the interests of the debtor and the estate would not be harmed by permitting the identified action to continue without leave of the court, or that the rights being enforced are important enough to permit continued enforcement without interruption from the stay.

(1) Criminal actions and enforcement: §365(b)(1). Criminal prosecution is conducted by the government for the protection of its citizens, and there is a strong policy that bankruptcy should not interfere with the government's power to enforce criminal law. A debtor may not evade or forestall criminal proceedings by filing bankruptcy. The exclusion of criminal enforcement from the stay is usually clear-cut. However, an issue does arise where criminal proceedings may have the ancillary purpose of compensating the victim. For example, a victim or prosecutor may hope that the initiation of criminal proceedings will put pressure on the defendant to pay a debt, or a court may suspend a sentence on condition that the defendant makes restitution to the victim. A common criminal proceeding of this kind is prosecution for passing a bad check. Where debt collection motives are intertwined in the criminal case, some courts will examine the motive of the prosecution and will stay the criminal proceedings if the debtor can prove that the true motivation of the proceedings is to coerce payment of the debt rather than to punish a violation of the law. See, for example, *In re Dorsey*, 373 B.R. 528 (Bankr. N.D. Ohio 2007). (In *Dorsey* the court found that the primary motive in prosecuting a bad check was criminal punishment because the creditor had followed a consistent policy of prosecuting all bad checks.) However, most courts refuse to conduct an inquiry into the motivation of the prosecution and adopt an absolute approach: The stay is inapplicable to all criminal proceedings, no matter how they may be intertwined with debt collection motives. See, for example, In re Gruntz, 202 F.3d 1074 (9th Cir. 2000); In re Bartel, 404 B.R. 584 (B.A.P. 1st Cir. 2009).

(2) Proceedings by governmental units to enforce police or regulatory powers: §362(b)(4). The stay does not apply to the commencement or continuation of an action or proceeding by a governmental unit to enforce its police and regulatory power. This includes the enforcement of a judgment other than a money judgment. This means that the government may pursue any enforcement up to the stage of judgment. If the judgment is not monetary in nature, the government may continue beyond the stage of judgment. However, if the judgment is for money, the proceedings must end at the point of judgment and the further enforcement is stayed. The government will then prove a claim in the estate for the monetary debt. For example, in In re Mystic Tank Lines Corp., 544 F.3d 524 (3d Cir. 2008), the state was held not to have violated the stay by obtaining a postpetition judgment against the debtor in state court for the cost of cleaning up petroleum contamination for which the debtor was responsible. The stay would apply to the collection of the judgment debt, but the state had not attempted to collect it, and had proved a claim in the estate based on the judgment.

Not every kind of action or proceeding by a governmental unit is an exercise of police or regulatory power. Governments often engage in commercial transactions. In this role their claims are no different from those of private creditors and are subject to the stay. It is a question of fact whether the government is acting as a regulator in the public interest, or is just in the position of a creditor, pursuing only its own interest. This factual question is determined by examining the nature of the transaction or relationship, its purpose, and its underlying policy motivation. The interrelated tests used by courts to determine if governmental action falls within or is outside the exception are the "pecuniary purpose" and "public policy" tests. The essential question is whether the government's action is aimed at protecting public safety or welfare or is merely taken for the pecuniary purpose of gaining advantage over other creditors in the collection of a debt. For example, in Lockyer v. Mirant Corp. 398 F.3d 1098 (9th Cir. 2005), the court held that action to overturn an antitrust violation by compelling the divestiture of electrical plants was a matter of public welfare and fell within the exception. In N.L.R.B. v. P.I.E. Nationwide, Inc., 923 F.2d 506, 511-512 (7th Cir. 1991) the court found the exception to apply to proceedings before the National Labor Relations Board to prevent an unfair labor practice. In Penn Terra Ltd. v. Department of Environmental Resources, 733 F.2d 267 (3d Cir. 1984), the court held that the exceptions covered an injunction compelling corrective measures to comply with environmental laws.

The fact that proceedings may ultimately result in a money judgment does not necessarily disqualify the proceedings as regulatory. Often, a monetary assessment is needed to penalize violations of policy or to effect a regulatory purpose. For example, in In re Commonwealth Companies, Inc., 913 F.2d 518 (8th Cir. 1990), a civil fraud action brought by the United States under the False Claims Act was held to be regulatory and excluded from the stay up to the point of enforcement under §362(b)(4). The court found that the goal of the suit was not merely to recover compensation for fraud, but also to penalize it and to deter such conduct by others. (The court made it clear that once a money judgment was obtained, the enforcement of that judgment is stayed. The exception to the stay in §362(b)(4) only permits enforcement of nonmonetary judgments.) See also California ex rel Brown v. Villalobos, 453 B.R. 404 (D. Nev. 2011), which found that fines and penalties for improperly influencing state pension fund officials served a public purpose and were regulatory, not pecuniary.

By contrast, in In re Corporation de Servicios Medicos Hospitalarios de Fajardo, 805 F.2d 440 (1st Cir. 1986), the Puerto Rican Department of Health was held not to be entitled to rely on §362(b)(4) to continue with an action arising out of a contract with the debtor to operate hospital services. In In re FV Steel Wire Co., 324 B.R. 701 (Bankr. E.D. Wis. 2005), the court found that enforcement of a consent decree to clean up hazardous waste involved nothing more than payment into a fund and was outside of the exception. In In re Nortel Networks, Inc., 669 F.3d 128 (3rd Cir. 2011), the court found the exception did not apply because the action to enforce a government-created scheme to protect pension funds was purely pecuniary. (In addition, the government-created entity that sought to enforce the scheme did not qualify as a governmental unit because it was not set up as a government entity.)

(3) Specified creditor action to consolidate nonbankruptcy rights: §362(b)(3).

The stay does not affect certain specified actions taken by a creditor under nonbankruptcy law to perfect or consolidate rights against the debtor or the estate. The rationale for these exceptions is that they are merely legal procedures that the creditor is entitled to take under nonbankruptcy law to validate a legitimate claim. For example, under §362(b)(3) a creditor may perform acts to perfect or to maintain or continue perfection if that action is recognized by §546 or 547 as binding on the estate (this is illustrated by Example 4).

(4) Family support obligations: §362(b)(2).

The impact of bankruptcy on the dependents of an individual debtor is a matter of ongoing concern. This is particularly so where the dependents are also creditors because the debtor has support obligations to them under a prior agreement or court order. To prevent a debtor from using bankruptcy to evade these support obligations, the Bankruptcy Reform Act of 1994 enacted a number of provisions giving these debts special treatment, including higher priority, exclusion from the operation of the exemptions, nonavoidability of a lien securing them, and nondischargeability. BAPCPA continued the trend started in 1994 by further strengthening support obligations in various ways. (Protections other than exclusion from the stay will be dealt with in the appropriate places.)

The exception to the stay in §362(b)(2) is one of these provisions designed to protect the debtor's dependants from the consequences of his bankruptcy. Under §362(b)(2)(A) the stay does not bar the commencement or continuation of a civil action or proceeding to establish paternity or to establish or modify a domestic support obligation.[1] BAPCPA expanded §362(b)(2)(A) to include proceedings concerning child custody or visitation, to dissolve a marriage, and regarding family violence. Section 362(b)(2)(B) also excludes from the stay the collection of a domestic support obligation from property that is not property of the estate (that is, from the debtor's own property).

§10.5 TERMINATION OF THE STAY

The stay of a particular activity may be lifted by the court following an application for relief from stay under §362(d). This is discussed in Chapter 11. Apart from that, §362(c)(1) and (2) provide for termination of the stay in the normal course of the bankruptcy proceedings. It treats the stay of acts against estate property differently from the stay of other acts. BAPCPA added §§362(c)(3) and (4) to grounds for terminating the stay. These subsections deal with abusive serial filings by providing for termination of the stay where the debtor has engaged in this improper strategy

§10.5.1 Termination of the Stay of Acts against Estate Property

Under §362(c)(1), the stay of acts against estate property continues until the property is no longer property of the estate. Property may be released by

---

1. The term "domestic support obligation" was substituted by BAPCPA for the phrase "alimony, maintenance, and support." Although the terms mean roughly the same thing, "domestic support obligation" is more comprehensive. It is defined in §101(14A) to include debts in the nature of alimony, maintenance, or support, established by a separation agreement, divorce decree, property settlement agreement, court order, or determination of a governmental unit. The debt must be owed to or recoverable by a spouse, a former spouse, a child, a party responsible for the child, or a governmental unit.

the estate for different reasons. For example, the trustee may sell it in the course of liquidation; it may be abandoned to a claimant because neither the debtor nor the estate has any equity in it; or it may be abandoned to the debtor as exempt. Section 362(c)(1) is of limited effect. It does not authorize proceedings against the property following release by the estate, but merely makes the stay inapplicable to the extent that it was grounded on the fact that the estate had an interest in the property. Although it is no longer property of the estate, it may still be protected from the stay on some other ground. For example, if property is abandoned to the debtor as exempt, it still cannot be subjected to the claims of prepetition creditors, who remain bound by the stay of actions against the debtor and the debtor's property (*see* Example 2). However, a postpetition creditor of the debtor could perfect a security interest in it or seize it in execution, because postpetition claims are not affected by the stay of acts against the debtor or the debtor's property.

§10.5.2 Termination of the Stay of Other Acts

The stay of all acts other than acts against property of the estate continues in effect under §362(c)(2) until the case is closed or dismissed or a discharge is granted or denied, whichever occurs first. If the reason for termination of the stay is the dismissal of the case, creditors can take action to enforce their claims under nonbankruptcy law following the dismissal. If the reason for termination of the stay is the grant of a discharge, the stay is immediately succeeded by the discharge injunction under §524(a)(2), which permanently enjoins the creditor from collecting whatever portion of the debt was not paid from the estate. The discharge may not extend to all debts. As discussed in Chapter 22, some debts may be excluded from the discharge and therefore are not covered by the discharge injunction. The creditor may proceed to recover an undischarged debt after the stay terminates. If the debtor is denied a discharge altogether (*see* Chapter 22), all creditors may proceed with enforcement actions under nonbankruptcy law.

§10.5.3 Termination of the Stay following Serial Filings

BAPCPA added §362(c)(3) and (4) in an attempt to address the problem of abusive serial filings by an individual debtor. As many courts have noted, the drafting of these provisions is appallingly poor, and their language is dense and almost incomprehensible. In broad terms, they are intended to make it much more difficult for an individual debtor to file successive petitions for the purpose of using the stay to frustrate creditor collection actions. Because §707(b) contemplates that a debtor whose Ch. 7 case is dismissed for abuse should have the opportunity to refile under Chs. 11 or 13, §362(c)(3) and (4) do not apply where the case had been dismissed under §707(b). (*See* section 9.8 for an explanation of the operation of §707(b).)

Section 362(c)(3) limits the duration of the automatic stay where the debtor had filed a prior case that was pending within the year preceding the petition and that case was dismissed. Unless the debtor can meet a stringent burden of proving that the current petition was filed in good faith, the automatic stay in the current case terminates 30 days after the case is filed. The precise language of the section is difficult to understand. It states that the stay "with respect to any action taken with respect to a debt or property securing such debt or with respect to any lease shall terminate with respect to the debtor on the 30th day after the filing of the later case." Section 362(c)(3) applies whether the current case is voluntary or involuntary. Because §362(c)(3) refers to "any action taken" it is unclear if it applies only to creditors who have actually taken action to enforce the debt prior to the filing of the second petition. Some courts have held that the use of this language indicates that the stay does not terminate in its entirety, but only terminates with regard to those creditors who had "taken action," that is, instituted judicial or other formal collection proceedings prior to the filing of the current petition. See, for example, In re Paschal, 337 B.R. 274 (Bankr. E.D.N.C. 2006); In re Stanford, 373 B.R. 890 (Bankr. E.D. Ark. 2007). Other courts disagree, and hold that the section terminates the stay entirely after the 30-day period with regard to all creditors, whether or not they have taken any action to enforce the debt. See, for example, In re James, 358 B.R. 816 (Bankr. S.D. Ga. 2007).

The words "with respect to the debtor" have also created interpretational difficulties. It is unclear whether §362(c)(3) terminates the stay only against the debtor and property of the debtor, or if it also applies to the property of the estate. Most courts have held that the reference to the debtor and the absence of any reference to estate property means that the stay terminates only as against the debtor and the debtor's property. See, for example, In re Stanford; In re Jump, 356 B.R. 789 (B.A.P. 1st Cir. 2006). Other courts have interpreted the words "with respect to the debtor" as having nothing to do with distinguishing estate property from the debtor and his property. Rather, they interpret these words as relating back to the beginning of §362(c)(3), which refer to both single and joint cases: the reference to the debtor merely makes it clear that in a joint case, the termination of the stay only effects the debtor who falls foul of §362(c)(3). The courts who favor this interpretation argue that it is reinforced by the legislative history and purpose of the section because it gives creditors the greatest degree of protection against bad faith serial filings. See In re Reswick, 446 B.R. 362 (B.A.P. 9th Cir. 2011).

To prevent expiry of the stay after 30 days, the debtor must apply to the court before the end of the 30-day period to extend the stay. If, after notice and a hearing, the court finds that the new filing is in good faith, the court may continue the stay, with or without conditions, against all or particular creditors. If the stay is to continue against a particular creditor, §362(c)(3)(ii) creates a presumption that the petition was not filed in good faith if that creditor had moved for relief in the prior case and the application for relief was still pending at the time of dismissal of the case, or the creditor had received relief from stay. Where the debtor seeks continuation of the stay as against all creditors, §362(c)(3)(C)(i) creates a presumption that the petition was not filed in good faith where the debtor filed more than one previous case in the preceding year, or the debtor has failed to perform properly in the prior case, or the debtor has not had a substantial change in his financial affairs since the prior dismissal, or there is no basis for believing that the current case will result in a discharge or a fully performed plan. The presumption can be rebutted only by clear and convincing evidence of good faith. Good faith is determined on the totality of the circumstances, including such factors as the timing of the filing of the later petition, how the debts arose, the reason for the dismissal of the prior case, any change in the debtor's circumstances, and the debtor's conduct and apparent motivation. In essence, the debtor has the onerous burden of convincing the court that the debtor's honesty and the equities justify allowing the stay to remain in effect. See In re Charles, 332 B.R. 538 (Bankr. S.D. Tex. 2005); In re Baldesssaro, 338 B.R. 178 (Bankr. D.N.H. 2006).

Section 362(c)(4) governs situations in which the debtor had filed two or more prior cases that were pending within the preceding year and were dismissed. The multiple prior filings more strongly suggest abuse, so the debtor does not get the 30-day grace period, and the stay does not go into effect at all. The court can order the stay to take effect with regard to all or some creditors if, within 30 days of the petition, the debtor is able to show that the filing was not in bad faith. Section §362(c)(4)(D) contains a presumption of bad faith similar to that in §362(c)(3) that can only be rebutted by clear and convincing evidence to the contrary.

§10.6 THE EFFECT OF THE STAY ON LIMITATION PERIODS — §108

Under nonbankruptcy law, creditors' claims are subject to statutes of limitation. Because the stay halts lawsuits and collection efforts, a creditor may be prevented from initiating suit within the time required by nonbankruptcy law. If the bankruptcy case is not dismissed and the claim is settled and discharged in the course of bankruptcy, the postpetition expiry of the limitation period is irrelevant. The discharge injunction under §524 precludes any further enforcement action and the creditor cannot commence proceedings in another court.

However, if the bankruptcy case is dismissed, relief from stay is granted, or the debt is excluded from the discharge, the creditor's right to continue nonbankruptcy enforcement proceedings revives. The stay does not toll the limitation period entirely. However, §108(c) gives the creditor an opportunity to commence suit after termination of the stay. It provides, in essence, that if the claim is subject to a limitation period (including not only a statute of limitations but also a period fixed by court order or contract) and that period had not expired before the petition was filed, it will not expire until the time fixed by nonbankruptcy law or 30 days after notice of the termination or expiry of the stay, whichever is later. In other words, if, when the creditor is notified of termination of the stay, the nonbankruptcy limitation period had not expired and has more than 30 days to run, suit must be commenced in the remaining limitation period. However, if the period expired during the stay or will expire within 30 days of notice of termination, the creditor has 30 days following notice to commence suit.

§10.7 THE EFFECT OF VIOLATING THE STAY

§10.7.1 The Nullification of Advantages Gained by the Violation

The stay binds creditors as soon as the petition is filed, whether or not they have knowledge of it, and any act in violation of the stay, whether innocent or deliberate, is ineffective to give the actor any advantage. Apparent legal rights acquired in violation of the stay are a nullity, and the creditor is obliged to restore any money or property (or its value). There is some difference of view on the legal effect of an act in violation of the stay. Some courts regard an act in violation of the stay as voidable, so that it remains effective unless the debtor or trustee moves in bankruptcy court to have it set aside. See, for example, Sikes v. Global Marine, Inc., 881 F.2d 176 (5th Cir. 1989); In re Siciliano, 13 F.3d 748 (3d Cir. 1994). However, the majority view is to treat the act as void, so that the actor gains no legal advantage from it, even if no motion for avoidance is made. See, for example, Ellis v. Consolidated Diesel Electric Corp., 894 F.2d 371 (10th Cir. 1990); In re Schwartz, 954 F.2d 569 (9th Cir. 1992); Jones v. Cain, 804 A.2d 322 (D.C. Cir. 2002); In re Kline, 472 B.R. 98 (B.A.P. 10th Cir. 2012). The latter approach gives the stay greater potency.

§10.7.2 Willful Violations: Compensatory Damages, Including Costs and Attorneys' Fees

Although an innocent violation of the stay renders the act ineffective, a deliberate violation has further consequences. It could result in an award of costs, attorney's fees, and compensatory and punitive damages under §362(k)[2] or a sanction for contempt of court. Section 362(k)(1) provides that an individual injured by a willful violation of the stay "shall recover actual damages, including costs and attorneys' fees and, in appropriate circumstances, may recover punitive damages." Section 362(k) uses the word "individual" rather than "debtor" or "entity," which, in its plain meaning, confines the remedy to natural persons. Some courts have interpreted it this way and have held that an artificial person, such as a corporation, has no remedy under §362(k). See, for example, In re Just Brakes Corporate Systems, Inc., 108 F.3d 881 (8th Cir. 1997), in which the court emphasized not only that "individual" is consistently used in the Code to refer to a natural person, but also pointed out that the subsection was originally enacted in 1984 as part of a package of amendments relating to consumers. In re Spookyworld, Inc., 346 F.3d 1 (1st Cir. 2003), is to the same effect. Other courts have extended the remedy to corporations. See, for example, In re APF Co., 264 B.R. 344 (Bankr. D. Del. 2001), which discusses court of appeals authority for this approach. Even if §362(k) does not provide a remedy to debtors other than individuals, a court has the power under §105 to award compensatory damages, as discussed below. However, it is not clear if the court's general powers under §105 extend to an award of punitive damages.

Section §362(k)(1) is most commonly used by individuals who are debtors. However, the language of the section does not, in its plain meaning, confine the remedy to debtors, so an individual other than the debtor may have standing to claim damages if he can show that the violation caused him loss. This was recognized in In re MD Promenade, Inc., 51 BCD 22 (Bankr. N.D. Tex. 2009), in which the debtor's landlord claimed damages resulting from the removal of property from the debtor's premises. (However, because the landlord was a corporation, the court awarded damages under §105 rather than §362(k).) See also St. Paul Fire & Marine Ins. Co. v. Labuzan, 579 F.3d 533 (5th Cir. 2009), in which the court held that individual creditors of the debtor could claim damages under §362(k) if they could establish injury distinct from the injury to the estate itself. (In that case, the creditors seeking relief under §362(k) also happened to be owners of the debtor. The court made it clear that it was their status as creditors, not as owners, that gave rise to the claim for damages.)

---

2. Section 362(k) was formerly numbered (h). The numbering was changed by BAPCPA.

To receive damages for a willful violation of the stay under §362(k)(1), the individual need only show that the creditor knew of the stay and intended the action that violated it. No specific intent to cause injury is required. It is no excuse that the creditor had a good faith belief that it was entitled to take the action. See, for example, In re Kaneb, 196 F.3d 265 (1st Cir. 1999) (the creditor was liable for damages even though it erroneously believed that it had obtained relief from stay); In re Johnson, 501 F.3d 1163 (10th Cir. 2007) (the creditor disbelieved information that the debtor had filed a petition, and thought it was a ruse to delay enforcement).

Upon a showing of willful violation of the stay, the individual is entitled to receive compensatory damages for any economic loss that resulted from the violation. To recover compensatory damages, the individual must provide concrete evidence of loss that can be ascertained with reasonable certainty. For example, in In re Frankel, 391 B.R. 266 (Bankr. M.D. Pa. 2008), the court refused to award compensatory damages to the debtor where both the fact and extent of loss was conjectural. As part of those compensatory damages, the debtor is entitled to costs and attorneys' fees. Courts are divided on the scope of the costs and attorneys' fees. In In re Repine, 536 F.3d 512 (5th Cir. 2008), the court held that they included all costs and fees incurred, including those relating to the debtor's action for damages. However, in Sternberg v. Johnston, 582 F.3d 1114 (9th Cir. 2009), the court read the words "actual damages" to cover only fees and costs incurred in challenging the stay violation but not to include those incurred in seeking a damages award.

§10.7.3 Emotional Distress Damages

Some courts have allowed emotional distress damages as part of the compensation for injury where the debtor can show that he has suffered unusual mental distress as a result of the willful violation. However, other courts have refused to award emotional distress damages unless the violation amounted to a tort. For example, in In re Kaneb (above) and In re Dawson, 390 F.3d 1139 (9th Cir. 2004), the courts recognized the availability of emotional distress damages under §362(k). In re Kaneb awarded the damages, but In re Dawson did not, because the debtor had failed clearly to establish that he had suffered significant emotional harm directly caused by the violation. By contrast, other courts have confined damages under §362(k) to economic injury. See, for example, United States v. Harchar, 331 B.R. 720 (N.C. Ohio 2005), Aiello v. Providian Financial Corp., 239 F.3d 876 (7th Cir. 2001). In Aiello the court refused such damages in the absence of a recognized tort, even though the creditor's attempts at collection were quite aggressive.

§10.7.4 Punitive Damages

Punitive damages are not appropriate in all cases of willful violation and are generally awarded only where the violation is malicious or particularly egregious. See, for example, In re Cullen, 329 B.R. 52 (Bankr. N.D. Iowa 2005) (the creditor, a credit union, had frozen the debtor's account to coerce the debtor into reaffirming the debt, and it was apparent that the credit union used this tactic pervasively against its bankrupt members).

§10.7.5 Sanctions for Contempt of Court

Although the stay is automatic, it is nevertheless a court order. Therefore, a deliberate violation of the stay is contempt of court, and sanctions for contempt can be imposed as an alternative to or in addition to a remedy under §362(k). The contempt power of the bankruptcy court is explained in section 7.5.2. Sanctions for contempt of court may be either civil or criminal in nature. The distinction between civil and criminal contempt is difficult and complex at the margins. However, it can be stated as a broad rule that contempt sanctions are civil if they are designed to compensate the other party for violation of the court order (by awarding damages for loss, much like an award of compensatory damages under §362(k)), or are intended to coerce compliance with the order (such as by imposing a fine on the contemnor for each day that it persists in the violation). They are criminal if their purpose is to punish disobedience. It is generally accepted that bankruptcy courts have civil contempt power under the general authority given to them by §105(a) to issue orders and judgments necessary or appropriate to carry out the provisions of the Code. There is considerable doubt over a bankruptcy court's power to impose criminal sanctions for contempt. Several courts of appeal have held that §105(a) authorizes only orders and judgments that are "necessary and appropriate to carry out" the provisions of the Code, to enforce or implement court orders, or to prevent an abuse of process. Civil contempt sanctions adequately meet these purposes, and criminal contempt sanctions, whose purpose is punishment, are not necessary to achieve them. In addition, these courts have held that criminal contempt sanctions are not within the bankruptcy court's inherent power. See, for example, In re Dyer, 322 F.3d 1178 (9th Cir. 2003); In re John Richards Homes Building Co., LLC, 475 B.R. 585 (E.D. Mich. 2012. The district court clearly has this power, and may impose criminal penalties for a deliberate violation of the stay.

Examples

1. DeLay & Co., Inc. defaulted on a loan from Blitzkrieg Bank. The bank commenced a collection suit, obtained default judgment, and issued a writ of execution. On June 1, the sheriff levied on office equipment owned by DeLay & Co. Under state law, a lien arose in the property upon levy. An execution sale is scheduled for June 15. On June 14, Blitzkrieg received notice from the clerk of the bankruptcy court informing it that DeLay & Co. had filed a voluntary Ch. 7 petition on May 31. Because the collection suit was so close to its conclusion, the bank decided that it made sense to proceed with the sale, thereby avoiding the need to become involved in the bankruptcy proceedings. Was that a good decision?

2. Last year, Debtor borrowed money from his bank. When he failed to repay the loan on its due date in February, the bank commenced suit to recover the amount of the loan. The bank obtained judgment at the end of June. Debtor filed a Ch. 7 petition on July 1. After the petition had been filed, the bank wished to execute on its judgment. There are two vehicles parked outside Debtor's home. One is an old car, abandoned to Debtor by the trustee because it is exempt, and the other is a motorbike purchased by Debtor from his postpetition income. Can the bank execute on either of these assets?

3. Debtor became involved in a dispute with his neighbor over a new fence erected by the neighbor. Debtor believed that the fence encroached on his property. During the dispute, Debtor became so enraged that he assaulted the neighbor and caused him serious personal injury. Debtor also threatened to destroy the fence. Shortly after the attack, the state initiated a criminal prosecution against Debtor for assault. In addition, the neighbor commenced proceedings in state court to recover damages for his injury and to enjoin Debtor from damaging or removing the fence. After these actions were commenced, Debtor filed a bankruptcy petition. At that time, both of the proceedings were pending. How will the stay affect them?

4. Two months prior to Debtor's bankruptcy, a contractor completed an alteration to his home. The contractor has not been paid. Under the state's mechanic's lien law, the contractor is entitled to a lien on the property to secure the price of the work. Under the statute, the lien attaches to the property with priority effective from the date of commencement of the work, provided that the claimant files a lien claim in the deeds registry within three months of completion. The claimant is required to commence action to foreclose the lien within six months of filing the claim. The contractor had not filed a lien claim by the petition date. Does the stay prevent the contractor from filing the lien and commencing suit in the periods prescribed by the state statute?

5. For several months before his bankruptcy, Debtor neglected to have his garbage hauled away. It has accumulated in piles in the front yard of his house. In June, the city health department warned Debtor that if he did not have the garbage removed, action would be taken against him. Debtor ignored the warning. Not only has he failed to clean up the existing garbage, but he continues to add new refuse to the heap.

   On July 1, Debtor filed a bankruptcy petition. On July 5, the city initiated suit in municipal court to enjoin further dumping and to compel Debtor to remove the existing garbage. In the event that Debtor fails to obey the cleanup order, the city asks the court for authority to clean up Debtor's yard itself and to charge him for the cleanup costs. Was the city allowed to commence this proceeding? If the municipal court grants the order, can the city enforce it without leave of the bankruptcy court?

6. Debtor failed to pay tuition due to the university she attends. She subsequently filed a bankruptcy petition. While her case was pending, she asked the university for a transcript. It refused to provide the transcript because Debtor had not paid her tuition. Is this a violation of the stay?

7. Percy Verence operates a debt collection agency. When he receives notice of a bankruptcy filing, his usual practice is to enter that information on his computer system so that his staff knows not to send dunning letters to the debtor. Tess De Stress is one of the debtors from whom Percy has been trying to collect money. Percy received notice that Tess had filed a petition and he entered the information in his system. However, because of a glitch in the system, the information did not show up in Tess's records. As a result, a staff member sent a dunning letter to Tess after the petition, had been filed. Tess is emotionally fragile as a result of her financial difficulties and bankruptcy. She was terribly upset to receive the dunning letter. Has Percy willfully violated the say? If so, can Tess recover damages for emotional distress?

Explanations

1. No. Blitzkrieg's correct response would have been to surrender the property to the trustee and to prove a claim in the estate for its unpaid debt, which would ultimately be paid at the rate payable to other general unsecured claims. The stay took effect on May 31 upon the filing of the petition. Any action taken subsequent to that is a violation of the stay. As noted in section 10.7, the majority view is that an act in violation of the stay is void, so any advantage obtained by the creditor is a nullity.

   The levy on June 1 violated §362(a)(2), which forbids enforcement of a prepetition judgment against the debtor or property of the estate. The levy also violates §362(a)(1), which bars the continuation of judicial proceedings against the debtor, and §362(a)(4), which prohibits any act to create, perfect, or enforce a lien against property of the estate. (The levy creates a judicial lien and DeLay & Co.'s property became property of the estate under §541 on the date of the petition.) The fact that Blitzkrieg did not know of the bankruptcy filing when it levied on June 1 does not validate the levy. The stay takes effect whether or not the creditor knew of it, so Blitzkrieg's execution lien is a nullity and the property or its proceeds must be returned to the estate.

By continuing with the sale in execution after acquiring knowledge of the bankruptcy, Blitzkrieg compounded its violation of the stay and became a willful transgressor. As discussed in section 10.7, this could lead to liability beyond the restoration of the property or its value to the estate. Damages and fees are not recoverable by the debtor under §362(k) because the debtor is a corporation, not an individual. However, Blitzkrieg could be subject to sanctions for contempt of court or could be held liable for compensatory damages under §105(a).

2. The bank is an unsecured judgment creditor. It may not move unilaterally to satisfy its claim but must wait for a pro rata distribution from the estate. The car has been abandoned to Debtor, so it is no longer property of the estate and is not subject to the stay on actions against estate property under §362(a)(2), (3), and (4). However, the car is now Debtor's property, and levy is stayed by §362(a)(1), which forbids the continuation of process to recover a prepetition claim against the debtor. The bike was never estate property, but levy against it is likewise stayed by §362(a)(1). Alternatively, §362(a)(5) applies: As the levy would create a judicial lien on the bike and car, it violates the bar on action to create a lien on the debtor's property to secure a prepetition claim.

3. The criminal case against Debtor is not stayed. Section 362(b)(1) excludes from the stay the commencement or continuation of a criminal action or proceeding against the debtor. The reason for this exclusion is that bankruptcy should not intrude upon the operation of the state's criminal law system.

The suit for personal injury damages is clearly stayed by §362(a)(1). The claim for the injunction does not aim to recover money or property from Debtor or the estate. Nevertheless, it is covered by the plain language of §362(a)(1), which does not confine actions or proceedings to suits for the payment of money but extends to the commencement or continuation of a proceeding that was or could have been commenced against the debtor before the petition, as well as to a proceeding to recover a prepetition claim. There is no statutory exclusion relating to injunctions in §362(b). A court adopting a plain-meaning approach to §362(a) would likely hold that the proceedings for the injunction are stayed, so that the neighbor must apply for relief from stay if he wishes to continue with his suit. However, a court that adopts a purpose-based approach may hold that the stay does not apply to the suit for an injunction, the aim of which is not to enforce a debt, but to restrain postpetition tortious conduct by the debtor.

4. Debtor's home became the property of the estate upon the filing of the petition. In the absence of an exception in §362(b), any attempt to perfect the lien by filing offends both §362(a)(4) and §362(a)(6). Commencement of the foreclosure suit is barred by §362(a)(1).

However, §362(b)(3) does provide an exception to the stay for perfection of the lien. It provides that the stay does not apply to any act to perfect or to maintain or continue perfection of an interest in property to the extent that the trustee's rights and powers are subject to such perfection under §546(b). (Section 546(b) is explained more fully in section 15.3.1.) In simple terms, it recognizes the effectiveness against the estate of a provision of nonbankruptcy law that permits perfection of an interest to backdate upon completion of the act of perfection. In the context of this case, §546(b)(1)(A) upholds the rule of state law that allows the builder to perfect the mechanic's lien by filing within three months of completion, thereby acquiring a lien effective as from the date of commencement of the work. Section 362(b)(3) excludes the act of perfection from the stay, so that it can be accomplished within the portion of the statutory period that remains unexpired after the petition has been filed. Perfection by filing is affected by the normal procedure prescribed by state law. However, if seizure of the property or commencement of suit is required to complete perfection, §546(b)(2)(A) requires that this act is substituted for by giving notice to the trustee.

Although the builder is able to proceed with the lien filing as if no bankruptcy has occurred, he cannot commence suit within the subsequent six-month statutory period. Instead, he must give notice to the trustee under §546(b) within that period, which will give him a valid lien and a secured claim. The purpose of these provisions is to protect statutory liens by deferring to extended perfection periods conferred under state law.

5. The stay under §362(a) applies to all entities, including governmental units. However, §362(b)(4) excludes from the stay the commencement or continuation of an action or proceeding by a governmental unit, defined in §101(27) to include a municipality, to enforce its police or regulatory power. The collection and disposal of waste is surely within the city's regulatory power. Section 362(b)(4) further permits the enforcement of a judgment other than a money judgment obtained for the purpose of exercising that power.

The city's suit aims to enjoin Debtor's violation of the law and to compel him to cure his prior noncompliance, or to pay the city for doing so. The judgment is both a prohibitory injunction forbidding future violations of the law and a mandatory injunction compelling rectification of a prior breach of the law. The bar on future violations is not a money judgment and is excluded from the stay under §362(b)(4). However, the cleanup order is a money judgment that requires the estate to spend money in doing the work itself or to pay the city to do it. The cleanup order is therefore not excluded from the stay under §362(b)(4), and the city cannot proceed beyond the judgment to enforce it unless it applies for and receives relief from stay.

6. If the refusal of a transcript is used as a means to persuade or coerce a debtor into paying a prepetition tuition debt, it is a violation of the stay — an act to recover a claim against the debtor barred by §362(a)(6). It should be noted, however, that qualifying debts for educational loans or benefits are nondischargeable under §523(a)(8) (discussed in Chapter 22). If the debt for tuition qualifies for exclusion from the discharge, action to recover it will cease to be stayed once the stay terminates upon the court's grant of the discharge to the debtor. However, until that happens, the university is bound by the stay, and any attempt to collect the debt will violate the stay. In re Parker, 334 B.R. 529 (Bankr. D. Mass 2005); In re Kuehn, 563 F.3d 289 (7th Cir. 2009).

7. Courts are generally not sympathetic to a defense that "the computer did it" and hold creditors accountable for properly functioning office systems. The simple fact that Percy had knowledge of the filing and deliberately sent out the dunning letter is enough to make the violation willful. No ill motive or specific intent to violate the stay need be shown. This was the approach taken in In re Wingard, 382 B.R. 892 (Bankr. W.D. Pa. 2008). Like Tess, the debtor in Wingard suffered no economic harm as a result of receiving the dunning letter, but sought emotional distress damages because he claimed that the letter aggravated the distress that he experienced as a result of the bankruptcy. The court recognized that emotional distress damages are recoverable under §362(k)(1), but to receive them the debtor must clearly establish significant psychological or emotional injury and must show a causal connection between the harm and the violation of the stay. Where the creditor's action is not egregious and aggressive, the debtor must produce corroborating evidence to prove the harm, and cannot rely only on self-serving testimony.

Relief from Stay and Adequate Protection

§11.1 INTRODUCTION

Chapter 10 described the breadth and impact of the stay and showed how it prevents activity to recover or secure prepetition debts or to assert interests in property of the estate. Sometimes the claimant's right to continue the stayed activity outweighs the interest of the estate or the debtor in suspending it. To enable the court to safeguard the rights of claimants in such circumstances, §362(d)-(g) provide a procedure under which the court can grant relief from stay if the claimant establishes grounds for it. Section 362(d), the central provision, sets out the forms and grounds for relief, while §362(e), (f), and (g) deal with ancillary procedural and evidentiary matters.

Because the stay is so wide-ranging and affects so many types of activity, applications for relief from stay are common. Although they are often made almost immediately after the petition has been filed, they could arise at any time during the case. If the court grants relief, the order benefits only the party who applied for it and covers only the activity in issue in the application. With regard to all other persons and all other matters, the stay remains in effect.

§11.2 THE PROCEDURE FOR RELIEF FROM STAY

A party who wishes to obtain relief from stay must file a motion requesting relief. Section 362(d) requires the court to grant relief after notice and a hearing if grounds for relief are shown. Under §102(1), the phrase "after notice and a hearing" means that appropriate notice must be given, but that a hearing need only be held if a party in interest requests it. The application is a "contested matter" (that is, a proceeding on motion rather than a trial) and is governed by Rules 4001 and 9014.

Other procedural and evidentiary matters are provided for in §362(e), (f), and (g). Section 362(e) is intended to encourage speedy disposition of applications for relief from stay. Section 362(e)(1) covers only applications for relief from stay of acts against property of the estate. In essence, it provides for an automatic grant of the application for relief unless the court acts on the application and orders a continuation of the stay within 30 days of the application. The court has some flexibility in postponing the final determination of the application by making a preliminary order in the 30-day period, but unless the parties otherwise consent or there are compelling circumstances, the application must be resolved finally within 30 days of the preliminary order. Section 362(e)(2), added by the Bankruptcy Abuse Prevention and Consumer Protection Act of 2005 (BAPCPA), applies to applications for relief from stay under all the provisions of §362(a) (not just of acts against property) where the debtor is an individual. The section provides that the stay terminates 60 days after a request for relief from stay unless the court makes a final determination within that 60-day period. The period can be extended only by consent of all parties in interest or by the court for compelling reasons. Section 362(f) permits the court to grant emergency relief following an ex parte application where the interest of the party seeking relief will be irreparably harmed if relief is not given immediately and there is no time for notice and a hearing. Section 362(g) deals with the burden of proof in applications for relief from stay. Because the burden is allocated differently on constituent elements of the grounds for relief, it is more conveniently discussed in section 11.4.

§11.3 FORMS OF RELIEF

Section 362(d) sets out four alternative forms of relief from stay: termination, annulment, modification, or conditioning. This allows the court flexibility in providing relief that is most appropriate to the circumstances.

Termination of the stay is the lifting of the stay so that the applicant can commence or resume the suspended activity. Termination ends the stay only from the time of the order, so it does not validate prior acts in violation of the stay.

Annulment terminates the stay retroactively, so that the stay is treated as if it was never in effect; prior acts in violation of the stay become valid. Annulment is therefore regarded as an extraordinary remedy and is usually used only in exceptional circumstances (*e.g.*, when the debtor has abused the system and the applicant's actions were in good faith and not in willful violation of the stay).

Modification of the stay is appropriate when the court decides to permit some activity but not to allow the applicant full rights to proceed with the enforcement of the claim. For example, the court may modify the stay by allowing the applicant to continue with litigation to the point of judgment, but not to proceed with enforcement of the judgment. Modification is a form of partial or limited relief.

If the court conditions the stay, it leaves the stay in effect, subject to the debtor or trustee satisfying some condition. For example, if the application for relief is based upon the grounds that the claimant's interest in property is deteriorating, the court may allow the stay to continue in effect on condition that the trustee takes steps to halt the deterioration or to compensate for it.

Diagram 11a summarizes the different dispositions of an application for relief from stay.

Relief from Stay — Alternative Dispositions

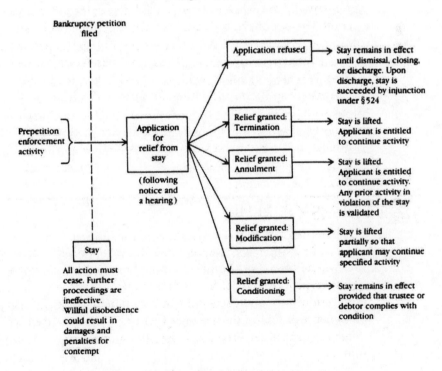

Diagram 11a

§11.4 GROUNDS FOR RELIEF

Section 362(d) sets out four separate grounds for relief from stay. The first, in §362(d)(1), is the broad ground, and is available as a basis for relief from the stay of any action described in §362(a) whether an act against the debtor, or against property of the debtor or the estate. The second, in §362(d)(2), is a narrower ground that applies only to the stay of acts against property. The two grounds are independent of each other. Only one of them need be satisfied for relief to be granted. The third, added to the section as §362(d)(3) by the Bankruptcy Reform Act of 1994, is a special basis for relief applicable only in "single asset real estate" cases. The fourth, added by BAPCPA, applies where the stay relates to real property subject to a secured claim. Each of these bases for relief is explained below.

§11.4.1 Relief from Stay for Cause (§362(d)(1))

Section 362(d)(1) requires the court to grant relief from stay if the applicant has cause for relief, including lack of adequate protection of the applicant's interest in property. Apart from stating one basis for cause (lack of adequate protection, discussed in section 11.5), §362(d)(1) does not specify what constitutes cause for relief. The other bases for cause under §362(d)(1) are as varied as circumstances may dictate. It is left to the court's discretion to grant relief whenever appropriate. For example, cause may arise from abusive behavior by the debtor, from the debtor's default under a plan, or because it is more efficient or fairer for another court to resolve the case. In deciding whether or not cause exists, the court weighs the harm that will be suffered by the applicant if the stay is continued against the interests of the estate or the debtor protected by the stay. For cases that discuss the various factors that may be relevant to a showing of cause for relief, see In re Robbins, 964 F.2d 342 (4th Cir. 1992); In re Mazzeo, 167 F.3d 139 (2d Cir. 1999).

In most motion proceedings, the applicant for relief bears the burden of proving cause. However, in applications for relief from stay §362(g) places the burden of proving lack of cause on the party opposing relief (i.e., the debtor or trustee). Thus, the applicant has the burden of going forward. It must allege cause and make out a prima facie case that cause exists, but the burden of nonpersuasion falls on the opposing party. The burden is allocated in this way because the stay is a form of injunction. As it is automatic, the trustee or the debtor do not have to apply for it and are initially relieved of the burden of establishing grounds for it. This places them in a better position than the normal applicant for an injunction, who must show grounds for relief. Therefore, once the continuation of the stay is challenged, the debtor or trustee must take up the burden of justifying its remaining in effect.

§11.4.2 Relief from Stay of Acts against Property on the Ground That the Debtor Has No Equity in the Property and the Property Is Not Necessary to an Effective Reorganization (§362(d)(2))

It is worth stressing again that §362(d)(2) applies only to the stay of acts against property and cannot be used to obtain relief from stay of acts against the debtor. Where acts against property are in issue, this ground is an alternative to relief for cause under §362(d)(1). Section 362(d)(2) has two conditions that both must be satisfied for relief to be granted: The debtor has no equity in the property and it is not necessary for an effective reorganization. In essence, the basis for relief is that neither the debtor nor the estate will obtain an economic advantage by keeping the property, so the applicant's right to enforce its claim to the property should not be further suspended.

Under §362(g), the applicant for relief bears the burden of proving that the debtor has no equity in the property, and the party opposing relief bears the burden on all other issues. This means that the applicant must establish that the value of the property does not exceed existing valid encumbrances. The applicant must allege and make a prima facie showing of the other elements of §362(d)(2), but the burden of nonpersuasion falls on the party opposing relief.

a. The Debtor's Lack of Equity in the Property (§362(d)(2)(A))

The debtor's equity is the value in the property in excess of all encumbrances on it. If there is an exemption in the property or it has revested in the debtor under a plan, this equity is wholly or partially owned by the debtor. Otherwise it is property of the estate. Thus, reference to the debtor's equity in property in §362(d)(2) includes both the debtor's and the estate's interests in the property.

The existence and extent of the debtor's equity is determined by valuation of the property. The Code's general policy on valuation is expressed in §506 concerning the valuation of secured claims: The court should try to place a realistic value on the property in light of the purpose of the valuation and the property's proposed use or disposition. (For example, if the property will be disposed of on the market by a private sale, market value should be used rather than foreclosure value.) Valuation is usually established by expert testimony. When the parties' witnesses disagree, the court must resolve the conflict by assessing the reliability, credibility, and relevance of their valuations. The court may accept one of the appraisals or make a determination of value based on the evidence taken as a whole. For examples of actual cases involving valuation issues in an application for relief from stay, see In re Castle Ranch of Ramona, 3 B.R. 45 (Bankr. S.D. Cal. 1980); In re Sutton, 904 F.2d 327 (5th Cir. 1990). See also Examples 1 and 2.

If the debtor is found to have equity in the property, relief from stay cannot be granted under §362(d)(2) because one of its two elements is not satisfied. Further inquiry into the role of the property in an effective reorganization is not necessary. However, if no equity exists, the second element of §362(d)(2) becomes relevant.

b. The Property Is Not Necessary to an Effective Reorganization (§362(d)(2)(B))

In a Ch. 7 case, no reorganization is contemplated so the property cannot be necessary to an effective reorganization. Therefore, in a Ch. 7 case the second test is satisfied as a matter of course: If the debtor has no equity in the property, relief from stay should be granted.

Reorganization is the principal goal of Ch. 11, and §362(d)(2)(B) was drafted with Ch. 11 cases in mind. (Its applicability to cases under Chs. 12 and 13 is discussed below.) In a Ch. 11 case, the debtor usually attempts to operate its business while formulating and effectuating a plan to restructure its debts and reorganize its operations. Therefore, if property is a necessary component of the debtor's business operations, depriving the debtor of the ability to use the property will damage its chances of overcoming its financial difficulties. For this reason, the fact that the debtor has no equity in the property is not enough to warrant relief from stay unless, in addition, the property does not advance the debtor's attempt at successful reorganization. Because §362(d)(2)(B) requires that the property be necessary to an "effective" reorganization, it is not enough for the debtor to show merely that the property will be used in its reorganization. The debtor must also establish that the proposed reorganization is feasible. This prediction can be difficult to make. While not addressing the issue in depth, the Supreme Court indicated a broad guideline by dictum in United Savings Association of Texas v. Timbers of Inwood Forest Associates, 484 U.S. 365 (1988): The debtor must show that there is a reasonable prospect of successful reorganization within a reasonable time.

Usually, the earlier in the case that the application for relief is made, the harder it is to make an accurate prediction of the debtor's prospects of successful reorganization. Therefore, courts tend to adopt a more lenient test when the application for relief is made early in the case. Even when there is doubt about the debtor's chances of successful reorganization, if some prospect for success exists, the court is likely to refuse relief from stay. However, if the reorganization has been limping along for some time and no longer looks promising, the court may be more readily persuaded that the reorganization is unlikely to be effective. For example, in In re Sun Valley Ranches, 823 F.2d 1373 (9th Cir. 1987), the application for relief was made after the debtor had been in Ch. 11 bankruptcy for three years, during which time it had suffered losses and the property had declined in value. It also had become clear that the debtor could not pay the amount proposed in the plan. The court lifted the stay. See also In re Tejal Investment, LLC, 2012 WL 6186159 (Bankr. D. Utah 2012) (the debtor's financial data and projections were speculative and did not show that a successful reorganization within a reasonable time was probable); In re Bowman, 253 B.R. 233 (9th Cir. B.A.P. 2000). For further illustrations of the application of §362(d)(2)(B), see Examples 1 and 2.

Because §362(d)(2)(B) uses the word "reorganization," there has been some question about whether it applies only in Ch. 11 cases or also in cases under Ch. 12 or 13. This is because Ch. 11 is officially entitled "reorganization," while Chs. 12 and 13 are headed "debt adjustment." If it does not apply under Chs. 12 and 13, then the effect of §362(d)(2) would be the same as in Ch. 7: Once the debtor has no equity in the property, relief from stay must be granted. Although some courts have taken this view, the more favored interpretation is to read "reorganization" broadly to include rehabilitation under Chs. 12 and 13. Thus, one should treat §362(d)(2)(B) as requiring that the property is not necessary to the debtor's fresh start, whether the debtor is in business or is a consumer who may need the property for personal rehabilitation, and irrespective of whether the case has been filed under Ch. 11, 12, or 13. (See Example 2.)

§11.4.3 Single Asset Real Estate Cases

Section 362(d)(3) was added in 1994 and was amended by BAPCPA. Its purpose is to deal with complaints by mortgage holders that the stay was being abused in "single asset real estate" (SARE) cases. Section 362(d)(3) applies only to a SARE case, which is defined in §101(51B) to be a case in which the debtor (other than a family farmer) derives substantially all of its gross income from the rental of a single piece of real property that is, essentially, either used as commercial premises or as an apartment complex larger than four units. Prior to 2005, the definition had a debt ceiling that confined it to smaller cases. However, the debt ceiling was eliminated by BAPCPA. In short, a case satisfies the definition of a SARE case if the debtor's only significant business is the ownership of a single piece of income-producing real estate, and the debtor is engaged only in the passive activity of collecting rent and conducting maintenance of the property and other activity incidental to business of renting the property. If the debtor conducts some other substantial income-producing business activity in addition to the rental business, the case does not qualify as a SARE case. See, for example, *In re Scotia Pacific Co., LLC*, 508 F.3d 214 (5th Cir. 2007).

The type of problem that §362(d)(3) is designed to deal with arises where the SARE debtor defaults on its mortgage and files a Ch. 11 petition to forestall foreclosure, without a realistic immediate prospect of successful reorganization. Although cases of this kind could be disposed of on the basis of relief from stay under §362(d)(1) or (2), Congress decided to address the problem more directly by enacting subsection (d)(3). Section 362(d)(3) is therefore a ground for relief completely separate from and alternative to the grounds in §362(d)(1) and (2). In essence, its purpose is to prevent dilatory behavior by putting pressure on the debtor to devise a workable plan within a relatively short period after the order for relief, usually 90 days, or if this has not been possible, at least to make payments equal to interest to the mortgage holder. If the debtor does neither of these things, the mortgagee may obtain relief from stay.

§11.4.4 *In Rem* Relief Relating to Real Property Collateral

BAPCPA added subsection (4) to §362(d) to counter a form of debtor abuse in which the debtor, sometimes with the collusion of related entities, files successive bankruptcy petitions to frustrate the foreclosure of a security interest in real property. The subsection provides for the grant of relief from the stay of an act against real property in favor of a creditor who has a claim secured by that property. The court may grant relief to the secured creditor if it finds "that the filing of the petition was part of a scheme to delay, hinder, or defraud creditors" that involved either a transfer of ownership (or some other interest) in that property without the approval of the secured creditor or the court, or involved multiple bankruptcy filings affecting the property. Section §362(4)(d) refers to a "scheme," which denotes that the debtor's abusive conduct must be part of a deliberate overall plot or plan to hinder, delay, or defraud creditors. As originally enacted, the section used the language "delay, hinder, and defraud," which led courts to conclude that it was not enough for the applicant to show hindrance and delay. It must also show fraudulent intent. The word "and" was replaced by "or" by an amendment in 2010, making it clear that Congress intended delay, hindrance, and fraud to be alternative bases for relief. In *In re Tejal Investment, LLC* the court observed that the 2010 amendment lowered the bar to granting *in rem* relief because the phrase must be read disjunctively, so the section applies either if the scheme was to delay, or to hinder, or to defraud.

To establish fraud, the applicant must prove that the debtor made fraudulent misrepresentations, knowing they were false, with intent to deceive, inducing reliance by the creditor to its detriment. See, for example, *In re*

Muhaimin, 343 B.R. 159 (Bankr. D. Md. 2006); In re Smith, 395 B.R. 711 (Bankr. D. Kan. 2008). In Muhaimin the court addressed the burden of proving the debtor's fraud under §362(d)(4). Although the debtor bears the burden of persuasion under §362(g), the applicant has the initial burden of going forward to establish prima facie grounds for relief for fraud.

If the creditor obtains relief from stay under §362(d)(4), it may file the order for relief in the appropriate real estate records under state law. The order will then be binding in any other bankruptcy case (whether filed by the debtor or someone else) that would affect the property for a period of two years after entry of the order. Because this order for relief from stay binds the real property upon being filed, it is referred to as an in rem order. An order of this kind is of particular value where, for example, the debtor files a bankruptcy petition and the creditor gets relief from stay but, before the foreclosure can proceed, an entity related to the debtor files a bankruptcy petition and claims an interest in the property. The in rem nature of the order makes it binding on any party that takes transfer of the property after the stay is lifted.

§11.5 LACK OF ADEQUATE PROTECTION AS CAUSE FOR RELIEF FROM STAY UNDER §362(d)(1)

§11.5.1 The Interests Entitled to Adequate Protection

As stated earlier, the lack of adequate protection is the only cause for relief from stay that is expressly mentioned in §362(d)(1). The concept of adequate protection plays a significant role in applications for relief from stay and also arises in connection with the trustee's dealings with encumbered estate property.[1]

Section 362(d)(1) permits relief from stay when the applicant's interest in property lacks adequate protection. Adequate protection is only available to holders of interests in property of the estate or the debtor and cannot be sought by unsecured creditors. Section 362(d)(1) is thus confined to claimants such as secured creditors, lessors who have leased property to the debtor, co-owners of the debtor's property, and others with a valid interest in property. The existence of such a valid interest in property is determined with reference to nonbankruptcy law. In the remainder of the discussion, the secured claim is used to exemplify an interest for which adequate protection is sought.

---

1. Adequate protection is raised again in Chapter 17.

§11.5.2 The Circumstances under Which the Need for Adequate Protection Arises

When the petition is filed, the debtor's property becomes property of the estate under §541. Because all the debtor's legal and equitable interests in property fall within the estate, property of the estate includes property that is subject to liens or security interests. Provided that these encumbrances are valid under nonbankruptcy law and do not have qualities that make them avoidable in bankruptcy (discussed in Chapters 14 to 16), they remain effective against the estate. At the appropriate time, the secured creditor is entitled to be paid out the full value of the secured claim (whether in a lump sum or by installments under a plan) or to have the property abandoned so that it can be foreclosed upon. In the interim, the stay prevents the secured creditor from taking any action to enforce the interest.

The stay creates a risk for the secured creditor. In the absence of the stay it could have foreclosed on the property immediately upon the debtor's default and applied the proceeds to satisfaction of its claim. Because the stay prevents immediate foreclosure, the creditor faces the risk that its collateral may decline in value while the stay is in effect, so that if the property eventually has to be realized, it may generate fewer proceeds. If the collateral value drops below the amount of the debt, the reduction in value eats away the security, reducing the secured portion of the claim and increasing the deficiency. This risk of delay in realization may sometimes be a problem in a Ch. 7 liquidation, but the nature of a Ch. 7 case usually makes adequate protection less of an issue because collateral is normally liquidated or abandoned quite promptly, and is not usually used extensively by the estate. The situation is different in cases under Chs. 11, 12, and 13, where the debtor or the estate usually proposes to keep and use the property while the claim is paid off under the plan. As plan payments can extend over some time, the secured creditor is exposed to a much more substantial risk of devaluation. If the debtor's rehabilitation is successful, the risk of loss does not materialize: The plan is consummated, and the secured claim is eventually paid in full. However, if the debtor's attempt at rehabilitation fails, the estate ends up in liquidation and the secured creditor is left to its recourse against the property for the unpaid balance of the debt. If the relationship between the debt and the value of the property has changed adversely during the period of the stay, the creditor has been prejudiced by having to wait. Adequate protection is intended to reduce the secured creditor's risk of loss from the stay by requiring the trustee to take action to protect the collateral's value so that if realization becomes necessary in the future, the creditor will not suffer a loss that would have been avoided by immediate foreclosure.

Note that the interest to be protected is the present value of the collateral. It is not the purpose of §362(d)(1) to allow the claimant to improve its position by making up a deficiency that previously existed. In addition, in *United Savings Association of Texas v. Timbers of Inwood Forest Associates, Ltd.*, 484 U.S. 365 (1988), the U.S. Supreme Court held that adequate protection does not cover any loss that the creditor may suffer as a result of not having the ability to reinvest the proceeds of the property on immediate foreclosure. The Court said that the interest in property to be protected is the value of the property itself, not the right to take possession of the property and realize it. (*See* Example 4.)

§11.5.3 Factors to Be Considered in Determining the Need for Adequate Protection

To decide whether the security interest is adequately protected, a comparison must be made between the present ratio of property value to debt and the predicted future ratio if the property is to be kept and used or disposed of as proposed by the estate. Three questions must be asked:

(1) If the stay is lifted and foreclosure proceeds, what is the claimant likely to receive?   This requires a factual determination of the present value of the property in relation to the debt.

(2) If the stay is left in effect and the estate deals with the property as proposed, what is likely to happen to the value of the property in relation to the debt?   This inquiry involves a calculation of the rate of increase or decrease of the debt and a comparison to the future value of the collateral. To predict future value, account must be taken of such factors as appreciation or depreciation of market value, deterioration of the property through use, hazards to the property, and insurance coverage.

(3) What is the likelihood of successful rehabilitation?   In a Ch. 7 case, the first two inquiries are sufficient to determine the need for adequate protection because the only issue is whether delay in liquidation will prejudice the secured claim. In rehabilitation cases, this third inquiry must be pursued. If there is a good chance that the debtor's plan will be consummated, the risk of eventual liquidation of the property under adverse circumstances is diminished. Therefore, if the debtor's prospects of recovery seem good, the lower probability of liquidation may offset some uncertainty about the future debt-collateral ratio.

As these factors indicate, the need for adequate protection is a factual issue that calls for an overall assessment of the vulnerability of the collateral. To make this assessment, the court must determine the present and predicted future value of the collateral (usually proven by expert testimony), must take into account any potential hazards to the property, and must evaluate the efficacy of the debtor's rehabilitation efforts. This factual determination can be difficult, particularly where conflicting testimony is offered by the parties.

The following simple example illustrates the process of comparison: Say that in a Ch. 11 case, the debtor owes $100,000 to the secured creditor. That debt is secured by a lien on a piece of machinery with a present value of $100,000. If foreclosure took place immediately, the secured claim would be paid in full (less the foreclosure costs, which are ignored here for the sake of simplicity). If the stay remains in effect and the estate uses the machine during the course of its rehabilitation efforts, the machine will depreciate by 20 percent per annum. If the rehabilitation fails in a year's time and the machine is then realized, the secured claim will be worth only $80,000. Unless the plan provides for reduction of the debt by at least $20,000 during this period or for some other means of offsetting the depreciation, the interest is not adequately protected and relief from stay should be granted. *See* section 11.5.4.

By contrast, say that the present value of the machine is $150,000 and the debt is $100,000. The claim is oversecured. This surplus of debtor equity in the property over the secured claim is called an "equity cushion."[2] The existence of the equity cushion means that even if the property depreciates at 20 percent per year and the depreciation is not offset by an immediate reduction in debt, the value of the property will exceed the debt for some time. If the rehabilitation fails in the next couple of years, the claimant will still receive full payment of the secured claim. Therefore, at this stage[3] the interest is adequately protected, and there is no cause for relief from stay. (Once again, complicating factors such as the accrual of interest and foreclosure costs are disregarded here.) An equity cushion is often important in adequate protection cases. If the property is valuable enough to provide a buffer of unencumbered equity to accommodate likely depreciation, the secured claim is protected. Of course, the question of whether such an equity cushion exists and how large it should be to assure protection can be difficult to resolve. For a useful example of a case concerning this issue, see In re *Alyucan Interstate Corp.*, 12 B.R. 803 (Bankr. D. Vt. 1981). *See also* Example 2.

As noted in section 11.5.2, it must be stressed that the secured creditor is only entitled to protection of the present value of its interest and cannot demand an improvement in its position. For example, if the debt is

---

2. *See* section 2.5.3. for a further explanation of this term.
3. Although the equity cushion may adequately protect the claimant at this stage, that protection will diminish as the cushion shrinks unless the estate makes payments to reduce the debt. Therefore, even if the claimant is not entitled to relief from stay at present, it may seek relief later.

$100,000, the present value of the collateral is $90,000 and depreciation is predicted to be 20 percent per annum, adequate protection requires maintenance of the nine-tenth's secured claim. It does not entitle the undersecured creditor to make up the $10,000 deficiency.

§11.5.4 The Means and Method of Furnishing Adequate Protection

Section 362(d)(1) merely refers to adequate protection without indicating what it is. There is in fact no definition of the term in the Code. However, §361 provides three examples of how adequate protection may be furnished.[4] Section 361 is not intended to be exclusive: Any means by which the trustee can assure protection of the claimant's interest can be tendered as adequate protection.

The three methods of providing adequate protection suggested by §361 are the following:

(1) Cash payments (§361(1)). If the estate has sufficient income, it can make cash payments to the claimant to reduce the debt and maintain the ratio between the claim and the property value.

(2) Additional collateral (§361(2)). If there is unencumbered property in the estate, the trustee can provide adequate protection by granting a lien on additional property or replacing the existing lien with a lien on property of greater value.

(3) The grant of an "indubitable equivalent" (§361(3)). The third suggested form of adequate protection is the most general. Section 361(3) authorizes the trustee to propose adequate protection by giving the claimant any form of relief that will result in realization of the "indubitable equivalent" of the claimant's interest in property. This quaint term, standing in sharp contrast to the otherwise pedestrian statutory prose, was lifted from an opinion by Learned Hand, who knew how to turn a phrase. The formulation sets a standard for measuring the protection, rather than suggesting a means of providing it. It requires the court to decide whether a means of protection proposed by the trustee ensures that the claimant will certainly receive no less than the value of its property interest.

Section 361(3) expressly excludes the grant of an administrative expense priority as a means of providing adequate protection. Congress

---

4. Section 361 does not apply in a Ch. 12 case. Section 1205 has its own list of ways in which adequate protection may be furnished in a Ch. 12 case.

felt that such a grant is too uncertain a means of protection, because the estate may not have sufficient assets to pay administrative expenses in full. (Administrative expenses are a second priority unsecured claim, so they are paid before most other unsecured creditors. Priorities are discussed in section 19.6.)

As stated in section 11.4.1, the trustee, as the party opposing relief from stay, bears the burden of proving that the interest is adequately protected. If the trustee believes that the interest is not at risk, he or she will seek to prove that nothing need be done to bolster it. If it seems that adequate protection is lacking, the trustee has the initiative of offering corrective measures of the kind suggested in §361. The court then determines whether or not the interest is adequately protected and grants relief from stay if it is not. See, for example, In re Blehm Land & Cattle Co., 859 F.2d 137 (10th Cir. 1988). Relief need not take the form of an immediate lifting of the stay. If the court determines that adequate protection is lacking and that any measures proposed by the trustee are insufficient to cure the problem, it can condition the stay on the trustee taking specified action to protect the interest. It is also possible for the trustee and claimant to settle the adequate protection issue by agreeing to the form of protection to be provided. Such an agreement can be made an order of the court.

§11.5.5 The Failure of Adequate Protection: Superpriority under §507(b)

As stated in section 11.5.3, the determination that the interest is adequately protected is based on evidence of present value and predicted future value. This evidence is speculative and could be wrong. If realization of the property eventually becomes necessary, it may turn out that deterioration of the property-debt ratio was worse than anticipated, so that the interest was not adequately protected.

Section 507(b) is intended to provide relief to the secured creditor under these circumstances. It states that if the trustee provided adequate protection to a claimant, and the protection turns out to be inadequate, the shortfall is treated as a priority claim that ranks at the top of the administrative expense priority category. As more fully explained in section 19.6.4, administrative expenses are paid as a second priority under §507(a)(2), just below qualifying first-priority domestic support obligations. The superpriority granted to the shortfall resulting from the misjudgment of adequate protection therefore places the claim for the shortfall in a position senior to administrative expenses and all other priority claims in §507 except for first-priority domestic support claims. As long as the estate has sufficient funds after settling secured claims and paying any first-priority claims, the superpriority assures payment of the shortfall.

Section 507(b) is not clearly drafted. Not only does it send the reader on a wild goose chase by a cryptic reference to §507(a)(2), but it also has some restrictive language that appears to confine superpriority relief to cases in which the trustee has actually furnished adequate protection. The section begins with the words, "If the trustee . . . provides adequate protection. . . ." Literally interpreted, it therefore appears to apply only if the trustee takes action to provide adequate protection, which may occur by consent, or may follow the court's determination that adequate protection must be furnished. It does not appear to apply when the court has refused relief from stay on the basis that adequate protection already exists without further bolstering by the trustee. In *LNC Investments v. First Fidelity Bank*, 247 B.R. 38 (S.D.N.Y. 2000), the court concluded that although a different interpretation of the labyrinthine and ambiguous language of §507(b) is plausible, the better approach is to give literal effect to the word "provides" and to exclude from the section situations in which the court found that the creditor was already adequately protected, and that no further steps were required to protect its interest. Notwithstanding that the plain meaning of the language points to this result, it seems unfair in principle to distinguish cases in which protection was provided from those in which the court found it to be unnecessary. In both cases, the miscalculation left the claimant with a deficiency. (*See* Example 3.)

Examples

1. Maladroit Manufacturing Co., Inc. has filed a bankruptcy petition under Ch. 7. Among the debtor's assets is a large piece of machinery that forms an integral part of its manufacturing plant. The machine was purchased on credit from Lien Machine, Inc. for $500,000 about two years prior to bankruptcy. At the time of sale, Lien Machine perfected a security interest in the machine to secure the price. The current balance on the debt is $200,000. Maladroit had defaulted in its payments prior to filing the petition, and Lien Machine had been about to foreclose on the machine when the petition was filed.

   Almost immediately after the petition was filed, Lien Machine applied for relief from stay under §362(d)(2) so that it could continue its foreclosure. At the hearing of the relief application, an appraiser hired by the estate testified that the market value of the machine is $250,000. Lien Machine offered evidence by two appraisers. The one testified that the market value of the machine is $195,000. The other testified that the value of the machine, if sold by auction in a foreclosure sale, is not more than $150,000.

   a. Is Lien Machine likely to obtain relief from stay under §362(d)(2) in this Ch. 7 case?

    b. Would the answer be different if Maladroit had filed a petition under Ch. 11?

    Note: Lien Machine seeks relief under §362(d)(2). This question is confined to grounds for relief under that provision and does not address the alternative ground for relief for cause under §362(d)(1).

2. Rocky Shoal filed a Ch. 13 petition last month. His prize possession, and his only asset of economic value, is a sailboat that he uses for recreation. He bought the boat on credit from High Seize Boating Co. two years ago. Under the sales contract, he undertook to repay the loan in monthly installments over five years and granted High Seize a security interest in the boat to secure the balance of the price. The security interest is validly perfected under state law and unavoidable.

    Rocky defaulted in his payments two months before filing the petition. High Seize had initiated foreclosure proceedings that have been suspended by the automatic stay. At the time of the filing of the petition, the balance due on the loan was $30,000.

    High Seize has applied for relief from stay under §362(d)(2) on the ground that Rocky has no equity in the property, and it is not necessary for an effective reorganization. As an alternative, High Seize also argues that it has cause for relief under §362(d)(1) because its interest in the boat is not adequately protected.

    There is conflicting evidence on the value of the boat. The appraiser testifying on behalf of High Seize places a present market value of $30,000 on the boat and predicts that it will depreciate 10 percent during the next year. The appraiser estimates that the boat would realize only $20,000 in a distress foreclosure sale. The trustee's appraiser estimates the market value of the boat to be $50,000 and its distress sale value to be $35,000. She disagrees that the boat will depreciate over the next year: Rocky has taken meticulous care of it, and the market for good used boats is vigorous.

    a. Does High Seize have grounds for relief from stay under §362(d)(2)?
    b. Does High Seize have grounds for relief under §362(d)(1) as a result of lack of adequate protection?

3. Assume that the court, in evaluating the evidence in High Seize's application for relief from stay, finds that the boat is indeed worth $50,000, leaving an equity cushion of $20,000. The court also determines that the value of the boat is likely to remain stable, that the boat is fully insured, and that Rocky has a good prospect of successful rehabilitation. Because the equity cushion is sufficient to accommodate interest that accrues on the claim and will also act as a buffer for any unexpected drop in market value, the court finds the interest to be adequately protected and refuses relief from stay under §362(d)(1). Because the debtor has equity in the property, relief is also refused under §362(d)(2).

Rocky's Ch. 13 plan is confirmed. Under the plan he proposes to pay High Seize its full $30,000 plus interest over a three-year period and to retain the boat, which remains subject to the lien until the plan is consummated. About a year after the plan confirmation, Rocky loses his job. He can no longer afford payments under the plan and converts the case to Ch. 7. At this time, the balance of the debt to High Seize is $22,000. The trustee attempts to liquidate the boat so that High Seize can be paid and any surplus can be placed in the estate's general fund. However, because of an economic recession, the used boat market has collapsed. The best offer received for the boat is $20,000. Because High Seize realizes that it will do no better itself, it does not object to the trustee's sale. The proceeds of the sale are paid out to High Seize. What can be done about the shortfall?

4. Asset Indigestion, Inc. recently filed a Ch. 11 petition. Its principal asset is a piece of real property subject to a mortgage held by Linger Longingly Loan Co. At the time of the petition, the debt secured by the mortgage was $450,000. The value of the property has declined over the last few years as a result of an economic slump in the region. The experts agree that its value at the time of the petition is $425,000 and that the property market has stabilized. Although there is little prospect of prices rising in the near future, they are not likely to decline either.

   Linger Longingly has applied for relief from stay on the ground that its interest lacks adequate protection. It argues that if the property were sold immediately, the proceeds of $425,000 would be realized and could be invested elsewhere to generate income. If the estate is allowed to keep the property, Linger Longingly will be delayed in realizing it and therefore loses the opportunity of reinvestment. Should relief from stay be granted?

5. Multilien Investments, Inc., a debtor in Ch. 11, owns a piece of real property worth $5 million. It owes $4.7 million to Premier Mortgage Co. on a first mortgage, $600,000 to Secundo Security Co. on a second mortgage, and $400,000 to Trinity Finance Co. on a third mortgage. Premier has moved for relief from stay under §362(d)(2) on the ground that the debtor does not have an equity in the property and that it is not needed for an effective reorganization. The debtor opposes the motion. It is joined in its opposition by the two junior lienholders, who realize that if Premier is allowed to foreclose now, Secundo will recover only portion of its undersecured debt from the proceeds and Trinity's lien will be wiped out. They feel that if the debtor is allowed to keep the property, a predicted upward trend in the market may benefit their interests. They argue that if one just takes into account the mortgage of Premier, the party seeking relief, the debtor does have an equity of $300,000 in the property, and this should preclude Premier from getting relief under §362(d)(2). Is this a good argument?

Explanations

1. a. Is Lien Machine likely to obtain relief from stay in this Ch. 7 case? Two elements must be satisfied for relief to be granted under §362(d)(2). First, the debtor must have no equity in the property. (Because the debtor's prepetition property becomes property of the estate, the debtor's equity is in fact the estate's equity in the property.) The equity is measured by the excess in the property's value over the amount of the debt secured by the property. There is no dispute that the debt is $200,000. The question in issue, to determine the debtor's equity in the property, is the value of the property. Under §362(g), Lien Machine bears the burden of proving that the debtor has no equity in the property.

   Valuation is a factual question that is often based on conflicting opinion evidence. If the evidence of the estate's appraiser is accepted, the debtor does have equity in the property; the creditor's evidence contradicts this. The court must attempt to determine a realistic valuation based on the credibility of the witnesses, the proposed use and disposition of the property, and any other relevant factors. One of the issues suggested by the question is whether market value or distress sale proceeds is a more realistic figure. The machine is to be liquidated, but there may be an opportunity to sell it on the market by private sale, rather than by auction.

   If the court finds that the property is worth more than $200,000, the debtor has equity in the property, and relief from stay cannot be granted under §362(d)(2). If the property is found to be worth $200,000 or less, the first element is satisfied, and the second must be determined: Because this is a Ch. 7 case, the property cannot be necessary for an effective reorganization, and this element is inevitably satisfied. Therefore, unless the debtor has equity in the property, the grounds for relief under §362(d)(2) are satisfied and the stay will be lifted.

   b. Is the answer different if Maladroit had filed under Ch. 11? The first part of the test remains the same, but the question of whether the property is necessary to an effective reorganization is now relevant. To decide this, two factors must be considered: (1) the debtor must need the property for its reorganization efforts, and (2) the debtor must have a prospect of successful reorganization. Section 362(g) places the burden on the debtor (as the party opposing the relief) to prove these matters. As this is a Ch. 11 case, the debtor in possession represents the estate.

   The question indicates that the machine is an integral part of the plant, thereby suggesting that the debtor may be able to satisfy this aspect of the test. No information is given on the prospects of

Maladroit's success in its effort to reorganize. However, because the application is made very early in the Ch. 11 case, the court is likely to lean in favor of giving the debtor a chance and will be less exacting in the level of proof required to show the likelihood of rehabilitation.

Even if relief from stay is refused at this stage, Lien Machine will be able to make a new application if circumstances change. Also, even though consideration of §362(d)(1) has been excluded by this question, it should be noted that any possible deterioration in the debt-collateral ratio could serve as grounds for relief under that section.

2. a. Relief under §362(d)(2). Rocky may or may not have equity in the property, depending on the valuation fixed by the court. As in Example 1, the experts clash on the valuation issue: On High Seize's evidence, Rocky has no equity in the property, but the trustee's figures show otherwise. Also, the choice between distress liquidation value and market value has to be made based on the likely disposition of the boat. Thus, the court must not only resolve the conflict on value, but must also decide what standard of valuation is most realistic. High Seize bears the risk of nonpersuasion under §362(g).

   If the debtor has no equity in the property, one of the two requirements for relief under §362(d)(2) is satisfied, and the question of whether the property is needed for an effective reorganization must be considered. Although there is some dissent on the question, §362(d)(2)(B) is generally regarded as being applicable in Ch. 13 cases, in spite of the use of the word "reorganization." In Ch. 13, the question is whether the asset is necessary for the debtor's rehabilitation — that is, whether it is needed to affect a fresh start. This is apparently purely recreational property that is not used to support or shelter Rocky or to enable him to earn income. It is therefore very likely that the court will find that the property is not necessary to the debtor's "effective reorganization."

   In summary, if the court determines that Rocky has no equity in the property, and also finds the property not to be necessary for an effective reorganization, relief from stay will be granted under §362(d)(2). However, even if these grounds for relief are not satisfied, High Seize may still have cause for relief under §362(d)(1) if its interest is not adequately protected.

   b. Relief for lack of adequate protection. The property interest to be protected here is High Seize's valid, perfected security interest in the boat. (Remember that it is the interest in property, not the debt, that requires protection.) If the property is worth as much or more than the debt, the interest in the property is the full amount of the debt. If the property is worth less than the debt, part of the debt is unsecured, and the right to adequate protection relates only to the portion secured by the property. Once again, the valuation of the property is an important factual issue.

To decide whether High Seize's interest is adequately protected, the present and predicted future relationship between the debt and collateral value must be compared. The process of determining current value for the purpose of §362(d)(1) is the same as it is for §362(d)(2). It must be decided whether market or liquidation value is the proper measure, and the evidence must be weighed to decide what that value is. Also, the probability and extent of future change in that value in relation to the debt must be determined.

Assume that the testimony of the trustee's appraiser is accepted, and that High Seize usually resells repossessed property on the retail market, making market value the proper measure. The market value of the boat is $50,000 and the debt is $30,000. An immediate foreclosure would yield enough to pay the secured claim in full with costs and interest, and a surplus would remain for the estate. As the trustee's appraiser predicts a stable or rising value for the boat, this position will not deteriorate. An oversecured creditor is entitled to receive interest on its claim and costs until the surplus equity is exhausted, but there is a large enough equity cushion to accommodate increase in the debt by the addition of interest and costs. In short, on the trustee's evidence, the interest is adequately protected.

High Seize's appraiser fixes the current market value at the same level as the debt — $30,000. An immediate sale would give High Seize almost full payment of its claim after deducting sale costs. However, as there is no equity cushion and the appraiser predicts a decline in the value of the boat, a delay in foreclosure will prejudice High Seize. Even though Rocky will pay off the debt over time under his plan, it is not clear that those payments will be high enough or will begin soon enough to offset the decline in collateral value. If not, relief from stay must be granted unless the trustee is able to offer additional protection under §361. This could take the form of an immediate cash payment to reduce the debt, the provision of additional collateral, or any other means of ensuring that High Seize will receive the indubitable equivalent of its interest. The facts indicate that Rocky has no other valuable property, so augmentation of the collateral may not be possible. It is not clear whether the other means are open to him.

Of course, the court is not obliged to accept either of the two conflicting appraisals. It could decide a figure and rate of depreciation somewhere between those offered by the parties. The court would then decide, based on its factual finding, whether there is a sufficient equity cushion to protect the interest from deterioration. Although present and future value are very important considerations in deciding adequate protection, they are not the only factors to be taken into account. The debtor's prospects of rehabilitation are also relevant, and a strong likelihood of success may counteract some doubt in valuation. Also, because Rocky will retain and use the boat while the Ch. 13 plan is being consummated, adequate protection also requires that High Seize's interest is protected by insurance from loss or destruction of the collateral.

3. Assuming that the court's estimate of value at the time of the application was correct (it may not have been, but this will never be known), there has been a gross miscalculation of market trends. As a result, the protection of the interest was not adequate. Section 507(b) states that if the trustee "provides" adequate protection but that protection ultimately turns out to have been inadequate, the shortfall is to be given priority over all administrative expenses. (Section 507(b) is obscurely drafted, but this is its basic meaning.) Therefore, if §507(b) applies, its effect would be to elevate the unsecured claim for the shortfall to rank at the top of administrative expenses, which are a second priority claim. That is, the deficiency would be paid immediately after any qualifying first-priority domestic support obligations and before any other unsecured claims, including other second-priority administrative expenses. Unless Rocky owes qualifying first-priority domestic support obligations that are large enough to eat up the entire value of the estate, there is a good prospect that the deficiency would be paid. High Seize's problem is that the language of §507(b) may not cover its situation. which same courts read the subsection to cover situations in which the court finds no need to provide adequate protection, others emphasize the word "provides" and hold that the subsection covers only situations in which the trustee has actually provided adequate protection. In the present case, the trustee was not called on to provide any protection because the court concluded that the interest was already adequately protected.

4. Linger Longingly's argument sounds plausible because it will not be paid interest on its undersecured claim by the estate pending confirmation of the plan,[5] so estate retention of the property deprives it of the immediate opportunity to invest the property proceeds gainfully. However, as noted in section 11.5.2, the U.S. Supreme Court held in *United Savings Association of Texas* that the interest in property to be protected is the value of the property itself, not the economic benefit of realizing it and using the

---

5. Section 506(b) is discussed in section 19.5. In a Ch. 11 case, prior to confirmation of a plan, an unsecured or undersecured creditor is not entitled to receive interest on its claim. These creditors can demand that they are paid interest after confirmation so that they receive the present value of their claims. Present value is calculated by adding interest to the face amount of the debt. This is explained in Chapters 20 and 21.

proceeds gainfully. The court reasoned that undersecured creditors are not entitled to receive interest on their claims under §506, so §362(d) should not be available to allow an undersecured creditor to circumvent §506. If the loss of interest was to be a ground for adequate protection, undersecured creditors could obtain relief from stay as a matter of course under §362(d)(1).

The inability to get pendency interest places undersecured creditors in a difficult position and causes them losses where the prospects for successful reorganization are uncertain and the debtor is struggling (with attendant delay) to devise a confirmable plan. This may motivate them to look more carefully at the possibility of seeking relief either for cause (such as that the poor prospects of reorganization call into question the debtor's good faith in filing the Ch. 11 case), or on the basis of §362(d)(2). By definition, the debtor has no equity in the property where the mortgage is undersecured, and the poor prospects of success may establish that the property is not needed for an effective reorganization.

The ground for relief in §362(d)(3) may be available because this is a single asset real estate case as defined in §101(51B). Linger Longingly will be able to obtain relief from stay if Asset Indigestion cannot devise a feasible plan of reorganization within the prescribed period after the order for relief (which is 90 days, subject to some qualifications), or if that cannot be done, if Asset Indigestion fails to make interest payments to Linger Longingly from the end of that period.

5. Some courts have accepted this argument where junior lienholders have opposed the senior lienor's motion for relief from stay under §362(d)(2). However, this approach is difficult to reconcile with the plain language of §362(d)(2). Although the Code does not itself define what is meant by debtor's "equity," it is generally understood to mean the debtor's (or estate's) remaining economic interest in property — the surplus owned by the debtor (or estate) — after all liens on the property have been satisfied. If there is more than one lien on the property, the debtor is entitled only to what is left after all have been satisfied. It therefore goes against common usage, and is not supported by any statutory language, to define "equity" for purposes of §362(d)(2) as meaning whatever is left after the senior lien is satisfied. This was the view taken in In re Indian Palms Associates, Ltd., 61 F.3d. 197 (3d Cir. 1995), which insisted on using the plain and accepted meaning of "equity." The court noted that it is appropriate to disregard junior liens for the purposes of deciding whether the senior lienholder has an equity cushion that will adequately protect its interest. The reason for this is that from the perspective of the senior lienor, it does not matter if the debtor himself, or other junior interests, are entitled to the value in the property in excess of the lien. In either event, the excess value is available to act as a cushion

to the senior lien. However, just because "equity cushion" is used to describe value in the property that may not actually qualify as debtor's equity in the usual sense does not mean that a similar meaning is appropriate in §362(d)(2). The role that debtor's equity plays in that section is quite different. There, the fact that the debtor (or estate) has an economic interest in the property is one of the justifications for allowing the estate to keep it.

Of course, the finding that the debtor has no equity in the property does not end the inquiry. The next question to be decided is whether the property is necessary for an effective reorganization. The example does not provide facts to decide this.

12

Property of the Estate

§12.1 THE CREATION OF THE BANKRUPTCY ESTATE AND DEBTOR'S NEW ESTATE

Section 541(a) states that an estate is created by the commencement of the bankruptcy case. The bankrupt estate is a new legal entity, separate from the debtor. In a Ch. 7 liquidation of an individual debtor, the break between the debtor and the estate is most complete. The debtor's property, as at the date of the petition, passes to the estate. In due course, all this property (with the exception of property that is abandoned by the trustee as discussed in section 12.4) is liquidated and its proceeds distributed to creditors.

At the same time as the bankruptcy estate is created, the individual Ch. 7 debtor[1] begins to accumulate a new estate. This new estate consists of earnings and property acquired after the filing as well as property that has been released to the debtor from the estate as exempt or abandoned by the trustee as having no economic value. These postpetition assets of the debtor are the basis of his or her fresh start. As mentioned in sections 10.4.1 and 10.6, prepetition creditors cannot reach them because they are stayed from doing so pending the debtor's discharge. Upon discharge of a pre-petition debt, the creditor is permanently enjoined from collecting that debt.

---

1. A corporation in liquidation cannot be rehabilitated. (*See* sections 8.2.1 and 22.1). It therefore does not acquire a new estate. When the corporation's bankrupt estate has been liquidated, the corporation ceases to operate and is ultimately de-registered.

Diagram 12a shows the flow of property into and out of the Ch. 7 estate of an individual debtor, and the birth of the debtor's postbankruptcy estate.

Flow of Property in a Ch. 7 Case

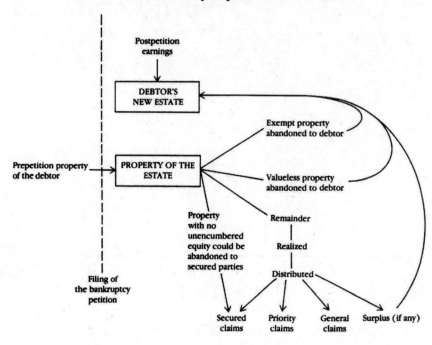

Section 541 applies in cases under Chs. 11, 12, and 13, as it does in Ch. 7. Like a Ch. 7 filing, a petition under any of the rehabilitation chapters creates a bankruptcy estate as a legal entity separate from the debtor. However, because rehabilitation bankruptcy is aimed at preservation of the estate for the debtor rather than its liquidation, the break between the bankruptcy estate and the debtor's fresh start estate is not as complete or final. Chs. 11, 12, and 13 enable the debtor to reacquire prepetition property from the estate by committing postpetition earnings or other property or value to the payment of claims that would otherwise have been settled by the liquidation of the property. In effect, by using property or postpetition income that would not have been part of the Ch. 7 estate, the debtor is able to save property that would have been liquidated under Ch. 7. The debtor is usually able to keep and use estate property pending confirmation of the plan. Upon confirmation, all property in the estate that is not otherwise disposed of under the plan revests in the debtor. If the plan is ultimately consummated, the debtor keeps this property, which forms part of the debtor's new estate.

However, if the debtor's attempt at rehabilitation fails and the case is converted to Ch. 7, the debtor's right to keep estate property ends, and the property is surrendered to the trustee for liquidation.

Flow of Property in a Ch. 13 Case

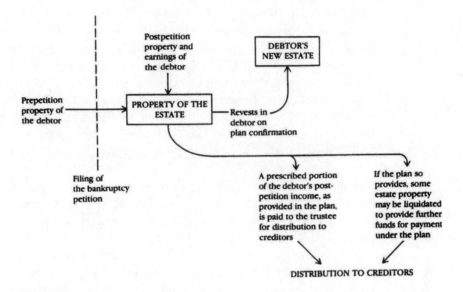

There are differences between the treatment of property under Chs. 11, 12, and 13 that are not taken into account in the above description. One important difference is that postpetition property of the debtor continues to enter the estate in a Ch. 12, 13, and individual Ch. 11 case, but not in a corporate Ch. 11 case. This is explained in section 12.2.3. Despite such differences, the following broad outline of the relationship between the bankrupt estate and the debtor's new estate makes the essential distinction between rehabilitation and liquidation cases. Diagram 12b reflects the flow of property in a Ch. 13 case. Comparison with Diagram 12a illustrates this distinction.

§12.2 THE COMPOSITION OF THE ESTATE

§12.2.1 Legal and Equitable Interests of the Debtor at the Time of the Petition

As stated in section 12.1, the bankruptcy estate is created at the commencement of the case. In both voluntary and involuntary cases, the date of filing the petition is the crucial date for determining the debtor's property interests that pass to the estate. Section 541 prescribes the composition of the estate: §541(a) states what is included in the estate, and §541(b) and (d) make some specific exclusions from it. The exclusions relate to specific and specialized types of property that are not detailed in this book. The Bankruptcy Abuse Prevention and Consumer Protection Act of 2005 (BAPCPA) added several new exclusions to §541(b) covering property such as educational savings accounts, tuition benefit funds, and contributions to employee benefit plans. The broadest and most far-reaching provision is §541(a)(1), which includes in the estate "all legal or equitable interests of the debtor in property as of the commencement of the case." The remaining provisions of §541(a) deal with ancillary categories of property such as community property, property recovered by the trustee in the exercise of avoidance powers, certain bequests acquired by the debtor within a pre-scribed time of the petition, proceeds of estate property, and property acquired by the estate itself.

Although §541(a)(1) brings into the estate all the debtor's legal and equitable property interests at the time of the petition, it does not define what these interests are. The question whether or not the debtor has an interest in property and the determination of the nature and extent of that interest must be resolved under nonbankruptcy law. That is, bankruptcy law provides for the estate's succession to the debtor's property rights, but nonbankruptcy law governs the issue of whether and to what extent a particular asset is the debtor's property. If the debtor's interest in property is limited or qualified, the estate acquires the property subject to that limitation or qualification. The estate generally can acquire no greater right to property than the debtor had.[2] Therefore, if property of the debtor is subject to a valid encumbrance, it enters the estate subject to that encumbrance. Also, if the property in question is a claim against another person, the estate acquires the claim subject to any defense that the other person could have asserted against the debtor. For example, in *Mosier v. Callister, Nebeker, & McCullough*, 546 F.3d 1271 (10th Cir. 2008), the court allowed a party sued by the estate to assert the *in pari delicto* defense against the estate where that defense could have been raised had the debtor initiated the suit. Example 1 illustrates some of the inclusions and exclusions of §541 in conjunction with nonbank-ruptcy law.

---

2. In some circumstances, the trustee has the power under various provisions of the Code to avoid a claim to or interest in estate property. (*See* Chapters 14 to 16.) In a sense, the result of this is that in some cases the trustee may have greater rights in relation to the property than the debtor had. However, the trustee's avoidance powers must be distinguished from the estate's succession to the debtor's property rights.

§12.2.2 Restrictions on the Transfer of Property Rights under Nonbankruptcy Law or Contract

Although the debtor's interest in property is determined by nonbankruptcy law, the deference to nonbankruptcy law is not absolute. Section 541(c) invalidates any provision of nonbankruptcy law as well as any condition created by contract or transfer instrument that restricts the transfer of property rights so that they do not pass to the estate on bankruptcy. Therefore, if the debtor has a property right under nonbankruptcy law but a contract or state law declares that right nontransferable to the estate or forfeited upon the debtor's bankruptcy, the restriction is ineffective. Section 541(c) is intended to prevent a state or a private party from circumventing §541(a).

An important exception to this rule is set out in §541(c)(2), which validates in bankruptcy a "restriction on the transfer of a beneficial interest of the debtor in a trust that is enforceable under applicable bankruptcy law." The plain meaning of this provision makes it applicable to a retirement fund that is subject to an antialienation provision under nonbankruptcy law. However, some courts of appeal refused to apply it to such funds on the basis that the legislative history of §541(c)(2) indicates that Congress intended this exception to apply only to spendthrift trusts recognized as nonexecutable under applicable state law. The U.S. Supreme Court rejected this approach in *Patterson v. Shumate*, 504 U.S. 753 (1992). The Supreme Court held that because the meaning of §541(c)(2) was clear, there was no occasion to resort to legislative history. In its plain meaning, §541(c)(2) covers all trusts, including retirement funds, that are subject to restrictions on alienation enforceable under nonbankruptcy law. The Court therefore held that a retirement plan that qualified as tax exempt under the Employee Retirement Income Security Act (ERISA) did not enter the estate because ERISA requires a qualifying plan to preclude assignment or alienation of benefits under the plan. The Court considered that this plain-meaning approach was also consistent with ERISA's policy of protecting pension benefits, which outweighed the bankruptcy policy of broad inclusion in the estate. Lower courts have applied *Patterson* to include retirement plans that are not ERISA-qualified, provided that the plan qualifies as a trust subject to restrictions on transfer under state or other federal law. See *In re Williams*, 290 B.R. 83 (Bankr. E.D. Pa. 2003); *In re Laher*, 496 F.3d 279 (3d Cir. 2007). In *Laher* the court noted that the Code does not define "trust" so nonbankruptcy law determines if a pension plan qualifies as a trust, and §541(c)(2) covers a fund that is functionally equivalent to a trust. See Example 1(e).

§12.2.3 Property Acquired after the Filing of the Petition

Section 541 focuses primarily on the property interests held by the debtor at the time of the petition. In most cases, the debtor continues to acquire property after the petition has been filed, such as new income from employment or business, or returns from prepetition transactions, investments, or assets. It is necessary to decide whether this new property falls into the estate or is retained by the debtor as part of the new fresh start estate. The chapter under which relief is sought affects this question.

a. Chs. 7 and Corporate Ch. 11 Cases

In a Ch. 7 liquidation and a Ch. 11 reorganization, the general rule is that all earnings and property acquired by the debtor subsequent to the filing from sources that are not related to prepetition property remain property of the debtor and do not become property of the estate. (postpetition property in an individual Ch. 11 reorganization is dealt with in the same way as in Chs. 12 and 13.) However, §541(a)(6) and (7) include in the estate proceeds and profits of estate property and property acquired postpetition by the estate itself. In some cases, it is easy to determine whether postpetition property belongs to the debtor or the estate. For example, a salary that the debtor earns from employment subsequent to filing is clearly his own property. By contrast, income or products generated by estate property (say, rent earned from the lease of estate property) fall within the estate. However, in some cases the link between prepetition and postpetition property is more ambiguous, and has to be determined by careful examination.

A few examples illustrate these more difficult situations: In *In re Marvel*, 372 B.R. 425 (Bankr. N.D. Ind. 2007), the debtor received a postpetition tax refund relating to an overpayment of taxes on income received both prior to and subsequent to the petition. The court apportioned the refund so that the portion relating to prepetition period was property of the estate, and the portion relating to postpetition period was property of the debtor. In *In re Burgess*, 438 F.3d 493 (5th Cir. 2006), the debtor received a disaster relief payment for a crop loss. Although the payment was received postpetition, the crop loss had occurred prepetition. The statute awarding the disaster relief payment was enacted postpetition. The court held that the payment was not property of the estate. The estate never acquired any interest in the crop because the crop had been destroyed prior to bankruptcy, and the debtor had no right in the relief payment at the time of filing because the statute granting relief was enacted only after the petition. In *In re McLain*, 516 F.3d 301 (5th Cir. 2008), the debtors converted bank accounts to cash prior to filing and deliberately failed to list the cash as an asset in their schedules. Subsequent to filing, they bought a life insurance policy with the cash. The court held the policy and its proceeds to be property of the estate. The debtors had wrongfully concealed the cash when they filed the petition, and under state law constructive trust doctrine, they were deemed to have held the cash in constructive trust for the estate. Therefore, the policy purchased with the cash became property of the estate, even though the policy was acquired postpetition. *See also* Example 2.

b. Ch. 12, 13, and Individuals Ch. 11 Cases

In Chs. 12 and 13, the general rule is different. In terms of §§1207 and 1306, property of the Ch. 12 or 13 estate includes not only property qualifying under §541 at the time of petition but also all property (as defined in §541) acquired and all remuneration for services earned by the debtor up to the time that the case is closed, dismissed, or converted. In other words, §§1207 and 1306 provide for property and income of the debtor to continue entering the estate until the case comes to an end, either because the plan is consummated or because the debtor's plan of rehabilitation fails. Section 1115, added by BAPCPA, extended this rule to an individual Ch. 11 case.

Postpetition property and earnings are included in the Ch. 12 or 13 estate so that the trustee has supervisory power over them while the debtor is performing under the plan. Because the property vests in the debtor upon confirmation of the plan, and the debtor retains possession of it, the trustee's control of the property is legal rather than physical. *See* §§1207(b), 1227, 1306(b), and 1327. The trustee does handle property that is to be distributed under the plan so that installments due by the debtor under the plan are paid to the trustee for distribution. Because thers is usually no trustee in a Ch. 11 case, the debtor in possession contracts the property.

c. The Effect of Conversion from Ch. 12 or Ch. 13

Because property of the Ch. 7 estate is fixed at the date of the petition while property and earnings continue to enter the Ch. 12 or 13 estate after the petition, conversion from Ch. 12 or 13 to Ch. 7 gives rise to the question of whether the converted Ch. 7 estate includes property acquired by the debtor after the petition but before the conversion.

Section 348 deals with the effect of conversion. Its general rule, in §348(a), is that although the conversion constitutes the order for relief under the chapter to which the case is converted, the original petition date remains the effective date of commencement of the case for all purposes except those specified in the section. Section 348(f) was added to the Code in 1994 to resolve a split among courts over the question of whether property of the Ch. 7 estate, in a case converted from Ch. 12 or 13, was to be determined at the time of conversion or at the time of the original Ch. 12 or 13 filing. Section 348(f) governs only conversions from Ch. 13 to Ch. 7 and does not resolve the uncertainty where the debtor converts from Ch. 12. Section 348(f) provides that if the debtor's conversion is in good faith, the property of the Ch. 7 estate includes only the property of the original Ch. 13 estate that is still in the debtor's control or possession at the time of conversion. If the conversion is in bad faith, the Ch. 7 estate expands to include all the property acquired by the debtor (and hence by the Ch. 13 estate) up to the time of conversion.

§12.3 THE TRUSTEE'S POWER TO COMPEL DELIVERY OF PROPERTY OF THE ESTATE ("TURNOVER")

Section 521(a)(4) obliges the debtor to surrender all property to the trustee when the petition is filed. Under §542, any property of the debtor in the possession of other persons must be delivered to the trustee or its value accounted for; likewise, a debt due to the debtor must be paid to the trustee. The duty to deliver property to the estate ("turnover") under §542 applies even if the estate's equity in the property is small. Section 542(a) expressly applies to all property that may be used, sold, or leased by the trustee, or that may be exempted by the debtor. The link between this turnover requirement and the automatic stay is apparent. Even a creditor with an interest in property is obliged to relinquish possession to the trustee. If the creditor wishes to recover the property so that the interest can be enforced, application must be made for relief from stay. Section 542(a) makes an exception to the duty of delivery to the trustee for property that is of inconsequential value or benefit to the estate.

If the property is in the hands of a custodian, including an assignee for the benefit of creditors or a receiver or trustee who was appointed in non-bankruptcy law to administer any property of the debtor, then §543 applies rather than §542. Section 543 requires the turnover of and accounting for all the debtor's property or its proceeds in the control of the custodian. As soon as the custodian receives knowledge of the bankruptcy, the administration of the nonbankruptcy insolvency proceedings end and no further distributions may be made. The purpose of §543 is to ensure that upon bankruptcy, the trustee supersedes any nonbankruptcy trustee of the debtor's property. The section protects certain parties to whom the custodian has incurred obligations in the course of administering the property, and it provides for compensation to be made to the custodian for services rendered.

Provisions in both §§542 and 543 protect persons who have transferred property or made payments to third parties or to the debtor in good faith and without knowledge of the bankruptcy filing. Unless those exceptions apply, if a person fails to deliver estate property voluntarily the trustee is able to compel delivery by court order. In addition, §502(d) provides for the disallowance of the entire claim of a creditor who has failed to turn over property recoverable by the trustee.

§12.4 ABANDONMENT OF PROPERTY BY THE TRUSTEE

Some property that enters the estate is of no value or benefit to the estate. This may be because it is fully encumbered and is not needed for the debtor's rehabilitation, because it is fully exempt and cannot be liquidated for the benefit of creditors, because it costs more to maintain than it is worth, or simply because it has no economic value. The efficient administration of the estate and fairness to the debtor (and any other holder of an interest in the property) dictate that such property should be given up by the estate. Section 554 permits the court to authorize or order its abandonment. The initiative to abandon property may be taken by the trustee under §554(a) or applied for by a party in interest under §554(b). In either event, notice and a hearing are required. Under §102, this means that notice must be given to parties in interest, but a hearing is only held if objection is made. Section 554 does not indicate to whom the property is abandoned. However, abandonment divests the estate of all interest in the property, and it reverts to the debtor, whose rights in the property are restored as if no bankruptcy had occurred. Upon abandonment, the property remains subject to the automatic stay as property of the debtor. If someone other than the debtor has a possessory interest in the property (for example, a secured creditor who had lawfully seized the property prior to the filing) the court may abandon the property to that party. However, because the debtor still has a legal or equitable interest in the property, the party with the possessory interest must seek relief from the stay to foreclose on it.

To illustrate, say that property worth $5,000 entered the Ch. 7 estate of an individual debtor. The debtor has an exemption of $1,000 in the property, and it is subject to a valid, unavoidable lien of $4,000. There is therefore no value for the estate in the property, so the trustee will abandon it to the debtor. Unless the debtor is able to make arrangements with the creditor to keep the property and pay off the debt, the creditor will likely apply for relief from stay so that it can foreclose on its security interest.

The trustee cannot abandon property as of right. As noted before, if a party in interest objects, a hearing must be held at which the court must authorize the abandonment. A common reason for objection is a creditor's contention that the property does in fact have value for the estate. An objection may also be grounded on the basis that abandonment of the property places a burden on the public that outweighs the estate's interest in abandoning the property. This has happened where the estate has sought to abandon polluted property because the high costs of remedying the pollution render the property valueless to the estate. Although abandonment serves the estate's interest, it offends the public policy that the owner, not the public, should be responsible for the cleanup. In *Midlantic National Bank v. New Jersey Department of Environmental Protection*, 474 U.S. 494 (1986), the

Court balanced the estate's interest in abandoning polluted property against the public interest in having the owner remedy the pollution. The Court held that where state law is reasonably designed to protect the public from imminent and identifiable harm, the protection of the public health outweighs the bankruptcy policy of maximizing the value of the estate. Since *Midlantic*, lower courts have grappled with this balance. For example, in *In re Guterl Special Steel Corp.*, 316 B.R. 843 (Bankr. W.D. Pa. 2004), the court allowed the trustee to abandon radioactively contaminated property even though to do so would violate state law, because the state had not demonstrated that the pollution was severe enough to pose an imminent threat to public health.

Section 554(c) provides that at the close of the case, property that was included in the debtor's schedule but was not administered in the estate will be abandoned to the debtor. If it happens that any property is left in the estate at the end of the case, it is returned to the debtor. This situation is only likely to occur if the estate was not insolvent, so that all the property was not needed to pay claims, or if a particular item of property was worthless and unrealizable but was not abandoned to the debtor earlier in the case.

Examples

1. At the time of filing a petition for Ch. 7 relief, an individual debtor has the various interests described below. Which of these interests become property of the estate under §541?

   a. **Tort claim.** A year before the petition, the debtor was injured by a negligently driven automobile. At the time of the petition, the debtor's claim against the driver had not yet been litigated. Is the tort claim property of the estate?

   b. **Refrigerator.** About five months before bankruptcy, the debtor borrowed money from Newgate Loan Co. to finance the purchase of a refrigerator. When the funds were advanced, Newgate properly perfected a security interest in the refrigerator in accordance with state law. One month before bankruptcy, the debtor defaulted on the loan payments, and Newgate took possession of the refrigerator for the purpose of foreclosing on its security interest. By the time the petition was filed, Newgate had not yet held its foreclosure sale. Is the refrigerator property of the estate?

   c. **Furniture.** Two weeks before bankruptcy, the debtor held a garage sale at which she sold a well-worn dining room suite to Reese Cycle. Reese could not take delivery of it immediately because he needed to borrow a truck from a friend to haul it away. Nevertheless, he paid for it in cash at the time of the sale.

   Before Reese managed to arrange for the truck, the debtor filed the bankruptcy petition. Is the dining room suite, which is still in the debtor's possession, property of the estate?

    d. **Retirement plan.** Some years prior to filing, the debtor began to participate in a tax-exempt retirement plan under the Employee Retirement Income Security Act (ERISA). For the purpose of meeting the statute's requirements for tax-exempt status, the plan contained an antialienation provision that precluded the assignment or alienation of benefits under the plan. The benefits under the plan have not matured. Is the debtor's retirement nest egg property of the estate?

    e. **Season tickets.** Prior to filing, the debtor subscribed to baseball season tickets. The contract under which she bought the tickets clearly states that the subscription is not transferrable. However, season subscriptions are often sold by holders, and the team does not usually challenge the sales. On this occasion, it does claim that the tickets are not property of the estate. Is it correct in its assertion?

2. Although property acquired by a Ch. 7 debtor after the petition is generally part of the debtor's new estate, §541(a) includes certain postpetition receipts in the estate if they have an appropriate connection with prepetition property. Consider whether the following postpetition acquisitions are property of the estate:

    a. **Kittens.** At the time of the petition, the debtor owned a highly pedigreed pregnant cat. The cat produced a litter three weeks after the filing. Who owns the kittens?

    b. **Postpetition income.** The debtor sold her business about 11 months before filing the petition. At the time of sale, the debtor entered into a noncompetition agreement with the purchaser under which the debtor agreed, for an additional consideration of $100,000 per year (separate from the consideration paid for the business), not to compete with the business in a specified area for a period of five years. The annual payments were to be made at the end of each of the five years. About a month after the petition, the debtor received the first payment. Is it property of the estate?

    c. **Inheritance.** Three weeks after the petition the debtor's Uncle Lucrum died, leaving her a generous bequest. What happens to the debtor's inheritance?

Explanations

1. Sections 541 and 542 should be applied as follows:

    a. **Tort claim.** Do not forget that state law determines if and when a property right arises. As a general rule of state law, tort liability is created as soon as the tort is committed, so the debtor had a property right in his claim for damages when he filed the petition. It does not matter that the debtor had not yet sued on it and it is unliquidated. The inclusive language of §541 is broad enough to include unliquidated claims for damages. The claim is therefore property of the estate. Although the assertion just made about the creation of tort liability is sound in most cases, In re WitKo, 374 F.3d 1040 (11th Cir. 2004), shows how important it is to know the exact rules of state law. The debtor had a malpractice claim against an attorney who had represented him in a prepetition alimony suit in which the debtor had received an adverse ruling. The act of malpractice had occurred in the suit prior to the petition, but the debtor had appealed, and the appeal was pending at the time of the petition. The state appellate court affirmed the lower court's ruling after the debtor had filed for bankruptcy. State law treated malpractice claims differently from other tort claims—a malpractice claim arises not when the incompetent representation occurs, but only upon the final adverse ruling in the case. The malpractice claim was therefore not property of the estate.

b. **Refrigerator.** The foreclosure sale has not yet taken place, and it is stayed upon the advent of bankruptcy. Even though the debtor defaulted on the loan, and foreclosure proceedings had begun prior to the petition, the debtor still owned the fridge under state law, and this ownership interest passed to the estate under §541(a)(1). (Of course, the debtor's ownership interest may not be very valuable if the secured debt is close to or equal to the value of the collateral. Nevertheless, it exists, and had the sale occurred prior to bankruptcy the debtor would have been entitled to any surplus sale proceeds or to a redemption right under state law.) Newgate may apply for relief from stay so that foreclosure can proceed. Until such relief is granted, the estate is entitled to the refrigerator and the trustee can demand turnover under §542.

Again, it must be stressed that the existence and extent of the debtor's property interest is a matter of state law. In In re Kalter, 292 F.3d 1350 (11th Cir. 2002), the secured party had repossessed vehicles prepetition but had not yet sold them at the time of the debtor's bankruptcy. The court determined that under state law, ownership of the collateral passed to the secured party on repossession, so the debtor had no property interest in the vehicles at the time of the petition. By contrast, in In re Moffett, 356 F.3d 518 (4th Cir. 2004), the court found on similar facts, under a different state's law, that the debtor's right of redemption and to any surplus that might exist after the sale only expires upon the sale of the vehicle. The debtor therefore had a property interest that passed to the estate.

c. **Furniture.** Although §541 affects transfer of the debtor's property to the estate, nonbankruptcy law—in this case UCC Article 2—determines the nature and extent of the debtor's rights in property. Article 2 provides for the passage of title when the goods were identified to the contract, so the sale passed title to Reese and the suite does not become property of the estate.

d. **Retirement plan.** The fund in the retirement plan is prepetition property of the debtor that would enter the estate under §541(a)(1) unless the prohibition on transfer is effective in bankruptcy. Section 541(c)(1) generally overrides restrictions on the transfer of property under contract or nonbankruptcy law, so that such property passes to the estate in spite of the restriction. However, §541(c)(2) provides an exception to §541(c)(1) where the restriction on transfer relates to the debtor's beneficial interest in a trust and the restriction is enforceable under nonbankruptcy law. As discussed in section 12.2.2, a retirement plan with valid restrictions on transfer under nonbankruptcy law, such as those imposed by ERISA, is covered by §541(c)(2) and does not enter the estate.

e. **Season tickets.** The facts of this example are based on In re *Platt*, 292 B.R. 12 (Bankr. D. Mass. 2003), in which the trustee claimed that the debtor's Boston Red Sox season tickets were property of the estate. The trustee ultimately lost on an issue of proof—he could not show that the debtor actually owned the tickets in his personal capacity. However, the court said that had the trustee been able to prove this, the tickets would have become property of the estate. The nontransferability clause in the season ticket subscription contract would not have been upheld under §541(c)(1) because the team's practice was to permit transfers.

2. The postpetition acquisitions are dealt with in the following way:

a. **Kittens.** The cat became property of the estate upon the debtor's bankruptcy. Although the litter was born after the petition, it is property of the estate under §541(a)(6), which includes in the estate all proceeds, product, offspring, rents or profits of or derived from estate property.

b. **Postpetition income.** Although the earnings from the noncompetition agreement accrue postpetition, the agreement creating the right to the earnings was entered into prepetition. In In re *Andrews*, 80 F.3d 906 (4th Cir. 1996), the debtor argued that the payments due after bankruptcy under such an agreement are not property of the estate, but are earnings from services performed by the debtor after the commencement of the case, excluded from the estate under §541(a)(6). The debtor's reasoning was that he became entitled to the payments by refraining from competing, and this forbearance did constitute an ongoing service that he performed for the purchaser after the petition. The court disagreed, observing that it was too much of a stretch to include inaction in the concept of performance of services under §541(a)(6). Furthermore, the court reasoned that the purpose of the exclusion in §541(a)(6) was to facilitate the debtor's fresh start by separating from the estate whatever new income he may earn by postfiling endeavors. The proceeds from the noncompetition agreement were not of this nature, but arose out of and were ancillary to the sale of an asset before bankruptcy. As such, the earnings derived from the debtor's prepetition activities, and were more properly viewed as proceeds of estate property. (A dissent in the case agreed with the debtor's argument that the payments should be treated as earnings from the postpetition service of forbearing from competition.)

c. **Inheritance.** Section 541(a)(5) includes in the estate any property that the debtor acquires or becomes entitled to by bequest, devise, or inheritance within 180 days after the petition, if such property would have qualified as property of the estate had the debtor an interest in it at the time of the petition. The inheritance would have been property of the estate had Uncle Lucrum died before the debtor filed the petition, so it satisfies §541(a)(5) and is estate property.

CHAPTER 13

Exemptions, Redemption, and Reaffirmation

§13.1 THE CONCEPT OF EXEMPTIONS

Exemptions were first introduced in the explanation of executability in section 3.2.1, and have since been mentioned in a number of different contexts. For example, in section 5.3, they were mentioned to illustrate that uniformity in bankruptcy law has some tolerance for variety, and they were identified in sections 5.5.2 and 8.3.1 as an important component of the debtor's fresh start. Although exemptions are discussed here in connection with bankruptcy, they are also available in collection proceedings under state law. As explained in section 3.2.1, state exemption statutes designate specific property or types of property that cannot be levied upon by creditors in state debt collection proceedings.

Exemptions are only available to individual debtors. Whether under state law or in bankruptcy, the goal of exemptions is to insulate certain of the debtor's property from the claims of creditors[1] so that the debtor is not rendered destitute by seizure or liquidation. In bankruptcy, property released to the debtor as exempt forms part of the debtor's new estate, thereby helping the debtor to gain a fresh start.

Exemptions are provided for in §522. They are claimable by individual debtors in all cases, whether under Ch. 7, 11, 12, or 13. Exemptions are used most directly in Ch. 7 cases, where fully exempt property is released and the

---

1. An exemption does not avail against a valid and unavoidable consensual lien on the exempt property. This is also usually true of statutory liens. *See* section 13.5.

cash value of partial exemptions is paid out from the estate to the debtor. In cases under Chs. 11, 12, and 13, estate property vests in the debtor upon confirmation of the plan, except as otherwise provided for in the plan. (*See* section 12.2.) Therefore, the debtor does not directly use exemptions to reacquire estate property; instead, exemptions help the debtor because they are deducted from the liquidation value of the estate. This liquidation value is one of the factors taken into account in determining the minimum level of payment required for plan confirmation. (Standards for plan confirmation are explained in Chapters 20 and 21.) Exemptions are also relevant in all cases for the purpose of lien avoidance under §522(f), which is discussed in section 13.5.

§13.2 EXEMPTIONS APPLICABLE IN BANKRUPTCY CASES

§13.2.1 Uniformity of Exemptions — State Opt-Out

Although the Bankruptcy Act of 1898 granted exemptions to individual debtors in bankruptcy, it did not designate which property of the debtor would be exempt. Instead, it completely deferred to state exemption laws so that the exemptions available to the debtor in the bankruptcy case would be whatever exemptions were allowed to the debtor under the law of the debtor's state. Soon after the enactment of the Bankruptcy Act, the constitutionality of its deference to state exemption laws was challenged on the grounds that this violated the requirement of Art. VI, cl. 2 that Congress establish a uniform law of bankruptcy throughout the United States. As explained in section 5.3, the U.S. Supreme Court upheld the Act's incorporation of state exemption law in *Hanover National Bank v. Moyses*, 186 U.S. 181 (1902). The Court set out the fundamental principle that absolute and literal uniformity is not required. Although the provisions of federal bankruptcy law must themselves be uniform throughout the United States, they inevitably operate in the context of state law rights and can take into account variations in state law. The test is not whether bankruptcy law will lead to the same outcome in every state, but whether the superstructure of bankruptcy law is evenly imposed. As explained below, while the Code does provide a set of exemptions applicable in bankruptcy cases, it continues to defer to state exemption law by allowing states to enact legislation that substitutes state law exemptions for those provided for in the Code. As a result, the exemptions available to debtors in bankruptcy still vary depending on the debtor's state of domicile. A few years after the Code was enacted, the Code's continued deference to state law exemptions was again challenged on the grounds that Congress had failed to comply with the constitutional requirement of uniformity in bankruptcy law. In re Sullivan, 680 F.2d 1131 (7th Cir. 1982), cert. denied, 459 U.S. 992 (1983) rejected this argument on the precedent of Hanover National Bank, and it now seens settled that there is no constitutional bar on adopting state exemptions in bankruptcy. However, the controversy over whether this is good policy has continued.

When the Bankruptcy Reform Act (the current Code) was enacted in 1978, there was a debate over the way in which the Code should treat exemptions. Advocates of uniform bankruptcy exemptions argued that the Code should provide a standardized set of exemptions applicable to all individual debtors, irrespective of their state of domicile. Others preferred to maintain the approach of the old Bankruptcy Act, which had made applicable in bankruptcy the exemptions granted to the debtor in the law of the debtor's state of domicile. Section 522 was a compromise between these opposing views. Section 522(d) provides a set of uniform bankruptcy exemptions, but §522(b) allows a state to elect to substitute its own exemptions for those listed in §522(d). This has come to be known as the "opt-out." There are two important limitations on the states' power to opt-out of §522(d). First, a state cannot use its opt-out right to enact different sets of exemptions applicable in bankruptcy and in collection cases under state law. If the state opts out, the same exemptions available under state law become the bankruptcy exemptions for debtors domiciled in that state. (In re Wallace, 347 B.R. 626 (Bankr. W.D. Mich. 2006).) Second, the opt-out relates only to §522(d), which lists the property that the debtor may exempt. It does not apply to other provisions of §522, which cannot be varied by the states.

The state opts out of §522(d) by enacting a statute that specifically does not authorize debtors domiciled within its jurisdiction to use the exemptions listed in §522(d). Those debtors are confined to exemptions provided by state law, together with any applicable federal nonbankruptcy exemptions (such as exemptions provided for Social Security benefits or other protected benefits conferred by federal statutes other than the Code). If a state has not opted out, a debtor domiciled in that state may choose to claim either the exemptions provided in §522(d) or the applicable nonbankruptcy exemptions, and will claim whichever set of exemptions gives him the greatest benefit. (The debtor must choose either the state exemptions or the §522(d) exemptions. He cannot pick some exemptions from the state set and others from the federal set.)

The majority of states have opted out, so debtors are commonly not entitled to claim the exemptions set out in §522(d); they are confined to the same exemptions in bankruptcy as are available in collection proceedings in nonbankruptcy law. Many states have exemption laws that are roughly similar to the exemptions in §522(d), so it sometimes does not make a dramatic difference if state exemptions apply rather than the exemptions listed in §522(d). However, some state exemption laws are very different from the set of exemptions provided for in §522(d). Therefore, if the state has opted out, a debtor domiciled in that state may have exemptions that are dramatically better or worse than those listed in §522(d) or claimable by a debtor domiciled in another state.

The issue of uniform exemptions was revisited by the 1994 National Bankruptcy Review Commission. In its 1997 report, the majority of the Commission criticized the widely divergent treatment of debtors that resulted from deference to state law, and recommended that Congress eliminate the states' right to opt out of the standard exemptions in §522(d). Congress declined to follow this recommendation in enacting the Bankruptcy Abuse Prevention and Consumer Protection Act of 2005 (BAPCPA), so the Code continues to allow states to opt out.

§13.2.2 Determining Which State's Law Governs Exemptions — the Debtor's Domicile

The law of the state of the debtor's domicile determines which set of exemptions applies in the bankruptcy case. Domicile requires both actual residence and a present intent to remain. (Temporary removal to another jurisdiction does not defeat domicile if the debtor intends to return.)

Because the debtor's domicile at the time of the petition can have a significant impact on what property the debtor can claim as exempt, a debtor may make the strategic decision to move to and establish domicile in a state with favorable exemptions in anticipation of the filing. Prior to the passage of BAPCPA in 2005, the rule in §522(b) for determining domicile for exemption purposes was quite lenient. The section applied the exemption law of the state in which the debtor was domiciled for the 180 days (about six months) prior to the petition. If the debtor had not been domiciled in a single state during the period, the law of the place of longest domicile in the 180-day period was used. This provision made it too easy for a debtor to establish domicile in an advantageous state just before filing. BAPCPA amended §522(b) to impose more stringent control. Section 522(b)(3) now provides that the law that governs the debtor's exemption rights is the law of the state in which the debtor was domiciled for the 730 days (two years) immediately preceding the petition. If the debtor has not been domiciled in any single state for that 730-day period, the applicable exemption law is that of the state in which the debtor was domiciled in the 180 days immediately preceding the 730-day period, or for a longer portion of that 180 days than any other place. That is, if the debtor has been domiciled in a state for the two years immediately before the petition, that state's exemption law applies. If the debtor has not been domiciled in the same state for the two years immediately before the petition, we must then look back to the six-month period immediately before those two years to determine domicile. Section 522(b)(3)(C) contains a safety net for a debtor who cannot establish the requisite domicile in any state under the section — in that case federal exemptions in §522(d) apply.

Section 522(b)(3) makes it very difficult for a debtor to move to a hospitable state for the purpose of enhancing her exemptions. In close cases, the determination of the proper domicile can be tricky. For example, in In re Dufva, 388 B.R. 911 (Bankr. W.D. Mo. 2008), the debtors were domiciled in Missouri. However, before moving to Missouri, they had been domiciled in Nevada, which had more generous exemptions. The debtors claimed Nevada exemptions on the grounds that they had established domicile in Missouri only 729 days before filing, and had been domiciled in Nevada during the 180-day period before that. To resolve the issue, the court had to go through a tortuously finicky counting and interpretational exercise, which led it to conclude that the debtors were in fact domiciled in Missouri for the 730 days before filing.

§13.2.3 Exemption Planning and Controls on Abuse of the Homestead Exemption

The legislative history of §522 indicates that a debtor should be able to plan for bankruptcy and take advantage of available exemptions by selling non-exempt property and using the proceeds to buy exempt property before filing the petition. In light of this, courts have recognized that the prepetition conversion of nonexempt assets into exempt property is not per se wrongful. However, because this kind of activity can easily be abused, they have policed it by applying a good faith test. If the conversion is fraudulent or improperly manipulative, that is, if the debtor has behaved dishonestly or deceptively in making the conversion, the exemption could be denied. Alternatively, the court may permit the exemption to be claimed but take the debtor's fraud into account in deciding whether to limit or deny the debtor's discharge. The line between permissible bankruptcy planning and dishonest behavior is not always easy to draw. This creates a hazard for the debtor's attorney, who must be careful about how she advises the debtor before the petition is filed. The attorney must inform the debtor of the permissible scope of prepetition planning while not encouraging or collaborating in dishonest dealings.

Courts take several factors into account to decide if prepetition planning has been legitimate. Some of the indicia of dishonesty and manipulation include the use of credit to acquire or enhance an interest in exempt property, the concealment of the activity, and other conduct designed to mislead creditors. In In re McCabe, 280 B.R. 841 (Bankr. N.D. Iowa 2002), the court found that in the absence of any of these indications of dishonesty, the debtor's prepetition acquisition of exempt property was permissible. (The debtor bought a valuable gun prior to filing his petition because he knew that Iowa exemption law provided for an unlimited firearm exemption, and he wished to take advantage of it.)

One of the most glaring abuses of prepetition exemption planning and manipulation of the nonuniform exemption system has related to the homestead exemption. Although BAPCPA did not go as far as the Commission recommended in tackling this problem by standardizing exemptions, it did enact new provisions in §522 designed to restrain the abuse. Section 522(d) and most state exemption statutes give the debtor a limited and often modest exemption in the value of her residence. For example, the homestead exemption in §522(d)(1) is in the amount of $22,975.[2] Many state homestead exemptions are similarly of small amount in relation to the value of the home. This means that a debtor cannot claim the home as exempt in full; he is limited to a relatively small portion of his equity in the home. A few states have considerably larger homestead exemptions, and a handful provide for an unlimited homestead exemption — that is, the complete exemption of the debtor's equity in the home. This means that debtors in some states are treated far more generously than in others. It has also given some debtors the means to manipulate the system by shifting wealth into a homestead before they file bankruptcy. There have been cases in which a debtor who was domiciled in a state with a generous homestead exemption greatly enlarged his homestead exemption prior to filing by realizing all his nonexempt property and using the proceeds to buy a homestead or to pay down the mortgage on his existing homestead. This manipulation has not been confined to debtors who already live in a state with a generous or unlimited homestead exemption. There have been cases in which a debtor who lived in a state with a small or limited homestead exemption realized nonexempt assets, moved to a state with a generous or unlimited homestead exemption, and invested those proceeds in a home. Where the debtor was wealthy and the state had an unlimited homestead exemption, the homestead exemption created by this process could shelter millions of dollars from creditors.

Section 522(o), (p), and (q) create controls to curb these abuses of the homestead exemption. These subsections are written in the mind-boggling form common to so many of the provisions in BAPCPA. In essence, they do not cap overly generous state homestead exemptions in most cases. However, they do provide for controls on high homestead exemptions in certain circumstances in which the debtor has behaved dishonestly or manipulatively. Remember, as discussed in section 13.2.2, that in addition

---

2. This amount is subject to periodic adjustment under §104. This is the amount promulgated with effect from April 1, 2013. The amount will be adjusted again with effect from April 1, 2016. See section 5.4.3.

to the controls in §522(o), (p), and (q), the domicile provisions of §522(b)(3) prevent the debtor from moving to a state on the eve of bankruptcy to take advantage of desirable exemptions (including a generous homestead exemption). The controls that are imposed on the homestead exemption under §522(o), (p), and (q) boil down to this:

Section 522(o) reduces the debtor's homestead exemption under state law to the extent that the value of the debtor's interest in the homestead is attributable to the disposition of nonexempt property in the ten years before the petition, with intent to hinder, delay, or defraud creditors. The basic idea is that if the debtor had sold nonexempt property in the ten years before bankruptcy and had invested the proceeds in exempt homestead property, the exemption will be reduced by the amount of that investment if intent to hinder, delay, or defraud creditors can be shown. It is not itself fraud for the debtor to realize nonexempt property and to use the proceeds to enlarge his exemptable equity in the homestead. For §522(o) to apply, the party challenging the debtor's exemption claim must show that this activity was for the purpose of hindering, delaying or defrauding creditors. That is, that the debtor engaged in this activity with the intent to evade the payment of debt or to deceive and defraud creditors. Deception may be present, for example, where the debtor seeks to conceal transactions, makes misrepresentations to creditors, or realizes the nonexempt property well below its value. Because the language in §522(o) is the same as that used in §548 in relation to fraudulent transfers and in §727 in relation to denial of the discharge, the tests of fraudulent intent developed by the courts under those sections, including the use of badges of fraud, are applicable here. See In re Maronde, 332 B.R. 593 (Bankr. D. Minn. 2005); In re Anderson, 386 B.R. 315 (Bankr. D. Kan. 2008), aff'd 406 B.R. 79 (D. Kan. 2009).

Section 522(p) limits the debtor's interest in a homestead exempted under state law to an amount of $155,675[3] if the debtor acquired the homestead within 1,215 days (about three years and four months) of the petition. The purpose of the section is to place a restriction on the kind of exemption planning in which a debtor buys an expensive home in a state with an unlimited homestead exemption. The application of the section is relatively clear where the debtor buys new property. However, it is less clear where the debtor newly establishes a homestead on property that he already owns. Section 522(p) applies to an "interest" that the debtor "acquired" during the 1,215-day period. In In re Greene, 583 F.3d 614 (9th Cir. 2009), the debtor had owned a parcel of undeveloped land for about ten years. About a year before he filed a Ch. 7 petition, he brought a trailer onto the property, began to live in it, and recorded a declaration of homestead with

---

3. This is the amount in effect with effect from April 1, 2013. The amount will be adjusted again under §104 in 2016.

the county. In his Ch.7 case, he claimed the full value of the land ($240,000) as exempt under the state homestead exemption. A creditor challenged the exemption and argued that even if the property was a homestead, the debtor had acquired the homestead within the 1,215-day period and should be confined to the limit in §522(p). The court conceded that §522(p) is ambiguous on the question of when the debtor acquires an exemptible interest, but it concluded that the acquisition of interest means when the debtor acquired ownership of the property, not when he began to use it as a homestead. The court distinguished a homestead claim, which is a personal right granted by statute, from an interest in property on which the exemption is dependent.

There are some exceptions to the limitation imposed by §522(p), the most notable of which is that it does not apply to the extent that proceeds of a prior home acquired before the 1,215-day period are transferred into the new home. In re Summers, 344 B.R. 108 (Bankr. N.D. Ariz. 2006), illustrates how §522(p) operates: The debtors were domiciled in Arizona, which has opted out of §522(d). The Arizona homestead exemption was $150,000. The debtors had bought a home worth $465,000 in the 1,215-day period. After deducting the amount owing on the home mortgage, the debtors had an equity of $210,000 in the home. Although Arizona law would have allowed an exemption of $150,000, the debtors would normally have been confined to an exemption of $125,000[4] under the limit imposed by §522(p). However, $54,000 of the purchase price of the house was proceeds from the sale of the debtor's previous homestead, so this amount could be added to the $125,000 limit under §522(p). This did not mean, however, that the debtors would have been entitled to an exemption of $179,000, because the state exemption of $150,000 was the upper limit of the amount of the exemption.

Section 522(q) caps the homestead exemption at $155,675[5] where the debtor has been guilty of certain kinds of misconduct. Section 522(q)(1)(A) confines the debtor's homestead exemption to $155,675 if the debtor has been convicted of a felony that, under the circumstances, demonstrates that the filing of the bankruptcy case was an abuse of the Code. Section 522(q)(1)(B) imposes that cap if the debtor owes a debt that arises from specified kinds of wrongful act, including fraud or deceit in a fiduciary capacity or any criminal act, intentional tort, or willful or reckless misconduct that caused serious physical injury or death. In In re Larson, 513 F.3d 325 (1st Cir. 2008), the court held that negligent vehicular homicide qualified as a criminal act that caps the homestead exemption under §522(q)(1)(B).

---

4. $125,000 was the dollar amount of the cap under §522(p) at the time of the case. (As indicated in the text, it is now higher.)
5. Again, as adjusted with effect from April 1, 2013.

The section does not require mens rea, nor does it have the prerequisite (as does §522(q)(1)(A) that the debtor has been convicted of the crime.

Subsections (p) and (q) begin with unfortunately chosen language. They are stated to apply where the debtor "as a result of electing under subsection (b)(3)(A)" exempts property under state or local law. The word "electing" suggests that the subsections only apply where the state has not opted out, because if the state has opted out, the debtor is bound by state exemptions and has no right to make any election. At least one court has given the language this literal interpretation. See In re McNabb, 326 B.R. 785 (Bankr. D. Ariz. 2005). The problem with this literal interpretation is that it renders §522(p) and (q) virtually useless because so few states allow for the election. Other courts have rejected this approach. They have found the language of the subsections to be ambiguous, and have consulted legislative history, which indicates congressional intent to cap the exemption in all states in which state law has an exemption in excess of $155,675. See, for example, in In re Kaplan, 331 B.R. 483 (Bankr. S.D. Fla. 2005); In re Summers (above).

§13.3 THE NATURE OF EXEMPT PROPERTY

Exemptions are granted at the expense of creditors, whose recourse is limited to nonexempt assets. Because exemptions detract from creditor interests, they are limited and controlled so that they are no more generous than they need to be to accomplish their goal of preventing the debtor's impoverishment. As explained in section 13.2.1, the list of exemptions claimable by an individual debtor in bankruptcy is set out in §522(d). However, because most states have opted out of that section and substituted their own exemptions, the actual exemptions allowed by §522(d) are commonly inapplicable. This variation of exemptions, depending on the state of the debtor's domicile, is mitigated to some extent by the fact that many state statutes follow a similar pattern and have been influenced by what Congress provided for in §522(d). As mentioned in section 13.2.1, the majority report of the 1994 National Bankruptcy Review Commission recommended that Congress establish a uniform set of bankruptcy exemptions by eliminating the states' right to opt out of §522(d). It also recommended that Congress move away from the current format of §522(d), which lists specific types of property that may be exempted, with a dollar limit on most categories. The objection to this format is that a debtor's ability to take advantage of exemptions is dependent on the extent to which her property coincides with the exemptions provided for in §522(d). (For example, a debtor who owns a car or tools of trade can claim exemptions for those items, but a debtor who does not own property of that kind cannot substitute other property and so ends up with fewer exemptions.)

The Commission proposed, instead that the list of exempt property in §522(d) be replaced with a lump sum dollar limit, so that a debtor could pick whatever property she wanted to exempt up to that limit. This change would have eliminated the problem of disparate treatment of debtors with different types of property and would have allowed all debtors the same total exemption amount, irrespective of the type of property they own. Congress did not follow this recommendation, and the categories of exempt property in §522(d) were not changed by BAPCPA except for the addition of one new category.

Although §522(d) is not applicable in most bankruptcy cases because of the opt-out, it serves as a model of what a common set of exemptions looks like. It specifies the types or classes of property that may be claimed as exempt and imposes a value limit on most categories of exempt property. Most of the assets that qualify for exemption are ordinary necessities such as household furnishings and goods, a motor vehicle, tools of trade on which the debtor depends for a livelihood, the debtor's homestead, professionally prescribed health aids, and various pension, disability, or alimony payments. Almost every category has a value limitation. Some have a specified dollar limitation[6] that is quite modest, and some require the court to make a determination of the amount reasonably necessary for the support of the debtor and dependents. To be exempt, an asset must fit within one of the specified categories. To the extent that the asset is worth more than the exemption limit (or to the extent that the debtor has more assets in that category than may be claimed as exempt) the exemption is only partial, and the value over the exempt amount falls into the estate. The only category that allows the debtor the ability to select an asset to exempt (that is, provides for a general exemption in an asset of the debtor's choice) is the so-called "wildcard exemption." It has a relatively small dollar limit that can be increased to a limited extent if the debtor does not claim the homestead exemption. (Example 4 provides an exercise in determining how the exemption categories would be applied to a debtor's assets.)

§13.4 THE PROCEDURE FOR CLAIMING EXEMPTIONS

Exemptions do not automatically take effect. To claim them, the debtor must file a list of exempt property under §522(l). If the debtor fails to file the list,

---

6. The dollar limits in §522(d) stayed constant for almost 20 years from the enactment of the Code in 1978 to 1994. The Bankruptcy Reform Act of 1994 updated the amounts and provided in §104 for their administrative adjustment every three years based on increases in the Consumer Price Index. (*See* section 5.4.3.) The last adjustment took effect on April 1, 2013, and the next will be on April 1, 2016.

a dependent of the debtor may do so, thereby safeguarding the exemptions. The claim of exemptions is provided for in Schedule C of Official Form 6. Rules 1007 and 4003(a) require the schedule to be filed with the petition or within 14 days after the order for relief. Under Rule 1009, the debtor is able to amend the schedule of exemptions at any time up to the closing of the case.

The trustee or a creditor has the right to challenge the debtor's claim of exemptions. Rule 4003(b) requires objection to be filed within 30 days of the creditors' meeting. Rule 4003(c) places the burden on the objector to prove that the exemption is improperly claimed. Section 522(l) states that unless such an objection is made, the property is exempted as claimed. Therefore, if the trustee and creditors are not vigilant, the debtor could get away with an excessive exemption claim. In *Taylor v. Freeland & Kronz*, 503 U.S. 638 (1992), the Supreme Court held that if the creditor or trustee fails to file the objection within the 30-day period (or within such extended period as the court allows), the right to object is barred and the exemption stands, even if the debtor had no colorable basis for claiming it. In *Schwab v. Reilly*, 130 S.Ct. 2652 (2010) the court qualified its holding in *Taylor*. The debtor had conducted a catering business and filed a Ch. 7 petition when the business failed. In her schedule of exemptions, she claimed kitchen equipment which she valued at $10,718. This value would be fully exempt because the value asserted was less than the dollar limit under the combined tools of trade and wildcard exemptions. The trustee did not object to the exemption claim, but later determined that the property was worth more than the debtor had asserted, and moved to auction it, pay out the debtor's claimed exemption, and retain the balance for the estate. The debtor objected to the trustee's motion to auction the equipment, arguing that by failing to object to the exemption claim, the trustee had accepted the debtor's value and her claim of a full exemption of the property. The lower courts held in favor of the debtor on the basis of *Taylor*. However, the Supreme Court reversed, stating that the lower courts had misinterpreted the decision in *Taylor*. Section 522(l) imposes the duty on the party in interest to object to the property listed as exempt. It does not require him to object to the estimated value assigned by the debtor to that property if, on the face of the schedule, that property and the amount of exemption claimed falls within an exemption category. The exemption covers only the debtor's interest in the property, not the property itself, so the trustee is not bound by the debtor's valuation if it turns out that the property is worth more than the debtor asserted. The court distinguished *Taylor* on the basis that the debtor's schedule in that case stated that the value of the property (the proceeds of a suit for lost wages) as "unknown." By failing to assign any value to the claimed exemption the debtor in *Taylor* appeared to claim the entire extent of the property, irrespective of value. Because the claim was subject to a value limitation in §522(d), this rendered the exemption claim facially questionable and put the trustee on notice to object to the claimed exemption.

It is unclear if a second 30-day objection period is created if the debtor converts the case from one chapter to another. Some courts have held that a second 30-day objection period arises after the creditors' meeting following conversion, while others hold that conversion does not create a second objection period. In re Brown, 375 B.R. 362 (Bankr. W.D. Mich. 2007), discusses the conflicting case law and chooses the former approach.

§13.5 THE DEBTOR'S POWER TO AVOID CERTAIN INTERESTS THAT IMPAIR EXEMPTIONS

§13.5.1 General Scope and Purpose of the Debtor's Avoidance Power

As a general rule, a debtor's exemption in property does not avail against the holder of a valid consensual security interest in that property. By granting the interest, a debtor has effectively waived the right to assert the exemption against the consensual lienholder. Statutory liens, conferred by the legislature to protect persons who have enhanced or preserved the value of the property, are also usually immune from exemption claims. By contrast, an exemption normally does take precedence over a judicial lien that attaches to the property. Judicial liens are acquired by the very process of seizure or judgment against which exemptions are meant to protect the property.

The purpose of §522(f)(1)(A) is to give effect to the primacy of the debtor's exemptions over judicial liens, by empowering the debtor to avoid them to the extent that they impair her exemptions. Section 522(f)(1)(B) creates a limited exception to the general rule that exemptions cannot be used to avoid consensual security interests. It extends the debtor's avoidance power to nonpossessory, nonpurchase-money security interests in specific classes of exempt property. This exception reflects Congress's determination that these types of security interest are predatory and should not be permitted to undermine the debtor's exemptions.

§13.5.2 Judicial Liens

Section 522(f)(1)(A) allows the debtor to avoid a judicial lien in exempt property to the extent that the lien impairs an exemption to which the debtor would have been entitled in the absence of the lien. With an exception relating to domestic support obligations, §522(f)(1)(A) applies to all judicial liens, whether created by prejudgment proceedings, by recording of the judgment, or by postjudgment proceedings such as execution. Also, unlike §522(f)(1)(B), it applies to all types of exempt property.

The exclusion of domestic support obligations (as defined in §101(14A)) from the debtor's avoidance power reflects a strong policy, manifested in a number of provisions enacted by the Bankruptcy Reform Act of 1994 and reinforced by BAPCPA, that a debtor should not be able to use bankruptcy to evade domestic support obligations. We have already seen in section 10.4.2 that the enforcement of domestic support obligations is not subject to the automatic stay, and we will see later that these obligations are also given top priority over other unsecured claims and are nondischargeable. In the present context, §522(f)(1)(A) does not permit the debtor to avoid a judicial lien that enforces a domestic support obligation, even if that lien impairs an exemption to which the debtor would otherwise be entitled.

§13.5.3 Avoidable Nonpossessory, Nonpurchase-Money Security Interests

Section 522(f)(1)(B) creates a narrow exception to the general rule that consensual liens take priority over an exemption in the collateral: The debtor may avoid a nonpossessory, nonpurchase-money security interest in specified household or consumer goods, tools of trade, or professionally prescribed health aids to the extent that the security interest impairs an exemption in such property.[7] The scope of §522(f)(1)(B) is very limited. The security interest can be avoided only if all three requirements of the section are satisfied: The secured party must not have perfected the interest by taking possession of the collateral, the loan or credit must not have been provided to enable the debtor to acquire the collateral, and the impaired exemption must relate to one of the three types of property specified. Section 522(f)(1)(B) is aimed at a particular type of transaction under which a creditor secures the debt by filing a security interest in household goods or other necessities already owned by the debtor. In many cases, the property is likely to be worth more to the debtor than its realization value, so that the threat of foreclosure gives the creditor great power over the debtor. Congress was concerned about abuses in transactions of this type, which it regarded as manipulative and unethical. It therefore subordinated them to the debtor's exemption.

The Bankruptcy Reform Act of 1994 added §522(f)(3), a limited qualification to the debtor's power to avoid a nonpossessory, nonpurchase-money lien in tools of trade where state law exemptions apply and the

---

7. BAPCPA added §522(f)(4), which defines "household goods" for the purpose of §522(f)(1)(B). It contains a long list of what does and does not qualify as household goods. The definition is expressly for the purpose of §522(f)(1)(B), so its restrictions should not be applicable to the term as it is used in §522(d)(3). That is, an item that may qualify as a household good for the purpose of claiming an exemption for it may not qualify as a household good for the purpose of avoiding a nonpossessory, nonpurchase-money security interest in it.

state either has no monetary limit on the exemption or prohibits the avoidance of consensual liens on exempt property. The subsection is obscurely drafted and its purpose unclear. It imposes a dollar limit on the extent to which the debtor may avoid the lien, so its apparent effect is to limit the amount of the debtor's avoidance under these circumstances.

§13.5.4 Avoidance "to the Extent" of Impairment

Section 522(f) does not necessarily result in the total avoidance of offending judicial liens and security interests. It permits avoidance only to the extent necessary to preserve the exemption. Therefore, if the debtor's equity in the property exceeds the exemption, the lien or security interest remains a valid charge on the nonexempt portion of the equity. For example, assume that the debtor owns a piece of equipment used as a tool of trade. The value of the equipment is $3,000. The debtor's exemption under §522(d)(6) is $2,300.[8] If a judicial lien attached to the property securing a judgment of $1,000, it would impair the debtor's exemption to the extent of $300 (That is, if the judicial lien was allowed in full, the debtor's equity in the property would be reduced from $3,000 to $2,000, but the debtor's exemptible interest in the property is $2,300.) The lien can therefore be avoided to the extent of $300 and becomes a secured claim for $700 and an unsecured claim of $300. If the value of the collateral is $2,300 or less, the lien is avoided entirely, and if the collateral is worth $3,300 or more, it is not avoidable at all. *See* Example 1.

§13.5.5 A State Cannot Override the Avoidance Power in its Opt-Out Statute

As explained in section 13.2, states have the power under §522(b) to enact legislation substituting nonbankruptcy exemptions for those provided in §522(d). In conferring this power on the states, §522(b) refers only to the substitution for exemptions listed in §522(d). It does not authorize states to override any other provisions of §522. Nevertheless, courts had reached contrary results on the question of whether a state, in substituting its own exemptions under §522(b), could negate the debtor's avoidance power under §522(f) by making an exemption subject to liens that would otherwise be avoidable. This controversy was settled in *Owen v. Owen*, 500 U.S. 305 (1991), in which the Supreme Court held that the debtor may avoid a lien under §522(f) even though state law gives the lien precedence over the exemptions. The Court focused on the language of

---

8. This is the amount with effect from April 1, 2013. The amount will be adjusted again under §104 in 2016.

§522(f), which allows avoidance of the lien to the extent that it "impairs an exemption to which the debtor would have been entitled" under §522(b). The Court reasoned that the inquiry called for by this language is not whether the lien impairs an exemption to which the debtor is actually entitled under the state statute, but whether it impairs one to which the debtor would have been entitled if no lien existed. In *In re Cleaver*, 407 B.R. 354 (B.A.P. 8th Cir. 2009), the court, applying *Owen*, held that a truck qualified as a tool of trade for purposes of §522(f) where federal exemption law recognizes it as such, but state law does not. Even though the state had opted out of the federal exemptions, the opt-out pertains only to the selection of exemptions, and not to the federal remedy of lien avoidance.

§13.5.6 How Impairment Is Measured

Although *Owen* set the basic meaning of "impairment," it did not resolve the question of how that impairment is measured. Congress attempted to provide some guidance on this issue in the Bankruptcy Reform Act of 1994 by adding §522(f)(2). Section 522(f)(2)(A) defines "impairment" by setting out an arithmetical formula. To find the amount of impairment:

(1) Determine what the value of the debtor's interest in the property would be — that is, the full interest or equity that the debtor would have in the property — in the absence of liens. (When the debtor is the sole and absolute owner of the property, this is equivalent to the full value of the property.)

(2) Add together:

(a) the lien to be avoided plus
(b) other liens on the property plus
(c) the amount of the debtor's exemption.

(3) Compare 1 and 2. The exemption is impaired to the extent that 2 is greater than 1.

Where there is more than one lien on the property, §522(f)(2)(B) makes it clear that once any lien is avoided, the avoided lien is not taken into account in calculating the total of "other liens" for the purpose of avoiding any remaining lien.

The formula seems quite easy to work with in an uncomplicated case. However, it does raise some questions and present interpretational difficulties, under some circumstances. The following three examples show the basic operation of the formula in two easy cases and then in one more difficult one.

Say that a homestead worth $200,000 is subject to an exemption of $50,000. There is only one judicial lien of $180,000 on the property. The lien can be avoided to the extent that:

The total of
the amount of the lien itself ($180,000) plus
other liens ($0) plus
the exemption ($50,000)
= $230,000
exceeds
the value that the debtor's interest would have in the property in the
absence of liens ($200,000).

Therefore, the lien is avoided by $230,000 − $200,000 = $30,000. As a result, it remains a lien on the property to the extent of $150,000.

Say that the same property is subject to two judgment liens, the senior is for $100,000 and the junior is for $80,000. Although §522(f)(2)(A) does not say so, the avoidance must be directed at the junior avoidable lien first. (If this were not so, the avoidance of the senior lien first would elevate the junior lien in priority, because under §522(f)(2)(B), the avoided senior lien would not be taken into account in that second avoidance action.) The calculation is therefore:

First, apply the calculation to the junior lien.
The total of
the junior lien ($80,000) plus
"all other liens" — the senior lien ($100,000) — plus
the exemption ($50,000)
= $230,000
exceeds
the debtor's equity interest ($200,000).

Therefore, the junior lien is avoided, by $230,000 − $200,000 = $30,000. As a result, it survives only to the extent of $50,000.

Next, apply the calculation to the senior lien.
The total of
the senior lien ($100,000) plus
"all other liens" — the remaining unavoided portion of the junior lien
($50,000) — plus
the exemption ($50,000)
= $200,000.

This is exactly equal to the debtor's unencumbered equity, and it, therefore, does not impair the exemption at all and is unavoidable.

Say that the homestead, worth $200,000 and subject to an exemption of $50,000, has three liens on it. The first is a consensual first mortgage of $70,000, perfected a year before bankruptcy. The second is a judgment lien of $80,000, recorded eight months before bankruptcy. The third is consensual second mortgage of $60,000, perfected six months before bankruptcy. If this was nonexempt property, the priority of the three interests would simply be based on the first-in-time rule. This would mean that the first mortgage would be entitled to full payment of $70,000, then the judgment lien would be entitled to full payment of $80,000. Finally, the second mortgage would be third in line. It would only be paid what is left of the value of the property, $50,000, and would have an unsecured deficiency of $10,000.

As the property is exempt, the debtor is able to use §522(f)(1)(A) to avoid the judicial lien, but not the consensual liens. (The consensual liens cannot be avoided under §522(f)(1)(B) because the homestead is not one of the exemptions protected by that subsection.) Therefore, the assumption that we made in the prior illustration, that the junior lien must be avoided first, cannot apply to the second mortgage. The avoidance is directed at the judgment lien only. The calculation is as follows:

The total of
the amount of the judgment lien ($80,000) plus
all other liens ($130,000) plus
the exemption ($50,000)
= $260,000
exceeds
the value that the debtor's interest would have in the property in the absence of liens ($200,000).

Therefore, the judicial lien is avoided to the extent of $60,000. It becomes a secured claim of $20,000 and an unsecured claim of $60,000. The twist here is that this does not mean merely that the debtor's exemption is preserved. It also has the effect of elevating the second mortgage above the judicial lien. That is, avoidance under §522(f)(1)(A) benefits not only the debtor, but also the unavoidable consensual lien that would otherwise be junior to the judicial lien. This can be seen if we set out the distribution of the proceeds of the property: first mortgage, $70,000; second mortgage, $60,000; exemption $50,000; unavoided portion of judgment lien, $20,000. On similar facts, the court in In re Kolich, 328 F.3d 406 (8th Cir. 2003), found this apparent anomaly to be a little unsettling, but nevertheless consistent with the intent of Congress in enacting the formula in §522(f)(2). The bankruptcy court had excluded the junior mortgage from the calculation, thereby holding that the judgment lien did not impair the exemption. The bankruptcy appellate panel (BAP) reversed, and the court of appeals affirmed the BAP. The court of appeals reasoned that Congress deliberately included "all other liens" in the impairment formula, so there was no justification, on the plain wording of the subsection, to disregard the junior mortgage. The holder of the judgment lien argued

321

that the literal application of the formula gave a windfall to the junior mortgagee, but the court was not persuaded. It said that Congress could have drafted the formula to exclude junior consensual lines from the calculation, but did not. This demonstrates congressional intent to treat consensual liens more favorably, even if it means that avoidance of the judicial lien would have the effect of elevating their priority. See also In re Brinley, 403 F.3d 415 (6th Cir. 2005) cert. denied, 126 S. Ct. 1164 (2006), in which the court likewise avoided the second-priority judgment lien to the extent of its impairment of the exemption, even though this benefited a third-priority second mortgage.

§13.6 THE INDIVIDUAL DEBTOR'S REDEMPTION RIGHT IN CH. 7 CASES

Under §722, when property is subject to a lien that secures a dischargeable consumer debt, an individual debtor in a Ch. 7 liquidation may redeem the property from the lienholder. The property must be tangible personal property intended primarily for personal, family, or household use and it must have been either exempted or abandoned. As the above restrictions show, redemption is available only in narrow circumstances. Under §521(a)(2) the debtor must file a statement of intention within 30 days of the petition indicating whether or not the property will be redeemed. See section 9.3. Section 521(a)(3) requires the redemption to be affected within 30 days of the first date set for the meeting of creditors unless the court grants additional time for cause.

By redeeming the collateral, the debtor in effect buys it from the secured creditor for the amount of the allowed secured claim. If the value of the collateral is equal to or exceeds the debt, the debt will be fully allowed as a secured claim provided that is valid and unavoidable. To redeem, the debtor must pay the claim in full. However, if the collateral is worth less than the debt (so that the creditor is undersecured), the allowed secured claim, and hence the redemption price, is limited to the value of the collateral.

Section 722 requires the property to be abandoned or exempt. Unless the lien is avoidable under §522(f), the existence of an exemption does not reduce the redemption price to be paid to the lienholder. As noted in section 13.5, exemptions do not avail against liens except to the extent provided in §522(f). The requirement of abandonment or exemption relates to the existence or extent of the estate's interest in the unencumbered equity in the property. If the collateral value is exactly equal to or less than the secured debt, the estate has no interest in the property, so it is likely to be abandoned, thereby allowing the debtor to redeem it by settling the secured claim.

Similarly, if the property is worth more than the debt but the equity is fully exempt, the estate has no interest in it and redemption can be affected by paying the secured claim. However, if the equity exceeds the debtor's exemption, the estate does have an interest in the property, and redemption is not possible unless the debtor first pays out the estate's interest so that the trustee will abandon the property. Following abandonment, the debtor may redeem by paying the redemption price to the secured claimant. (Example 5 illustrates this point.)

Prior to 2005, §722 did not say expressly that a debtor must redeem in cash. Most, but not all, courts did not allow a debtor to redeem by installments. BAPCPA added the words "in full at the time of redemption" to the end of §722 to make it clear that the debtor has no right to redeem by installments. This means that redemption is not practical for a debtor who has no means to raise the necessary cash after having filed bankruptcy. A debtor in that position cannot salvage encumbered property in a Ch. 7 case unless a reaffirmation agreement can be negotiated with the secured creditor.

The debtor's right to redeem is provided for only in Ch. 7 cases because redemption is not needed in Chs. 11, 12, and 13. Under those chapters, the debtor is able to retain desired property upon confirmation of a plan providing for protection of the security interest and periodic payments on the debt. The rehabilitation process under Chs. 11, 12, and 13 in fact permits the debtor to "redeem" collateral by installments under the plan. Therefore, a debtor who wishes to keep property, but cannot afford to redeem it for cash, has an incentive to choose rehabilitation rather than liquidation under Ch. 7. However, even in a Ch. 7 case, the debtor may have alternatives to redemption, as discussed in the next two sections.

§13.7 REAFFIRMATION

§13.7.1 The General Principles of Reaffirmation

A reaffirmation agreement is a contract between the debtor and a creditor under which the debtor agrees to pay a debt that would otherwise be discharged. Reaffirmation agreements are governed by §524. Section 524, has always been a big section, but it was extended to unbearable length by BAPCPA, which added several new provisions, including a lengthy standard disclosure that must be provided to the debtor by the creditor at or before the time of signing the agreement.

Sometimes the debtor may initiate negotiations for a reaffirmation agreement and sometimes the creditor may be the party that first proposes reaffirmation to the debtor. A creditor who approaches the debtor to suggest reaffirmation takes the risk that the debtor will object to the overture and claim that the creditor has violated the stay. Most (but not all) courts do not consider a mere suggestion of reaffirmation to be a per se violation of the stay, and recognize that by providing for a reaffirmation process in §524, the Code must be somewhat tolerant of creditor-initiated proposals for a reaffirmation agreement. But if the creditor's conduct is overbearing, coercive, deceptive, or harassing, a court may well find that the creditor has overstepped the mark and is using §524 as a pretext for trying to evade the strictures of the stay. As discussed in section 10.7, this could render the creditor liable for costs, fees, and damages under §362(k) (formerly (h)) or for sanctions for contempt of court under §105(a). This distinction between legitimate negotiation and disregard for the stay can be illustrated by a couple of cases. In In re Duke, 79 F.3d 43 (7th Cir. 1996), the creditor sent a letter to the debtor's attorney, with a copy to the debtor, offering to reinstate the debtor's credit line if he elected to reaffirm the debt. The court found that this approach did not violate the stay. There was no coercion or threat in the creditor's conduct, and the offer to reinstate the credit line was merely an incentive for reaffirming, rather than a penalty for not doing so. In re Seelye, 243 B.R. 701 (Bankr. N.D. Ill. 2000), followed In re Duke, but took a strict approach and confined it to the narrowest terms. It found a violation of the stay because the creditor did not notify the debtor's attorney of the proposed reaffirmation and did not send the debtor a covering letter adequately explaining the nature and effect of the reaffirmation. In In re Estrada, 439 B.R. 227 (Bankr. S.D. Fla. 2010), the court held that the creditor had violated the stay by intimating in a standard reaffirmation letter that the debtor could avoid the consequence of negative credit reporting by reaffirming. However, because the creditor argued convincingly that it had not intended to threaten the debtor, and had since changed the wording of its standard reaffirmation letter, the court did not impose sanctions on the creditor for contempt.

Even where the debtor initiates negotiations, the creditor's reaction could be a violation of the stay, so the creditor must be cautious in its response. In In re Jamo, 283 F.3d 392 (1st Cir. 2002), the debtor, not the creditor, initiated contact, offering to reaffirm a debt secured by a home mortgage. The creditor refused to enter a reaffirmation agreement for the mortgage debt unless the debtor also agreed to reaffirm some unsecured debts that the debtor owed to the creditor. The debtor claimed that this was a violation of the stay, but the court disagreed. It noted that reaffirmation is a contract, and the creditor can take advantage of its bargaining leverage and refuse to make the contract unless the debtor agrees to its terms. This is not a violation of the stay as long as the creditor does not engage in coercive or harassing conduct.

Because the debtor's discharge is such an important consequence of bankruptcy, the Code places a number of restrictions on reaffirmation agreements. To be enforceable, the agreement must comply with the following conditions set out in §524(c) and (d).

(1) The agreement is valid only to the extent that it is enforceable in nonbankruptcy law. At common law, the debtor's promise to pay a discharged debt does not require consideration because the original consideration given by the creditor creates a "moral obligation" sufficient to support the new promise. However, statutory or common law policing doctrines such as unconscionability, fraud, and duress may make the agreement avoidable under nonbankruptcy law.

(2) The agreement must have been made before the discharge is granted and it must be filed with the court.

(3) The debtor may rescind the agreement at any time before the discharge is granted, or within 60 days of the agreement having been filed in the court, whichever is the later. The agreement must conspicuously express this rescission right.

(4) The creditor must provide the debtor with a disclosure statement containing the information set out in §524(k) at or before the time of signing the agreement.

(5) If the debtor was represented by an attorney when the agreement was negotiated, the attorney must file a declaration with the agreement stating that the debtor's consent was informed and voluntary, that the agreement does not impose an undue hardship on the debtor or a dependent, and that the attorney fully advised the debtor of the legal effect and consequences of an agreement of that kind, and of default under it. Where a debtor is legally represented, her attorney may be in the awkward position of having to go against her wishes. The debtor may want to reaffirm, but the attorney cannot certify that the reaffirmation will not impose an undue hardship on the debtor. The attorney cannot simply give in to the debtor's wishes; she must conduct a proper assessment of her financial situation. If the attorney signs the certificate without justification, she could be sanctioned. See, for example, In re Vargas, 257 B.R. 157 (Bankr. D.N.J. 2001), in which an attorney who failed to conduct a proper hardship evaluation was required to disgorge his fees. (Some courts may allow the attorney to withdraw where she feels that she cannot give the certificate, so the duty of vetting the agreement falls to the court. See, for example, In re Brown, 95 B.R. 35 (Bankr. E.D. Va. 1989).)

Section 524(m) creates a presumption of undue hardship where the scheduled payments on the debt exceed the debtor's disposable monthly income, as reflected in the debtor's financial data submitted in support of the reaffirmation. The debtor can rebut the presumption by showing additional sources of income. If the presumption does not apply and the other requirements of §524 are met, the agreement becomes effective as soon as it is filed with the court. However, if the presumption applies, the court must conduct a hearing on notice to determine the question of undue hardship.

(6) If the debtor was unrepresented at the time of negotiating the agreement and is an individual, the agreement needs court approval that is granted only if the agreement does not impose undue hardship on the debtor or a dependent and is in the debtor's best interests. (This requirement of court approval does not apply to a "consumer debt secured by real property" — that is, a mortgage reaffirmation on the debtor's home.) The court evaluates undue hardship and the best interests of the debtor only where the debtor is unrepresented or the presumption of undue hardship applies. Otherwise the attorney's declaration is sufficient. See In re Morton, 410 B.R. 556 (B.A.P. 9th Cir. 2009).

(7) At the time for the individual debtor's discharge, the court may hold a discharge hearing at which the debtor must be present in person. If the debtor had not been represented by an attorney at the time of negotiating the agreement, the court must use the occasion of the discharge hearing to tell the debtor that the agreement is not required by law. The court must explain its effect and must determine whether or not the agreement satisfies all the requirements described above. An amendment to §524(d) in 1994 makes it clear that this procedure is not to be followed if the debtor was legally represented in entering the agreement.

The consequences of failing to comply with the requirements of §524(c) and (d) is illustrated by In re Sandburg Financial Corp., 446 B.R. 793 (S.D. Tex. 2011. The creditor had entered into a reaffirmation agreement with the Ch. 11 debtor. However, the agreement did not comply with §524 in that it was made after the discharge, did not contain the required disclosures, and was not filed with the court. The court found the reaffirmation agreement invalid and held that the creditor's attempt to enforce it was a willful violation of the discharge injunction. The court found the creditor in contempt and imposed a compensatory contempt sanction, awarding the debtor damages. The creditor had argued that it should not have had to comply with §524 because it had given the debtor new and independent consideration for entering into the agreement. Like other courts, the court held that the furnishing of new consideration does not excuse the creditor from complying with §524 where the agreement also reaffirms a dischargeable debt.

The restrictions in §524(c) and (d) apply only to reaffirmation agreements, that is, to contracts under which debtors undertake the obligation to pay the debts. Under §524(f), they do not apply when, instead of promising payment, the debtor actually makes a voluntary payment of the debt.

Section 524 makes no express distinction between secured and unsecured debts, and both are capable of being reaffirmed if the requirements of the section are satisfied. However, as explained below, there is a very important practical difference between the reaffirmation of these two classes of debt which makes courts much more wary of approving the reaffirmation of unsecured debt.

§13.7.2 The Reaffirmation of Secured Debt as an Alternative to Redemption

Reaffirmation of secured debt is commonly used by a debtor to save the collateral from liquidation. As stated in section 13.6, redemption under §722 is available only in very narrow circumstances. If the property does not qualify for redemption or the debtor cannot find the cash to redeem, reaffirmation could be an alternative means of keeping collateral that would otherwise be liquidated in a Ch. 7 case. Because reaffirmation is consensual, the debtor cannot force the secured creditor to reaffirm. The debtor must negotiate with the secured creditor and must usually provide an incentive — some benefit beyond that expected from liquidation of the property — to persuade the creditor to assent. (*See* Example 7.) If the debtor intends to reaffirm a secured debt, the statement of intent under §521(a)(2) must so indicate, and the debtor must perform that intent within 30 days after the first date set for the meeting of creditors, unless the court has extended that period for cause.

Unlike redemption, reaffirmation is not confined to Ch. 7 cases. However, because Chs. 11, 12, and 13 allow the debtor to retain property by providing for payments under a plan, the debtor does not need to use reaffirmation to keep property. In fact, if the debtor's primary goal is to prevent the liquidation of encumbered property, bankruptcy under Ch. 11, 12, or 13 may be easier and less expensive than attempting to negotiate reaffirmation agreements in a Ch. 7 case.

§13.7.3 The Reaffirmation of Unsecured Debt

Where reaffirmation is used by a debtor as a means of keeping property that would otherwise be liquidated, the rationale for the reaffirmation is clear. However, there is less obvious advantage to a debtor who reaffirms an unsecured debt. There are various reasons why a debtor may wish to pay an unenforceable unsecured debt: for example, creditor pressure, the desire not to damage a relationship, the hope of future credit, or guilt. Where there is no clear economic benefit to the debtor for the reaffirmation, the court should look even more carefully at the transaction to ensure that the requirements of §524 have been satisfied.

Reacting to abuse by large providers of consumer credit, which were found to have routinely bullied bankrupt customers into entering reaffirmation agreements, the majority report of the 1994 National Bankruptcy Review Commission recommended that reaffirmation should be confined to secured debt, and no longer permitted to the extent that a debt is unsecured. Congress did not adopt this recommendation in BAPCPA and decided, instead, to strengthen the creditor's disclosure requirements relating to reaffirmation and to provide for more rigorous enforcement to ensure that creditors follow them.

§13.8 THE CH. 7 DEBTOR'S RETENTION OF THE COLLATERAL UNDER THE ORIGINAL CONTRACT — THE "RIDE-THROUGH"

As noted earlier, §521(a)(2) requires the debtor to file a statement of intention concerning the retention or surrender of property securing a consumer debt, and to state whether redemption or reaffirmation will be sought. Section 521(a)(2) expressly provides only for surrender, redemption, or reaffirmation. However, some (but not all) courts have recognized an additional way for a debtor to keep property subject to a security interest. If the debtor has not defaulted on payments on the secured debt, some courts have allowed the debtor to retain the collateral while continuing to pay installments to the secured party as required by the contract. This is known as a "ride-through" because the secured transaction rides through the bankruptcy without being formally administered and dealt with as part of the estate. Where a court permits the ride-through the creditor must allow the debtor to keep the collateral as long as she remains current on the payments required by the contract. If the debtor later defaults, the creditor can foreclose on the collateral, but any deficiency would be discharged. (That is, although the creditor could enforce the security interest by foreclosing on the debt, the debtor would not be liable to the creditor for any deficiency.)

BAPCPA did not directly address the question of whether the ride-through is a permissible alternative to surrender, redemption or reaffirmation, but it enacted provisions that prohibit it under certain circumstances. Although courts have continued to allow the ride through in some cases, the changes enacted by BAPCPA have curtailed it. Section 521(a)(6) states that in a Ch.7 case, an individual debtor shall not retain personal property as to which a creditor has a secured claim for its purchase price unless the debtor has entered into a reaffirmation agreement or has redeemed the property. Section 521(a)(6) therefore makes it clear that if all its elements are satisfied, redemption for cash or reaffirmation are the only courses available to an individual debtor, and the ride-through is not a permissible alternative. Note the several restrictions on the application of §521(a)(6): the case must be under Ch. 7, the debtor must be an individual, the property securing the debt must be personal property, and the creditor's interest must secure the purchase price of the collateral (that is, it must be a purchase money interest). Because the section is written in narrow terms, courts have found that BAPCPA did not entirely eliminate the ride-through and have allowed it in cases that do not satisfy all the elements of the section. For example, in In re Hart, 402 B.R. 78 (Bankr. D. Del. 2009), the court allowed a ride-through in relation to real property.

Where §521(a)(6) applies and the ride-through is not permitted, the debtor must make a timely election under §521(a) to redeem or reaffirm and must follow through with a timely exercise of that intention. If he does not, §362(h) terminates the automatic stay with regard to the property that secures the claim and removes it from the estate so that the creditor can proceed to foreclose on it.[9] Notwithstanding, some courts have permitted the debtor to use the ride-through despite §521(a)(6) where the debtor did enter into a reaffirmation agreement, but the court declined to approve it. See, for example, In re Baker, 400 B.R. 136 (D. Del. 2009) and In re Moustafi, 371 B.R. 434 (Bankr. D. Ariz. 2007). However, in In re Dumont, 581 F.3d 1104 (9th Cir. 2009) the court stressed that this exception does not apply where the debtor has not made an effort to reaffirm.

Examples

The Examples involving exemptions are based on the list of exempt property in §522(d). The federal exemptions provided in §522(d) are used for convenience and illustrative purposes even though, in most cases, state law exemptions substitute for those in §522(d), either because the state has opted out under §522(b) or the debtor elects state law exemptions. Even if the exemptible property in a particular case differs from that set out in §522(d), the Examples based on that section raise principles applicable to exemption issues generally. The Examples use the exemption amounts in §522(d), as adjusted under §104 with effect from April 1, 2013. The amounts will be adjusted again with effect from April 1, 2016.

1. Melody is a composer by profession. She has managed to sell some of her musical compositions, but she has struggled for recognition in the world of music. She lives in a cold rented garret and owns no property of value except for a concert grand piano on which he composes. Despite her poor credit rating, Melody was able to procure a loan of $5,000 from Flesh-pound Finance Co., secured by a security interest in the piano. The security interest was properly perfected under state law.

---

9. Section 362(h) permits the trustee to retain the property in the estate and to forestall foreclosure by showing that the property is of consequential benefit or value to the estate. If this is established, the court must order the debtor to deliver the property to the trustee, and the creditor is entitled to adequate protection.

About a year later, Melody filed a Ch. 7 petition. At the time of the filing, the balance of the loan is $3,500. The piano is worth $6,000. Can Melody avoid the security interest under §522(f)?

2. An individual Ch. 7 debtor owns a small house valued at $250,000, subject to a security interest of $240,000. She earns her living by house-sitting for people when they travel. She usually has about ten housesitting jobs a year, which means that she lives in other people's homes for a total of about 30 weeks in a year. When she is not housesitting, she lives in her own house. Is the debtor entitled to an exemption in the house? If so, how much can she exempt? What would her exemption be if the house was not subject to a mortgage?

3. The value of the house was given in Example 2. It is the prerogative of law professors to fabricate convenient facts. Courts are not supposed to exercise the same creativity with regard to factfinding. How would the value of the debtor's home be decided in a bankruptcy case?

4. The property in the Ch. 7 estate of Earnest Everyman is valued at $52,000. It consists of the following assets: Earnest's equity of $30,000 in his home; furniture, appliances, household goods, and personal effects, with a total value of $16,000 (none of these items is worth over $575); a car worth $4,000; and carpentry tools worth $2,000, used by Earnest in his job.

   Aston Martin, another Ch. 7 debtor, loves old cars. Instead of buying a house, furniture, and other items of ordinary personal property, he has chosen to live modestly in a cheap furnished apartment. He has used all his savings to buy a vintage sports car worth $48,000. As a result, his Ch. 7 estate consists of household and personal effects worth $4,000 (none of these items is worth over $575) and the car.

   What is the maximum that each of these debtors can exempt under §522(d)? What does the comparison of their exemptions say about the emphasis, underlying policy, and possible inequity of the Code's exemption scheme?

5. Given the answer to Example 4, should Aston have sold his sports car before filing his bankruptcy petition and used the proceeds to buy property that qualifies as exempt?

6. One of the assets in the Ch. 7 estate of Eva Porate is a diamond ring. About a year before bankruptcy, Eva had obtained a loan from Unrequited Loan Co. to buy the ring and had granted Unrequited Loan Co. a valid security interest in the diamond ring to secure the loan.

   At the time of bankruptcy, the balance of the loan is $5,000. The ring is valued at $6,500. Eva would like to redeem the ring. Can she do so? How does the answer change if the ring is valued at $4,500 or $7,000?

7. Eva Porate, the debtor in Example 6, cannot raise the cash needed to redeem the ring. Eva wishes to enter into a reaffirmation agreement with Unrequited Loan Co. under which she will repay the debt in installments and keep the ring.

   Eva's salary is just sufficient to support herself and a minor child. If she scrimps very hard and forgoes a few meals a week, she can put aside $200 per month to pay Unrequited Loan Co. This is $75 less per month than she was obliged to pay under the original security agreement, so she needs an extension of time to pay off the debt. Eva is willing to pay interest at the rate fixed in the original contract, and Unrequited would retain its security interest. The balance of the debt is $5,000. The ring is worth $6,500. Is Eva able to use the reaffirmation process to keep the ring?

8. Another of Eva Porate's debts was an amount of $5,000 owed on a credit card. After the issuer of the card received notice of Eva's bankruptcy filing, it wrote a letter to her in which it noted the outstanding balance on the card and stated, "We realize that you have the right to discharge this debt in your bankruptcy case. However, before you do this, we urge you to bear in mind that bankruptcy can have a serious impact on your ability to obtain credit in the future. We therefore invite you to consider entering into the attached reaffirmation agreement. If you elect to make this agreement and you repay the outstanding balance due to us in installments as reflected therein, we will reinstate your credit card with your former credit limit. Please discuss this with your attorney, who will explain the procedure you must follow to reaffirm this debt." Has the credit card issuer done anything wrong in sending this letter?

Explanations

1. The piano should qualify as a tool of trade in which Melody may claim an exemption of $2,300 under §522(d)(6). Property qualifies as a tool of trade if it is used by the debtor to earn her livelihood. Although Melody uses the piano to compose, and not to perform, she is a composer by profession and needs the piano to do her work, from which she is trying to earn a living. (Compare In re Gregory, 245 B.R. 171 (10th Cir. B.A.P. 2000), in which the court refused to allow the debtor, a security guard, to claim a pistol as a tool of trade. The debtor argued that he used the pistol for practice, but the debtor's employer supplied another pistol that the debtor used on the job, and the employer did not require him to have another pistol for practice.) Although some courts have questioned whether expensive equipment should qualify as a tool or implement

of trade and have interpreted the exemption to apply only to small hand implements or devices of modest value, most courts do not adopt such a restrictive approach.

Fleshpound's security interest in the piano is a nonpossessory, nonpurchase-money interest, and tools of trade are one of the three categories of property covered by the avoidance provisions of §522(f)(1)(B). Melody can avoid the security interest to the extent that it impairs her exemption. If only the tools of trade exemption in §522(d)(6) is used, the lien cannot be avoided. That exemption is limited to $2,300, and she has a $2,500 equity in the piano beyond the amount of the security interest. Thus, the interest does not impair the exemption, which can be fully paid out of the equity with a surplus over for the estate.

However, §522(f) states that the security interest can be avoided to the extent that it "impairs an exemption to which the debtor would have been entitled" in a tool of trade. It does not say that the exemption is confined to the amount allowed for a tool of trade under §522(a)(6). A debtor is able to apply the general exemption in §522(a)(5) to property that is otherwise nonexempt, or to augment an existing exemption. If Melody applies the general exemption to the piano, she will be able to exempt its full value, because the general exemption is $1,225, plus up to $11,500 of the unused homestead exemption, which is available to Melody because she does not own a home. In In re McNutt, 87 B.R. 84 (9th Cir. B.A.P. 1988), the court allowed the debtor to apply the general exemption to a tool of trade to increase the extent of avoidance under §522(f). If Melody is able to avoid the security interest in its entirety, she will be able to keep the piano, and Fleshpound will be left with a general unsecured claim.

2. The debtor may claim the homestead exemption under §522(d)(1), provided that the debtor or a dependent uses the property as a residence. The value of the exemption is $22,975. (A debtor is able to increase it to $24,200 by adding the $1,225 general exemption provided for in §522(d)(5). Assume for the sake of this question that the debtor has used the general exemption for another asset, so the amount of the homestead exemption is $22,975.)

The general rule is that the debtor's temporary absence from the homestead, with a specific intent to return, does not prevent the debtor from claiming the exemption. Although the debtor's absences do add up to more than half a year, they are temporary and the debtor does always return to her home, which is her permanent abode.

This property, worth $250,000, is subject to a mortgage of $240,000, so the debtor's equity in the home is worth only $10,000. Unless §522(f) applies — which it clearly does not in this case — the debtor's exemption is subordinate to a valid consensual security interest in the property. By granting the mortgage, the debtor is taken to have waived the exemption as against the mortgagee. This is recognized by §522(c)(2).

Therefore, the debtor may claim an exemption in the house to the extent of the equity of $10,000. However, the debtor does not necessarily lose the full unused balance of the homestead exemption. Section 522(d)(5) allows her to add to the general exemption up to $11,500 worth of unused homestead exemption. Because the amount of unused homestead exemption is $12,975, she is able to apply almost all of it to exempt other property. Because the mortgage and the exemption consume the entire value of the house, there is no value in it for the estate, so it should be abandoned by the trustee.

Had there been no mortgage on the house, the debtor would have been entitled to claim the full exemption of $22,975. Because the house is only partially exempt, the trustee would have sold it, paid out the exemption amount to the debtor, and retained the balance of the home's value for the estate.

3. Section 522(a)(2) defines value for the purposes of §522 as the fair market value of the property at the date of the petition, or when property enters the estate after the petition, at the date that the estate acquires the property. The determination of fair market value is a factual issue to be decided on all the available evidence. This can in itself be a difficult question to resolve. (Some of the difficulties in valuing property are discussed in relation to relief from stay in section 11.4.2 and in Examples 1 and 2 of Chapter 11.)

In addition, courts have had difficulty in interpreting what is meant by fair market value in the bankruptcy context. If the facts suggest that the property will not be sold on the open market but will be liquidated, the use of market value results in artificially high appraisal. The impact of an unrealistic appraisal could be to the advantage or disadvantage of the debtor, depending on the facts. For example, in some cases a high valuation could harm the debtor by leading to the conclusion that the equity in the property exceeds the debtor's exemption. In other cases, a low valuation could make it appear that the debtor has no equity over a security interest, so that the property is abandoned to the secured claimant, or an application for relief from stay is granted. For this reason, some courts have been influenced by liquidation value where this has seemed more realistic, in spite of the reference to market value in §522(a)(2).

4. Each of the estates is worth $52,000, yet Earnest's exemptions are greater than Aston's. Earnest can claim exemptions in a total amount of $42,425, made up as follows:
   a. Homestead under §522(d)(1), limited to $22,975
   b. Household goods and personal effects under §522(d)(3) to a maximum aggregate value of $12,250. (Because no item is worth

more than §575, this amount is not reduced by the cap on individual item value in §522(d)(3).)

c. Motor vehicle under §522(d)(2), limited to $3,675

d. Tools of trade under §522(d)(6). He can claim the full $2,000 value because it is under the cap of $2,300.

e. General exemption of $1,225 under §522(d)(5), to be applied to nonexempt property or to enhance an existing exemption category

Aston can exempt all his personal and household goods. Their total value is $4,000, which is under the $12,250 cap, and no item is worth more than $575. He can partially exempt the sports car to the extent of $14,425 by adding together his motor vehicle exemption of $3,675 under §522(d)(2) and his wildcard exemption under §522(d)(5). Because Aston does not claim a homestead exemption, the wildcard is $12,725 ($1,225 plus $11,500 not used for the homestead exemption). Aston's total exemptions are therefore $20,400.

The advantage of specifying exemption categories with dollar limits is that the legislature can control exemptions and confine them to property and amounts that the legislature deems essential to the debtor's subsistence. The drawback of this approach is that it can result in groundless discrimination between debtors whose needs and interests vary from the generalized preconception of the legislature. The problem of unequal treatment can be avoided by allowing debtors to choose any property to exempt, up to a maximum lump sum amount. Congress declined to follow the recommendation of the 1994 National Bankruptcy Review Commission to make this change.

5. As noted in section 13.2.3, courts, relying on the legislative history of §522, have been willing to countenance the prepetition conversion of nonexempt assets into exempt property provided that the conversion does not constitute bad faith. A debtor's ability to engage in prepetition exemption planning mitigates the concern about the unequal treatment of debtors raised in Explanation 4. Provided that Aston simply makes the conversion by selling the car at market value and reinvesting the proceeds in exempt property, his conversion is likely to be permissible. However, if he goes beyond that and engages is deceptive or manipulative transactions (for example, if he uses credit to buy or increase the value of exempt property) he could be denied the exemption or, in a severe case, may be denied a discharge.[10]

---

10. Had the exempt property been a homestead, the basis for policing the conversion for impropriety would have been governed by §522(o). It reduces the amount of the debtor's homestead exemption to the extent that, with intent to hinder, delay, or defraud creditors, the debtor acquired or increased an exempt homestead interest in the ten years before the petition by converting nonexempt property.

6. The ring can be redeemed only if all the requirements of §722 are satisfied. If the ring is worth $6,500, all are satisfied: Eva is an individual. The ring is tangible personal property. The ring is apparently intended primarily for personal use, and the debt is a consumer debt, incurred to buy the ring. The debt is dischargeable. (Discharge is discussed in Chapter 22. Assume that none of the exclusions from discharge are applicable on the facts of this case.) The property must be exempt or abandoned. If the ring is worth $6,500, the claim is fully secured with a surplus of $1,500 (less any costs and additional interest) that constitutes the debtor's equity in the property. The equity is exemptable by Eva under §522(d)(4), which provides for a $1,550 exemption in jewelry held for personal, family, or household use. Provided that Eva has claimed the ring as exempt, she may redeem the ring by paying Unrequited the amount of its secured claim of $5,000. The redemption price must be paid in cash. Eva may not redeem by installments. (She also cannot reduce the secured claim below $5,000 by avoiding it under §522(f) because it is a purchase money interest.)

   If the ring is worth $4,500, Unrequited is undersecured. Because §722 permits redemption by payment of the secured claim, the value of the collateral sets the upper limit on the redemption price.

   If the ring is worth $7,000, the redemption price is set at the amount of the debt ($5,000) as in the first example. However, unlike in the first example, the debtor's equity of $2,000 exceeds the $1,550 exemption. The estate has a $450 interest in the property, so that it is not fully exempt and will not be abandoned by the trustee. To satisfy the requirements of §722 and effect redemption, Eva must pay the estate $450 so that the trustee will abandon the property. This means that Eva must be able to raise $5,450 in cash to redeem the property.

7. Reaffirmation is a consensual arrangement, and Unrequited will likely not have much incentive to agree to enter a reaffirmation agreement if immediate liquidation would fully settle its claim. Because the collateral is worth $6,500, Unrequited's secured claim will be settled in full upon impending liquidation of the property with a surplus of $1,500 (less costs and any additional interest). For this reason, Eva may not be able to persuade Unrequited to forgo immediate liquidation in exchange for a promise of extended payments from a debtor who will struggle to make payments.

   Had the value of the ring been less than the debt, Eva would have been in a better bargaining position because she could have offered to reaffirm the debt in full. The creditor would have an incentive to agree because in the absence of reaffirmation, the deficiency is an unsecured claim that would most likely receive partial payment, at best, from the estate, with the balance being discharged. This, combined with other factors (such as an attractive interest rate and a likelihood that the ring would not depreciate in value over the term of payment so that later foreclosure will not result in loss), could outweigh the risk of default under the reaffirmation agreement.

Even if Unrequited could be persuaded to enter into a reaffirmation agreement, the provisions of §524(c) and (d) must be satisfied. These restrictions are intended to protect the debtor from the coerced or uninformed assumption of liability for a discharged debt. In addition to imposing requirements to ensure that the debtor acted voluntarily and was fully informed in entering into the reaffirmation, §524 requires an impartial review of the agreement. If Eva was represented by an attorney when negotiating the reaffirmation, the attorney must certify that the agreement is informed and voluntary and that it does not impose an undue hardship on her or her dependent. If Eva was not legally represented when negotiating the reaffirmation, the court cannot approve the agreement unless it is satisfied that it is in the debtor's best interests and does not impose an undue hardship on her or her dependent.

Reaffirmation agreements under which the debtor receives some advantage, such as the right to retain property that would otherwise be liquidated, are generally regarded as more justifiable than those that merely reaffirm unsecured debts. However, the facts indicate that Eva cannot afford the reaffirmation and that the proposed payments will impose a strain on her household budget. The ring is not a necessity, and Eva's efforts to keep it seem irresponsible. If Eva is legally represented, her attorney would be hard-pressed to certify the reaffirmation as not imposing an undue hardship on her and her child. If she is not legally represented, the court would have similar difficulty and would in addition be likely to find that the agreement does not serve her best interests.

Where a debtor cannot use redemption or reaffirmation to keep property in a Ch. 7 case, Ch. 13 may be an alternative if the debtor can afford to pay under a Ch. 13 plan. Ch. 13 enables a debtor to force creditors to allow him to retain property and to accept payment of the debt by installments.

8. As discussed in section 13.7.3, a creditor who approaches the debtor to propose reaffirmation takes the risk that its action may be construed as an attempt to recover a claim against the debtor in willful violation of the automatic stay. (§362(a)(6).)

Most courts will not find a violation of the stay if the creditor's proposal for reaffirmation is not aggressive, coercive, or harassing. Also, it is wiser for the creditor to make the approach through the debtor's attorney, and to make sure that the debtor is fully informed about the nature and effect of the reaffirmation. Any deception or nondisclosure could cause problems for the creditor. Although the distinction between an incentive and a threat can be quite subtle, the letter in Eva's case may not overstep the mark and violate the stay. The warning of a bad credit rating could be construed as vaguely threatening, but it does not seem strong enough to be coercive. It does not really indicate that this creditor would take any action adverse to the debtor if the offer is refused. Further, as the creditor would have no obligation to extend credit to the debtor in the future, the hint that it may not do so unless the debtor reaffirms is not properly regarded as a threat.

CHAPTER 14

The Trustee's Avoidance Powers: General Principles and Policies

§14.1 INTRODUCTION

In general terms, the avoidance powers enable the trustee to set aside certain transactions entered into by the debtor prior to the filing of the petition. (All of the Code's avoidance provisions relate to the prepetition period except for §549, which is concerned with postpetition transactions.) The avoidance powers are aimed primarily at transfers of property by the debtor, but some are also applicable to obligations assumed by the debtor. "Transfer" is defined very broadly in §101(54) to include every mode of disposing of property or an interest in it. A transfer may be voluntary or involuntary, direct or indirect, or absolute or conditional. It may be an outright disposition of property, such as a sale or a gift, or the grant of a lien or security interest, or other interest in it.

The avoidance of prepetition transfers and obligations is part of the trustee's function of collecting estate property and maximizing the estate's value. The discussion of property of the estate in section 12.2 expresses the general rule that property enters the estate only to the extent that the debtor has an interest in it, as determined under nonbankruptcy law. The trustee's avoidance rights qualify that general rule in that they enable the trustee to avoid transactions and recover property that the debtor had no right to reverse or recover under nonbankruptcy law.

Some of the trustee's avoidance rights are unique to bankruptcy law while others have counterparts that may be used by a creditor outside of bankruptcy law. The trustee's array of avoidance rights, both created by the

Code and derived from principles of nonbankruptcy law, place the trustee in a much stronger position than any creditor could occupy outside of bankruptcy.

Each of the trustee's avoidance powers is examined in Chapters 15 and 16. This chapter introduces them generally, outlines some procedural issues and common themes, and explains their basic concept and rationale.

§14.2 THE STRUCTURE OF THE AVOIDANCE PROVISIONS

Before discussing the trustee's avoidance powers, it is helpful to identify the following provisions in the Code that bear on these powers and to indicate their functions.

1. The trustee's power to avoid prepetition transactions is conferred by §§544, 545, 547, 548, and 553, which prescribe the transactions that are avoidable and specify prerequisites for avoidance.
   a. §544 allows the trustee to avoid transfers and obligations that could have been avoided under nonbankruptcy law by an actual unsecured creditor or by specified hypothetical claimants.
   b. §545 gives the trustee limited power to avoid certain kinds of statutory liens.
   c. §547 allows the trustee to avoid preferential transfers that occurred within 90 days (or in the case of insiders, within one year) before the petition.
   d. §548 gives the trustee the power, similar to that available to creditors under state fraudulent transfer law, to avoid fraudulent transfers and obligations that occurred within a year before the petition.
   e. §553 allows the trustee to avoid setoffs to the extent they involve disallowed claims or arose out of certain transactions within 90 days prior to the petition.
2. Although §552 is not an avoidance provision strictly speaking, it does have the effect of partially avoiding floating liens[1] to the extent that they would otherwise cover collateral acquired after the petition has been filed. Under §552, a security interest in after-acquired collateral is confined to such collateral acquired up to the time of bankruptcy and proceeds of that collateral. It does not attach to property acquired by the estate or the debtor after the petition.

---

1. This type of transaction is explained in section 2.2.4.

3. Although it is also not an avoidance power in the same sense as the others, §558 should be included in this list. It allows the trustee to succeed to any defense that the debtor may have against any entity. Hence, if the debtor has an avoidance right under nonbankruptcy law (*e.g.*, the right to rescind a transfer on grounds of the transferee's fraud), the trustee may exercise that right for the benefit of the estate.

4. Section 549 permits the trustee to avoid unauthorized postpetition transfers.

5. Section 546 imposes limitations on the avoidance powers. It contains a statute of limitations and also subjects the trustee's avoidance rights to provisions of nonbankruptcy law that confer protection on certain transferees in specified transactions.

6. The effect of avoidance is governed by §§550 and 551. Section 551 allows the estate to take over the rights the defeated transferee had in estate property, so that avoidance benefits the estate rather than the holders of junior interests in the property. Section 550 provides for the recovery of property by the estate following avoidance of the transfer. Section 502(d) adds further force to the obligation to surrender property by providing for the disallowance of the claim of a transferee who fails to turn over property to the estate.

7. The provisions discussed here are concerned with the trustee's avoidance power. Remember, however, that the debtor has the right under §522(f) to avoid certain liens that impair exemptions. (*See* section 13.5.)

8. Finally, this list of relevant statutory provisions would be incomplete without a reminder that §101 must be consulted for the definition of many terms used in the avoidance sections.

§14.3 APPLICABILITY OF THE AVOIDANCE POWERS IN LIQUIDATION AND REHABILITATION CASES

The avoidance powers are applicable in all cases under the Code, whether filed under Ch. 7, 11, 12, or 13. However, they have a somewhat different effect in rehabilitation and liquidation cases. In a case under Ch. 7 the trustee's exercise of the avoidance powers directly benefits the creditor body. Recovered property swells the value of the fund to be distributed, and the avoidance of encumbrances and obligations adjusts the share in the fund by eliminating claims against the estate or demoting claims from secured to unsecured status.

In cases under Chs. 11, 12, and 13, the link between the creditors' interest and the avoidance power is not as direct, because much (if not all) of the estate property ultimately reverts to the debtor. Therefore, the debtor may be the principal beneficiary of avoidance actions. The advantage to creditors from avoidance derives from the fact that the liquidation value of the estate sets a minimum level of payment under the plan. The recovery of property enlarges that liquidation value and thereby raises the minimum standards for confirmation of the plan. Also, as in liquidation cases, the avoidance of encumbrances or obligations expands the value of the estate to the benefit of creditors generally.

§14.4 EXERCISE OF THE AVOIDANCE POWER BY A DEBTOR IN POSSESSION OR OTHER PARTIES

All the avoidance provisions specifically confer the avoidance power on the trustee. As noted in section 6.2, in Ch. 11 cases the debtor in possession normally exercises all the powers of a trustee. It is therefore common for the debtor in possession to represent the estate in avoidance litigation. This leads to the paradoxical result that it is frequently the very debtor who made the transfer or incurred the obligation that later seeks to avoid it. Although this anomaly has occasionally caused courts to balk at allowing avoidance by a debtor in possession, the usual approach is to recognize that the debtor in possession is really operating in a new capacity.

Avoidance rights cannot normally be exercised by anyone other than the trustee or debtor in possession. There are some narrow exceptions to this. In a Ch. 11 case, the court might authorize a creditors' committee to avoid a transfer if the debtor in possession unjustifiably fails to do so. Although the creditor's committee cannot simply take the initiative and sue, the court has the discretion to authorize suit. See In re The V Companies, 292 B.R. 290 (6th Cir. B.A.P. 2003); Official Committee of Unsecured Creditors of Cybergenics Corp. v. Chinery, 330 F.3d 548 (3d Cir. 2003). Also, §522(h) provides for another limited exception for individual debtors. If a transfer of exempt property is avoidable and the trustee does not attempt to avoid it, the debtor may do so provided that the transfer was involuntary and the debtor did not conceal the property.

§14.5 THE AVOIDANCE SUIT AND THE ENFORCEMENT OF A JUDGMENT OF AVOIDANCE

To seek the avoidance of a transfer or obligation, the trustee must commence suit in the bankruptcy court. The suit takes the form of an adversary proceeding — essentially, a civil lawsuit within the bankruptcy case.

Avoidance suits are included in the list of core proceedings in 28 U.S.C. §157(b)(2)(F), (H), and (K). This indicates that Congress considered them to be centrally related to the bankruptcy process and fully within the jurisdiction of the bankruptcy courts. However, as discussed in section 7.3, Congress's determination of whether or not a matter is a core proceeding is not dispositive; the Supreme Court has cast doubt on the characterization of avoidance actions as core proceedings because they involve the adjudication of rights under nonbankruptcy law.

If the avoidance action concerns an obligation incurred by, or an interest in property granted by, the debtor, the court's determination of avoidability results either in disallowance of the claim against the estate or in invalidation of the claim to the property. If the action is aimed at the avoidance of a transfer of property by the debtor, judgment in favor of the trustee obliges the transferee to return the property or its value to the estate. Section 550 governs the enforcement of this obligation. Section 550(a) allows the trustee to recover the property (or its value, if the court so orders) from the initial transferee who received or benefited from the transfer and from any subsequent transferee. Although this means that there may be more than one person liable for the property or its value, §550(d) makes it clear that the estate can only obtain a single satisfaction.

Section 550(b) limits the trustee's right to recover from a subsequent transferee who takes the property for value, in good faith, and without knowledge of the voidability of the transfer (i.e., a bona fide purchaser). A bona fide purchaser is not liable to return the property or its value; any later transferee who takes in good faith is also protected from avoidance. Section 550(b) applies only to subsequent transferees and cannot be used as a defense by the person who acquired the property from the debtor. Once grounds for recovery are established, the trustee's power to recover from the initial transferee is absolute.

Under §550(e), any transferee who acquired the property in good faith but who is not entitled to protection under §550(b) is given a lien on the property to secure the lesser of the net cost of any improvement made to the property after transfer (offset by profits from the property) or the increase in value resulting from the improvement. This lien is available to both the initial transferee and to any subsequent transferee who does not satisfy the requirements of §550(b), provided that the transferee acted in good faith in acquiring the property.

In many cases, the initial transferee of property is a creditor who acquired the property in satisfaction of a debt. When the transfer is avoided, the previously settled indebtedness becomes an unpaid claim once again. To encourage such transferees to surrender property to the estate following avoidance of the transfer, §502(d) provides for the disallowance of the transferee's claim against the estate unless the property is returned. In In re Davis, 889 F.2d 658 (5th Cir. 1989), the court observed that this provision is intended to be coercive rather than punitive: It is supposed to put pressure on the creditor to turn over the property to the estate within a reasonable time after having been ordered to do so.

§14.6 PRESERVATION OF THE TRANSFER FOR THE BENEFIT OF THE ESTATE

Section 551 states that any avoided transfer is preserved for the benefit of the estate with respect to property of the estate. This means that when the trustee avoids an interest in estate property, the estate automatically succeeds to the avoided rights in the property. This allows the trustee to assert those rights against any other interest in the property that is junior to the avoided interest. Say, for example, that there are two security interests in a piece of estate property. Both are valid under state law, and the first security interest has priority over the second. If the senior interest is avoidable in bankruptcy[2] but the junior interest is not, the trustee avoids the senior interest and is then able to assert its priority over the junior one. Were it not for §551, the avoidance of the superior interest would simply promote the junior lien, so that it becomes first in line as claimant to the proceeds of the property. Section 551 ensures that when the trustee exercises the avoidance power, it is the estate, rather than the holder of the junior interest, that benefits from the avoidance.

§14.7 THE STATUTE OF LIMITATIONS AND "REACH-BACK" PROVISIONS

Two statutes of limitation pertain to the period within which the trustee must act to assert the avoidance powers.

First, §546(a) requires that actions or proceedings for avoidance be commenced at the latest before the case is closed. However, the closing of the case is the outside limit for the commencement of avoidance proceedings. Even if the case has not yet closed, the limitation period ends on the later of two years from the order of relief, or (provided that the first trustee is appointed or elected within that two-year period) one year from the first trustee's appointment or election.

---

2. Section 16.1 explains how an interest could be avoidable in bankruptcy notwithstanding its validity under state law.

Second, §550(f) requires that actions or proceedings to recover property following avoidance be commenced within the earlier of one year after the transfer has been avoided or by the time that the case is closed or dismissed.

These provisions recognize that avoidance proceedings consist of two distinct stages: the action of avoidance itself and the enforcement of the judgment of avoidance by proceedings to compel turnover of the property under §550. Of course, the trustee is able to make the avoidance and turnover claims in the same suit, so that judgment on these issues is granted simultaneously.

These limitation periods must be distinguished from so-called "reach-back" provisions contained in the avoidance sections themselves. Some powers of avoidance apply only to transfers that occurred within a specific period before the petition. That is, the trustee can "reach back" only so far into the prebankruptcy period to avoid certain transfers. These periods are noted in the discussion of the different avoidance powers in Chapters 15 and 16. While the reach-back provisions prescribe the retrospective temporal range of the avoidance power, limitation periods require the trustee to initiate avoidance proceedings within a specific period during the bankruptcy case. (*See* section 15.1.3 for further discussion of this distinction.)

§14.8 THE GENERAL PURPOSE AND GOALS OF THE AVOIDANCE POWERS

Before becoming involved in the intricacies of the avoidance powers, it is useful to identify the principal policies that motivated their enactment and that continue to influence courts in their interpretation. These broad policy themes are not served equally by all the avoidance provisions. Each section is designed to achieve specific ends with regard to particular types of transactions. However, there are common threads, and a survey of them at the outset helps create a perspective from which the detailed rules may be viewed. The themes raised here will arise again in a more concrete context in Chapters 15 and 16.

(1) Most avoidance powers are intended to facilitate the bankruptcy goals of preservation of the estate and collective treatment of claims. Two of the fundamental bankruptcy policies identified in section 5.5 are the preservation of the estate and collective treatment of claims, leading to the optimum distribution to creditors in the order of priority prescribed by law. These policies could not be effectively realized if the trustee was able to look no further than the remnants of the debtor's

estate at the time of the filing of the petition. In many cases, the debtor's bankruptcy is preceded by a period of financial crisis in which creditors jostle for advantage by collection activity and the debtor responds to pressure by making payments to particular creditors or by disposing of property. Much activity in this period could be abnormal or contrary to regular business practices; some of it could be dishonest or manipulative.

By permitting the trustee to go back into the prebankruptcy period and to avoid dispositions made and obligations incurred irregularly or illegitimately, the Code gives the trustee's power of preservation some retrospective effect. The trustee is able, to some extent at least, to ameliorate the harm caused by disruptions prior to the filing of the petition. The avoidance enhances the value to the estate by restoring property to the estate or reducing claims against it. In addition, the avoidance of a transfer to a creditor deprives that creditor of the inappropriate advantage obtained in the period preceding bankruptcy and brings the creditor into bankruptcy's collective process. The argument is also made that the avoidance powers have a preventative function that goes beyond the case at hand. If it is generally understood that certain advantages will be avoidable if the debtor becomes bankrupt, creditors and other recipients may be discouraged from pursuing them, because gains will be short-lived and futile. Of course, to some creditors, the possibility of avoidance may be no disincentive at all, because the risk of having to return the avoided transfer will be outweighed by the prospect of benefit if bankruptcy does not occur in the near future.

(2) The avoidance provisions attempt to differentiate between legitimate and illegitimate transactions. It will become clear when the prerequisites for avoidance are discussed in Chapters 15 and 16 that the avoidance powers do not extend to every prepetition transfer or obligation. They are aimed at transactions that are perceived by Congress to be irregular or illegitimate, in that they unfairly or unjustifiably diminish the estate or undermine the proper order of distribution in bankruptcy. This limitation on the avoidance powers is very important. If every prepetition transfer or obligation could be overturned, the risk of a debtor becoming bankrupt would make all credit transactions hazardous and unappealing. Furthermore, it is one of the fundamental policies of bankruptcy that rights under nonbankruptcy law should be interfered with only to the extent necessary to affect the essential goals of bankruptcy such as estate preservation and evenhanded treatment of creditors. In creating the avoidance provisions, Congress was sensitive to the tension between effecting the goals of bankruptcy and protecting legitimate rights under nonbankruptcy law. Accordingly, the avoidance provisions constantly call for the distinction to be drawn between legitimate and illegitimate transactions.

(3) The avoidance powers are frequently used to invalidate unpublicized rights. In a sense, this point is really a subcategory of the previous one, but the issue of unpublicized rights is important enough to be highlighted as a distinct policy concern. The law requires that certain rights must be publically recorded so that their existence can be ascertained by any person who searches the public records. For example, title to real property and some personal property (such as motor vehicles) must be recorded in the appropriate public repository. Similarly, as we saw in chapter 2, most liens and encumbrances must be recorded or otherwise publicized to be perfected — that is, effective against parties other than the debtor. The public record protects those persons who deal with the debtor by informing them of the debtor's ownership in the property and of any limitations on it. A "secret lien" — that is, an unpublicized encumbrance in the debtor's property — creates a potential for abuse by the debtor and a danger of misplaced reliance by third parties. For this reason, where an interest in property is required to be publicized by recording or otherwise, but it is not, the unpublicized right will not avail against a creditor who was unaware of it when extending credit, and it will not avail against the trustee if the debtor becomes bankrupt.

The failure to publicize a lien or other interest may be the result of deliberate collusion between a debtor and the creditor where the parties do not want it to be known that the interest has been granted. However, more commonly the failure to publicize is the result of inadvertence, error, or delay. Whether or not the lack of publicity is deliberate, the law does not generally protect unpublicized interests.[3] Therefore, as a general rule, when nonbankruptcy law requires an act of publicity to perfect a lien or right in property, failure to complete the act makes the lien or right avoidable unless particularly strong equities favor the holder.

---

3. In some narrow circumstances, equity may recognize an interest that is not properly recorded, giving rise to an equitable lien or interest. (*See* section 2.4.5.) However, even an equitable lien or interest is based on some form of publicity that substitutes for proper recording. (*See* sections 2.4.5 and 15.1.2(3).)

The Trustee's Avoidance Powers: Unperfected Interests and Statutory Liens

---

§15.1 THE AVOIDANCE OF UNPERFECTED INTERESTS UNDER §544

§15.1.1 Introduction

The basic idea behind §544 is that the trustee should have the same avoidance rights that would be available in nonbankruptcy law to the classes of persons identified in the section. Section 544 does not create rights of avoidance that are peculiar to the bankruptcy trustee, but rather confers a status on the trustee under which avoidance rights under nonbankruptcy law may be exercised. However, the concentration of these nonbankruptcy rights in the hands of the trustee, combined with the operation of legal fictions, gives the trustee a collection of powers that would not be held by actual creditor under nonbankruptcy law. The two subsections of §544 are distinct and provide different avoidance powers.

§15.1.2 The Trustee's Status as a Hypothetical Lien Creditor, Execution Creditor, or Bona Fide Purchaser of Real Property under §544(a)

Section 544(a) is known as the "strong arm" clause — a nickname inherited from its predecessor in the Bankruptcy Act. It confers three hypothetical roles on the trustee: those of judicial lienholder, unsatisfied execution creditor, and bona fide purchaser of real property.

Section 544(a) expressly declares that the trustee's assumption of any of these hypothetical positions is not dependent on the existence of an actual creditor or purchaser. The trustee is not a successor to the existing rights of any person, but obtains the status as a matter of law. This means that even though there was no actual creditor or purchaser in existence who could have exercised these rights prior to the petition, the bankruptcy filing brings the avoidance rights into effect. Section 544(a) also states expressly that the trustee's rights of avoidance are not affected by any knowledge that the trustee or any creditor may have. This is because the trustee acts in an official capacity and occupies the applicable status hypothetically. Any knowledge that would affect the equities against a real purchaser or lien creditor should therefore not be applicable to the trustee. (*See* Example 3.)

(1) The trustee as judicial lienholder under §544(a)(1). Section 544(a)(1) gives the trustee the power to avoid any transfer of property or any obligation incurred by the debtor that would be avoidable in non-bankruptcy law by a creditor who has a judicial lien on all the debtor's property as at the date of the petition.[1] "Judicial lien" is defined in §101(36) to mean a lien arising out of judgment, levy, or some other judicial process. Section 544(a)(1) places the trustee in the position of a hypothetical lien creditor as at the date of the petition, but it actually gives the trustee greater powers than an actual lien creditor would have. Despite the use of the term "voidable" in §544, a lien creditor who has priority over a claimant under state law does not in fact avoid a junior claim. It just takes priority over that claim to the extent of the lien. The claim remains valid and can still be asserted in the proceeds of the property that are left after the senior lien creditor is paid. To illustrate: On January 5 a secured party lends $100,000 to the debtor and enters into a security agreement with the debtor under UCC Article 9. The security agreement gives the secured party a security interest in the debtor's equipment, which is valued at $100,000. The secured party fails to file a financing statement as required by Article 9, so it never perfects the interest. On February 1, a lien creditor, who obtained judgment against the debtor for $60,000, levies execution on the equipment and thereby acquires a judicial lien. Under state law (UCC §9.317(2)), the lien creditor takes priority over the secured party's unperfected security

---

1. The actual language of §544(a)(1) is rather more convoluted. It refers to a creditor who extends credit and gets a lien at the time of the commencement of the case. This language was intended to make it clear that the Code meant to overturn some pre-Code case law that is no longer of concern to us. The reference to "simple contract" merely signifies that the judicial lien to be used in the hypothesis must be an ordinary one and not one that is given special priority under nonbankruptcy law.

interest. This means that the lien creditor is paid first out of the proceeds of the equipment and receives $60,000. However, the secured party's security interest, although subordinate to the lien, does not disappear. It remains valid to the extent of the surplus value of the collateral and gives the secured party the right to recover the $40,000 balance of the proceeds. By contrast, if there is no judicial lienholder, but instead the debtor had filed bankruptcy on February 1, the trustee avoids the security interest entirely under §544(a)(1), the full value of the property belongs to the estate, and the secured party loses its security interest and becomes a general unsecured claimant. (This is further illustrated by Example 1.)

(2) The trustee as a creditor with a nulla bona return under §544(a)(2). §544(a)(2) gives the trustee the avoidance power that would be available in nonbankruptcy law to a creditor who obtains a nulla bona return on an execution as at the date of the petition. This provision is not much used because it only applies where state law gives a creditor special avoidance rights after a nulla bona return. Few states have such a law, and this subsection is seldom used.

(3) The trustee as a hypothetical bona fide purchaser of real property under §544(a)(3). Section 544(a)(3) gives the trustee the avoidance power that would be available in nonbankruptcy law to a bona fide purchaser of real property from the debtor who obtained and perfected that status on the date of the petition. Under state law a bona fide purchaser often has more powerful rights than a judicial lienholder. This is because some unperfected interests in real property are given priority over a subsequent judicial lien in the property, but not over a later bona fide purchaser. Where interests in real property are vulnerable to avoidance, the hypothetical bona fide purchaser status therefore augments the trustee's power beyond that of a hypothetical lien creditor. (The value of this hypothetical status of the trustee is illustrated by Example 3.)

Like the other provisions of §544(a), this subsection is expressly not dependent upon the existence of an actual bona fide purchaser. Simply stated, §544(a)(3) employs the fiction that the trustee is a perfected bona fide purchaser of real property as of the date of the petition. If, under nonbankruptcy law, such a bona fide purchaser of real property would take precedence over the preexisting interest in it, the trustee can avoid the debtor's transfer of that interest.

To qualify as a bona fide purchaser under state law, a person must purchase the property in good faith, for value, and without knowledge or constructive notice of the prior rights in the property. Of course, as a hypothetical bona fide purchaser, the trustee is legally presumed to satisfy these requirements, and §544(a) expressly states that the avoidance rights under the section are not effected by any actual knowledge that the trustee or a creditor may have. Although actual knowledge of interest is not legally relevant, constructive notice is. The rights of the estate should not be affected by what the trustee or a creditor might know because the trustee is merely an official representing the estate, not an actual participant in a purchase transaction whose knowledge may affect the equities of the case. However, constructive notice is a legal fiction imputed to a person irrespective of what he actually knows for the purpose of protecting an earlier equitable interest that has achieved a level of publicity sufficient to be treated as quasi-perfection. For this reason, it should bind the trustee as hypothetical occupant of the status, in the same way as it would bind an actual party. This was the conclusion reached in *McCannon v. Marston*, 679 F.2d 13 (3d Cir. 1982). Constructive notice is most obviously present where the interest has been properly recorded (called "record notice"). However, it may also be furnished by some form of publicity that falls short of proper recording, but that would give notice of the interest to a reasonable purchaser (called "inquiry notice"). In *In re Polo Builders*, 433 B.R. 700 (Bankr. N.D. Ill. 2010), the deed conveying the property to a buyer was not recorded at the time of the petition, so there was no record notice of the buyer's interest. However, inquiry notice could be attributed to the trustee because the buyer had moved into the property and was in possession of it. By contrast, the court did not attribute notice of the rights of an unrecorded mortgagee in *In re Deuel*, 594 F.3d 1073 (9th Cir. 2010). The holder of the unrecorded mortgage argued that the trustee had constructive notice of it and therefore could not avoid it under §544(a)(3) because the debtor had disclosed the mortgage in her schedule which was filed with the petition. The court rejected this argument: The trustee's status as a bona fide purchaser arises on commencement of the case, and even if the schedules are filed simultaneously with the petition, the moment of commencing the case must be distinguished from the filing of the schedules, which cannot be taken as filed until after there is a case to file them in. Therefore, notice of matter in the schedule cannot be attributed to the trustee as of the commencement of the case. The court distinguished this case from an earlier case that involved an involuntary bankruptcy. In that case, the petition itself alleged the lien, giving constructive notice of it immediately upon commencement of the case.

§15.1.3 The Trustee's Status as Successor to an Actual Unsecured Creditor under §544(b)

Section 544(b)(1) states that the trustee may avoid any transfer made or obligation incurred by the debtor that is avoidable in prevailing nonbankruptcy law by a creditor holding an allowable unsecured claim. Unlike §544(a), this subsection does not create a hypothetical status. Rather, it provides for the trustee's succession to the avoidance rights of an actual unsecured creditor. Note that the rights conferred on the trustee are those of an unsecured creditor. The trustee cannot use this provision to acquire the more powerful rights of a lienholder. Although an actual unsecured creditor must be in existence, the creditor need not have proved a claim in the estate. All the subsection requires is that the claim would be allowable if proved. The power of avoidance under §544(b)(1) is not deemed to arise on the date of the petition. Although the trustee succeeds to the avoidance right on the petition date, the effectiveness of the right against the transferee is determined as at its actual effective date, that is, the date that the real-life creditor became entitled to exercise it.

As discussed in sections 1.4 and 4.1, unless the debtor has transferred property fraudulently, unsecured creditors have very little power to avoid transactions entered into by the debtor. For this reason, §544(b)(1) is of limited use to the trustee. In fact, most of the cases decided under §544(b)(1) involve fraudulent transfers. Even when fraudulent transfers are involved, §544(b)(1) is often not needed to avoid them because §548 gives the trustee the nonderivative power to avoid fraudulent transfers. (*See* section 16.3.) Section §544(b)(1) may be helpful, however, if the state's fraudulent transfer law provides broader powers of avoidance than §548 or if it allows the trustee to reach back earlier into the prebankruptcy period than §548 does. More specifically, §548 allows the trustee to avoid fraudulent transfers made within two years before the petition.[2] However, the statute of limitations under the Uniform Fraudulent Transfer Act (UFTA) is four years. Therefore, if a transfer occurred, say, three years before the petition, the trustee cannot use §548. But if there is an actual creditor who has the right to avoid the transfer under the UFTA, the trustee can use §544(b) to take over that creditor's avoidance rights, on which the UFTA limitation period has not yet run. (*See* Example 2.)

Where the trustee uses §544(b), the state law statute of limitations therefore operates as an alternative reach-back period. This must be distinguished from the statute of limitations under the Code, which limits the period during which the trustee must bring an avoidance suit after the bankruptcy case has been filed. For example, in *In re American Energy Trading, Inc.*, 291 B.R. 159 (Bankr. W.D. Mo. 2003), the fraudulent transfers occurred in August 1999. The Ch. 11 case was filed in September 1999, and the trustee brought the suit to avoid the transfer under §544(b) in July 2002. Under state law there was a four-year statute of limitations, which would have allowed the trustee to reach back to avoid the transfer. However, the trustee failed to bring the avoidance suit within two years of the commencement of the case, as required by §546(a), so the court dismissed the trustee's suit as time-barred.

---

2. The period used to be one year, but was extended to two years by the Bankruptcy Abuse Prevention and Consumer Protection Act of 2005 (BAPCPA).

Although the trustee's avoidance right under §544(b) is based on the right of an actual creditor, there is one respect in which the trustee's avoidance power is more extensive than that of the creditor. Where a creditor has the right to avoid a fraudulent transfer under state law, the creditor can avoid it only to the extent of the debt due to that creditor. For example, if the debtor fraudulently transferred property worth $10,000, and the debt due to the creditor is $2,000, the creditor can avoid the transfer only to the extent of $2,000. This means that the creditor would either get a money judgment of $2,000 against the transferee, or if the property is returned, the creditor would execute upon it and would get only $2,000 of its proceeds (and costs) and the rest would go to the debtor. However, if the trustee uses §544(b) to succeed to the rights of the creditor, an old doctrine, derived from *Moore v. Bay*, 284 U.S. 4 (1931), extends the trustee's avoidance power to the entire transfer. The legislative history of §544(b) indicates that Congress intended the *Moore v. Bay* doctrine to continue to apply under the Code. For some recent cases that apply the doctrine, see *In re DLC, Ltd.*, 295 B.R. 593 (8th Cir. B.A.P. 2003); *In re JTS Corp.*, 617 F.3d 1102 (9th Cir. 2010).

The fact that the trustee has used the rights of an actual creditor to avoid a transfer and recover property for the estate does not mean that the creditor who had the avoidance rights under nonbankruptcy law is entitled to special treatment. *Moore v. Bay* held that if the trustee recovers a transfer by using the rights of an actual creditor under §544(b), the transferred property is returned for the benefit of the estate as a whole. The creditor whose rights were used continues to have merely a nonpriority unsecured claim against the estate. (*DLC, Ltd.*, recognizes this principle as well.)

Section 544(b)(2), added to the Code by an amendment enacted in 1998, qualifies the trustee's right to avoid a transfer by having recourse to state law under §544(b)(1). If the transfer satisfies the definition of a "charitable contribution" in §548, so that it would be exempted from avoidance as a fraudulent transfer under §548, it cannot be avoided by the trustee's use of state law either. As more fully explained in section 16.3, this amendment is intended to protect charitable organizations, particularly churches, from having to return to the estate tithes and contributions of limited amount, made by the debtor without actual intent to defraud creditors.

§15.2 THE AVOIDANCE OF STATUTORY LIENS UNDER §545

The nature and purpose of statutory liens was discussed in section 2.4.3. Section 101(53) defines them as liens "arising solely by force of a statute on specified circumstances or conditions. . . ." The definition includes common law liens of distress for rent, and it expressly excludes consensual security interests and judicial liens even if they are provided for by statute. The bankruptcy definition comports with the general meaning of the term under nonbankruptcy law.

The trustee's power to avoid statutory liens is provided for and delimited by §545, which is narrow in its scope. As a general rule, a statutory lien that is validly obtained and perfected under nonbankruptcy law is fully effective upon the bankruptcy of the debtor and cannot be avoided unless it fits into one of three categories specified by §545:

Under §545(1), a statutory lien is avoidable if it is specially created to take effect only upon the debtor's insolvency, bankruptcy, or financial distress. By providing for a lien that arises upon the debtor's financial distress, the state turns a formerly unsecured claim into a secured one, thereby tampering with the order of priority in bankruptcy and infringing upon the federal bankruptcy power.

Under §545(2), a statutory lien is avoidable if it is not perfected or enforceable against a hypothetical bona fide purchaser who is deemed to have purchased the property on the date of commencement of the case. This subsection is similar to §544(a)(3), in that it gives the trustee the hypothetical status of a bona fide purchaser as at the petition date so that the trustee can avoid the lien if it could have been avoided under nonbankruptcy law by a bona fide purchaser of the property. Unlike §544(a)(3), it is not confined to real property.

Under §§545(3) and (4), statutory liens for rent or of distress for rent are avoidable in bankruptcy. ("Distress" in this context stems from the word "distraint," which means the seizure or detention of a chattel.) This subsection invalidates landlord's liens in bankruptcy, whether created by statute or common law. The discrimination against liens for rent or distress of rent predates §545, and stems from the policy decision made some time ago that lessors should be treated as unsecured creditors and not be given any special rights in bankruptcy unless they have obtained a consensual security interest in the lessee's property. The traditional landlord's lien is not protected in bankruptcy, even though it is generally still available in state law to a landland of nonresidential property.

The trustee's limited power to avoid statutory liens reflects the policy goals outlined in section 14.8. Most statutory liens are conferred on particular classes of creditor by state law or federal nonbankruptcy law because the legislature has determined that these claimants have a special need for protection. If the Code allowed the trustee to overturn statutory liens that were validly obtained under nonbankruptcy law, it would undermine this protection. Hence, apart from landlord's liens, statutory liens are avoidable only where they are an usurpation of the bankruptcy power or are insufficiently perfected for protection under nonbankruptcy law. Section 545 is illustrated by Example 4.

§15.3 THE EFFECT OF §546 ON THE TRUSTEE'S AVOIDANCE RIGHTS UNDER §§544 AND 545

Section 546 contains a number of different restrictions on the trustee's avoidance rights. The statute of limitations in §546(a) has already been discussed in section 14.7. Two other provisions of §546 are also relevant to the trustee's avoidance powers under §§544 and 545.

§15.3.1 The Preservation of Nonbankruptcy Backdating Rules by §546(b)

The operation of §546(b) (introduced in the context of the automatic stay — *see* Example 4 in Chapter 10) effectuates rules of nonbankruptcy law that provide a grace period to a lienholder within which to perfect its interest in property. If nonbankruptcy law has a generally applicable rule that permits perfection of an interest to backdate, the trustee's powers of avoidance are subject to the rule. Therefore, if the interest is unperfected at the date of the petition but the period prescribed by nonbankruptcy law for perfection has not yet expired, the holder of the interest may perform the act of perfection at any time before the expiry of the applicable period. Upon perfection, the interest backdates to the earlier effective date prescribed by nonbankruptcy law. The requirement that the backdating must be "generally applicable" means that the law authorizing the backdating must apply generally to the lien or interest in question and cannot be geared to the debtor's bankruptcy or insolvency. Example 4 provides a further illustration of the application of §546(b).

§15.3.2 The Preservation of the Seller's Reclamation Rights by §546(c)

As stated in section 1.2, an unsecured seller of goods has no special interest in the goods once title has passed to the buyer. If the buyer fails to pay, the seller is in the position of a general unsecured creditor. A limited exception to this rule, derived from common law, is provided for in UCC §2.702. Under common law, a buyer is deemed to make an implied representation of solvency when purchasing goods; if the buyer was insolvent upon receiving the goods, and the seller was unaware of this, the seller may rescind the contract and reclaim the goods on grounds of fraud. UCC §2.702 codifies this right, although in qualified form: If a buyer receives goods on credit while insolvent, and the seller did not know of the insolvency at the time, the seller may demand return of the goods within ten days of receipt unless the buyer has made a written misrepresentation of solvency within three months of delivery.

Section 546(c) subjects the trustee's right of avoidance to any right of reclamation available to a seller under statute or common law, provided that the subsection's requirements are met: The delivery of the goods to the debtor must have occurred no earlier than 45 days before the petition, the debtor must have been insolvent at the time of delivery, and the seller must have sold the goods to the debtor in the ordinary course of the seller's business. If these requirements are satisfied, the seller may reclaim the goods in writing by a demand made not later than 45 days after the date of the debtor's receipt of the goods. If the 45-day period expires after the commencement of the bankruptcy case, the written demand must be made within 20 days of the commencement of the case.[3] The requirements of §546(c) differ from those of UCC §2.702 in a number of respects: The time within which the seller may claim reclamation is longer; he sale must have been in the ordinary course of the seller's business; and the demand for reclamation must be in writing. Also, the definition of insolvency in bankruptcy is stricter than under the UCC. Section 101(32) applies a balance sheet test (liabilities exceed the fair value of assets), whereas UCC §1-201(23) permits insolvency to be established either on a balance sheet test or an equity test (failure to pay debts as they fall due). The operation of §546(c) is illustrated by Example 5.

If the seller fails to give notice to the buyer, the seller is able to claim the price of the goods as a priority administrative expense under §546(c)(2) read with §503(b)(9) if the goods were delivered to the buyer within 20 days of bankruptcy.

Examples

1. Rock Bottom has just filed a voluntary petition under Ch. 7. About a year ago he borrowed money from Confidential Credit Corp. and secured the loan by granting Confidential a security interest in equipment used in his business. A security agreement and financing statement were properly executed by the parties, but Confidential neglected to record the interest because of a clerical oversight. This error was only discovered after Rock had become bankrupt. Rock still owes a substantial balance on his loan.

   Can the trustee in Rock's estate use §544 to avoid Confidential's security interest?

2. Rock Bottom had been in financial difficulty for some years before his bankruptcy. Two years and three months before his petition, when

---

3. The time periods in §546(c) were amended by BAPCPA.

threatened by impending judgments in collection suits, he transferred a valuable antique desk to a friend. Although the desk was worth $15,000, Rock gave it to his friend as a gift, subject to the understanding that the friend would donate it back when Rock's financial position became less hazardous.

One of Rock's creditors, who has an unsecured claim of $1,000 allowable against Rock's estate, had the right to avoid the disposition of the desk under the state's fraudulent transfer law but never exercised that right.

a. Can the trustee take over the creditor's avoidance right under §544?

b. If so, to what extent can the transfer of the desk be avoided?

c. If the trustee avoids the transfer and recovers the desk, is the creditor whose rights were assumed entitled to any priority in the proceeds of the desk?

3. a. Manny Fest bought a condominium from No Con Do, Inc., a property developer. The parties executed a contract of sale in terms of which Manny paid a down payment and obliged himself to pay the balance of the price in monthly installments. The sale should have been recorded, but it was not, so the real estate records reflected No Con Do, Inc. as the owner of the condominium.

Manny moved into the condominium immediately after the contract was signed. He remained in possession of the property, and continued to pay his monthly installments. About a year after he bought the condominium, No Con Do, Inc. filed a voluntary Ch. 7 petition.

Under state law, a written but unrecorded purchase of real property makes the purchaser an equitable owner of the property. Equitable ownership is superior to all interests except for those of a bona fide purchaser of the property from the owner of record. To qualify as a bona fide purchaser, a person must purchase the property in good faith, for value, and without knowledge or constructive notice of the prior rights to the property. Clear and open possession of the property serves as constructive notice of the equitable owner's interest. Can the trustee avoid Manny's equitable ownership of the condominium under §544?

b. Change the facts in (a) as follows: Manny Fest paid the down payment but never occupied the condominium. He had purchased it as an investment and left its management as a rental unit in the hands of No Con Do, Inc. No Con Do, Inc. subsequently filed a Ch. 11 petition and, acting in its capacity as debtor in possession, seeks to avoid Manny's interest under §544(a)(3).

Should it succeed?

4. Ownerous Investments, Inc. filed a Ch. 7 petition on July 1. During the previous May it had entered into a contract with Jerry Bilt, a building contractor, to execute an alteration to a building that it owned. Jerry began work in early May and completed the job near the end of June. Although Jerry was to be paid in full on completion of the work, Ownerous failed to pay him. Jerry had taken no action to enforce his claim by the time Ownerous filed its petition.

   Under the state's construction lien statute, Jerry is entitled to a lien to secure his claim. He is not obliged to take any action to create the lien at the time of commencing work. The statute gives him three months following completion of the work in which to file a claim of lien. He must then institute action to foreclose the lien within six months of filing the claim. Provided that the claim is filed and suit is commenced within the prescribed periods, the lien is effective from the date on which construction commenced. What is the status of Jerry's claim against the estate?

5. On June 25, Red Alert sold his expensive propane barbecue and meat smoker to Pearl Loin, a coworker. Pearl took delivery of the barbecue on that day. The parties agreed that she would pay for it at the end of the month. On June 28, Pearl filed a bankruptcy petition. On June 30, Pearl told Red of this, and informed him that she could not pay for the barbecue. Red immediately demanded its return, and Pearl referred him to her trustee. Should the trustee accede to Red's demand?

Explanations

1. Quite inadvertently, Confidential's loan to Rock was much more confidential than anticipated. It failed to publicize its interest by filing, and thereby became the holder of a "secret lien." As mentioned in section 14.8, there is a general policy against the enforcement of unrecorded interests in bankruptcy as well as under nonbankruptcy law because unrecorded interests are potentially prejudicial to third parties who may deal with the debtor in reliance on the appearance that no encumbrance exists. With some exceptions, this policy precludes enforcement of the unpublicized interest, even if the failure to record was not deliberate against a third party.

   The unperfected interest is avoidable under §544(a)(1), which gives the trustee the hypothetical status of an ordinary judicial lienholder who acquired a lien on all Rock's lienable property (including the business equipment) on the date of the petition. This status enables the trustee to avoid Confidential's unperfected interest, because applicable nonbankruptcy law — in this case, UCC §9.317(2) — gives a judicial lien priority over a security interest that was unperfected at the time that the lien arose. The effect of avoidance is to leave Confidential with a general unsecured claim against the estate.

Section 544(a)(1) can only be used when the interest remains unperfected at the time of the petition. Had Confidential realized its error and perfected the interest before the petition was filed, the interest could not have been avoided under §544(a). (However, if the last-minute filing had occurred within 90 days of the bankruptcy, the perfected security interest would have been avoidable as a preference under §547, discussed in section 16.1 and in Example 3 of Chapter 16.)

2. The facts in this Example illustrate the trustee's succession to the rights of an actual creditor under §544(b).

a. Although §548 also empowers the trustee to avoid fraudulent transfers, it cannot be used in this case because it reaches back only two years before the petition date. By taking over the creditor's avoidance power under nonbankruptcy law, the trustee is subject to the statute of limitations applicable to the creditor's suit, which may extend back further in time. For example, it is four years under the UFTA. This allows the trustee to reach back four years to avoid transfers in that time. (Note, however, as explained in section 15.1.3, the trustee must bring the suit within two years of the order for relief as required by §546(a).) It is not necessary that the creditor has proved a claim in the estate, provided that the claim is an allowable unsecured claim. The facts indicate that it is. Under the principles discussed in section 4.3, the actual creditor could have avoided the transfer, and the trustee can therefore do likewise.

b. It is clear that if the creditor had exercised the avoidance rights under state law, the transfer could have been avoided only to the extent necessary to satisfy the claim, that is, $1,000. However, if the trustee uses §544(b) to succeed to the rights of the creditor, the *Moore v. Bay* doctrine (explained in section 15.1.3) extends the trustee's avoidance power to the entire transfer.

c. Under the *Moore v. Bay* doctrine, the trustee's recovery of property under §544(b) is for the benefit of the estate as a whole. The creditor whose rights were used remains a general unsecured creditor.

3. a. Under the rules of state law outlined in the Example, the trustee cannot avoid Manny's interest by assuming any of the roles provided in §544. State law does not give priority to a hypothetical lien creditor or a creditor with a nulla bona return, so the trustee has no right to avoid under §544(a)(1) or (2). No actual creditor has avoidance rights to which the trustee could succeed under §544(b). The trustee would have been able to avoid the interest as a hypothetical bona fide

purchaser of real property under §544(a)(3) but for the fact that Manny's open possession constitutes constructive notice of his rights. It may seem at first glance that the constructive notice should not affect the trustee's avoidance power because §544(a) states that the avoidance power may be exercised regardless of any knowledge of the trustee or of any creditor. However, this applies only to any actual knowledge, not to constructive knowledge of the trustee, which is merely a legal fiction based on a finding that an equitable interest is sufficiently publicized to be protected.

b. Because, under the changed facts, there is no constructive notice of Manny's interest, the trustee can avoid the interest under §544(a)(3) as a hypothetical bona fide purchaser of real property. In a Ch.11 case, the debtor in possession exercises the trustee's powers, including the power to avoid transfers and obligations under §544. This creates an anomaly where the debtor, the very corporation that sold the interest and has full knowledge of it, now seeks to avoid it as a debtor in possession. Some courts have refused to allow a debtor in possession to use §544(a)(3) to avoid an unrecorded interest arising out of a transaction in which it participated prior to the time that it became bankrupt. However, most courts permit a debtor in possession to use §544(a)(3) on the reasoning that when a debtor becomes a debtor in possession, it acts in a new capacity as representative of the estate. The avoidance of the transfer does not merely further its own interests, but the interests of creditors as well. See, for example, In re Eads, 69 B.R. 730 (Bank. 9th Cir. 1986), aff'd in part sub nom In re Probasco, 839 F.2d 1352 (9th Cir. 1988); In re Sandy Ridge Oil Co., 807 F.2d 1332 (7th Cir. 1986).

4. Statutory liens are generally upheld in bankruptcy provided that they are valid and perfected under nonbankruptcy law. This principle is reflected in §545(2), which allows the trustee to avoid a statutory lien only if it would be avoidable by a bona fide purchaser of the property as at the time of bankruptcy. As in §544(a), the hypothetical status in §545(2) requires reference to the nonbankruptcy law governing the lien. The construction lien statute protects Jerry from a bona fide purchaser of the property provided that he complies with the requirements for perfection within the statutory time limits. The statute backdates Jerry's lien, so that if someone had purchased the property from Ownerous on the petition date, the purchaser's interest would have been junior to the inchoate construction lien, provided that Jerry thereafter made the lien filing in the prescribed three-month period and commenced suit to foreclose the lien within six months from the recording date.

The advent of bankruptcy before the end of the statutory perfection period does not detract from Jerry's right to complete the perfection requirements. Section 546(b) preserves the backdating rules of nonbank-ruptcy law as long as they are generally applicable and are not created to take effect only upon the debtor's insolvency or bankruptcy. However, §546(b) changes the procedure to be followed to complete perfection. The filing of the claim of lien takes place as normal under state law and is excluded from the stay by §362(b)(3). (*See* Example 4 in Chapter 10.) However, instead of commencing the foreclosure suit thereafter, Jerry must give notice to the trustee within the period prescribed by the state statute for the commencement of suit.

This example shows that the policy against unrecorded interests is not absolute because the construction lien statute, in effect, allows Jerry to have an unrecorded lien on the property for some months. This reflects a legislative policy that the protection of the lienholder outweighs the need to protect persons who subsequently deal with the debtor. In fact, some statutory liens do not require recording at all, but arise automat-ically and avail against all subsequent purchasers of the property. Such liens are protected in bankruptcy under §545. This is illustrated by In re *Loretto Winery Ltd.*, 898 F.2d 715 (9th Cir. 1990) (an automatically per-fected, unpublicized statutory lien in favor of grape growers was effective against a bona fide purchaser under §545(2) and therefore unavoidable in bankruptcy.).

5. Outside of bankruptcy, Red is entitled to reclaim the goods under UCC §2.702 if he can show that Pearl was insolvent when she received the barbecue and he only discovered this afterward. Red made a reclamation demand for the barbecue within about five days after it was received by Pearl, which is well within the ten-day period under UCC §2.702. Section 546(c) gives effect to the seller's reclamation right in bankruptcy if the additional requirements of that section are satisfied. In this case two con-ditions are satisfied, but two are not. Pearl received the goods in the 45-day period before the petition, and Red reclaimed them within 20 days of the petition. However, the demand was not in writing, and Red, being a consumer, did not sell the goods in the ordinary course of his business.

Although the reclamation right does not qualify for protection under §546, that section does not itself avoid the right. (That is, §546 merely protects qualified rights from avoidance by the trustee under the listed sections of the Code.) Having not qualified for protection, Red's recla-mation is subject to avoidance if avoidable under any of those sections. It might be avoidable under §544(a)(1) if state law gives a lien creditor priority over an unsecured seller with a reclamation right. Alternatively, it might be avoidable under §545(1) if the seller's reclamation right qualifies as a statutory lien. (Some courts have found it not to be a statutory lien.)

The Avoidance of Preferences, Setoff, Fraudulent Transfers, and Postpetition Transfers

§16.1 PREFERENTIAL TRANSFERS UNDER §547

§16.1.1 Introduction

Section 547 is a frequently used provision that generates volumes of case law. Although it ties into nonbankruptcy law, it is unlike §544 in that it does not base the trustee's avoidance power on the nonbankruptcy rights of actual or hypothetical parties. It goes beyond rights recognized in nonbankruptcy law and allows the avoidance of transfers that are fully effective outside of bankruptcy. This is because nonbankruptcy law generally permits the preferential treatment of a creditor. Outside of bankruptcy, a debtor may choose to prefer one creditor over others, say by allocating her limited resources to paying that debt in full while making no payment on other due debts.[1] Under nonbankruptcy law, the disfavored creditors have no grounds to overturn that preferential payment (transfer). However, the preferential treatment of a creditor offends the bankruptcy goal of collective and even-handed treatment of creditors. To effectuate this policy, it is not enough that creditors are treated evenhandedly after the petition has been filed. It is also necessary that the trustee has the power to examine prepetition transfers and

---

1. As noted in section 3.9.3, there is one area of nonbankruptcy law in which a debtor is not permitted to treat a creditor preferentially. Where the debtor makes an assignment for the benefit of creditors, the preferential treatment of a creditor could make the assignment invalid.

to avoid preferential transfers by the debtor in the period immediately preceding the bankruptcy filing.

Section 547 therefore permits the avoidance of transfers made by the debtor in the 90 days (or, in the case of insiders, one year) before the petition that give the creditor an advantage to which it is not entitled in bankruptcy. It does not allow the trustee to impugn every transfer to creditors in this period—only those that satisfy all its elements. The basic purpose of these elements is to identify transfers that illegitimately prefer the creditor, thereby upsetting the bankruptcy goal of evenhanded treatment of creditors.

Section 547 is aimed at creditors who have previously given consideration to the debtor for the transfer. Therefore, unlike §548 or state fraudulent transfer law, it is not concerned with the recovery of dispositions that were made with fraudulent intent or for inadequate value. Under §547, there is no requirement that the court take into account the state of mind of the debtor or transferee. It has no requirement of bad faith, knowledge, or deliberate advantage-taking. In fact, the grounds for avoidance under §547 are entirely objective: If the transaction has the external attributes set out in §547, it is avoidable.[2]

Section 547 has two operative subsections: §547(b) confers the power of avoidance on the trustee, listing five elements that must be satisfied for the transfer to be avoidable. Every one of these elements must be satisfied. If any one is not, the transfer cannot be avoided. Section 547(c) contains exceptions to the trustee's avoidance power. Even if a transfer meets all the requirements of §547(b), it cannot be avoided to the extent that it fits within one of the exceptions in §547(c). Section 547(c) only becomes relevant if all the elements of §547(b) are satisfied. If they are not, the transfer is unavoidable, and recourse to §547(c) is not necessary.

In addition to §547(b) and (c), there are a number of other subsections of §547 that are discussed in this chapter:

(i) Section 547(a) supplements the definitions in §101 by defining some terms that are not included in the general definition section.

(ii) Section 547(e) is also definitional in a sense, in that it sets out a formula for determining when a transfer takes place. This determination can be crucial in avoidance suits, and it is explained in section 16.1.3.

(iii) Sections 547(f) and (g) are concerned with the burden of proof in avoidance suits. Section 547(g) requires the trustee to prove all the elements of avoidance under §547(b), but this burden is alleviated in part by §547(f), which rebuttably presumes the debtor's insolvency in the 90

---

2. Preference rules have not always been as objective as they are under §547. Under the Bankruptcy Act, the trustee had to show that the transferee had reasonable cause to believe that the debtor was insolvent at the time of transfer. This standard survived partially in the 1978 Bankruptcy Reform Act, but was eliminated entirely in 1984.

days preceding the petition. Under §547(g), the transferee must prove the grounds for nonavoidability if it invokes one of the exceptions in §547(c).

§16.1.2 The Elements of §547(b)

To be avoidable under §547(b), the transfer must satisfy every one of the following requirements.

(1) There must have been a transfer of an interest in property of the debtor to or for the benefit of a creditor (§547(b)(1)). The transfer is the transmission of value from the debtor to the creditor, either directly or in an indirect way, so as to confer a benefit on the creditor. "Transfer" is defined in §101(54) in very broad terms to cover a wide variety of dispositions. It includes all dispositions of property, whether direct or indirect, absolute or conditional, voluntary or involuntary. It also includes the creation of liens on property. (*See, e.g.,* Example 7.) "Creditor" is defined in §101(10) to mean, essentially, the holder of a claim against the debtor that arose at the time of or before the order for relief. "Claim," in turn, is given a wide-ranging definition in §101(5). In short, it includes all rights to payment in law or equity.

The property interest transferred must have been property of the debtor. In most cases where a debtor makes a transfer, it is clear that the debtor transferred her own property. However, where a third party provides funds to the debtor for the purpose of paying a specific debt, the debtor's use of those funds to pay the designated debt may not constitute a transfer of the debtor's property. For example, the debtor owes $100,000 to Creditor 1. The debtor borrows $100,000 from Creditor 2 for the expressly agreed purpose of using that money to settle the debt to Creditor 1, and does use the money for that purpose. Under the judicially created "earmarking" doctrine, a court may find that this transaction is simply a substitution of creditors so that the payment of $100,000 to Creditor 1 was, in effect, made with property of Creditor 2 rather than the debtor's property. Courts use somewhat different tests to decide if it is appropriate to find earmarking. For some courts, the determinative question is whether the debtor had dispositive control over the funds used to pay Creditor 1. If the debtor acquires control and actual ownership of the funds, so that the debtor has the power to use them for other purposes, the funds do not qualify as earmarked and there has been a transfer of the debtor's property. Other courts treat the payment as earmarked if there is a clear and express agreement between the new lender and the debtor that the funds will be used only to pay the specific debt, the debtor does perform the agreement in accordance with its terms, and the transaction as a whole did not result in any diminution of the debtor's estate. See, for example, In re Entringer Bakeries, Inc.,

548 F.3d 344 (5th Cir. 2008) (no earmarking because the funds were deposited in the debtor's general bank account, giving it legal title, all indicia of ownership, and control of the funds); In re Wells, 561 F.3d 633 (6th Cir. 2009) (an advance to the debtor by one credit card issuer was not earmarked to pay down the balance on another credit card because the debtor had complete control of the funds and the discretion to use them for purposes other than paying down the other credit card); In re Adbox, Inc., 488 F.3d 836 (9th Cir. 2007) (earmarking could not be used because there was no proof of an agreement under which the debtor clearly committed to use the funds to pay the designated debt).

(2) The transfer must have been for or on account of an antecedent debt (§547(b)(2)). "Debt" is defined in §101(12) to mean liability on a claim. (As mentioned above, "claim" is comprehensively defined in §101(5)). Although the Code defines debt, it offers little guidance on the meaning of "antecedent," except for the apparently tautologous language in subsection (b)(2): "owed by the debtor before such transfer was made." The intent is clear: If the debt arose before the transfer was made, it is antecedent. This is true even if the period of time between the two sides of the exchange is very short. (If there is only a short delay between the creation of the debt and the transfer, one of the exceptions in §547(c) will probably apply, as discussed in section 16.1.4. However, for the purposes of satisfying §547(b), all the trustee needs to establish is that the debt arose at some time before the transfer was made.)

The Code does not provide rules for determining when the debt came into being. The question of when the debt arose — that is, when the debtor became legally obligated to the creditor — must be determined under non-bankruptcy law. The creation of the debt must not be confused with the due date for payment of the debt. It is common for a debt to arise (that is, for liability to be created) some time before the time that this liability is fixed, mature, and unconditionally payable. (For example, in a loan transaction, the debt arises as soon as the money is advanced, but the debt does not become payable until the due date for the loan to be repaid.)

(3) The debtor must have been insolvent at the time of the transfer (§547(b)(3)). "Insolvent" is defined in §101(32), which uses the balance sheet test (liabilities exceed assets at fair valuation) rather than the equity test (not generally paying debts as they fall due) to determine insolvency. Because the value of both assets and liabilities must be established to determine insolvency, difficult valuation issues can arise. This is illustrated in In re Trans World Airlines, Inc., 134 F.3d 188 (3d Cir. 1998), in which the court had to decide if the debtor had been insolvent at the time transfers had been made. Because liquidation was not imminent at that time, the court said that the reference to fair valuation in the insolvency definition in §101(32) required that the debtor's assets be valued as if the business was a going concern and the assets were being sold on the market without pressure to dispose of them quickly. Although the reference to fair valuation in the section qualified only assets and not liabilities, liabilities must also be calculated as if the business was a going concern, and not discounted to take into account that the debtor may not remain in business. Because §547(f) presumes the debtor to have been insolvent during the 90 days before the petition, the trustee's burden of proving this element is eased. The presumption is not conclusive and may be rebutted by the transferee.

(4) The transfer must have occurred within the prepetition avoidance period (§547(b)(4)). The avoidance period is 90 days before the filing of the petition, unless the transferee is an insider (the meaning of which is explained below), in which case it is one year before the petition. It is not clear if one should count the avoidance period backward from the bankruptcy date (which seems the most sensible approach, and accords best with the language of §547) or forward from the transfer date. In most cases, this would not be a crucial issue, but it could be determinative where the transfer is on the borderline of the period.

Where the transfer was made more than 90 days before the petition but within a year of it, the transfer is avoidable against an insider. "Insider" is defined in §101(31) to include a variety of persons with a close relationship to the debtor, such as relatives of an individual debtor and officers of a corporate debtor. The word "includes" in the definition indicates that the list of insiders expressly identified in the definition is not exclusive. Any other person who had a close and influential relationship with the debtor could qualify. Courts distinguish between statutory or per se insiders—those who are expressly mentioned in §101(31) and are conclusively presumed to be insiders—and nonstatutory insiders, who are encompassed in the definition by the word "includes." To decide if a person should be found to be a nonstatutory insider, courts take all the circumstances of the relationship into account, including the intimacy of the relationship, knowledge of the debtor's affairs, access to inside information, and the degree to which the person could control or influence the debtor. For example, in In re McIver, 177 B.R. 366 (Bankr. N.D. Fla. 1995), the debtor's live-in companion was held to be a nonstatutory insider. Even a creditor could be a nonstatutory insider if it had a sufficiently close connection to the debtor. However, courts will not generally find a creditor to be an insider unless the relationship was unusually close and it allowed the creditor to exercise control over the debtor, to influence the debtor's decision making, and gave it access to inside information. For example, in In re U.S. Medical, Inc., 531 F.3d 1272 (10th Cir. 2008), the creditor was held not to be a nonstatutory insider, even though it had an exclusive distributorship agreement with the debtor, was the sole supplier of the debtor's product, could designate a director on the debtor's board, and held 10 percent of the debtor's stock. The court found that the creditor did not use its position to exercise control over or unduly influence the debtor. In *In re QuVis*, 446 B.R. 490 (Bankr. D. Kan. 2011) a creditor was held not to be a nonstatutory insider by virtue of its power to appoint a director and to inspect the debtor's books where the creditor was one of several similarly situated lenders, and its rights gave it no unique insider information.

Section 550(c), added to the Code in 1994, and §547(i), added by the Bankruptcy Abuse Prevention and Consumer Protection Act of 2005 (BAPCPA), make it clear that the one-year reach-back period applies only to an insider; it cannot be used against a noninsider even if the transfer to the noninsider indirectly benefited an insider. These provisions overturn prior caselaw (named the "Deprizio rule" after the case that created the rule), which permitted a transfer to be avoided against a creditor who was not an insider if the transfer to that creditor conferred an incidental benefit on someone else who was an insider. For example, if the debtor pays a debt to a noninsider that is guaranteed by an insider, the payment of the debt confers an indirect benefit on the insider by eliminating the insider's liability under the guarantee. The one-year reach-back does not apply to the payment merely because the insider was indirectly benefited.

(5) The transfer must have improved the creditor's position (§547(b)(5)). The transfer must have enabled the transferee to receive more than it would have received if the transfer had not been made and the debt had been paid at the appropriate rate under a Ch. 7 distribution. This element, called the "improvement-in-position test", is the heart of §547(b). Its basic purpose is to test whether the prebankruptcy transfer gave the creditor a higher level of payment on its claim than it has the right to receive. It is this attribute of the transfer that makes the creditor's advantage illegitimate and undermines bankruptcy's collective process.

Irrespective of whether the case had been filed under Ch. 7, 11, 12, or 13, the test requires a hypothetical Ch. 7 liquidation to be calculated. A comparison must then be made between the total payment that the transferee would receive if the transfer is left intact and the total payment that it would receive if the transfer was restored to the estate and the transferee proved a claim in the estate for the debt that had been reduced or eliminated by the transfer. If the first figure is higher than the second, the improvement-in-position test is satisfied. The hypothetical liquidation is calculated as at the petition date, and the trustee must establish the hypothetical liquidation distribution by a reliable, rationally based analysis of the financial situation as at that date. This may require the testimony of an accountant or other qualified expert. See *In re Falcon Products*, 381 B.R. 543 (B.A.P. 8th Cir. 2008); *In re Connolly North America LLC*, 398 B.R. 564 (Bankr. E.D. Mich. 2008).

In most cases involving a transfer to an unsecured creditor, it does not take complex calculations to determine that the improvement in position test is satisfied: Unless the estate is solvent enough to pay unsecured creditors in full, a transfer to the creditor that eliminates or reduces its unsecured claim will easily be established as preferential. For example, in In re Polo Builders, 433 B.R. 700 (Bankr. N.D. Ill. 2010), the debtor settled the unsecured creditor's debt in full within 90 days of the petition. Just a rough tally of the debtor's debts and assets made it clear that unsecured creditors would not receive any more than 22 percent of their claims, so the 100 percent received by the transferee clearly improved its position.

In calling for the comparison between what the creditor received as a result of the transfer, and what it would have received without the transfer, §547(b)(5) does not state specifically that the improvement in position must be determined only by taking into account the distribution that would have been received from the estate itself, and must not factor in any possible payment that the creditor may have been able to receive from other sources. However, the court read the section this way in United Rentals v. Angell, 592 F.3d 525 (4th Cir. 2010). The debtor had entered into a subcontract with the creditor for the supply of equipment on a construction project and had executed a payment and performance bond under which a surety undertook to pay the creditor if the debtor defaulted. The debtor made payments to the creditor during the 90-day prepetition period which clearly satisfied the other elements of §547(b). The question in issue was whether the payments satisfied the improvement-in-position test of §547(b)(5). The creditor argued that the payments did not improve its position because had the debtor not paid, it would have been able to enforce its rights under the bond and claim full payment from the surety. The court rejected this argument, holding that the critical question was not whether the creditor would have been able to receive payment from another source had the transfer not been made, but rather whether, in the absence of the transfers, the creditor would have been entitled to a distribution of as much from the estate.

The operation of the improvement-in-position test is illustrated in Examples 1, 2, 4, and 7.

§16.1.3 The Timing of the Transfer

(1) The general rule governing timing of the transfer under §547(e). The timing of the transfer is crucially important for a number of purposes. For example, the date of the transfer must be known to decide if it falls within the avoidance period, if it was for an antecedent debt, or if the debtor was insolvent when it was made. Section 547(e) provides the formula for determining the date of the transfer.

In broad terms, §547(e) treats the transfer as having occurred on the date on which it became effective between the parties under nonbankruptcy law. However, if, under nonbankruptcy law, some act is required to perfect the transfer (e.g., the filing of a financing statement to perfect the transfer of a security interest in the debtor's property), the transfer will occur only on the date of perfection, unless the act of perfection is completed within 30 days of the transfer taking effect.[3] (Examples 1, 3, and 4 address timing issues.)

(2) Under §547(e)(3) the transfer does not occur until the debtor acquires rights in the property. Section 547(e)(3) provides a further qualification. It states that for the purposes of the section, a transfer is not made until the debtor has acquired rights in the property transferred. This means that even if the act of perfection (such as the public filing) occurs within 30 days of the transfer taking effect, the timing of the transfer is delayed if the debtor has not yet acquired an interest in the property. That is, the 30-day rule does not apply to property that the debtor does not own at the time of perfection, even though he may anticipate acquiring it in the future. The date of transfer is delayed until he actually does acquire the property. The significance of this is illustrated by In re Morehead, 249 F.3d 445 (6th Cir. 2001). The creditor obtained judgment against the debtor in 1995 and served a continuing wage garnishment on the debtor's employer in 1997, under which the employer automatically deducted the garnished amount from the debtor's wages in each future month. The debtor filed his Ch. 7 petition in November 1997. The issue was whether the wage garnishments during the 90 days before bankruptcy were avoidable preferences. The bankruptcy court held that they were not because, under state law, the creditor obtained a perfected garnishment lien on all the garnished wages as soon as it served the garnishment order on the employer in 1997. The court of appeals reversed on the basis of §547(e)(3): Even though the transfer was perfected outside the 90-day period, the debtor did not acquire rights to the wages until he earned them. (The court rejected the theory, adopted by other courts, that once garnishment occurs, the debtor loses the right to the portion of his wages that have been garnished.)

(3) The definition of "perfection" in §547(e)(1). Because the timing of the transfer is often dependent on the date it was perfected, the meaning of "perfection" is important. Section 547(e)(1) defines perfection for the purposes of §547 with reference to nonbankruptcy law. In the case of real property, perfection is complete as soon as a subsequent bona fide purchaser "cannot" acquire a superior interest in the property, and

---

3. Prior to 2005, the period was ten days. It was increased to 30 days by BAPCPA.

perfection of all other property is complete as soon as an ordinary judicial lienor "cannot" acquire superior rights. In the usual situation, this means that perfection will only occur under nonbankruptcy law from the time that the act required for perfection (for example, filing the proper document in the correct records office) is accomplished.

However, with regard to certain types of interest, nonbankruptcy law permits the effective date of the interest to backdate to some specified earlier time. (For examples of backdating *see* Example 6 in Chapter 2, Example 5 in Chapter 15, and section 3.5.) As noted in section 15.3.1, §546 generally recognizes and preserves these backdating rules in bankruptcy. However, the Supreme Court held in *Fidelity Financial Services v. Fink*, 522 U.S. 211 (1998), that the same rule does not apply in §547(e), because the language of that section indicates that "perfection" is used there in a different sense. In §546, it is used to mean the legal conclusion that the interest is perfected, but in §547(e) it is used to mean the act necessary to effect that perfection. The court found this meaning to be apparent from the fact that §547(e) says that perfection occurs when a creditor on a simple contract "cannot acquire" a superior judicial lien. The court reasoned that a creditor *can* acquire a superior judicial lien at any time during that gap period, even though that lien would lose priority to the transferee if the transferee thereafter performed the act of perfection that would give it retrospective effect. Unless and until that act is performed, the judicial lienholder "can" acquire a superior lien, and it is only when the act of perfection is complete that it "cannot" any longer achieve priority. For this reason, §547(e)(1) must be interpreted to date perfection only from the time that the final act of perfection, and not from any earlier date to which it would relate back under state law.

In *In re Taylor*, 599 F.3d 880 (9th Cir. 2010), the court held that under *Fidelity Financial Services* the grace period allowed by state law for perfection of a security interest in a vehicle did not apply. As a result, the transfer of the security interest occurred on the date of actual filing of the interest with the state, not on its backdated effective date under state law. In *In re Johnson*, 611 F.3d 313 (6th Cir. 2010), the court affirmed the B.A.P.'s application of *Fidelity Financial Services* where the final act of perfection was out of the hands of the creditor, and had to be accomplished by a state official. The security interest was in a motor vehicle, and had to be perfected by notation on the certificate of title. Even though state law treated the perfection as taking effect when the creditor filed the proper documentation with the Department of Motor Vehicles, the court held that perfection for purposes of §547(e) was a matter of federal law, and that the final act of perfection under §547(e) occurred only when the state actually made the notation. (The timing of perfection is discussed further in Example 4.)

§16.1.4 Exceptions to Avoidance under §547(c)

Section 547(c) provides nine exceptions to the trustee's avoidance power under §547(b). As stated before, the most efficient sequence of analysis is to determine first if the transfer is avoidable under §547(b). If it is not, there is no occasion to use §547(c); if it is, §547(c) should be consulted to determine if any of the exceptions apply. Once the trustee has established that the transfer is avoidable, the burden shifts to the transferee under §547(g) to prove that an exception is applicable.

The exceptions in §547(c) refine and qualify the avoidance power to distinguish legitimate ordinary-course business dealings from last-minute preferences. In this way, the Code preserves transactions that are technically preferential because they satisfy all the elements of §547(b) but do not truly confer an inappropriate advantage on the recipient. This abstract observation is more clearly demonstrated in the discussion of the specific exceptions.

All the exceptions apart from §547(c)(6), (8), and (9) preclude avoidance of the transfer only "to the extent that" it is covered by the exception. It is therefore possible for a transfer to be partially avoidable. The nine exceptions are as follows:

(1) A substantially contemporaneous exchange for new value (§547(c)(1)). Although it satisfies all the requirements for avoidance under §547(b), a transfer may not be avoided to the extent that it was intended by both parties to be a substantially contemporaneous exchange for new value given to the debtor. The protection of exchanges of this kind is consistent with the policies underlying the avoidance of preferences. The transaction is a regular commercial exchange that is reasonably thought of as concurrent, not a last-minute attempt by the creditor to thwart the order of distribution in bankruptcy. "New value" is defined in §547(a)(2) to mean money, goods, services, or new credit, and can also include the release of property previously transferred by the debtor, provided that the original transaction is unavoidable.

If the debt was created even a short time before the transfer, it is antecedent. This exception is therefore intended to protect transfers from avoidance on the technicality that they were made subsequent to the debt, where the parties intended an immediate exchange and the delay between the creation of the debt and the transfer is inconsequential. Section 547(c)(1) provides no guidance on what constitutes substantial contemporaneity, which must be decided by the court under all the circumstances of the case. A classic example of a substantially contemporaneous exchange (specifically mentioned in the legislative history) is a purchase of goods paid for by check on delivery. Although payment only occurs when the check is cleared by the bank, some days after the sale, the parties consider this to be a cash transaction, and the exchange is in fact substantially contemporaneous. Credit sales are not usually substantially contemporaneous, but they could so qualify. For example, in In re Hechinger Investment Co. of Delaware, Inc., 489 F.3d 568 (3d Cir. 2007), the court found that short-term credit was substantially contemporaneous where the parties understood that the price of goods shipped would be paid on or before they arrived at the buyer's premises.

(2) Ordinary-course payments (§547(c)(2)). Section 547(c)(2) excepts a transfer from avoidance to the extent that both the creation of the debt and its payment qualify as ordinary-course transactions. That is, two distinct requirements must be satisfied:

1. The debt itself must have been created by a transaction that was in the ordinary course of business or financial affairs of both the debtor and the transferee.

2. The payment of the debt was either in the ordinary course of business or financial affairs of the debtor and transferee, or it was made according to ordinary business terms.

Prior to 2005, this second requirement read differently. To satisfy it, the transferee had to show both that the payment was in the ordinary course of the parties' business or financial affairs (a more subjective test based on the attributes of the parties' own commercial practices) and that it was in accord with ordinary business terms (a more objective test based on practices in the market). BAPCPA, following the recommendation of the 1994 National Bankruptcy Review Commission, amended §547(c)(2) to make these requirements alternative rather than conjunctive. The reason for the change is that it is unnecessary to subject the payment to both a subjective and an objective test because a transfer that satisfies either is the kind of routine transaction to be protected.

Section 547(c)(2) is meant to prevent the avoidance of normal prebankruptcy transfers that conform to the debtor's pattern of dealing and can fairly be regarded as usual and routine. These are not the kinds of transfers intended to give the creditor an unfair advantage on the eve of bankruptcy, and they create a legitimate expectation that the transfer will not be disturbed if the debtor becomes bankrupt. It is a question of fact, to be determined under all the circumstances of the transaction, as to whether the debt was incurred and paid in the ordinary course. Many different types of transactions are protected from avoidance by the exception. For example, it covers regular trade purchases by a business debtor on short-term credit, payments made by a consumer for regular monthly expenses such as utilities or services, and regular monthly payments on long-term debt[4] incurred in the ordinary course of the debtor's affairs.

---

4. Since the decision of the U.S. Supreme Court in Union Bank v. Wolas, 502 U.S. 151 (1991), it is clear that ordinary-course payments on long-term debt can qualify for the exception under §547(c)(2).

Where the parties have had an ongoing relationship, their established course of dealings and past practices are taken into account to decide if the transfer is an ordinary-course payment. For example, in *In re Quebecor World (USA), Inc,* 491 B.R. 363 (Bankr. S.D.N.Y. 2013), the trustee sought to avoid a late payment made by the debtor to the creditor in the 90-day period. The debtor had generally paid the creditor late during the course of a lengthy relationship, so the court took into account the parties' routine practice of making and accepting late payments to establish a baseline for determining their ordinary course of business. In the pattern of dealing before the 90-day period, the debtor's average lateness in making payments was about 60 days. By comparison, the payment challenged by the trustee was made 90 days late. The court held that this delay went beyond a reasonable delay established by prior dealings and therefore did not qualify as within the ordinary course of business. In *In re Jan Weilert RV, Inc.,* 315 F. 3d 1192, *as amended,* 326 F. 3d 1028 (9th Cir. 2003), the court took a particularly flexible approach in deciding whether payments were on ordinary business terms. The court said that where a debtor is experiencing financial difficulty, the court should focus not merely on what would be ordinary patterns of dealing between financially secure parties but should also have regard to the usual way of dealing with financially distressed debtors. The transfer should only be avoided if it is so aberrant that it goes beyond the usual means by which a creditor might accommodate the needs of a financially shaky debtor.

Although a pattern of past dealings is helpful in establishing whether the transfer meets the test of §547(c)(2), this does not mean that the parties must have had an existing relationship to qualify a transfer as in the ordinary course. Where the transfer occurred in a first-time transaction, the test for deciding if it is in the ordinary course is whether the transaction would be ordinary for a person in the debtor's position and generally consistent with the debtor's prior practices. See *In re Ahaza Systems, Inc.,* 482 F.3d 1118 (9th Cir. 2007). In *In re Frey Mechanical Group, Inc.,* 446 B.R. 208 (Bankr. E.D. Pa. 2011), after a commercial lender refused to extend a line of credit to the financially troubled debtor, the parents-in-law of the debtor's president extended a line of credit to the debtor under which they made loans to the debtor to enable it to continue operating. The court held that the §547(c)(2) exception was inapplicable. Not only were the lenders not in the business of lending money to companies, but an unsecured line of credit to a financially unsound debtor did not accord with ordinary business terms. (Example 5 deals with this exception.)

(3) Purchase-money security interests (§547(c)(3)). A purchase-money security interest is one granted by the debtor to secure a loan or credit used to acquire the very collateral subject to the interest. (*See* section 2.2.5.) An interest qualifies as a purchase-money interest for the purposes of §547(c)(3) to the extent that it secures new value given by the transferee to the debtor at or after the execution of a security agreement describing the collateral, and the new value is both intended to be used and is in fact used to acquire the collateral. The rationale for making an exception for purchase-money interests is that the holder of the interest has enabled the debtor to obtain the property that secures the debt.

Section 547(c)(3) does not absolutely except purchase-money security interests from avoidance. It merely creates a limited protection to the secured party by providing a special grace period for perfection: The interest is unavoidable provided that it is perfected within 30 days[5] from the date on which the debtor received possession of the collateral. It is important to understand the limited scope of §547(c)(3). Where a secured party does not perfect its security interest within 30 days of its attachment, the transfer dates from the date of perfection under §547(e)(3). Because the transfer occurs only on the perfection date, the debt becomes antecedent and the later perfection could push the transfer into the 90-day period, making it avoidable. Section 547(c)(3) merely provides that if this occurs, a purchase-money security interest will be protected if perfected 30 days after the debtor received possession of the property. Therefore §547(c)(3) is only helpful to a secured party where the debtor receives possession some time after the date on which the interest attaches, and the perfection date is within 30 days of the possession date. (*See* Example 3.)

In *Fidelity Financial Services v. Fink*, 522 U.S. 211 (1998), the court held that where the grace period allowed under §547(c)(3) is shorter than that allowed under state law, the period provided for in §547(c)(3) governs, and the interest must be perfected within the shorter time allowed by §547(c)(3). On this principle, the lender in *In re Taylor* was not able to rely on the §547(c)(3) because its security interest was filed one day after the grace period provided for in that section.[6]

(4) The "net result" exception (§547(c)(4)).

If, after receiving an avoidable transfer, the creditor gives to the debtor new value that is not itself secured or paid for by a new transfer, the otherwise avoidable transfer

---

5. The grace period has increased over the years. It was originally 10 days but was amended to 20 days in 1994 and to 30 days by BAPCPA.

6. The grace period provided for in §547(c)(3) applicable in *In re Taylor* was the 20-day period in effect before the 2005 amendment that extended the period to 30 days. Because §547(c)(3) now provides for a 30-day grace period, it is less likely that the grace period under the section will be shorter than under state law. For example, the grace period for perfecting a purchase money security interest in UCC 9-324(a) is 20 days from the debtor receiving possession of the goods.

cannot be avoided to the extent of the new value. This exception in §547(c)(4) is known as the "net result" rule. The name, which was inherited from its predecessor section under the Bankruptcy Act, is a little deceptive because §547(c)(4) does not net out all transfers to and from the debtor in the 90-day period. It applies only to value given to the debtor after the preferential transfer.

The justification for the net result rule is that a creditor who extended new credit or other value to the debtor after payment of an older obligation was probably motivated by that payment to deal further with the debtor. If, upon bankruptcy, the earlier payment is reversed, the creditor's reliance is defeated. The earlier payment would have to be returned and a claim made against the estate for both the old debt and the new one. Apart from being unfair to the creditor, a rule like this would discourage persons from dealing with a debtor in financial difficulty, because they would not be able to rely on the payment of earlier obligations as a basis for extending new credit. See In re New York City Shoes, Inc., 880 F.2d 679, 680 (3d Cir. 1989). In addition, it could be argued that the later value, in effect, replenishes the estate by returning the preference to the estate, thereby reversing its prejudicial effect. It was pointed out in In re Frey Mechanical Group, Inc. (cited under heading (2), above) that the exception is commonly and appropriately applied where the debtor and creditor have an ongoing relationship in the form of a line of credit or a revolving credit transaction, under which the debtor makes periodic payments and withdrawals.

Note that for the new value exception to apply, the debtor must not have granted an unavoidable security interest to secure the new value and must not have made an "otherwise unavoidable transfer" to the creditor in exchange for it. The impact of this language is illustrated by In re Frey Mechanical Group, Inc. Although the court held that the ordinary course exception in §547(c)(2) did not exempt the loan payments from avoidance, they could be partially exempted by §547(c)(4). The fact that the debtor had repaid the new value (the advances made to the debtor under the line of credit) before bankruptcy did not disqualify them from the exception because the payments were avoidable (or, in the double-negative suggested by the language of the section, were not unavoidable). In fact, the trustee was in the process of moving to avoid them as preferences. In other words, the new value cannot be counted if it was secured or repaid by the debtor and that security interest or payment cannot be avoided. However, if the security interest or payment is avoidable, the fact that it was made is irrelevant because it can be undone, resurrecting the unsecured debt for the new value. See also In re Musicland Holding Corp., 462 B.R. 66 (Bankr. S.D.N.Y. 2011).

The scope of §547(c)(4) is narrow, and the protection given to creditors who deal with the debtor is quite restricted. Payments are protected only to the extent that new value is given by the creditor[7] after the payment without a corresponding new transfer by the debtor. The question of what constitutes new value involves an inquiry similar to that under §547(c)(1), and the definition of new value in §547(a)(2) applies here as well. For §547(c)(4) to be applicable, the value given must constitute a new benefit to the estate, which replenishes it after the transfer. A benefit that does not replenish the estate does not satisfy the exception. For example, in In re ABC-Nabco, Inc., 483 F.3d 470 (7th Cir. 2007), a creditor's agreement to forbear from taking action against the debtor in return for the payment was held not to be new value because it added nothing to the estate. In In re Armstrong, 291 F.3d 517 (8th Cir. 2002), a casino's grant of new line of credit to the debtor was not new value for the payment of a debt to the casino because the line of credit did not replenish the estate, but diminished it by enabling the debtor to incur more gambling debts. The operation of §547(c)(4) is illustrated by Example 6.

(5) Floating liens in inventory and receivables (§547(c)(5)).

Floating liens were introduced in section 2.2 and Example 3 of Chapter 2. In this type of transaction, the security interest secures all advances made by the secured party in the future and automatically attaches to all new collateral of a particular kind (typically, accounts or inventory) acquired by the debtor in the future. The parties contemplate that the secured party will advance funds to the debtor when inventory or accounts come into existence. As the inventory is sold or the accounts are paid, the loan will be reduced by the proceeds. When a further batch of inventory is acquired or accounts are generated, the secured party will again make an advance in proportion to the value of the new collateral. In this way, the relationship between the debt and the collateral is kept stable.

If the debtor becomes bankrupt in the course of such a continuing secured transaction, many transfers are likely to have been made to the secured party in the 90 days before bankruptcy. Every payment and every acquisition of new collateral would qualify as a transfer. To examine each one of these transfers for the purpose of determining avoidability would be an exhausting task because the total figures for each month may represent numerous transactions. Furthermore, such a painstaking examination of the multitude of transfers under the floating lien could unfairly undermine the secured party's reliance on the routine activity in its continuing relationship with the debtor.

To solve these problems, §547(c)(5) presents a simplified test for determining whether and to what extent the aggregation of all the transfers in the

---

7. In In re Musicland Holding Corp. the court pointed out that the plain language of §547(c)(4) requires the new value to be given by "such creditor" and is not available where the new value is given to the debtor by a third party (an affiliate of the creditor in that case), rather than by the creditor who received the earlier transfer.

90-day period should be avoided as a preference. The language of this section is convoluted, but the concept is quite straightforward: When a floating lien arrangement in accounts or inventory has been validly created (note that the section applies only to these two types of commercial collateral), each separate transaction in the 90-day period does not have to be examined. The transfers to the secured party are unavoidable except to the extent that all the transfers in the 90-day period caused a reduction in the shortfall between collateral and debt (i.e., in the deficiency) to the prejudice of unsecured creditors in the estate. If the secured party is an insider, the prebankruptcy period is, as usual, one year. If the transaction is first brought into effect within the applicable prebankruptcy period, the reduction of the shortfall must be measured from the time that new value was first given.

Therefore, the focus of §547(c)(5) is not on the individual transfers in the prebankruptcy period but on the transferee's overall improvement in position over the prebankruptcy period. If the collateral was worth less than the debt at the beginning of that period and transfers to the transferee during the period had the effect of eliminating or reducing that shortfall as at the date of the petition, the transfers are avoidable to the extent that they made up the shortfall.[8] Although the two-point comparison can involve complex issues, such as valuation questions, it greatly simplifies what could be a very arduous examination of each transfer in an ongoing relationship that involves many individual transfers. It therefore assists a creditor who has been keeping an eye on the debtor's business and making sure that the value of the collateral never drops below the debt. For example, in In re Smith's Home Furnishings, Inc., 265 F.3d 959 (9th Cir. 2001), the secured party had financed the debtor's inventory through a floating lien. When the debtor began operating at a loss, the secured party reduced its line of credit and required a substantial pay-down of the debt. In the 90 days before bankruptcy, the debtor paid about $12 million to reduce the debt. The court held that the trustee could not recover these payments because he could not discharge his burden of showing that the creditor had been undersecured as at the 90-day date.

In determining the transferee's improvement in position, transfers are not counted to the extent that they did not reduce the value of the estate to the prejudice of unsecured creditors. Therefore, for example, if the collateral is inventory that appreciated in value due to market conditions, or if it is

---

8. Note that §547(c)(5) is concerned only with transfers within the prebankruptcy period. Under §552(a), acquisitions of collateral after the petition are not transfers because they are excluded from the floating lien and are estate property. Proceeds of prepetition collateral are also not transfers. They generally belong to the secured party, even if they are received postpetition, provided that nonbankruptcy law recognizes an interest in such proceeds, and the transfer of the proceeds is not otherwise avoidable. §522(b).

accounts that turned out to be more collectable than originally supposed, this augmentation of the value of the collateral could reduce any shortfall without harming the estate.

In summary, §547(c)(5) is applied by taking the following steps.

1. *Determine the first date for comparison.* This is 90 days before the petition for a noninsider, a year for an insider, or the date of the first advance, if that occurred after the start of the applicable prebankruptcy period.

2. *Determine the amount of the debt and value the collateral on this first date.* If the secured party is undersecured (i.e., the collateral is worth less than the debt), calculate the shortfall.

3. *Determine the amount of the debt and the value of the collateral on the date of filing the petition.* Calculate any shortfall.

4. *Compare the shortfall on the two dates.* There is a voidable preference to the extent that the shortfall has been reduced, provided that the reduction has reduced the value of the estate to the prejudice of other creditors.

Like the other exceptions to avoidance, §547(c)(5) is designed to protect legitimate, routine transactions that do not enable the creditor to obtain an impermissible advantage on the eve of bankruptcy. A holder of a floating lien who monitors the debtor's dealings with the collateral is able to reduce the risk of a shortfall. However, a lienholder who permits the debt to become undersecured takes the risk that any attempt to redress the deficiency by payment or new collateral could fall within the prebankruptcy period and be avoidable. Because the prebankruptcy avoidance period can only be ascertained once the petition has been filed, the lienholder will not know when it has begun until after the attempt at bolstering the interest has been made. Therefore, a careful lienholder should treat every day as the potential comparison date, and try to ensure that no shortfall ever occurs. In re *HovdeBray Enterprises*, 483 B.R. 187 (B.A.P. 8th Cir. 2012), illustrates how careful a secured creditor needs to be in setting up and monitoring its security interest. A bank granted an operating loan to the debtor about three years before its bankruptcy and took a security interest in inventory and accounts to secure the loan. However, the bank did not perfect its security interest by filing until the debtor defaulted on the loan. As it happened, this occurred within the 90-day prebankruptcy period. The value of the property covered by the security interest exceeded the debt as at the 90-day date so that there would have been no shortfall, and payments to the creditor in the 90-day period would have been protected by §547(c)(5). However, because the creditor had delayed perfecting its interest, the interest itself was avoidable under §547, which meant that all transfers pursuant to that interest within the 90 day period were outside of the protection of §547(c)(5).

Because §547(c)(5) requires a comparison of debt-collateral ratios at two points, valuation of the collateral at each stage is often an important issue on which the trustee and transferee may disagree. The extent of avoidance is enhanced by a lower value on the comparison date and a higher value on the bankruptcy date, and is reduced by contrary trend. (But bear in mind that valuation, on its own, is not the sole determinative factor. As noted above, to the extent that an increase in value results from an increase in market price or other facts not to the prejudice of creditors, there is no transfer.) As always, valuation is a factual issue to be determined under the circumstances of each case.

Before evidence can be received on value, the standard of valuation must be determined. Valuation of accounts could be based on their face value, collection value (the amount actually paid by customers), market value (the amount for which the accounts could be sold in a factoring transaction), book value (the amount at which they would be valued in accordance with accepted accounting practices), or contract value (the value placed on the accounts by the parties themselves when entering the transaction). Similarly, inventory could be valued based on its retail, wholesale, liquidation, or going-concern value. In deciding on the standard for valuation, the court must try to make a realistic assessment of the use or disposition of the collateral. Whatever standard of value is chosen, it must be applied to both the comparison date and the bankruptcy date.

(6) Statutory liens (§547(c)(6)). Section 547(c)(6) simply provides that statutory liens must be dealt with under §545 and they are beyond the scope of §547. If a statutory lien is unavoidable under §545, the trustee cannot try to avoid it under §547, even if it arose in the prebankruptcy period and satisfies all the elements of §547(b).

(7) Payment of debts for domestic support obligations (§547(c)(7)). As mentioned in sections 10.4.2 and 13.5.2, the Bankruptcy Reform Act of 1994 added a set of provisions designed to protect claims for family support obligations from the bankruptcy of a debtor spouse or parent. BAPCPA reinforced and refined these provisions. One of its refinements was to create a statutorily defined term, "domestic support obligation," in §101(14A) to cover a variety of domestic obligations owed to different parties. In essence the definition includes debts in the nature of alimony, maintenance, or support established by a separation agreement, divorce decree, property settlement agreement, court order, or determination of a governmental unit. The debt must be owed to or recoverable by a spouse, former spouse, child, the guardian or other person responsible for the child, or a governmental unit.

To the extent that a transfer was the payment of a bona fide debt for a domestic support obligation, it is not avoidable as a preference. The statutory language makes it clear that the actual nature of the obligation (to be determined as a question of fact), not merely the way that the parties have labeled or structured it, is determinative, and that the payment must relate to that obligation.

(8)-(9) Small-value transfers (§547(c)(8) and (9)). Where the debtor is an individual whose debts are primarily consumer debts, §547(c)(8) excludes a transfer from avoidance as a preference if the aggregate value of the property included in that transfer is less than $600. Section 547(c)(9) excludes avoidance of a transfer up to a total value of $6,225[9] where the debtor's debts are not primarily consumer debts. Section 547(c)(9) is not confined to individual debtors. Section 547(c)(8) was added to the Code in 1984 to prevent the recovery of small preferences in consumer cases. Following the recommendation of the 1994 National Bankruptcy Review Commission, BAPCPA enacted §547(c)(9) to expand the protection to cover nonconsumer debtors.

§16.2 SETOFF UNDER §553

§16.2.1 Setoff in Nonbankruptcy Law

As a general principle of law, the debts of two persons who are mutually indebted may be set off against each other. To the extent of the smaller debt, they cancel each other out, and the only payment that need change hands is the remaining balance of the larger debt. For setoff to operate, the debts must be mutual: This means that each party is both a creditor and a debtor of the other in the same capacity. For example, setoff could not be affected where *A* is indebted to B in her personal capacity, but B is indebted to *A* in *A*'s capacity as trustee for a trust. (Mutual indebtedness is raised in Example 8.) In addition, both debts must be valid and enforceable. The debts need not have arisen out of the same transaction.

§16.2.2 The Effect of Setoff Rights in Bankruptcy

When one of the mutually indebted parties becomes bankrupt, the other party's exercise of the right of setoff permitted by nonbankruptcy law results

---

9. Section 547(c)(8) is not listed in §104, but §547(c)(9) is. Therefore, the dollar amount in §547(c)(9) is revised every three years, but the amount in §547(c)(8) is not. The figure in §547(c)(9) is that in effect from April 1, 2013. The next revision will take effect on April 1, 2016.

in full payment of the debt due from the bankrupt debtor to the extent that it is covered by the other debt. If §547 applied to setoffs, such a transaction could satisfy all its elements. For example, say that the debtor became indebted to the creditor for $1,000 four months before bankruptcy. Two months later, the debtor performed services for the creditor in an unrelated transaction for a fee of $1,000. Setoff simply cancels each debt. If the debtor was insolvent at the time of setoff, the transaction would satisfy all of the five elements of §547(b). It is a transfer to a creditor on account of an antecedent debt, made while the debtor was insolvent, during the 90-day prebankruptcy period. Except in the rare case where the estate has enough funds to pay all unsecured creditors in full, the setoff would prefer the creditor in position because it results in full payment of the debt. Had there been no setoff, the creditor would have had to pay the estate the $1,000 owed to the debtor and would have proved a claim for the $1,000 owed by the debtor. This claim would have been paid at the rate of distribution payable to general unsecured creditors. None of the exceptions in §547(c) apply.

Notwithstanding its potentially preferential effect, a right of setoff valid under nonbankruptcy law is not covered by §547 but is governed by §553, which generally upholds the setoff in bankruptcy provided that it does not fall within the limited grounds of avoidance under §553. A valid right of setoff may be exercised at any time up to the petition, and may also be asserted thereafter following relief from stay. (Setoff is subject to the stay under §362(a)(7) and cannot be exercised postpetition without relief being obtained.)

The policy of protecting the right of setoff is a longstanding one. It may seem like an exception to bankruptcy's general aim of evenhanded treatment of creditors because a creditor with a right of setoff is given more favorable treatment than one who just received payment of the debt during the prebankruptcy preference period. However, it is not really an exception at all because the right of setoff is treated as akin to a security interest — the mutual debt secures each party against the other's nonpayment. Section 506(a) expressly recognizes a right of setoff as a secured claim to the extent of the amount that is subject to setoff. (It is an unsecured claim to the extent that the amount due to the creditor is less than its claim.) For example, the debtor borrowed money from Bank, and the balance of the loan as at the petition dates is $10,000. The debtor also has a savings account at Bank, with a balance of $6,000 as at the petition date. A bank deposit is categorized in law as a debt due by the bank to its customer. Under nonbankruptcy law, if the debtor should default in repaying the loan, the bank would be entitled to set off the amount in the savings account against the debt due by the debtor. Section 553 upholds that setoff right in bankruptcy provided that none of the limitations in that section apply, and §506 treats the right of setoff as a secured claim. As a result, upon bankruptcy, Bank has a secured claim to the extent of the $6,000 deposit in the account, and an unsecured claim for the $4,000 balance of the loan in excess of that amount. *See* Example 8.

§16.2.3 Limitations on the Right of Setoff

The limitations on setoff in §553 are designed to prevent abuses and to ensure that a creditor does not try to manipulate setoff rights to obtain an inappropriate advantage. The right of setoff may not be exercised by a creditor to the extent that any one of the following conditions is satisfied.

(1) Section 533(a)(1). The creditor's claim has been disallowed as a claim against the estate. This is the most obvious restriction on setoff — if the court disallows the creditor's claim, the effect must necessarily be that the creditor cannot use that claim to reduce any debt that the creditor owes to the estate.

(2) Section 533(a)(2). The creditor has acquired the claim by transfer from another entity either during the 90-day prebankruptcy period while the debtor was insolvent or after the commencement of the case. As in §547, there is a presumption of insolvency during the 90-day prebankruptcy period (§553(c)). This exception is aimed at transactions in which a person who owes money to debtor of the estate takes over the claim of a creditor of the estate so that the debt and claim can be offset. Such a transaction would be prejudicial to the estate because the combination of the debt and claim in the hands of the estate's debtor it has the effect of reducing or eliminating the debt that would otherwise be payable to the estate. To illustrate: Finance Company made an unsecured prepetition loan of $10,000 to the debtor. Finance Company therefore has an unsecured claim of $10,000 against the estate. Buyer bought goods from the debtor on credit before the bankruptcy and had not paid the price of the goods, $10,000, by the time of the petition. Buyer therefore owes a debt of $10,000[10] to the estate. If these two transactions are kept separate, the trustee would be able to recover the full $10,000 from Buyer, but the estate would only pay Finance Company at the rate of distribution to unsecured creditors. If that rate is, say, 10 percent, Finance Company would receive only $1,000 on its claim. The net result is that the estate would be enhanced by $9,000. However, if Finance Company and Buyer enter into a transaction under which Finance Company sells its claim of $10,000 to Buyer, the effect would be that Finance Company gets payment of its claim from Buyer, and

---

10. For the sale of simplicity, the debt to the debtor and claim against the debtor are in the same amount in this example. This need not be so. If the debts are not of equal amount, setoff operates to the extent of the lesser amount.

Buyer acquires the right to set off its newly-acquired claim of $10,000 against its debt to the estate of $10,000. The effect of this setoff would be the same as if the estate had paid Finance Company's claim in full so that it loses the $9,000 that it would otherwise have gained. To avoid this kind of manipulation, §553(a)(2) invalidates a setoff right acquired from another entity within the 90 days before the petition, while the debtor was insolvent, or after commencement of the case.

(3) Section 553(a)(3). The debt due from the creditor was incurred during the 90-day prebankruptcy period, while the debtor was insolvent, and for the purpose of obtaining a right of setoff against the claim owed to the creditor. This subsection may sound repetitious of §553(a)(2), but it deals with a different situation. It does not aim at the creditor's acquisition of a setoff right from a third party, but rather at the deliberate creation of a setoff right between the debtor and a creditor on the eve of bankruptcy. For example, say that the debtor owed Bank $10,000 as a result of a loan. Bank became concerned about the debtor's financial situation. To give itself some protection from default, Bank insisted that the debtor open a savings account with it and maintain a deposit of not less than $4,000 in the account. A bank account constitutes a debt by Bank to the debtor, its depositor. The effect of this arrangement is that if the debtor became bankrupt, the bank would cut its losses by having a $4,000 right of setoff against the loan debt — that is, it would now have a partially secured claim instead of a completely unsecured claim, and the secured claim would be paid in full. Section 533(a)(3) invalidates the setoff right so created if this arrangement was made within 90 days of the petition, while the debtor was insolvent, and with the purpose of creating the setoff right. This situation is illustrated by *In re HovdeBray Enterprises,* (cited in section 16.1.4(5)). In addition to holding that the exception in §547(c)(5) did not save the creditor bank's floating lien, the court invalidated a setoff created by an arrangement between the bank and the debtor within 90 days of the petition, under which the debtor made a deposit with the bank. The court found that the deposit was not an ordinary course transaction, but rather was deliberately arranged for the purpose of giving the bank a right of setoff.

(4) Section 553(b). The setoff has enabled the creditor to improve its position in the 90-day prebankruptcy period by reducing an insufficiency between the the claim against and the debt due to the debtor. This is an improvement-in-position test similar in concept to that in §547(c)(5). Although there are differences in the rules of the tests in §§553(b) and 547(c)(5), both tests use a two-point comparison. Stated in the simplest terms (and without its qualifications and refinements), the test in §553(b) is intended to prevent a creditor from using setoff in the 90 days before bankruptcy in order to recover more of its claim than it could

have recovered if the mutual debts had been set off 90 days before the petition. The test requires measurement of the amount (if any) by which the creditor's claim exceeds its debt to the debtor on the 90-day date and on the date of setoff. If the insufficiency in the setoff — that is, the amount of the creditor's claim in excess of the debtor's claim — is reduced between the 90-day date and the setoff date, the offset is recoverable by the trustee to the extent of that reduction.

§16.3 FRAUDULENT TRANSFERS UNDER §548

§16.3.1 Avoidance under §548 as an Alternative to §544 and State Law

The trustee may avoid fraudulent transfers in the prepetition period either by using state fraudulent transfer law, which is accessible to the trustee under §544(b) (*see* section 15.1.3), or by employing the Code's own avoidance provision in §548. There are some striking similarities in language between §548 and the Uniform Fraudulent Transfers Act (UFTA), which has been enacted in many states and is representative of the typical state law that would be available to the trustee under §544(b). The similarity is deliberate. Section 548 was modeled on the Uniform Fraudulent Conveyance Act (UFCA), the predecessor to the UFTA, and when the UFCA was revised to become the UFTA, the revision was modeled on §548. (The influence of the Code on the UFTA can be particularly seen in the UFTA's definition of terms such as "insider," "creditor," and "transfer," and in its provisions relating to the determination of the effective date of the transfer.)

The trustee's choice to seek avoidance of a transfer under §548 or under §544(b) and state law will depend on which vehicle for avoidance gives the trustee stronger rights. Because the provisions of the UFTA and §548 are similar in so many ways, it may not make a significant difference which route the trustee selects. However, in some cases, there could be an important advantage to selecting one or the other. Bear in mind that not every state has enacted the UFTA, so the law of a particular state could be notably different from §548. Even where the state has enacted the UFTA, there are differences in detail (identified in the following discussion) between that statute and §548 that could be significant on the facts of a particular case. Overall, one of the most common reasons why a trustee may use §544(b) and the UFTA instead of §548 is because of a longer reach-back period. (This is explained in section 16.3.4).

This section does compare and contrast the provisions of the UFTA and §548, and it summarizes the UFTA provisions. However, because the UFTA and the general principles of state law relating to the avoidance of fraudulent transfers were covered in Chapter 4, the treatment here assumes familiarity with state law in this area and focuses more on the ways in which §548 differs from state law. You may therefore find it helpful to refer back to Chapter 4 as a background to the discussion in this section.

§16.3.2 Actual Fraud

Section 548(a)(1)(A) deals with actual fraud. It empowers the trustee to avoid any transfer made or obligation incurred by the debtor within two years before the petition, if the transfer was made or the obligation was incurred with the actual intent to hinder, delay, or defraud an entity to which the debtor was indebted on the date of the transfer or became indebted thereafter. Section 548(a)(1)(A) is equivalent to UFTA §4(a)(i), discussed in section 4.3. As explained in section 4.3.2, UFTA §4(b) lists indicia of fraud known as "badges of fraud." This is a nonexclusive codification of long-recognized inferences that have been recognized by courts as tending to prove actual fraud by circumstantial evidence. Unlike the UFTA, §548(a)(1)(A) does not expressly list badges of fraud. However, these inferences are recognized by judicial decision in the context of bankruptcy as well. Because fraudulent intent is seldom provable by direct evidence of the debtor's state of mind, the presence of conduct or circumstances that give rise to an inference of fraud are commonly used to establish that intent.

§16.3.3 Constructive Fraud

Section 548(a)(1)(B) covers constructive fraud. It empowers the trustee to avoid a transfer made or obligation incurred by the debtor within the two years prior to filing, even if actual fraud cannot be proved, if the debtor received less than equivalent value in exchange for it and one of four alternative additional grounds is satisfied. That is, like the UFTA, each ground of avoidance for constructive fraud under §548 has two elements. The element of lack of reasonably equivalent value is common to all of them. The analysis under §548 to determine the absence or presence of reasonably equivalent value follows the same lines as that under the UFTA: Although the comparison of economic values is an important consideration, courts go beyond this to look at all the circumstances of the transfer, including the parties' relationship, the economic environment, and the apparent motive for the transfer. (*See* section 4.4.2.)

The other element of constructive fraud in §548 identifies four separate situations, detailed below, of which three are the same as in the UFTA. If any one of these applies, and there has been a lack of reasonably equivalent value, the transfer is avoidable. (*See* Example 7, which presents an issue of constructive fraud under §548.)

(1) Insolvency: §548(a)(1)(B)(ii)(I). The transfer is avoidable by the trustee if the debtor received less than reasonably equivalent value and was insolvent at the time that the transfer was made or the obligation was incurred, or became insolvent as a result of the transfer or obligation. This is equivalent to UFTA §5. (*See* section 4.4.3.) The definitions of insolvency are similar in the UFTA and the Code, but under UFTA §2 equity insolvency creates a presumption of insolvency. There is no equivalent presumption in §548, in which the general definition of insolvency in §101(32), based on the balance sheet test, applies.

Recall from the discussion in Chapter 4 that under the UFTA, while actual fraud and other forms of constructive fraud may be used as a basis of avoidance by any creditor, constructive fraud on grounds of insolvency may be used as a basis of avoidance only by a creditor whose claim was in existence at the time of the transfer. Section 548 does not make any equivalent distinction between existing and subsequent creditors, because such a distinction is irrelevant where the avoidance remedy is exercised by the trustee for the benefit of the estate.

(2) Undercapitalization: §548(a)(1)(B)(ii)(II). The transfer is avoidable by the trustee if the debtor received less than reasonably equivalent value and was engaged in, or was about to engage in, a business or transaction for which the debtor's remaining property was unreasonably small capital. This is equivalent to UFTA §4(A)(2)(i), discussed in section 4.4.3.

(3) Intent to incur debts that will not be paid: §548(a)(1) (B)(ii)(III). The transfer is avoidable by the trustee if the debtor received less than reasonably equivalent value and intended to incur, or believed that he would incur debts that would be beyond his ability to pay as they matured. This is equivalent to UFTA §4(A)(2)(ii), discussed in section 4.4.3.

(4) Payment to an insider under an employment contract, not in the ordinary course of business: §548(a)(1)(B)(ii)(IV). The transfer is avoidable by the trustee if the debtor received less than reasonably equivalent value and made the transfer or incurred the obligation to or for the benefit of an insider under an employment contract and not in the ordinary course of business.

The rules relating to constructive fraud where the transfer is to an insider are different in the UFTA and §548. UFTA §5(b) allows avoidance of the transfer to an insider on grounds of constructive fraud if the transfer was made for an antecedent debt, the debtor was insolvent at the time, and the insider had reasonable cause to believe that the debtor was insolvent. Section 548 does not have an equivalent provision but provides specifically in §548(a)(1)(IV) for payments to insiders under an employment contract. It states that the trustee may avoid a transfer made or an obligation incurred by the debtor to or for the benefit of an insider within the two-year pre-bankruptcy period "under an employment contract and not in the ordinary course of business." In In re TransTexas Gas Corp., 597 F.3d 298 (5th Cir. 2010), the court upheld the trustee's right to avoid a large severance payment to its CEO as constructively fraudulent. The transferee argued that he had given reasonably equivalent value to the debtor by agreeing to resign and compromising his rights under the employment contract. However, the court held that because there were grounds to dismiss the CEO for cause, his resignation was not reasonably equivalent value. The CEO also argued that he was not an insider at the time of the transfer because he was no longer working for the debtor when the payment was made. The court rejected this argument because he was an insider at the time that the obligation was incurred.

§16.3.4 Reach-back and the Effect of Avoidance

One of the most important differences between the UFTA and §548 is their temporal range: §548 allows the trustee to avoid transfers that occurred within two years preceding bankruptcy,[11] and the UFTA generally allows creditors a period of four years from the transfer in which to commence an avoidance suit.[12] As noted in section 15.1.3, if the transfer occurred more than two years before the petition, the trustee may be able to avoid it by using state law under §544(b), even though it cannot be avoided under §548. Also, the avoidance remedy itself is different. Section 548 does not have the remedial alternatives of the UFTA, but it is subject to the general

---

11. BAPCPA increased the period from one year to two. As explained in section 14.7 and section 15.1.3, the two-year period in §548 is a reach-back period: It specifies the period of vulnerability of the transfer. It is not a statute of limitations (a period within which the trustee must act to avoid the transfer). The statute of limitations is provided in §546(a).

12. The four-year period under the UFTA is a statute of limitations, but it operates as a reach-back period for purposes of avoidance. Thus, the trustee can reach back four years to avoid the transfer if applicable nonbankruptcy law follows the UFTA statute of limitations and the trustee exercises the avoidance power under §544(b), or two years if the trustee seeks avoidance under §548. In either case, the trustee, but must commence suit within the limitations period under §546(a).

rules (outlined in section 14.5) governing the return of avoided transfers to the estate.

The UFTA contains detailed provisions for the protection of good faith transferees for value and subsequent transferees. Section 548(c) adopts a similar approach by granting lien rights in favor of a good faith transferee for value, and §550 protects good faith subsequent transferees. (*See* section 14.5.)

§16.3.5 The Fraudulent Transfer of Exempt Property

It is not clear if the transfer of exemptable property qualifies as a fraudulent transfer. Some courts have held that if the property is exemptable, its transfer does not harm creditors and should not be avoidable. Others (the majority, it seems) say that the fact that the debtor could have claimed the property as exempt should not be taken into account. For example, *Tavenner v. Smoot*, 257 F.3d 401 (4th Cir. 2001), followed this approach. The court based its reasoning on two factors. First, §522(g) contemplates the avoidance of transfers of property that could have been exempted and precludes assertion of the exemption after recovery of fraudulently transferred property unless the transfer was involuntary and the debtor did not conceal the property. Second, property is not inherently exempt, and the debtor has to claim it as exempt in her schedules. If she fails to claim an exemption, the property remains in the estate for the benefit of creditors. *In re Lumbar*, 457 B.R. 748 (B.A.P. 8th Cir. 2011) also found the transfer of exempt property to be available. It held that even if state exemption law treats the transfer of exempt property non-fraudulent, federal law governs avoidance under §548 and allows the trustee to avoid the transfer of property that the debtor may otherwise have claimed as exempt. In essence, by transferring the property voluntarily, the debtor abandons the exemption and loses the right to claim an exemption in it, even after it is recovered by the trustee.

§16.3.6 Charitable Contributions by an Individual Debtor

Section 548(a)(2) specifically provides that a charitable contribution to a qualified religious or charitable entity or organization is not to be treated as a transfer for less than a reasonable equivalent value provided that the contribution does not exceed 15 percent of the debtor's gross annual income for the year in which it was given, or if in excess of that percentage, the contribution was consistent with the debtor's practices in making such contributions. Section 548(d)(3) defines "charitable contribution" and "qualified religious or charitable entity" with reference to the definitions used for tax-deduction purposes, but it adds the further restrictions that the debtor must be an individual and the donation must be cash or a financial instrument. Because the exception relates only to constructive fraud, it does not shield a transfer made with fraudulent intent to a charity or religious organization.

These provisions were added to §548 in 1998 to resolve uncertainty about whether a charitable contribution should be treated as constructively fraudulent. Although they cover both charities and religious organizations, Congress was primarily concerned about protecting churches from having to return tithes and contributions upon the debtor's bankruptcy. By preventing the avoidance of gifts to charities and churches, §548(a)(2) allows an insolvent debtor to continue to be generous at the expense of creditors. Courts do not agree on the extent to which this generosity is to be allowed. Some courts read §548(a)(2) as applying to each individual contribution, not to the total of contributions that the debtor may make in a year. On this interpretation, the debtor could contribute all her income and assets as long as she did it in separate gifts, each of which is under 15 percent of her income. Other courts recognize the absurdity of this interpretation and hold that the intent of the section is that aggregate contributions in the year must not exceed 15 percent of the debtor's gross annual income. For example, this was so held in *Universal Church v. Geltzer*, 463 F.3d 218 (2d Cir. 2006) and in *In re McGough*, 467 B.R. 22 (B.A.P. 10th Cir. 2012). In *In re McGough*, the trustee argued that because the debtor's contributions exceeded the 15 percent cap in both of the two years before bankruptcy, the plain language of §548(a)(2) required that the full amount of the contributions be avoided. The court disagreed that the language of §548(a)(2) was that clear. It therefore consulted the legislative history, which indicated that Congress intended to protect up to 15 percent of the contributions, so that only the excess over that amount was avoidable.

§16.4 POSTPETITION TRANSFERS UNDER §549

The avoidance powers discussed up to now concern prepetition transfers. Section 549 gives the trustee the power to recoup estate property that has been transferred without authority *after* the petition has been filed. It is conceptually quite different from the other avoidance provisions: Its aim is not the reversal of prepetition harm, but the preservation of property of the estate. The central basis for avoidance under §549 is lack of authority to make the disposition. Therefore, if after the case has been commenced the debtor makes an unauthorized transfer of estate property to settle a prepetition debt, the trustee does not need to establish the elements of §547 to avoid the transfer, but simply relies on lack of authority under §549.

Section 549(a) allows the trustee to avoid postpetition transfers that are not authorized by the Code itself or by the court and to avoid transfers that are authorized only under §§303(f) and 542(c). The reference to the two other Code sections requires explanation:

Section 303(f) allows a debtor in an involuntary case to continue to operate its business and to use or dispose of estate property until the order for relief is granted. However, once the order for relief is granted and a trustee is appointed, the trustee can use §549(a)(2)(A) to overturn any transfers made by the debtor unless they were approved by the court or they satisfy the requirements of §549(b). Section 549(b) validates transfers during the gap period to the extent that the transferee gave something new of economic value in exchange for the transfer, whether or not the transferee knew of the bankruptcy.

Section 542 requires entities who have property of the estate or who owe debts to the debtor to turn over the property or to pay the debts to the estate. Section 542(c) protects an entity who, acting in good faith and without actual knowledge or notice of the commencement of the case, transfers the property or pays the debt to someone other than the trustee. The transfer is treated as fully effective for the purpose of discharging the transferor's obligations to the debtor, and the transferor is not liable to the estate as a result of the inadvertent disposition. Although the good faith transferor is protected by §542(c), the person who receives the payment or the property is not covered by that section. Section 549(a)(2)(A) makes that transferee vulnerable to attack by the trustee. For example, immediately after a petition is filed, and before the trustee takes control of the estate, the debtor draws a check in favor of a creditor. Upon presentment, the bank pays the check in good faith and without notice or knowledge of the filing. Section 542(c) excuses the bank from liability to the estate for the improper payment of funds that had become property of the estate. However, this protection does not extend to the payee of the check, who has received an unauthorized postpetition transfer avoidable under §549(a).

In addition to these avoidance powers, §549 contains two other provisions. First, §549(c) requires a copy or notice of the petition to be recorded with the title records pertaining to real property in the estate. If a bona fide purchaser (i.e., one who purchases the property for fair equivalent value, in good faith, and without knowledge of the bankruptcy) purchases the property under an unauthorized sale from the debtor, and that interest is perfected prior to the recording of the notice of bankruptcy, the transfer may not be avoided. If less than equivalent value was given, but the purchaser otherwise meets the standards of bona fide purchaser and the transfer was perfected before notice of the bankruptcy was recorded, the transfer is avoidable but the purchaser acquires a lien on the property to secure reimbursement of the value given.

The second provision is §549(d), which is a statute of limitations governing the avoidance of postpetition transfers. The trustee must commence avoidance proceedings before the earlier of two years after the transfer or the time that the case is closed or dismissed.

Examples

1. On January 1, Binow & Palater, Inc. sold and delivered goods to Gloria Transit Co., Inc. The price of the goods, $2,000, was to be paid within 30 days of delivery. Gloria Transit failed to pay on due date, February 1. After making demands for payment, Binow & Palater received a check for $2,000 from Gloria Transit on March 30. The check was deposited immediately and was paid by Gloria Transit's bank on April 5.

   Gloria Transit had been in financial difficulty for some time, and its liabilities had exceeded the value of its assets since November last year. On July 1, it filed a voluntary Ch. 7 petition. After secured and priority claims are paid, the fund remaining in the estate will be enough to pay 10 percent of unsecured general claims. Has there been a transfer avoidable under §547(b)?

2. On January 1, Gloria Transit Co., Inc. bought some other goods on credit from Prudential Purveyors, Inc. At the time of the sale, Prudential retained a security interest in the goods that was properly perfected by filing under UCC Article 9 on January 20. The price of the goods was $2,000. Gloria Transit was obliged to pay for the goods in two installments due at the end of February and March. It failed to make the payments on the due dates. Upon being threatened with foreclosure, it paid half the debt ($1,000) on April 10. No further payments were made, and Gloria Transit filed its Ch. 7 petition on July 1.

   If the collateral is worth $2,500 at the time of the petition, can the trustee avoid the payment of $1,000? What difference would it make if the collateral was worth $1,500 or $2,000?

3. On February 15, Gloria Transit Co., Inc. borrowed money from D. Laid Security, Inc. to purchase a piece of equipment. On that day, the parties executed a security agreement under which Gloria Transit gave a security interest in the equipment to D. Laid Security. D. Laid Security immediately remitted the loan funds to the supplier of the equipment, which delivered the equipment to Gloria Transit on the same day.

D. Laid Security normally perfects its secured transactions immediately. However, because of an oversight, no filing was made at the time of the agreement. The omission was discovered during a routine audit in May, and the filing was made on May 3.

Gloria Transit filed its bankruptcy petition on July 1. Is there an avoidable transfer here?

4. In January, a customer of Gloria Transit Co., Inc. commenced suit against it for damages arising out of a breach of contract. On January 15, the plaintiff obtained an order of attachment, and on January 20 it levied on a piece of equipment owned by Gloria Transit.[13] On June 1, the plaintiff obtained judgment against Gloria Transit. On June 10, it levied execution on the equipment that had been held in the sheriff's custody under the writ of attachment. A sale in execution was scheduled for July 3. On July 1, before the sale could take place, Gloria Transit filed its bankruptcy petition.

Has there been a transfer avoidable under §547(b)?

5. On February 15, Annie C. Dent borrowed $5,000 from Fallshort Finance Co. for the purpose of paying for some orthodontic treatment for her son. To secure the loan, Annie executed a security agreement granting Fallshort Finance a security interest in an artique cabinet that had been appraised at $6,000. Fallshort Finance filed a financing statement in proper form on February 20. Unknown to both parties, the cabinet had been incorrectly appraised, and its true value was only $2,500. This fact was not discovered until Annie's trustee had the cabinet reappraised after her bankruptcy.

In terms of the loan agreement, Annie was obliged to repay her debt to Fallshort Finance at the rate of $200 per month. She paid on time in the months of March, April, and May, and then defaulted, leaving a balance of $4,400 plus interest due to Fallshort Finance. Before Fallshort Finance could proceed to foreclose on its security interest, Annie filed her bankruptcy petition on July 1.

Are any of the transfers to Fallshort Finance avoidable under §547(b)? Will any exception in §547(c) protect such transfers from avoidance?

6. In February Chico N. DeMail borrowed $5,000 from his friend, Annette Result, promising to repay the loan in a month. When he failed to pay on due date, Annette began to nag him and eventually threatened never to

---

13. Attachment is explained in section 3.3.3. It is a remedy that is available in some cases (as in this one for a debt on a contract) in the period before the plaintiff has obtained judgment. Levy of attachment creates a lien on the attached property that secures the judgment that is ultimately obtained.

speak to him again unless he repaid her. Eventually, on May 15, Chico sent Annette payment of the $5,000. Unknown to Annette, Chico was insolvent at this time.

On June 1, Chico called on Annette with a hard luck story and a plea for another loan. Being softhearted, Annette loaned him $3,000, which he promised to repay in two weeks. As before, Chico failed to repay the loan on its due date and still owed the money to Annette when he filed a voluntary Ch. 7 petition on July 1. Shortly thereafter, Chico's trustee in bankruptcy demanded that Annette pay to the estate the $5,000 received from Chico on May 15.

Is the trustee justified in making this demand?

7. Several years ago, Erstwhile Enterprises, Inc. purchased a plot of land as an investment. To finance the purchase, it borrowed money from Promised Land Co. and granted a mortgage on the property to Promised Land to secure the loan. The mortgage was properly recorded at the time. After suffering losses on its investments for some years, Erstwhile Enterprises became insolvent and could no longer raise the funds to pay its debts. In January of this year it ceased payment of installments due on its mortgage. Promised Land commenced suit, obtained judgment, and foreclosed on the property. After complying fully with statutory notice and advertising requirements, Promised Land held a foreclosure sale on April 15. The sale was conducted in all respects in accordance with the law.

Shrewd Investment Co., a land speculator, attended the sale. Because bidding was light, it managed to buy the property for $30,000. At the time its fair market value was $50,000. The proceeds of the foreclosure sale were paid to Promised Land by the sheriff. They were just sufficient to settle the balance owing under the mortgage plus the costs of foreclosure.

Erstwhile Enterprises filed a bankruptcy petition on July 1. Can the foreclosure sale be avoided?

8. Two years ago, Mutual Obligation Co., Inc. entered into a contract with the U.S. Air Force in which it undertook to construct buildings on an air base. It breached the contract and became liable to pay damages to the Air Force. The Air Force sued to recover the damages, and the parties settled the suit a few months ago. In terms of the settlement, Mutual agreed to pay the Air Force $500,000. Last month, Mutual obtained a judgment in a case that had been pending in the U.S. Tax Court, obliging the Internal Revenue Service to refund $300,000 in overpaid federal taxes. Mutual had been struggling financially for some time, and it has now filed a petition under Ch. 7. It is badly insolvent, can no longer conduct its business, and will be liquidated. At the date of filing, it had not paid the damages due to the Air Force and had not received a refund of its overpaid taxes from the I.R.S.

Immediately after the filing, the government applied for relief from stay so that it could offset the tax refund of $300,000 due to Mutual against the $500,000 damages due by Mutual. It would then prove an unsecured claim of $200,000 against the estate. The trustee has challenged the government's claim of setoff on the grounds that there is no mutual indebtedness because Mutual's claim is against the I.R.S., not the Air Force. In the alternative, the trustee argues that even if the indebtedness was mutual, the setoff right is avoidable because it arose within 90 days of bankruptcy. Are these good arguments?

Explanations

1. The chronology of the transaction is as follows:

| | | | | ┌─90-day period─┐ | | |
Jan. 1	Feb. 1	Feb./Mar.	Mar. 30	Apr. 2	Apr. 5	July 1
Goods sold on credit and delivered	Payment due	Demands made	Check received		Check paid	Bankruptcy filing

First determine if the transfer qualifies as a preference under §547(b). If it does, then consider if any of the exceptions to avoidance in §547(c) apply. It does satisfy all five of the requirements for avoidance. First, the payment is a transfer of property of the debtor to the creditor. When payment is made by check, it is not the delivery of the check, which is merely an order to the bank, but its payment by the drawee bank that constitutes the transfer for purposes of §547(b). This was settled by Barnhill v. Johnson, 503 U.S. 393 (1992), following general principles of nonbankruptcy law.[14]

Second, the transfer is on account of an antecedent debt. In a sale of goods, the debt of the buyer normally arises when the goods are delivered. See In re Energy Co-Op, Inc., 832 F.2d 997 (7th Cir. 1987). Thus,

---

14. Barnhill focused on the question of whether delivery or payment of the check constituted the transfer for the purposes of §547(b). The Court expressly confined its opinion to §547(b) and left open the issue of whether a different rule should apply where the date of transfer must be determined for the purpose of establishing an exception under §547(c). There is substantial lower court authority that the date of delivery, rather than the date of payment, should be determinative where the transferee seeks to show that a transfer was substantially contemporaneous under §547(c)(1), or is made in the ordinary course of business under §547(c)(2), or constitutes a post-transfer payment of new value to the debtor under §547(c)(4). The Supreme Court acknowledged that the policy of protecting regular commercial practices could justify a different rule under these subsections.

the debt was created on January 1 and is antecedent to the transfer on April 15.

Third, Gloria Transit was insolvent at the time of the transfer. Under §101(32), insolvency is determined on the basis of the balance sheet test. The presumption of insolvency in §547(f) eases the trustee's burden of proving this element.

Fourth, the transfer — the payment of the check on April 2 — occurred within the prepetition avoidance period. Because Binow & Palater is not an insider of Gloria Transit Co., the preference period is 90 days before the petition. Counted back from the bankruptcy date, the 90-day period begins on April 2.

Fifth, the transfer improves the position of Binow & Palater. The improvement-in-position test requires a comparison to be made between the total amount Binow & Palater would receive in a Ch. 7 distribution if the transfer had not been made, and the total satisfaction it receives (combining the transfer and the Ch. 7 distribution on any balance of its claim) if the transfer is left undisturbed. If the transfer is not avoided, Binow & Palater is paid in full; if it is avoided, Binow & Palater, as a general unsecured creditor, will receive approximately 10 percent of its claim. (The percentage will increase slightly over 10 percent because the fund available to unsecured creditors will be enlarged by the value of the returned transfer.) Hence, the transfer has improved the position of Binow & Palater. Section 547(b)(5) is almost always satisfied when the transfer has been made to a general unsecured (or partially secured) creditor and the estate has insufficient funds to pay general unsecured creditors in full. Any portion of the debt that is satisfied by a prebankruptcy transfer is paid at a higher rate than it would be in bankruptcy.

Having determined that §547(b) is satisfied, one must now consider if one of the exceptions in §547(c) applies. None of them do. Most are not even remotely relevant, but §547(c)(1) and (2) merit some discussion. Section 547(c)(1) does not save the transaction because the transfer is not a substantially contemporaneous exchange for new value. Although §547(c)(1) was drafted with check transactions in mind, the kind of exchange contemplated was the immediate delivery of a check in payment of the goods or services. In the present case, the parties intended a credit transaction. Section 547(c)(2) protects ordinary-course transactions and covers regular payments on ordinary debts. In the present case, the debt may have been incurred in the ordinary course of business, but the payment was not routine or regular. It was overdue, and followed some pressure by the creditor. This is not the kind of payment that should be excepted from avoidance under §547(c)(2).

2. Chronological diagram:

Jan. 1	Jan. 20	Apr. 2	Apr. 10	July 1
Sale and creation of security interest	Perfection of security interest	90-day date	Overdue partial payment of $1,000	Bankruptcy filing

Unlike Binow & Palater in Example 1, Prudential has a perfected secured claim. (Although the creation of a security interest is expressly included in the definition of transfer in §101(54), that transfer is not within the preference period, and its avoidance is not in issue.) The payment of $1,000 on April 10 is also a transfer. It satisfies the first four requirements of §547(b) (*see* the analysis in the Explanation to Example 1). However, the fact that Prudential has a secured claim affects the improvement-in-position test of §547(b)(5).

If the collateral is worth $2,500 on the date of the petition, the payment to Prudential did not enable it to do better than it would have done in the absence of the transfer: Prior to the transfer it had a secured claim of $2,000 which would have been paid in full from the proceeds of the collateral. The transfer reduces the claim to $1,000, which would still be paid in full, with a large surplus left over for the estate. Either way, Prudential is paid in full. Because one of the requirements of §547(b) is not satisfied, the transfer is unavoidable. This shows that a valid security interest, perfected before the 90-day preference period, fully protects the creditor, provided that the collateral is sufficiently valuable to accommodate the entire debt. (Example 3 deals with the creation of a security interest within the 90-day period.)

If the collateral is worth only $1,500 at the time of the petition, the improvement-in-position analysis changes. The transfer reduced the debt to $1,000, so that it became fully covered by the collateral. Without the transfer, the debt would have been undersecured with a deficiency of $500. As the deficiency would have been paid as a general unsecured claim, Prudential would not receive full payment unless the estate has sufficient funds to pay general unsecured claims in full. Thus, by eliminating the deficiency, the transfer improved Prudential's position and is avoidable. None of the exceptions in §547(c) apply. As a result, Prudential is obliged to return the $1,000 to the estate and to prove a claim for its secured debt of $1,500 and its unsecured debt of $500. (By agreement with the trustee, Prudential may be permitted to keep the $1,000 and to deduct it from the secured claim, leaving it with a secured claim of $500 and an unsecured claim of $500.)

If the collateral is worth $2,000, the result may seem to be the same as it was in the first example: The transfer did not improve Prudential's position, because the secured claim would have been paid in full out of the collateral even in the absence of the transfer. However, the exact equivalence of the debt and collateral does change the answer: A secured claimant is entitled to interest, legal costs and attorney's fees under §506(b), to the extent of any surplus value in the collateral. *See* sections 19.5 and 19.6.3. Without the transfer, there would be no such surplus, so no interest, costs, and fees could be claimed. However, payment of the $1,000 creates a surplus by reducing the debt in relation to the collateral value. The right to interest, costs, and fees improves Prudential's position and makes the transfer avoidable. This demonstrates that a secured creditor does well to ensure that an equity cushion exists in the collateral so that payments on the debt are fully protected.

3. Chronological diagram:

Feb. 15	Apr. 2	May 3	July 1
Security agreement executed. Loan funds remitted to seller. Equipment delivered to debtor.	90-day date	Perfection	Bankruptcy filing

The facts mention no payments to D. Laid Security, so the only transfer in issue is the grant of the security interest, which, as stated before, constitutes a transfer under §101(54). Although D. Laid Security discovered its error before the petition was filed, thereby preventing avoidance of its interest under §544(a),[15] the perfection in the 90-day period could make the transfer avoidable under §547(b). The crucial issue is the date of the transfer: If it occurred at the time of execution of the security agreement, it is outside of the 90-day period and is contemporaneous with the debt. However, if it occurred when the interest was perfected, it falls within the 90-day period and is some considerable time after the creation of the debt.

Section 547(e)(2) sets out the rules for fixing the date of the transfer:

(1) The transfer normally takes effect for bankruptcy purposes on its effective date as between the parties under nonbankruptcy law.

(2) If an act of perfection is required by nonbankruptcy law, that act must be completed within 30 days of the effective date as between the parties. If so, the effective date remains the date of the transfer for

---

15. *See* section 15.1.2 and Example 1 of Chapter 15.

bankruptcy purposes. If perfection is delayed beyond the 30-day period, the date of perfection becomes the transfer date. (Under §547(e)(1), a transfer of real property is perfected when a bona fide purchaser of the property from the debtor cannot acquire an interest in the property superior to the transferee. A transfer of personal property is perfected when it is effective against an ordinary judicial lienholder.)

(3) If the transfer has not been perfected by the time the petition is filed, the transfer is deemed to have occurred immediately before the filing of the petition. However, if the 30-day period for perfection has not yet expired when the petition is filed, the transferee may complete the act of perfection within the 30-day period, in which case the transfer occurs on the date that it took effect between the parties.

Under UCC §9.203, a security interest takes effect between the parties (attaches) when the security agreement is authenticated in proper form, the debtor has rights in the collateral, and value is given by the secured party. This happened on February 15, when the agreement was executed, D. Laid Security advanced money to the seller, and the equipment was delivered to Gloria Transit. The perfection of the interest occurred on May 3, when the proper filing was made. Because the perfection is more than 30 days after the date on which the transfer took effect as between the parties, the transfer is deemed to have occurred on the perfection date. This places the transfer in the 90-day period, and it removes it in time from the debt, thereby making the debt antecedent. Therefore, assuming that the presumption of insolvency cannot be rebutted, the elements of §547(b) are satisfied — there is a transfer to D. Laid Security on account of an antecedent debt within the 90-day period. Because D. Laid Security would be a general unsecured creditor in the absence of the transfer (its unperfected security interest would be avoided under §544), the transfer does improve its position unless the estate is solvent and can pay all creditors in full. The 30-day grace period in §547(e), like the avoidance power in §544, is a manifestation of the policy against unrecorded interests. By placing the security interest in jeopardy if there is a delay in perfection beyond the fairly short period of 30 days, it encourages secured parties to record their interests expeditiously.

None of the exceptions to avoidance in §547(c) are applicable. Section 547(c)(1) is not likely to save the transfer. It would be a real stretch to argue that a delay of nearly three months is substantially contemporaneous. Section 547(c)(3) also does not save the transfer. Even though the interest was a purchase-money security interest, the special grace period for perfection, measured 30 days from the debtor's receipt of possession of the collateral, does not extend the time for perfection on the present facts because the delivery of the collateral to the debtor coincided with, and was not later than the effective date of the transfer.

4. Chronological diagram:

Jan. 15	Jan. 20	Apr. 2	June 1	June 10	July 1
Attachment authorized	Attachment writ levied	90-day date	Judgment	Execution levied	Bankruptcy filing
	attachment lien			execution lien	

As discussed in section 3.3.3, under general principles of state law, attachment gives rise to an inchoate lien that is effective on the date of the levy of the writ of attachment. When execution is ultimately levied after judgment, the execution lien merges with the earlier attachment lien and backdates for priority purposes to the date of the levy of attachment. Therefore, although the execution lien is a transfer[16] within the 90-day period, the prior attachment lien has already secured the debt so that the execution lien does not prefer the lienholder in position. Section 547(b)(5) is not satisfied, and the lien is unavoidable.

Although the execution lien backdates in priority, this example does not raise the issue dealt with by the Supreme Court in *Fidelity Financial Services, Inc. v. Fink*, 522 U.S. 211 (1998). As discussed in section 16.1.3, the court held that "perfection," as used in §547(e)(1)(B), means the act of perfection, not its retrospective priority date. For this reason, if a transfer was perfected outside the grace period allowed by that section, the perfection cannot be backdated to fit within the grace period, even if nonbankruptcy law permits such backdating for priority purposes. In the present case, we are not concerned with trying to backdate the perfection of the execution lien under §547(e) so as to avoid the problem of a transfer for a noncontemporaneous debt. This is simply a case in which the transfer of the execution lien does not prefer the creditor in position because the property is already secured by the preexisting, unavoidable, attachment lien. (Although the attachment lien is inchoate in the sense that it would lapse if the creditor failed to levy execution within the prescribed time after judgment, it did not in fact lapse and was immediately succeeded by the execution lien.)

5. There have been four transfers to Fallshort Finance in this case: the grant of the security interest and the three payments. The security interest and

---

16. The definition of *transfer* in §101(54) includes involuntary dispositions.

the first payment are outside the 90-day period and are not in issue. The payments for April and May are avoidable under §547(b) because they satisfy all the elements of that subsection. (Example 2 explains why the payment to an undersecured creditor satisfies the improvement-in-position test.)

The payments were not contemporaneous exchanges for new value, so §547(c)(1) is not applicable. However, §547(c)(2) likely protects from avoidance the regularly scheduled installment payments due under the loan agreement. As noted in section 16.1.4(2), §547(c)(2) is applicable to payments on a long-term debt provided that the debt was incurred in the ordinary course of business or financial affairs of both the debtor and the transferee and payment was in the ordinary course or according to ordinary business terms. The loan here is probably a one-time transaction because Annie does not regularly borrow money to pay for orthodontic treatment. However, a one-time transaction can qualify as a debt incurred in the ordinary course as long as it fits in with Annie's ordinary patterns of domestic consumption and is a normal transaction for a person in her position. The payments on the debt made up to the time of Annie's default also qualify as in the ordinary course because they were routine and regular payments made in terms of the loan agreement.

6. If it were not for §547(c)(4), the trustee would be entitled to demand return of the payment of $5,000 because it satisfies all the elements of a preference under §547(b). Annette would be obliged to return the money and prove a claim against the estate for the two loans totaling $8,000.

However, §547(c)(4) makes the transfer to Annette unavoidable to the extent that, after the transfer, Annette gave new value to Chico without receiving a new unavoidable transfer or security interest in exchange for it. After being paid the $5,000, Annette made a second loan of $3,000. Its value must be offset against the $5,000 preference, making only $2,000 of the payment avoidable. Annette may therefore keep $3,000 of the payment, but must return $2,000 to the estate. She must now prove a claim in the estate for $5,000 — the $2,000 balance on the original loan plus the $3,000 on the second loan.

7. The foreclosure sale is a transfer of the debtor's property. It is expressly included in the definition of "transfer" in §101(54). The foreclosure sale in fact constitutes two transfers: the payment of the sale proceeds to Promised Land and the conveyance of the property to Shrewd Investment. The transfer to Promised Land was on account of an antecedent debt and was made while the debtor was insolvent within the 90-day prebankruptcy period. However, Promised Land is a fully secured claimant. It received from the sale no more than the value of its perfected secured claim, and did no better than it would have done in a Ch. 7 distribution if the transfer had not been made. Therefore the

improvement-in-position test is not satisfied, and the transfer is not avoidable under §547.

The transfer to Shrewd Investment is not a preferential transfer to a creditor and is therefore not avoidable under §547. However, because the sale occurred within two years of the bankruptcy filing, it is vulnerable under §548. It is not suggested that the debtor, Erstwhile Enterprises, was guilty of actual fraud in this involuntary disposition. However, it was insolvent, so that if the foreclosure proceeds are less than reasonably equivalent value, the grounds of constructive fraud in §548(2) are satisfied. There had been some doubt over whether a low price received at a foreclosure sale should be treated as inadequate value, but this question was settled by the U.S. Supreme Court in BFP v. Resolution Trust Corp., 511 U.S. 531 (1994). The Court ruled that as long as the foreclosure sale is conducted in compliance with state law, the proceeds received from the sale are conclusively deemed to be reasonably equivalent value. The majority reasoned that as distress sales are seldom at market price, §548 could not be intended to allow courts to use a market standard of any kind to evaluate the price received at a foreclosure sale. The court found this interpretation to be supported by Congress's choice of wording in §548, which uses "reasonably equivalent value," and not "fair market value," as the basis of measuring adequacy of consideration for the purposes of §548.

BFP is expressly confined to the treatment of foreclosure sales under §548. Although its reasoning could persuade lower courts to adopt a similar rule in other distress sales, the case does not settle the divergence of views among courts of appeal in cases other than foreclosure.[17] As the proceeding under which Shrewd Investment acquired the property is a foreclosure sale, BFP governs, and as the sale fully complied with state law, it cannot be avoided as a fraudulent transfer.

8. Before Mutual obtained the Tax Court judgment, the Air Force had an unsecured claim of $500,000 against it. If the government cannot offset the debt to the estate for the tax refund against the Air Force's claim against the estate, it will have to pay the full $300,000 to the estate, and will prove its general unsecured claim of $500,000. Because the estate is badly insolvent, it may receive nothing or only a small fraction of its claim. However, if it can set off the debts, it could keep the $300,000 that would otherwise have been payable to the estate and apply it to the

---

17. It is also not clear if BFP applies outside of §548. For example, under defined circumstances, §549 precludes the avoidance of a postpetition transfer for which "present fair equivalent value" was given. Some courts have held that BFP should be applied to a foreclosure sale under §549 as well. However, others, such as In re Miller, 454 F.3d 899 (8th Cir. 2006), have held that BFP is inapplicable because "present fair equivalent value" in §549 is not the same as "reasonably equivalent value" in §548.

payment of its claim, which would be treated as secured to the extent of the $300,000. Only the balance of $200,000 would be an unsecured claim. Given the insolvency of the estate, the setoff would surely improve the government's position.

Setoff can only be used when the parties are mutually indebted. It may sound as if this requirement is not satisfied here because Mutual's debt is owed to the Air Force, but it is the I.R.S., not the Air Force, that is indebted to Mutual. However, the real creditor is the U.S. government, and the Air Force and I.R.S. are simply agencies of the creditor. They are not separate entities. In In re HAL, Inc., 122 F.3d 851 (9th Cir. 1997), the court permitted the setoff of debts owed by the debtor to some federal agencies against debts due to the debtor by others. It held that for the purposes of setoff, all agencies of the federal government must be treated as parts of a single governmental unit — a unitary creditor — and that a debt due to one agency of this unit can be offset by a debt owed by another. (The same principle would apply to agencies of the government of a single state, but obviously would not apply when agencies of different states or state and federal governments are involved.)

This conclusion makes sense as a matter of principle, because all these agencies derive their funding and authority from a centralized source, and do not operate autonomously. It has some support in the language of §553, read with the definitions in §101, but there is an ambiguity in §101(27) which could also justify a contrary argument: Section 553 refers to the setoff right of a "creditor," which is defined in §101(10) to be an entity with a claim against the debtor. "Entity" is in turn defined in §101(15) to include a governmental unit, which is defined in §101(27) to include the United States, states, and other local and regional authorities, as well as their departments, agencies, and instrumentalities. HAL read this as meaning that the U.S. government, including its agencies and constituent parts, must be deemed an indivisible governmental unit, but a glance at that section will demonstrate that it could just as easily be read to mean that each constituent part qualifies as a "governmental unit" on its own.

Once the issue of mutual indebtedness is resolved, we must look at §553 to see if any of its grounds for avoidance are satisfied. They are not. Contrary to the trustee's argument, there is no bar to setoff merely because the mutual debt was created within the 90 days before bankruptcy. For the setoff to be avoidable, the setoff must be tainted in one of the ways specified in §553, which involve a defect in the claim itself or conduct by the creditor designed to create an improper improvement in position in the 90 days before bankruptcy.

CHAPTER 17

The Trustee's Power to Deal with Estate Property and to Obtain Credit

§17.1 INTRODUCTION

Sections 363 and 364 are concerned with two central administrative functions of the trustee: The power to deal with estate property and to enter into credit transactions on behalf of the estate. Both sections are part of Ch. 3, which is applicable in all cases whether under Ch. 7, 11, 12, or 13. Of course, the powers are not equally relevant in every case, nor are they used in the same way or to the same extent in different types of bankruptcy. As a general matter, the trustee's sale of estate property is likely to predominate in Ch. 7 cases because the trustee is less likely to need the ability to lease and use property and to obtain credit where the estate is being liquidated. By contrast, in a rehabilitation case, especially one involving a business, the trustee (including a debtor in possession) is likely to use these powers much more extensively.

Sections 363 and 364 are meant to enable the trustee to conduct the affairs of the estate to best advantage, whether that involves liquidation or the conduct of the debtor's business or affairs. In Ch. 11 (and to some extent in Ch. 12) this role, like other trustee functions, is exercised by the debtor in possession who is not likely to approach estate administration with the same impartiality as a disinterested trustee. Therefore, the conduct of the estate's affairs by a debtor in possession is likely to attract closer monitoring by creditors and the court.

Both §§363 and 364 distinguish between actions that are and are not in the ordinary course of the debtor's business. The trustee has wider discretion to enter into ordinary-course transactions and normally conducts such activity routinely without special permission of the court. However, extraordinary activity can only be undertaken with court authority, obtained after notice and a hearing. (As stated before, "notice and a hearing" is defined in §102 to mean that parties in interest must receive notice, but that a hearing need not be held unless a party in interest requests it.)

§17.2 THE USE, SALE, OR LEASE OF ESTATE PROPERTY UNDER §363

§17.2.1 The Distinction between Ordinary and Extraordinary Transactions

Section 363 provides authority for the trustee's dealings with estate property, sets out some general principles governing the exercise of this power, and places limits on the trustee's discretion for the protection of creditors and other parties whose interests may be affected by the trustee's activities. Section 363 encompasses a wide range of activity, including the disposition of estate assets, the operation of equipment, the use of resources and premises, and the routine conduct of daily operations.

As noted in the introduction, §363 makes a fundamental distinction between transactions in the ordinary course of business, which may be conducted within the trustee's discretion, and those outside the ordinary course, which require notice to interested parties and, where requested, a hearing and court approval. The basic idea behind this distinction is that the trustee should be able to maintain routine business operations with a minimum of interference but should not be permitted to enter extraordinary transactions without giving notice to creditors and other interested parties and, if need be, justifying the transaction to the court.

The trustee may only enter into ordinary-course transactions without notice and a hearing under §363 if the debtor had been engaged in business at the time of the petition and the postpetition conduct of business operations is generally allowed in the chapter under which the petition has been filed. Section 363(c)(1) is expressly premised on the trustee's underlying statutory authorization to operate the debtor's business under §721, 1108, 1203, 1204, or 1304. In rehabilitation cases, if the debtor had a business at the time of the petition, authority to continue its operation is the norm. Sections 1108, 1203, 1204, and 1304 allow the trustee to continue business activities unless the court orders otherwise. Therefore, in rehabilitation cases, the trustee may continue the debtor's ordinary business operations under §363(c)(1) without notice or court approval unless such activity has been curtailed by court order. (The exception to this rule, for cash collateral, is discussed in section 17.2.5.)

In liquidation cases the opposite is true. Because Ch. 7 is aimed at the expeditious liquidation of the estate, the continuation of the debtor's business is not normally contemplated. Section 721 requires court approval for any business activity by the trustee, and stipulates that such approval should be granted only for a limited time and only upon a showing that further business operations are in the best interests of the estate and consistent with orderly liquidation. In a Ch. 7 case, therefore, there can be no ordinary-course business activity without notice and a hearing under §363(c)(1) unless the conduct of the business has first been authorized by the court under §721.

In short, unless the debtor conducted business at the time of the petition and the continuation of the business is permitted under the chapter governing the petition, notice and a hearing is required for any use, sale, or lease of estate property, whether or not in the ordinary course of business. If the continuation of ordinary business operations is authorized, ordinary-course transactions may proceed at the trustee's discretion, but any transaction involving the extraordinary use, sale, or lease of estate property must be preceded by notice and a hearing. (*See* Example 1.)

To know if notice must be given, the trustee must decide if a transaction fits within the scope of ordinary business operations. In some situations this is not a difficult question to resolve. For example, if the debtor's business is the retail sales of goods, a routine sale of inventory to a customer is obviously in the ordinary course of business, but the sale of all the debtor's inventory or the disposition of one of its branches is not. In cases where there is doubt, the determination of the ordinary or extraordinary character of the transaction is a factual question to be resolved under all the circumstances of the case. Courts have developed a two-pronged test for deciding if a transaction is in the ordinary course of the debtor's business. Both parts of the test must be applied to the transaction, and if it satisfies both, it is in the ordinary course of business. One part of the test, sometimes called the "vertical dimension," focuses on the reasonable expectations of parties in interest. The court views the transaction from the perspective of a hypothetical creditor and asks whether the transaction would impose economic risks on that creditor beyond those reasonably expected in light of the debtor's prepetition business activities. The other, sometimes called the "horizontal dimension," looks more broadly at the commercial context in which the debtor's business is operated, and asks whether the postpetition transaction is of a type that may be expected in a business similar to the debtor's. Overall, the purpose of the two-pronged inquiry is to ascertain whether parties in interest could reasonably have anticipated a transaction of this type, given the range and scope of the debtor's business and the normal practices in the business environment in which the debtor participates. If not, the transaction is outside the ordinary course of the debtor's business, and interested parties must be informed of it and given an opportunity to demand a hearing. See In re Dant & Russel, Inc., 853 F.2d 700 (9th Cir. 1988); In re Straightline Investments, Inc., 525 F.3d 870 (9th Cir. 2008). See also Example 1.

§17.2.2 The Approval of Transactions outside the Ordinary Course of Business under §363(b)(1)

If the use, sale, or lease of property is outside the ordinary course of business, the court must determine whether it should be approved under §363(b)(1). The standard for approval is that the transaction serves the best interests of the estate and furthers the legitimate ends of the bankruptcy. This is a factual determination, to be made in the context of the case as a whole. The factors evaluated by the court include the adequacy of the price, the business efficacy of the transaction, and its overall benefit to the estate. See, for example, In re Exaeris, Inc., 380 B.R. 741 (Bankr. D. Del. 2008). In a Ch. 11 case, the court will view the transaction in light of the larger scheme of rehabilitation envisioned for the estate to determine if the transaction is likely to further or hamper the debtor's rehabilitation strategy. Section 363 is meant to be used for extraordinary dealings with estate property prior to the confirmation of the Ch. 11 plan. Therefore, if there is no need for immediate action, or if the transaction involves the sale of a significant portion of the debtor's assets, or if it is very complex, the court may refuse approval under §363 and require the transaction to be dealt with in the plan so that it can be subjected to the scrutiny of the confirmation process. This process contains safeguards more stringent than those available under §363.[1] Examples 1(e) and 2 illustrate the factors to be considered by a court in approving sales outside the ordinary course of business.

§17.2.3 The Protection of Interests in Property That Is to Be Used, Sold, or Leased

Sales at low prices and disadvantageous use or lease of estate property diminish the value of the estate. Unsecured creditors may therefore object to transactions that appear to be undesirable. Secured creditors or other

---

1. These safeguards are explained in Chapter 21. They include the publication of a disclosure statement detailing plan provisions, voting on the plan by creditors, and compliance with statutory confirmation requirements. The notice and hearing process in §363(b)(1) does not provide safeguards of equal strength.

persons who have an interest in estate property usually have an even more immediate stake in preventing the sale, use, or lease of the property in which they have an interest. Section 363 has a number of provisions designed to protect these interests in estate property. In terms of §363(d), the trustee's power to deal with property must be consistent with any relief from stay granted under §363. In addition, the holder of the interest in estate property may seek adequate protection under §363(e) if the proposed use or disposition of the property jeopardizes that party's interest in it. The right to adequate protection applies to all proposed transactions under §363, whether or not they are in the ordinary course of business and irrespective of the nature of the property. Under §363(o), the party who demands adequate protection bears the burden of proving the interest, but the trustee must prove that the interest is adequately protected. The factors that are evaluated by the court in deciding if adequate protection exists (such as the presence of an equity cushion and the debtor's prospects of successful reorganization) are the same as those discussed in connection with relief from stay, as are the standards for evaluating the adequacy of any additional protection offered by the trustee under §361. As in the case of relief from stay, the court has discretion in selecting an appropriate remedy. Section 363 allows the court to permit or prohibit the use, sale, or lease of collateral absolutely or subject to conditions. Apart from the protection of interests in property generally, §363 has special rules to preserve cash collateral, discussed below.

Sections 363(f) through (k) impose restrictions and qualifications on the trustee's power to sell property of which the estate is a co-owner or which is subject to a lien or interest held by another. Like §363(e) on adequate protection, most of these provisions apply to both extraordinary sales and to sales in the ordinary course of business. In essence, they permit the sale of property free and clear of interests, or the sale of both the estate's and the other party's undivided interests only under specified conditions. If such a sale occurs, the holder of the interest is paid out the value of the interest from the sale proceeds. In some situations, the co-owner must be given a right of first refusal to purchase the property at the proposed sale price. When property is sold outside the ordinary course of business under §363(b), the holder of a lien in the property is entitled to bid at the sale, and if the lienholder purchases the property, to offset its claim against the purchase price.

§17.2.4 Insolvency or Bankruptcy Clauses in Prepetition Contracts or Nonbankruptcy Law

In dealing with property of the estate, section 11.2.1 indicated that §541(c) invalidates ipso facto clauses — provisions in contracts or nonbankruptcy law that restrict transfer or provide for the forfeiture of property rights on bankruptcy — so that private parties or states cannot circumvent bankruptcy law by making the debtor's property interests nonassignable to the trustee. Similar considerations exist with regard to the trustee's power to use, sell, or lease property. To prevent states or private parties from negating the trustee's power to deal with property under §363, §363(l) disregards contractual or statutory provisions that provide for the forfeiture or modification of the debtor's property rights upon insolvency or bankruptcy.

§17.2.5 Restrictions on Dealing with Cash Collateral

Section 363 treats cash collateral differently from other property of the estate. The essential difference is that cash collateral may not be dealt with by the trustee, even in the ordinary course of business, unless the holder of the interest in that collateral consents or the court authorizes the transaction after notice and a hearing. "Cash collateral" is defined in §363(a) to mean cash or a cash equivalent that is subject to an interest held by someone other than the estate. The most common form that this interest takes is a security interest in the cash collateral, either as original collateral or as proceeds of original collateral. Of course, the security interest must be valid under nonbankruptcy law, and if the cash collateral is proceeds of original collateral, the security interest must validly extend to such proceeds under nonbankruptcy law. Quite a wide range of property is considered to be the equivalent of cash under §363(a). The definition includes not only banknotes and bank accounts, but also various kinds of negotiable or readily transferable commercial paper such as negotiable instruments, documents, and securities. These are treated as cash equivalents because they can be liquidated easily by being sold to purchasers who take free of the rights of the secured party. Example 3 illustrates different types of cash collateral.

The liquid nature of cash and cash equivalents explains the stricter approach in §363 to the trustee's dealings with cash collateral. Because the debtor's business needs cash to operate, it is very tempting for the estate to spend these assets, thereby dissipating them in the ongoing conduct of the business. A creditor who has a security interest in such assets is therefore in much greater danger than other secured creditors of having its collateral frittered away in the payment of daily business expenses. For this reason, §363(c)(2) freezes the use of cash collateral even when this normally would be in the ordinary course of running the business, until the trustee either obtains permission from the interest holder or authority from the court to deal with it. In addition, §363(c)(4) obliges the trustee to keep cash collateral separate and to account for it, unless the creditor or court dispenses with this requirement. Sections 363(d) and (e) make it clear that the authorization to deal with cash collateral is subject to any relief from stay that has been granted and is conditional upon adequate protection of the interest.

In many cases, a debtor's only source of the cash needed to continue operating is cash collateral, and the debtor will need access to this cash immediately after filing the petition. It is therefore common for the debtor to negotiate an agreement with the secured party under which it gives permission to the debtor to use the cash collateral, subject to terms that protect the secured party's interest. If the debtor cannot obtain creditor consent, it must apply to court for authorization. Because the need for access to the cash may be pressing, §363(c)(3) requires the court to act promptly on any request that the debtor makes to use cash collateral.

§17.3 POSTPETITION CREDIT UNDER §364

§17.3.1 The Rationale of §364

Section 364 deals with credit given to the estate after the petition has been filed. In these transactions the estate is the debtor, and is liable for payment of the debt. (Such estate debts qualify as administrative expenses with top priority for payment.) A Ch. 7 estate does not usually need to borrow money. However, a debtor that is undergoing rehabilitation and is attempting to operate and reorganize its business often requires credit to support its operations. In some cases, financing is vital to the debtor's survival and successful reorganization. To obtain credit, the debtor needs to convince the prospective financer that it has good prospects of rehabilitation. In addition, because of the risk that the debtor will not overcome its financial difficulties, the postpetition lender is likely to require some security or an assurance of priority if the debt is not repaid. Section 364 assists the trustee in obtaining postpetition credit by providing the means for securing or otherwise protecting financial transactions entered into by the estate.

Like the ordinary use, sale, or lease of estate property, the routine creation of postpetition unsecured debt is within the discretion of the trustee. However, credit transactions outside the ordinary course of business and the creation of secured debt must be authorized by the court following notice and a hearing. The assumption of new debt by the estate is potentially detrimental to existing unsecured creditors. If the reorganization ultimately fails, new creditors with secured or priority claims will consume assets or funds that would have been available to pay the prepetition claims. Thus, postpetition financing creates a dilemma: If the debtor obtains new credit, its chances of successful rehabilitation are improved, and prepetition unsecured creditors have a chance to receive a higher level of payment than they would have received in liquidation. However, if new credit is obtained and the debtor fails in the end, the estate's assets will have been further encumbered, the expenses of administration will have increased, and the source of funds formerly available to unsecured creditors will have been reduced or eliminated. Because prepetition creditors bear a large part of the risk of failure, courts are usually careful to try to protect their interests when called upon to approve a postpetition credit transaction. Fully secured prepetition creditors are not as vulnerable as unsecured creditors because their claims are protected by their liens. However, proposed postpetition financing can, under some circumstances, affect the security of a prepetition secured creditor. If this is a possibility, the prepetition creditor can demand adequate protection as a precondition to the court approving the financing.

§17.3.2 The Credit Arrangements Permitted by §364

Section 364 is based on the policy that the trustee should be required to find the least onerous financing available. For example, if unsecured credit is available, it is to be preferred to secured credit. If secured credit is necessary, unencumbered property should be used as collateral rather than property subject to an existing interest. This policy is expressed in the hierarchical organization of the section. It proves for the possibility of four different levels of credit transaction that are progressively more burdensome for the estate, and makes it clear that credit on more stringent terms should not be approved unless easier terms are unavailable.

The four levels of transaction are as follows:

(1) Unsecured debt incurred in the ordinary course of business (§364(a)). If continuation of the debtor's business is authorized under §721, 1108, 1203, 1204, or 1304, the trustee has the power to obtain unsecured credit in the ordinary course of business. The debts so incurred are given the priority of an administrative expense, so that they will be paid before most other unsecured claims. (*See* section 19.6.) This provision is similar in concept to §363(c)(1), which was discussed in section 17.2.1. Unless the court orders otherwise, these routine credit transactions do not require notice or a hearing. The test for deciding whether or not a transaction is in the ordinary course of business is the same as that applicable to the use, sale, or lease of estate property.

(2) Unsecured debt outside the ordinary course of business (§364(b)). If the unsecured credit transaction does not fall within the normal course of the debtor's business (or if there is no authority to operate a business under the applicable chapter of the Code), the trustee must obtain court permission, following notice and a hearing, to incur the unsecured credit. The approved credit is given administrative expense priority. The general grounds for approving the credit transaction are similar to those for approving the use, sale, or lease of estate property outside the ordinary course of business: The court must be satisfied that the transaction is on fair and reasonable terms, that it is likely to further the interests of the estate, and that it will not impose an unjustifiable burden or risk on parties in interest.

(3) Secured or superpriority credit (§364(c)). If the trustee cannot obtain unsecured credit allowable as an administrative expense, §364(c) allows the court, after notice and a hearing, to approve security or special priority for the debt. Section 364(c) provides the court with three alternatives: It may authorize superpriority for the debt, placing it ahead of administrative expenses so that it is paid in preference over priority and general unsecured claims,[2] or it may allow the trustee to secure the debt by a lien on unencumbered property or by a junior lien on encumbered property. See Example 5. The court is not confined to any one of the alternatives and can approve a transaction that combines them. In addition to determining that unsecured credit is unavailable, the court takes into account the same factors as those identified for §364(b), in deciding whether to approve a transaction under §364(c).

(4) Credit secured by a senior or equal lien on encumbered property (§364(d)). The credit terms in the prior categories do not infringe upon the rights of existing secured claimants. Only if the credit is unobtainable by any other means and the need for it is demonstrated by the trustee can the court (after notice and a hearing) approve credit that is secured by a lien senior or equal to an existing lien on estate property. This kind of lien is commonly called a "priming lien' because it primes an existing lien on the property.

The grant of such a lien endangers the valid preexisting security interest in the property and the holder's legitimate expectation of full satisfaction of its secured claim. It therefore should only be approved in compelling circumstances. Section 364(d) also requires the existing interest to be adequately protected. The trustee has the burden of proving adequate protection, and the principles discussed in section 11.5 apply — adequate

---

2. Prior to 2005, administrative expenses were a first-priority claim, paid before all other categories of priority claims. The Bankruptcy Abuse Prevention and Consumer Protection Act of 2005 (BAPCPA) elevated domestic support obligations to first priority, so administrative expenses are now in second place. (See section 19.6.) Because postpetition credit is more commonly used in business bankruptcy cases, this change in the priority structure will often have no impact on the rank of a superpriority claim. However, if postpetition credit is given to an individual debtor who owes domestic support obligations, superpriority is no longer as super as it was.

protection may be afforded by a sufficient equity cushion, new collateral, payment to reduce the debt, or other means. The fact that the equity cushion is large enough to accommodate both the existing and the proposed liens may not, on its own, be enough to adequately protect the existing interest. For example, in *In re Stoney Creek Technologies, LLC*, 364 B.R. 882 (Bankr. E.D. Pa. 2007), the court refused to approve credit secured by a senior lien despite an adequate equity cushion because the Ch. 11 debtor's prospects of successful reorganization were poor and the proposed financing would not have improved them.

§17.3.3 Cross-Collateralization

Because a bankrupt debtor is usually a poor credit risk, it may be unable to entice a new lender to extend credit. It may therefore approach an existing creditor for further advances. Because the existing creditor has a stake in the debtor's rehabilitation, it has some incentive to provide new financing if it believes that the debtor's reorganization may be successful as a result. The creditor has an even stronger incentive to provide postpetition financing if its prepetition claim is unsecured or undersecured, and the debtor is willing to provide collateral to secure both the new credit and the unsecured prepetition credit. Such an arrangement is known as cross-collateralization. In short, it is the provision of postpetition credit to the estate on condition that the collateral securing the new credit also covers the unsecured or undersecured prepetition claim. For cross-collateralization to benefit the lender, there must be a present or anticipated excess equity in the collateral beyond the amount of the new debt. For example, suppose a creditor is owed a prepetition debt of $5 million, secured by collateral worth $4 million. The creditor agrees to make a new postpetition loan of $2 million to the debtor to enable it to reorganize. As a condition of this postpetition loan, the creditor demands a security interest in unencumbered property of the estate worth $3 million, which will secure both the postpetition loan and the prepetition debt. If this arrangement is authorized by the court, the creditor not only secures the new financing, but also bolsters the security for its prepetition debt and eliminates its unsecured deficiency. In essence, the creditor uses its bargaining power in negotiating postpetition financing to improve the position of its undersecured prepetition debt at the expense of other unsecured creditors. This offends the bankruptcy policy of even-handed treatment.

It is not clear whether cross-collateralization is permissible. Some bankruptcy courts have allowed it, albeit reluctantly, when the debtor in possession can show that the business will not survive without the proposed financing, the estate cannot obtain better financing, the proposed lender will not agree to better terms, and the transaction is in the best interests of the estate and creditors. See In re *Vanguard Diversified*, 31 B.R. 364 (Bankr. E.D.N.Y. 1983). Other courts have held that a court may not sanction a postpetition financing scheme involving cross-collateralization. In In re *Saybrook Mfg. Co., Inc.*, 963 F.2d 1490 (11th Cir. 1992), the court noted that §364 authorizes only the granting of liens for postpetition loans and gives the court no power to extend the lien to a prepetition debt. Although bankruptcy courts do have general equitable powers to adjust claims to avoid unfairness, this does not entitle them to authorize the preferential treatment of a claim in contravention of the Code's priority scheme and the fundamental policy of evenhanded treatment of creditors.

§17.3.4 Protection on Appeal

A party in interest may appeal the court's approval of postpetition credit. If the estate needs the advance urgently, the delay resulting from an appeal could be damaging. Therefore, provided that the court has not stayed action pending appeal, §364(e) allows the parties to proceed with the transaction immediately after approval, notwithstanding appeal. As long as the creditor has acted in good faith, the debt and its supporting lien or priority authorized by the court remain valid and enforceable even if the approval is reversed or modified on appeal. The lender fails to act in good faith if it commits fraud, attempts to take unfair advantage of others, or acts with an improper purpose, but the mere fact that the creditor knows that an appeal is pending does not constitute bad faith. In In re *Foreside Management Co., LLC*, 402 B.R. 446 (B.A.P. 1st Cir. 2009), the court noted that the protection afforded to a good faith lender under §364(e) is broad and substantial, so the appellate court cannot second-guess or modify the bankruptcy court's approval. The sole issues for consideration on appeal are whether the lower court stayed action pending appeal, and if not, whether the lender acted in good faith in extending the credit.

Examples

1. Carrion Business, Inc., which operates a chain of three retail stores, has recently filed a voluntary Ch. 11 petition. Are the following proposed transactions within the ordinary course of the debtor's business?
    a. The debtor keeps the stores open and continues selling inventory to customers.
    b. The debtor proposes to conduct a mammoth clearance sale at which it plans to sell all its slow-moving inventory at greatly reduced prices, to reduce stock and improve its cash flow.
    c. The debtor proposes to use the cash generated by its sale of inventory to pay salaries, rent for its premises, and other operating expenses.

d. One of the debtor's three stores has never made a profit. The debtor enters into an agreement with one of its competitors under which it proposes to sell the unprofitable store to the competitor for cash.

e. The debtor has filed the petition under Ch. 7 rather than Ch. 11. The trustee wishes to keep the stores open for a few months and to continue selling inventory to customers to liquidate the inventory at its retail value.

2. Joyful Trifles, Inc. is a toy manufacturer. Its toys contain electronic components manufactured by Sound Bytes, Inc., a profitable and financially stable company in which Joyful Trifles is the majority shareholder. These shares are Joyful Trifle's most valuable asset. After suffering losses for several years, Joyful Trifles filed a Ch. 11 petition in an attempt to restructure its business. While it was formulating its plan of reorganization, it received an offer for the purchase of its shares in Sound Bytes, Inc. The prospective buyer has offered a very good price for the shares, provided that the sale can be executed speedily. Joyful Trifles wishes to accept the offer so that it can use the proceeds in the reorganization of its manufacturing business, but some creditors objected upon being notified of the proposed sale. What factors should the court take into account in deciding whether or not to approve the sale?

3. Fiscal Jam Co., Inc. operates a berry farm, makes its produce into jam, and sells the finished product to supermarkets. Fiscal Jam owns its farm, a cannery, and a warehouse building. It does not need the entire warehouse for its own product, and leases a portion of the building to a tenant.

Fiscal Jam has filed a petition under Ch. 11. At the time of filing the petition, Fiscal Jam's estate included the property listed below. Which of these assets satisfies the definition of cash collateral?

a. The debtor's inventory of jam, subject to a security interest in favor of a lender.

b. Proceeds of the sale of jam, received prior to the bankruptcy filing and deposited in a special proceeds account, as required by the security agreement between the debtor and the inventory financer.

c. Proceeds of the sale of jam, received after the bankruptcy filing and deposited in the special account.

d. Accounts receivable, representing debts due to the debtor by its customers for jam sold on credit.

e. Undeposited checks received from customers in payment of jam sold.

f. Other funds in the general bank account, derived from sources other than sales of inventory and rent. The bank in which this account is maintained had made a loan to the debtor prior to the petition, and the loan remains unpaid.

4. One of the assets in a Ch. 7 estate is the debtor's undivided half-share ownership in a piece of real property. The property is subject to a valid mortgage. The trustee has not been able to find a buyer for the half-interest, but has found a buyer who wishes to buy the entire property free of all encumbrances. The price offered is sufficient to pay off the mortgage, leaving a substantial equity to be divided between the estate and the co-owner. Can the trustee accept the offer?

5. Last year, Receding Airlines, Inc. filed a Ch. 11 petition. Shortly thereafter, one of its secured creditors, Mayday, Mayday & Co., applied for relief from stay on the grounds that its collateral (some equipment owned by the debtor) was not adequately protected. In response to the application, the debtor augmented the collateral by including some additional equipment. The court found that the increase in collateral adequately protected Mayday's interest, and it refused relief from stay. A few months ago, the court approved a loan to the estate from Mortimer Post, Inc. and authorized its payment in priority over all administrative expenses, as provided for in §364(c)(1).

   Receding Airline's attempt at reorganization has failed and the company is in liquidation. It now appears that the additional collateral given to Mayday was not enough to offset depreciation. Although it was fully secured at the time that it applied for relief from stay, its collateral now falls short of its debt by $200,000. The balance due to Mortimer Post on its loan is $2 million.

   After secured claims are paid, the fund remaining in the estate for distribution to all creditors is $1.5 million. How will this fund be distributed?

Explanations

1. a. The continued routine operation of the retail stores is clearly in the ordinary course of its business. Unless the court has ordered otherwise, this activity is authorized by §1108 and encompassed within §363(c)(1). The debtor's ability to conduct its business in the usual way is often central to the Ch. 11 debtor's effort to reorganize and revitalize its business. Therefore, unless there is some good reason to restrict the debtor's normal income-producing endeavors, the debtor should be able to get on with its business without the disruption and inefficiency of notifying interested parties of its routine activities and seeking court approval in the event of objection.

   b. The mammoth clearance sale is not as obviously in the ordinary course of business as the day-to-day dealings with customers. To decide whether this transaction is in the ordinary course of business, the court must consider the reasonable expectations of parties in interest in light of the commercial context in which the debtor operates. If periodic clearance sales are part of the debtor's business practice, and such sales are not inconsistent with expected activity in the debtor's trade, this may qualify as an ordinary-course transaction. In addition, the degree of markdown, the inventory included in the sale, and the period of the sale should not be dramatically different from usual.

c. The use of proceeds of inventory to pay business expenses qualifies as an ordinary-course transaction provided that the payments are not abnormal or accelerated. See, for example, In re James A. Phillips, Inc., 29 B.R. 391 (S.D.N.Y. 1983). Note, however, that if the inventory was subject to a security interest, the funds generated by the sale of inventory would be cash collateral, and cannot be used even to pay ordinary-course business expenses without notice and a hearing or the consent of the secured party.

d. The sale of the unprofitable store is not in the ordinary course of business. Although it may be a good idea for the debtor to dispose of the unprofitable store as part of its Ch. 11 reorganization, this must, at a minimum, be done with notice and an opportunity for a hearing under §363(b). Even this procedure may not be appropriate. Unless there is a good reason to authorize the sale under §363 because, for example, the debtor needs to dispose of the store without delay, it is more appropriate for the debtor to provide for the sale in the plan of reorganization so that it is subject to the safeguards of the plan-confirmation process.

e. The operation of the stores by a Ch. 7 trustee does require court approval. Even though the operation of the stores is in the ordinary course of the debtor's business, §363(c)(1) only allows the trustee to conduct the business of the debtor without notice and a hearing if continued operation is authorized in the chapter under which the bankruptcy is filed. In Ch. 7 cases, §721 allows the short-term operation of the business only if the court authorizes it as being in the best interests of the estate and consistent with orderly liquidation. Therefore, in a Ch. 7 case, the trustee may not continue running the stores, even in the ordinary course of business, unless the court has given permission to keep the stores open for a limited period in order to realize the most advantageous price for the inventory.

2. This question is inspired by In re Lionel Corp., 722 F.2d 1063 (2d Cir. 1983). Like Joyful Trifles, Lionel Corp.'s most valuable asset was stock that it owned in a profitable corporation that manufactured electronic components for its toys. In the Lionel case, the proposed sale was motivated not by an attractive offer to buy the shares but by pressure exerted by major creditors to sell the shares for the purpose of realizing a substantial cash fund. The proposed sale was objected to by stockholders

in the debtor and by the Securities and Exchange Commission (SEC) which is also an interested party in Ch. 11 cases involving public corporations. The court of appeals reversed the bankruptcy court's approval of the sale on the grounds that there was no articulated business justification for selling the shares at this stage instead of dealing with the disposition of the shares in the Ch. 11 plan, subject to the safeguards of the plan-confirmation process.

The court articulated the factors to be considered in deciding when it is appropriate for a sale of a significant asset to be conducted under §363, rather than in the Ch. 11 plan. The court must be concerned not only with the merits of the transaction (i.e., whether it is advantageous, represents good business judgment, and will further the ends of successful reorganization) but also with its timing: Under all the circumstances of the case, an immediate sale must be based on a reasonable business judgment and must be likely to further the best interests of the estate. Some of the questions to be asked in making this determination are the following: Is the proposed sale on such attractive terms that they are not likely to be repeated if the sale is not executed? Is the asset likely to depreciate or appreciate? Will the management of the asset constitute a drain on the resources of the estate? Is the sale of the asset at this stage consistent with the debtor's plans for rehabilitation? The court concluded that there was no good business reason to sell the shares in the electronics company at that time: They were not depreciating, the price was not adequate, and no emergency required disposition. By contrast, in *Stephens Industries, Inc. v. McClung*, 789 F.2d 386 (6th Cir. 1986), the court did permit the sale under §363 of all the debtor's assets. The debtor was a radio station and one of its principal assets was a Federal Communications Commission (FCC) license. The estate no longer had the capacity to keep its radio station operational and risked revocation of its license for going off the air. The immediate sale was therefore necessary to prevent loss of the license which was the estate's most valuable asset. In effect, the sale amounted to the liquidation of the estate, which is not an appropriate use of §363 except in the most pressing circumstances.

The facts of this question do not suggest a dire emergency like that in *Stephens Industries* but they do suggest some business justification that was absent in *Lionel* — an advantageous price. However, this may not, on its own, be enough to justify an immediate sale in advance of plan confirmation.

3. The classification of the collateral is as follows:
   a. The inventory, although readily disposable property, is not cash collateral. It is neither commercial paper nor a cash equivalent as required by §363(a). Therefore, because the debtor is authorized to

continue its business under §1108, sales of inventory in the ordinary course of business may continue without notice and a hearing under §363(c)(1).

b. The funds in the special bank account are identified as proceeds of inventory. The inventory is subject to a security interest. UCC Article 9, which governs such security interests, automatically extends the interest to identifiable proceeds received by the debtor in exchange for the original collateral. Hence, the funds in the special account are cash collateral under §363(a). They cannot be used by the debtor unless court authority or creditor consent is given under §363(2).

c. The only difference between these proceeds and those described in question (b) is that these were received after the petition was filed. Postpetition proceeds of estate property are included in the estate. §541(a)(6). In terms of §552(b), they are subject to the security interest because they are proceeds of prepetition collateral under a valid prepetition interest that extends to proceeds under nonbankruptcy law. In defining cash collateral, §363(a) expressly includes postpetition proceeds in which a security interest is recognized by §552(b). Therefore, like the funds deposited in the special account before commencement of the case, these identifiable cash proceeds of inventory, received after the filing of the petition, are cash collateral.

d. Like the inventory in question (a), these accounts are not commercial paper or cash equivalents. They are simply intangible claims that the debtor has against its customers. They do not fall within the definition of cash collateral. However, the accounts are identifiable proceeds of original collateral in which the security interest continues under §552(b). When the accounts are paid, the payments are likewise identifiable proceeds and will be cash collateral.

e. The checks are negotiable instruments under UCC Article 3, and are cash collateral under §363(a).

f. These funds are not proceeds of original collateral. However, because the debtor is indebted to the bank, and the bank has a right of setoff against the account, the funds are treated as collateral of the bank to the extent of its unpaid claim. (See §553, discussed in section 16.2.) A deposit account is included in the definition of cash collateral in §363(a). This question illustrates one of the ways in which an original interest in cash collateral may arise.

4. This question merely introduces §363(f), (h), (i), and (j). It is not a comprehensive treatment of those subsections, which are full of difficult issues. The facts suggest that the estate will benefit from the sale of the entire property, free of the mortgage. Under appropriate circumstances,

§363 gives the trustee the power to sell not only the debtor's interest but the co-owner's interest as well, using the proceeds of the sale to pay off the mortgage and to pay out the co-owner's share of the property, keeping the balance for the estate.

The sale free of the mortgage is governed by §363(f), which permits such a sale only if one of five conditions is satisfied. There is some doubt about the scope and meaning of certain of these alternative requirements, but in essence they are the following: the mortgagee consents; the mortgage's validity is in genuine dispute; nonbankruptcy law provides a means of sale free and clear of the mortgage; the mortgagee can be compelled by litigation to accept money satisfaction; or the sale price of the property exceeds the aggregate value of all liens on the property. Notwithstanding the existence of any one of these grounds, there remains the general requirement under §363(e) that adequate protection of the mortgagee's interest be provided. If the property does qualify for sale free and clear of the mortgage, the mortgagee's interest will attach to and will be paid out in full from the proceeds.

The co-owner's share of the property may be sold only if all four of the conditions in §363(h) are satisfied: Partition is impracticable; the sale of the estate's interest alone would realize significantly less; the benefit to the estate outweighs the detriment to the co-owner; and the property is not used for the production or supply of electrical energy or gas. In addition, §363(i) gives the co-owner the right of first refusal at the sale price, and §363(k) requires the trustee to pay over to the co-owner her share of the sale proceeds.

5. Section 11.5.5 and Example 3 of Chapter 11 deal with Mayday's situation. If adequate protection is provided, and it later turns out to have been inadequate to protect the interest, the shortfall is given superpriority by §507(b). It takes precedence over all other claims allowable as administrative expenses.

However, Mortimer Post's claim has also been given a heightened level of priority under §364(c)(1), and this priority is senior to that granted by §507(b). This is apparent from a comparison of the wording of §§507(b) and 364(c)(1). While §507(b) gives Mayday's claim "priority over every other claim allowable under [§507(a)(2)]," §364(c)(1) gives Mortimer Post's claim "priority over any or all administrative expenses of the kind specified in . . . §507(b)." In other words, Mortimer Post's claim is placed above all administrative expenses, including Mayday's superpriority claim. The fund of $1.5 million is less than Mortimer Post's $2 million claim. As a result, the full fund is paid to Mortimer Post, leaving an unsatisfied balance of $500,000. Mayday receives no payment at all on its deficiency of $200,000, so the backup to its adequate protection failed. In addition, unsecured creditors of the estate, both priority[3] and general, have borne the risk of the debtor's failure, because the payment of the postpetition loan has consumed the entire fund and left nothing for the payment of claims.

---

3. As noted in section 17.3.2, BAPCPA elevated domestic support obligations to first priority over administrative expenses. This has no impact in this case because the debtor is a corporation. However, if the debtor had been an individual who owes domestic support obligations, both superpriority claims would have ranked below those obligations.

Executory Contracts and Unexpired Leases

§18.1 INTRODUCTION

The trustee's duties and powers in dealing with executory contracts and unexpired leases are set out in §365 — a long, confusing section, full of detail, subtleties, and gaps. It consists of general provisions as well as subsections that relate to particular types of contract, including, amongst others, leases of nonresidential real property, shopping centers, and nonconsumer personal property. This book focuses on general principles and does not cover these specific types of contract.

The essential goal of §365 is similar to that of §§363 and 364: to empower the trustee to take best advantage of the rights and assets of the estate while affording some protection to the countervailing interests held by other parties. Many of the provisions of §365 attempt to balance the good of the estate against the other party's right to receive the benefit of its bargain.

Being part of Ch. 3, §365 applies in all forms of bankruptcy, but its operation and importance in each case depends on the nature of the debtor's prepetition affairs and the form of bankruptcy relief sought. Although §365 is often most significant in Ch. 11 cases, because Ch. 11 debtors often have many outstanding contractual relationships, one should fully expect to find it arising in bankruptcies under other chapters as well. When §365 is used in a Ch. 11 case, the usual rule applies that the trustee's function is exercised by the debtor in possession unless the court orders the appointment of a trustee for cause. In most situations, the court must approve the assumption or

423

rejection of an executory contract. The estate is obliged to notify the other contracting party of its election, and the other party has the opportunity to object to the proposed action.

§18.2 THE MEANING OF "EXECUTORY CONTRACT" AND "UNEXPIRED LEASE"

The Code does not define "executory contract" and "unexpired lease." The standard definition of executory contract, known as the "Countryman definition," derives from a test expounded by Professor Countryman in a 1973 law review article: A contract is executory if the obligations of both parties are so far unperformed that the failure of either to perform would be a material breach. In other words, a contract only qualifies as executory for bankruptcy purposes if, at the time of bankruptcy, both parties had material obligations outstanding. If either had fully or substantially performed, the contract is no longer executory and should not be dealt with under §365. Similarly, if the contract had terminated prior to bankruptcy, either because its term had ended or because one of the parties rightfully canceled it, it is not executory. The Countryman test can be difficult to apply and its results can be unpredictable where the materiality of the outstanding obligations is unclear. A contract is less likely to be treated as executory where one of the parties has paid its monetary obligations in full, but this is not dispositive. As the court pointed out in In re Aerobox Composite Structures, LLC, 373 B.R. 135 (Bankr. D.N.M. 2007), there could still be significant nonmonetary obligations to be performed by that party.

The Countryman definition is approved in the legislative history of §365 and is the standard test for executory contracts used by many courts. However, some courts have moved away from the test in favor of a more functional approach that looks not only at the materiality of the unperformed portion of the contract, but also takes into account the impact on the estate of allowing the trustee to assume or reject the contract. This approach is motivated by the concern that a rigid test of materiality, that examines only the contractual significance of outstanding mutual performances, may make some contracts unassumable because one side has substantially performed. As the principal goal of assumption or rejection of an executory contract is to benefit the estate, a court should consider not merely if there has been substantial performance, but also what effect the determination of executoriness will have on the estate, the interests of creditors, and the debtor's prospect of rehabilitation. This thinking is expressed, for example, in In re Riodizio, Inc., 204 B.R. 417 (Bankr. S.D.N.Y. 1997). For an example of a contrary case that rejects the functional approach and continues to apply the Countryman test, see BNY *Capital Funding, LLC*, 345 B.R. 549 (E.D. Va. 2006).[1] (*See also* Example 1.)

Section 365 refers to both executory contracts and unexpired leases, which is redundant because an unexpired lease is a form of executory contract. Some specific types of leases are given special treatment, as mentioned in section 18.3, but except for that, the same general principles apply whether the executory contract is a lease or some other kind of agreement. To avoid constant repetition of the whole phrase "executory contracts and unexpired leases," this chapter uses the term "executory contracts" to include both leases and other contracts.

§18.3 THE SPECIAL TREATMENT OF SELECTED TRANSACTIONS

As mentioned earlier, §365 contains general rules applicable to most executory contracts, as well as special rules applicable to specific types of contracts such as leases of premises in shopping centers, leases of nonresidential real property, leases of equipment and other goods used in business, timeshares, and intellectual property. The special treatment of particular types of transactions is generally justified on the basis that they present unique issues. For example, nonresidential leases and equipment leases are typically long-term contracts of high economic value, so the way in which they are treated could have a significant impact on the debtor's ability to rehabilitate its business and on the rights of the other contracting party. It must be recognized, however, that successful lobbying by particular industry groups is not entirely irrelevant to the creation of special rules.

This chapter focuses on the general principles applicable to executory contracts; it does not discuss any of these narrower transaction-specific provisions. However, it is worth noting that some of the specialized rules have caused interpretational difficulties in the general provisions. The most common problem is that where a particular rule is expressed in a specialized subsection but not in the general provisions, it is not always clear if that

---

1. The 1994 National Bankruptcy Review Commission recommended a far-reaching change in the concept of executory contracts. The Commission considered that the issue should not be whether a contract is executory, but whether its assumption or rejection best serves the interests of the estate. The Commission considered that if Congress declined to make this fundamental change, it should at least formulate a statutory definition of executory contract to dispel the confusion that has arisen in the judicially recognized definitions. Congress did not adopt these recommendations. The Bankruptcy Abuse Prevention and Consumer Protection Act of 2005 (BAPCPA) makes some amendments to matters of detail in §365, but it does not offer any guidance on the meaning of "executory contract" and does not change the basic concepts in §365.

articulation of the rule is just an express codification of a principle that applies to all executory contracts, or if expressing it in the specialized section means that, by negative implication, it is applicable only to that kind of transaction. The 1994 National Bankruptcy Review Commission recommended the streamlining of §365 to get rid of the clutter of specialized provisions, but Congress did not follow this recommendation and the Bankruptcy Abuse Prevention and Consumer Protection Act of 2005 (BAPCPA) did not make far-reaching changes to the section.

§18.4 THE ESTATE'S RIGHT TO ASSUME OR REJECT EXECUTORY CONTRACTS

In making provision for executory contracts, the Code distinguishes bilateral contractual relationships from unilateral contract rights. If one party to a contract has fully or substantially performed, all that remains is the other party's claim for counterperformance. Therefore, if the debtor had fully performed its contractual obligations by the time of bankruptcy, the outstanding performance due by the other party is simply a right of the debtor's which becomes property of the estate under §541. Conversely, if the other party has fully performed, the debtor's remaining obligation gives rise to a prepetition claim, to be proved in the estate and paid at whatever rate of distribution is due to claims of that class.

However, when material performance is due on both sides at the time of the petition, so that the contract qualifies as executory, the Code recognizes this not simply as a set of claims by and against the estate, but as a live relationship between the debtor and the other party. Section 365 gives the trustee the option of honoring this relationship or repudiating it. If the trustee elects to keep the relationship in existence, the estate assumes the contract, thereby adopting it so that it becomes the estate's contract. The estate is entitled to receive the other party's performance and is liable for the obligations undertaken by the debtor. The performance due by the estate qualifies as an administrative expense and is thus entitled to priority under §507(a)(2). See section 19.6.4.

The trustee's election to reject the contract constitutes a breach that is treated by §365(g)(1) as a prepetition breach by the debtor. When the estate rejects the contract, it rejects it in its entirety. It cannot reject some aspects of the contract while retaining the benefit of others. However, this does not mean that rejection is the same as rescission of the contract. Although the rejection is a breach, giving rise to a claim for damages and a discharge of any future performance obligation by the other party, it does not reverse the contract *ab initio*. Therefore, depending on the nature of the contract, it may be appropriate in some transactions for rejection to terminate performance only prospectively, so that the parties retain any performance that has already been rendered under the contract, and property that has already passed to the debtor under the contract to becomes property of the estate. See *Thompkins v. Lil' Joe Records, Inc.*, 476 F.3d 1294 (11th Cir. 2007). See also section 18.11. Upon rejection, the other party to the contract becomes a creditor (it is specifically included in the definition of "creditor" in §101(10)(B)), and its claim for damages for breach of contract is classed by §502(g) as a general unsecured prepetition claim. It is paid in the bankruptcy distribution at whatever fractional rate is due to such claims. Some claimants do even worse than this: §502(b)(6) and (7) limit damage claims for the unexpired period of real property leases and employment contracts so that the rejection of these long-term contracts does not result in excessive claims against the general fund of the estate. Because the estate pays damages at the reduced rate payable to unsecured claims, the estate is able to commit a more profitable breach than the debtor would have been able to do outside of bankruptcy.

If the estate first assumes a contract and later rejects it, the rejection is the estate's breach and the other party's damages are treated as an administrative expense under §365(g)(2). These damages are measured at the time of rejection or, if a rehabilitation case was converted to Ch. 7 between assumption and rejection, at the time of conversion.

In deciding whether to assume or reject the contract, the trustee tries to serve the best interests of the estate. If the contract is advantageous and profitable or if, in a rehabilitation case, it advances the debtor's plans for economic recovery, the trustee should assume it. Conversely, if the contract is not on favorable terms, the estate could do better by using its resources elsewhere, or the contract imposes an unacceptable burden or risk on the estate, the trustee should reject it. It should be noted, however, that the trustee does not have absolute discretion to adopt an opportunistic approach to the contract. As indicated below, courts sometimes refuse to approve a rejection unless it is clear that performance would place an undue burden on the estate.

§18.5 THE PROCEDURE AND STANDARDS FOR ASSUMPTION OR REJECTION

Section 365(d)(1) requires the trustee in a Ch. 7 case to assume or reject the contract within 60 days of the order for relief or in such extended period as the court may for cause allow. If action is not taken by the end of that period, the contract is deemed to have been rejected. In cases under the other chapters, unless the contract is a lease of nonresidential real estate,[2] the trustee may make the decision to assume or reject at any time up to confirmation of the plan. Upon application of the other party to the contract, the court can require the trustee to make an earlier decision.

An affirmative decision to assume or reject must be approved by the court following a motion by the trustee on notice. However, if the contract is deemed rejected because of the trustee's failure to act within the prescribed period, the rejection is automatic and does not require court approval.

The most widely accepted standard for the court's approval of the trustee's decision to assume or reject is the business judgment rule. The court will not interfere with the trustee's decision if it was based on a good faith, reasonable business judgment that appears beneficial to the estate.[3] *See* Example 2. In *In re Pomona Valley Medical Group, Inc.*, 476 F.3d 665 (9th Cir. 2007), the court said that the bankruptcy court's review of the trustee's rejection of the contract under the business judgment standard should be cursory, and focused merely on ensuring that the decision benefited the estate, and was not capricious or in bad faith. A more exacting review would put the court in the position of having to second-guess the trustee's judgment, which it is not equipped to do. Other courts have engaged in a more stringent review, particularly where the trustee seeks to reject a contract. They have refused to approve rejection unless assumption of the contract would be unduly burdensome to the estate. Where the bankruptcy filing was motivated primarily by the desire to use the rejection power to escape an unwanted contract, rejection may well not satisfy the good faith test. *See* Example 3.

§18.6 INTERIM PERFORMANCE

In many cases, performance may be suspended on both sides pending the trustee's decision to assume or reject. However, some contracts may involve continuing performance by the other party in the period before the decision is made and there is nothing in §365 that allows the nondebtor party to withhold performance pending the estate's decision to assume or reject the contract. For example, the estate may retain possession of leased property during this period. If the contract is ultimately rejected, the general rule is

---

2. As noted in section 18.3, we do not consider the special rules relating to nonresidential real property leases. These rules are designed to give lessors of commercial real estate (often high-value transactions) special protection.
3. Section 1113 provides special rules for the rejection of collective bargaining agreements in a Ch. 11 case.

that the other party is entitled to compensation, payable as an administrative expense, for the reasonable value of any benefit received. Reasonable value may be less than the contract rate, and it is only payable to the extent that the estate was actually enriched. Therefore, for example, if the estate retained residential premises but did not use them, no compensation is payable.[4]

§18.7 THE ASSUMPTION OF CONTRACTS IN DEFAULT

To assume a contract that is in default, the trustee must comply with §365(b)(1) by curing the default, compensating for any loss caused by it, and giving the party adequate assurance of future performance under the contract. The question of whether there has been a default is determined with reference to the contract terms and nonbankruptcy law.

Under §365(b)(2) two types of default need not be cured:

1. If the default is simply the violation of an ipso facto clause (explained in section 18.11), the default really cannot be cured without the debtor dismissing the bankruptcy case and becoming solvent. It would, therefore, be an absurdity to demand such cure, and §365(b)(2) does not require it.
2. If the default consists of the failure to pay a penalty rate or it consists of some nonmonetary default (for example, the debtor's failure to keep a business open during the hours specified in the contract), cure of that default is not needed for assumption.

Section 365(b)(3) goes to some length in expressing what is required for adequate assurance of performance in connection with leases of premises in shopping centers, but it does not otherwise offer guidance on what assurances of cure, compensation, or future performance are adequate. It is left to the court to evaluate the trustee's proposals for rectifying the breach and assuring future performance. The concept of adequate assurance of future performance is taken from UCC §2.609, which entitles a party to a sales agreement to demand such assurances when there are grounds for insecurity about the other party's ability to perform. Both under the UCC and in §365(b)(1)(c), assurance is provided by showing that resources are likely to be available for the discharge of the contractual obligations and performance appears to be commercially feasible. (There is some conceptual affinity between adequate assurance of performance and adequate protection, in

---

4. Section 365(d) contains exceptions to this general rule for leases of nonresidential real property and equipment leases.

that they both aim to reduce the risk to the other party of the estate's continuing commercial activity.)

§18.8 NONASSUMABLE CONTRACTS

Section 365(c) denotes three types of executory contracts that may not be assumed. The bar on assumption arises as a matter of law and does not depend on the existence or absence of a clause in the contract forbidding or restricting assignment.

§18.8.1 Contracts That Are Not Assignable in Nonbankruptcy Law

In the absence of consent by the other party, §365(c)(1) prevents the assumption of a contract if applicable law (that is, nonbankruptcy law) excuses the other party from accepting performance from or rendering performance to someone other than the debtor or the debtor in possession. Section 365(c)(1) therefore respects rights of nontransferability under nonbankruptcy law and enables the other party to resist assumption by the estate if transfer of the contract could have been prevented outside of bankruptcy. It is a general rule of contract law that contractual rights and duties can be transferred. (The transfer of rights is called "assignment", and the transfer of duties, "delegation".) However, the common law recognizes exceptions to this rule. For example, if the contract contemplates personal performance by a party, that party cannot delegate the duty to perform. Similarly, rights to performance cannot be assigned if this would reduce the other party's expectation of proper counter-performance. In addition to rules of contract law, other policies may motivate statutory prohibition on the transfer of certain contractual rights and duties. For example, contracts with the government can usually not be transferred by the other party.

The reference in the section to laws that excuse the nondebtor party from accepting performance from or rendering it to an "entity other than the debtor or debtor in possession" (with no mention of the trustee), raises the question of whether the estate's assumption rights are different depending on whether it is represented by a debtor in possession or a trustee. Some cases have held that they are not. If nonbankruptcy law bars the assignment of the contract to a hypothetical third party, it cannot be assumed by the estate, whether administered by a trustee or a debtor in possession. The reasoning of these courts is that the debtor in possession is a different legal entity from the debtor. This approach is called the "hypothetical test" because it focuses not on whether the party to perform the contract (that is, the debtor in possession) is functionally the same as the debtor, but asks instead whether a hypothetical third party would be allowed to take over the contract. For cases that adopt this approach, see *In re West Electronics, Inc.*, 852 F.2d 79 (3d Cir. 1988); *In re Catapult Entertainment, Inc.*, 165 F.3d 747 (9th Cir. 1999). Other cases have disagreed. For example, in *In re G.P. Express Airlines, Inc.*, 200 B.R. 222 (Bankr. D. Neb. 1996), the court reasoned that although the debtor in possession is a legal entity distinct from the debtor for all other purposes, it is functionally the same entity as the debtor where the performance of the contract is concerned. Therefore, if the debtor in possession will perform the contract itself, and does not intend to assign it, it is artificial to refuse assumption merely because the contract could not be assigned to a hypothetical third party. See also *Institute Pasteur v. Cambridge Biotech Corp.*, 104 F.3d 489 (1st Cir. 1997); *In re Aerobox Composite Structures, LLC* (cited in section 18.2); *In re Jacobsen*, 465 B.R. 102 (Bankr. N.D. Miss. 2011).

§18.8.2 Loan and Financing Transactions

Section 365(c)(2) forbids the trustee from assuming a contract to make a loan, to extend other debt financing or financial accommodations to the debtor, or to issue a security of the debtor. Limited in its scope, it does not cover all credit transactions but is confined to loan and financing contracts. Therefore, for example, it does not include many types of transactions in which the debtor is given credit, such as leases or credit sales of goods or services. Courts construe §365(c)(2) strictly and refuse to extend it to contracts whose primary purpose is not the provision of a loan or financing. For example, in *In re UAL*, 368 F.3d 720 (7th Cir. 2004), the court held that a credit card processing agreement between the debtor (United Airlines) and a bank was not a contract that extended financial accommodations to the debtor and therefore was assumable. Although some extension of credit was involved, it was incidental to the contract's primary purpose of enabling the debtor to make credit card sales of tickets to its customers.

You may wonder why §365(c)(2) is necessary, because most financing contracts would probably be nonassumable under §365(c)(1) — the identity of the debtor is material and a lender would be excused from accepting transfer of the contract. However, the rule against assumption in §365(c)(2) is stricter than that in §362(c)(1) because it does not even allow assumption with the consent of the other party. The reason for this is explained in *In re Sun Runner Marine, Inc.*, 945 F.2d 1089 (9th Cir. 1991): The assumption of a financing contract is tantamount to postpetition credit, so assumption under §365 cannot be allowed to circumvent the creditor protections in §364.

§18.9 BANKRUPTCY TERMINATION OR IPSO FACTO CLAUSES

A provision in a contract that allows the nondebtor to declare default or to terminate the contract on the grounds of the insolvency, financial condition, or bankruptcy of the debtor (a bankruptcy termination or ipso facto clause) is ineffective in bankruptcy. The disregard of such clauses and provisions of nonbankruptcy law has already been discussed in connection with property of the estate (section 12.2.1), the avoidance of statutory liens (section 15.2), and the trustee's power to deal with estate property (section 17.2.4). These provisions reflect the general policy of preventing states or private parties from undermining the bankruptcy process through laws or contractual terms that are designed to take effect on bankruptcy.

Section 365 refers to ipso facto provisions four times: §365(b)(2) does not require cure of a breach of an ipso facto clause in a contract: §365(c)(1) makes such contract terms ineffective in deciding whether contract rights are transferable under nonbankruptcy law; §365(e)(1) prevents termination or modification of an executory contract after the petition on grounds of an ipso facto clause in the contract or in nonbankruptcy law; §365(f)(3) prevents termination or modification under such a clause or provision of nonbankruptcy law when the trustee assigns an executory contract after assuming it. Note that §§365(b)(2) and 365(c)(1) apply only to contractual clauses, while §§365(e)(1) and 365(f)(3) cover provisions of nonbankruptcy law as well.[5] The bar on enforcing ipso facto termination rights comes into effect once the petition has been filed. If the ipso facto clause covered the debtor's insolvency or other adverse financial circumstances, and the other party validly exercised the termination right on those grounds prior to bankruptcy, the termination is effective to end the contract so that it is no longer executory when the bankruptcy case is commenced.

---

5. At first glance, §365(e)(1) and (f)(3) may seem to conflict with §365(c)(1), which generally upholds rules of nonbankruptcy law that preclude the transfer of contractual rights and obligations. However, the rules of nonassignability upheld in §365(c)(1) are general rules of law, while the ipso facto provisions in §365(e)(1) and (f)(3) are geared to take effect only on bankruptcy. *See also* section 18.13.

§18.10 POSTPETITION TERMINATION BY THE OTHER PARTY ON GROUNDS OTHER THAN AN IPSO FACTO CLAUSE

A contract may provide grounds for termination other than the bankruptcy or financial condition of the debtor. If valid in nonbankruptcy law, termination rights not based on an ipso facto clause are effective against the estate.[6] Also, some contracts (e.g., leases) create obligations that continue until the expiry of a set term. If the contract can be validly terminated after the commencement of the case, the other party has the right to take the necessary steps to bring it to an end. However, because the debtor's contract rights are property of the estate, the other party must, in most cases, apply for relief from stay before exercising termination rights.[7] See In re Carrol, 903 F.2d 1266 (9th Cir. 1990).

§18.11 PROBLEMS OF REJECTION IN PARTIALLY EXECUTED CONTRACTS

If a contract is entirely executory, rejection is a clean break: Contractual rights and obligations terminate on both sides, save for the nondebtor party's unsecured prepetition claim for damages. However, the nondebtor party may have begun performance prior to the debtor's bankruptcy and may be fairly regarded as having earned rights under the contract by the time of the petition. Where this has happened, it must be determined whether rejection operates retrospectively, terminating all rights under the contract, or prospectively, leaving vested rights in place and cancelling only rights to future performance.

In a few select situations, §365 protects vested contractual rights and confines the effect of rejection to the estate's prospective performance. If the debtor is the lessor of real property, §365(h) allows the lessee to elect either to treat the rejection as a termination of the lease or to remain in possession of the property until the end of the lease term. If the lessee chooses to continue in occupation, §365(h)(1)(A)(ii) preserves all the lessee's rights under the lease, such as those relating to the due dates for rent and other payments, the right to occupy and use the premises, and to sublet them. However, even though all the lessee's rights remain intact, the lessor is

---

6. Remember, however, that §365(b) permits the estate to cure defaults, so termination on grounds of default is subject to the estate's right to cure.

7. There is a narrow exception to this rule for leases of nonresidential real property.

relieved from performing any of its future obligations such as the provision of services and the maintenance of the premises. The lessee must still pay rent, which is offset against any damages suffered as a result of the non-performance of the lessor's duties. Similar protection is made available by §365(i) to a possessory vendee who purchased real property from the debtor under an installment sale.[8] (*See* Example 1.)

The fact that Congress has provided specifically for these transactions creates uncertainty with regard to all other contracts in which substantial rights have been earned by the nondebtor party prior to the petition. Application of the *expressio unius* rule of statutory construction suggests that rejection of other contracts terminates all rights under them, leaving the other party with nothing but an unsecured prepetition claim for damages. However, a better approach seems to be for the court to interpret the contract to ascertain whether it is severable into executed and executory portions. If so, rejection can be confined to the executory portion of the contract, leaving vested rights in effect. This seems to have been the approach in *Leasing Services Corp. v. First Tennessee Bank*, 826 F.2d 434 (6th Cir. 1987). That case was distinguished and not followed in *In re Register*, 95 B.R. 73 (Bankr. M.D. Tenn. 1989).

§18.12 ASSIGNMENT

In many situations, the estate performs the contract itself after assumption. However, it often happens that the most desirable way for the estate to realize the value of an advantageous contract is to sell it. Contract rights are property, and as a general rule, the debtor would have had the right to transfer property of this kind under nonbankruptcy law. (The word "assignment" is used to describe the transfer of a contract in its entirety. The assignment of a contract includes both the assignment of rights due under the contract and the delegation of duties owed under the contract.) Under §365(f) the trustee succeeds to the debtor's right to assign the contract. Upon assignment of the contract, the purchaser of the contract (the assignee) acquires all the estate's rights under the contract, and assumes all its duties of future performance. Section 365(k) relieves the estate of all liability for postassignment breaches. (The estate is therefore in a better position than a delegating party would be under nonbankruptcy law. Outside of bankruptcy, delegation does not usually release the delegator

---

8. *See also* §365(h) and (i) and §365(n), which contain similar provisions for time-shares and intellectual property licenses.

from its responsibility under the contract, and it could be liable for damages if the delegate fails to perform properly.)

To assign the contract, the estate must first assume it, so that all the limitations on and qualifications for assumption apply. Section 365(f) imposes an additional requirement on the trustee where the contract is assigned after assumption: The trustee must provide adequate assurance of future performance to the other party to the contract that is to be assigned. This requirement protects the other party from being forced into a contractual relationship with an assignee who is financially unstable or otherwise unlikely to provide a performance that conforms to the contract. This is important because, as noted above (unlike the general rule in nonbankruptcy law), the other party to the contract has no recourse against the estate if the assignee breaches. Adequate assurance of performance must cover not only the monetary provisions of the contract, but must extend to all the debtor's material future obligations under the contract, so that the other party to the contract is assured of receiving the full benefit of the bargain. See In re Fleming Companies, Inc., 499 F.3d 300 (3d Cir. 2007). The test for deciding whether the assignee's performance is adequately assured is transaction-specific and based on all the circumstances of the case, including the nature of the contract, the assignee's business, and its financial ability to perform. The assurance does not have to be an absolute guarantee of performance but is merely a showing, on the preponderance of the evidence, that the assignee is likely to perform. In In re Resource Technology Corp., 624 F.,3d 376 (7th Cir. 2010) the court applied this test, and found that there was no adequate assurance of performance where the assignee would have to secure substantial funds to perform the contract and it could not be shown that the assignee would be able to secure such funds.

As stated in section 18.8, §365(c)(1) prohibits assumption (and consequent assignment) of a contract by the trustee if, irrespective of the contract terms, applicable law excuses the nondebtor party from accepting performance from or rendering it to a person other than the debtor. Section 365(f)(1) is expressly made subject to §365(c), yet it appears to contradict §365(c) by making a contract assignable notwithstanding a provision in the contract or in applicable law that prohibits assignment. Clearly, both subsections override contractual antiassignment clauses, but §365(c) appears to uphold antiassignment rules of nonbankruptcy law while §365(f) appears to render them ineffective.

Courts have had trouble reconciling these provisions. Although there are a number of cases that offer somewhat differing approaches to the question of how they are to be read consistently, courts do in fact succeed in accommodating the conflicting language of the two sections. In broad terms, without attempting to account for the more subtle distinctions between the cases, the difference between the sections lies in the distinction between the general and the particular. Section 365(f) invalidates contractual antiassignment clauses, and also overrides nonbankruptcy laws that generally uphold antiassignment clauses in contracts, or generally prohibit the assignment of contract rights. By contrast, section 365(c) gives effect to nonbankruptcy law that makes certain specific types of contract unassignable, whether or not the contract contains an antiassignment clause. In short, although §365(f) generally renders ineffective antiassignment clauses and nonbankruptcy laws that preclude assignment, this disregard of nonbankruptcy law is not absolute. It is qualified by §365(c) when the rule of nonbankruptcy law is designed to protect the legitimate expectations of the nondebtor party in circumstances where the transfer of a particular type of contract would damage those expectations. For some cases that discuss this issue, see In re Pioneer Ford Sales, Inc., 729 F.2d 27 (1st Cir. 1984); In re Magness, 972 F.2d 689 (6th Cir. 1992); In re Claremont Acquisition Corp., 186 B.R. 977 (C.D. Cal. 1995); In re CFLC, Inc., 89 F.3d 673 (9th Cir. 1996). See also Example 5.

Examples

1. Alice N. Vendorland sold a house to Wendy Vendee under a land sale contract. In terms of the contract, Wendy is obliged to pay the price of the land in installments over several years. Wendy occupied the property immediately after execution of the contract. Alice has no duty under the contract to maintain the property or perform other services. Her only outstanding obligation is to transfer title to the property when all payments have been made.

   Alice has become bankrupt. The contract still has a few years to run before Wendy is due to complete her payments. The property has appreciated since the sale, and Alice's trustee wishes to reject the contract so that the property can be recovered by the estate and resold at a higher price.
   a. Is this contract executory?
   b. If so, can the trustee reacquire the property by rejecting the contract?

2. Jack Pott owned some land on which he decided to build a house. He entered into a construction financing contract with Fairweather Funding, Inc., under which Fairweather agreed to lend him funds to pay for the building. The contract provided for advances to be made in the form of direct payments to the contractor as work progressed. Fairweather recorded a mortgage on the property at the time of the contract to secure the advances to be made. Jack then contracted with Housebound, Inc. for construction of the house.

   After the house had been half built and Fairweather had advanced about half of the loan, Jack filed a Ch. 11 petition. Property values have appreciated, and if the house is completed, the property can be sold for a good profit. Jack, as debtor in possession, would like to assume both the financing contract and the construction contract so that he can finish the house. May he do so?

3. Martin A. Idle is an actor. He recently contracted with a public broadcasting station to perform the role of Hamlet in a television production of that play. Shortly before filming was to begin, Martin received an irresistible offer to play the principal heartthrob in a prime-time soap opera, which would give him national exposure, fame, and fortune. He cannot work on both productions at the same time.

   Martin filed a Ch. 11 petition and, as debtor in possession, he immediately rejected the contract with the public broadcasting station so that he can accept the offer of the other contract. Can he do this?

4. Sandy Trapp is a member of a country club. To avoid congestion on its golf course, the club distinguishes general membership from golf membership and restricts golf privileges to a strictly limited number of people. Golf membership has been fully subscribed for decades, and new admissions can only occur when existing members leave. As a result, golf privileges are prized, and people who desire them have to wait for years. To ensure an equitable and orderly succession to vacancies, the club maintains a waiting list and fills openings in golf membership in order of seniority.

   Sandy holds a coveted golf membership. He has filed a Ch. 7 petition. His trustee has discovered that several people who are not near the top of the list are eager to buy Sandy's membership and are willing to bid against each other for it. The trustee realizes that the sale of the membership will bring substantial funds into the estate. The trustee seeks to assume Sandy's golf membership and to sell (assign) it to the highest bidder. The country club objects.

   May the trustee assume and assign Sandy's golf membership?

Explanations

1. a. The standard traditional test for deciding whether a contract is executory is that there are material unperformed obligations on both sides. In this contract, Wendy still has to pay the balance of the purchase price and probably has other obligations as well concerning the maintenance and protection of the property. Her outstanding performance is surely material. Alice's only remaining obligation is to transfer title to the property when payment is complete. Some courts have held that the transfer of title is a legal formality that is not significant enough to make the contract executory. See, for example, *In re Streets & Beard Farm Partnership*, 882 F.2d 233 (7th Cir. 1989). Other courts have disagreed,

and have held that because a failure to deliver title would be a material breach, the duty to transfer title makes the contract executory. See, for example, In re *Ravenswood Apartments, Ltd.*, 338 B.R. 307 (B.A.P. 6th Cir. 2006). This difference of opinion shows that the materiality of an outstanding performance is a matter of contract interpretation on which courts can differ.

Because a focus on nothing more than the materiality of the outstanding obligations can be very rigid, some courts have moved away from the traditional test in favor of a more flexible "functional approach." This continues to take the materiality of outstanding obligations into account, but treats this as a guideline rather than a firm test, and also examines the nature of the contract and the impact on the estate of classifying it as executed or executory.

It has been argued that a land sale contract should not be treated as an executory contract at all because it is analogous to a credit sale of the property secured by a mortgage and should therefore be regarded simply as a secured claim by or against the estate and not be dealt with under §365. Some courts have accepted this argument, and others have not. In In re *Terrel*, 892 F.2d 469 (6th Cir. 1989), the court, while conceding the merit of the analogy, pointed out that the transactions are legally quite distinct and should not be treated alike in the absence of Code authority. Whatever approach is taken, if the contract is executory, it must be dealt with under §365. If not, the contract rights are property of the estate.

b. If the contract is executory, it falls within the special rule in §365(i) for the protection of a possessory purchaser of real property. Even if the trustee rejects the contract, Wendy is entitled to remain in possession of it and to complete her purchase under the terms of the contract. Therefore, in the present case the characterization of the contract as executory does not enable the trustee to reacquire the property. (If the contract was not covered by §365(i), the question raised in section 18.11 would have arisen: Could the estate terminate all Wendy's contract rights by rejection, thereby reacquiring the property for resale at a better price and leaving Wendy with a claim for damages to be paid at the rate payable to unsecured prepetition creditors? To avoid the harshness of such a result, the court might sever the contract into executed and executory portions, so as to give rejection prospective effect only. In other words, the court could reach the same result as that prescribed expressly by §365(i).)

2. Both contracts are unquestionably executory. The estate cannot assume the financing contract; it clearly falls within the exception to assumption in §365(c)(2). As the financing contract cannot be assumed, Fairweather cannot be compelled to provide further funds. The advances already

made are a secured prepetition claim against the estate. Section 365(c)(2) does not authorize assumption, even with the consent of Fairweather. However, if the property has in fact appreciated so that Fairweather is assured of the full benefit of its bargain, Jack may be able to persuade it to provide the remaining funds under a new credit agreement negotiated and approved in terms of §364.

The construction contract is assumable, but if the estate cannot obtain the needed financing it may not be able to perform its obligations to Housebound. There apparently has not been a default in the contract, so Housebound is not entitled to adequate assurance of performance under §365(b). However, to obtain court approval of the assumption on the business judgment standard, Jack must show that the estate has the means to perform its obligations under the contract and that assumption is likely to benefit the estate. Ultimate benefit to the estate can be established by evidence of appreciating value, but unless Jack can arrange postpetition financing, either with Fairweather or with another lender, he cannot demonstrate a source of funding for progress payments under the contract. (In assuming the contract, the estate cannot modify its terms, so Jack cannot force Housebound to defer payment until the property is sold.)

3. Good try, sweet prince, but this tactic may not work. Martin, in his capacity as debtor in possession, is using §365 to reject the *Hamlet* contract so that he can accept the offer, in his personal capacity, to star in the soap opera. The issue is whether it should be treated as an abuse of the Code for a debtor to file bankruptcy for the primary purpose of using §365 to escape an unwanted contract. In *In re Carrere*, 64 B.R. 156 (Bankr. C.D. Cal. 1986), which inspired this Example, the court refused to approve the rejection. Although the court relied on a rather technical analysis to find that the trustee had no standing to reject a personal services contract, the underlying principle of the decision is that §365 is supposed to be used to benefit the estate, not to let the debtor out of a contract for personal services. Other courts have allowed the estate to reject such contracts, at least where the debtor was genuinely in need of relief from financial adversity and was not solely motivated by the purpose of getting rid of the contractual obligation. See, for example, *In re Taylor*, 913 F.2d 102 (3d Cir. 1990); *All Blacks B.V. v. Gruntruck*, 199 B.R. 970 (W.D. Wash. 1996). BAPCPA did not make any amendment to the Code to address this issue. However, a court may find some guidance in §707(b)(3).[9] That section includes, as one of the factors to be considered

---

9. Section 707(b)(3) is discussed in section 9.8.5. It deals with the grounds for dismissing a Ch. 7 consumer case for abuse where the presumption of abuse (the means test) is inapplicable or rebutted.

in deciding if a Ch. 7 consumer case should be dismissed for abuse, whether the debtor seeks to reject a personal services contract and the financial need for such rejection. Although this provision is not directly relevent here because Martin's debts may not be primarily consumer debts, it does signal Congress's approach to this kind of conduct.

4. This question is a simplified version of the facts in In re Magness, 972 F.2d 689 (6th Cir. 1992), cited in section 18.12. In that case, the court characterized the debtor's golf membership as an executory contract in which both parties had material outstanding obligations: the debtor's payment of dues and the club's provision of golfing facilities. The court's central focus was the reconciliation of §362(c)(1), which upholds rules of nonbankruptcy law excusing the nondebtor party from accepting the assignment and assumption of a contract, and §362(f)(1) which overrides antiassignment provisions in contracts and nonbankruptcy law. The court held that while §362(f) sets out the general rule disregarding barriers to assignment in bankruptcy, §362(c) recognizes an exception to this rule where the assignment of the contract in question would have an adverse impact on the rights of the nondebtor party, and nonbankruptcy law protects those rights by permitting the nondebtor party to refuse assignment.

The court found that assignment of the golf membership would adversely affect the club's maintenance of an orderly method of filling golf vacancies, and would force it into a breach of its obligations to members on the waiting list. State law upholds reasonable rules developed by voluntary associations and hence would excuse the club from accepting the assignment of a golf club membership. Therefore, the court concluded, §362(c)(1) precludes the trustee's assumption and assignment of the debtor's golf membership without the club's consent.

Claims against the Estate

§19.1 INTRODUCTION

The subject of creditor claims and their ranking has arisen frequently in earlier chapters. This chapter focuses more systematically on the rules and principles governing the assertion of claims against the estate and the distribution of estate funds or property to creditors. It begins with an explanation of the different types of claim that may be proved against the estate. It then surveys the process of claim submission and allowance, and examines the ranking of claims.

§19.2 WHAT IS A CLAIM?

§19.2.1 The Definition of "Claim"

Section 101(5) defines "claim" very broadly to include any secured or unsecured right to payment arising in law or equity. The claim need not be fixed, settled, and due at the time of the petition, but it may be unliquidated, contingent, unmatured, or disputed. To qualify as a claim, the obligation must give rise to a right to payment. A nonmonetary right (such as an injunction that merely mandates or restrains some conduct of the debtor without any alternative for a monetary remedy) is not a claim. Of course, many injunctions and other judicial and administrative orders do provide for a payment alternative because they might permit recourse to compensation if the debtor fails to obey the order. The question of whether an obligation of the debtor represents a right to payment, thereby qualifying as a claim, has two important consequences. First, if the obligation is not a claim, the obligee has no right to participate in the bankruptcy distribution. Second, liability on a claim is dischargeable in bankruptcy, but obligations that are not claims are not subject to the discharge. Therefore, the debtor's ongoing responsibility to perform the obligation after bankruptcy is dependent on the determination of whether the obligation is classified as a claim.

The significance of determining whether an obligation is a claim is illustrated by the problem of dealing with the debtor's liability for environmental pollution. In *Ohio v. Kovacs*, 469 U.S. 274 (1985), a state agency had obtained a court order, prior to the debtor's bankruptcy, authorizing it to clean up pollution caused by the debtor and to claim the cleanup cost from the debtor. The Supreme Court held that the debtor's liability to the state for the cost of remedying pollution qualified as a claim because it constituted a right to payment under §101(5). The situation in which the debtor has monetary liability to the government arising from environmental harm must be distinguished from that in which the government has obtained an injunction against the debtor prohibiting future pollution. The bar on prospective action is not a claim because it cannot be translated into money — the state agency does not have the authority to permit the pollution to continue in exchange for compensation. In applying *Kovacs*, courts have developed refinements on the question of when liability for pollution translates into a claim. In *In re Industrial Salvage, Inc.*, 196 B.R. 784 (Bankr. S.D. Ill. 1996), state law did not empower the agency to perform the cleanup itself and claim reimbursement, but confined the state to seeking a cleanup order. The cleanup order did not give rise to a claim, even though the estate would have to spend money to comply with the order. However, in *In re Torwico Electronics, Inc.*, 8 F.3d 146 (3d Cir. 1993), the agency had the power either to obtain a cleanup order or to perform the work itself and seek reimbursement. The state's option of performing the cleanup and claiming reimbursement qualified the obligation as a claim. In *In re Mark IV Industries, Inc.*, 459 B.R. 173 (S.D.N.Y. 2011), the state statute under which the agency ordered the debtor to perform environmental remediation did not provide for the alternative remedy of a monetary compensation. The debtor argued that its obligation to remedy the pollution nevertheless constituted a claim because the agency had a choice of statutes under which to proceed, and some of the applicable statutes did permit the agency to remedy the pollution and claim reimbursement. The court rejected this argument: The question of whether monetary relief is available as an alternative to a cleanup order must be based on the statute used by the agency, not on remedies that might be available under different statutes that the agency could have used but did not invoke. (Examples 2 and 3 deal with the determination of whether an obligation is a claim, and this issue is also discussed in connection with the discharge in section 22.2.)

§19.2.2 Unliquidated, Contingent, Unmatured, and Disputed Claims

Section 101(5) expressly includes unliquidated, contingent, unmatured, and disputed claims. A claim is unliquidated if its amount is not fixed and certain and cannot be calculated arithmetically from known data. For example, a tort claim arises upon commission of the tort, but is unliquidated until determined by adjudication or settlement. A claim is contingent if the debtor's liability is conditional upon the happening of a future uncertain event. The possibility of this contingency occurring is in the actual or presumed contemplation of the parties when their relationship is created. For example, when a surety guarantees the debt of the principal debtor, the surety's debt comes into existence upon execution of the suretyship, but liability on the debt only arises if the principal debtor defaults. (*See also* Examples 2 and 3.) A claim is unmatured until the time for payment comes about. For example, when goods are purchased on 30-days' credit, the debt is created on delivery of the goods, but it only matures at the end of the 30-day credit period. (Because the passage of 30 days is not an uncertain event, the debt cannot be considered contingent.) A claim is disputed if the debtor challenges the existence or extent of liability. The fact that a debt is disputed does not, in itself, make the debt unliquidated or contingent if the underlying debt itself is of fixed amount and unconditional.

A debt that is subject to one or more of these barriers to enforcement at the time of the petition is nevertheless a claim against the estate. During the course of the case, the issue or issues affecting enforcement will be resolved by negotiation or litigation: Disputes will be settled or adjudicated, and a value will be placed on unliquidated or contingent claims, as discussed in section 19.3. Bankruptcy inevitably alters contractual due dates for unmatured debts. Some may be accelerated, especially in liquidation cases, while others may be extended in terms of a plan of rehabilitation.

In re Rodriguez, 629 F.3d 136 (3d Cir. 2010) illustrates how a claim might exist even though there is no right to payment as at the petition date. The holder of a mortgage on the debtor's property argued that the debtor's obligation to pay funds into an escrow account to cover future disbursements by the mortgagee for tax and insurance payments was not a claim. The basis of this argument was that until the disbursements were made by the mortgagee, there was no debt due to it, and hence no claim. The court rejected that argument: Although the debt had not yet arisen, the terms of the mortgage obliged the debtor to make the payment into escrow. Therefore although the mortgagee's right to payment out of the escrow account was contingent on its paying the taxes and insurance premium, the debtor's obligation was nevertheless a claim in existence at the time of the petition.

§19.2.3 Prepetition and Postpetition Debts

Although the claim may not yet be enforceable at the time of the petition, it must, in most cases, have come into existence before bankruptcy. As a general rule, only prepetition debts of the debtor are claims against the estate. Debts incurred by the debtor after the petition are charges against the debtor's fresh start estate.

However, the estate itself does incur postpetition debts arising from the administration of the estate or the conduct of its business. Those debts are claims against the estate and, provided that they were authorized, are paid from the estate as second-priority administrative expenses. (This is explained in section 19.6.4.)

There are some claims that arise only after the petition but are treated as prepetition claims because they are linked to a prepetition transaction. For example, the rejection of an executory contract occurs after the petition, but it gives rise to a claim deemed by §365(g)(1) to have arisen prepetition. Similarly, a claim created by the avoidance of a transfer is deemed to be a prepetition claim by §502(h).

There are two situations, applicable only in Ch. 13 cases, where the debtor's personal postpetition debts may be included as claims against the estate. In the first, §1305(a)(1) permits governmental units to prove claims in the estate for postpetition taxes owing by the debtor.

In the second situation, §1305(a)(2) enables a proof of claim to be filed in the estate by a person who has extended credit to the debtor in a postpetition consumer transaction for the debtor's purchase of "property or services necessary for the debtor's performance under the plan." The property or services must be essentials such as medical treatment or the repair of vital property, and they must relate to the debtor's personal or domestic affairs, not to business activity. The creditor does not have to prove this postpetition claim against the estate. It has the option of treating the debt as a nondischargeable claim against the debtor's fresh start estate and collecting it from the debtor personally. However, the claim may be hard to collect. The debtor may have little cash to spare after making payments to the trustee under the plan, and the creditor cannot enforce the debt against estate property until the close of the case, by virtue of the stay under §362(a)(3). Therefore, the creditor may elect to prove the claim in the estate to ensure payment under the plan. The drawback to the creditor is that if the debtor obtained prior approval of the transaction from the trustee, or such approval was impractical, any balance of the debt unpaid in the Ch. 13 distribution is discharged by §1328(d). The creditor is barred from proving a claim in the estate if the creditor knew or should have known that the debtor could have obtained the trustee's advance approval and failed to do so.

§19.2.4 Claims against the Debtor's Property

When one thinks of prepetition claims against the estate, one usually assumes these are debts on which the debtor was personally liable at the time of bankruptcy. In most cases this assumption is correct, but §102(2) extends "claim" to cover not only the debtor's personal obligations but also claims against the debtor's property. It is possible that a right to payment constitutes a charge on property of the debtor even though the debtor has no personal liability on it. This may happen, for example, when a secured party holds a nonrecourse security interest in the debtor's property. (That is, the secured party's claim is limited to the collateral, and the debtor is not responsible for any deficiency.) It could also occur with some statutory liens, such as construction liens, which attach to real property even though the work was ordered by the prime contractor rather than the owner. Because the lienholder and owner have no contractual relationship, the owner has no personal debt to the lienholder. However, if the claim is not paid, the lienholder is entitled to foreclose on the property to recover payment. Section 102(2) makes it clear that such claims against the debtor's property are to be treated as claims in bankruptcy.

§19.2.5 Determining When a Claim Arises

As explained in section 19.2.3, the date on which a claim arises (comes into existence) is important. If the claim arose prepetition, it is a claim against the estate. If it arose postpetition it may be either an administrative expense or a claim against the debtor's postbankruptcy estate. The Code does not prescribe any specific test for deciding when a claim arises, and this must be decided with reference to nonbankruptcy law. The general rule under nonbankruptcy law is that a claim comes into existence as soon as the act giving rise to liability takes place. In most situations, it is not difficult to determine the date on which liability was created. However, in some cases, the question can be complex, particularly where the conduct that creates potential liability occurs some time earlier than the date on which liability actually arises. For example, say that the debtor, an industrial corporation, causes pollution prior to its bankruptcy. At the time of filing the petition, the pollution has not been rectified, and a government agency will clean it up during the course of the administration of the estate. If the government's claim for the cleanup costs arose at the time that the pollution occurred (the act giving rise to liability), it is an unsecured prepetition claim, but if it arises only when the cleanup work is performed, it is a postpetition claim. Liability for potential injury from a hazardous product provides a second example: Say that a customer bought a carpet from the debtor some time before the debtor's bankruptcy. Unknown to the customer, the carpet was impregnated with a toxic chemical that made the customer ill. However, the illness only manifested postpetition. If the claim arises at the time of exposure, it is prepetition, but if it arises at the time of the onset of the illness, it is a postpetition injury and not a claim against the estate. Courts have struggled with the question of when the claim arose in situations like this. Most courts believe that a test based simply on the date liability was created, or on the date that the debt was actually incurred, is not sophisticated enough to balance the fresh start policy of bankruptcy against the policy of holding the debtor accountable for injurious acts. To fix the claim at too early a date tends to favor the debtor's fresh start too heavily by making most liability for prepetition wrongs into dischargeable general unsecured claims. Conversely, to fix the claim as arising only when the debt is actually incurred tends to give special preference to the claim, either by treating it as an administrative expense or by treating it as a nondischargeable charge against the fresh start estate. To attempt a better policy balance, these courts have favored a more complex test under which the claim comes into existence at some point between these poles.

In re Chateaugay Corp., 944 F.2d 997 (2d Cir. 1991), involved a claim for cleanup costs by the Environmental Protection Agency (EPA). The court drew an analogy to contract law, because it felt that the EPA as regulator has a relationship with the debtor similar to that between parties to a contract. On this theory, the claim arises as soon as EPA becomes aware of the problem site and can reasonably contemplate the need for cleanup. Since Chateauqay was decided, many other courts have adopted a test based on relationship and reasonable contemplation to find that the claim arose at some point in the prepetition period. For the debt to arise prepetition, there must have been some identifiable prepetition relationship between the claimant and the debtor, either because they had a contract or were in some other form of privity or because the claimant had already been exposed to tortious conduct by the debtor before the filing. This was the test adopted in In re Piper Aircraft Corp., 58 F.3d 1573 (11th Cir. 1995), and followed in relation to future sex abuse claimants in In re Roman Catholic Archbishop of Portland in Oregon, 2005 WL 148775 (Bankr. D. Or. 2005) (not reported in B.R.). Some courts have refined the test further by adding a requirement of fairness. For example, in *Signature Combs, Inc. v. U.S.*, 253 F. Supp. 2d 1028 (W.D. Tenn. 2003), the court held that a claim for environmental cleanup arose, not when the EPA had a general awareness that there was a pollution problem, but when it became aware and could fairly have contemplated that the site would require remediation. In *In re Zilog, Inc.*, 450 F.3d 996 (9th Cir. 2006), the court applied the "fair contemplation" test to a sex discrimination claim. (*See also* Example 3.)

The problem of fixing the date on which a claim arose is particularly difficult where it is not clear, on the date of the petition, whether a claim will actually come into being. That is, there is a potential liability, but that liability is contingent on an injury that has not yet manifested itself and may never do so. For example, in *In re Grossman's, Inc.*, 607 F.3d 114 (3d Cir. 2010), the court had to determine when the debtor's liability to its customer arose. The customer's claim was for personal injury caused by asbestos in building products. The products were sold to her by the debtor some years prepetition, but the asbestos-related disease only manifested itself about ten years after the debtor's Ch. 11 plan had been confirmed. The court, overruling its precedent that a claim arises only when the injury manifests itself, and adopting the "relationship" test, held that the claim arose prepetition. Because the customer and the debtor had a prepetition relationship under which the product was sold, the claim arose when the customer was exposed to the harmful product.

§19.3 DETERMINING AND ESTIMATING CONTINGENT AND UNLIQUIDATED CLAIMS

In the normal course of events outside of bankruptcy, liability on an unliquidated or contingent claim is settled with the passage of time. An unliquidated debt will be made certain by negotiation or litigation, and a contingent debt will either become due or fall away, depending upon whether or not the future contingency occurs. In bankruptcy it is not always possible to allow the resolution of contingent or unliquidated liability to take its normal course, because the process of resolution may hold up the bankruptcy case. Therefore, §502(c) requires contingent or unliquidated claims to be estimated where necessary to prevent undue delay in the administration of the estate.

In some situations, the estimation can be provisional — for example, where the claim is likely to be resolved by normal means during the future course of a Ch. 11 case but an immediate determination of the claim is needed to fix the claimant's voting rights. In other situations, when the prospect of timely resolution is poor, estimation may have to be a final determination that fixes the claimant's distribution from the estate. A provisional estimation for voting purposes is a core proceeding, but the final estimation for distribution purposes is noncore and must be finally decided by the district court unless all parties consent to the bankruptcy court's jurisdiction. See *In re Roman Catholic Archbishop of Portland in Oregon*, 339 B.R. 215 (Bankr. D. Or. 2006). (This case also contains a helpful discussion of the process of claim estimation.)

If estimation is required, §502(c) leaves it to the court to decide on the most efficient and reliable means of making the estimation. This may involve a truncated trial, arbitration, a summary evaluation by the court, appraisal, or negotiation. The goal is to make as accurate an estimate as possible while keeping delay to a minimum. To liquidate an unliquidated claim, the court evaluates testimony on the debt or loss. The fixing of a contingent claim can be more awkward, because a contingent claim by its nature depends on the occurrence of an uncertain future event. Even if the amount of the contingent claim is certain (i.e., it is liquidated), the ultimate liability could be for the full debt or nothing, depending upon whether or not the event occurs. The court has to decide on the probability of the event occurring and must try to value the contingent claimant's chance of having a realized claim against the estate. If the contingent claim is also unliquidated, the uncertainty is greater still, and the court must resolve both the probability of actualization and the extent of the debt.

The estimation of contingent claims becomes particularly difficult and important in cases involving extensive potential liability for prepetition actions of the debtor that have caused actual or potential injury to a large group of people. One of the problems in these situations involves notifying potential claimants of the bankruptcy where the identity of many of them may not be known or ascertainable. Another problem involves the handling of potential claimants who may have been exposed to the harm, but who do not yet manifest injury. For example, workers in a factory may have been exposed to a harmful substance such as asbestos. Some may have already become ill at the time of the petition, but others do not yet show signs of illness, and it is not certain if they will become ill in the future. That is, the harmful act has been committed, but it has not yet manifested in injury, and it may never do so. These potential claimants could be treated as having claims contingent upon the advent of illness, or they could be treated as having no claim unless and until an actual injury develops. This latter approach seems particularly compelling where the contingency is very remote. However, its effect is to exclude the claims of the potential victims from participation in the estate, and to leave them with the possibility of a postbankruptcy claim against the debtor, provided that the debtor survives bankruptcy. (*See* Example 2.) The tests adopted by courts for determining when a claim arose, discussed in section 19.2.5, also have a bearing on the question of whether a potential claim can be treated as a contingent claim at all. As explained there, most courts apply some version of the "relationship" and "reasonable contemplation" tests to determine if a claim should be treated as arising prepetition. Where it is not yet certain that any liability will arise from the harmful act, these tests are helpful in deciding the question of whether potential liability that may arise from the act should be handled in the bankruptcy case as a contingent prepetition claim. The device of the trust fund has been used in some cases involving prepetition tortious conduct that has caused injury and may still cause injury to multiple victims. The trust fund, established under the plan, is intended to provide for the compensation of victims while permitting the rehabilitation of the debtor. All tort claims, both existing and future, are channeled into the trust as they arise. The debtor is discharged from liability, and the court issues an injunction compelling all future claims to be made against the trust. Although the creation of a trust ameliorates some of the difficulties mentioned above, it does not solve a number of problems. One of the most serious concerns is that the size of the fund must be estimated, and there is a danger that it will prove inadequate to cover all claims that arise. Furthermore, it is not clear that future victims who have not proved claims in the fund should be bound by the discharge.

In the Bankruptcy Reform Act of 1994, Congress recognized the need to make some provision for the handling of mass tort claims in bankruptcy, and enacted §524(g). However, §524(g) falls short of providing any kind of detailed or comprehensive system for dealing with mass claims. It does nothing more than authorize the issuance of an injunction to supplement the discharge injunction in cases involving asbestos-related injury, in which a trust has been set up in the plan of reorganization. Because the section does not deal with other types of mass claims, and does not fully provide for the creation of a trust, it does not make it clear that the trust device can be generally used to deal with mass claims in bankruptcy. However, the section says nothing to preclude the use of this device either and could be read to recognize it implicitly. In its 1997 report, the 1994 National Bankruptcy Review Commission noted the inadequacy of existing legislation and recommended that the Code be amended to include an express recognition of the power to deal with mass claims in bankruptcy, and to provide for a structure for dealing with them. Congress did not follow this recommendation, and the Bankruptcy Abuse Prevention and Consumer Protection Act of 2005 (BAPCPA) did not address this issue.

§19.4 THE PROOF AND ALLOWANCE OF CLAIMS

A proof of claim is the creditor's formal submission of a claim against the estate. After the debtor files the list of creditors, the clerk notifies them of the bankruptcy and calls for the submission of claims. (If it is clear that the estate is too insolvent to make any distribution to unsecured claims, the clerk informs them to save them the trouble of proving claims.) In a Ch. 11 case, a creditor need not prove a claim unless its claim is listed as disputed, contingent, or unliquidated, or the claim is unlisted and the creditor otherwise comes to know of the bankruptcy. In cases under all other chapters, unsecured creditors must prove claims to be included in the distribution. Unless there are good grounds for excusing the delay, claims must be filed by the date specified (the "bar date") to be allowed.

Because a secured claim encumbers specific property of the estate, a secured claimant need not prove a claim to protect the lien. Even though the debtor's personal liability is discharged in bankruptcy, the lien (that is, the right in the property) survives the discharge. This principle is codified in §506(d), which states the general rule that a lien is void to the extent that it secures a claim that is not allowed. It then goes on, in §506(d)(2), to validate a claim that was not allowed only because it was not proved. An undersecured creditor must prove a claim to receive a distribution on its deficiency.

Section 502 deals with the allowance of claims. Once a claim is proved, it is allowed automatically unless a party in interest files a timely objection to it.

Section 502(b), (d), and (e) set out the grounds for disallowing the claim. Most of the grounds apply only to the extent that the claim falls within their terms, so it is possible for a claim to be reduced, rather than completely disallowed. The ground in §502(b)(1) — that the claim is unenforceable against the debtor and the debtor's property under an agreement or applicable law — is the most general one, and allows objections on the merits of the claim under nonbankruptcy law. The other grounds are much more specific (but are not covered here); two of them, mentioned in previous chapters, serve as examples: §502(b)(6) and (7) limit damages claimable by lessors and employees whose contracts have been rejected (*see* section 18.9), and §502(d) bars claims by a transferee who has failed to return property to the estate after the transfer has been avoided (*see* section 14.5). The disallowance of claims for unmatured interest under §502(b)(2) is considered in section 19.5. Even after a claim has been allowed or disallowed, §502(j) permits it to be reconsidered for cause, so that the objector or the claimant can apply for a new ruling if new evidence, fraud of the other party, or other grounds exist for reopening the matter.

As a general rule, claims in a Ch. 7 case are paid near the end of the bankruptcy proceedings, after claims have been determined and assets liquidated. In rehabilitation cases, most payments begin after confirmation of the plan, and continue over time as provided for in the plan but payments could be made earlier if appropriate. (For example, administrative expenses are often paid for when incurred, and payments to a secured party may be needed to ensure adequate protection.)

§19.5 INTEREST ON CLAIMS

Section 502(b)(2) disallows claims for unmatured interest (i.e., interest on the debt that had not yet been earned when the petition was filed). This sets out the basic rule that creditors do not normally receive interest on their claims between the time the petition is filed and the distribution is made on the claim. However, this rule is subject to three significant qualifications:

1. The rule does not apply to fully secured claims, to the extent of any equity cushion. Section 506(b) (discussed in section 19.6.3) permits interest to be paid on fully secured claims to the extent that the value of the collateral exceeds the secured debt. That is, Section 506(b) permits a secured claimant to recover postpetition interest as long as there is an equity cushion in the collateral against which it can be charged. Once accumulated interest has consumed this surplus equity, the right to interest ceases.

2. Postpetition interest must not be confused with "present value" payments under plans of rehabilitation. As explained in Chapters 20 and 21, one of the standards for confirming a plan under Ch. 11, 12, or 13 is that the plan proposes to pay creditors at least the present value of what they would have received if the estate had been administered and distributed under Ch. 7. Because the plan provides for payment over time, this present value is calculated by increasing the amount payable on the claim to compensate for the delay in payment. Although this compensation is analogous to interest, it is not covered by the bar on interest in §502. In rehabilitation cases, §502 is essentially confined to the period between the petition and confirmation of the plan.

3. The reason that interest is not payable on claims is that where the estate is insolvent, so there are not enough funds to pay the principal amount of claims, it is pointless to pay interest on those claims. However, where the estate is solvent enough to pay the principal amount of claims in full, §726(a)(5) allows interest to be paid on unsecured claims to the extent that funds are left over after principal has been fully paid to all claimants. Therefore, it is more correct to think of a claim for unmatured interest not as absolutely barred, but as a low priority claim that is usually too low in rank to receive payment. Section 726 is part of Ch. 7 and therefore not directly applicable in other forms of bankruptcy. However, as discussed in

Chapters 20 and 21, rights to distribution in Ch. 7 form a yardstick for confirmation of rehabilitation plans, so the question of whether or not a claim is entitled to interest in Ch. 7 does have an effect on the rights of creditors in other chapters.

§19.6 CLAIM CLASSIFICATION AND PRIORITIES

§19.6.1 General Principles

The dichotomy between secured and unsecured claims is thoroughly familiar by now. In summary, secured claims are satisfied by the collateral or its proceeds. If there is more than one lien on a piece of property, the secured claims are ranked in accordance with priority prescribed by non-bankruptcy law, as discussed in Chapter 2. The general rule is that the most senior lien (usually measured by date of perfection) has first claim to the collateral, and junior liens are covered by the collateral only to the extent that there is any value left in it after more senior claims have been paid. In bankruptcy, ranking is not confined to secured claims: Unsecured claims are also divided into different priority categories. Section 507(a) lists ten priority classes in descending order. They are followed by general (that is, nonpriority) unsecured claims, which are in turn followed by low priority categories such as unmatured interest on unsecured claims.

The ranking of claims is the same in all forms of bankruptcy, whether under Ch. 7, 11, 12, or 13, but the rules governing the treatment of claims in Ch. 7 are different from those applicable in other chapters. In a Ch. 7 case, the fund realized from the liquidation of estate property is applied in turn to each class of priority claims in order of rank. A senior class must be paid in full before the next class is entitled to any distribution. The fund travels down the hierarchy until it is exhausted. If the fund is insufficient to pay all claims in a class in full, it is shared pro rata in that class. Because most bankrupt estates are insolvent, the fund is seldom large enough to cover all claims. Often, the insolvency is so severe that only claims in the top priority class or classes receive payment. Because general unsecured claims are fairly low in the order of priority, it is quite usual for them to receive only minimal payment or no payment at all from an insolvent estate.

The standards for plan confirmation in Chs. 11, 12, and 13 require all §507 priority claims to be paid in full unless holders of the claims agree to the contrary. Therefore, the ranking of different classes of priority claims does not have the same significance in rehabilitation cases as it has in Ch. 7. In the absence of the agreement of the holders of priority claims, a plan cannot be confirmed unless it proposes to pay them in full. However, this does not mean that the priority ranking of claims is unimportant in a rehabilitation case. As explained in section 20.7.2, the rate of distribution under Ch. 7 has an impact on the question of whether full payment is made at face value or present value. Even if the plan provides for full payment of priority claims and it is confirmed, the ranking of priority claims could later become directly relevant if the rehabilitation fails and the debtor is ultimately liquidated.

The existence of priority claims has a further impact on a rehabilitation case, in that it affects the minimum payment required for unsecured claims. As explained further in Chapters 20 and 21, the amount that would have been paid on unsecured claims, if the debtor had been liquidated, is used as one of the yardsticks to decide if the plan may be confirmed: General unsecured claims must receive at least as much under the plan as the present value of what they would have received in a Ch. 7 liquidation. This means that if priority claims would have consumed all or a significant portion of the fund if the debtor had been liquidated, the minimum payment required for general unsecured claims in the plan is correspondingly lessened.

§19.6.2 The Order of Distribution

Diagram 19a summarizes the order of distribution. The different categories of claim are explained thereafter. (*See also* Example 5.) Secured and priority claims are governed by §§506 and 507, respectively. The order of distribution for general unsecured claims and lower-ranking orders is provided for in §726, which, as noted earlier, only applies to Ch. 7 cases, but is indirectly applicable in other cases.

The Order of Distribution in Bankruptcy

A. Secured claims

Fully secured debts____Secured claim____Paid in full plus interest and costs (to extent of equity cushion)

Partially secured debts____Secured portion____Paid in full to extent of collateral

└─Deficiency____General unsecured claim

B. Priority claims

Note that the priority classes denoted with an asterisk have dollar limits. To the extent that the claim exceeds the limit, it is a general unsecured claim.

(1) Domestic support obligations
(2) Administrative expenses
First rank — superpriority claims under §364(c)(1)

> Second rank — superpriority claims under §507(b)
>
> Third rank — other admin. expenses under §503

(3)   Ordinary-course business expenses in gap period between filing and order for relief, in involuntary cases

(4)   Wages and salaries (limited)*

(5)   Employee benefits (limited)*

(6)   Grain producers and fishermen — claims against processor or storehouse (limited)*

(7)   Deposits for consumer goods or services (limited)*

(8)   Various taxes (limited)*

(9)   Claims arising out of federal depository insurance

(10) Claims for wrongful death or personal injury resulting from debtor's driving while intoxicated

C.   General unsecured claims

(Includes the balance of undersecured or limited priority claims together with all other claims proved and allowed and not covered by a priority category)

(1)   Timely filed general unsecured claims and late claims where creditor had no notice or knowledge of the case to file in time but filed early enough to be able to participate

(2)   Other tardily filed general unsecured claims

D.   Claims for fines, penalties, forfeiture, or punitive damages, which are not compensation for actual pecuniary loss

E.   Interest on priority and general unsecured claims

F.   Any surplus remaining goes to the debtor

Diagram 19a

§19.6.3 Secured Claims

a. The Definition and Nature of Secured Claims

The nature and effect of security has been given much attention in prior chapters. In summary, a lien that is valid under nonbankruptcy law and unavoidable under the Code is fully effective in bankruptcy, and is satisfied in full to the extent of the value of the collateral. Although the lienholder's right to foreclose is subject to the automatic stay, and the estate may retain the collateral in furtherance of its efforts at rehabilitation, the lienholder is entitled to adequate protection of its interest and to ultimate full payment of its secured claim. Priority between competing liens in the same property is determined under the principles of nonbankruptcy law.

Section 506(a)(1) defines "secured claim" as "[a]n allowed claim of a creditor secured by a lien on property in which the estate has an interest," or an allowed claim that is subject to setoff under §553. "Lien" is expansively defined in §101(37) to include any "charge against or interest in property to secure payment of a debt or performance of an obligation" The definition therefore encompasses all encumbrances, whether consensual or not. The requirement that the underlying claim be allowed reflects the principles introduced in Chapter 2 that a lien cannot exist in the abstract—it must secure a valid debt. Therefore, if the claim supporting the lien is invalid and therefore disallowed, the lien that purported to secure that debt cannot be treated as a secured claim. Section 506(d) reinforces this by voiding the lien on a claim that was proved but disallowed. Note (as explained in section 19.4) that the lien is not voided if the claim was not allowed solely because it was not proved. A lienholder is entitled not to prove a claim against the estate, whereupon the lien survives as a charge against the property even though personal liability of the debtor is discharged. (*See* Example 1.)

b. Deficiency in Collateral Value: "Strip Down" and "Strip Off"

Section 506(a)(1) states that a claim is secured to the extent of the collateral's value and is unsecured as to any deficiency. Because security is necessarily limited by the value of collateral, §506(a)(1) splits an undersecured debt into a secured and unsecured claim. If a secured party forecloses on collateral under nonbankruptcy law, the value of the collateral at the time of foreclosure determines how much of the debt is secured. It does not matter that at some time before foreclosure the collateral value was lower than at the time of foreclosure. In bankruptcy, however, the court may determine the value of the collateral at some time before foreclosure, so that there is a delay between the judicial determination of value and the price actually received at the ultimate foreclosure sale. Where that happens, and the collateral has increased in value since the valuation, the issue is whether the increase in value benefits the creditor by increasing the secured amount of the claim. That is, if the debt was undersecured at the time of the valuation, it bifurcated into a secured debt to the extent of the value of the collateral and an unsecured debt for the deficiency. Had the property been liquidated immediately, the secured claim would have been confined to the collateral's value. However, if foreclosure does not occur immediately, and the property increases in value between the time of the valuation and the foreclosure, the question is how to deal with this increase in value. It could be added to the secured claim, thereby reducing the unsecured deficiency, or the secured claim could be treated as having been pegged at the value fixed by the court, so that the appreciation redounds to the debtor's benefit. To illustrate this, imagine the collateral is a sculpture securing a claim of $6,000. Based on an appraisal, the court fixes the value of the sculpture at $5,000, which gives the creditor a secured claim of $5,000 and an unsecured claim of $1,000. Because the sculpture has no value for the estate, the Ch. 7 trustee abandons it to the debtor. The creditor has the right to apply for relief from stay and to foreclose on the security interest immediately, but it does not do this for six months. In the interim, the value of the sculpture has risen to $5,500. If the increase in value is added to the secured claim, it reduces the unsecured deficiency to $500. However, if the secured claim is pegged at the $5,000 value of the collateral originally fixed by the bankruptcy court, the appreciation of $500 belongs to the debtor. This is known as "lien stripping" or "strip down."

In *Dewsnup v. Timm*, 502 U.S. 410 (1992), the U.S. Supreme Court held that a debtor cannot strip down a consensual lien in a Ch. 7 case. The Ch. 7 debtor argued that because §506(a)(1) bifurcates an undersecured claim, the deficiency cannot be classified as an "allowed secured claim." This means that it must be void under §506(d), which voids a lien "[t]o the extent that [it] secures a claim . . . that is not an allowed secured claim." The court rejected this argument and found that the language of §506(d) was only intended to cover situations in which the secured claim itself had been disallowed, not where the secured claim was allowed, but a deficiency remains that becomes an unsecured claim. In reaching its decision, the court was influenced by the fact that pre-Code law treated liens as passing through bankruptcy unaffected, and that if Congress had intended to change that result, it would have more clearly provided so. The effect of *Dewsnup* is that a Ch. 7 debtor cannot use §506(d) to reduce an undersecured claim to the present value of the collateral as judicially determined in the bankruptcy case. However, the court was concerned only with a consensual lien in a Ch. 7 case and did not indicate if the same rule would apply outside of Ch. 7 or to a nonconsensual lien. Most subsequent lower court decisions have extended it to nonconsensual liens in Ch. 7 cases. See, for example, In re Concannon, 338 B.R. 90 (B.A.P. 9th Cir 2006). However, subsequent caselaw has not generally applied *Dewsnup* to rehabilitation cases. Courts have pointed out that *Dewsnup* is not reconcilable with the different approach to under-secured claims in a Ch. 11 case and should therefore not be extended beyond its Ch. 7 context. See, for example, In re Johnson, 386 B.R. 171 (Bankr. W.D. Pa. 2008); In re Heritage Highgate, Inc., 679 F.3d 132 (3d Cir. 2012). (We will see in Chapter 20 that in a Ch. 13 case, the U.S. Supreme Court has adopted an approach consistent with *Dewsnup* in relation to security interests in real property that is the debtor's principal residence. But that is based on the reading of a particular provision in Ch. 13.)

Since *Dewsnup*, a number of courts have grappled with its impact on secured claims that have completely lost all the value of their collateral. This occurs where there are two liens on property, and the value of the property is so low that it is sufficient to pay only the senior interest (in whole or in part) so that there is no value remaining to cover the junior interest. Debtors have argued that *Dewsnup* applies only to an undersecured lien, and that if a lien is totally unsecured on the debtor's bankruptcy the claim cannot be treated as secured at all and the lien must be void. (This is known as "strip off," as opposed to "strip down.") Courts have reacted differently to this argument. Some courts have accepted it, but others have held that there is no principled distinction between this situation and that addressed by *Dewsnup*. Therefore, provided the lien is otherwise valid and unavoidable, the debtor should not be able to strip it off merely because the collateral does not have enough value to support it at the time of bankruptcy. See, for example, *Ryan v. Homecomings Financial Network*, 253 F.3d 778 (4th Cir. 2001); *In re Concannon* (above).

c. Interest, Costs, and Fees on Secured Claims

We have already encountered the principle that if the collateral is worth more than the debt, the surplus is applied to any junior claims to the property or, if there are none, belongs to the estate. This principle is subject to the oversecured claimant's right to interest and costs under §506(b) that was alluded to in section 19.5. Once the surplus is exhausted, the secured claim's right to interest, fees, and costs ends.

Under §506(b) a secured claimant is entitled to postpetition interest[1] on its claim to the extent of any surplus value in the collateral. Since *United States v. Ron Pair Enterprises*, 489 U.S. 235 (1989), it is clear that interest is not confined to consensual lienholders but is also available to oversecured nonconsensual liens. The rate of interest is the contract rate. In *In re Payless Cashways, Inc.*, 287 B.R. 482 (Bankr. W.D. Mo. 2002), the court noted that while §506(b) applies a reasonableness standard to costs and fees, it says nothing about reasonable interest. Therefore, the court should apply the contract rate, and as long as that rate is permissible under nonbankruptcy law, should not inquire into its reasonableness.

If the lien is consensual and the agreement so provides, the claimant can also recover reasonable costs and fees from the surplus. Unlike interest, these costs and fees are subject to a test of reasonableness and the court can reduce them if it considers them unreasonable, even if the contract authorizes them in the amount claimed. In *In re Welzel*, 275 F.3d 1308 (11th Cir. 2001), the court said that even if fees provided for in the contract are reduced as unreasonable, this does not mean that they are disallowed. The unreasonable portion of the costs and fees cannot be paid out of the surplus, but they can be proved in the estate as an unsecured claim.

---

1. Although it does not expressly say so, §506(b) applies only to postpetition interest. Interest that had accrued prior to the petition is added to the claim. If the underlying contract or statute so provides, and if the collateral is valuable enough to accommodate it, the prepetition interest forms part of the secured debt.

d. The Costs of Realizing or Preserving the Collateral

The trustee may need to take action to preserve or realize collateral. If so, §506(c) permits the reasonable and necessary costs and expenses of doing so to be recovered from the collateral to the extent of any benefit to the secured claimant. To be recoverable from the collateral, the expenses must be directly related to its preservation or disposition so that the secured claimant benefits by the protection or realization of its interest. (*See* Example 4.) If the expenditure benefits the claimant in part, a pro rata share of it is chargeable against the collateral. Expenses payable under §506(c) take precedence over the claimant's right to recover interest and costs and reduce any surplus that would otherwise be available for those charges.

Although the trustee is able to recover these costs from the secured party, the U.S. Supreme Court held in *Hartford Underwriters Ins. Co. v. Union Planters Bank*, 530 U.S. 1 (2000), that §506(c), by its clear terms, is only available to the trustee. Therefore, if the trustee does not claim the expenses, the party who provided the services has no direct cause of action against the secured party for their recovery.

e. Valuation of the Collateral

The valuation of collateral is obviously crucial to the extent and treatment of a secured claim. Section 506(a)(1) states the general principle that collateral must be valued in light of the purpose of the valuation and of the proposed disposition or use of the property. That is, §502(a)(1) prescribes a rational, fact-based valuation that takes the circumstances and purpose of the valuation into account. For example, if it is apparent that the property is to be liquidated, liquidation value should be used, but if the property is to be used by the debtor or sold on the market, a market-based value makes more sense. Although this general principle is easy to grasp in the abstract, it has proved very difficult to apply. It is not always obvious how the proposed disposition or use is to be defined. Even where a market standard is appropriate, there is often no single market standard, which raises the question of which market standard to use. Finally, once the standard is determined, value is a factual question on which experts can differ.

The U.S. Supreme Court tackled the issue of valuation in *Associates Commercial Corp. v. Rash*, 520 U.S. 953 (1997). In *Rash*, the Ch. 13 debtor proposed to keep a truck that was subject to a security interest. Under Ch. 13, the plan must provide for the payment of the present value of the secured claim. To peg the truck's present value as low as possible, the debtor argued that the liquidation value of the truck was the proper measure because if the debtor's Ch. 13 plan did not provide for his retention of the truck, the creditor would foreclose on it and would sell it at a distress sale. The Court rejected this argument. Because the debtor proposed to keep the truck, the "proposed disposition" under §506(a) was the truck's replacement value — a market standard based on what the debtor would have to pay to acquire the truck on the market. The Court suggested that in calculating the replacement value, it may be appropriate to deduct the seller's costs of sale because the debtor already owned the truck and would not actually be buying it. The opinion in *Rash* was confined to the valuation of collateral in a Ch. 13 case for the purpose of determining the amount to be paid on the claim in the Ch. 13 plan. Although its standard of valuation is based on the general guideline set out in §506(a)(1) and is therefore potentially applicable in all cases, it is not clear how far it extends beyond those facts.

BAPCPA further confused the scope of *Rash* by adding a new subsection (2) to §506(a). Subsection (a)(2) partially codifies *Rash* and partly deviates from it. Also, the subsection is confined to a narrow situation — where the valuation relates to personal property that is collateral for a secured claim in an individual debtor's case under Ch. 7 or 13. It follows *Rash* by providing that the value of property in those circumstances must be based on the replacement value of the property at the date of the petition. However, it does not accept the suggestion in *Rash* that it may be appropriate to deduct the costs of sale and marketing from the replacement value. That is, in the situations in which it applies, §506(a)(2) calls for the use of the actual replacement cost on the market, without any deduction for the costs of sale or marketing. Notwithstanding, some lower courts have taken the saving of these costs into account to some extent by pointing out that "replacement value" is not synonymous with "retail value." Therefore, where the property could be replaced in the market through purchase from a private individual, rather than a dealer, the replacement value could be lower than what a dealer would have to charge to cover its overhead. See, for example, In re *Henry*, 457 B.R. 402 (Bankr. E.D. Pa. 2011).

Section 506(a)(2) does not contain a generally applicable definition of "replacement value," but it does define that term in relation to personal property acquired for personal, family, or household purposes (consumer goods). Where the property securing the debt is consumer goods, replacement value is the price that a retail merchant would charge for property of that kind considering its age and condition at the time of valuation. This has led courts to conclude that the valuation standard differs, depending on whether or not the personal property collateral was bought by the individual Ch.7 or 13 debtor for personal, family, or household purposes: If the property is not consumer goods, the replacement value must be determined from the debtor's perspective — the price must be based on what a willing debtor would pay to obtain the property on the market. However, if it is consumer goods, the replacement value must be measured from the seller's perspective. See In re *Henry*. This could lead to different values, depending on the purpose for which the debtor purchased the property.

Because §506(a)(2) is only a partial codification of *Rash*, and does not cover exactly the same ground, it leads to the confusing situation in which rules have been established for valuations in some circumstances that may or may not apply in others. In essence, the combined effect of *Rash* and §506(a)(2) seems to be that in cases under Ch. 7 or 13 involving an individual debtor, personal property collateral must be valued under §502(a)(2) by replacement value, not taking costs of sale into account. (*Rash* involved an individual debtor in Ch. 13, so §502(a)(2) affirms the holding but parts company with the Court on the deduction of the seller's costs of sale.) In all other cases, such as those involving real property in a Ch. 13 case, or real or personal property in a case under Ch. 7 or 11 where the debtor is not an individual, §502(a)(2) does not apply, but *Rash* might. Because *Rash* interprets the meaning of the words "intended disposition or use" in §502(a)(1), a good argument can be made that its interpretation is relevant beyond the narrow confines of the facts of the case. Nevertheless, some courts have applied *Rash* narrowly and have held that replacement value is not always the correct standard. For example, in *In re Henderson*, 235 B.R. 425 (Bankr. C.D. Ill. 1999), the court used liquidation value to decide the redemption price of goods under §722 because if the debtor did not redeem, the property would be foreclosed upon. See also *In re Zell*, 284 B.R. 569 (Bankr. D. Md. 2002).

§19.6.4 Priority Claims

While secured claims are satisfied by the collateral or its proceeds, all other claims are paid from the general fund of the estate. The Code recognizes ten classes of priority unsecured claims which are payable, in descending order, before general unsecured claims are entitled to any share in the estate. It is worth stressing again (as noted in section 19.6.1) that the general rule is that all claims in a class rank equally and are paid pro rata if the fund in the estate is insufficient to pay them in full. As you will see when we look more closely at the various priority categories, there are two exceptions to this general rule in relation to domestic support obligations and administrative expenses.

Prior to 2005, the expenses of administering the estate were given the highest priority. However, BAPCPA elevated claims for domestic support obligations, which formerly had seventh priority, to the position of first priority. As explained in sections 10.4.3 and 13.5.2, the Bankruptcy Reform Act of 1994 enacted a set of provisions designed to ensure that a debtor cannot use bankruptcy to escape domestic support obligations. As part of that package of protections, debts due to a spouse, ex-spouse, or children for alimony, maintenance, or support were given a seventh priority. BAPCPA enhanced this protection by ranking those debts (now encompassed within the statutory definition of "domestic support obligations" in §101(14A)) above all other priority claims. (As explained below, there are still some administrative expenses that have first-priority status — those incurred in relation to administering assets that are available to pay the domestic support claims.)

Administrative expenses (apart from those just mentioned) now occupy the second priority level. As discussed in section 17.3.2 and below, super-priority claims for postpetition financing under §364(c)(1) are at the top of this category and are paid first, followed by superpriority claims under §507(b) to compensate for a failure of adequate protection, followed by other administrative expenses.

The remaining nine priority categories are listed in rank order in §507(a). Every subsection of §507(a) uses the word "allowed" to qualify the claims in each priority class. If a claim is disallowed, it does not partic-ipate in the estate as a priority claim or otherwise. Also, many of the priority categories have monetary limits. To the extent that a claim exceeds the limit, it is a general unsecured claim. It is therefore possible for a single debt to be partly a priority claim and partly a general claim. Where a priority category has a dollar limit, that limit is administratively adjusted every three years based on changes in the Consumer Price Index. Section 507(a) is one of the sections included in §104, which provides for these periodic administrative adjustments. (See section 5.4.3 for a fuller explanation.) The amounts were last changed with effect from April 1, 2013, and will be next changed with effect from April 1, 2016.

The more common and important priority categories are explained below.[2] Congress has chosen to give these claims priority because it believes that the claims are worthier of payment than claims in a lower class. The policy of preferring administrative expenses makes practical sense because if they were not given a high priority it would be difficult to find people who would be willing to perform services for the estate. The other classes of priority claims are given priority because Congress decided that these types of claims should be singled out from other unse-cured claims and given special treatment. Although these priority claims are surely deserving, it is not always easy to see why they are more deserving than some other types of claims that have not been elevated. It is also not obvious why Congress has chosen to rank them in the particular order selected.

---

2. Other priority categories that are not discussed further are sixth-priority claims of grain farmers and fishermen for produce deposited with the debtor; seventh-priority claims for a deposit paid by a consumer to the debtor for future goods or services that were not provided (for example, a down payment or possibly even a full advance payment to a retailer or provider of services); ninth-priority claims based on a debtor depository institution's com-mitment to governmental units that insure deposits; and tenth-priority claims for death or personal injury resulting from the debtor's driving of a vehicle while under the influence of alcohol or drugs.

Priority rules interact with the provisions relating to discharge, discussed in Chapter 22. Where a priority debt is also nondischargeable, the debtor is benefited by the priority status of the debt. Because the debt has priority, it is more likely to be paid in the bankruptcy, which means that there is a better chance that the debtor will not have responsibility for it after the case.

First-priority domestic support obligations (§507(a)(1)). As noted above, "domestic support obligation" is defined in §101(14A). To qualify for this first-priority status, the debt has to satisfy the requirements of the definition, which covers debts in the nature of alimony, maintenance, or support, established by a separation agreement, divorce decree, property settlement agreement, court order, or determination of a governmental unit. The debt must be owed to or recoverable by a spouse, former spouse, child, the guardian or other person responsible for the child, or a governmental unit. The definition makes it clear that it is a question of fact whether a debt qualifies as a domestic support obligation irrespective of how the parties may have labeled or structured it. The types of obligation covered by the definition of "domestic support obligation" are quite wide. They extend beyond obligations payable directly to the spouse or dependent to include obligations to governmental agencies and others who have furnished support or assistance to the dependents. Courts have tended to read the definition broadly. For example, in *Wisconsin Dept. of Workforce Development v. Ratliff*, 390 B.R. 607 (E.D. Wis. 2008), the court granted first-priority status to the government agency's claim for repayment of food stamp overpayments made to the debtor, and used for the support of the debtor's dependent children. In *In re Rose*, not reported in B.R., 2008 WL 4205364 (Bankr. E.D. Tenn. 2008), the court adopted the majority view that first-priority status should be given to the fees of a guardian ad litem appointed to represent the debtor's minor child.

Section 507(a)(1) does not follow the usual principle of treating all claims in the same-priority category equally. It breaks the first priority into three subcategories, (A), (B), and (C), and prioritizes those categories. The claims that must be satisfied first are those listed last in subsection (C) — administrative expenses under §503(b)(1)(A), (2), and (6) — that is, the actual necessary costs and expenses of the trustee and the trustee's fee "to the extent that the trustee administers assets that are otherwise available for the payment of . . ." claims in subsections (A) and (B). While the exact meaning of this convoluted language is elusive, the idea seems to be that although other administrative expenses are paid after domestic support obligations, the trustee's fees and expenses that are directly related to the administration of assets used to pay domestic support obligations must be paid as a very top priority. Claims under subsection (A) are paid next. These are, in essence, allowed claims for domestic support obligations owed directly to the spouse, ex-spouse, child, or the child's legal guardian or responsible relative. Claims under subsection (B) are paid last. These are allowed claims for domestic support obligations that are assigned to or owed directly to a governmental unit.

Second-priority administrative expenses (§507(a)(2)). Unlike most other claims against the estate, administrative expenses are incurred after the petition has been filed. They are given high priority because the costs of administering the estate are meant to benefit creditors as a whole, and also because it would be difficult to find anyone to provide services or supplies to the estate without a reasonable assurance of being paid. The kinds of claims that are entitled to administrative priority are described in §503(b). The broadest group of expenses are the actual and necessary costs of preserving the estate referred to in §503(b)(1)(A). This encompasses all manner of expenditures deemed by the court to be reasonable in advancing the estate's interests, preserving or enhancing its assets, or furthering the debtor's efforts at rehabilitation. In addition to this general species of expense, §503(b) includes items such as trustee compensation, fees for professional services, and postpetition taxes due by the estate. Also, as mentioned in Chapters 17 and 18, the estate's obligations for postpetition credit and the performance of executory contracts are administrative expenses. The list in §503(b) is not definitive, and the court has the discretion to approve other expenses for inclusion in this category. (Administrative expense claims are illustrated in Examples 4 and 5(f).) Civil liability for wrongful acts by the estate's representative are commonly treated as administrative expenses because they are committed in the course of the estate's business. However, it is not clear that every liability for wrongful conduct by the estate's representatives should be treated as an administrative expense. For example, in *Pennsylvania Dept. of Environmental Resources v. Tri-State Clinical Laboratories, Inc.*, 178 F.3d 685 (3d Cir. 1999), the court refused to give administrative expense priority to a fine imposed on the estate for the unlawful disposal of waste, because this would have the effect of making junior creditors pay the penalty for the estate's unlawful activity.

For the most part, all administrative expenses rank equally in accordance with the general principle that all claims in a class are of equal rank. However, recall that there are two classes of superpriority claim that take precedence over administrative expenses. Superpriority claims for postpetition financing under §364(c)(1) occupy the most senior position, and are given "priority over any or all administrative expenses." Next in line are superpriority claims under §507(b), which have "priority over every other claim allowable under [§507(a)(2)]."[3] Thereafter, all administrative

---

3. These superpriority categories are explained in section 17.3.2 and Example 5 of Chapter 17.

expenses are of equal rank. The ranking of administrative expenses breaks into two priority categories where a rehabilitation case under Ch. 11, 12 or 13 is converted to Ch. 7. Section 726(b) subordinates the preconversion administrative expenses to the postconversion Ch. 7 administrative expenses. The reason for this is that the administrative expenses of the failed reorganization could be significant, and unless the expenses of liquidating the estate are given preference, there may not be enough funds in the estate to cover them. Most courts that have considered the question have held that when a case is converted to Ch. 7, the priority given to the Ch. 7 administrative expenses by §726(b) takes precedence over all priority claims arising prior to the conversion, including superpriority claims under §§364(c)(1) and 507(b). See In re Visionaire Corp., 290 B.R. 348 (Bankr. E.D. Mo. 2003),[4] in which the court held that the language of §726(b) is absolute in giving postconversion expenses priority over a preconversion superpriority claim under §364(c)(1). However, some courts read the language of §§726(b) and 364(c)(1) differently. See In re Mayco Plastics, Inc., 379 B.R. 691 (Bankr. E.D. Mich. 2008) (by giving a superpriority claim priority over all administrative expenses, §364(c)(1) elevates the claim over both preconversion and postconversion administrative expenses.)

Third-priority "gap" administrative expenses (§§502(f) and 507(a)(3)). In an involuntary case, the debtor is entitled to continue operating its business or conducting its financial affairs in the period between the petition and the order for relief or appointment of a trustee. (See section 9.6.3.) Expenses incurred by the debtor in the ordinary course of business or financial affairs are allowed as a claim against the estate by §502(f). Section 503(b) expressly excludes these expenses from second priority administrative expenses, but §507(a)(3) gives them third priority so they are paid immediately after administrative expenses. (See Example 5(c).)

Fourth-priority salary and wage claims (§507(a)(4)). The fourth priority provides limited protection to claims of the debtor's employees for wages, salary, or commission (including vacation, severance, or sick-leave pay) that was unpaid at the time of bankruptcy. (See Examples 5(c) and 6.) The Bankruptcy Reform Act of 1994 added to this category individuals (or corporations with only one employee) who, while they are independent contractors and not technically employees, earn a large portion of their livelihood (75 percent or more of their income) from commissions paid to them by the debtor for the sale of goods or services.

---

4. This case was affirmed as to this aspect of the opinion by the bankruptcy appellate panel at 299 B.R. 530 (B.A.P. 8th Cir. 2003).

The extent of fourth-priority claims is curtailed by both time period and amount. The modest dollar limit and relatively short temporal limit mean that the protection of priority will provide only a modicum of security to workers whose wages are unpaid at the time of bankruptcy. There is a $12,475[5] limit on each claim, and the remuneration must have been earned within 180 days of the petition or, if the debtor ceased business before that, within 180 days of the closing of the business. To the extent that the employee's claim exceeds these limits, it is a general unsecured claim. The fourth priority includes not only the employee's net earnings but also taxes due by the employee on those earnings, which should be withheld from her pay. These fourth-priority taxes due by the employee must be distinguished from employment taxes due by the debtor-employer and taxes that have already been withheld by the debtor-employer, both of which fall into the eighth-priority category. The fourth priority covers only prepetition earnings: If the debtor's business is operated by the trustee after the petition, the salary of employees for that period is an administrative expense, entitled to first priority. (*See* Example 5(c).)

Fifth-priority contributions to employee benefit plans (§507(a)(5)).

The fifth priority must be taken in conjunction with the fourth. The purpose of the fifth priority is to cover fringe benefits that complete an employee's pay package, but which do not count as wages or salary under the fourth priority. It includes contributions to employee benefit plans, such as pensions, life insurance, or health insurance. It is not always clear if a particular program provided by an employer for its employees qualifies as an employee benefit plan. For example, in *In re Howard Delivery Service, Inc.*, 547 U.S. 651 (2006), the Court held that premiums owed to an employment compensation insurer did not qualify as contributions to an employee benefit plan, but were rather in the nature of liability insurance premiums. Although the insurance did benefit the workers, it also benefited the employer by indemnifying it from liability to its workers for employment-related injuries. In *In re Consolidated Freightways Corp. of Delaware*, 564 F.3d 1161 (9th Cir. 2009), the court found that the reimbursement claims of the administrator of a self-funded medical plan did qualify for fifth priority.

Payments to employees for salary or wages under the fourth priority reduces the amount payable under the fifth because the fourth- and fifth-priority categories have a combined $12,475[6] cap per employee, with wage and salary claims paid first. Each plan's priority is limited to contributions

---

5. This is the amount as adjusted under §104 as from April 1, 2013. It will be adjusted again with effect from April 1, 2016.
6. This is the amount as adjusted under §104 as from April 1, 2013. It will be adjusted again with effect from April 1, 2016.

relating to services rendered by covered employees in the 180 days before the earlier of the filing of the petition or the cessation of the debtor's business. The priority is also limited in amount. It cannot exceed $12,475 multiplied by the number of employees covered by the plan, less the aggregate amount paid to covered employees as salary or wages under the fourth priority. If there is more than one employee benefit plan, then the total payable to all plans under the fifth priority, together with amounts paid to covered employees under the fourth priority, cannot exceed the number of covered employees multiplied by $12,475.

Eighth-priority taxes (§507(a)(8)). The eighth priority covers a variety of taxes due to governmental units, defined in §101(27) to include federal, state, and local governments. Taxes that receive priority under §507(a)(8) are nondischargeable under §523(a)(1). In rehabilitation cases, these priority taxes must be paid in full under the plan unless the taxing authority agrees otherwise. In a Ch. 7 case, if the fund is inadequate to pay eighth-priority taxes in full, the debtor remains liable after bankruptcy for any unpaid balance. When there are enough funds in the estate to pay claims up to and including the eighth priority, but not enough to pay general unsecured claims as well, the debtor benefits and general creditors are prejudiced by the eighth-priority status of non-dischargeable taxes. Payment of the taxes from the estate exhausts the fund that would otherwise have been distributed to the general creditors, while eliminating or reducing the debtor's undischargeable liability for the taxes. Under the right circumstances, therefore, the debtor's taxes are, in effect, paid by unsecured creditors. Although this may sound outrageous, bear in mind that federal and state governments have powerful collection rights under nonbankruptcy law too, and can usually trump unsecured creditors by perfecting a statutory lien on all the debtor's property.

A number of different taxes are included in the eighth priority. Many of them have priority only to the extent that they became due within a specified time before bankruptcy. Roughly speaking (and without examining the intricate qualifications of §507(a)(8)), eighth priority is given to income taxes for three to four years prior to the petition; property taxes payable in the year before bankruptcy; "trust fund" taxes that the debtor withheld from its employees' salaries but failed to transmit to the taxing authority; employment taxes due by the debtor itself and payable by the debtor within approximately three years of bankruptcy (which differ from withholding taxes in that the debtor, rather than the employee, is liable for them); certain excise and customs duties; and compensatory penalties due on other eighth priority taxes. (Example 5(e) illustrates the tax priority.)

§19.6.5 General Unsecured Claims and Lower Classes

As stated already, general unsecured claims share pro rata in any fund remaining after all priority claims have been paid. All unsecured claims that do not qualify for any priority fit into this category, as well as any deficiency due on undersecured claims and any amount over the limit on priority claims. (*See* Example 5.) Because most bankrupt estates are insolvent, general unsecured claims often receive only a partial distribution or are discharged with no payment at all. When the estate is solvent and general claims are paid in full, any remaining funds are distributed to the lowest priority claims listed in Diagram 19a.

§19.7 SUBORDINATION AND RECHARACTERIZATION OF CLAIMS

Subordination is the demotion of a claim. In nonbankruptcy law, subordination may result from agreement or it may be imposed upon a claimant by a court of equity. Section 510 recognizes both these forms of subordination in bankruptcy. Recharacterization of a claim could have a similar impact to subordination, but it is a distinct remedy.

§19.7.1 Consensual Subordination

A senior claimant may agree to subordinate its claim to induce another person to enter into a desirable transaction with the debtor. Say, for example, that a secured party has a security interest in the debtor's equipment. The debtor wishes to borrow money from another lender to upgrade the equipment, and the second lender will only advance the funds if it is given a first-priority security interest in the equipment to secure the loan. If the senior secured party believes that the equipment in its present state may not be worth enough to fully cover its loan, and that the renovations will enhance the equipment's value beyond the amount of the second secured loan, it may be willing to make an agreement with the second lender to subordinate its otherwise senior lien to that of the second lender. Section 510(a) recognizes such subordination agreements and makes them enforceable in bankruptcy to the extent that they are enforceable in nonbankruptcy law.

§19.7.2 Equitable Subordination

Courts of equity have the power to subordinate a claim where the equities so dictate. Section 510(c) authorizes the bankruptcy court to use principles of equitable subordination to reduce the rank of all or part of an allowed claim. If the subordinated claim is secured, the court may transfer the lien to the estate.

The most common basis for subordination is inequitable or dishonest conduct by the claimant that results in unfair advantage or prejudice to other creditors. Courts require both the elements of wrongful conduct and prejudice to be present. Subordination is meant to be an adjustment of rank to correct for the inequitable conduct, rather than a punishment, so the general rule is that the claim is subordinated only to the extent necessary to rectify the harm. For example, if a senior secured claimant caused harm to a junior lienholder by making a misrepresentation to it, the appropriate remedy is to subordinate the senior claim to the junior one. However, particularly harmful and inequitable conduct could justify a dramatic reduction in rank. For some illustrative cases, see In re Fabricators, Inc., 926 F.2d 1458 (5th Cir. 1991); In re Lemco Gypsum, Inc., 911 F.2d 1553 (11th Cir. 1990); In re Giorgio, 862 F.2d 933 (1st Cir. 1988).

Although the use of equitable subordination is clearly warranted where harm is caused by inequitable conduct, it is not clear if a court has the discretion to subordinate a claim on general equitable considerations in the absence of wrongful conduct by the subordinated creditor. In United States v. Noland, 517 U.S. 535 (1996), the U.S. Supreme Court cast doubt on the propriety of equitable subordination in the absence of inequitable conduct by the creditor. The claim subordinated by the bankruptcy court was an administrative expense claim for nonpecuniary tax penalties owed by the estate to the I.R.S. The bankruptcy court subordinated the claim, even though the I.R.S. had not behaved inequitably, on the grounds that it was unfair to pay nonpecuniary penalties ahead of the claims of general creditors. Although the Court did not decide if creditor misconduct must always be found as a basis for equitable subordination, it did hold that a court should not simply subordinate a claim because it considers it unfair to pay it in priority over claims in a lower class. Congress has set the priorities for payment, and it is not up to a court to use the equity powers recognized by §510(c) to reorder these priorities because it perceives the Code's ranking to be unfair.

§19.7.3 Recharacterization

Recharacterization has a superficial resemblance to equitable subordination but is conceptually different and distinguishable. Equitable subordination is the demotion of a claim in rank, based on the inequitable conduct of the creditor. Recharacterization is a determination by the court that a claim asserted by a claimant is not properly characterized as a claim but is more appropriately treated as an investment in the debtor. That is, recharacterization does not lower the rank of a claim because of the claimant's conduct, but finds that the claimant is not a creditor at all because the underlying purpose of the transaction was not a loan to the debtor, but an investment in the debtor. The focus here is not on inequitable conduct, but on the underlying substance of the transaction. For example, prior to the debtor's bankruptcy, an existing shareholder in the debtor provided funds to the debtor to enable it to keep operating. This transaction was structured as a loan. If it is established that despite the appearance of the transaction, its true nature was an investment in the debtor, a court can use its equitable power to declare the transaction as creating equity, not debt. The significance of this is that the advance of the funds to the debtor is removed as a claim, and is treated like an ownership interest. Unlike subordination, this does not just demote the claim in rank, but it reclassifies it so that it ceases to be a claim at all. The significance of the change is profound. As mentioned before, the interests of owners of the debtor rank below the claims of creditors so owners are unlikely to salvage any part of their ownership interest in the bankrupt debtor unless there is a surplus after all creditors' claims have been paid in full.[7] The test used to decide whether to recharacterize a transaction as equity rather than debt involves the examination of the entire context of the transaction to ascertain the true nature of the funding and the intent of the parties at the time that it was provided.

Section 510 does not mention recharacterization, so it is does not provide express authority to the court to recharacterize a claim. However, courts have held that the power to recharacterize a claim inheres in the court's general authority to disallow claims under §502 and to issue orders under §105. See, for example, In re Atlanticrancher, Inc., 279 B.R. 411 (Bankr. D. Mass. 2002); In re Official Committee of Unsecured Creditors for Dornier Aviation (North America) Inc., 453 F.3d 225 (4th Cir. 2006); In re Airadigm Communications, Inc., 616 F.3d 642 (7th Cir. 2010).

Examples

1. Included in the Ch. 7 estate of Lester Pay is a house worth $100,000, subject to a mortgage held by Mori Bond Co. securing a debt of $120,000.
   a. Must Mori Bond Co. prove a claim in the estate to preserve its rights or to receive payment of its claim?
   b. Assume that the trustee abandoned the property as having no value or benefit to the estate. Because the property has been abandoned, Mori Bond may apply for relief from stay and foreclose on it immediately,

---

7. This statement sets out the general principle. As you will see in section 21.7.3, there are some means in a Ch. 11 case for the owners of the debtor to salvage their interests.

or wait to foreclose after the case is closed. Lester commences proceedings to have the mortgage declared void under §506(d) to the extent that the debt exceeds the value of the collateral (i.e., by $20,000), and to peg the value of the secured claim at $100,000. Can Lester do this?

2. Cess Pools, Inc. manufactures pool chemicals. Some years ago it developed a revolutionary chemical that kept water clearer and brighter than any competing product. After the chemical had been marketed successfully for several years, it was discovered to be carcinogenic. Because it had been so popular, countless people had been exposed to it. Several hundred had already become ill, and an unknown number of people will probably develop cancer in the future as a result of contact with the chemical. In the face of this widespread tort liability, Cess Pools, Inc. has filed a Ch. 11 petition. Do the people with cancer have claims against the estate? How about the people who have been exposed to the chemical but do not have cancer?

3. In the course of manufacturing the chemicals described in Example 2, Cess Pools, Inc. discharged hazardous substances into the ground. These discharges occurred prior to Cess Pools' bankruptcy and have since ceased because Cess Pools no longer makes the chemicals. Shortly before Cess Pools filed its Ch. 11 petition, the EPA identified the polluted land as requiring cleanup. Although the EPA could have ordered Cess Pools to clean up the waste, it exercised its statutory right to restore the site itself and to claim reimbursement from Cess Pools. No cleanup work had begun by the time of Cess Pools' bankruptcy, and the exact extent of the pollution and the cost of restoration are not yet known.

   The EPA contends that its future claim for reimbursement following cleanup is not a dischargeable claim against Cess Pools' Ch. 11 estate, but will become a debt payable in full from the assets of the reorganized debtor. Is the EPA correct?

4. Prior to its bankruptcy under Ch. 7, Withering Heights, Inc. owned and operated an office building. The property is subject to a mortgage securing a debt that exceeds the building's market value. The trustee continued to manage the building for a few months after the petition was filed, pending a determination of its value and a decision on what should be done with it. Eventually the building was abandoned to the mortgagee as having no value or benefit to the estate. During the period that the estate operated the building, the power company continued to supply electricity that was needed to keep the building habitable by tenants and to allow its electronic security system to function. The electricity bills for this period have not been paid. How should they be treated?

5. Trickle Downs, Inc. owned and managed an apartment complex. A group of its creditors petitioned to place it in Ch. 7 bankruptcy. A week after the petition, an interim trustee was appointed. The order for relief was granted a few weeks later. The trustee has sold the apartment complex as well as other estate property, and the estate will soon be distributed. Rank the following claims that have been proved and allowed in the case:

   a. A first mortgage on the apartment complex, recorded ten years ago.

   b. A second mortgage on the complex, recorded five years ago.

   c. Salary due to the manager of the complex for the month prior to the petition and the month thereafter.

   d. The manager's claim for breach of contract, arising from the estate's termination of his employment contract a month after the petition. At that time, the term of the contract had two more years to run.

   e. Property taxes on the complex for the two years prior to the petition.

   f. An attorney's fee for services rendered to the trustee in connection with the sale of the complex.

   g. A claim by a landscaping service company for maintenance work done in the months before the petition and for damages for breach of contract arising out of the trustee's rejection of the contract for future services.

   h. Various claims by trade creditors that provided services and supplies to Trickle Downs in the months before bankruptcy.

Explanations

1. a. Must Mori Bond prove a claim? A secured claim need not be proved to preserve the lien. Even though the debtor's personal obligation is dischargeable, the lien survives the bankruptcy provided that it is valid and not disallowed on grounds other than the lienholder's failure to prove a claim. However, Mori Bond is undersecured. If it wishes to receive a distribution on its deficiency (provided, of course, that non-bankruptcy law permits a mortgagee to claim a deficiency), it must prove a claim.

   b. Is the mortgage void under §506(d) to the extent of the deficiency? Lester's purpose is to peg the mortgage debt at the level of the current value of the property — that is, to have the court declare that the undischarged mortgage survives the bankruptcy only to the extent of $100,000, not to the full extent of the debt of $120,000. The advantage to Lester is that if the property appreciates before foreclosure so that it realizes more than $100,000, any surplus will belong to Lester and cannot be claimed by the mortgagee up to the amount of $120,000. Another advantage would be that if Lester was able to redeem the property, the redemption price would be $100,000 rather than $120,000, irrespective of any appreciation in the property. The tactic being tried by Lester is called "lien stripping". As discussed in section 19.6.3, *Dewsnup v. Timm* precludes a Ch. 7 debtor from stripping down a consensual mortgage. Even though the reach of the case is uncertain beyond that, it clearly applies here, and the mortgage survives to the full extent of $120,000, even though Lester's personal liability is discharged.

2. The people who are already stricken clearly have claims against the estate. These claims may still be unliquidated or disputed, but they qualify as claims under §101(5). During the course of the case, their claims will be resolved by litigation or negotiation. Under §502(c), the claims can be estimated if the normal process of resolution would cause undue delay in the administration of the case.

The people who have been exposed to the chemical but are still healthy are potential claimants: The harmful act has been committed, but it has not yet caused physical injury. Some of these people will become ill, and others will not. As explained in section 19.3, they could be treated as the holders of contingent claims against the estate, but they might be treated as having no claim against the estate at all, which would leave them with a postbankruptcy claim against the debtor if and when they do become ill. Different courts have developed the different tests identified in section 19.3 for trying to resolve this issue.

The decision on whether to treat potential liability as a prepetition contingent claim or a postbankruptcy claim has significant consequences for claimants, the estate, and the debtor. If Cess Pools, Inc. has a good prospect of successful reorganization, potential victims may do better if their claims are treated as arising postpetition, because they can be asserted against the rehabilitated debtor when they arise, and need not be proved in the estate for fractional distribution. This classification creates serious trouble for Cess Pools, Inc., which cannot settle its liability in the bankruptcy case. If Cess Pools' prospects of survival following reorganization are not good, potential claimants are better served by having their claims treated as contingent. This allows them to prove claims in the estate so that they can share in the fund. (The same would be true if the debtor is to be liquidated: Because it will not survive the bankruptcy, the characterization of the incipient claims as contingent prepetition claims allows the potential victims to participate in the estate.) If the claims are treated as contingent, they must be estimated by taking into account both the likely extent of injury and the probability of contracting the disease.

3. Because the EPA has chosen to restore the site and claim the costs of doing so, its reimbursement claim is a right to payment under §101(5), and therefore a claim as determined by the U.S. Supreme Court in *Ohio v.*

Kovacs, discussed in section 19.2.1. If the EPA's claim is treated as a prepetition claim, it is a general unsecured claim against the estate. However, if it arose postpetition, it could be classified as an administrative expense or a postpetition claim against the reorganized debtor. It is therefore important to determine when the claim arose. As explained in section 19.2.5, the dating of the claim can be difficult in situations like this. It could be seen as arising postpetition, when the cleanup costs are incurred, or it could arise prepetition, when liability was created by the act of pollution. If it arises prepetition, it is a contingent claim (conditional on the EPA performing the cleanup), but a contingent claim does qualify as a claim under §101(5). In deciding when a claim such as this arises, most courts do not use a mechanical test to select one or the other of these times, but use a more sophisticated test based on the reasonable or fair contemplation of the parties, as explained in section 19.2.5: The claim arose when the EPA became aware of the pollution and could reasonably or fairly have contemplated that the site would require remediation. Our facts are not full enough to enable us to decide at what point the EPA can be taken to have contemplated that Cess Pools' site would require remediation, which shows that this standard is much more complex than a test based on an identifiable, discrete event. To answer the question, the court will have to conduct a factual inquiry into the history of the EPA's relationship with the debtor and the site, including the extent of its investigation and the action taken over a period of time.

The court's effort to date the claim performs the kind of policy balancing that was mentioned in Example 2 of Chapter 5 and in section 5.5: When bankruptcy policy pulls in a different direction from the policies served by another federal statute, the court must try to balance and reconcile the conflicting aims of the statutes as well as it can. The inclusion of the cleanup obligation as a claim in the estate serves at least two bankruptcy goals. It permits the debtor a fresh start by discharging the claim, and it advances the aim of evenhanded treatment of creditors by according the environmental claim no higher status than any other claim of its class. This must be balanced against the dominant goal of environmental legislation to ensure that the person responsible for pollution, rather than the public treasury, pays for its remediation. Treating the cleanup responsibility as a postbankruptcy claim will usually best serve this goal unless the debtor has no assets and no likelihood of rehabilitation.

4. Provided that the trustee had court authority to operate the debtor's business under §721 for the purpose of orderly liquidation, the electricity charges qualify as an administrative expense under §§364(a), 503(b)(1), and 507(a)(2). However, the trustee may argue that the

consumption of electricity was a reasonable, necessary expense for the preservation of the building that was incurred for the benefit of the mortgagee. As such, it is recoverable from the property under §506(c).

In In re Delta Towers, Ltd., 924 F.2d 74 (5th Cir. 1991), the case on which this question is based, it was conceded that the expenses were necessary and reasonable, which is probably true in the present case as well. The focus was therefore on the issue of whether they were beneficial to the mortgagee. The court emphasized that the expenses must be primarily for the benefit of the secured claimant, and that the benefit must be quantifiable and direct — it is not enough that some tangential or speculative benefit is conferred. The court concluded that no such direct benefit was received by the mortgagee. Its interest extended only to the property itself, and was not enhanced or protected by the continued supply of utilities that were not needed to prevent deterioration of the property or to maintain its realizable value.

The question of benefit is a factual one, and it does not inevitably follow that the present case would be resolved the same way as Delta Towers was. The facts indicate that power was needed to operate a security system and to allow tenants to inhabit the building. It could be argued that the security system protected the building itself (rather than only the tenants), and that failure to provide the tenants with services would have resulted in lease cancellations that would have reduced the building's value. The facts would need to be examined more fully to decide if these arguments are tenable. If the electricity costs were partially beneficial to the mortgagee, they must be apportioned so that only those attributable to the preservation of the property are charged against it.

5. These claims should be ranked as follows.
   a-b. The first and second mortgages are secured claims that will both be paid in full out of the proceeds of the apartment complex — provided that the property realizes enough to cover them both. If the property's proceeds are sufficient to cover both mortgages, their relative priority is not practically significant because they are both paid in full. As there do not appear to be interests in the property junior to the mortgages, any surplus goes into the general fund of the estate for ultimate distribution to unsecured creditors. However, if the property is not valuable enough to pay both claims in full, they must be ranked. The order of priority between them is determined by nonbankruptcy law, which most likely follows the first-in-time rule based on the date of recording the mortgages. Therefore, for example, if the proceeds are sufficient to pay the first mortgage in full but only to satisfy the second in part, the deficiency due to the second mortgagee is a general unsecured claim. Of course, the claims set out in (c) through (h) will only

be paid to the extent that there are funds in the estate. Therefore, once the priority rank of the claims is determined, each class will be paid in order until the fund runs out.

c. The manager's salary for the month prior to the petition is a fourth-priority claim under §507(a)(4), but only to the extent of $12,475. If the claim is larger than that, the excess is a general unsecured claim. The manager's salary for the month after the petition should be split into two. The salary for the week between the petition and the appointment of the trustee is a claim under §502(f). It seems to be an ordinary-course expense incurred by the debtor in operating its business before the trustee's appointment in an involuntary case. As such, it is excluded from administrative expenses by §503(b) and is given third priority by §507(a)(3).

The claim for salary for the period following the trustee's appointment arises out of the trustee's short-term operation of the debtor's business in the course of liquidation. Provided that the court authorized this operation under §721, the claim results from the ordinary course of operating the debtor's business as permitted by §364(a), and it is a second-priority administrative expense claim under §507(a)(2).

In summary, the salary debt due to the manager splits into three separate claims, having second, third, and fourth priority. In addition, if the prepetition claim exceeds $12, 475, the debt also produces a fourth claim that is a nonpriority general claim.

d. The manager's damages claim for breach of contract arises out of the estate's rejection of the executory employment contract. As discussed in section 18.4, §365(g) treats the rejection as a prepetition breach and §502(g) provides for the damages claim to be handled as if it arose prepetition. Section 502(b)(7) disallows the claim for damages to the extent that it exceeds one year's compensation measured from the petition date or the date on which the employee's performance terminated. Therefore, not only is this claim a general unsecured claim, but it will also be reduced to the extent that it exceeds the limits imposed by §502(b)(7).

e. Property taxes qualify for eighth priority under §507(a)(8)(B) provided that they were assessed before the petition and were last payable, without penalty, within a year of the petition. The tax claim represents two years' unpaid property taxes. Although the latest year probably satisfies the conditions for priority, the tax for the prior year only does so if the debtor could have paid it in the year before bankruptcy without being liable for a penalty. The state tax statute must be consulted to determine this. To the extent that the tax claim does not qualify for eighth priority, it is a general unsecured claim.

(The exception to discharge in §523(a)(1) does not apply to the portion of the tax that does not qualify for priority status.)

f. The attorney's fee relating to the sale of the complex is a cost of administering and liquidating the estate. It qualifies as an administrative expense under §503(b)(2), provided that the trustee's employment of the attorney is authorized under §327 and the fee is awarded by the court under §330. As an administrative expense, it is given second priority under §507(a)(2).

g. The landscape company's claim for prepetition work fits into no priority category. It is a general unsecured claim. The same is true of the damages claim for breach arising out of the rejection of the executory contract which, like the manager's claim, is deemed to be a general unsecured prepetition claim. Unlike the manager's claim, there is no limit imposed by §502 on the extent of damages claimable.

h. The trade claims are all general unsecured claims.

In summary, the claims are ranked in the following order:

Secured Claims (to the extent of the proceeds of the collateral):
1. First mortgage
2. Second mortgage

Priority Claims:

Second	Manager's salary for period after trustee's appointment attorney's fee
Third	Manager's salary during gap between petition and trustee's appointment
Fourth	Manager's prepetition salary, up to $12, 476
Eighth	Property taxes, to the extent that they qualify under §507(a)(8)(B)

General Unsecured Claims (all of equal rank):

Deficiency on mortgages, if any
Property taxes, to the extent not qualified for eighth priority
Manager's prepetition salary above $12,476
Manager's claim for breach of contract, subject to limit in §507(b)(7) Landscape company's claims for prepetition work and for damages for breach of contract
Trade claims

CHAPTER 20

The Chapter 13 Plan

§20.1 INTRODUCTION AND REVIEW

Although principles applicable in Ch. 13 cases have been discussed in each of the preceding chapters, the focus here is on the details of Ch. 13 bankruptcy, especially on the proceedings themselves and the mandatory and permissive standards for confirming a Ch. 13 plan.[1] It is a useful starting point to list the features of Ch. 13 that have already been dealt with in prior chapters.

1. Unlike Ch. 7, in which the debtor's nonexempt assets are liquidated and the proceeds distributed to creditors, Ch. 13 is designed to enable the debtor to keep all or most of her property and to use part of future income over a period of years to pay creditors at least as much as — and ideally more than — they would have received from the liquidation of prepetition assets.

2. It is a general policy of bankruptcy law to favor rehabilitation under Ch. 13 over liquidation under Ch. 7, on the theory that creditors are likely to do better in a Ch. 13 case. Whether or not this assumption is correct, it motivates many provisions of the Code that

---

1. Refer back to section 8.6.1 for a summary of the principal differences between Ch. 13 and the other forms of bankruptcy. Note, also, that although Ch. 12 does have variations from Ch. 13, it is largely based on Ch. 13, so its underlying concepts are the same and many of its provisions are identical. The rules and principles discussed in this chapter will therefore give you a very good idea of how a Ch. 12 case is handled.

provide incentives to the debtor to choose Ch. 13 over Ch. 7. The addition of the means test of §707(b) by the Bankruptcy Abuse Prevention and Consumer Protection Act of 2005 (BAPCPA) (discussed in section 9.8) is intended to go beyond incentives by restricting the use of Ch. 7 as an alternative to Ch. 13 where a consumer debtor is deemed able to afford a Ch. 13 plan.

3. Eligibility for Ch. 13 relief is restricted. Only an individual with regular income, whose debts fall within the limitations of §109(e), can be a debtor under Ch. 13. (These limitations are discussed in section 8.4.2.) Commonly, the source of a Ch. 13 debtor's earnings is salary or wages, and her debts were incurred for personal, family, or household purposes (consumer debts). However, Ch. 13 is not confined to wage-earning consumers. Any individual debtor with a source of regular income and debts below the ceiling can file under Ch.13, including self-employed individuals, business owners, and people whose debts are business-related.

4. A Ch. 13 case must be commenced voluntarily. Creditors have no right to petition for an involuntary Ch. 13 bankruptcy. Similarly, only the debtor may convert a case to Ch. 13. Under §1307, the debtor has the right to convert the Ch. 13 case to Ch. 7 or to have it dismissed, subject to the court's discretion to refuse a bad faith voluntary dismissal or conversion. Creditors may convert a Ch. 13 case to Ch. 7 or have it dismissed for cause, which includes dilatory, abusive, or noncompliant behavior by the debtor. Section 1307 does not expressly include lack of good faith as a cause for dismissal, but courts have recognized that this is a basis for cause, as discussed in section 20.6.

5. In a Ch. 13 case, the automatic stay is extended by §1301 to any individual who is codebtor or surety of the debtor on a consumer debt.

6. Under §1306, the Ch. 13 estate consists not only of property covered by §541 but also of all such property, including postpetition earnings, acquired by the debtor between commencement of the case and its close. Postpetition property is included in the Ch. 13 estate because the debtor's performance under the plan is dependent on it. On confirmation of the plan, the property vests in the debtor, except as provided for in the plan. (This is explained further in section 20.2.)

7. A trustee is appointed in all Ch. 13 cases. Districts with a large volume of Ch. 13 cases have a standing Ch. 13 trustee. The principal duty of the Ch. 13 trustee is the collection and disbursement of payments under the plan. In addition, under §1302, the trustee must account for property of the estate, investigate the debtor's affairs, examine and object to proofs of claim, help the

        debtor to formulate the plan, and participate in the confirmation and discharge hearings.

8.   Ch. 13 does not recognize the concept of a debtor in possession. However, if the debtor operated a business at the time of the petition, §1304 permits the debtor to continue to run the business after bankruptcy. The debtor retains control of the business under §1304 and performs the trustee's functions under §§363 and 364 with regard to the sale, use, and lease of estate property and post-petition credit. Other trustee's powers are exercised by the trustee who is required under §1302(c), read with §1106(a)(3) and (4), to monitor the debtor's business activities until the close of the case.

9.   The exemptions available to an individual debtor are less directly applicable in Ch. 13 than they are in Ch. 7, because the general effect of Ch. 13 is to enable the debtor to keep all property that is not designated for liquidation in the plan. However, exemptions are relevant in a Ch. 13 case, in that they are taken into account in deciding how much the debtor must pay under the plan to meet minimum requirements for confirmation. This is discussed in section 20.7.

10.   Finally, remember that all the provisions in Chs. 1, 3, and 5 apply in a Ch. 13 case unless specifically excluded.

§20.2 OUTLINE OF THE CH. 13 PROCEEDINGS

A Ch. 13 case begins much like the Ch. 7 case described in section 9.3, with a voluntary petition and supporting documents that are much the same, except for the plan.

Section 1321 requires the debtor to file a plan. Under Rule 3015(b), the plan must be filed with the petition or within 14 days thereafter unless the court extends the time. Only the debtor may file a plan. (Unlike Ch. 11, creditors have no right to file competing plans.) Section 1323 allows the debtor to modify the plan before confirmation without court approval. This enables the debtor to respond to any objections informally before the plan is submitted to the court for confirmation.

A trustee is appointed after the petition has been filed. There is no provision for the trustee's election at the meeting of creditors, as there is in a Ch. 7 case. Rule 2003(a) requires the meeting of creditors to be called within 21 to 40 days after the petition, and under Rule 3002 claims must be proved within 90 days of the meeting.

Unless the court orders otherwise, §1326(a)(1) requires the debtor to begin making payments within 30 days of the order for relief or the filing of the plan, whichever is earlier. The debtor must make payments to the trustee in the amount proposed by the plan, except for any current lease payments for personal property leased and any payments to ensure adequate protection of a purchase-money security interest in personal property, which must be made directly to the lessor or secured party. Section 1302(b)(5) imposes the duty on the trustee to ensure that the debtor makes the payments. Under §1326(a)(2), the trustee retains the payments made to her until the plan is confirmed, and then, as soon as practicable after confirmation, the trustee transmits payments to creditors in accordance with the plan. If the plan is not confirmed, the trustee refunds the payments that she has been holding to the debtor, less administrative costs.

Section 1324 deals with the confirmation hearing. It provides that the hearing must take place not less than 20 days nor more than 45 days after the meeting of creditors. The court is able to hold the hearing earlier if it determines this to be in the best interests of creditors and the estate and there is no objection to the earlier date. Rules 2002(b) and 3015(d) provide for notice of the hearing and the transmission of the plan or a summary of it to creditors. Even if no one objects to the plan, the hearing must be held, and the court must scrutinize the plan to ensure that it complies with the statutory standards. (The term of art "after notice and a hearing" is not used in §1324, so the hearing is not dispensed with in the absence of objections.) If confirmation is refused, the debtor has the opportunity to correct objectionable elements in the plan by amendment. If the plan is not satisfactorily amended, a party in interest can apply under §1307 for dismissal of the case or its conversion to Ch. 7.

Upon confirmation of the plan, the trustee distributes the debtor's pre-confirmation payments under §1326(a)(2), and the debtor begins the course of payments required by the confirmed plan. If necessary, the court is able to issue a form of garnishment order under §1325(c), compelling the person from whom the debtor receives income to transmit the plan payments to the trustee. Section 1326 contemplates that the debtor makes payments provided for in the plan to the trustee, who disburses them in accordance with the plan after deducting trustee's fees and other administrative expenses. However, in appropriate circumstances the court has the discretion to confirm a plan that provides for the debtor to make some payments directly to particular creditors. The debtor's default in the performance required under the plan is grounds for dismissal or conversion under §1307.

Section 1327(a) states the effect of confirmation: The plan binds the debtor and all creditors, whether or not their claims are provided for by the plan or whether they accepted or rejected it. The reference to acceptance or rejection of the plan by creditors is confusing because creditors do not vote on the Ch. 13 plan, as they do in a Ch. 11 case, and they are not called on to accept or reject it.[2] Their only opportunity to challenge the plan is to try to prevent its confirmation through an objection on the grounds that the plan does not meet statutory standards. However, if the plan is confirmed, it binds creditors whether they like it or not. It is imposed on them ("crammed down"' in bankruptcy jargon), provided that it satisfies the prerequisites for confirmation.

Under §1327(b) and (c), confirmation of the plan vests all property of the estate in the debtor, free and clear of any claim or interest in it, except as otherwise provided in the plan or the order of confirmation. Although the debtor's postpetition property continues to enter the estate under §§1306 and 541, all the estate property passes back to the debtor upon confirmation except for that property or income committed to performance of the plan. The estate therefore continues to exist as a legal entity, separate from the debtor, even though the bulk of its property vests in the debtor.

Unlike Ch. 11, in which confirmation of the plan discharges preconfirmation debts, the Ch. 13 confirmation does not operate as a discharge. The debtor is only discharged under §1328 after the plan has been consummated, unless cause exists for an earlier discharge on grounds of hardship (discussed more fully in Chapter 22). Therefore, if the debtor defaults on the plan and the case is dismissed, the balance of the claims against the debtor remains recoverable. If the case is converted to Ch. 7, the discharge is as provided for in a Ch. 7 case.

In appropriate circumstances, the plan may be revoked or modified after confirmation. Revocation may be ordered under §1330 after notice and a hearing if a party in interest applies for it within 180 days after the entry of the order of confirmation and shows that the confirmation was fraudulently procured. Modification may be applied for under §1329 by the debtor, the trustee, or an unsecured claimant, if the debtor's circumstances change after confirmation. This is discussed in section 20.10.

§20.3 OVERVIEW OF THE PLAN AND THE PREREQUISITES FOR CONFIRMATION

The plan is the debtor's proposal for the resolution of the Ch. 13 case. Its provisions are based on the information disclosed in the schedules filed in connection with the petition. Broadly speaking, the plan has three components: It states what income and assets will be used to fund the plan, it proposes the treatment to be given to claims, and it provides for various

---

2. An exception to this is where the plan proposes to give a secured or priority claim less than its statutory entitlement. The creditor's consent is then required for confirmation of the plan.

optional matters, such as the election on whether to assume or reject executory contracts. Sections 1322 and 1325 contain the crucial provisions on the contents of the plan and the standards for its confirmation. Both these sections were amended in several respects by BAPCPA. In summary, they are as follows.

(1) Optional provisions under §1322(b).   Section 1322(b) lists optional provisions that may be included in the plan. It covers matters such as the classification of unsecured claims, the modification of claims, the cure of default, and other terms that may be useful to the debtor and appropriate in the case. The list in §1322(b) is not exclusive: §1322(b)(11) allows the debtor to include in the plan any provision that is not inconsistent with the Code.

(2) Mandatory provisions under §1322(a).   Section 1322(a)(1), (2), and (3) state that the plan "shall" contain the following provisions:

1. Section 1322(a)(1)—it must bind the debtor to pay future earnings in an amount sufficient to execute the plan. (*See* section 20.4.)
2. Section 1322(a)(2)—it must provide for the full payment of priority claims unless the claimant agrees otherwise. This rule is qualified by §1322(a)(4), added by BAPCPA. The plan may provide for less than full payment of those first priority domestic support obligations that are assigned to or owed directly to a governmental unit (that is, claims under §507(a)(1)(B)), but only if the plan commits all the debtor's disposable income for the five years of the plan. (*See* section 20.7.2.)
3. Section 1322(a)(3)—if the plan classifies claims, it must treat claims in the same class equally. (*See* section 20.7.3.)

(3) Confirmation requirements under §1325(a).   Section 1325(a) states that the court "shall" confirm a plan if it meets the criteria set out in the section and if confirmation is not precluded by §1325(b). In its plain meaning, the section appears to give the court no discretion to refuse confirmation of a plan that meets all of the requirements of §1325. However, the court does have considerable discretion in determining whether each of the individual requirements set out in §1325(a) is satisfied, and therefore can refuse confirmation on the basis that the plan failed to meet one or more of the listed requirements. Similarly, the language of §1325(a) it does not indicate whether a court has the discretion to confirm a plan that falls short of those criteria. This has led some courts to hold that they have the discretion to confirm a plan that does not fully meet the requirements of §1325(a), provided that the deviation from the requirements is trivial or the parties whose rights are infringed acquiesce. See, for example, In re *Escobedo*, 28 F.3d 34 (7th Cir. 1994). Other courts have reached the opposite

conclusion, and have held that the requirements of §1325(a) are mandatory and should be understood as requirements for confirmation. See, for example, *Shaw v. Aurgroup Financial Credit Union*, 552 F.3d 447 (6th Cir. 2009).

Section 1325(a) is examined more fully in the following sections. In summary, its criteria are the following.

1. §1325(a)(1). The plan must comply with Ch. 13 and all other applicable provisions of the Code.
2. §1325(a)(2). All fees required to be paid before confirmation must have been paid.
3. §1325(a)(3) and (7). The debtor must both have filed the petition and proposed the plan in good faith, and the plan must not violate the law. (*See* section 20.6.)
4. §1325(a)(4). The distribution to be paid to each unsecured claimant under the plan must be at least equal to what it would have received had the estate been liquidated under Ch. 7. Because the payments under the plan will be made over time, interest must be added to the amount distributed to each claimant so that the claimant receives the present value of its hypothetical Ch. 7 distribution. (*See* section 20.7.3.)
5. §1325(a)(5). Unless a secured claimant accepts different treatment, the plan must either provide for the collateral to be surrendered to the claimant, or it must preserve the claimant's lien and provide for full payment of the present value of the secured claim. Present value is determined by adding interest to the face amount of the claim. (*See* section 20.7.1.)1
6. §1325(a)(6). The plan must be feasible. Based on the financial data furnished in the schedules, it must be apparent that the debtor will be able to make all payments under the plan and to comply with it. (*See* section 20.4.)
7. §1325(a)(8). The debtor must have paid all domestic support obligations required to be paid, by court or administrative order or by statute, that became due after the petition was filed.

(4) Confirmation requirements under §1325(b).   Section 1325(b) contains a further requirement for confirmation that cannot be enforced by the court of its own accord but must be raised by objection by the trustee or an unsecured claimant. In the simplest terms, the trustee or an unsecured creditor who would receive less than full payment under the plan may object to the plan if the debtor has not committed to payment of unsecured claims under the plan all of her disposable income for the "applicable commitment period," which is up to five years. This disposable income test is explained in section 20.7.3.

§20.4 THE FUNDING OF THE PLAN AND THE DEBTOR'S OBLIGATION TO MAKE PAYMENTS

As stated before, the Ch. 13 debtor usually seeks to keep the property that would otherwise have been liquidated under Ch. 7 and to substitute a series of payments to be distributed by the trustee to creditors. Although the premise of Ch. 13 is that the plan will be funded from the debtor's future income, it does not have to rely exclusively on that source. The debtor may liquidate some property to supplement the monies contributed from income, and is authorized to do so by §1322(b)(8). Also, §1325(a) permits the debtor to surrender property subject to a security interest, rather than retain the property and pay off the debt. Whatever the source of funding may be, the plan must specify it as well as set out the proposed periodic payments to be made by the debtor and the length of the payment period. Section 1322(a) requires the plan to provide for income to be submitted to the trustee sufficient to support the plan, §1302 obliges the trustee to ensure that payments are commenced, and §1326 regulates payments by the trustee.

Because the debtor's payments are the lifeblood of the plan, the court must be satisfied at the outset that the debtor can afford to make the payments. As stated in section 8.4.2, a debtor must have regular income to be eligible for Ch. 13 relief. A debtor with unpredictable or unstable income cannot be permitted to undertake Ch. 13 bankruptcy. This principle is also reflected in §1325(a)(6), which includes as one of the criteria for confirmation that the debtor appears to be able to make payments under the plan. Sections 109(e) and 1325(a)(b) impose a minimum standard of affordability on the debtor. At the other end of the scale, §1325(b) enables the trustee or an unsecured creditor to insist that the debtor commits all disposable income to the plan. This is discussed in section 20.7.3.

§20.5 THE LENGTH OF THE PLAN

When it enacted Ch. 13 in 1978, Congress felt there should be a limit on the length of time that a debtor could be committed to payments under a Ch. 13 plan. Section §1322(d) absolutely forbids payments under a plan to extend beyond five years. Prior to 2005, a plan could not extend beyond three years unless a court, for cause, approved a longer period, up to the maximum of five years. BAPCPA amended §1322(d) to confine this rule to low-earning debtors, using the concepts of current monthly income and median family income that are used in the means test of §707(b).[3] If the combined current annual income of the debtor and spouse[4] is less than the median family income for a household of the debtor's size,[5] the plan cannot go beyond three years without the court's approval for cause. However, if the combined current annual income of the debtor and spouse is higher than the median family income for a household of the debtor's size, the plan may extend to five years. As discussed in section 20.10, a plan may be modified after it is confirmed. However, the modification cannot extend a plan beyond the statutory limit, which continues to be measured from the original date, not from the modification date.

No minimum period of payment is prescribed. Courts disagree on whether the disposable income test has the effect of making the maximum payment period into a minimum period as well by requiring the debtor to make payments for the full three- or five-year period. (This is discussed in section 20.7.3.) Quite apart from this, a debtor who proposes to pay relatively small amounts over a short period will probably not satisfy the good faith and best interests tests described below.

§20.6 GOOD FAITH

Section 1325(a)(3) requires the plan to be proposed in good faith and not by any means forbidden by law. BAPCPA added §1325(a)(7), which requires also that the filing of the petition must be in good faith. That is, the court may refuse to confirm a Ch. 13 plan if the debtor lacked good faith either in filing the case or in proposing the plan. Even prior to the enactment of §1325(a)(7), courts recognized a pervasive requirement of good faith in Ch. 13, both in relation to the filing of the case and the proposal of the plan. However, §1325(a)(7) makes it clear that a lack of good faith in filing the

---

3. Although the means test applies only to consumer debtors, the rule in this section applies to all Ch. 13 debtors, whether or not their debt is primarily consumer debt. The means test of §707(b) is explained in section 9.8.

4. Section 101(10A) defines "current monthly income" to mean the average income that the debtor receives from all sources for the six-month period ending on the last day of the calendar month preceding the petition. (*See* section 9.8.4.) Because the median family income is an annual figure, the debtor's income must be annualized for comparison purposes. Therefore, the current monthly income must be multiplied by 12 to get current annual income. Note that for purposes of §1322(d), the current annual income is the combined income of the debtor and spouse, even though the case is not a joint case and the debtor's spouse has not also filed for bankruptcy.

5. "Median family income" is defined in §101(39A) to mean the median family income as reported by the Census Bureau for the most recent year for the "applicable state," which is presumably the state in which the debtor resides. If the Bureau has not reported the median income for the current year, the figure for the most recent year is used, with adjustments to reflect changes in the Consumer Price Index. (*See* section 9.8.4.)

case is grounds not only for dismissing a Ch. 13 case under §1307, but also for refusing confirmation of the plan. The practical difference between dismissal and refusal to confirm the plan is that dismissal terminates the bankruptcy case, while refusal of confirmation allows the debtor the opportunity of coming forward with an amended plan that cures the problem of lack of good faith. See In re Lancaster, 280 B.R. 468 (Bankr. W.D. Mo. 2002). Courts have used the same standards to measure good faith, whether they are dealing with a motion to dismiss or to convert the case or an objection to plan confirmation.

The scope and meaning of good faith is not defined by the Code, but it has been developed judicially. The inquiry is directed at the debtor's state of mind in seeking Ch. 13 relief or in proposing the plan. The debtor's honesty is a factual issue to be decided under all the circumstances of the case. There is no definitive list of factors to be considered. However, the following are some of the areas that are often the subject of inquiry: the accuracy and honesty of the debtor's financial disclosures; the circumstances under which debts were incurred (e.g., whether they arose from tortious or dishonest conduct); the debtor's prepetition dealings with creditors (e.g., whether the debtor had used delaying tactics to avoid payment or had otherwise misled or deceived creditors); the debtor's dealings with property (e.g., whether there had been avoidable preferences, fraudulent transfers, or attempts to conceal assets); the reason for the debtor's financial distress (e.g., whether it was caused by unfortunate circumstances or by irresponsible or dishonest dealings); the advantages sought by the debtor in choosing relief under Ch. 13 instead of under Ch. 7 (e.g., whether there is a substantial debt that is dischargeable under Ch. 13 but not under Ch. 7, as illustrated by Example 2); the debtor's financial history (including, for example, the frequency with which the debtor has sought bankruptcy relief in the past); the degree of effort undertaken by the debtor to pay claims and to give creditors fair treatment.

The last factor has to be approached with caution. As discussed in section 20.7, §1325 has objective criteria—the best interests test and the disposable income test—for deciding if the debtor's proposed payments under the plan are sufficient. If the payments are not enough to satisfy these minimum standards, that is in itself grounds for refusing confirmation of the plan, so an inquiry into the debtor's good faith is not needed. However, these payment standards do prescribe a minimum commitment, and the circumstances could show that the debtor could in fact pay more or that the Ch. 13 plan is not a sincere effort to treat creditors fairly. If this is so, it is one of the factors to be taken into account in deciding if good faith exists in the totality of the circumstances. See, for example, In re LeMaire, 898 F.2d 1346 (8th Cir. 1990); In re Keach, 243 B.R. 851 (B.A.P. 1st Cir. 2000); In re Lancaster (above).

§20.7 THE CLASSIFICATION OF CLAIMS AND THE STANDARDS APPLICABLE TO EACH CLASS

The plan deals with secured, priority, and general claims separately. In addition, §1322(b)(1) allows the debtor to divide unsecured claims into classes. The treatment of claims in each of the three principal classifications is subject to different rules.

§20.7.1 Secured Claims

a. The Debtor's Three Alternatives for the Treatment of Secured Claims under §1325(a)(5)

The debtor has three alternatives for the treatment of secured claims[6] in a Ch. 13 plan[7]: consensual treatment under §1325(a)(5)(A), payment of the claim and preservation of the lien while payment is pending under §1325(a)(5)(B), or surrender of the collateral under §1325(a)(5)(C). The last two do not require the creditor's acquiescence, and can be crammed down provided that the plan meets the statutory requirements.

(i) The consensual treatment of a secured claim under §1325(a)(5)(A). Section 1325(a)(5)(A) allows the debtor to handle the secured claim in a manner different from that provided for in §1325(a)(5)(B) or (C) if the holder of the claim accepts the plan. Acceptance is indicated most clearly by an affirmative act, but the claimant may be held to have accepted the plan if it fails to object.

(ii) Payment of the claim and preservation of the lien while payment is pending under §1325(a)(5)(B). The amount to be paid is the allowed amount of the secured claim, valued as at the effective date of the plan. As noted in section 19.6.3, *Associates Commercial Corp. v. Rash*, 520 U.S. 953 (1997), requires replacement value, not foreclosure value, to be used in determining the value of the collateral, which will in turn determine if the

---

6. Recall that under §506, a partially secured claim bifurcates. The claim is secured only to the extent of the collateral's value and is unsecured as to the deficiency. This rule applies fully in Ch. 13. However, in the case of a mortgage on the debtor's principal residence, it is a precondition to the debtor's retention of the home under the plan that the actual debt, not just the secured portion of it, be fully paid. *See* section 20.8.3. As discussed in section 20.7.16, an obscure amendment enacted by BAPCPA may extend this principle to certain purchase-money mortgages in personal property.

7. As a fourth alternative, the debtor can simply not provide for the claim in the plan, in which case it is not affected by the bankruptcy and survives the discharge.

claim is fully secured, and if it is not, the amount of the secured portion of the claim. (*See* section 19.6.3 for a fuller discussion of the determination of replacement value.) The value as of the effective date of the plan (present value) is calculated by adding interest to the face value of the claim to compensate for the payment over time under the plan. The calculation of the amount of interest to be added to reach present value must also be based on a market standard. Disagreement among courts on how to calculate market interest was settled by *Till v. S.C.S. Credit Corp.*, 541 U.S. 465 (2004), in which the Court adopted a "formula" approach that uses an objective interest rate (the national prime rate) adjusted to take the creditor's risk into account.[8]

If the plan provides for the payment of the secured claim, it must also preserve the holder's lien to secure payment. Section 1325(a)(5)(B) makes it clear that the secured claimant retains the lien until the grant of the discharge under §1328, or the full payment of the debt under nonbankruptcy law, whichever is earlier. This provision, added by BAPCPA, overrules cases that allowed the debtor to get the lien released as soon as the secured portion of a bifurcated claim was paid. The creditor therefore becomes entitled to foreclose to the extent of the full balance of the debt if the debtor should default before consummation of the plan, and the case is converted or dismissed without completion of the plan.

Except in the case of home mortgages, the payment schedule under the plan may be different from the original payment terms governing the secured debt. Also, the plan may provide for the cure of default and for the payment of long-term debt beyond the period of the plan. This is discussed in sections 20.8 and 20.9. BAPCPA added language to §1325(a)(5)(B) that requires periodic payments under the plan to be in equal monthly installments. If the collateral securing the claim is personal property, the amount of the periodic payments must be enough to provide the secured claimant with adequate protection during the period of the plan.

(iii) Surrender of the collateral under §1325(a)(5)(C). If the debtor so choses, she may surrender the collateral to the holder of the claim, thereby disposing of the secured claim and freeing the debtor of the obligation to pay it under the plan. Of course, if the collateral is worth less than the debt, the deficiency is provable as an unsecured claim, provided that the creditor is entitled to claim the deficiency under nonbankruptcy law.

---

8. Note that *Till* was a Ch. 13 case, so the court's choice of rate is clearly applicable in a Ch. 13 case, but is not necessarily applicable in a Ch. 11 case. See *In re American Homepatient, Inc.*, 420 F.3d 559 (6th Cir. 2006).

b. Restrictions on Strip Down under the "Hanging Paragraph" of §1325(a)

BAPCPA added some obscure language following §1325(a)(9), which is not part of subsection (9) but rather floats at the end of §1325(a). This poorly drafted and sloppily incorporated provision therefore has no subsection number and has come to be called the "hanging paragraph." The exact intent of this language is unclear. It says that §506 will not apply to a claim for purposes of §1325(a)(5) in two separate situations: The first is where the claim is secured by a purchase-money interest in a vehicle acquired by the debtor for personal use, and the debt was incurred within the 910 days prior to the petition. The second is where the claim is secured by a purchase-money in "any other thing of value," and the debt was incurred within the one-year period before the petition.

The apparent purpose of this provision is to protect the rights of secured creditors who entered into secured personal property transactions with the debtor within a fairly recent time before the petition — 910 days (about two and a half years) for purchase-money security interests in a motor vehicle bought for personal use, or one year in the case of a purchase money interest in other personal property of value. Because the transaction occurred relatively close to the bankruptcy and the motor vehicle or other valuable personal property could depreciate quite quickly, the debtor is not permitted to strip down the lien. For example, the debtor bought a car for personal use on secured credit two years before the petition and financed the purchase by a secured loan, repayable over four years. Because cars depreciate relatively quickly after being removed from the showroom, the car's value at the date of the petition has dropped below the outstanding amount of the debt — for example, the car is worth $20,000, but the debtor still owes $23,000 on the loan. In the absence of the hanging paragraph, the amount owed to the creditor would be bifurcated under §506 into a secured claim of $20,000 and an unsecured deficiency of $3,000. The debtor would thereby strip down the lien to the car's current value. The hanging paragraph is intended to prevent this by excluding the application of §506 in this situation. The problem with the hanging paragraph is that its clumsy drafting has raised questions on how to apply it in some situations. It seems to be clear that where the debtor elects to retain the collateral under §1325(a)(5)(B), the claim cannot be bifurcated and has to be treated in its entirety as secured, even if the collateral is worth less than the debt. It seems, furthermore, that because the entire claim is treated as secured, the creditor is entitled to present-value interest calculated on the whole claim. See In re Dean, 537 F.3d 1315 (11th Cir. 2008); In re Jones, 530 F.3d 1284 (10th Cir. 2008). However, where the debtor elects to surrender the collateral under §1325(a)(5)(C), courts disagree on the effect of excluding the application of §506. Some courts have held that because the hanging paragraph eliminates recourse to §506, there is no bifurcation of the claim, so that the surrender of the vehicle extinguishes the claim for a deficiency. Other courts have disagreed, reasoning that §506 merely defines the nature of a secured claim, but it does not create the creditor's right to a deficiency. That right derives from nonbankruptcy law, so that if the creditor is entitled to a deficiency under the contract and state law, the creditor may prove a claim for it even though the collateral has been surrendered. See, for example, In re Rodriguez, 375 B.R. 535 (B.A.P. 9th Cir. 2007); Capital One Auto Finance v. Osborne, 515 F.3d 817 (8th Cir. 2008).

While the one-year rule for other things of value applies to a purchase money interest any type of collateral, the 910-day rule applies only to purchase-money interests in motor vehicles bought for personal use. The creditor must establish each of these elements to prevent strip down. One of the crucial elements is whether a security interest qualifies as a purchase-money interest. Although it is usually quite easy to establish whether the debt was incurred to enable the debtor to acquire the collateral, this is not always clear. For example, in In re Trejos, 374 B.R. 210 (B.A.P. 9th Cir. 2007), the debtor argued that a car loan lost its status as a purchase-money interest when the original lender assigned it to the creditor who held it at the time of the petition. The court rejected the argument.

§20.7.2 Priority Claims

Section 1322(a)(2) requires all priority claims to be paid in full by deferred cash payments unless the holder agrees to different treatment. As mentioned in section 20.3, BAPCPA enacted a narrow exception to this rule in §1322(a)(4), which allows less than full payment of first priority domestic support obligations that are assigned to or owed directly to a governmental unit (that is, claims under §507(a)(1)(B)), but only on condition that the plan commits all the debtor's disposable income for the five years of the plan. The purpose of this rule is to alleviate the burden on a debtor who owes such a significant amount to a governmental agency for support obligations that it would be impossible for the debtor to pay this debt in full over the period of the plan. Provided that the debtor commits all disposable income to the plan for five years, the plan can reduce the total payment on this support debt by the appropriate amount.

Because priority claims must be paid in full, the order of priority in §507 is not as directly relevant in a Ch. 13 case as it is in Ch. 7. However, the ranking has some impact on the treatment of claims. If a class of priority claims would have received nothing had the case been filed under Ch. 7 (because the fund would have been exhausted by senior classes), the plan need provide only for full payment of the face amount of claims in that class. However, if the class would have been paid in full under Ch. 7, the best interests test described in section 20.7.3 requires that the class receives the present value of the Ch. 7 distribution, which includes interest on the face amount of the claims. If the priority class would have been treated somewhere between these extremes had the case been filed under Ch. 7 so that the claims would have received a pro rata payment, the amount paid under the plan must be the greater of the face value of the claims and the present value of the hypothetical pro rata Ch. 7 distribution. That is, if the Ch. 7 distribution plus interest is higher than the face value of the claim, this higher amount must be provided for in the plan to satisfy the best interests test.

§20.7.3 Unsecured Claims

The standards for confirmation relating to unsecured claims are prescribed by §1325(a)(4) and (b). Section 1325(a)(4) sets a minimum level of payment for unsecured claims — unsecured creditors must receive at least as much under the plan as they would have received if the debtor had filed for liquidation under Ch. 7. This requirement has traditionally been called the "best interests" test. Section 1325(b), added to the Code in 1984 and significantly amended by BAPCPA, requires the debtor to commit to payments under the plan all disposable income for an "applicable commitment period" not to exceed five years. As mentioned before, this requirement only applies if invoked by the trustee or by an unsecured claimant whose claim is not to be paid in full under the plan.

a. The Best Interests Test

Section 1325(a)(4) requires that the amount paid on each allowed unsecured claim have a value as of the effective date of the plan that is no lower than what would have been paid on the claim had the estate been liquidated under Ch. 7. To determine present value, a hypothetical Ch. 7 distribution must be calculated based on the value of estate property at the petition date, and to that amount a market interest rate for the period of payments under the plan must be added. The principle here is similar to that applicable to secured claims, in that interest must be added to compensate the claimant for payment over time. Note, however, that the formula for calculating present value differs between secured and unsecured claims. The present value of a secured claim is determined by adding interest to the allowed amount of the claim (i.e., its face value); the present value of an unsecured claim is confined to the Ch. 7 distribution plus interest. This is because secured claims are paid in full out of the collateral in a Ch. 7 case, but unsecured claims receive only a partial distribution unless the estate is solvent.

If the Ch. 7 estate would have been so badly insolvent that general unsecured claims would have received no distribution, the best interests test provides no relief to them. As they would have received nothing under Ch. 7, a plan that provides for no distribution to general creditors satisfies the test. In such a case, a creditor cannot complain of inadequate payments unless there are grounds for invoking the disposable income test or the good faith standard.

b. The Disposable Income Test

The disposable income test is brought into effect on the objection of the holder of an allowed unsecured claim that is not to be paid in full under the plan, or the objection of the trustee. In essence, §1325(b) forbids court approval of the plan unless the plan commits all the debtor's projected disposable income for a three-year period, or in some cases a five-year period, to the payment of unsecured claims. Prior to 2005, the court determined the debtor's disposable income by evaluating the debtor's budget and deducting the debtor's reasonable expenses from her income. To satisfy the disposable income test, the debtor had to commit to pay under the plan all her disposable income (the amount left over after reasonable expenses had been deducted from income) for three years. The court had considerable discretion in evaluating the debtor's budget, and some courts were less rigorous than others in disallowing expenses claimed by the debtor. BAPCPA made significant changes to the disposable income test, making it more rigid and complex, curtailing court discretion in evaluating both income and expenses, and holding the debtor to a more rigorous repayment effort. In essence, BAPCPA made three important changes to §1325(b):

1. It increased the total amount of disposable income to be committed to the plan from three years' worth to five years' worth where a debtor's income exceeds the median family income.
2. It created a more rigid formula for determining the debtor's projected disposable income.
3. Where the debtor earns more than the median family income, it limited the court's discretion in evaluating the debtor's budget by using the same standardized formulae for both income and expenses that have been adopted for means testing under §707(b).

In many ways, §1325(b), as amended by BAPCPA, is a companion measure to §707(b), so you may find it helpful to reread the discussion of the means test in section 9.8. Criticism of the means test in §707(b) is mirrored in criticism of the disposable income test in §1325(b): First, as a matter of technique, the BAPCPA amendments are poorly drafted and have caused interpretational difficulty. Second, as a matter of policy, the method of calculating disposable income can lead to unrealistic results, making it an unreliable solution to the problem of inadequate payment efforts by debtors. Although the toughening of standards may help to prevent some abuse of the Code, the more rigorous approach and the use of quite rigid and artificial formulae make it more difficult for the debtor to propose a confirmable plan with reasonable prospects of consummation.

(1) The total amount of money committed to the plan: the "applicable commitment period." Prior to BAPCPA, §1325(b) provided that a debtor must commit all disposable income for the three years beginning on the date of first payment under the plan. BAPCPA replaced the simple three-year rule with a two-tiered commitment period, called the "applicable commitment period," which distinguishes between debtors whose income exceeds or is less than the family median income. "Applicable commitment period" is defined in §1325(b)(4). In essence, the period is three years (as it was before BAPCPA) unless the combined current annual income of the debtor and spouse exceeds the median family income for a household of the debtor's size in the "applicable state," in which case it is five years. (Although "applicable state" is not defined, §707(b)(2)(A)(ii) indicates that this is the state in which the debtor resides.) For example, say that the debtor's monthly disposable income is calculated to be $200. If the debtor's current annual income is over the state median, he must pay a total of $200 × 60 months ($12,000) over the term of the plan. If his current sannual income is under the state median, he must pay a total of $200 × 36 months ($7,200).

Subsection (b)(4)(B) allows the applicable commitment period to be less than the three- or five-year period (whichever is applicable) only if the plan provides for payment in full of allowed unsecured claims over a shorter period. This provision has caused confusion over the relationship between the "applicable commitment period" and the maximum length of the payment period under the plan, provided for in §1322(d) and discussed in section 20.5. Section 1322(d) prescribes the maximum plan length, but does not set out any minimum payment period. Some courts have held that §1325(b)(4) does not change this. It is merely a monetary provision — that is, it simply prescribes the total amount that the debtor must pay under the plan, but does not require the plan to last the full three or five years. That is, as long as the plan provides for the payment of the total amount of disposable income projected to be received over the three- or five-year period, it does not actually need to last for that amount of time. See, for example, In re Fuger, 347 B.R. 94 (Bankr. D. Utah 2006) (§1325(b)(4) merely requires a set return, but does not require the debtor to commit to a specific time period for payment). Other courts have held that §1325(b)(4) is both a monetary and a temporal provision — that is, it not only requires the debtor to pay the amount calculated under the test, but it also requires the plan to last no less than the three- or five-year period unless unsecured payments are to be paid in full under the plan. See, for example, In re Davis, 348 B.R. 449 (Bankr. E.D. Mich. 2006) (the "applicable commitment period" is a temporal concept). This may seem like a pointless debate. After all, whatever the temporal length of the plan, the amount of disposable income due to creditors is determined by the amount of the debtor's disposable income for three or five years, even if payment of that amount is accelerated so that it is paid in a shorter time. However, there is a practical consequence of the temporal length of the plan: Under §1329, an unsecured creditor may request modification of the plan during the plan payment period if the debtor's income improves beyond the amount anticipated when projected disposable income was originally calculated. (See section 20.10.)

Some courts have adopted a hybrid approach, in which the "applicable commitment period" does normally set the minimum temporal duration of the plan, but this does not apply where the calculation of the debtor's projected disposable income shows that the debtor will have no disposable income to make any payment to unsecured creditors. For example, in In re Flores, 692 F.3d 1021 (9th Cir. 2012), the calculation of projected disposable income showed that the above-median debtors had a negative disposable income after payments to secured and priority creditors. The debtors proposed to pay one percent of allowed general unsecured claims for 36 months, but the trustee objected on the grounds that the plan had to last 60 months. The court, reaffirming its own precedent, held that the "applicable commitment period" applied only to payments of projected disposable income, and that if the debtor proposed to make some payments to unsecured creditors beyond that mandated by the disposable income test, they were not required to have the plan extend to the full "applicable commitment period."

(2) The debtor's projected monthly income.   As stated already, the basic rule is that the debtor must commit all projected disposable income to the payment of unsecured creditors under the plan for the applicable commitment period. Prior to BAPCPA the court conducted a purely factual evaluation of the debtor's expected monthly income and expenses to determine how much the debtor would need to maintain a reasonable standard of living. The excess was disposable income and had to be committed for at least three years to payments under the plan. Although courts would base the determination of the debtor's monthly income on her current and historic earnings, the concept of projected disposable income invited the court to take into account how the debtor's income might change over the period of the plan.

Section 1325(b)(2) still uses the term "projected disposable income" to mean an excess of income over necessary expenses. However, the section does not define "projected disposable income." It does define "disposable income" in §1325(b)(2) to mean the "current monthly income received by the debtor" (excluding certain payments such as child support or other payments made on account of a child) less reasonably necessary expenses as explained in (3) below. As we have seen, "current monthly income" is defined in §101(10A) to mean the average income that the debtor receives from all sources for the six-month period ending on the last day of the calendar month preceding the petition. It includes amounts contributed regularly by someone else for the debtor's household expenses but excludes various government benefits such as social security payments.[9] Sometimes this snapshot of the debtor's income in the six months immediately preceding the bankruptcy will be a reasonably reliable basis for making a projection of the debtor's prospective income over the period of the plan, but sometimes it will not be. For example, it does not take into account whether the debtor's earnings in that period were atypical (say, because the debtor did not work for part of the period, or conversely, because he worked more than usual or received income from sources that are not likely to continue into the future).

Because the concept of current monthly income does not allow for adjustment to income based on potential increases in the debtor's earning capacity, it seems to pull in the opposite direction from the concept of projected disposable income, which seems to call for a forward-looking calculation. Courts had struggled with this inherent conflict in §1325(b)(2). Some had held that the section requires a purely mechanical approach, so that projected disposable income must be calculated purely on the basis of the disposable income shown after necessary expenses are deducted from current monthly income. Others held that the section's use of the word "projected" signals a forward-looking approach that uses current monthly income as a base but calls for the court to examine the debtor's actual income potential over the term of the plan. In *Hamilton v. Lanning*, 130 S. Ct. 2464 (2010), the Supreme Court settled this conflict by rejecting a purely mechanical approach. The debtor had received a lump sum payment from her former employer during the six-month prepetition period, which inflated her current monthly income. If a mechanical approach was followed, this would have resulted in an unrealistically high projected disposable income that would have required plan payments that the debtor clearly could not afford. The court noted that although §1325(b) defines "disposable income," it does not define "projected disposable income." In ordinary usage, a projection, while based on current data, must take anticipated future circumstances into account. Therefore,

---

9. The definition of current monthly income applies to both above- and below-median debtors. The distinction between these two types of debtor is relevant to the expense side of the calculation of disposable income, not to the income side. See *Mort Ranta v. Gorman*, cited in the text, below.

while the debtor's disposable income, based on the deduction of reasonably necessary expenses from current monthly income, is the starting point for calculating projected disposable income, the court may take into account changes in the debtor's income or expenses that are known or virtually certain at the time of confirmation. To hold otherwise would lead to a senseless situation in which an abnormally low current monthly income would deprive creditors of higher payments, and an abnormally high current monthly income would make it impossible for the debtor to propose a realistic plan. The court noted that this interpretation is in accord with other language in §1325 and with practice prior to the enactment of BAPCPA. It is not to be assumed that Congress intended to overturn established practice in the absence of a clear indication that it meant to do so.

Note that the definition of current monthly income in §101(10A) excludes social security benefits received by the debtor. That is, any social security payments that the debtor receives in the six-month prepetition period are not counted in determining current monthly income, and hence are not included in the calculation of projected disposable income. In *Mort Ranta v. Gorman*, 2013 WL 3286252 (4th Cir. 2013), the debtor excluded social security payments from his current monthly income, which resulted in his disposable monthly income being insufficient to make any payment to unsecured creditors. Nevertheless, so that the debtor could meet the feasibility standard, he proposed in the plan to use some of his social security income to make a minimal payment on unsecured debts. The bankruptcy court (affirmed by the district court) refused to confirm the plan because it felt that the debtor could afford to make a greater payment. If the debtor declined to include social security income in his disposable income, it could not be taken into account in the determination of whether the plan was feasible. Therefore, if the social security income was disregarded, the plan did not meet the feasibility standard. The court of appeals reversed. It held that because social security income was statutorily excluded from current monthly income, it was necessarily excluded from projected disposable income. This was not affected by the forward-looking approach mandated by *Hamilton*, which recognizes the court's discretion to take into account foreseeable changes in the debtor's income but does not permit the court to ignore the statutory formula for determining that income. The court also held that the lower courts erred in refusing to take the social security income into account in the feasibility determination: Nothing in the Code precluded the debtor from funding the plan from a source other than his disposable income. In *In re Ragos*, 700F.3d 220 (5th Cir. 2012), the court likewise held that the debtor properly excluded social security benefits from current monthly income, and that *Hamilton* was inapposite because it involved the entirely different circumstance of a disparity between current monthly income and anticipated actual disposable income. The court affirmed the bankruptcy court's confirmation of the plan, rejecting the trustee's argument that the debtor failed to propose a plan in good faith by refusing to use social security income to pay creditors.

(3) The debtor's reasonably necessary expenses. To calculate the debtor's projected disposable income, the amounts necessary to be expended for the maintenance or support of the debtor or a dependent must be deducted from income. As amended by BAPCPA, §1325(b) curtails the factual inquiry into expenses where a debtor earns more than the median family income by imposing a formula for determining those expenses. This formula is essentially the same as that used in deciding if a presumption of abuse applies for the purpose of dismissing a Ch. 7 case under §707(b).

To determine what amounts qualify as necessary to be expended for the maintenance or support of the debtor or any dependents, we must combine §1325(b)(2) and (3). Section 1325(b)(2) sets out three types of expenses that are claimable in all cases. They include domestic support obligations that first become payable postpetition, qualifying charitable contributions, and if the debtor is in business, any amounts reasonably necessary to pay the expenses of continuing, preserving, or operating the business.

Section 1325(b)(3) sets out the basis of determining other expenses. If the debtor's current annual income is less than the applicable family median income, the determination of the debtor's remaining allowable monthly expenses is conducted as it was prior to BAPCPA. That is, the court evaluates the debtor's budget and decides, using its discretion as before, whether the claimed expenses are appropriate. If the debtor's current annual income exceeds the applicable family median income, §1325(b)(3) adopts the expense formula used in §707(b)(2)(A) and (B). That is the list of expenses based on the National and Local Standards promulgated by the I.R.S. for the area of the debtor's residence, combined with those additional expenses authorized by §707(b)(2)(A) and adjusted for special circumstances established by the debtor under §707(b)(2)(B). (*See* section 9.8.6 for a fuller explanation of these provisions.)

As discussed in (2), above, in *Hamilton v. Lanning* the U.S. Supreme Court rejected a mechanical calculation of projected disposable income in favor of a forward-looking approach that allows the court to take into account known or virtually certain changes in income. Although *Hamilton* focused on the income side of the calculation, the court indicated that the same approach should be adopted with regard to expenses. Therefore, although the formula prescribed by §707(b)(2) is the starting point for calculating expenses, and it creates a presumption that expenses will be as determined under the formula, the court has some discretion to make adjustments based on realities that are known or strongly anticipated.

The awkward drafting of §§707(b) and 1325(b) has led to uncertainty about the treatment of priority claims. Section 1325(b)(1)(b) requires that the disposable income be applied to the claims of unsecured creditors.

It does not specify that this means general unsecured creditors, so it could include priority claims, which are also unsecured. However, the calculation under §707(b) allows the debtor to deduct payments on priority claims as an expense. In In re Wilbur, 344 B.R. 650 (Bankr. D. Utah 2006), the court held that the reference to unsecured creditors must mean only general unsecured creditors because to include priority claims would result in these claims being taken into account twice, which would be absurd. However, in In re Williams, 394 B.R. 550 (Bankr. N.D. Colo. 2008), the court reached the opposite conclusion. It noted that an approach that avoids double-counting for above-median debtors would have a negative impact on below-median debtors because the formula in §707(b) does not apply to them, and they do not deduct priority claims as expenses. In re Puetz, 370 B.R. 386 (Bankr. D. Kan. 2007) opted for a more flexible approach to "unsecured claims" that would include priority claims that are not deducted as expenses.

Courts had disagreed on whether the above-median debtor's calculation of disposable income may include expenses allowed under §707(b) where the debtor's actual expenses in that category are less than the allowed amount, or are nonexistent. For example, §707(b) makes an allowance, based on I.R.S. standards, for transportation expenses relating to vehicle ownership. The question is whether the debtor can claim this expense in full even though her actual expenses are less than the allowed amount, or she has no such expenses at all. The U.S. Supreme Court settled this question with regard to a debtor who has no such expenses in Ransom v. F.I.A. Card Services, N.A., 131 S.Ct. 716 (2011). The court held that a debtor who has no actual loan or lease expenses on a car cannot claim the car ownership expense. The court based its decision on the use of the word "applicable" in §707(b), which confined expense claims to those that corresponded to the debtor's actual circumstances.[10] The court also made it clear that a debtor whose actual expenses exceeded the I.R.S. standards is confined to the standard amount and cannot claim more. However, the court did not decide if a debtor whose actual expenses are less than the standard could claim the full standard amount. Courts have disagreed on the approach to be taken in this situation. In In re Scott, 457 B.R. 740 (Bankr. S.D. Ill. 2011), the court held that as long as the debtor had some car ownership expenses, the I.R.S. standard is "applicable," as required by Ransom, so that the debtor is entitled to claim the full standard expense, even if his actual expense is lower. However, in In re Schultz, 463 B.R. 492 (Bankr. W.D. Mo. 2011), the court said that the essence of Ransom is that a debtor should not be allowed to claim expenses that were essentially fictional, so that debtors whose car

---

10. Although the court resolved this issue in relation to the disposable income calculation under §1325(b), its holding extends to the same calculation that is required for the presumption of abuse under §707(b). See section 9.8.6.)

operating expenses[11] were lower than the standard amount were confined to their actual expenses.

(4) The formula, in summary. In simple terms, the formula for determining projected disposable income can be charted as follows.

STEP 1

Calculate the debtor's **current monthly income** as defined in §101(10A):

This is calculated by taking the debtor's actual earnings from all sources for the six months before bankruptcy, divided by six to get the average monthly income. Then multiply the monthly figure by 12 to compare the debtor's income to the annual median income.

STEP 2

Ascertain the **median family income** for a household of the debtor's size in the state of the debtor's residence.

This is an annual income figure obtained from the Census Bureau report.

STEP 3

If the debtor's current annual income is less than the median family income, do the following:

(a) The disposable monthly income calculation:

(i) Calculate the debtor's monthly income. This is presumptively the debtor's current monthly income (excluding child support payments received), but where it is known or virtually certain that the debtor's prospective monthly income will be higher or lower, the court has the discretion to take the anticipated increase or decrease into account.

(ii) Calculate the actual expenses reasonably necessary to support the debtor and any dependents, as well as postpetition expenses for domestic support, charitable contributions, and running a business. There is no statutory formula for calculating these expenses, which the court must evaluate on the facts, using its discretion to allow, reduce, or disallow claimed expenses.

---

11. This case involved car operating expenses, as opposed to ownership expenses. Both types of expense are covered in the standards.

(iii) Deduct the expenses from the income. This gives the debtor's monthly disposable income.

(b) *Determine disposable income for three years:*

Multiply the debtor's monthly disposable income by 36 to determine the debtor's projected disposable income for three years. This is the total amount that the debtor must commit to the plan to satisfy the disposable income test.

If the debtor's current annual income is more than the median family income, do the following:

(a) *The disposable monthly income calculation:*

(i) Calculate the debtor's monthly income. This is presumptively the debtor's current monthly income (excluding child support payments received), but where it is known or virtually certain that the debtor's prospective monthly income will be higher or lower, the court has the discretion to take the anticipated increase or decrease into account.

(ii) Determine the debtor's allowed expenses. The debtor is entitled to deduct only those expenses allowed under §707(b)(2)(A) and (B) as well as postpetition expenses for domestic support, charitable contributions, and running a business. The debtor may only deduct §707(b)(2)(A) expenses that he actually incurs. Although expenses calculated under the formula are presumptively applicable, where it is clear that they are not realistic, given the debtor's circumstances, the court has discretion to make adjustments.

(iii) Deduct the expenses from the income. This gives the debtor's monthly disposable income.

(b) *Determine disposable income for five years:*

Multiply the debtor's monthly disposable income by 60 to determine the debtor's projected disposable income for five years. This is the total amount that the debtor must commit to the plan to satisfy the disposable income test.

One of the items that can be claimed as an expense is a bit odd. Although the debtor is in severe financial trouble, is struggling to pay creditors, and is held to a stringent budget for her living expenses, §1325(b)(2)(A) permits her to include charitable contributions up to an amount of 15 percent of the debtor's annual gross income made to a charitable or religious organization that meets the qualifications of §548(d)(4) and the Internal Revenue Code. Because these contributions come out of the disposable income that would otherwise go to the payment of creditors, the debtor is permitted to be charitable at their expense. This subsection was part of a set of provisions enacted in 1998 for the primary purpose of protecting tithes and other contributions to churches and other religious organizations. Other charities were included to avoid First Amendment problems. (These contributions are also protected from avoidance as prepetition transfers under §544(b)(2) or as fraudulent transfers under §548(a)(2), and are not to be taken into account by the court in deciding whether to dismiss a debtor's Ch. 7 cases for abuse under §707(b)(1).) The language of §1325(b)(2)(A)(ii) gives the court very little flexibility to question the reasonableness of contributions of up to 15 percent of the debtor's gross income, but the court is able to examine the debtor's motive in making the contribution under the good faith requirement of §1325(a)(3). For example, in In re Cavanagh, 250 B.R. 107 (B.A.P. 9th Cir. 2000), the court inquired into the debtor's good faith where the debtor, who had not previously paid church tithes, amended his Ch. 13 plan to reflect an increase in earnings offset by a new contribution of tithes to his church. (Despite these suspicious circumstances, the court concluded that the debtor had undergone a genuine religious conversion.)

c. The Classification of Unsecured Claims

Section 1322(b)(1) gives the debtor the discretion to place unsecured claims in separate classes. There are three guidelines that apply to claim classification: Claims in the same class must be treated alike (§1322(a)(3)), the plan must not discriminate unfairly against any class (§1322(b)(1)), and claims can only be classed together if they are substantially similar (§1322(b)(1) read with §1122). In addition, the best interests and disposable income tests require that even the class of claims that is treated least generously in the plan receives the level of payment required by §1325.

Section 1322(b)(1) expresses only one justification for separate classification: If an individual is liable with the debtor on a consumer debt, that claim may be separated from other unsecured claims. The purpose of this provision is to allow the debtor to treat a consumer debt preferentially to eliminate or reduce the liability of a friend or relative who is codebtor or surety. The rationale behind the provision is that it prevents financial hardship to the codebtor and eliminates any pressure that the debtor would otherwise feel to pay the debt outside the plan, thereby endangering his or her rehabilitation.

The separate classification of guaranteed or joint consumer debts is presumptively fair, since §1322(b) specifically mentions this basis for discrimination. However, this does not mean that it is conclusively fair, so it is still subject to scrutiny by the court. There is no statutorily recognized justification for other types of claim, so the debtor must provide a good reason for any classification and discriminatory treatment. A court is likely to approve a claim classification only if it is necessary to the execution of the plan and the debtor's rehabilitation, it is reasonable and proposed in good faith, and the degree of discrimination is no greater than it needs to be to achieve its purposes. Most courts adopt an evaluation that centers around these questions, recognizing that the determination of whether discrimination is fair involves the exercise of reasonable court discretion. See In re Crawford, 324 F.3d 539 (7th Cir. 2003); In re Pracht, 464 B.R. 486 (Bankr. M.D. Ga. 2012). For example, courts have generally held that discrimination based purely on nondischargeability is unfair. That is, the debtor may not devote a disproportionate amount of her disposable income toward the payment of the dischargeable claim, thereby reducing the fund that would otherwise be available to pay other creditors. However, in In re Pracht the court found that the debtor's separate classification and higher rate of payment of a nondischargeable student loan debt was fair discrimination. The reduction on payments to other creditors was modest but the maintenance of contract payments on the student loan during her Ch. 13 case would make the debtor eligible for a student loan forgiveness program that would allow her to write off a significant amount of the otherwise nondischargeable debt. For a further illustration of claim classification, see Example 6.

§20.8 THE MODIFICATION OF A CLAIMANT'S RIGHTS AND THE CURE OF DEFAULT

§20.8.1 Introduction and General Note on Cure

Section 1322(b)(2) allows the plan to modify the rights of all claimants except those whose claims are secured only by a security interest in real property used by the debtor as a principal residence. Section 1322(b)(3) allows the plan to provide for the cure or waiver of any default; this cure or waiver of default applies to all debts, including an otherwise nonmodifiable home mortgage.

The cure of default is a pervasive concept in §1322. It is permitted both by §1322(b)(3), which covers claims to be fully disposed of during the plan period, and by §1322(b)(5), which covers long-term debt to be paid off beyond the period of the plan. (Long-term debt is discussed in section 20.9.) This note states some general principles of cure, but the subject recurs in the remainder of this section and in section 20.9. As noted earlier, the cure of default is not regarded as a modification of the contract, so it applies, both under §1322(b)(3) and §1322(b)(5), to specially protected, nonmodifiable home mortgages. Although §1322(b)(3) provides in general terms for the cure of any default, its primary use is in connection with a secured debt in default. The debtor's motivation to propose the cure is her desire to retain property subject to a security interest. To do this, she is obliged, not only to pay the amounts due prospectively on the secured claim, but also to pay arrears or to remedy other breaches. That is, if the debtor has fallen into arrears in payments or has otherwise breached the contract, the right to cure enables her to reinstate the agreement by providing in the plan for payments or performance to remedy the breach. That is, of course, in addition to provisions in the plan (or in and beyond the plan for long-term debt) for the payment of future installments.

There is a difference of opinion among courts on whether §1322(b)(3) and (5) apply only to prepetition defaults, or if they can also be used by a debtor who defaults during the course of the case by failing to perform the obligations assumed in the plan. If the cure right is available postpetition, a debtor who stumbles in making plan payments could then apply for a modification of the plan to include a cure of the default, thereby preventing dismissal or conversion to Ch. 7. In re Mendoza, 111 F.3d 1264 (5th Cir. 1997), is one of the cases that interpreted the cure provisions as applicable to postpetition default. The court noted that the general policy of §1322 is to encourage and facilitate the cure of default, and there is nothing in the language of the section that confines it to prepetition defaults. The court did recognize, however, that the debtor would be precluded from curing a postpetition default if the plan contained a "drop-dead" clause, which allows the creditor to foreclose in the event of default.

§20.8.2 The Modification and Cure of Claims Other Than Specially Protected Home Mortgages

The ability to modify rights enables the debtor to extend contractual installment periods that would otherwise have ended before the proposed period of the plan. This is most helpful when the debtor wishes to keep property subject to a security interest. Say, for example, that the debtor purchased a car on secured credit prior to bankruptcy, and the contractual payment period has two years to run. If the debtor proposes a three-year plan, §1322(b)(2) allows the payment period to be extended an extra year, thereby reducing the size of the monthly payments. In addition, if the debtor defaulted on the contract, §1322(b)(3) permits cure of the default so that the plan may provide for the payment of arrears as well as future installments. In effect, §1322(b)(2) and (3) give the debtor the opportunity to redeem collateral by installments — something that cannot be done in a Ch. 7 case. The debtor's ability to modify a claimant's rights is limited by the confirmation criteria in §§1322 and 1325. So, for example, unless the claimant accepts the plan, the debtor cannot modify a security agreement by canceling the lien, substituting collateral, or giving the secured claimant less than it is entitled to receive under §1325(a)(5).

§20.8.3 The Special Treatment of Claims Secured Only by a Security Interest in Real Property That Is the Debtor's Principal Residence

Section 1322(b)(2) excludes from the debtor's ability to modify secured claims, a claim that is "secured only by a security interest in real property that is the debtor's principal residence." Section 101(13A) defines "debtor's principal residence" to mean a residential structure and incidental property used by the debtor as a principal residence. The structure may or may not be attached to real property, and it could be an individual condominium, a co-operative unit, a manufactured or mobile home, or a trailer. However, because §1322(b)(2) applies only to real property, a security interest in a mobile home, trailer or other unattached property would not be subject to the bar on to modification if state law did not classify the structure as real property. The bar on the modification of a security interest in the debtor's principal residence is intended to protect home mortgagees on the theory that its absence would discourage them from providing home financing to individuals. Even though the debtor has some flexibility in restructuring other debts, the terms of the debtor's home mortgage must be complied with if the debtor wishes to keep the home. The plan cannot alter the payment schedule or otherwise propose to ease the debtor's commitments under the security agreement.

The prohibition on modification applies only to future payments. Default on the mortgage may be cured under §1322(b)(3) and (c)(1) by providing in the plan for payment of the arrears by installments. Section 1322(c)(1), added by the Bankruptcy Reform Act of 1994, makes it clear that the cure provisions in §1322(b)(3) and (5) are not affected by the antimodification rule in §1322(b)(2). Section 1322(c)(1) also specifies that the right to cure is not cut off by foreclosure until such time as the foreclosure sale has been completed. In states that recognize a statutory redemption period, courts have held that the right to cure extends even beyond the sale, until the end of the redemption period. (See Example 4.) The debtor has the right to cure defaults whether the mortgage is a short-term loan payable within a period of the plan, or a long-term loan that may be dealt with under §1322(b)(5), as discussed in section 20.9.

The language used in §1322(b)(2) to exclude home mortgages from the debtor's modification power covers claims that are "secured only by a security interest in real property that is the debtor's principal residence." The word "only" means that if the mortgage covers other property in addition to the debtor's home (such as a second piece of real property, or personal property and appliances on the premises) or a multifamily dwelling, the antimodification rule does not apply. See, for example, In re Scarborough, 461 F.3d 406 (3d Cir. 2006) (the antimodification provision did not apply to a two-unit residence where the debtor lived in one unit and rented the other). However, in In re Ferandos, 402 F.3d 147 (3d Cir. 2005), the court held that the inclusion of rents arising from the property in the mortgage did not change it from being secured only by a security interest in the home. The rents were merely incidental to and stemmed from the property itself and were not separate collateral. Section 1322(b)(2) does not apply to a security interest in, say, a mobile home if state law does not classify it as real property, nor to property that is not the debtor's principal residence (e.g., a summer beach cottage).

Section 1322(c)(2), also added in 1994, creates another situation in which the antimodification rule is inapplicable. If the final payment under the mortgage falls due within the period of the plan (that is, the original contractual due date for the final payment occurs within the plan period), the payment schedule can be amended by the plan so as to stretch out the mortgage payments over the entire length of the plan.

Section 1322(b)(2) refers to "secured claims," so it had been unclear how it applies where the value of the home is worth less than the debt and the mortgagee's claim bifurcates into a secured claim to the extent of the collateral's value and an unsecured claim for the deficiency. The U.S. Supreme Court resolved this question in Nobelman v. American Savings Bank, 508 U.S. 324 (1993), by holding that an undersecured mortgage on the debtor's principal residence is protected to the full amount of the debt. The court based this conclusion on the wording of §1322(b)(2), which prohibits modification of the rights of the holder of the mortgage, not merely of the claim secured by the mortgage. The effect of Nobelman is to extend the principle of Dewsnup v. Tim, 502 U.S. 410 (1992), to a mortgage on the debtor's principal residence under Ch. 13. (Dewsnup, discussed in section 19.6.3, held that a debtor cannot use §506(d) to strip down an undersecured lien on real property in Ch. 7 by pegging its value at the judicially determined valuation at the time of bankruptcy.) The combined effect of Nobelman and Dewsnup is that a debtor cannot strip a lien on real property in a Ch. 7 case, or a mortgage on his principal residence in a Ch. 13 case. The U.S. Supreme Court has not addressed lien stripping with regard to other secured claims, and lower courts have generally held it to be permissible. See In re Davis, 716 F.3d 331 (4th Cir. 2013).

Although Nobelman settles the issue of strip down in relation to a partially secured mortgage on the debtor's principal residence, it does not cover the question of whether a debtor may "strip off" a completely unsecured second mortgage. A second mortgage becomes completely unsecured if the home has no excess value after the senior mortgage has been paid. The strip-off issue was discussed in relation to *Dewsnup* in section 19.6.3b, in which it was noted that courts have been divided on whether *Dewsnup* extends to strip off. Courts dealing with the issue under §1322(b)(2) have likewise been divided, but the weight of opinion is that *Nobelman* was premised on the creditor having at least some interest in the property at the time of bankruptcy, so that if there is no equity left in the property to support the mortgage, it cannot qualify as a secured claim entitled to protection under §1322(b)(2). See, for example, In re *Zimmer*, 313 F.3d 1220 (9th Cir. 2002); In re *Samala*, 295 B.R. 380 (Bankr. D.N.M. 2003); In re *Davis*.

§20.9 LONG-TERM DEBT

While §1322(b)(2) enables the plan to extend payments on short-term debt, §1322(b)(5) allows the debtor to take advantage of a contract payment period that is longer than the period of the plan. Section 1322(b)(5) applies to all long-term debts, including those secured by a home mortgage. Note, however, it applies only to long-term debts — that is, debts whose last payment is due after the date of the final payment on the plan. If the due date of the debt is within the plan payment period, the debtor may not use §1322(b)(5) to extend the payments beyond the plan period. For example, in In re *Pierotti*, 645 F.3d 277 (5th Cir. 2011), the debtor owed arrear taxes to the IRS, secured by a tax lien on the debtor's real property. The debtor proposed to pay off the arrear taxes over a 15-year period. The court held this to be impermissible because the tax debt was already mature, payable, and in default. It was therefore not a debt due only after the final payment under the plan.

The following example illustrates how §1322(b)(5) operates where the final payment of the debt is due, under the original contract, only after the final payment under the plan. The debtor bought a piece of equipment on credit two years before bankruptcy. Under the contract of sale, the seller retained a security interest in the equipment, which the debtor undertook to pay off in installments over ten years. The debtor proposes a five-year plan, but the remaining contractual payment period is eight years. This is so even if the debtor had defaulted on the payments, and the contract allows the creditor to accelerate payments under nonbankruptcy law. The debtor's right to cure the default reverses any acceleration, so that the final date of payment is the unaccelerated contractual due date. Section 1322(b)(5) allows the debtor to adhere to the contractual payment schedule, rather than accelerating it to bring it within the term of the plan. The debtor maintains regular installment payments while the plan is pending (these may be paid through the trustee or directly to the claimant) and continues to make contract payments after the conclusion of the plan until the debt is satisfied. Because payments on the claim will extend beyond the period of the plan, §1328(a)(1) excludes the debt from the Ch. 13 discharge. (For a further illustration of the use of §1322(b)(5), see Example 4.)

If the debtor had defaulted on the debt, §1322(b)(5) requires cure of the default within a reasonable time. Therefore, in addition to paying the regular installments as they become due, the debtor must provide in the plan for payments to be made on the arrears. The question of what time is reasonable for affecting the cure depends upon the circumstances of the case. The debtor is not necessarily entitled to spread the cure payments over the whole length of the plan.

§20.10 MODIFICATION OF A CONFIRMED PLAN

As mentioned in section 20.2, before confirmation, §1323 permits the debtor to modify the plan easily, and without court approval. Modification after confirmation is a more onerous process that does require an application to court. Section 1329 provides for the modification of a confirmed plan, at any time before completion of payments, on request of the debtor, the trustee or the holder of an unsecured claim. Under §1329(a), the modification may either increase or reduce payments to a particular class, alter the time period for such payments, or change the amount of the distribution to a creditor to take account of payments outside of the plan. BAPCPA added to this list the modification of a plan to allow the debtor to reduce payments for the purpose of buying health insurance under specified circumstances. For the modification to be approved, §1329(b) states that the plan as modified must satisfy the same standards and requirements under §§1322 and 1325(a) as govern the original confirmation of a plan (such as the full payment of priority claims, the good faith and feasibility standards, and best interests test — as discussed in sections 20.3 through 20.7). Section 1329(b) does not say that the modified plan must also satisfy §1325(b) — the disposable income test. This is odd, especially because a creditor's right to apply for modification under §1329 was added to the Code in 1984, at the same time as the disposable income test. (Prior to 1984, §1329 allowed only a debtor to seek modification of the plan.) The effect of this omission is unclear. For example, in In re Sunahara, 326 B.R. 786 (B.A.P. 9th Cir. 2005), the court held that on the plain language of §1329(b), the disposable income test in §1325(b) is not directly applicable in a modification, but a change in the debtor's disposable income could be taken into account in the analysis of the debtor's good faith. In re Keller, 329 B.R. 697 (Bankr. E.D. Cal. 2005), disagreed with this approach, holding that even though

§1329(b) does not expressly mention §1325(b), it does not exclude it either.

Upon approval of the modification, the modified plan substitutes for and supersedes the original. Under §1329(c), even if a plan is extended by modification, it cannot exceed the permissible length measured from the date of the first payment under the original plan. That is, the modification cannot increase the payment period beyond the maximum applicable commitment period prescribed by §1322(d) from the time of the first payment made in the case.

Most applications for modification are brought by debtors who seek to reduce or extend the payment of obligations undertaken in the original plan on the basis that the commitments in the confirmed plan are too onerous or have become so as a result of changed circumstances. However, it is not uncommon for a creditor or trustee to apply for modification on the grounds that the debtor's financial situation has improved. Some courts treat the confirmed plan as res judicata with regard to any circumstances that existed or were foreseeable at the time of confirmation, so they require a substantial unanticipated change to justify modification. Other courts adopt a more lenient test, and do not require the applicant to demonstrate a significant unexpected change in circumstances. See, for example, In re Brown, 219 B.R. 191 (B.A.P. 6th Cir. 1998); Barbosa v. Soloman, 235 F.3d 31 (1st Cir. 2000); In re Thomas, 291 B.R. 189 (Bankr. M.D. Ala. 2003).

Section 1329(a) expressly permits modifications to adjust the amount or period of payments, but it does not say whether or not a debtor may modify the substantive provisions of the plan to achieve other purposes. Some courts have held that the debtor's ability to use §1329 to make substantive changes to the confirmed Ch. 13 plan is restricted, especially where the modification would result in unfairness to a creditor. For example, in In re Nolan, 232 F.3d 528 (6th Cir. 2000), the court held that where collateral has depreciated in value, the debtor cannot modify the plan to surrender the collateral and reduce the amount of the secured claim based on the lower value. In In re Adkins, 425 F.3d 296 (6th Cir. 2005), the court applied this same rule where the debtor had defaulted on plan payments and the collateral had been repossessed and sold at a lower value following relief from stay. That is, the court held in these cases that once a claim has been classified as secured in a fixed amount in the original plan, the plan cannot be later modified to reduce the amount of the secured claim and increase the unsecured deficiency. Not all courts agree with this approach. For example, in In re Mellors, 372 B.R. 763 (Bankr. W.D. Pa. 2007), and In re Disney, 386 B.R. 292 (Bankr. D. Colo. 2008), the courts held that because §502(j) allows reconsideration of an allowed claim for cause, it is permissible to reduce the amount of a secured claim under §1329 where cause for the modification is shown.

§20.11 SUCCESSIVE FILINGS UNDER CHS. 7 AND 13: THE "CHAPTER 20" TACTIC

Under certain circumstances, a debtor may benefit from the tactic of first filing a Ch. 7 case to gain advantages available under Ch. 7 and, immediately thereafter, filing a Ch. 13 case to obtain advantages under Ch. 13 that were not available under Ch. 7. Because this tactic involves the combination of Chs. 7 and 13, it has come to be called "Chapter 20." BAPCPA made some amendments to the Code that, while they do not directly prevent a "Chapter 20" serial filing, erect three significant barriers to the "Chapter 20" strategy. First, a consumer debtor has greater difficulty in filing the initial Ch. 7 case because §707(b) makes the debtor more vulnerable to dismissal of the Ch. 7 case, either because the presumption of abuse applies or because the court finds abuse under the totality of the circumstances. Second, as explained below, BAPCPA amended §1328 to prevent a debtor from getting a Ch. 13 discharge within four years of getting a discharge in another case filed under Ch. 7, 11, or 12, effectively eliminating the use of "Chapter 20" for the purpose of discharging debt that is only dischargeable in Ch. 13. Third, BAPCPA added grounds for relief from stay under §362(d)(4)(b) which authorizes the court to grant relief from stay to a creditor whose claim is secured by real property where the court finds that the filing of the petition was part of a scheme to hinder, delay, or defraud creditors that involved multiple bankruptcy filings against the property. (*See* section 11.4.4.)

A debtor used to be able to use "Chapter 20" to gain the advantage of liquidation under Ch. 7 while enjoying the wider discharge of Ch. 13. As we will see in Chapter 22, some debts are nondischargeable in a Ch. 7 case but can be discharged in Ch. 13. A debtor who wished to liquidate under Ch. 7 but needed Ch. 13 to handle a debt that was dischargeable only in Ch. 13 could file a case under Ch. 7 to handle the bulk of his debt by liquidation, and then file a Ch. 13 case to dispose of the debt that could not be discharged in Ch. 7. The use of "Chapter 20" for this purpose is no longer possible because BAPCPA amended §1328 to prevent a debtor from getting a Ch. 13 discharge within four years of getting a discharge in another case filed under Ch. 7, 11, or 12. (*See* Chapter 22.) Apart from this, there are other reasons why a debtor may choose the "Chapter 20" strategy: One is that if the debtor wishes to file under Ch. 13, but his debt exceeds the Ch. 13 debt ceiling, he can make himself eligible for Ch. 13 relief by reducing his debt through a Ch. 7 discharge. The other is that "Chapter 20" may help a debtor to handle liens that survive a Ch. 7 discharge. The use of "Chapter 20" to deal with a lien that survived the Ch. 7 discharge works as follows: The debtor first files a Ch. 7 case and receives a discharge of personal liability on her debts. One of these discharged debts is secured by a mortgage on real property. Although the debtor's personal liability on the claim is discharged, the security interest is not affected by the discharge. (*See* section 19.4.) After the close of the Ch. 7 case, the mortgagee commences foreclosure proceedings, but before the foreclosure sale is held, the debtor files a Ch. 13 petition in which she proposes to retain the property and pay off the mortgage claim in installments. The debtor is thereby able to use Ch. 13 to force the secured claimant into accepting the equivalent of a redemption by installments, which she would not have been able to do in the Ch. 7 case. The prior Ch. 7 discharge also gives the debtor the advantage of keeping her payments under the Ch. 13 plan to a minimum because she has shed her dischargeable debt in the prior Ch. 7 case.

The U.S. Supreme Court held in *Johnson v. Home State Bank*, 501 U.S. 78 (1991), that this practice is permitted by the Code. The court said that a mortgage still qualifies as a claim under §101(5), even after the debtor's personal liability has been discharged, and the Code has no restriction on filing a Ch. 13 case immediately after receiving a Ch. 7 discharge. The Court did recognize, however, that the good faith standard in §1325 could be used to refuse confirmation of the plan if, under the totality of the circumstances, the Ch. 13 plan was filed as part of a scheme to undermine the policy and purposes of the Code. Since *Johnson*, several lower courts have applied the good faith standard to "Chapter 20" serial filings. For example, *In re Cushman*, 217 B.R. 470 (Bankr. E.D. Va. 1998), found a lack of good faith where, in the totality of the circumstances, the debtor had planned the Ch. 13 filing before he filed the Ch. 7 case to force the secured claimant to accept what amounted to a redemption by installments, he discharged all his debt under Ch. 7 without making any payment to unsecured creditors, and he planned to pay the secured claim off over four years even though he could have afforded to pay the debt more quickly.

A debtor may also use "Chapter 20" to strip down a partially secured claim or to strip off a formerly secured claim that is no longer backed with any collateral value. As explained in section 19.6.3, under §506(a)(1) a claim is treated as secured to the extent of the value of the collateral and is unsecured as to any deficiency. Strip down is the process whereby the debtor uses §506(a)(1) to fix the amount of the secured claim at the value of the collateral at the time of bankruptcy. As a result, any increase in the value of the collateral thereafter will not be added to the secured claim, which is pegged at the original value determined by the court. Strip off is similar to strip down, but it relates to situations where the value of the collateral at the time of determining secured status is so low, that there is nothing to secure the claim. This typically occurs where the claim is a junior lien on the property, and the collateral value is less than the amount of the senior lien. *Dewsnup v. Timm*, 502 U.S. 410 (1992) held that a debtor cannot strip down an undersecured consensual lien in a Ch. 7 case. Courts have differing views on whether *Dewsnup* applies to nonconsensual liens, or to strip off, so it is possible that a court in a particular venue will treat all strip downs and strip offs as impermissible in a Ch. 7 case. Where the debtor wishes to file under Ch. 7, but is precluded from stripping down or stripping off a lien under Ch. 7, the debtor may seek to use the "Chapter 20" tactic to first dispose of debt under Ch. 7, and then to strip down or strip off surviving liens in Ch. 13. The majority of the court in *In re Davis* (cited in section 20.8.3) held that this use of "Chapter 20" is permissible. The debtors initially filed a case under Ch. 7 and received a discharge. However, they were unable in the Ch. 7 case to strip off junior liens on property[12] where those liens had become completely unsecured because the senior lien exceeded the value of the collateral. The court held that even though the amendment of §1328 precluded the debtors from getting a discharge in the Ch. 13 case, this did not prevent the debtors from using the "Chapter 20" tactic to strip off liens that had become valueless. The court rejected the trustee's argument that the debtors were using "Chapter 20" to evade *Dewsnup's* bar on Ch. 7 lien stripping and concluded that the debtors were merely taking advantage of a mechanism made available under the Code. (The dissenting judge considered the majority's conclusion to be anomalous because the liens had survived the Ch. 7 bankruptcy, and should be treated as allowed secured claims in the Ch. 13 case.)

Although *Johnson* holds that the Code does not prohibit serial filings, it does not address the situation in which a debtor files Ch. 7 and then files a Ch. 13 case while the Ch. 7 case is still pending. Some courts have permitted this where, even though the Ch. 7 case was still pending at the time of the Ch. 13 petition, the Ch. 7 discharge had already been granted. However, courts generally agree that the Ch. 13 petition cannot be filed before the Ch. 7 discharge because a debtor may not maintain two concurrent cases relating to the same debts. See *In re Sidebottom*, 430 F.3d 893 (7th Cir. 2005).

Examples

1. Buster Budgett has filed a petition under Ch. 13. He works as the manager of a store and earns a gross salary of $5,000 per month ($60,000 per year). However, three months before he filed his petition, he took two months' unpaid leave to care for his father, who had been seriously ill. Buster is unmarried and lives alone. The applicable median family income in Buster's state is $40,000 per annum. Buster's schedules reflect his current monthly income as $3,333. As required by §1325(b)(2), this is based on his average income for the six months prior to the petition

---

12. The property in question was the debtor's principal residence, but the court held that *Nobelman* did not bar strip off because the lien did not qualify as a secured claim entitled to protection from modification under §1322(b)(2). See section 20.8.3.

(four month's earnings of $5,000) divided by six. His schedules show monthly expenses of $2,733, which include payments on his house and car, utilities, property taxes, insurance, gas, parking, food, clothing, entertainment, medical and dental expenses (including the cost of health in surance), and state and federal taxes. The monthly expenses of $2,733 are well supported and documented, entirely reasonable, and not in excess of appropriate living standards. After his monthly expenses are deducted from his current monthly income, Buster is left with $600 a month, which he proposes to allocate for five years to the payment of unsecured claims under his Ch. 13 plan. There are no priority claims in Buster's estate except for administrative expenses. Had Buster filed under Ch. 7, the realizable value of his nonexempt property after the full payment of administrative expenses would have been $36,000, which would have been enough to pay 10 percent of the claims of general unsecured creditors.

a. Does Buster need court approval for a five-year payment period?

b. Based on the figures given above, does the proposed plan satisfy the financial standards for plan confirmation in §1325?

c. Change the facts of this Example to the following extent: Buster did not take the two months unpaid leave, and earned the full $5,000 a month for the six months prior to filing. In addition, because his employer was temporarily short-staffed during two of those six months, Buster was called upon to work overtime, for which he received additional salary of $2,000 for each of those two months (that is, $4,000 in total overtime pay). This was an unusual circumstance. Buster's employer does not normally ask staff to work overtime. The addition of his overtime pay makes his current monthly income $5666 ($30,000 plus $4,000 divided by six). Buster's actual reasonable expenses are $4,000, but the standardized expenses allowed under §707(b)(2)(A) and (B) are $3,500. Buster asserts that his projected disposable income is $1,000 per month ($5,000 income less $4,000 reasonable expenses) and he proposes a plan under which he will allocate this amount for 60 months, with a total payout of $60,000 to general unsecured creditors. The trustee objects, arguing that Buster has not committed all his disposable income to payments under the plan. In the trustee's view, Buster's disposable income is actually $2,166 ($5,666 current monthly income less $3,500 standardized monthly expenses), so he is required to make a total 60-month commitment of $129,960 to the payment of unsecured creditors. Can Buster's proposed plan be confirmed over the trustee's objection?

2. Fido Semper had been fired by his ex-employer, Fire and Casualty Co., Inc. and bore a deep grudge against the company. One night Fido broke

into the offices of Fire and Casualty Co. and set a fire that destroyed furniture and equipment worth $100,000. Shortly afterward, Fido filed a Ch. 13 petition. His plan proposes to pay 20 percent of his monthly income over 30 months in payment of his debts. His largest debt by far is the tort claim of Fire and Casualty Co. Fido's annualized current monthly income is far below the applicable median family income, and it is clear that Fido cannot pay more than the 20 percent of his income that he proposes in his plan. This amount will pay general unsecured creditors, including Fire and Casualty Co., 2 percent of their claims.

Fido has so few assets that if his nonexempt property had been liquidated under Ch. 7, there would not have been enough proceeds to pay anything to general unsecured creditors. However, the claim of Fire and Casualty Co. would not have been discharged in the Ch. 7 case because it arose from willful and malicious injury to property and would have been excluded from the discharge under §523(a)(6). This claim is dischargeable in a Ch. 13 case because §1328, the discharge provision of Ch. 13, does not apply the exclusion to willful and malicious injury to property in a Ch. 13 case.[13] As a result, Fido will be able to discharge Fire and Casualty Co.'s claim after paying 2 percent of it under the plan. (*See* Chapter 22 for a fuller discussion of this discharge issue.)

What grounds, if any, does Fire and Casualty Co. have for objecting to Fido's plan?

3. Mo DeFied filed a Ch. 13 petition two years ago. At the time, he was employed as a sales representative and earned $50,000 per annum in salary and commission. He proposed a plan under which general unsecured creditors would receive payment of 20 percent of their claims. The plan met the standards of §§1322 and 1325 and was confirmed.

One of Mo's unsecured creditors has now discovered that Mo was recently promoted to sales manager, and that his annual earnings have increased to $100,000. The creditor has applied for modification of the plan under §1329, asking for the size of the payments to be doubled. Mo opposes the modification. He argues that the modification would be unfair because he earned the extra income by working hard. He also says that if modification is allowed under these circumstances, debtors would have no incentive to better themselves because any increase in income simply enlarges the commitment under the preexisting plan.

Should the court approve the modification?

---

13. A claim for damages arising out of a judgment for willful and malicious action resulting in personal injury or death is excluded from the Ch. 13 discharge, as discussed in Chapter 22. However, a claim for willful and malicious damage to property is not excepted from the Ch. s13 discharge.

4. Bill Overdew owns a home subject to a mortgage. The home is his principal residence. He defaulted on his monthly mortgage payments, and the mortgagee accelerated the debt, initiated foreclosure proceedings, and eventually obtained a judgment of foreclosure. The mortgage would have had 20 more years to run had it not been accelerated. The house is worth considerably more than the balance of the debt.

   Shortly after the judgment, and before a foreclosure sale took place, Bill filed a Ch. 13 petition. In his plan, he proposes to pay the arrears owing on the mortgage over a few months. (Assume that the period of the proposed cure is reasonable.) He will also pay the current installments on the mortgage as required in the mortgage note. These payments will extend beyond the period of the plan, for the remaining term of the mortgage.

   Is this provision in the plan acceptable?

5. Sal Vage borrowed money secured by a mortgage on a piece of land. Sal defaulted on the loan, and the mortgagee began suit to foreclose on the collateral. While the foreclosure proceedings were pending, Sal filed a Ch. 7 petition. The value of Sal's nonexempt property was sufficient to pay general unsecured creditors five percent of their claims. The rest of his unsecured debt was discharged. In addition, he discharged his personal liability on the loan, but the mortgage on the property was not affected by the discharge. (See section 19.4.) After the close of the Ch. 7 case, the mortgagee resumed its foreclosure action. However, before the foreclosure sale could be held, Sal filed a Ch. 13 petition. In his Ch. 13 plan, Sal proposes to retain the property and to pay off the mortgage claim in installments. Is this permissible?

6. Katie Gorize, a debtor under Ch. 13, has proposed a plan that meets the best interests and disposable income tests. The lowest class of unsecured claims will receive a total distribution of ten percent of the value of their claims. These claims would have received no payment in a Ch. 7 liquidation. Although the plan seems to be acceptable in other respects, the treatment of three claims raises questions. Is there a basis for objecting to this treatment?

   a. Three years ago, Katie bought a car on credit, and gave the seller a security interest to secure the debt. The term of the loan is five years, so it has two years to run. The car is worth less than the balance of the debt. Katie proposes to keep the car. The plan provides for the seller's retention of its lien, and for payment of the full balance owing on the car over the five years of the plan.

   b. Katie failed to pay the property taxes due on her house for the tax year ending prior to her petition. The taxes had been assessed, and they should have been paid a few months before the petition to avoid penalties. The state did not file a lien, so the claim is unsecured.

Katie has classified it with other unsecured claims, and will pay ten percent of it over the five years of the plan.

c. A short time before Katie's bankruptcy, a friend loaned her some money to help her cope with her financial difficulties. Katie is grateful to the friend, and feels bad about not having repaid the loan. She has therefore classified the friend's claim separately and proposes to pay 100 percent of it over the five years of the plan.

7. a. Prior to Leanne Stripper's bankruptcy, Junior Loan Co. lent her $25,000, secured by a second mortgage on her home. At the time of the transaction, the home, Leanne's principal residence, was subject to a first mortgage in favor of Senior Security Co. Leanne has now filed a petition under Ch. 13. The balance due to Senior under the first mortgage is $180,000, and the balance of the debt due to Junior is $20,000. The value of the home has been reliably appraised at $160,000. In her plan, Leanne proposes to treat Senior's first mortgage as a secured claim to the extent of $160,000, and an unsecured claim to the extent of the deficiency of $20,000. The proposed plan treats Junior's claim in its entirety as a general unsecured claim. The plan provides for a 10 percent distribution on general unsecured claims. Does either Senior Security Co. or Junior Loan Co. have grounds to object to the plan?

b. Would your answer change if, at the time of the transactions, Leanne was using the home as her principal residence, but by the time of the petition, she had moved out of the house to live elsewhere, and was renting it to a tenant?

Explanations

1. Although Buster's actual monthly income is $5,000, his current monthly income as defined in §101(10A), calculated as the average of his earnings over the six months before the petition, is only $3,333. (He earned salary for only four of the last six months, so his average income for the period is $20,000 divided by six.) To compare this with the family median income, an annual figure, his current monthly income must be multiplied by 12, which comes to $39,996. This leads to the strange result that Buster's income, according to the statutory definition, is below the median, even though his real income is above it. Under the plain meaning of the provision, the confirmation standards that apply to him are therefore those applicable to a debtor who earns below the median family income. *Hamilton v. Lanning*, discussed in section 20.7.3b allows for a court to exercise discretion in adjusting projected disposable income to accord with reality, but it does not extend to determining

current monthly income, which must conform to the statutorily-prescribed calculation.

a. **The five-year payment period.** Had Buster's current monthly income exceeded the median, §1322(d)(1) would have authorized a five-year plan without the court needing to approve the period for cause. However, because Buster's income is below the median, §1322(d)(2) applies, and Buster can only propose a plan with a payout period of more than three years if the court approves the longer period for cause. If Buster's projected disposable income is based purely on a mechanical multiplication of his current monthly income, his payments of disposable income over three years would have been insufficient to satisfy the best interests test. However, because (as explained below) a court is likely to find that Buster's projected disposable income is higher than it would be under a mechanical calculation based on current monthly income, the amount that he is required to pay under the disposable income test over three years will satisfy the best interests test, and his plan will also satisfy the feasibility test. Therefore, there does not appear to be cause to extend the plan to five years.

b. **The financial standards.** In this question we are not interested in secured claims, which you should assume are properly dealt with under the standards of §1325(a)(5). Also, the priority administrative expenses would have been paid in full had Buster filed under Ch. 7, and §1322(a)(2) requires them to be paid in full in the Ch. 13 case. Assume that they will be. We are therefore concerned only with the financial standards relating to the payment of general unsecured claims. There are three financial standards for confirmation in §1325: the best interests test in §1325(a)(4), the feasibility test in §1325(a)(6), and the disposable income test in §1325(b).

The best interests test — §1325(a)(4). To satisfy the best interests test, the total amount of payments to unsecured claims under the plan must be not less than the present value of amounts that would have been paid on those claims had the debtor filed under Ch. 7. Had Buster filed under Ch. 7, there would have been a fund of $36,000 to distribute to his unsecured creditors, paying 10 percent of their claims. Therefore, to satisfy the best interests test, the total payments to unsecured creditors under the plan must be at least $36,000 plus interest to compensate the unsecured creditors for having to wait for their money over the plan payout period. Buster's proposed payment to general unsecured creditors of $36,000 over the proposed five years of the plan ($600 multiplied by 60) is exactly equal to the face value of the Ch. 7 payment to unsecured claims. This is not enough because it does not include the interest necessary to give the claims their present value.

To satisfy this test, Buster's payments must be high enough to cover interest.

The feasibility test — §1325(a)(6). The court should not confirm a plan unless it is apparent that the debtor will be able to make all payments and comply with the plan. Had Buster's actual projected earnings been no more than $3,333 a month, he would have had trouble meeting the feasibility standard, because his disposable income would not realistically have been enough to support the plan payments including interest. However, the reality is that Buster has more actual disposable income than the amount based on current monthly income. A plan that uses his actual disposable income should satisfy the feasibility test.

The disposable income test — §1325(b). Buster's projected disposable income must be determined by deducting his projected expenses from his projected income. Where, as in Buster's case, the debtor's current monthly income is lower than the median, actual expenses are used, rather than the standardized expenses allowed by §707(b).[14] Buster's expenses sound reasonable and are likely to be approved. However, the income figure is the problem here. If the court allowed the use of the current monthly income figure to determine projected income, the disposable income test would not require Buster to pay more than the $600 per month that he proposes. However, *Hamilton* calls for a forward-looking approach to projected disposable income that allows the court to take into account known or virtually certain changes in income. As in *Hamilton*, the debtor's current monthly income is artificial because it is skewed by circumstances that are not likely to recur, so the court is likely to adjust Buster's projected monthly income upwards to reflect the expectation that he will earn $5,000 per month, rather than $3,333. Because he is a below-median debtor, his actual reasonable expenses are used, rather than the standardized expenses. Because his expenses are stated to be reasonable, assume that the court approves them. This gives him a monthly projected disposable income of $2,267 (income of $5,000 less actual reasonable expenses of $2,733). The total that he would be obliged to pay under a 3-year plan as a below-median debtor is $81,612 ($2,267 multiplied by 36). This is more than enough to satisfy the best interests test — it will pay unsecured creditors a considerably higher percentage of their claims than the present value of what they would have received under

---

14. Had Buster been an above-median debtor, his expenses would have been based on the standardized expenses allowed under §707(b)(2)(A) and (B). Most of his expenses seem to be of the kind and may be in the amount allowed by the National Standards and Local Standards promulgated by the I.R.S., supplemented by the other expenses allowed by §707(b)(2)(A) and (B). This is illustrated in Example 1c.

a Ch. 7 distribution. In short, the court is not likely to approve Buster's proposed plan because it satisfies neither the best interests test nor the disposable income test. To have his plan confirmed, Buster will have to make the greater commitment of projected disposable income for three years, as indicated above.

c. Buster's current monthly income now exceeds the median, so he is subject to the confirmation standards applicable to above-median debtors. He may propose a plan with a five-year payment period without court approval. (As noted in section 20.7.3b, some courts hold that he is obliged to commit to a five-year payment period.) As in the original version of the facts, there is an obvious discrepancy between his projected disposable income in reality and as determined mechanically from his current monthly income. In this case, his earnings in the six-month prepetition period are inflated by unusual income, rather than reduced by an unusual loss of earnings. Nevertheless, the principle is the same, and this is an appropriate case for a court to use its discretion to disregard the unusual earnings in projecting his disposable income, which should be $5,000 per month. Because Buster is an above-median debtor, he cannot deduct his actual expenses of $4,000, even if the court finds them reasonable, but is confined to the standardized expenses of $3,500. (There do not seem to be facts that suggest that the standardized expenses are so obviously not an accurate predictor of future expenses that the court should use its discretion to increase them.) This means that the projected disposable income that he must commit to the plan is $90,000 ($5,000 - $3,500 = $1,500 × 60). Because this is more than the present value that general unsecured creditors would receive in a Ch. 7 distribution, the best interest test is also satisfied.

2. There are three possible grounds on which Fire and Casualty Co. could object to confirmation of the plan.

a. The best interests test. Fido's proposed plan satisfies the best interests test because the plan unquestionably pays more than the present value of zero, which is what unsecured creditors would have received had the case been filed under Ch. 7. Even though the claim of Fire and Casualty Co. would have been nondischargeable under Ch. 7, §1325(4) requires only that the claim receive what it would have been paid by the estate on liquidation. It does not take into account what the creditor may have ultimately recovered from the debtor's fresh start estate on an undischarged debt.

b. The disposable income test. The facts state that Fido earns below the median income and that his disposable income has been properly determined. The only issue here is that Fido proposes a 30-month plan. Section 1325(b)(1)(B) requires the debtor to apply all his disposable income in the applicable commitment period to payment under the plan. Where the debtor earns less than the median income, §1325(b)(4)(A) prescribes a three-year commitment period. To satisfy the disposable income test, Fido would have to pay the equivalent of 36 months of disposable income. Some courts would allow him to do this over 30 months if he can afford it, but others read §1325(b)(4)(A) to require a 36-month commitment period.

c. Good faith. Sections 1325(a)(3) and (7) require the debtor to have been in good faith both in filing the petition and in proposing the plan. Good faith is a factual matter to be decided under all the circumstances of the case. It is not necessarily bad faith for a debtor to select Ch. 13 to take advantage of its broader discharge — this is just the exercise of a choice that Congress has conferred. However, where a Ch. 13 plan proposes to pay only a small portion of a debt that would not have been discharged under Ch. 7, the plan must be given particular scrutiny to decide if it is in good faith. See In re Caldwell, 895 F.2d 1123 (6th Cir. 1990); In re Francis, 273 B.R. 87 (B.A.P. 6th Cir. 2002).

Section 20.6 sets out the considerations that courts take into account in deciding whether the totality of the circumstances demonstrates a lack of good faith. The relevant facts here are that Fido filed his petition very soon after he had deliberately and maliciously done extensive property damage; had he filed under Ch. 7, he could not have escaped liability for this debt, which constituted the greater part of his indebtedness; and his payments under the plan are a tiny fraction of what he owes. For examples of cases that apply the totality of the circumstances test, see In re Norwood, 178 B.R. 683 (Bankr. E.D. Pa. 1995); In re Lancaster, 280 B.R. 468 (Bankr. W.D. Mo. 2002); In re Schaitz, 913 F.2d 452 (7th Cir. 1990); In re Sidebottom, 430 F.3d 893 (7th Cir. 2005).

3. Section 1329(a)(1) allows an unsecured creditor to apply for modification of the plan to increase the amount of the payments. As noted in section 20.10, §1329(b) applies the standards of confirmation in §1322(a) and (b) and §1325(a) to a modification but fails to mention the disposable income test in §1325(b), which suggests that the disposable income test does not apply to a modification. Notwithstanding, courts have not hesitated to approve modifications where the debtor's income has increased significantly under circumstances that were not anticipated in the plan. Mo's argument that the modification would be unfair and would create a disincentive to betterment is not persuasive. Similar arguments were rejected by the court in In re Arnold, 869 F.2d 240 (4th Cir. 1989). The court pointed out that the fresh start is supposed to begin after the debtor has consummated the plan, and

that a responsible debtor should be willing to increase payments to creditors if she can afford it.

4. Although the home is Bill's principal residence, §1322(b)(2) is not implicated because Bill does not seek to modify the rights of the mortgagee. Under §1322(b)(5), the curing of a default is not treated as a modification of the mortgagee's rights. In addition, §1322(c)(1) (enacted in 1994 to overturn case law to the contrary) makes it clear that cure is possible until such time as the property has been sold at a properly conducted foreclosure sale. This provision overrides any rule of state law that would have the effect of extinguishing the debtor's right to cure at a stage before the completion of the foreclosure sale.[15]

5. Sal is using the "Chapter 20" tactic described in section 20.11. He seeks to first discharge his personal liability on the debt in the Ch. 7 case, and then to use Ch. 13 to prevent foreclosure on the surviving lien so that he can keep the property and force the lienholder to accept payment of the secured claim under the plan. Had he simply filed the initial petition under Ch. 13, he would have been able to prevent the foreclosure, cure the default, and cram down the installment payments. However, by discharging all his unsecured debt in the previous Ch. 7 case, Sal gets the additional advantage of having eliminated the need to provide in the plan for any payment of that unsecured debt. This frees him from the need to commit his future disposable income to the payment of those debts. Although the U. S. Supreme Court held "Chapter 20" to be permissible in *Johnson v. Home State Bank*, the debtor's conduct and motivation in filing the successive petitions are subject to evaluation under the good faith test. Amendments to the Code by BAPCPA have not precluded the use of "Chapter 20" but they have erected barriers to its use, as discussed in section 20.11.

6. a. The claim secured by the car. This claim is not covered by the hanging paragraph of §1325(b). Although this is a purchase-money security interest in a car bought for personal use, the transaction occurred more than 910 days before the petition. Katie proposes to pay this claim under §1325(a)(5)(B) after modifying the payment period under §1322(b)(2). If the claim was fully secured, this treatment would be unobjectionable, provided that the full payment amount is adjusted to present value. The problem with the proposal is that the car is worth less than the debt, so part of the claim is unsecured. Katie has in fact

---

15. The impact of §1322(c)(1) is not clear where state law gives the debtor a postsale right of redemption. Some courts have held that the debtor has the right to cure up to the end of the state law redemption period. See, for example, In re Sims, 185 B.R. 853 (Bankr. N.D. Ala. 1995). Other courts have disagreed, and have held that §1322(c)(1) unambiguously designates the completion of the foreclosure sale as the termination of the debtor's right to cure. See, for example, In re Cain, 423 F.3d 617 (6th Cir. 2005).

classified the seller's secured and unsecured claims together and is proposing full payment of both. This could be challenged under §1322(b)(1) by another creditor or the trustee, or disapproved by the court of its own accord. The secured and unsecured claims are not substantially similar as required by §1122, and the discrimination is unfair because there is no appropriate justification for treating this unsecured claim differently from others.

b. The property taxes. The property tax meets the qualifications for priority under §507(a)(8)(B): It was assessed before the petition and was last payable without penalty within a year before the petition. Section 1322(a)(2) requires full payment of priority claims unless the holder agrees to a different treatment. This claim has been misclassified, and the proposed payment is inadequate.

c. The friend's loan. The friend's claim is a general unsecured claim which Katie has placed in a separate class. She is entitled to do this by §1322(b)(1), as long as the discrimination is not unfair. For discrimination to be fair, there must be a reasonable basis for the separate classification, and the discrimination should serve some legitimate purpose in the debtor's attempt at rehabilitation. The desire to favor a friend should not be adequate justification for paying him more at the expense of other creditors, who are being paid only a tenth of their claims, and whose distribution will be reduced by the higher payment to the friend.

7. a. Leanne's proposal to bifurcate Senior's mortgage and to treat the deficiency as an unsecured claim, payable at the rate of 10 percent, is a clear contravention of *Nobelman v. American Savings Bank*, 508 U.S. 324 (1993). The mortgage is a claim secured only by a security interest in real property that is the debtor's principal residence, and §1322(b)(2) forbids any modification of the rights of the holder. *Nobelman* held that the section's use of the word "rights" extends the protection beyond the portion of the debt that qualifies as a secured claim, and includes any deficiency that would otherwise qualify as an unsecured claim. Leanne's attempt to strip Senior's lien to correspond to the present appraised value of the property is not allowed, and Senior has grounds to object.

Junior's position is less clear because the senior lien covers the entire value of the property, leaving nothing over for Junior. Its mortgage is therefore not merely undersecured, but completely unsecured. As noted in section 20.8.3, courts differ on whether a completely unsecured mortgage is protected from "strip off" by §1322(b)(2).

b. Section 1322(b)(2) gives no indication of the point in time at which the use of the property must be determined. This issue had to be resolved in *In re Smart*, 214 B.R. 63 (Bankr. D. Conn. 1997), in which the court held that the time of the original transaction, not the time of the petition, was the proper point for determining the property's use. The court reasoned that the purpose of §1322(b)(2) was to encourage lenders to make home loans, and this incentive would be undermined if they could not rely on the state of affairs that existed at the time of the loan. It imports a risk, inconsistent with the goals of the section, to deprive a lender of the protection from modification if, after the transaction, the debtor converts the use of the property from that of principal residence. On this reasoning, the answer to question (a) would not change merely because Leanne was no longer using the home as her principal residence at the time of her bankruptcy.

21

The Chapter 11 Plan

§21.1 INTRODUCTION TO CH. 11 AND ITS DEBTORS

§21.1.1 General Introduction

Remember that the general provisions in Chs. 1, 3, and 5 are applicable in all forms of bankruptcy, so that much of the discussion throughout this book on topics covered by those Chapters has relevance to a case under Ch. 11. On many occasions in previous chapters of this book, there have been specific references to the operation of sections in Chs. 1, 3, and 5 (such as the petition for relief, property of the estate, avoidance powers, the estate's dealings with property, postpetition credit, executory contracts, and the treatment of claims) in a Ch. 11 case. In this chapter, we focus on the Ch. 11 process, including the creation, confirmation, and execution of the plan. Ch.11 bankruptcy is an intricate and complex topic, worthy of an entire book on its own. All that can be attempted here is a broad overview and basic explanation of the central issues relating to the Ch. 11 process and the plan.

It is useful to begin this discussion of Ch. 11 with reference to Ch. 13, its simplified equivalent for individual debtors with relatively small debt. Although there are many significant differences between Chs. 11 and 13, they have close conceptual and structural affinities. The differences between them are necessitated by their intended scope of application: While Ch. 13 is designed to fit the needs of an individual — a consumer or a person who owns a business as a sole proprietor — with relatively small debt, Ch. 11 accommodates debtors with more complex affairs, such as individuals whose debts exceed the Ch. 13 limitations or commercial enterprises, ranging from small privately held corporations to large publically held corporations.

§21.1.2 Eligibility for Ch. 11 and Distinctions between Ch. 11 Debtors, Particularly Individuals and Small Businesses

(1) Eligibility. Section §109(d) makes Ch. 11 relief available to most debtors who qualify for Ch. 7. (*See* section 8.4.2.) Although Ch. 11 is generally associated with corporate debtors or other commercial entities such as partnerships or associations, it may be used by individuals as well. Any doubt that may have existed on this point was put to rest by the Supreme Court in *Toibb v. Radloff,* 501 U.S. 157 (1991). Ch. 13 is generally more appropriate for an individual than Ch. 11 unless the debts exceed the Ch. 13 limitations or the debtor has affairs that are complex enough to require the flexibility of Ch. 11.

(2) The treatment of individual debtors in a Ch. 11 case. Although many of the rules and procedures in Ch. 11 apply equally to individuals and to corporate debtors, there are some provisions, many enacted by the Bankruptcy Abuse Prevention and Consumer Protection Act of 2005 (BAPCPA), that treat individuals differently. These rules are generally intended to cut down on the differences between Chs. 11 and 13 in cases involving individual debtors and to ensure that an individual debtor does not use Ch. 11 to evade duties or to nullify creditor protections that are provided for in Chs. 7 and 13. The different rules applicable to individual debtors are the following.

(a) *Property of the estate.* Where the Ch. 11 debtor is not an individual, property of the Ch. 11 estate is determined by the general rule in §541 — estate property consists of property in which the debtor had a legal or equitable interest at the time of the petition. However, where the debtor is an individual, §1115, added by BAPCPA, adopts the same approach as Ch. 13. The debtor's postpetition property continues to enter the estate after the petition until the case is closed, dismissed, or converted. The debtor remains in possession of estate property while the case is pending except to the extent provided for in the plan, or unless a trustee is appointed.

(a) *Domestic support obligations.* As noted frequently before, the Bankruptcy Reform Act of 1994 enacted several provisions of the Code to enhance the protection of the debtor's spouse, ex-spouse, and children to whom the debtor owes domestic support obligations. In addition to the other provisions that give special treatment to domestic support obligations (for example, in relation to the automatic stay, exemptions, and discharge), §1129(a)(14) provides that if a debtor fails to pay any domestic support obligation that first became due after the petition was filed (that is, current payments, as opposed to arrears), the debtor's plan does not qualify for confirmation under §1129(a)(14), and §1112(b)(4)(P) allows for dismissal of the case on this ground. (*See* section 21.7.1.)

(c) *The disposable income test.* BAPCPA introduced the disposable income test of Ch. 13 to an individual's Ch. 11 case. It added a rather cryptic requirement in §1123(a)(8) that an individual debtor must commit earnings from personal services to the payment of creditors under the plan to the extent necessary for execution of the plan. (*See* section 21.6.2.) More directly, if the holder of an unsecured claim objects to confirmation of the plan, §1129(a)(15) subjects the plan to the disposable income test of §1325(b). (*See* section 21.7.2.)

(d) *The absolute priority rule.* Where a debtor cannot get all classes of creditors to accept her plan, she can only obtain confirmation of the plan by satisfying the standards for cramdown (discussed in section 21.7). The absolute priority rule is one of the requirements for cramdown confirmation. The effect of the rule is that the debtor is not entitled to retain any property from the estate unless classes of unsecured creditors who did not accept the plan are paid in full. BAPCPA added a proviso to §1129(b)(2)(B)(ii) that makes the absolute priority rule inapplicable to an individual, at least with regard to postpetition property brought into the estate under §1115. This means that in a cramdown, an individual debtor's plan can provide for the debtor to retain some property, even if unsecured creditors will not be paid in full. (The absolute priority rule and its application to an individual debtor, is explained in section 21.7.3.)

(e)*Plan modification.* BAPCPA added a provision to §1127 that is similar to §1329. Where the debtor is an individual, the plan may be modified at any time between confirmation and the completion of payments, at the request of the debtor, the trustee, the U.S. Trustee, or an unsecured creditor, to increase or reduce the amount of payments or the time period for payments. (*See* section 21.4.7.)

(f) *Discharge.* Section 1141(d)(2) specifies that the Ch. 11 discharge of an individual debtor is fully subject to the exclusions from discharge in §523. The general rule in §1141(d) is that the Ch. 11 discharge takes effect on confirmation of the plan. Section 1141(d)(5), added by BAPCPA, changes the timing of the Ch. 11 discharge of an individual. The section postpones the discharge (unless the court otherwise orders for cause) until the debtor has completed all payments under the plan. Section 1141(d)(5) includes a discharge on grounds of hardship similar to that provided for in Ch. 13. (*See* section 21.4.9 *and also* sections 22.6 and 22.7.)

(3) Small business debtors. When the Code was enacted in 1978, Congress decided that Ch. 11 should consist of a single set of rules applicable to all debtors irrespective of their size. This was a change from the old Bankruptcy Act, which had provided separate chapters for large public corporations (Ch. X) and smaller businesses (Ch. XI). This unitary approach has never been entirely satisfactory because Ch. 11 was drafted to cater for the reorganization of large enterprises, and many of its rules and procedures were too complex for smaller ones. Congress recognized this when it enacted Ch. 12, which provided a simpler, expedited reorganization process for smaller family-owned farm operations with relatively low amounts of debt. Although Ch. 12 has been successful at creating a streamlined procedure for small farming businesses, it is confined to family farmers and is not available to other small businesses. There was an attempt in the early 1990s to enact an equivalent of Ch. 12 for other small businesses, but a proposed bill to create a new chapter of general application to small businesses (which would have been numbered Ch. 10) turned out to be too controversial and failed.

The Bankruptcy Reform Act of 1994 enacted a more modest and limited set of amendments to Ch. 11, designed to make simpler procedures available to small businesses in Ch. 11. If a debtor satisfied the definition of a small business, an expedited procedure was followed in the Ch. 11 case. The problem was that most of the small business procedures only applied if the debtor elected to be treated as a small business. As a result, a small business that did not want to subject itself to speedier procedures did not exercise the election. The 1994 National Bankruptcy Review Commission recommended strengthening the small business provisions enacted in 1994, making them mandatory, and expanding the U.S. Trustee's supervisory role in small business cases to compensate for less active creditors' committees in small cases. Congress accepted these recommendations, and BAPCPA amended the small business provisions of Ch. 11 to eliminate the debtor's election, to greatly expand the statutory oversight of the U.S. Trustee in small business bankruptcies, and to reinforce the simplified small business procedures enacted in 1994.

"Small business case" is defined in §101(51C) to mean a Ch. 11 case in which the debtor is a "small business debtor," which is in turn defined in §101(51D). In simplified terms (disregarding some qualifications and limits in the definition), a "small business debtor" is a person engaged in commercial or business activities whose noncontingent, liquidated secured and unsecured debt at the time of the petition is less than $2,490,925.[1] (Note that the definition uses the term "person," which is defined in

---

1. The debt limit is subject to adjustment under §104. The dollar amount in the text is as adjusted with effect from April 1, 2013. It will be next adjusted with effect from April 1, 2016.

§101(41) to include individuals, partnerships, and corporations.) For the small business provisions of Ch. 11 to apply, there must be no committee of unsecured creditors appointed in the case,[2] or the court must have decided that the committee has not been active enough to provide effective oversight of the debtor.

Where a Ch. 11 case qualifies as a small business case, a number of special rules and procedures take effect. These are outlined in broad terms here, without any attempt to be comprehensive, and just to provide an idea of the impact of the classification. Some of these small business variations are mentioned again in the applicable sections below.

(a) *The supervisory role of the U.S. Trustee.*   Section 1116 and 28 U.S.C. §586(a)(3)(H) and (6) set out the duties of the U.S. Trustee and the debtor in possession in a small business case. The U.S. Trustee's supervisory function can be divided into two stages:

(i) *The U.S. Trustee's duties at the outset of the case.*   One of the principal underlying goals of the small business procedures is to have the U.S. Trustee focus on a small business case at its initial stages and to identify as early as possible those cases in which the debtor does not have a reasonable prospect of reorganization. The U.S. Trustee must conduct an initial interview with the debtor, must investigate the debtor's viability, and must generally counsel and supervise the debtor. If the U.S. Trustee finds that the debtor will not be able to get a Ch. 11 plan confirmed, she must move for dismissal of the case. The debtor is required to attach financial information to its petition and must attend meetings scheduled by the court or the U.S. Trustee.

(ii) *The U.S. Trustee's oversight of the debtor in possession while the case is pending.*   As the definition of "small business debtor" indicates, a Ch. 11 case only qualifies as a small business case if the court authorizes the U.S. Trustee not to appoint an unsecured creditors' committee, or the court finds it to be ineffectual. One of the rationales for creating small business procedures is that unsecured creditors are generally not likely to participate actively in a small business case, so unsecured creditors' committees are seldom effective in such cases and do not exercise adequate supervision of the debtor in possession. The U.S. Trustee's supervisory role, once the case has passed the initial stage and proceeds through plan confirmation and consummation, is therefore largely intended to substitute for the role that would normally be exercised by a creditors' committee. To aid the U.S. Trustee in her supervision, the debtor has extensive reporting requirements during the course of the case, which are intended to reveal the state of the

---

2. Under §1102(a)(3) on request of a party in interest, the court may dispense with an unsecured creditors' committee for cause.

debtor's management of the business and its financial affairs. These reports include information on such matters as cash receipts and disbursements, tax payments, and profitability.

(b) *The disclosure statement and plan.* Simplified procedures relating to the disclosure statement and plan apply to a small business debtor. The disclosure statement is a crucial and usually complex document that contains a great deal of information about the debtor's financial history, financial affairs, and proposed strategy for rehabilitation. It must be approved by the court and disseminated to creditors before the debtor begins to seek approval of its Ch. 11 plan. (*See* section 21.4.4). In a small business case the debtor is able to use a simplified standard form disclosure statement, and the process of approving and disseminating the disclosure statement is quicker and easier. Also, the time limits for filing and confirming the plan are shorter. (*See* sections 21.4.3 and 21.4.6.)

§21.2 THE PURPOSE OF A CH. 11 CASE

It has been reiterated throughout this book that the goal of a Ch. 11 case is the rehabilitation of the debtor. The rehabilitative function of Ch. 11 is particularly important to corporate debtors, which cannot survive liquidation bankruptcy. By filing a Ch. 11 petition, the debtor is able to continue the operation of its business under the shelter of the automatic stay. It is thereby able to preserve its profitable activities and assets while it negotiates with creditors and attempts to develop a strategy for the satisfaction of debts and the revitalization of its failing enterprise. If the negotiations are fruitful, the debtor formulates a plan, which is the blueprint for its rehabilitation. The plan contains proposals for the treatment of debt and sets out the course to be taken by the debtor in seeking financial recovery.

If the plan satisfies the requirements of the Code, it is confirmed by the court. The debtor then tries to implement the plan. A successful consummation depends on the accuracy of the business judgments underlying the plan, the competence of the debtor's management, and the prevailing economic conditions. If all these factors are favorable, the terms of the plan will be performed, the Ch. 11 case will eventually be closed, and the debtor will emerge from bankruptcy freed of its prepetition debts and in fiscal health. From the perspective of creditors, a successful reorganization holds the promise of a greater recovery on their claims. For the owners of the debtor, rehabilitation offers a chance of preserving some or all of an investment that would have been lost in liquidation. Society as a whole is benefited by the preservation of the profitable elements of the enterprise with its jobs and products. Of course, not all Ch. 11 debtors can be rehabilitated. Many Ch. 11 cases end up in liquidation, which may be accomplished by converting the case to Ch. 7 or by remaining in Ch. 11 and modifying the plan to provide for the debtor's liquidation.

Apart from liquidation following an unsuccessful attempt at reorganization, a debtor can choose from the outset to liquidate under Ch. 11. Section 1123(a)(5)(D) expressly permits liquidating plans. Although the end result of liquidation under Ch. 11 is legally the same as liquidation under Ch. 7, a Ch. 11 liquidation can provide practical advantages to the debtor and creditors. For example, the debtor can usually retain greater control of the liquidation process, take more time to wind up its affairs, and enhance the ultimate liquidation value of its estate.

§21.3 THE IMPORTANCE OF NEGOTIATION AND BUSINESS JUDGMENT IN A CH. 11 CASE

Ch. 11 is much more intricate than Ch. 13 because the affairs of a Ch. 11 debtor can be very complex and require greater flexibility and more extensive participation by parties in interest. Two aspects of a Ch. 11 case stand out and distinguish it dramatically from the other forms of bankruptcy. The first is the great leeway given to the debtor and other parties in interest to negotiate during the case for the purpose of reaching agreement on the terms of the plan. Provision is made for representative committees, for the communication of information, and for voting. Ideally, a Ch. 11 plan should be a consensual document, although Ch. 11 does have some mechanisms for overriding opposition to it and imposing its terms on unwilling parties. The role played by Code provisions in encouraging negotiation or providing bargaining leverage to one or another party is a constant theme in any discussion of Ch. 11.

The second distinguishing feature of Ch. 11 is the extent to which it interacts with difficult issues of corporate and business law and business strategy. Particularly in corporate reorganizations, the Code provisions, complex as they may be, are mere skeletal structures. They are augmented by nonbankruptcy laws such as those governing corporations, labor relations, commercial law, securities, and taxation. Of course, nonbankruptcy law and economic considerations are relevant in all forms of bankruptcy, as has often been pointed out before. However, the scope and scale of the application of nonbankruptcy business law and business judgment is typically much greater in a complex Ch. 11 case.

§21.4 OUTLINE OF THE CH. 11 CASE

The progress of the Ch. 11 case is set out in this section, which provides a broad description of essential features in an approximate chronological sequence. (Many of the issues mentioned have been dealt with previously and are included for the purpose of review.) In sections 21.6 and 21.7 the contents of the plan and the requirements for confirmation are explained more fully. Diagram 21a charts the Ch. 11 process.

§21.4.1 Commencement of the Case

A Ch. 11 case may be commenced either voluntarily or involuntarily. Under Rule 1007, the debtor must file a schedule of assets and liabilities, a statement of financial affairs, and a statement of executory contracts, as described in section 9.3. In addition, a corporate debtor must file a list of equity security holders, and all Ch. 11 debtors must file a list of the 20 largest unsecured creditors, so that the U.S. Trustee can appoint a creditors' committee.

A case can be converted involuntarily to Ch. 11 only from Ch. 7, and it can be dismissed or converted to Ch. 7 by a party other than the debtor for cause. Section 1112 gives the debtor broader rights of conversion to and from Ch. 11.

The automatic stay goes into effect on commencement of the case. Prepetition property enters the estate as in a Ch. 7 case. Where the debtor is an individual, postpetition property becomes property of the estate as it does under Chs. 12 and 13. Where the debtor is a corporate entity, postpetition property does not automatically enter the estate.

§21.4.2 The Roles of the Debtor in Possession, Creditors, and Interest Holders

As mentioned before, the debtor in possession normally exercises the trustee's functions in a Ch. 11 case and operates the debtor's business under §1108.

However, a trustee may be appointed if the court so orders under §1104. The order for appointment of a trustee must be based on an application by the U.S. Trustee or a party in interest who must show cause (usually in the form of dishonesty or mismanagement by the debtor in possession) or that the appointment serves the interests of creditors and equity security holders. After the court orders the appointment of a trustee,

The Progress of a Ch. II Case

VOLUNTARY PETITION

INVOLUNTARY PETITION

ORDER FOR RELIEF

PLAN FORMULATION — Debtor has initiative to file plan.* Period of negotiation

Some of the other activity during this period:
- Relief from stay litigation
- Applications for the appointment of trustee or examiner, if appropriate
- Continued operation of business
- Creditors' meeting
- Appointment of committees

DISCLOSURE — Hearing for approval of disclosure statement → Statement approved → Statement and plan disseminated

SOLICITATION — Votes are solicited from parties in interest

VOTING — Parties vote to accept or reject the plan

CONFIRMATION HEARING — Debtor seeks confirmation. Objections to the plan are heard

ORDER OF CONFIRMATION — The plan must satisfy confirmation requirements under §1129

Under §1129(a) (accepted plan)   Under §1129(b) (cramdown)

EFFECT OF CONFIRMATION — Discharge and vesting of property

IMPLEMENTATION OF PLAN

CONSUMMATION AND CLOSE OF CASE

*If the debtor is unable to develop an accepted plan within the period of exclusivity, other parties in interest may file plans. This diagram does not reflect the possibility of competing plans.

Diagram 21a

the U.S. Trustee makes the appointment unless, within 30 days of the order, a party in interest requests under §1104(b) that the trustee be elected. If an election is requested, the U.S. Trustee must call a meeting of creditors and the election follows the procedures set out for the election of a Ch. 7 trustee. In cases where the maladministration is not dire enough to justify the appointment of a trustee to take over the administration of the estate, but there are questions of competence or honesty to be investigated, the court may, on the application of a creditor or the U.S. Trustee, and for cause, order the appointment of an examiner to conduct the appropriate investigation.

The creditors' committee plays a significant role in many Ch. 11 cases, particularly when the case is large enough to warrant the attention and interest of an influential group of creditors. However, in smaller cases, especially where creditors do not have large debts at stake, or have little optimism about getting substantial payment, it can be difficult to establish and maintain an active committee. Section 1102 requires the U.S. Trustee to appoint at least one committee of unsecured creditors as soon as practicable after the order for relief. If appropriate, the U.S. Trustee may appoint additional committees of creditors and equity security holders. However, when the debtor qualifies as a small business (see section 21.1.2), the U.S. Trustee's duty to appoint a committee is qualified by §1102(a)(3), which allows the court to dispense with the appointment of a committee on request of a party in interest and for cause.

Where a committee is appointed, its purpose is to represent the creditors' interests and to keep an eye on the debtor's conduct of estate affairs. Section 1103 sets out the committee's powers. Among other things, it may hire attorneys and accountants, investigate the conduct of the business, participate in the plan formulation, raise and be heard on any issue in the case, and otherwise participate in the case to protect the interests of its constituency.

Many Ch. 11 debtors are corporations, and shareholders in the debtor have an obvious stake in the reorganization. Because their shares constitute an ownership interest in the debtor, they would be the last to receive any distribution in a liquidation. Although they risk loss of their investment in a Ch. 11 case, they may be able to salvage all or part of it if the debtor is successfully reorganized. Shareholders fall within the definition of equity security holders in §101(16) and (17), and they are included as parties in interest in a Ch. 11 case. Ch. 11 constantly refers not merely to claims but to "claims and interests," signifying that shareholders are entitled to be full participants in the case. They may be represented by an equity security holders' committee, which is appointed by the U.S. Trustee, and their interests are dealt with in the plan.

Creditors and equity security holders are divided into different classes in the plan, as explained in section 21.6.2. Bear in mind that a class of claims or interests is treated as a unit for many purposes in a Ch. 11 case. This is particularly significant in the context of voting when the time comes for the approval or disapproval of a proposed plan.

In a Ch. 11 case, a creditor does not need to prove a claim unless its claim is omitted from the debtor's schedule or is listed as disputed, contingent, or unliquidated (§1111(a) and Rule 3003). If the claim is so listed, or is not scheduled at all, the creditor must file a proof to vote and participate in the distribution. Section 1111(a) also refers to a proof of interest, which reflects the rights of equity security holders. Under Rule 3003, equity security holders do not have to file proofs of interest. Their participation and voting in the case is based on the official records of ownership in the debtor.

§21.4.3 The Formulation of the Plan by the Debtor or Other Parties in Interest

Section 1121(a) says that the debtor may file a plan with the petition or at any time thereafter. It is possible that the debtor may have formulated a plan before the petition has been filed.[3] (*See* section 21.5.) However, unless the debtor has been able to negotiate the terms of the plan with creditors before filing the petition, the debtor needs to file the petition and get the protection of the automatic stay while it negotiates with creditors and solicits support for the plan.

As stated in section 20.2, in a Ch. 13 case the debtor is the only person who may file a plan, and it must be done within a prescribed period after the petition. The approach in Ch. 11 is very different. It has no absolute time limit for the filing of the plan. Section 1121 gives the debtor the exclusive right to propose a plan in the 120 days after the order for relief. If a trustee is appointed in the case, this period is cut short and ends upon the trustee's appointment. If the debtor does not file a plan in the exclusivity period, any party in interest may file a plan. If the debtor filed a plan in the 120-day period, and it was accepted during that period by each impaired class (*see* section 21.6.2), no one else may file a plan: The debtor's plan is the only one available for confirmation. If the plan was filed but not accepted by the end of the 120-day period, the debtor has a further 60 days to try to get the plan (or an amended version of it) accepted. If the debtor fails, any party in interest may propose a plan. The court is able to reduce or increase the exclusivity period after notice and a hearing, provided that a party in interest applies before the expiry of the period and shows cause. BAPCPA amended §1121 to impose outer limits on the period of extensions.

---

3. In fact, it is possible that the debtor may have negotiated a plan before the petition has been filed, so that it has a "prepackaged" plan in hand at the time of the petition. This is discussed in section 21.5.

Where the debtor qualifies as a small business, §1121(e) provides shorter time periods for proposing the plan. As explained in section 21.1.2, this provision was added in 1994 for the purpose of expediting bankruptcies involving business debtors with relatively small liabilities. As enacted in 1994, the provision applied only if the debtor elected to be treated as a small business. BAPCPA eliminated the debtor's power to elect application of the section and made it mandatory if the debtor meets the definition of a "small business debtor" in §101(51C). Section 1121(e), as amended by BAPCPA, gives the debtor an exclusivity period of 180 days and imposes an outer limit for the proposal of all plans, whether by the debtor or otherwise, of 300 days from the order for relief. Section 1129(e) requires the plan to be confirmed within 45 days after a plan complying with the Code is filed. The court's power to extend these time limits is circumscribed. It may grant an extension only if the application is made before the end of the time limit, for cause, and upon a showing that a confirmable plan will be proposed within a reasonable time. If the court does grant an extension, it must impose a new deadline.

The possibility for competing plans gives creditors negotiating power and puts pressure on the debtor to devise an acceptable and feasible plan as quickly as possible. The debtor knows that if it does not produce a plan that satisfies creditors, less advantageous alternative plans may be put forward. They may provide for the sale of desirable assets, the elimination of ownership interests, or even the debtor's liquidation. When the plans are voted on, dissatisfied creditors may favor a plan that the debtor does not want. Therefore, even if no competing plan emerges, the threat of alternative plans has an impact on the debtor's thinking as it deals with creditors in the negotiating process.

If competing plans are proposed, each must comply with the disclosure requirements and confirmation standards discussed below. If, in the end, there are two or more plans that satisfy the requirements for confirmation, §1129(c) requires the court to consider the preferences of creditors and equity security holders in deciding which to confirm. Only one plan can be confirmed. (Although the possibility is raised here that a plan may be proposed by someone other than the debtor, the remainder of this chapter operates on the assumption, for the sake of simplicity, that no competing plan has been proposed.)

§21.4.4 Disclosure

In a Ch. 11 case, creditors and equity security holders vote to accept or reject the plan, as described in section 21.4.5. To ensure that these parties are given sufficient information on the plan and the debtor's affairs before they vote, §1125 requires the proponent of the plan to draft a disclosure statement containing "adequate information." The statement must be approved by the court after notice and a hearing, and it must then be transmitted to all creditors and equity security holders, together with a copy of the plan or a summary of it. Section 1125 prohibits the postpetition[4] solicitation of acceptances or rejections of a plan prior to the dissemination of the plan and the court-approved disclosure statement.

Section 1125(a)(1), as amended by BAPCPA, defines adequate information very loosely to give the court discretion in evaluating a disclosure statement in light of the complexity of the debtor's affairs and the circumstances of the case: Enough information must be given, as far as reasonably practicable in light of the debtor's nature and history and the state of its records, to enable a hypothetical reasonable investor with attributes of the members of the class in question to make an informed judgment about the plan. Typically, a disclosure statement provides a history of the debtor and a description of its business operations. It explains the plan (which has been formulated by this time) and alerts parties to any options available under the plan. It describes the proposed course of consummation of the plan and provides financial information so that the debtor's prospects of rehabilitation can be evaluated and its liquidation value assessed.

The disclosure statement is analogous to the prospectus published by a corporation in connection with the issuance of stock. If the Ch. 11 case involves a corporation and the plan is complex, the disclosure statement could be as lengthy and intricate as a prospectus. If the debtor is an individual or a smaller business, the statement is likely to be considerably shorter and simpler.

If the debtor qualifies as a small business (*see* section 21.2.1), §1125(f), as amended by BAPCPA, provides for a less stringent process for approval of the disclosure statement. If the court concludes that the plan itself provides adequate information, it can dispense with a separate disclosure statement, or the court can approve a standard form disclosure statement. The statement can be conditionally approved by the court, and the debtor can immediately begin to solicit acceptances and rejections based on the conditionally approved disclosure, as long as the debtor provides adequate information to those holders of claims and interests who are solicited. Final approval of the statement may be combined with the confirmation hearing.

Outside of bankruptcy, the disclosure required by a corporate prospectus is subject to securities regulation. Section 1125(d) allows regulatory agencies such as the Securities and Exchange Commission (SEC) to address the court on the adequacy of disclosure, but makes it clear that the standards

---

4. Section 1125 applies only to postpetition solicitation of votes. Sometimes the debtor may negotiate a plan with creditors before filing the petition. BAPCPA added §1125(g) to make this clear by permitting prepetition solicitation if it complies with nonbankruptcy law. This is discussed in section 21.5.

of bankruptcy law ultimately determine the extent of disclosure required. A statement that does not fully satisfy nonbankruptcy standards could be adequate for Ch. 11 purposes.

Section 1125(c) allows different statements to be approved for different classes, but all members of a particular class must receive the same statement. Variations in the statement sent to different classes may be appropriate based on the nature of the claims or interests in that class and the depth of information that they require to exercise informed judgment.

Section 1125(e) contains what is called a "safe harbor" provision, which protects persons who violate nonbankruptcy regulations in the solicitation of votes or the issuance of securities under the plan, provided that they act in good faith and in accordance with the Code. The effect of this provision is to protect parties, such as creditors' committees, attorneys, or creditors, who solicit votes on the plan by using the court-approved disclosure statement. The protection only applies if the party acts in good faith, without knowledge of some defect or omission in the statement, and in compliance with the solicitation requirements of the Code.

§21.4.5 Voting on the Plan

When the court approves the disclosure statement, it fixes the period for voting on the plan. Holders of claims or interests who are eligible to vote on the plan receive ballots with the disclosure statement and must return them within the prescribed time, indicating acceptance or rejection of the plan. (Rules 3017, 3017.1, and 3018.) Acceptance of the plan is not based on a simple majority of all the votes. Instead, all claims and interests are divided into classes as explained in section 21.6.2. Each class forms a voting block. If the requisite majority of members of that class votes in favor of the plan, the class as a whole accepts it, even though some of its members may have voted to reject the plan. It is the vote of the class that is significant for confirmation purposes, and the outvoted dissenters are bound by the majority. However, when the class has accepted the plan, the minority who favored rejection is given some protection by provisions that set minimum standards for the treatment of their claims and interests. (This is discussed in section 21.7.2.)

The voting majority for acceptance by a class of claims is slightly different from that for a class of interests. Under §1126(c), a class of claims accepts the plan if at least two-thirds in amount and more than half in number of the voting creditors with allowed claims in that class have accepted the plan. (Voting majorities are illustrated in Examples 2, 3, and 4.) Note that the majority is determined on the basis of voting members of the class and does not take into account the claims of members who decline to vote. Therefore, for example, if the class consists of twenty creditors, but only one of them votes, that vote will carry the class, irrespective of the size of the claim. Under §1126(d), a class of interests accepts the plan if at least two-thirds in amount of the voting holders of allowed interests in that class have accepted the plan. Section 1126(e) allows the court, on request of a party in interest and after notice and a hearing, to exclude from the vote any entity whose acceptance or rejection was not in good faith or was not solicited or procured in good faith or in accordance with the provisions of the Code.

In two situations, the vote of a class is presumed as a matter of law, so no actual voting takes place. First, a class that is unimpaired does not vote on the plan, but is conclusively deemed by §1126(f) to have accepted the plan. (As explained in section 21.6.2, a class is impaired unless the rights of its members are left unaltered by the plan, except for the cure of default.) Second, a class of claims or interests that will receive or retain no property under the plan is deemed under §1126(g) to have rejected the plan and is not required to vote.

§21.4.6 Confirmation

After the period for voting has closed and notice of hearing has been given, §1128 requires a confirmation hearing to be held. Parties in interest may object to confirmation. An objection to confirmation differs from a vote to reject the plan: Rejection is motivated by the preference of the holder, and its perception of its best interests; objection must be based on the legal ground that the plan fails to meet the requirements for confirmation prescribed by §1129. (*See* section 21.7.) If the plan satisfies those requirements, the objection fails and the court issues an order of confirmation under Rule 3020. As noted in section 21.4.3, in a small business case, §1129(e), enacted by BAPCPA, requires the court to confirm a plan that complies with the provisions of the Code not later that 45 days after the plan is filed, unless the court has approved a time extension under §1121(e)(3).

§21.4.7 Modification of the Plan

Section 1127 permits the proponent of a plan to modify it before or after confirmation. Any modification must comply with the requirements applicable to the original plan under §§1122 and 1123 and a disclosure statement must be approved by the court and disseminated for the modified plan in accordance with §1125. A holder of a claim or interest who accepted or rejected the original plan is deemed to have voted the same way on the modified plan unless the holder changes its vote.

Prior to confirmation, §1127(a) allows the proponent to modify the plan simply by filing a modified plan with the court. This gives the proponent some flexibility to make changes in the plan to overcome opposition and achieve a higher degree of acceptance. The modified plan must comply with all the provisions of §§1121 through 1129, and there must be disclosure of the modified plan under §1125. Modification after confirmation is more disruptive, so §1127(b) imposes restrictions on postconfirmation modification. The plan may only be modified with court approval following notice and a hearing and upon a showing that circumstances warrant modification. In addition, the modification must be made before "substantial consummation" of the plan. This is defined in §1101(2) to mean the transfer of all or substantially all of the property proposed to be transferred by the plan, assumption by the debtor or its successor of the business or of the management of all or substantially all of the property dealt with by the plan, and commencement of distribution under the plan.

As noted in section 21.1.2, where the debtor is an individual, BAPCPA added §1127(e), which is similar to §1329(a). The plan can be modified at the request of the debtor, the trustee, the U.S. Trustee, or the holder of an unsecured claim to reduce or increase the amount of payments or to alter the length of the payment period. As in Ch. 13, payments under a Ch. 11 plan can be changed to take into account a significant unforeseen change in the debtor's financial circumstances.

§21.4.8 The Effect of Confirmation

The effect of confirmation is stated by §1141. In general, §1141(a) makes the provisions of the confirmed plan binding on all parties in interest—including the debtor, creditors, and shareholders—whether or not their claims were impaired and whether or not they accepted the plan. This general rule is subject to the exceptions to discharge mentioned below. Under §1141(b) and (c), confirmation also vests all the estate's property in the debtor, free and clear of all claims and interests except to the extent that the plan provides otherwise. (The plan may provide otherwise for the purpose of preserving liens pending payment of secured claims or because some property is to be transferred or liquidated to settle claims.)

Where the debtor is not an individual, §1141(d)(1) discharges the debtor upon confirmation of the plan, so that the debtor's original obligations fall away and are replaced by the commitments under the plan. This used to be the rule for all debtors, but BAPCPA changed it for individuals in Ch. 11, apparently to conform more closely to the Ch. 13 discharge. Where the debtor is an individual, §1141(d)(5) states that unless the court, after notice and a hearing, orders otherwise for cause, confirmation of the plan does not discharge any debt provided for in the plan until the court grants a discharge on completion of all payments under the plan. The language of §1141(d) is different from that of §1328(a), Section 1328(a) says that the court "shall" grant a discharge to the debtor as soon as practicable after the completion of payments under the plan. By contrast, §1141(d)(5) states that confirmation of the plan does not discharge debts "until the court grants a discharge on completion of all payments under the plan," but it gives the court some discretion to grant an earlier discharge under specified circumstances.

Whether or not the debtor is an individual, the discharge relates to all prepetition debts as well as postpetition debts allowed under §502(g), (h), and (i), whether or not a proof of claim was filed, the claim was allowed, or the plan was accepted by the holder. The discharge is subject to the provisions of the plan and the confirmation order, which may curtail its scope and exclude otherwise dischargeable debts. Quite apart from the provisions of the plan, §1141(d)(2) and (3) contain exceptions to discharge: §1141(d)(2) excepts from the discharge of an individual debtor any debts that are nondischargeable under §523. Section 1141(d)(3) denies a discharge to debtor, whether it is an individual or a corporation, if the plan liquidates all or substantially all of its property, the debtor does not engage in business after consummation of the plan, and it would not have been entitled to a discharge if the case had been filed under Ch. 7. (This is explained further in section 22.6.)

Section 1141(d)(1)(B) deals with the effect of confirmation on ownership interests in the debtor: Except as otherwise provided in the plan or the confirmation order, confirmation terminates the rights and interests of equity security holders and general partners provided for by the plan. In other words, §1141(d)(1)(B) sets out a general rule that ownership interests in the debtor cannot survive Ch. 11 bankruptcy unless the debtor is able to have a plan confirmed that preserves them in whole or in part. To achieve confirmation of a plan with such provisions, the debtor must provide sufficient payment to gain acceptance of the plan by creditors, or to meet the stringent cramdown standards explained in section 21.7.3.

§21.4.9 The Effective Date of the Plan, Performance, and Consummation

Unlike Ch. 13, Ch. 11 prescribes no time limit for performance of the obligations under the plan. The payment periods and the timetable for implementation of the plan are stipulated by the plan itself. These periods are settled in the preconfirmation negotiation process and are based on the business realities of the debtor's situation. Section 1142 requires the debtor to proceed with implementation of the plan following its confirmation. (The plan takes effect on a specified date shortly after confirmation, referred to in several sections of Ch. 11 as the "effective date" of the plan.) If the plan is successfully consummated, the case is closed. Otherwise, the debtor's failure to perform is grounds for dismissal or conversion to a Ch. 7 under §1112.

§21.5 PREPACKAGED PLANS

The above outline presupposes that the plan is developed and votes are solicited after the petition has been filed. This is the conventional approach, but the debtor may be able to work out a plan with creditors before filing the petition. The Code recognizes this possibility and accommodates it in §1121(a), which allows the debtor to file a plan with the petition; §1125(g), which allows for prepetition solicitation; and §1126(b), which treats prepetition acceptances and rejections as valid, provided that proper disclosure was made under nonbankruptcy disclosure regulations or, if none exist, under the "adequate information" standard of §1125(a).

A plan that is wholly or substantially settled prior to the petition is called a "prepackaged plan." It is essentially an out-of-court settlement between the debtor and creditors (or at least the most important creditors), followed by a Ch. 11 filing so that the Code can be used to effectuate the settlement, to deal with dissenters, and to obtain the court's imprimatur. If a prepackaged plan can be formulated, the reorganization usually proceeds much more quickly, which reduces the risk, delay, and uncertainty of the postpetition process.

Of course, a prepackaged plan is not a possibility for every debtor. The prospect of settling the reorganization before filing is only open to those debtors who are in a position to approach creditors without the protection of the bankruptcy stay. In addition, the feasibility of prepetition resolution of the plan is affected by factors such as the scope and complexity of what is to be achieved in the reorganization and the range of claims and interests to be accommodated.

§21.6 THE CONTENT OF THE PLAN

§21.6.1 Overview

As stated before, Ch. 11 favors consensual plans formulated by negotiation. Section 1123(a) therefore gives the debtor considerable flexibility to develop a plan that best meets its needs while accommodating the legitimate demands of creditors and other parties in interest. Section 1123 contains eight mandatory provisions for the plan, and §1123(b) sets out a range of permissive provisions that may be included in it. The content of the plan is also affected by §1129, which prescribes the standards that it must meet for confirmation. While some of the mandatory provisions and standards are absolute, others may be varied by consent so that they give bargaining power to a party whose consent is sought.

Ch. 11 plans vary greatly. Some are quite short and simple, while others are lengthy and complex. Obviously, this depends on the size of the debtor and the scale of its operations. Notwithstanding, the plan is likely to follow a typical pattern: It begins with an introductory section that defines terms and provides background material. It may provide some historical data to explain the debtor's situation, and it may offer a synopsis of the plan provisions and a justification for the decisions that have been made. It then classifies claims and interests into classes, states which classes are impaired, and specifies the treatment to be given to each class. This is a crucial part of the plan and is one of its mandatory components. The plan then sets out the means for implementation and the terms, time periods, and undertakings regarding performance. This is another vital component. Finally, the plan contains a variety of optional provisions, governing such matters as the treatment of executory contracts, the sale or liquidation of assets, any amendments to the debtor's charter, the employment of professionals, the retention of jurisdiction by the bankruptcy court to resolve certain postconfirmation matters, and so on.

§21.6.2 The Mandatory Provisions under §1123(a)

Section 1123(a) requires the plan to deal with the following matters.

(1) Designation of classes of claims and interests (§1123(a)(1)). The basic principles of claim classification were addressed in section 19.6, which described the tripartite classification into secured, priority, and general claims, and in section 20.7, which discussed the classification of unsecured claims in a Ch. 13 plan. The classification of claims and interests assumes a particularly important role in the Ch. 11 case because it not only affects the distribution to be received, but also the voting power of the creditor or interest holder. Section 1123(a)(1) requires the plan to designate classes of claims. All secured and unsecured must be placed in classes, except for those that qualify for second, third, and eighth priority under §507(a)(2) (administrative expenses), §507(a)(3) (gap administrative expenses in an involuntary case), and §507(a)(3) (priority taxes). The principles governing classification are set out in §1122 and in caselaw (and are illustrated in Examples 1 and 2). Because classification has an impact on the substantive and voting rights of parties, the debtor's discretion in establishing classes is controlled to prevent unfair discrimination and manipulation of voting power. The following principles apply.

1. Section 1122 requires claims and interests in a class to be substantially similar. The Code does not say what constitutes substantial similarity, but this is generally taken to mean that the claims must be of the same

priority and quality. Therefore, for example, a debtor cannot place in the same class a secured and an unsecured claim, or claims having different priorities. Although unsecured claims of equal rank are often placed in the same class, each secured claim is usually given a class of its own because secured claims are not substantially similar to each other—they are either secured by different collateral or have a different priority in the same collateral.

One group of dissimilar claims may be combined in a single class under §1122(b). Unsecured claims of relatively low value may be classed together for convenience, so that they can be dealt with in the same way. This classification requires court approval, which is granted only if the ceiling amount is reasonable and the classification is necessary for administrative convenience.

2. Although §1122 prevents the inclusion of dissimilar claims in a class, neither §1122 nor any other section of Ch. 11 forbids the debtor from placing similar claims in different classes. However, courts have held that the debtor's ability to classify similar claims separately is subject to the requirement that the classification has a reasonable basis, comports with the best interests of creditors, and facilitates the debtor's legitimate efforts to reorganize. This is intended to prevent manipulation of the classification process for the purpose of diluting the votes of unsympathetic creditors or providing preferential treatment for favored creditors.

3. Three types of priority claims are not subject to classification in the plan. Administrative expenses of the Ch. 11 case, given second priority by §507(a)(2); operating expenses incurred by the debtor in the gap period in an involuntary case, given third priority under §507(a)(3); and tax claims given eighth priority under §507(a)(8) are not classified. Claims under §507(a)(2) and (3) are not classified because §1129(a)(9)(A) requires all these claims to be fully paid in cash on the effective date of the plan. Because they are settled before the plan goes into effect, no purpose is served by classifying them. The rights of the holders of such claims cannot be impaired without their consent, and they do not vote on the plan. Eighth-priority tax claims are not classified either because §1129(a)(9)(C) permits their full payment in installments, subject to controls on the period and terms of payment. As with administrative expenses, the debtor has no discretion to impair these claims without the consent of the holder, so classification serves no purpose. Other priority claims may be classified because, as explained in section 21.7.2, §1129(a)(9)(B) contemplates the possibility that claims in other priority categories may accept a plan that provides for installment payments, rather than immediate cash payment.

4. Like claims, interests may also be divided into classes. For example, a corporate debtor may have issued preferred stock that has priority

over common stock. The same rules apply to prevent the placing of dissimilar interests in the same class or dividing up similar interests into arbitrary or manipulative classifications.

(2) Specification of unimpaired classes of claims and interests (§1123(a)(2)). Impairment is a central concept in Ch. 11. It has already been referred to in connection with voting, and its significance in the confirmation of the plan is discussed in section 21.7. Section 1123(a)(2) requires the plan to specify any class of claims or interests that is not impaired under the plan. It follows that it will also be apparent from the plan which classes are impaired.

The meaning of impairment is set out in §1124, which states that a class of claims or interests is impaired unless each claim or interest in the class is treated in one of the two ways specified in the section. Notice that although it is the class that is impaired, the test for nonimpairment is applied to each claim or interest in the class. In short, for a claim or interest to be unimpaired, the rights of the holder must be unaltered, or they must be unaltered except for cure of a default and deceleration of the debt, with full compensation for any damages incurred in reasonable reliance on the default or acceleration clause.[5] More specifically, these requirements mean the following.

1. *No alteration of rights* (§1124(1)). A claim or interest is not impaired under the plan if the legal, equitable, and contractual rights of the holder are left unaltered. In other words, the plan proposes to give the holder exactly what it is entitled to receive under the terms of its contract or applicable nonbankruptcy law. Any change in those rights (apart from those described in the next paragraph) is an impairment.
2. *No alteration of rights except for the cure of a default and deceleration with compensation for loss* (§1124(2)). If the debtor defaulted on an obligation prior to bankruptcy, §1124(2) allows it to provide in the plan for cure of the default and reversal of the acceleration. If the holder of the claim or interest is compensated for any damages resulting from reasonable reliance on the term of the contract or on nonbankruptcy law that permitted acceleration, and if all other rights of the holder of the claim or interest are left intact, the provision for cure and reinstatement of the original maturity date does not constitute an impairment.

(3) Specification of the treatment of impaired classes of claims or interests (§1123(a)(3)). The preceding explanation of impairment shows that, as a general matter, almost every deviation from the nonbankruptcy rights of a claimant or interest-holder results in impairment of the claim or interest. Because impaired parties will not receive exactly what they

---

5. Impairment is illustrated in Example 3.

had the right to expect under nonbankruptcy law, the plan must set out precisely how they are to be treated: what value they will receive, if any, and when and in what form they will receive it. A plan that fails to do this cannot be coherent or competent.

Section 1123(a)(3) merely requires the plan to specify the treatment of the impaired classes. Section 1129 sets out some minimum standards for that treatment, which are discussed in section 21.7. Subject to those standards, the debtor, as proponent of the plan, decides how impaired claims are to be provided for. Of course, to secure confirmation of the plan, the debtor needs to consult and negotiate with impaired parties in devising provisions that are practicable, affordable, and acceptable.

There are many different ways in which impaired claims could be treated. For example, the plan may undertake full or partial payment over an extended time or in a lump sum; it may propose that a class of claims be paid pro rata out of a particular fund or the proceeds of specified property; it may propose to issue stock or to transfer property to creditors in satisfaction of their claims; it may even provide for no distribution at all to a particular class or classes.

(4) Equal treatment of claims or interests in a class (§1123(a)(4)). The principle of equal treatment of members of a class was introduced in the Ch. 13 context in section 20.7.3. Once claims or interests have been classified together, they must be treated the same unless the holder of a particular claim or interest agrees to a less favorable treatment.

(5) Adequate means for the plan's implementation (§1123(a)(5)). A plan is meaningless unless it has provisions for its implementation. Section 1123(a)(5) requires the plan to set out the manner in which the plan will be funded and the course that will be followed to bring the reorganization to a successful conclusion. Section 1123(a)(5) has a nonexclusive list of some of the implementation provisions that may be included in the plan. Creation of the means of implementation is one of the important areas of flexibility in Ch. 11. It gives a wide range of options to the debtor for devising a reorganization scheme that best satisfies claims, while allowing the debtor to take advantage of resources available for the salvation of its business. The plan's implementation provisions can range from a simple funding scheme derived from future income and the liquidation of unwanted assets to a much more complex arrangement involving such strategies as the issuance of new stock, the creation of new investment or credit, or merger with another entity.

(6) Voting powers for corporate debtors (§1123(a)(6)). If the debtor is a corporation, the plan must provide for matters of voting power in the charter of the debtor and of any corporations with which it proposes to become associated. The charter of the reorganized debtor must forbid the issuance of nonvoting securities. If there are different classes of security, the voting power among them must be appropriately distributed.

(7) The selection of officers (§1123(a)(7)). The provisions in the plan concerning the selection of any officer, director or trustee must be consistent with public policy and the interests of creditors and equity security holders.

(8) The commitment of earnings of an individual debtor (§1123(a)(8)). BAPCPA added subsection (a)(8) to the mandatory requirements for a plan in a case where the debtor is an individual. The subsection is rather vague. It states that the debtor must "provide for the payment to creditors under the plan of all or such portion of earnings from personal services performed by the debtor after the commencement of the case, or other future income of the debtor as is necessary for the execution of the plan." Note that the provision does not require the commitment of all disposable income, or indeed of any particular portion of the debtor's income. It requires these payments only to the extent necessary to execute the plan. Although the enactment of this subsection at the same time as the means test in §707(b) and the toughened version of the disposable income test in §1325(b) would suggest that it must have some relationship to those tests, the relationship is hard to see. On its face, all this provision says is that to the extent necessary, the debtor must fund the plan from postpetition income. Notwithstanding the vagueness of this subsection, BAPCPA also added a new subsection (15) to §1129(a) that makes it clear that the disposable income test is a confirmation requirement for an individual Ch. 11 debtor. (See section 21.7.2.)

§21.6.3 Permissive Provisions under §1123(b)

Section 1123(b) is similar in tone to §1322(b) in that it provides a broadly drafted list of provisions that can be included in the plan if the proponent so desires. The decision on which classes of claims to impair or leave unimpaired is one example. Other matters that may be provided for include the assumption or rejection of executory contracts or the sale of property.

In short, the plan may deal with any appropriate matters that are not inconsistent with the Code. As mentioned before, the range and detail of these optional provisions can be far-reaching in the reorganization of a large debtor.

Section 1123(b)(5) duplicates in a Ch. 11 case the modification-of-rights provision of §1322(b)(5). Section 1123(b)(5) was added by the Bankruptcy Reform Act of 1994 to incorporate into the Ch. 11 case of an individual the same rule as applies in Ch. 13: The debtor can modify the rights of holders of unsecured claims and secured claims, except for the rights of the holder of a claim secured only by a security interest in real property that is the debtor's principal residence. The addition of §1123(b)(5) overrules case law that held that the protection from strip down, available to home mortgagees under Ch. 13, was not available in a Ch. 11 case. An individual debtor may therefore not use Ch. 11 to get around the prohibition on modification discussed in section 20.8.3.

§21.7 CONFIRMATION REQUIREMENTS

§21.7.1 Overview

Section 1129 imposes the standards and requirements for plan confirmation. It provides for two alternative means of confirmation: §1129(a), which sets out the prerequisites for confirmation when the plan has been accepted by all impaired classes, and §1129(b), which governs confirmation in the absence of universal acceptance by all impaired classes, known as "cramdown." Cramdown confirmation under §1129(b) is subject to all the requirements of §1129(a), except for §1129(a)(8), which specifies acceptance by all classes. In addition, the further requirements of §1129(b) must be satisfied. Diagram 21b shows these alternative means of confirmation.

Diagram 21b

§21.7.2 Confirmation under §1129(a) Where All Impaired Classes Have Accepted the Plan

There are 16 requirements for confirmation in §1129(a).[6] Some are applicable to all Ch. 11 plans, but some apply only in particular cases. For example, §1129(a)(14) and (15), added by BAPCPA, apply only to individual debtors. Some of the requirements are quite technical, and are omitted from this overview. Coverage is confined to those that are necessary to an understanding of confirmation under §1129(a).

(1) Lawfulness and good faith (§1129(a)(1), (2), and (3)). Both the plan itself and the proponent's conduct in proposing it must comply with the Code. In addition, the standard of good faith that was discussed in connection with the Ch. 13 plan applies to a Ch. 11 plan as well. The court has the power to refuse confirmation of a plan that is abusive, manipulative or counter to the spirit and purpose of Ch. 11.

(2) The treatment of impaired claims and interests (§1129(a)(7)). Unimpaired classes are deemed to have accepted the plan, so their consent is presumed as a matter of course. Impaired classes vote on the plan. Those members of the class that vote for acceptance are also treated as having consented to the plan. Even though an impaired class may have accepted the plan by the requisite majority, some class members may have voted against the plan. Section 1129(a)(7)(A) protects these dissenters by imposing a best interests test for their claims and interests that is similar to the test discussed in section 20.7 in connection with §1325(a): If a class is impaired, each member of that class who did not vote to accept the plan must receive a distribution under the plan at least equal to the present value, on the effective date of the plan, of what would have been received had the debtor been liquidated under Ch. 7. Although the best interests test applies only to the claims of those members of the class who have voted against accepting the plan, its effect is usually broader as a practical matter. A plan that proposes to pay unsecured creditors less than the present value of what they would have received had the debtor been liquidated is not likely to be well received by creditors in that class, and will probably not gain enough votes to be accepted by the class.

Section 1129(a)(7)(B) prescribes the minimum distribution to be provided for undersecured claims who have made the election under §1111(b). *See* section 21.7.4.

---

6. Section 1129(d) sets out a seventeenth requirement that allows a governmental unit to object to the plan if the plan's principal purpose is the avoidance of taxes or the application of security laws. This requirement is not discussed further here.

(3) Acceptance by classes of claims and interests (§1129(a)(8)).
Section 1129(a)(8) sets out the acceptance requirements that must be satisfied for a plan to be confirmed under the consensual standards of
§1129(a): Each class of claims or interests must either be unimpaired or
must have accepted the plan. Remember that an unimpaired class does not
vote because its acceptance is presumed, and a class who receives no value
under the plan is deemed to have rejected it. If even one impaired class does
not accept the plan §1129(a)(8) is not satisfied, and confirmation can only
be achieved by complying with the additional requirements for cramdown
confirmation under §1129(b).

(4) The required treatment for priority claims (§1129(a)(9)). Except to
the extent that the holder of a particular claim has agreed to a different
treatment, §1129(a)(9) specifies how priority claims must be treated.
Section 1129(a)(9) breaks priority claims into three categories, each with
a different rule, as explained below. (*See also* Example 1.)

1. Administrative expenses (that is, second priority claims under
   §507(a)(2)) and claims arising out of the conduct of the debtor's
   business during the gap period in an involuntary case (that is, third
   priority claims under §507(a)(3)) must be paid in cash, to the extent
   of the allowed amount of the claim, on the effective date of the plan.
2. All other priority claims, apart from priority tax claims, must be paid
   in full. If a class of priority claims has accepted the plan, the claims in
   that class may be paid in installments. (Note that it is the class as a
   whole that must agree to accept the plan.) The amount paid must
   equal the present value of the allowed claim as at the effective date of
   the plan. If a class does not accept the plan, claims in that class must
   be paid in cash on the effective date of the plan.
3. The present value of priority tax claims under §507(a)(8) must be
   paid in full in installments. Although priority tax claims are entitled
   to be paid in full, the holders of those claims cannot insist on cash
   payment, but must accept payments by installments if the plan so
   provides. Section 1129(a)(9) sets a limit of five years from the order
   for relief for the installment payment of priority tax claims.

(5) Acceptance by at least one impaired class (§1129(a)(10)). If any
class of claims is impaired under the plan, §1129(a)(10) requires that at
least one impaired class of claims has accepted the plan. In counting votes for
this purpose, the affirmative votes of any insiders in that class are disregarded. (*See* Example 3.)

This provision is of limited effect in a confirmation under §1129(a),
because §1129(a)(8) requires acceptance by all impaired classes. In most
cases, compliance with §1129(a)(10) follows as a matter of course from

satisfaction of the requirements of §1129(a)(8), but this is not always so. Section 1129(a)(10) excludes the acceptance votes of any insiders in the class. Therefore, if the acceptance of impaired classes was achieved only by the affirmative vote of insiders in those classes, the plan cannot be confirmed.

In cramdown under §1129(b), §1129(a)(10) serves as a control by ensuring that there is some modicum of creditor support for the plan. Although dissenting classes may exist, at least the majority of noninsider creditors in one impaired class has voted in favor of the plan.

(6) The feasibility standard: The plan must have a reasonable prospect of success (§1129(a)(11)). Section 1129(a)(11) requires, as a condition of confirmation, that the plan not be likely to be followed by liquidation or further financial reorganization, except as provided for by the plan. (The caveat makes it clear that this standard does not prevent a liquidating plan when that is the resolution contemplated by the plan.) This requirement places the burden on the proponent to satisfy the court that the plan has a reasonable prospect of achieving its goals and allows the court to refuse confirmation if the plan is impracticable or over-optimistic.

(7) Domestic support obligations of an individual debtor (§1129(a)(14)). BAPCPA added this additional prerequisite to plan confirmation for an individual in Ch. 11 as part of the set of provisions intended to ensure that the debtor cannot use bankruptcy to evade domestic support obligations, as defined in §101(14A). (*See* section 10.4.3 for background.) In essence, §1129(a)(14) makes it a condition of plan confirmation that the debtor is current on all postpetition domestic support obligations that the debtor is required to pay by court or administrative order or by statute. (If there are any domestic support obligations owing in arrears from the prepetition period, they may be provided for in the plan.)

(8) The disposable income test for an individual debtor (§1129(a)(15)). Prior to 2005, the disposable income test was confined to Ch. 13. In addition to making that test tougher in Ch. 13 cases, BAPCPA added §1129(a)(15), which adopts the test where the Ch. 11 debtor is an individual. The effect is to prevent a debtor from filing under Ch. 11 to avoid the application of the disposable income test. The disposable income test is only applied upon objection to confirmation by the holder of an allowed unsecured claim that is not to be paid in full under the plan. If such an objection is made, §1129(a)(15) requires that the debtor commit all projected disposable income, as defined in §1325(b)(2), for the longer of five years from the due date of the first payment under the plan or the duration of the plan payments.

The disposable income test may not operate in exactly the same way under Ch. 11 as it does under Ch. 13. Section 1129(a)(15) cross-references only to the definition of "disposable income" in §1325(b)(2). That section defines "disposable income" to mean current monthly income less amounts reasonably necessary to be expended for the maintenance and support of the debtor or a dependant, as well as necessary business expenses and allowable charitable contributions. Section 1129(a)(15) does not specifically refer to §1325(b)(3), which requires expenses to be calculated on the basis of the standardized expenses formula of §707(b) where the debtor's current monthly earnings exceed the median income. (For further details on the calculation of disposable income under §1325(b)(2), *see* section 20.7.3b.) It is therefore not clear if the standardized expenses are to be used in a Ch. 11 case. The cross reference to §1325(b)(2) may include §1325(b)(3) by implication, but the inference to be drawn from the omission of §1325(b)(3) suggests that in a Ch. 11 case, the debtor's expenses are determined on the basis of actual, reasonably necessary expenses. This was the conclusion reached in In re Roedemeier, 374 B.R. 264 (Bankr. D. Kan. 2007).

The amount of disposable income that the debtor has to commit to the plan under §1129(a)(15) is potentially greater than under §1325(b) because if the plan payments are to extend beyond five years (which may occur in Ch. 11, but not in Ch. 13), the disposable income for the entire plan payment period must be committed to the plan.

§21.7.3 Cramdown Confirmation under §1129(b)

The purpose of §1129(b) is to give the debtor a means of confirmation even though some classes of creditors or interest holders have refused to accept the plan. Essentially, §1129(b) prescribes a minimum level of treatment for claims and interests that was considered by Congress to be fair enough to justify imposition of the plan on unwilling classes.

In short, the plan will be confirmed by the cramdown method under §1129(b) if the following requirements are met.[7]

1. All the standards of confirmation in §1129(a) are satisfied, except for §1129(a)(8) which requires acceptance by all impaired classes.
2. The plan does not discriminate unfairly against any impaired class that has not accepted the plan.
3. The plan is fair and equitable with respect to each impaired class that has not accepted the plan.

The latter two additional standards for cramdown require explanation.

---

7. *See also* Examples 2, 3, and 4 for illustrations of the general standards for cramdown.

a. Unfair Discrimination (§1129(b)(1))

The question of whether a dissenting class has been unfairly discriminated against is largely a factual one that involves some degree of discretionary evaluation by the court. In general terms, the class that has rejected the plan must receive treatment under the plan consistent with that being given to other classes who have comparable legal rights. Thus, the treatment given to the dissenting classes must be compared with that of others with claims or interests of similar rank. If the dissenting class is not treated as well, this is discrimination. However, discrimination is permissible if it is not unfair. The question of fairness has to be resolved by evaluating the need and motive for the discrimination. If it is justifiable—it has some reasonable basis, it is not motivated by bad faith, and it is necessary to the success of the reorganization—it will likely not be unfair.

b. Fair and Equitable (§1129(b)(1) and (2))

The requirement that impaired classes must be treated fairly and equitably covers an even broader range of considerations than the unfair discrimination standard. However, some specific content is given to the meaning of "fair and equitable" by §1129(b)(2), which prescribes the minimum level of treatment to be given to secured claims, unsecured claims, and interests for the plan to qualify as fair and equitable. Note that these are minimum standards: If they are not satisfied, the plan is not fair and equitable. However, even if they are met, this does not dispose of the issue. Other factors may lead to the conclusion that the plan is still not fair and equitable to an impaired class that has not accepted the plan.

i. Secured Claims

To be fair and equitable to an impaired class of secured claims,[8] the plan must at a minimum contain provisions that satisfy one of three alternative tests:

(1) Retention of the lien and deferred payments (§1129(b)(2)(A)(i)).
To satisfy the first alternative test, the liens of the claimants in the class must be preserved to the full allowed amount of their secured claims. In addition, each claimant in the class must receive deferred cash payments totaling at least the allowed amount of its secured claim having a value, as at the effective date of the plan, at least equal to the value of the holder's interest

---

8. As mentioned in section 21.6.2, it is usual for the plan to place each secured claim in its own separate class. Therefore, although §1129(b)(2) applies to a class of secured claims and refers to claims in the plural, there is often only one claim in each class.

in the property. (As explained in section 20.7.3 in connection with Ch. 13, present value is the face value plus interest to compensate for the delay in payment.)

In other words, the first alternative test requires that claimants in the class retain their liens and also receive payment that cannot be less than the allowed amount of the claim, adjusted upward to compensate for deferred payment. When the claimant is fully secured, these two tests mean that it must receive deferred payments equal to the present value of its fully secured claim. If the claimant is undersecured, matters become a little more complicated because of an election provided for under §1111(b). That is dealt with in section 21.7.4.

(2) Sale free and clear of liens, and a lien on the proceeds (§1129(b)(2)(A)(ii)). The second alternative test applies if the debtor wishes to sell the property free and clear of liens, so that the lien cannot be preserved as required by §1129(b)(2)(A)(i). The debtor is permitted to sell the property free and clear of the lien under §363(K), which allows the claimant to bid at the sale. In *RadLAX Gateway Hotel, LLC v. Amalgamated Bank.* 132 S.Ct. 2065 (2012), the Ch. 11 plan proposed to sell the debtor's assets at auction but provided that the bank, which had a security interest in the property, could not bid at the auction. The bank objected because it wished to credit-bid at the auction (that is, to bid for the property, and if it won, to offset the debt it is owed against the purchase price). The Supreme Court held that if a debtor chooses to satisfy the fair and equitable standard by a sale free and clear of the lien, it is bound by the requirements of §1129(b)(2)(A)(ii), which, read with §363(k), entitle the secured party to bid at the sale. The court rejected the debtor's argument that because proceeds of the sale would be applied to paying off the lien, its proposed sale process would give the bank the indubitable equivalent of its claim under §1129(b)(2)(A)(iii). The court held that the alternative of indubitable equivalence in subsection (iii) is a general provision, which applies only to situations not covered by the more specific provisions of subsections (i) and (ii).

Where property is sold free and clear of the lien, the lien attaches to the proceeds of the sale. The claimant is given the same rights to preservation of the lien in the proceeds and to payment, as are provided in §1129(b)(2)(A)(i) and (iii).

(3) Indubitable equivalent (§1129(b)(2)(A)(iii)). The third alternative is a broad provision that gives the court discretion to approve some other treatment of the secured claim that assures the claimant of receiving the indubitable equivalent of the claim. This term is also used in §361(3). *See* section 11.5.4. As in that context, the question to be decided is whether some alternative treatment proposed in the plan will result in the holder of the claim receiving value that is unquestionably equal to its claim. For example, a proposal to surrender the collateral may satisfy this test. As mentioned above, in *RadLAX* the Supreme Court made it clear that this third alternative is a general provision, designed to give the debtor some discretion to come up with a means of satisfying the fair and equitable standard as an alternative to retention of the lien and deferred payments under subsection (i) or a sale free and clear of the lien under subsection (ii). Therefore, a debtor cannot argue that the lienholder receives the indubitable equivalent of its claim where the plan proposes treatment of the secured claim under either subsections (i) or (ii), but falls short of complying with the requirements that subsection.

ii. Unsecured Claims

For the plan to be fair and equitable to a dissenting class of unsecured claims, it must satisfy one of two alternative requirements:

(1) Payment of the allowed amount of the claim (§1129(b)(2)(B)(i)). The plan must provide that each holder of a claim in the class receives property of a value, as of the effective date of the plan, equal to the allowed amount of the claim. This is the present value test again: If deferred payments are to be made, the amount of the distribution must equal the full face amount of the claim plus interest.

(2) The absolute priority rule: No junior claim or interest receives or retains any property on account of its claim or interest (§1129(b)(2)(B)(ii)). As an alternative to full payment of the claims in the class, the plan can satisfy the fair-and-equitable standard by providing for no distribution or retention of property by anyone whose claim or interest is junior to the dissenting impaired class. This alternative is known as the "absolute priority rule", because it is similar to a rule under the Bankruptcy Act that required senior classes to be fully paid before junior classes received anything. The effect of the rule is that if the senior nonaccepting class is not paid in full, the plan can only be crammed down if the debtor is willing to deprive all junior classes of all value.

(aa) The impact of the absolute priority rule on ownership interests. Shareholders and other holders of ownership interests in the debtor are junior to creditors. Under the absolute priority rule, holders of equity in the debtor cannot remain owners unless general unsecured creditors are paid in full—they are "wiped out." Because cramdown results in the sacrifice of ownership equity, the debtor usually has a strong incentive to avoid this course, and to try to negotiate acceptance of the plan. However, if the debtor is willing to pay this price, or if no other alternative is feasible, the

absolute priority rule allows cramdown of a plan that pays the nonaccepting class little or nothing on its claims. (*See* Example 4.) Even where equity holders sacrifice their investment in the debtor because of inability to satisfy the absolute priority rule, dissenting unsecured claimants are still protected by the best interests test of §1129(a)(7). Therefore, the amount paid to dissenting unsecured creditors in the class must be at least the present value of what they would have received in a Ch. 7 liquidation.

(bb) The applicability of the absolute priority rule to individual debtors. Where the debtor is an individual, BAPCPA amended §1129(b)(2)(B)(ii) by adding a qualification to the absolute priority rule. It states that an individual debtor "may retain property included in the estate under section 1115" provided that the debtor has paid all domestic support obligations that arose postpetition, as required by §1129(a)(14). As explained in section 21.1.2, §1115 alters the general rule relating to property of the estate where the debtor is an individual. The general rule is that property of the Ch. 11 estate consists of that property in which the debtor had a legal or equitable interest at the time of the petition. However, if the Ch. 11 debtor is an individual, §1115 expands the property of the estate to include property acquired by the debtor post-petition, including earnings from services. The purpose of the provision is to bring Ch. 11 more closely in accord with Ch. 13 with regard to the individual debtor's postpetition property and earnings.

The problem is that the impact of the proviso to §1129(b)(2)(B)(ii) is not clear. Some courts have held that it abolishes the absolute priority rule with regard to the entire estate where the debtor is an individual. This basis of this interpretation is that §1115 states that property of the estate consists of property under §541 as well as postpetition property. Therefore, the reference to property "included in the estate under §1115" in §1129(b)(2)(B)(ii) covers all the property of the estate. This interpretation is plausible because Congress intended to bring an individual Ch. 11 case more closely in accord with Ch. 13, which has no absolute priority rule. Creditors have the protection of the disposable income test in an individual Ch. 11 case, and it would be too harsh to subject the debtor to the rule in light of the expansion of property of the estate to include postpetition property and earnings. See *In re Roedemeier* (cited in section 21.7.2, item (8)); *In re Shat,* 424 B.R. 854 (Bankr. D. Nev. 2010). However, the view that now seems more prevalent is that the proviso does not completely abolish the absolute priority rule with regard to an individual debtor, but, by its terms, applies only to postpetition property and earnings brought into the estate by §1115. Therefore, the plan may provide for the debtor's retention of postpetition property, to the extent not needed for implementation of the plan, even if a dissenting class of unsecured creditors is not paid in full. See *In re Lively,* 717 F.3d 406

(5th Cir. 2013); In re *Stephens*, 704 F.3d 1279 (10th Cir. 2013); In re *Maharaj*, 681 F.3d 558 (4th Cir. 2012). The facts of *Maharaj* illustrate the impact of interpreting §1129(b)(2)(B)(ii) to apply only to postpetition property. At the time of the petition, the debtors owned an auto body repair shop. Their plan proposed to retain the business and to use income from the business to fund payments under the plan, which would pay general unsecured creditors 1.7 cents on the dollar. Because the unsecured class voted against the plan, the debtors could only gain confirmation by cramdown and could not have the plan confirmed under the absolute priority rule if they retained the auto body repair business, which was prepetition property.

(cc) *The new value exception to the absolute priority rule.* There is one situation in which some courts have allowed equity holders to retain their interests even though a senior nonaccepting class has not received full payment: If the equity holders contribute new capital to the debtor, that is equal to or greater than the value of their interests, they can retain stock in the debtor in exchange for this new value. This is known as the "new value exception." (Some commentators argue that it is not an exception at all, but a corollary to the rule, implicit in the wording of §1129(b).) The new contribution must be in money or money's worth; it cannot take the form of a promise of managerial services or other intangible benefits. The effect of the exception is that equity holders can preserve their equity by making a contribution of capital reasonably equivalent to the value of their interests in the debtor.

The new value exception was recognized under the Bankruptcy Act, but it is not expressly adopted in the Code. Courts disagree on whether the exception continues to exist under the Code. Several courts of appeal have considered the new value exception. Some have found that it still exists, and others have held that it does not. Even among courts that recognize the exception, there is a difference of opinion on its nature and extent. The Supreme Court has had opportunities to resolve this conflict, but it has not done so. In the most recent case in which the question was presented, In re *203 La Salle Street Partnership*, 526 U.S. 434 (1999), the court skirted the question of finally deciding if the new value exception exists under the Code by holding that even if it did exist, the equity holders had not given new value under circumstances that satisfied the language of §1129(b). The 1994 National Bankruptcy Review Commission recommended an amendment to the Code expressly recognizing the exception and setting forth specific standards to be met for its application. Congress did not follow this recommendation.

iii. Interests

The fair-and-equitable standard applicable to classes of interests that have not accepted the plan is similar to that relating to unsecured claims. If the class does not receive the present value of its interest, no junior interest may receive or retain any property under the plan. The present value of the interest must be based on the greater of the fixed liquidation preference or the fixed redemption price to which the holder is entitled, or the value of the interest. §1129(b)(2)(C)(i) and (ii).

§21.7.4 Undersecured Creditors and §1111(b)

Section 1111(b) provides a protective device for undersecured creditors that is not available under any other chapter of the Code. You cannot discern the meaning of §1111(b) by reading it. In essence, its purpose is to provide a strategy for undersecured creditors that will allow them, under some circumstances, to gain greater bargaining leverage in the Ch. 11 case and to prevent the stripping of their liens. As is often the case in Ch. 11, it is not necessarily the exercise of the election but the possibility of its exercise that is important. The debtor's realization that the election is available could make the debtor more amenable to negotiating a consensual plan. Section 1111(b) does two things. First, it treats an undersecured nonrecourse claim as if it were a recourse claim. Second, it allows any class of undersecured claims (whether or not with recourse) to elect to be treated as fully secured for the purpose of applying the "fair and equitable" standard. The operation of §1111(b) is complex and is subject to a number of restrictions that are not detailed here. This overview is merely intended to explain its basic operation and purpose.

(1) Nonrecourse undersecured claims. A nonrecourse claim is one for which the debtor has no personal liability. The holder of the lien is confined (usually by contract or by a rule of state law) to the collateral for payment and has no recourse against the debtor to recover any deficiency. A nonrecourse claim would therefore not normally bifurcate under §506. The creditor has a secured claim only to the extent of the collateral's value but has no unsecured claim for the balance. Section 1111(b) disregards nonrecourse provisions in contract and under nonbankruptcy law and gives the nonrecourse creditor a deficiency claim. The reason for this is that the nonrecourse creditor is particularly vulnerable to a low appraisal of the property in the Ch. 11 case, which would strip down its lien to the current value and prevent it from recovering any enhanced value of the collateral if the debtor ultimately defaults. (Under nonbankruptcy law the nonrecourse creditor can better protect itself by bidding at the foreclosure sale and acquiring the property at current depressed value, which it could later resell once the value increases.)

(2) The election under §1111(b).   The election under §1111(b) must be made by the class as a whole. (Often, the requirement that the class as a whole makes the election is not important because the claim is placed in a class by itself.) A class of undersecured creditors can make the election, whether the claims in that class have recourse under nonbankruptcy law or are nonrecourse claims treated as having recourse under §1111(b). Where the class of undersecured creditors makes the election, the unsecured deficiency is eliminated and the claim is treated as secured to the full amount of the debt. As a result, the class of creditors loses its unsecured claims, which means that it loses its right to vote as a class of unsecured claims and to receive any distribution on those claims. In exchange, the members of the class now have secured claims for the full amount of the debt. As a result, the debtor cannot satisfy the "fair and equitable" test of §1129(b)(2)(A) by paying only the present value of the collateral. Instead, the debtor must pay at least the full face value of the secured claims in the class, having a present value equal to the value of the collateral. (Note that this treatment differs from that accorded to a fully secured claim, which must be paid at the present value of the allowed secured claim. Upon the §1111(b) election, the undersecured claim must be paid the greater of the face value of the allowed secured claim, or the present value of the collateral.) By adding the deficiency to the claim, its face value is increased, so if the deficiency is large enough it can inflate the face value of the claim beyond the present value of the collateral, and the plan can meet the "fair and equitable" standard only if the debtor provides for the full payment of this amount.

The election is particularly useful to avoid strip down where the collateral is temporarily depressed in value or undervalued. If the reorganization is unsuccessful and the collateral is ultimately liquidated, the election preserves the claim for the full amount of the debt and is not confined to the value of the collateral at the effective date of the plan.

The election will not always benefit a class of undersecured creditors. The loss of the distribution that would have been made on the unsecured deficiency claims, and the loss of voting power on those claims (which could have given the class the power to reject the plan and to force a cramdown) must be weighed against the benefit of enhancing the value of the secured claims. Example 5 illustrates the basic operation of §1111(b).

Examples

1. The debtor, a small corporation, is seeking to reorganize under Ch. 11. The following are some of its debts:

   (a) $50,000 in administrative expenses incurred to date in the Ch. 11 case.

(b) $40,000 owed to five employees for salary earned the month before the petition. None of the five claims exceeds $12,475.

(c) $100,000 owed to the I.R.S. for income taxes due for the tax year that ended just before the petition

(d) $500,000 due to six trade creditors who sold inventory to the debtor on credit in the three months before the petition.

What general rules does Ch. 11 prescribe for the treatment of these claims in the plan?

2. A corporate Ch. 11 debtor owes a total amount of $600,000 to three finance companies from whom it had received unsecured lines of credit for operating expenses. One of these creditors, Co-operative Credit Co., is owed $220,000 of this total debt. It has become apparent that Co-operative is very hostile to the debtor and will not accept the debtor's proposed reorganization plan, under which creditors in the class will receive payment of 60 percent of their claims. The other two finance companies are sympathetic and have indicated that they will support the plan. Assume that the three claims are substantially similar and can be placed in the same class under §1122. If the plan places all three of these creditors into a class, does it seem that the debtor can gain the vote of the class to accept the plan? If not, can the debtor place Co-operative in a different class? If the debtor can do this, what advantage, if any, will it get?

3. The corporate Ch. 11 debtor's plan classifies claims and proposes the following treatment of each class of creditor:

(a) Class 1. A secured creditor that has a fully secured mortgage on real property. The creditor will retain its lien and will be paid in accordance with the original loan agreement.

(b) Class 2. The president and major shareholder in the debtor who made a loan to the debtor, secured by a security interest in the debtor's equipment. The equipment is worth less than the balance of the loan, so the plan proposes to bifurcate the claim. Class 2 consists of the secured claim, which will be paid in full to the value of the collateral. The unsecured deficiency is included in class 5, with other general unsecured claims.

(c) Class 3. A secured creditor that has a security interest in the debtor's truck, which is worth more than the balance of the debt. The creditor will retain its lien and will be paid in full, with interest. However, the plan proposes to extend the payment period, so that is is a year longer than provided for in the original loan agreement.

(d) Class 4. Administrative expenses, to be paid in cash on the effective date of the plan.

(e) Class 5. General unsecured claims, which will receive a distribution of 20 percent of their claims.

Classes 1, 2, and 4 voted to accept the plan, but classes 3 and 5 voted not to accept. Can the debtor get the plan confirmed?

4. A corporate Ch. 11 debtor has proposed a plan under which general unsecured creditors are classified together and will receive installment payments equal to sixty percent of their claims. This amount is quite generous, and it satisfies the best interests test because general unsecured creditors would not receive anything close to that if the debtor was liquidated under Ch. 7. Therefore, some of the creditors in the class are willing to vote in favor of the plan. However, the two largest creditors in the class, whose claims together constitute half of the amount of claims in the class, refuse to accept anything less than full payment, and will not vote to accept a plan that provides for anything less. These two creditors are the only dissenters in the entire creditor body. All other classes are willing to accept the plan. The president of the debtor, who is also the principal shareholder in the debtor, does not believe that the debtor can afford to pay unsecured claims in full. What will happen if the debtor declines to increase the proposed distribution?

5. The real property of a Ch. 11 debtor is subject to a nonrecourse mortgage that secures a debt of $500,000. Because of a slump in property values, the collateral is appraised at $400,000, but it will likely appreciate in the future. The debt owed to the mortgagee therefore bifurcates into a secured claim of $400,000 and an unsecured claim of $100,000. Under nonbankruptcy law, because this is a nonrecourse mortgage, the unsecured deficiency is not recoverable from the debtor. Under §1111(b) a class of creditors that is undersecured is entitled to elect under §1111(b) to eliminate the deficiency and to have the entire $500,000 claim treated as secured. (Assume that the mortgagee is the only creditor in this class.) What are the advantages and drawbacks of so electing?

Explanations

1. (a) The administrative expenses are entitled to second priority under §507(a)(2), but in a corporate Ch. 11 case they are actually first-priority claims because the claims entitled to first priority under §507 — domestic support obligations — are not implicated. Unless the holder of the claim has agreed to different treatment, §1129(a)(9)(A) requires the allowed amount of administrative expense claims to be paid in full in cash on the effective date of the plan.

(b) The $40,000 owed to the employees qualifies as a fourth priority claim under §507(a)(4) because the salary was earned within 180 days before the petition and no claim exceeds the maximum priority amount of $12,475. Under §1129(a)(9)(B) the allowed amount of these claims must also be paid in cash on the effective date of the plan unless the plan provides for payment by installments and the class has accepted the plan. Because the claims of the five employees are similar, the debtor is likely to be required to classify them together and treat them equally under §1122 and 1123(a)(4). The class as a whole must accept the plan, for which §1126(c) requires an affirmative vote of two-thirds of the claims in amount and more than half in number.

(c) The tax debt is an eighth priority claim under §507(a)(8) because it is for a tax measured by income for a taxable year ending before the petition for which a return was last due after three years before the filing of the petition. Section 1129(a)(9)(c) treats priority tax claims differently from other priority claims. Unless the I.R.S. has agreed to a different treatment, the claim must receive the present value of the full allowed amount of the claim. However, the claim can be paid in installments over a period not to exceed five years and need not be paid in cash on the effective date of the plan.

(d) The trade creditors have general unsecured claims. If the claims are similar, the debtor may classify them together under §1122, but may place them in separate classes provided that the classification has a reasonable basis and is not for the purpose of manipulation. The plan will propose the treatment of these claims, and if the class is impaired (that is, it its members will receive less than their entitlement under nonbankruptcy law) the class will vote on whether to accept the plan. If the class votes not to accept the plan, the debtor can only have the plan confirmed by the cramdown method, which will require compliance with the requirements of §1129(b) that the plan must not discriminate unfairly against the dissenting class, and must be fair and equitable. (*See* section 21.7.3.) If the class as a whole votes to accept the plan, any dissenting members of the class have the protection of the best interests test under §1129(a)(7)(A).

2. If Co-operative refuses to accept the plan, the debtor will lose the favorable vote of the entire class. For a class of creditors to accept the plan, §1126(c) requires that at least two-thirds in amount and more than one-half in number of creditors in the class must vote to accept it. Although more than half in number of the creditors in the class appear willing to accept the plan, the total of their claims comes to $380,000, which falls $20,000 short of the necessary two-thirds of the total amount of claims in the class.

It is not clear if the debtor would be permitted to classify Co-operative's claim separately. There is no provision in Ch. 11 that forbids the placing of similar claims into separate classes, but courts refuse to allow this if the purpose of the separate classification is to manipulate voting or to achieve some end that is contrary to the interests of creditors and not reasonably needed to achieve the legitimate goals of reorganization. The debtor's principal benefit from classifying the claim separately would be to ensure that at least one class of impaired claims accepts the plan, which is required for confirmation under §1129(a)(10). This will be an important benefit if there is no other class of claims that has voted to accept the plan. Whether Co-operative is classified with the other two claims and its negative vote prevents that class from accepting, or it is placed in its own class and votes against the plan, its refusal to accept the plan creates a dissenting class that will preclude consensual confirmation under §1129(a) and require the debtor to satisfy the cramdown requirements of §1129(b).

3. We begin by determining which of these classes is impaired. Section 1124(1) states that a class is impaired unless the plan "leaves unaltered the legal, equitable, and contractual rights" to which each claim in the class is entitled. Therefore, the only unimpaired classes are class 1, the secured claim that will be treated exactly as provided for in the loan agreement, and class 4, the administrative expenses to be paid in cash on the effective date of the plan. Because it is unimpaired, class 1 is deemed to accept the plan and does not vote on it. Class 4 does not vote on the plan either. As explained in section 21.6.2, the administrative expense claim does not even have to be classified at all because it has to be paid in cash on the effective date of the plan. This leaves classes 2, 3, and 5, all of which are impaired because there has been an alteration of the legal rights that they have under nonbankruptcy law: Class 2 is impaired because the lien has been stripped down — the claim has been bifurcated and only the secured portion will be paid in full. Class 3 has been impaired. Even though the claim will be paid in full, the payment period will be longer than provided for in the loan agreement. Class 5 is impaired because creditors in that class will not be paid in full.

Because two classes (3 and 5) voted not to accept the plan, it does not qualify for consensual confirmation under §1129(a). Consensual confirmation is only possible under §1129(a)(8) if each class is either unimpaired or has accepted the plan. If §1129(a)(8) is not satisfied, the plan can only be confirmed by cramdown under §1129(b). However, all the requirements of §1129(a), apart from (a)(8), must be satisfied for a cramdown confirmation. One of those standards is that at least one class of impaired claims has accepted the plan, determined without including any acceptance of the plan by an insider. The only impaired class that has accepted the plan is class 2, but the creditor in that class is the president of the debtor, and as an officer of the debtor, qualifies as an insider under §101(31). Therefore, there is insufficient support of the plan by noninsider impaired classes to allow for confirmation under §1129(b).

4. If the debtor does not meet the demands of the holdout creditors, and cannot persuade them to accept a plan that pays less than they demand, their negative votes on the plan will preclude acceptance by the class under §1126(c), because the rest of the creditors in the class hold only one-half in amount of the claims in the class. This will prevent the debtor from confirming the plan as consensual under §1129(a), and will require a cramdown confirmation under §1129(b). The plan can only be confirmed in a cramdown if it qualifies as fair and equitable. To satisfy this test with regard to a class of unsecured claims, §1129(b)(2)(b) requires either that each holder of a claim that class receives the present value of the allowed amount of its claim, or if not, that no claim or interest junior to that class receives any property under the plan. (This is the absolute priority rule.) The effect of this is that if the debtor declines to pay the unsecured claims in full, equity interests, which are junior to debt, are wiped out. That is, the president will lose his ownership interest in the debtor.

5. Under §1111(b) the unsecured deficiency is recognized in the Ch. 11 case even if the mortgage was without recourse.

If the mortgagee does not make the §1111(b) election and the debtor proposes to keep the property, §1129(b)(2)(A) requires the debtor to pay at least the full value of the secured claim ($400,000), having a present value equal to the value of the collateral ($400,000 plus interest). The unsecured claim of $100,000 is entitled to a distribution and to a vote, so there may be both economic and strategic value to the claim. However, the drawback to not making the election is that if the Ch. 11 case is not successfully consummated and the collateral is liquidated, the secured claim is confined to payment of the balance of the $400,000 collateral value fixed in the plan, and gets no advantage of any appreciation of the collateral's value.

If the mortgagee makes the election under §1111(b), it loses the $100,000 deficiency claim as well as its voting rights as an unsecured claimant and has a secured claim for the full amount of $500,000. The plan must now provide for the greater of the face value of the claim ($500,000) or the present value of the collateral ($400,000 plus interest). If the Ch. 11 reorganization fails, the mortgagee's claim to the liquidation proceeds of the property is the balance of the $500,000 secured claim. Thus, the effect of the election is to prevent the debtor from stripping the lien.

22

CHAPTER

The Debtor's Discharge

§22.1 INTRODUCTION

The debtor's discharge has been referred to frequently in prior chapters. The discharge is the statutory forgiveness of the balance of debts that are not paid in full in the bankruptcy case. The debtor's right to receive a discharge as a matter of law, even in the absence of creditor assent, is one of the features that distinguishes bankruptcy from insolvency proceedings under state law. For many debtors, it is the principal incentive for seeking bankruptcy relief. The discharge is one of the most important manifestations of bankruptcy's fresh start policy. However, as was observed in the general discussion of bankruptcy policy in Chapter 5, the goal of providing a fresh start to the debtor must be balanced against other public policies served by the Code. To give due deference to these policies, limits and qualifications are imposed on the debtor's right to a discharge. Before covering the detailed rules of the discharge, it is useful to identify some of the broad themes that arise from the Code's attempt to balance the debtor's right to a fresh start against other bankruptcy goals.

Bankruptcy's fresh start is meant to help the honest debtor and not to provide a means for the unscrupulous evasion of debt. For this reason, there are provisions in the Code that deny or limit the discharge where the debtor has dealt dishonestly with creditors or has tried to abuse the spirit and purpose of the Code. However, these penalties are not comprehensive. They cover only specified conduct in particular situations. They also do not apply equally in all forms of bankruptcy; for example, some of the rules applicable in Ch. 7 do not apply in Ch. 13. Therefore, although one can state as a general proposition that undeserving conduct may affect the debtor's discharge, one has to examine the Code provisions carefully to determine whether particular behavior has an impact on the discharge.

As an alternative to denying or restricting the discharge to penalize bad faith conduct, the court has the power, upon cause being shown by a party in interest, to dismiss the bankruptcy case. (*See* section 9.7.) Dismissal denies all bankruptcy relief to the debtor, including the discharge, and is therefore another means of preventing abuse of bankruptcy's discharge privilege. Of course, grounds for dismissal must be present, and not all forms of unworthy conduct constitute a basis for dismissal.

Wrongful conduct is not the only basis for denying or limiting the discharge. Some debts are excluded from the discharge because Congress has decided that the claims in question should not be forgiven. This is exemplified by the nondischargeability of certain taxes, domestic support obligations, and student loans. These limits on dischargeability are very specific and only apply to debts that meet the statutory qualifications.

The extent and scope of the discharge varies between the different chapters of the Code. Each chapter has its own discharge provisions, namely §§727, 1141, 1228, and 1328. In addition, §§523, 524, and 525 apply to all chapters except to the extent that they are excluded by the specific provisions of a particular chapter. These variations in the discharge result in part from the policy favoring rehabilitation over liquidation. (This is most strikingly apparent in the comparison between discharge under Chs. 7 and 13.) However, divergence in the discharge provisions also reflects the particular structure of each chapter and the premises on which it is based.

Distinctions are also made in the Code between the availability of the discharge to individuals and to corporate entities. Unless there are grounds for denial of the discharge (and subject to any applicable exclusions from the discharge), an individual may obtain a discharge irrespective of which form of bankruptcy relief has been chosen. However, a corporation can only receive a discharge if it undergoes rehabilitation under Ch. 11 or 12. If it is liquidated under Ch. 7 or 11, it becomes a mere shell. Bankruptcy does not actually terminate its existence (this is left to nonbankruptcy law), but if the corporation is not deregistered under nonbankruptcy law, the Code provides a strong disincentive to the revitalization of the corporate shell: Its undischarged prepetition debts remain in existence and are claimable from its new assets. (For an example of a case in which a successor to a defunct corporation was held liable for its prepetition debt, see In re *Goodman*, 873 F.2d 598 (2d Cir. 1989).)

§22.2 THE SCOPE OF THE DISCHARGE

The discharge applies only to debts that fall within the bankruptcy case. As a general rule, this covers only prepetition debts that were or could have been proved in the estate. Of course, the estate itself incurs debts in the course of administering the estate. Although these debts are obligations of the estate and handled in the bankruptcy case, they are postpetition debts, and may not be subject to the discharge, depending on the chapter under which the debtor has filed. However, the question of whether they are discharged is seldom relevant because administrative expenses are usually paid in full out of the estate. Most postpetition debts incurred by the debtor (as opposed to debts incurred by the estate itself) are obligations of the debtor's fresh start estate and are not affected by the discharge. There are exceptions to this rule. In an involuntary Ch. 7 case, §727(b) includes in the discharge all debts incurred in the gap period between the petition and the adjudication of bankruptcy; in a Ch. 11 case, §1141(d)(1) includes in the discharge all debts that arose before the order of confirmation; and in cases under Chs. 12 and 13, the discharge covers all claims provided for in the plan (§§1228 and 1328).

Only debts are discharged: §§727, 1141, 1228, and 1328 all specifically refer to this term in providing for the discharge. "Debt" is defined in §101(12) to mean liability on a claim, which is in turn defined, in very broad terms, in §101(5). (*See* section 19.2.) Although most obligations are encompassed by this broad definition, some prepetition obligations of the debtors do not qualify as claims. If they are not claims, they are not covered by the discharge. The Supreme Court dealt with this issue in *Ohio v. Kovacs*, 469 U.S. 274 (1985). (*See* section 19.2.1.) In *Kovacs* the court held that a prepetition court order directing the debtor to clean up hazardous waste was a claim because the state agency had the alternative, under the state environmental statute, to conduct the cleanup itself and to seek reimbursement from the debtor. The court indicated that if there had been no alternative of a monetary remedy, the order compelling the debtor to clean up the site would not have been a claim. In *Pennsylvania Department of Public Welfare v. Davenport*, 495 U.S. 552 (1990), the Supreme Court held that the debtor's obligation to make restitution as a condition of probation in a criminal case is a right to payment and hence a debt. (Congress responded to *Davenport* by making the debt nondischargeable in a Ch.13 case, as discussed in section 22.7.3 and Example 2.) Since *Kovacs* and *Davenport*, lower courts have followed this distinction in a variety of different cases. For example, in *Kennedy v. Medicap Pharmacies, Inc.*, 267 F.3d 493 (6th Cir. 2001), the court held that an injunction to enforce a covenant not to compete did not constitute a claim under *Kovacs* because the plaintiff had no alternative right to payment. The equitable relief of an injunction was premised on the absence of an adequate legal remedy for damages.

As explained in sections 19.4 and 19.6.3, because the discharge only covers debts, it affects only the debtor's personal liability on a secured claim. It does not terminate any lien on the debtor's property. Therefore although a debt secured by a lien is discharged and cannot be collected from the debtor as a personal liability, the lien survives the discharge. Therefore, once the automatic stay is lifted, the lienholder is able to foreclose on the property to satisfy the discharged debt to the extent of the collateral's value.

§22.3 THE EFFECT OF THE DISCHARGE

The discharge of debts eliminates all the debtor's personal liability on those debts. The discharge is personal to the debtor. Section 524(e) makes it clear that the discharge of the debtor does not operate as a discharge in favor of any other person who is liable on the debt. Section 524(a) enjoins all further proceedings and activity to collect or recover the debt. The injunction created by the discharge succeeds the automatic stay that had been in effect during the case and turns the temporary bar of the stay into a permanent prohibition on collection activity in respect of a discharged debt.

The enforcement of the injunction is by means of the court's civil contempt power under §105. This is because the injunction, although imposed by statute, is equated to an order of court. Therefore, deliberate and knowing violation of the injunction subjects the creditor to sanctions, which could include coercive contempt sanctions (that is, those designed to compel obedience) as well as compensatory contempt sanctions, which include compensatory damages, attorney's fees, and in an egregious cases, even punitive damages. In In re Sandburg Financial Corp., 446 B.R. 793 (S.D. Tex. 2011) the creditor sought to enforce a reaffirmation agreement that did not comply with §524.[1] The court found this to be a willful violation of the stay and awarded the Ch. 11 debtor compensatory contempt damages of $500,000. In Walls v. Wells Fargo Bank, N.A., 276 F.3d 502 (9th Cir. 2002), the court held that a civil contempt order is the only remedy available to the debtor, who is granted no independent private right of action under §524. However, the court pointed out that no remedy beyond a contempt order is needed because the court can make a compensatory contempt order to reimburse the debtor for any loss suffered as a result of the violation. The awesome power of the contempt remedy is illustrated by In re Vivian,

---

1. See section 13.7

150 B.R. 832 (Bankr. S.D. Fla. 1992). Although the creditor knew of and tried to obey the discharge, it apparently could not get its computer to stop sending monthly dunning letters to the debtor. The court found the creditor's computer to be in contempt and fined it 50 megabytes of hard drive memory and 10 megabytes of R.A.M.

Section 525(a) prohibits discrimination against a person that is or has been a debtor, or a person associated with the debtor, by governmental units, and §525(b) prohibits discrimination by a private employer against an individual debtor or an indivdual associated with the debtor, solely on the ground of the debtor's bankruptcy, insolvency, or nonpayment of a discharged debt. The bar on discrimination by a governmental unit in §525(a) covers "persons" (so includes corporate debtors) and encompasses licenses, permits, and other grants as well as the denial of employment and termination or discrimination in employment. The bar on discrimination by a private employer in §525(b) is worded differently. It covers only individuals and is confined to termination of employment or discrimination with respect to employment. In In re Burnett, 635 F.3d 169 (5th Cir. 2011), the court held that different language relating to the scope of prohibited discrimination means that while a governmental unit cannot discriminate against a debtor in both hiring and employment, the bar on discrimination by a private employer covers only existing employees, and does not preclude discrimination in hiring. A private employer is therefore entitled to refuse to hire a person solely on the ground of bankruptcy, insolvency, or failure to pay a discharged debt.

The word "solely" allows a governmental unit or employer to justify adverse treatment by showing that it was based on grounds other than the debtor's bankruptcy or the nonpayment of a discharged debt. Courts have disagreed on the meaning and effect of "solely." Some have given it an interpretation favoring the debtor, and find discrimination if the bankruptcy played a significant role in the decision to refuse government services or to dismiss an employee. Others have adopted a plain-meaning approach and require only that the government or employer shows that the action was motivated by legitimate reasons other than the debtor's bankruptcy. For a discussion of these two approaches, see Laracuente v. Chase Manhattan Bank, 891 F.2d 17 (1st Cir. 1989), in which the court adopted the latter interpretation of §525. There is some difference of opinion about whether §525 extends to discrimination against a debtor who intends to file bankruptcy. In In re Majewski, 310 F.3d 653 (9th Cir. 2002), the court held that §525 does not preclude an employer from dismissing an employee who revealed that he was in financial difficulty and planned to file a petition.

Section 525(c) (added in 1994) makes it clear that a debtor, ex-debtor, or person associated with a debtor who seeks a student loan or loan guarantee is included in the protection from discrimination under §525. Section 525(c) merely clarifies that applications for student loans are included in the protection against discrimination, and does not confer any higher level of protection on them. Therefore, although the debtor cannot be discriminated against solely because of the bankruptcy or discharge, the loan or guarantee can still be denied for other, legitimate, reasons. That is, the debtor's eligibility for the loan or guarantee must be evaluated as if the bankruptcy or discharge never existed.

§22.4 WAIVER OF THE DISCHARGE AND REAFFIRMATION OF THE DEBT

Section 524(a)(2) states that the injunctive force of the discharge and the release of the debtor from liability is not affected by any waiver of the discharge. This provision generally invalidates waivers, but it is qualified by §§727(a)(10), 1228(a), and 1328(a), which give effect to a waiver executed by the debtor in writing after the order for relief and approved by the court. Although Ch. 11 does not have a provision with the same wording, §1141(d) has the same effect, in that it permits the debtor to waive a discharge in the plan. The discharge relating to a specific debt can also be waived by a reaffirmation agreement covering that debt, discussed in section 13.7. Reaffirmation is subject to controls even more stringent than waiver. Although waiver or reaffirmation is unenforceable unless the prescribed requirements are satisfied, §524(f) allows the debtor to repay a debt voluntarily. (Of course, if the creditor puts undue pressure on the debtor to pay, this would violate the injunction.)

§22.5 THE CH. 7 DISCHARGE

§22.5.1 Procedure and Scope

As stated before, the Ch. 7 discharge is available only to an individual debtor. Unlike other chapters of the Code, Ch. 7 does not specify the point in the proceedings at which the discharge occurs. Rule 4004 requires objections to the discharge to be filed within 60 days of the creditors' meeting. If an objection is filed, or there is a motion pending to dismiss the case for abuse, the discharge is granted only after the court hears the matter and determines the debtor's right to a discharge. In the absence of such challenges, the discharge is granted as soon as possible after the expiry of that period. Under §524(d), after the court grants or denies the discharge, it may hold a discharge and reaffirmation hearing at which the court deals with any reaffirmation agreement that the debtor has made.

Under §727(b), the discharge covers all prepetition debts as well as postpetition claims treated as prepetition debts by §502. (This includes, for example, claims arising out of the rejection of an executory contract or the avoidance of a transfer, as explained in section 19.2.) A creditor cannot avoid the discharge by not proving a claim. The discharge covers all debts, whether or not proved, subject to an exception noted in section 22.5.2(3) for debts omitted from the schedule. The debtor's right to a discharge is qualified by §727, which deprives the debtor of a discharge completely, and by §523, which excludes certain debts from it.

§22.5.2 Denial of the Discharge under §727

The denial of a discharge deprives the debtor of one of the most important (for some debtors, the most important) benefits of bankruptcy — forgiveness of the unpaid balance of debts provable against the estate. The grounds for denial of a discharge are set out in §727(a), which states that the court "shall grant the debtor a discharge unless" one of the grounds for denial applies. If any one of them is applicable, the trustee, a creditor, or the U.S. Trustee may object to the grant of the discharge. Many of the grounds for denial are intended to penalize wrongful conduct or to prevent abuse of the fresh start policy, but some are motivated by other concerns. The grounds for denying the Ch. 7 discharge can be grouped into the following categories.

(1) Debtors who are not individuals cannot receive a discharge under Ch. 7. As noted before, §727(a)(1) precludes the Ch. 7 discharge of a debtor that is not an individual. A corporation, association, or other legal entity must reorganize to obtain a discharge. If the entity is liquidated, the debt that was not paid in the liquidation remains with the corporate shell.

(2) Waiver. Section 727(a)(10) validates a written waiver of discharge executed by the debtor after the order for relief and approved by the court.

(3) Improper debtor conduct in or in anticipation of the Ch. 7 case. Section 727(a)(2) through (6) require the court to deny the discharge if the debtor has been guilty of specified dishonest, unlawful, or uncooperative conduct either during the case or in anticipation of it. The conduct listed in these subsections includes the fraudulent transfer of property, concealment of or damage to property, unjustified failure to keep

records, destruction or falsification of records, inability to explain a loss or deficiency in assets, refusal to obey a court order or to answer questions, or unjustified refusal to testify.

A debtor has the affirmative duty to document business dealings and to preserve records, so the debtor's unjustified failure to produce proper and complete business records is a common basis for denial of the discharge. The denial of the discharge on this ground is usually reserved for cases of serious inadequacy that makes it difficult or impossible to ascertain the debtor's financial situation or relevant financial history, or calls into question the debtor's honesty in conducting and disclosing his affairs. In determining what constitute adequate records, courts take into account the degree and seriousness of the deficiency as well as the nature and complexity of the debtor's financial affairs and the debtor's business sophistication. For example, see In re Schifano, 378 F.3d 60 (1st Cir. 2004). The creditor makes out a prima facie case for denial of the discharge by showing the lack of adequate records, upon which the burden shifts to the debtor to justify his failure to produce the documentation. See In re Caneva, 550 F.2d 755 (9th Cir 2008). (Examples 1 and 3 illustrate some of the grounds for denial of the discharge under §727(a) through (6).)

(4) Improper conduct in relation to another case.   Where the debtor's financial affairs are tied up with those of another entity, their fortunes may be so closely linked that the bankruptcy of one of them could lead to the bankruptcy of the other. For example, the failure of a corporation could lead not only to its bankruptcy, but to the bankruptcy of its principal shareholder as well. Section 727 recognizes that where two cases are closely related, the debtor in the one case may have the ability to influence what happens in the other and may use that power for improper ends. Therefore, §727(a)(7) authorizes the court to deny a discharge to a debtor who has committed any of the acts specified in §727(a)(2) through (6) in connection with the bankruptcy of an insider while the debtor's own case is pending or within a year before the debtor's petition.

(5) Successive bankruptcy filings.   Ideally, once a debtor has received a discharge, he should not need bankruptcy relief again, especially in the near future. Serial bankruptcy filings within a short period are likely to be more than the result of just bad management or economic misfortune; they begin to look like an abuse of the system. To discourage abuse of this kind, §707(a)(8) and (9) preclude the debtor from getting successive discharges within a relatively short period of years. The approach, of §707(a)(8) and (9) is therefore not to prohibit successive bankruptcy filings but rather to discourage them by precluding the discharge in the later filing, thereby

depriving the debtor of that important advantage of bankruptcy.[2] Section 727(a)(8) precludes a debtor from a Ch. 7 discharge in a case commenced within eight years of the filing of an earlier case under either Ch. 7 or Ch. 11 in which the debtor received a discharge. Section 727(a)(9) bars the debtor from a discharge under Ch. 7 for a period of six years after the commencement of a case under Ch. 12 or 13 in which the debtor received a discharge unless the Ch. 12 or 13 plan paid unsecured claims in full, or paid at least 70 percent of unsecured claims, was proposed in good faith, and was the debtor's best effort.

(6) Failure to take the required course on financial management. The Bankruptcy Abuse Prevention and Consumer Protection Act of 2005 (BAPCPA) added §727(a)(11), which denies a Ch. 7 discharge to a debtor until she has completed the instructional course on personal financial management required by §111 and approved by the U.S. Trustee. Section 8.4.1 describes the prepetition debt counseling required of an individual debtor under §109(h). The financial management course required by §727(a)(11) is different, and must be taken subsequent to filing the petition. (BAPCPA added the same language to §1328(a), making this a condition to the grant of the Ch. 13 discharge as well.) Section 727(a)(11) excuses the debtor from this requirement if the U.S. Trustee has determined that there are not sufficient courses available for "additional individuals" who are required to take the course, or if the debtor is excused from taking the course under §109(h)(4) because of severe incapacity or disability, or because of active military duty in a combat zone.

(7) Pending proceedings to determine reduction of the homestead exemption. BAPCPA added §727(a)(12), which forbids the granting of a Ch. 7 discharge until the court finds, after notice and the opportunity for a hearing, that there is no reasonable cause to believe that §552(q)(1) is applicable, or that there is any proceeding pending in which a debtor may be found guilty of a felony of the kind described in §522(q)(1)(A) or liable for as debt of the kind described in §522(q)(1)(B). The primary purpose of §522(q), enacted by BAPCPA, is to cut down on the size of the homestead exemption

---

2. As discussed in section 8.4.1(b), there is a situation in which the Code does prohibit successive bankruptcy filings. Section 109(g)(1) and (2) preclude an individual debtor or a family farmer from being a debtor in a successive case if, within 180 days of the filing, the debtor's prior case was dismissed for willful failure to obey a court order or to appear before the court in proper prosecution of the case, or the debtor requested and obtained a voluntary dismissal of the case following the filing of a request for relief from stay. Section 109(g) makes the debtor temporarily ineligible to file a petition for the for the 180-day period following the dismissal. By contrast, even where §109(g) does not bar the debtor from filing, §727(a)(8) and (9) provide for the denial of a discharge in a successive case under the stated circumstances.

where the state of the debtor's domicile allows a large or unlimited exemption and the debtor has been guilty of improper conduct. Section 522(q) places a limit of $155,675[3] on the homestead exemption where the debtor has been convicted of a felony that demonstrates that the filing of the bankruptcy case was an abuse of the Code or where the debtor owes a debt arising from various wrongful, criminal, or tortious acts. (The limitation on the homestead exemption is discussed in section 13.2.3.) Section 727(a)(12) is awkwardly and inconclusively worded. It seems to provide merely that before granting the discharge, the court must be satisfied that it is not likely that §522(q)(1) is applicable to the debtor and that there is no reasonable basis for believing that a proceeding under §522(q)(1) is pending. Section 727(a)(12) does not preclude the discharge if the debtor has been guilty of the conduct covered by §522(q)(1). The effect of that conduct is dealt with by limiting the homestead exemption. Rather, the effect of §727(a)(12) is to delay, rather than to deny the discharge permanently. If there is cause to believe that §522(q)(1) is applicable, the discharge must be suspended until the §522(q)(1) question is resolved and the extent of the homestead exemption is settled.

§22.5.3 Revocation of the Discharge

Section 727(d) allows a creditor, the trustee, or the U.S. Trustee to apply for revocation of the debtor's discharge on various grounds. The most general grounds are that the debtor obtained the discharge through fraud that was not discovered by the applicant until after the discharge was granted; the debtor deliberately withheld or concealed property that would have been property of the estate; or the debtor committed an act specified in §727(a)(6) — that is, disobeyed a court order or refused to testify or respond to a material question without justification based on the privilege against self-incrimination. Section 727(e) requires an application for revocation for fraud to be made within a year after the grant of the discharge, and an application on either the grounds of withholding property or of disobedience to a court order to be made within the later of one year after the grant of the discharge or the close of the case.

§22.5.4 Exclusions from the Individual Debtor's Ch. 7 Discharge by §523

Even when the debtor is entitled to a discharge under §727, the discharge may not include all the debts that are provable against the estate. Section 523

---

3. This is one of the dollar amounts adjusted every three years under §104. This amount is in effect from April 1, 2013. The next adjustment will be made with effect from April 1, 2016.

excludes several types of debt from the individual debtor's discharge. As noted in section 22.1, the reasons for these exclusions differ. Some of them are primarily aimed at penalizing wrongful conduct by the debtor, while others are more concerned with the protection of debts which Congress felt should not be reduced or eliminated in bankruptcy. There are several categories of nondischargeable debts listed in §523(a). The most generally applicable exclusions are summarized below, and some of them are illustrated by Examples 2, 3, 4, and 5.

All the exclusions in §523 are applicable in a Ch. 7 case. (Their applicability under other chapters is discussed below.) Most of the exclusions do not have to be adjudicated during the bankruptcy case and simply take effect if the debt meets the criteria for exclusion. This means that, with regard to many of the types of debt that qualify for exclusion from the discharge under §523, the debt automatically survives the bankruptcy and can be enforced by the creditor in the normal course, even after the debtor has received the discharge. In fact, disputes over whether a debt qualifies as nondischargeable often arise, not in the bankruptcy case itself, but at some time afterwards, when the creditor takes action to enforce it. However, this general rule is subject to an important qualification with regard to three types of nondischargeable debt. Section 523(c)(1) requires creditors whose debts qualify for exclusion under §523(a)(2), (4), or (6) (generally speaking, these are grounds relating to fraud or intentional wrongs) to apply to the court on notice for a determination of dischargeability. Rule 4007 governs this application, which must normally be filed within 60 days of the creditors' meeting unless the court grants an extension of the time. When a determination of nondischargeability is required, the debt is not automatically excluded from the discharge, and its exclusion from the discharge must be determined by the court. The creditor loses the right to exclude the debt from the discharge if the matter is not brought before the court for determination in time. The creditor's responsibility to make timely application for a dischargeability determination presupposes that the creditor knew or should have known of the bankruptcy. If the debt was not scheduled or listed and the creditor did not otherwise obtain knowledge of the bankruptcy in time to apply for the determination, §523(a)(3) excludes the debt from the discharge despite the lack of a court determination.

Some of the categories of exclusion are quite narrow and specialized. The following are those that are most likely to arise. (To remind you of the need for the creditor to seek a determination of nondischargeability for some of these categories of debt, the heading for each category indicates whether or not such action is required.)

(1) Priority taxes (§523(a)(1)). [A nondischargeability determination is not required.]   Taxes that are entitled to priority under §507(a) (see section 19.6.4) are not discharged. In addition, taxes are excluded from the

discharge if a required return was not filed, if it was filed late within two years before bankruptcy, or if the debtor filed a fraudulent return or tried to evade the tax. Under §523(a)(14), if the debtor borrows money to pay a nondischargeable tax, the loan itself becomes nondischargeable.

(2) Obligations incurred fraudulently (§523(a)(2)). [A nondischargeability determination is required.]   Section 523(a)(2) must surely be the most extensively invoked exception to discharge. It has slightly different rules for two distinct types of fraudulent misrepresentation made by the debtor to induce the debt. The first, dealt with in subsection (A), is the more general ground of fraud covering debts induced by the debtor's false representations, whether made orally or in writing. In cases involving last-minute consumer spending sprees, subsection (A) is augmented by a presumption set out in subsection (C). The second, dealt with in subsection (B), is a more specific basis for nondischargeability when the debt was induced by a materially false written financial statement. (Examples 2 and 5 raise the issue of nondischargeability for fraud.)

Section 523(a)(2) is one of the subsections listed in §523(c)(1), so the debt is not automatically excluded from the discharge, and the creditor must seek a determination of dischargeability from the court following notice and a hearing. At the hearing, the creditor has the burden of proving that the debt qualifies for exclusion from the discharge.[4] In *Grogan v. Garner*, 498 U.S. 279 (1991), the Supreme Court made it clear that fraud must be proved on the normal preponderance-of-the-evidence standard, and need not be established on the more rigorous clear-and-convincing standard.

Where the debt in question is a consumer debt, the creditor faces a hazard in seeking to have it excluded from the discharge on grounds of fraud. To discourage creditors from making vexatious or groundless applications under §523(a)(2) for the nondischargeability of consumer debts, §523(d) gives the court the discretion to award costs and attorneys' fees for the proceedings to the debtor if the creditor's application for nondischargeability was not substantially justified and there are no special circumstances that would make the award unjust.

(a) *Nondischargeability for actual fraud under* §523(a)(2)(A).   Section 523(a)(2)(A) excludes from the discharge a debt for money, property, services or new or renewed credit to the extent that it was obtained by false pretenses, a false representation, or actual fraud. This covers all types of oral or written fraudulent misrepresentations by the debtor except for one, which is explicitly excluded: a statement representing the debtor's or an insider's financial condition. This form of representation in writing is

---

4. This burden is relieved by the presumption of fraud in §523(a)(2)(C) where the debtor has engaged in a last-minute consumer spending spree, as explained below.

dealt with separately in §523(a)(2)(B). Note, however, that an oral misrepresentation of financial condition is not covered in either subsection and is therefore not a basis for exclusion from the discharge under §523(a)(2). The reason for confining nondischargeability to written misrepresentations of financial condition is because oral representations of financial condition lack the formality necessary for financial statements. Because there is no basis for finding a debt nondischargeable based on an oral misrepresentation of financial condition, courts have made some fine distinctions to decide if an oral misrepresentation relates to financial condition (so the debt is dischargeable) or to some other inducing factor (so that it is excluded from the discharge under §523(a)(2)(A)). For example, in In re Joelson, 427 F.3d 700 (10th Cir. 2005) and In re Bandi, 683 F.3d 671 (5th Cir. 2012), the court gave the narrowest possible meaning to "financial condition," confining it to statements relating to the debtor's overall financial situation or net worth. As a result, in both these cases the court found that the debtors' misrepresentations about their ownership of assets and ability to repay did not constitute statements relating to financial condition. The misrepresentations were therefore not excluded from §523(a)(2)(A), and qualified as fraudulent misrepresentations under that subsection. In In re Sharpe, 351 B.R. 409 (Bankr. N.D. Tex. 2006), the court gave a more expansive meaning to "financial condition." It held that the debtor's ostentatiously extravagant lifestyle, combined with oral misrepresentations of wealth, did constitute false representations of financial condition, and the debt induced by that representation was not covered by the exclusion from the discharge in §523(a)(2)(A). Because the representations were not in writing, the debt was also not excluded from the discharge by §523(a)(2)(B).

Section 523(a)(2)(A) specifically requires that the fraud or false pretenses relates to a debt for money, property, services, or credit. That is, the fraud or false pretenses must have tricked the creditor into furnishing the money, property, services, or credit. It is not enough merely that the debt arises from the debtor's fraud. Therefore, for example, in In re Rountree, 478 F.3d 215 (4th Cir. 2007), the court held that §523(a)(2)(A) did not apply to exclude a debt from the discharge where the debtor's deception did not induce the creditor to furnish money, property, services, or credit, but instead resulted in tortious injury in the form of emotional distress.

The type of conduct that will make a debt nondischargeable under subsection (2)(A) is equivalent to common law fraud. Although the elements to be satisfied are not expressly stated in the subsection, they are well established under common law: The debtor must have made a materially false representation with knowledge of its falsity and intent to deceive, and the misrepresentation must have justifiably induced the creditor to have provided the debtor with money, property, services, or credit, resulting in loss to the creditor. There must be a causal link between the fraudulent misrepresentations and the creditor's loss. Intent to defraud is determined under the totality of the circumstances. Some of the relevant factors are the length of time between the creation of the debt and the petition, whether the debtor had been contemplating bankruptcy at the time of incurring the debt, the debtor's employment status and prospects, whether the charges were for luxuries or necessities, whether the spending was unusual or frenetic, and the degree of the debtor's financial sophistication. See, for example, In re Ward, 857 F.2d 1082 (6th Cir. 1988) (the debtor went on a buying spree on receiving a credit card); In re Burdge, 198 B.R. 773 (B.A.P. 9th Cir. 1996) (a few weeks before her petition, the debtor made 47 purchases of luxury goods totaling about $8,600 when she was not earning enough to cover her living expenses); In re Hashemi, 104 F.3d 1122 (9th Cir. 1996) (the debtor charged $60,000 to her card for a six-week European vacation at a time when she already owed $300,000 on other credit cards). Compare In re Shartz, 221 B.R. 397 (B.A.P. 6th Cir. 1998) (there was no fraudulent intent where the debtor incurred $67,000 in credit card debt to buy necessities to support herself after losing her job, and while she was trying to find new employment); In re Kountry Korner Store, 221 B.R. 265 (Bankr. N.D. Okla. 1998) (the debtor did not commit fraud in incurring about $3,800 in credit card charges in the three weeks before her bankruptcy in an effort to keep her struggling business in operation and in the unrealistic but genuine hope that she would eventually repay her debt). Sometimes a court may give too much credence to a debtor's optimism. In In re Rembert, 141 F.3d 277 (6th Cir. 1998), the court found that dishonest intent was not established where the debtor used his credit card to obtain a cash advance so that he could gamble. The debtor hoped that he would win and would use some of his winnings to repay the debt. The debtor in In re Herrig, 217 B.R. 891 (Bankr. N.D. Okla. 1998), was not so lucky. The court found fraudulent intent where the debtor used his card to its credit limit in a short period of time to fund his gambling.

Even if fraudulent intent is established, the debt is not excluded from the discharge under §523(a)(2)(A) unless the creditor justifiably relied on the false representation. According to Field v. Mans, 516 U.S. 59 (1995), justifiable reliance is not as strict a test as the purely objective reasonable reliance standard, and it does allow account to be taken of some subjective attributes of the creditor, such as knowledge, experience, and other circumstances.

In Cohen v. De La Cruz, 523 U.S. 213 (1998), the Supreme Court held, based on a grammatical reading of §523(a)(2), that if a debt is excluded from the discharge under §523(a)(2)(A), the exclusion covers full liability on the debt, which includes both the original debt and any award of punitive damages traceable to the fraud and made by a court to penalize the debtor for the fraudulent conduct. Because Cohen requires the penal award to be traceable to the fraud, it must arise from the fraud. Therefore, in In re Sabban, 600 F.3d 1219 (9th Cir. 2010), the court found that a statutory penalty that required an unlicensed contractor to disgorge his fee did not arise from the debtor's fraud. Although the debtor had fraudulently misrepresented that he was licensed, the disgorgement penalty under the statute punished the lack of a license and was not dependant on a finding of fraud.

In *Archer v. Warner*, 538 U.S. 314 (2003), the Supreme Court held that a fraudulently induced debt does not change character where it is later included in a settlement agreement and released in exchange for a promise to pay the amount stipulated in the settlement. The settlement is not a novation, so the debt retains its fraudulent character and is not extinguished and replaced by a mere contract claim.

On a literal reading, §523(a)(2) does not actually say that the debtor must have himself been guilty of the fraud. The language of the section focuses on the character of the debt, not necessarily on the conduct of the debtor. As a result, the debt may be nondischargeable where it was induced by the fraud of another person (such as an agent or a partner of the debtor) whose conduct can be imputed to the debtor. This is so even if the debtor was not himself guilty of the fraud, had no knowledge of it, and did not benefit from it. See In re *M.M. Winkler & Associates*, 239 F.3d 746 (5th Cir. 2001) (the debt was nondischargeable as a result of the fraud of the debtor's partner because of the partnership relationship and the joint and several liability of the partners); In re *Quinlivan*, 434 F. 3d 314 (5th Cir. 2005) (a debt induced by the fraud of another is only nondischargeable if the other party is the debtor's partner or agent, as determined under principles of state law).

(b) *The presumption of fraud in last-minute consumer spending sprees under §523(a)(2)(C).* As discussed below, the creditor normally bears the burden of proving fraud. However, §523(a)(2)(C) makes one exception to this by creating a presumption of fraud for the purposes of §523(a)(2)(A) when, shortly before filing the petition, the debtor went on a consumer spending splurge. The presumption only applies to consumer debt incurred by an individual. It takes effect in one of two alternative circumstances.

First, the presumption applies if, within 90 days before the order for relief, the debtor incurred consumer debts for luxury goods or services (defined in the subsection as those not reasonably necessary for the support or maintenance of the debtor or her dependent), aggregating more than $650 owed to a single creditor.[5] There can be an interpretational issue about what constitute luxuries, and one debtor's luxury may be another's necessity. For example, in In re *Hall*, 228 B.R. 483 (Bankr. M.D. Ga. 1998), the court held that while credit given to a debtor by a casino is a luxury when the

---

5. BAPCPA lowered the threshold for the presumption to take effect by increasing the period of the presumption from 60 days to 90 days and decreasing the amount of the debt. Section 523(a)(2)(c) is one of the sections subject to §104(b), so the amount of the debt is adjusted administratively every three years. It was last adjusted with effect from April 1, 2013. The next adjustment will be made with effect from April 1, 2016.

gambling is recreational, it does not so qualify when the debtor is a long-time, high-stakes gambler trying to save his business by making a big win.

Second, fraud is presumed if within 70 days before the order for relief, the debtor obtained cash advances aggregating more than $925 and constituting an extension of consumer credit under an open-end credit plan.[6] (This is a plan under which the debtor is given a line of credit and repeated transactions are contemplated.) This provision is worded so as not to include the requirements that the advances be used to buy luxury goods or services, or that they all be obtained from the same creditor.

It is worth stressing that §523(a)(2)(C) does not make debts incurred under the stated circumstances automatically nondischargeable; it merely establishes a presumption that a debt so incurred is fraudulent. This places the burden on the debtor to prove that the elements of fraud are not satisfied despite the suspicious circumstances.

(c) *Nondischargeability for materially false financial statements under §523(a)(2)(B).* Section 523(a)(2)(B) applies only to situations in which money, property, services, or new or renewed credit is obtained by a materially false written statement "respecting the debtor's or an insider's financial condition." This subsection is only applicable to statements respecting financial condition, so courts often have to grapple with the question of whether a false statement relates to financial condition. As noted above, some courts define "financial condition" narrowly, to include only statements relating to the debtor's overall financial situation or net worth. If the statement does not meet this narrow definition, its nondischargeability for fraud should be evaluated under §523(a)(2)(A) rather than (a)(2)(B). In *In re Kosinski*, 424 B.R. 599 (B.A.P. 1st Cir. 2010) the creditor was induced to lend money to the debtor for the development of a nightclub project on the strength of a profit and loss projection furnished by the debtor. The court held that this did not qualify as a statement respecting the debtor's financial condition. Although the statement covered by §523(a)(2)(B) need not be a formal financial statement, it must at least describe the debtor's financial condition in some way.

Unlike subsection (a)(2)(A), this subsection does set out the required elements: The statement must be written; it must be materially false; the debtor must have published it or caused it to be published with intent to deceive; and the creditor must have reasonably relied on it. As you can see, the elements are quite similar to those for common law fraud, with two differences: Only written statements are covered, and the test for reliance is the more stringently objective reasonableness standard. The legislative history of §523(a)(2)(B) and *Field v. Mans* (above) explain why this subsection

---

6. BAPCPA expanded the scope of this presumption as well, by increasing its period from 60 to 70 days and decreasing the amount of the debt. This subsection is also subject to periodic adjustment in amount under §104.

articulates the elements of a false financial statement and imposes the stricter reasonable reliance standard: Congress did not want a creditor to claim nondischargeability on the basis of some unimportant misstatement or inaccuracy in a credit application or financial statement.

Because the elements of the subsections are similar in many respects, it may often not matter which of the two apply. However, in some cases, one of these two differences in the subsections could have a significant effect. For example, as noted above, in In re Sharpe the court's determination that the oral misrepresentation related to financial condition excluded it from §523(a)(2)(A), and because it was oral, it failed to meet the requirements of §523(a)(2)(B). The difference between the more subjective "justifiable reliance" standard and more objective "reasonable reliance" standard could also be important. The impact of this difference was pointed out in In re Kosinski. The test of reasonable reliance is more stringent than justifiable reliance because it focuses factors that would alert a reasonable creditor to the falsity of the representation, rather than on the individual attributes of this particular creditor, which may justify him in being less vigilant. Section §523(a)(2)(B) does not differ from §523(a)(2)(A) in the extent to which the debt will be excluded from the discharge. Both subsections are subject to the prefatory language that the debt is excluded from the discharge "to the extent obtained by" the fraud. Therefore, although Cohen v. De La Cruz was concerned with a case involving §523(a)(2)(A), its interpretation that the exclusion covers full liability on the debt, including punitive damages, is equally applicable to §523(a)(2)(B).

(3) Unlisted or unscheduled debts (§523(a)(3)). [A dischargeability determination is not required.]

Although the discharge normally extends even to those debts for which no proof of claim was filed, §523(a)(3) protects creditors who did not know of the bankruptcy in time to file a claim. If the debtor did not timely list or schedule the debt, so that the creditor did not receive notice of the bankruptcy and did not otherwise find out about it in time to file a proof of claim, the debt is excluded from the discharge.

As mentioned earlier, §523(a)(3) also precludes discharge of a debt covered by §523(a)(2), (4), or (6) where the creditor's failure to make timely application for a nondischargeability determination resulted from lack of knowledge of the bankruptcy because the debtor failed to list or schedule the debt.

(4) Debts arising out of the debtor's dishonesty as a fiduciary, or from embezzlement or larceny (§523(a)(4)). [A dischargeability determination is required.]

If, while acting in a fiduciary capacity, the debtor committed fraud or defalcation or if, acting in any capacity, the debtor embezzled money or committed larceny, the liability arising from that wrongful act is excluded from the discharge. This is one of the exclusions for which a determination of dischargeability must be requested. Note that the requirement that the debtor was acting in a fiduciary capacity qualifies only fraud and defalcation. The exclusion also applies to debts arising from embezzlement or larceny even when the debtor was not a fiduciary. Therefore, if fiduciary capacity cannot be established, embezzlement may be an alternative ground for nondischareability under §523(a)(4). This does not always work. In In re Thompson, 686 F.3d 940 (8th Cir. 2012) a general contractor failed to remit to a subcontractor funds that the owner had paid to the contractor on account of the subcontractor's work. The subcontractor sought to have the contractor's debt excluded from the discharge under §523(a)(4), but the court held that the debt was dischargeable: The debtor was not acting in a fiduciary capacity because, although a state statute declared such funds to be held in trust by the contractor, the obligation to remit the funds was merely contractual and the statute did not actually create a real trust relationship. The debtor could also not be treated as having embezzled the fund because the payment from the owner was the debtor's property, and he had merely a contractual obligation to pay the subcontractor. A person cannot embezzle his own funds. (See also Example 2.)

Courts disagree on the scope of that portion of §523(a)(4) that applies to fraud or defalcation committed in a fiduciary capacity. Some restrict it to trusts in the formal sense — that is, express or technical trusts. See, for example, In re Burress, 245 B.R. 871 (Bankr. D. Colo. 2000); Hunter v. Philpott, 373 F.3d 873 (8th Cir. 2004); In re Thompson. Other courts interpret "fiduciary capacity" more broadly to include any relationship in which the debtor stands in a position of trust and confidence toward the creditor which demands a duty of loyalty and care. See, for example, In re McDade, 282 B.R. 650 (Bankr. N.D. Ill. 2002). An attorney-client relationship is an example, and some courts have been willing to apply §523(a)(4) when the debt arose as a result of the attorney's faithless conduct, even if the wrong did not involve the misappropriation of trust funds. However, even among courts that adopt the broader approach, there seems to be general agreement that there must at least be some kind of actual relationship of trust between the parties, so it is not appropriate to apply §523(a)(4) when the debtor is deemed by equity or statute to be a constructive trustee purely for the sake of affording a remedy to the victim of the fraud or defalcation. As mentioned above, this was the conclusion reached by the court in In re Thompson. In re Marchiando, 13 F.3d 1111 (7th Cir. 1994) was to the same effect. The debtor, who owned a convenience store, failed to remit to the state the proceeds of lottery tickets that she had sold. The state statute provided that the proceeds of ticket sales would constitute a trust fund until paid to the state. The state sought to have the debt for the unpaid proceeds excluded from the debtor's discharge under §523(a)(4), but the court found the section inapplicable. Although the court agreed with a wider definition of fiduciary capacity, the debtor here was merely a ticket agent without any special power, expertise, or duty of loyalty. The statutory device of deeming the funds to be in trust was really nothing more than the creation of a constructive trust for a remedial purpose — a collection device.

There had been some confusion in the caselaw over the meaning of "defalcation." Some courts interpreted it broadly to cover all misappropriations or failures to account, whether or not deliberate. Others required the conduct to have been consciously wrongful, or even egregiously wrongful. The U.S. Supreme Court settled this conflict in the case law in Bullock v. BankChampaign, N.A., 133 S.Ct. 1754 (2013), in which it held that "defalcation" requires an intentional wrong. This includes not only conduct that the fiduciary knows to be improper, but also reckless conduct of the kind commonly treated as equivalent in criminal law. To qualify as defalcation where the trustee acts recklessly without actual knowledge of wrongfulness, the trustee must have grossly deviated from the conduct that a law-abiding person would observe, and must have been willfully blind to the substantial and justifiable risk that his conduct would violate his fiduciary duty.

Because §523(a)(4) covers fraud and defalcation, it has some commonality with §523(a)(2), which excludes fraudulently incurred obligations from the discharge. Therefore, where the facts satisfy the elements of §523(a)(2), that ground for excluding the debt from the discharge could be an alternative to §523(a)(4). If the exclusion is sought under §523(a)(2), the creditor does not need to show fiduciary capacity, but does need to show that money, property, services, or credit was obtained by the fraud. The question of which of these two bases for nondischargeability fits best will depend on the relative difficulty of proving fiduciary capacity or the link between the fraud and the giving of value.

(5) Domestic support obligations (§523(a)(5)). [A dischargeability determination is not required.]

Section 523(a)(5) excludes domestic support obligations, defined in §101(14A), from the discharge. Domestic support obligations have been discussed several times before.[7] Unlike the other provisions that prevent the debtor from evading domestic support obligations, §523(a)(5) was not created by the Bankruptcy Reform Act of 1994; it has been part of the Code since its enactment in 1978. It was amended by BAPCPA, which substituted the newly defined term "domestic support obligation" for the prior language "alimony, maintenance, or support." In essence, the definition covers prepetition and postpetition support debts established by court or administrative order or by divorce decree or

---

7. See, e.g., sections 10.4.3, 13.5.2, 16.1.4, and 19.6.4.

separation or property settlement agreement, and owing to a spouse, ex-spouse, child, person responsible for a child, or a governmental unit.

The debt must actually be for support. The protection does not extend to a debt arising from some other obligation merely because it has been characterized or labeled as for support. The way in which the parties have chosen to label the debt may be relevant to showing their intent, but it is merely one factor to consider, and is not dispositive. The issue of whether the debt is actually for support is a factual one, determined under federal bankruptcy law, not state law. The determination is made on all the facts, taking into account factors such as the mutual intent of the parties, their respective financial situations, and the purpose to be served by the obligation. See In re Johnson, 397 B.R. 289 (Bankr. M.D.N.C. 2008). Johnson also held that a debt payable to a third party, other than the dependent or a governmental unit, could qualify as domestic support. The debt in that case was the debtor's obligation, incorporated into a divorce decree, to pay to the mortgagee installments due under a deed of trust on the former marital home. The court said that this was in the nature of domestic support because the debtor's payments were intended to relieve his ex-wife of the obligation to pay.

(6) Debts for willful and malicious injury (§523(a)(6)). [A dischargeability determination is required.] A debt resulting from the debtor's willful and malicious injury to another entity or the property of another entity is excluded from the discharge. This is one of the exclusions for which a determination of dischargeability must be requested.

Although the precise scope of the term "willful and malicious" is subject to doubt, it is clear that this exclusion applies to liability for deliberate wrongful conduct. It is concerned with intentional rather than negligent behavior. Any doubt on this issue was settled by the Supreme Court in Kawaauhau v. Geiger, 523 U.S. 57 (1998), in which the claim arose from the debtor's medical malpractice. It was apparent that the debtor's conduct had been reckless. The court stressed that §523(a)(6) requires that the injury be both willful (that is, deliberate and intentional rather than reckless or negligent) and malicious (that is, inflicted with the intent to harm or with the callous realization that harm would be caused). These are separate and distinct elements. Willfulness encompasses the debtor's volition in taking the action, and malice focuses on the debtor's motivation in acting. The court found that it would violate the plain meaning of §523(a)(6) to read the subsection as covering reckless conduct, or even intentional conduct that is not accompanied by the intent to do the harm. The court said that such a reading would also render superfluous other subsections that cover reckless injury, namely §523(a)(9) (debts for injury caused by driving while intoxicated) and §523(a)(12) (malicious or reckless failure to fulfill commitments due to a federal depository institution regulatory agency). In applying *Kawaauhau* lower courts have emphasized the need to find both the elements of intent to commit the act and intent to cause harm. See, for example, In re *Sicroff*, 401 F.3d 1101 (9th Cir. 2005) (defamation was both deliberate and with malicious motive); In re *Moore*, 357 F.3d 1125 (10th Cir. 2004) (the debtor's false representation to an employee that the debtor carried liability insurance was deliberately intended to deceive but was not malicious, so the employee's claim for uninsured personal injury was not excluded from the discharge); *Ball v. A.O. Smith Corp.*, 451 F.3d 66 (2d Cir. 2006) (an attorney committed willful and malicious injury by bringing a suit that he knew to be unreasonable and without prospect of success). In In re *Patch*, 526 F.3d 1176 (8th Cir. 2008), the court held that although reckless or negligent injury is not enough, it is not necessary that the debtor desires to bring about the harmful consequences, provided that the act is done deliberately and the debtor realizes that the resulting harm is substantially certain.

Willful and malicious injury is normally associated with intentional tortious conduct in the form of acts that cause physical harm, but it could be inflicted in relation to commercial activity where the conduct that caused the economic injury qualifies as deliberate and malicious. The exact scope of §523(a)(6) in relation to commercial activity is not clear. For example, in In re *Jercich*, 238 F.3d 1202 (9th Cir. 2001), the court applied it to a breach of contract that was both deliberate and motivated by a desire to harm the other party. In In re *Trantham*, 304 B.R. 298 (B.A.P. 6th Cir. 2004), the court applied it to a purposeful and malicious infringement of patent rights. However, in *Lockerby v. Sierra*, 535 F.3d 1038 (9th Cir. 2008), the court refused to apply §523(a)(6) to a deliberate breach of contract unless there was tortious conduct involved in the breach.

If the claim has already been adjudicated in state court, and that court had made a finding as to willfulness and malice, the bankruptcy court may adopt that finding on the principle of collateral estoppel, so that the creditor does not have to prove these elements again in the dischargeability hearing. For example, in In re *Braen*, 900 F.2d 621 (3d Cir. 1990), damages for malicious prosecution were held nondischargeable without further evidence because the necessary elements had already been proven in the tort case. However, for collateral estoppel to apply, the prior state court judgment must have disposed of all the elements required for nondischargeability. In In re *Stage*, 321 B.R. 486 (B.A.P. 8th Cir. 2005), the state court judgment settled the question of whether an injury arising from deliberate tort was willful but did not address whether it was malicious because malice was not an element of the tort. The court therefore held that the creditor did not have to prove willfulness in the discharge hearing but did have to establish malice to have the debt excluded from the discharge.

As noted in the discussion of §523(a)(2), *Cohen v. De La Cruz* (above) held that the language of §523(a)(2) covered punitive damages as well as the original debt. Although the court did not address whether the same result would be called for by §523(a)(6), its reasoning, based on a grammatical interpretation of §523(a)(2), would be equally applicable to §523(a)(6) because the structure of the language is the same. In fact, if anything, the language of §523(a)(6) even more strongly leads to the conclusion that punitive damages are covered, because it simply excludes from the discharge "any debt . . . for willful and malicious injury," without the qualifying "to the extent" language found in §523(a)(2). In *Jendusa-Nicolai v. Larson*, 677 F.3d 320 (7th Cir. 2012), the debtor physically attacked his ex-wife and had been convicted of attempting to murder her. In addition to the criminal conviction, the ex-wife obtained a civil tort judgment against the debtor in state court for compensatory and punitive damages arising out of the assault, and her current husband and daughter obtained judgments against him for loss of consortium. In the debtor's subsequent bankruptcy, the bankruptcy court held that all these claims were nondischargeable under §523(a)(6). The court of appeals affirmed. There was no question that the injury qualified as both willful and malicious, and all the damages were nondischargeable. As regards the ex-wife's damages: Although the purpose of punitive damages is to punish the defendant, they are nevertheless due to the creditor and are consequent upon the willful and malicious injury. As regards the ex-wife's husband and daughter. The court held that it was not relevant that the debtor did not insert to harm thest parties. Although the damages for loss of consortium were derivative from the injury to the ex-wife, they nevertheless were suffered as a result of the debtor's willful and malicious act. (Section 523(a)(6) is illustrated in Examples 3 and 4.)

(7) Governmental fines, penalties, and forfeitures (§523(a)(7)). [A dischargeability determination is not required.]

Debts due to the government for fines, penalties, or forfeitures that are not compensation for actual pecuniary loss are excluded from the discharge. This category includes penalties on taxes that are nondischargeable under §523(a)(7), but does not include penalties on dischargeable taxes or on a transaction that occurred more than three years before the petition.

Section 523(a)(7) sets out four conditions for a debt to qualify as nondischargeable under the subsection: the debt must be a fine, penalty, or forfeiture; it must be payable to a governmental unit; it must be payable for the benefit of the governmental unit; and it must not be compensation for actual pecuniary loss. It can be a difficult factual question to decide whether a debt due to the government qualifies for exclusion from the discharge under §523(a)(7). *Kelley v. Robinson*, 479 U.S. 36 (1986), examined this question in relation to restitution payments imposed by a court as a condition of the debtor's probation following conviction of welfare fraud. Although the restitutionary obligation did have the purpose of compensating the state for the loss caused by the fraud, the Court nevertheless found that the restitution obligation was excluded from the discharge under §523(a)(7). The Court characterized the claim as a noncompensatory penalty because a criminal restitution obligation goes beyond mere compensation of the victim and serves the state's broader goal of punishing and rehabilitating offenders and enforcing its criminal law.[8] See also In re Thompson, 418 F.3d 362 (3d Cir. 2005). (See also Example 2.)

Since Kelley, lower courts have continued to grapple with the question of when a debt to the government is a penalty or forfeiture, rather than compensation for pecuniary loss. For example, In re Taggart, 249 F.3d 987 (9th Cir. 2001), a California statute allowed the state bar to collect the costs and fees of disciplinary proceedings from an attorney who was disciplined. The court found the claim for the costs and fees to be dischargeable because it was for compensation of pecuniary loss — a simple fee-shifting provision — and not a punishment. The court distinguished cases that interpreted statutes from other states, in which the payment of costs had a punitive purpose. After the case was decided, the California legislature amended the statute to recharacterize the award of costs and fees as a punishment to protect the public. In In re Findley, 593 F.3d 1048 (9th Cir. 2010), the court found that the statutory amendments focused the statute on the protection of the public and the maintenance of standards in the profession, and therefore moved the costs and fees beyond mere compensation for pecuniary loss and rendered them nondischargeable.

In Kelley the restitutionary obligation was for the repayment of fraudulently obtained welfare benefits, so restitution was payable to the state. Some courts have therefore distinguished cases where the restitution imposed in the criminal sentence or the other financial award is payable to a private party, rather than the government. Applying the plain meaning of the subsection, which uses the words "payable to and for the benefit of a governmental unit," these courts have held that the debt is dischargeable where payment is due to a private party. See, for example, In re Rashid, 210 F.3d 201 (3d Cir. 2000) (a restitution obligation payable directly to the victim is not within §523(a)(7)); In re Griffin, 491 B.R. 602 (Bankr. S.D. Ga. 2013) (although the purpose of civil contempt sanctions is to uphold the court's authority, the award of monetary sanctions in favor of the creditor is not payable to a governmental unit, and therefore not covered by §523(a)(7).). Other courts have adopted a more flexible approach and have been willing to apply §523(a)(7) to an award to a private litigant where the award has a

---

8. In a dictum, the Court expressed doubt that a restitution obligation is a debt at all under §101(12). If it does not qualify as a debt, it cannot be discharged, even if none of the exclusions in §523 apply. However, in Pennsylvania Department of Public Welfare v. Davenport, 495 U.S. 552 (1990), the Court reversed itself on its dictum in Kelley and held that a restitution obligation is a debt and is therefore dischargeable unless one of the grounds for nondischargeability in §523 applies.

penal basis or is criminal in nature. See, for example, In re Verola, 446 F.3d 1206 (11th Cir. 2006).

In addition to fines and penalties, §523(a)(7) refers to forfeitures. The meaning and extent of this word is not entirely clear. In In re Nam, 273 F.3d 281 (3d Cir. 2001), the debtor had posted bail for his son, who jumped bail and fled the country. The court held that the bail bond (in favor of the city) was excluded from the discharge as a forfeiture. By using the word "forfeiture" in the section, Congress indicates that it is not necessary that the debt arise from punishment. It was clear that the bond was not compensation for pecuniary loss. (The court confined its decision to bonds given by family members, recognizing that different considerations may apply to a professional bail bond agent.)

(8) Educational loans and benefits (§523(a)(8)). [A dischargeability determination is not required.] Section 523(a)(8) excludes from the discharge educational loans and other repayable educational benefits if they were made, insured, or guaranteed by the government, were made under a program wholly or partially funded by the government or a nonprofit institution, or otherwise qualify as educational loans or benefits as enumerated in the section. The obvious intent of this provision is to protect governmental and institutional student loan programs by preventing graduates from using bankruptcy to discharge liability for loans. Section 523(a)(8) used to be confined to loans whose first payment date occurred within seven years of bankruptcy. This was eliminated by an amendment in 1998, which bars the discharge of student loans, no matter how old they may be, in all cases commenced after the effective date of the amendment.

Even if the debt is nondischargeable under §523(a)(8), the section gives the court the discretion to discharge the debt if exclusion from the discharge would cause undue hardship to the debtor or dependents. The hardship determination is an adversary proceeding to be initiated by the debtor seeking the discharge, and the court should not discharge any part of non-dischargeable student debt in the absence of a hardship determination. In United Student Aid Funds, Inc. v. Espinosa, 130 S.Ct. 1367 (2010), the debtor's Ch. 13 plan proposed to pay the principal of a student loan and to discharge the accrued interest. The debtor did not file a complaint to initiate a hardship hearing, but the bankruptcy court nevertheless confirmed the plan. The debtor paid off the principal of the debt over five years, following which the court discharged the debt for accrued interest. About three years after the discharge, the creditor sought to enforce payment of the discharged portion of the debt, and the debtor moved for an order holding the creditor in contempt for violating the discharge injunction. The Supreme Court held that the bankruptcy court should not have confirmed the plan. However, its error was not jurisdictional, and the creditor's due process rights had not been violated because it had received notice of the filing and contents of the plan. Therefore, despite the bankruptcy court's error, its confirmation of the plan was not void, and the discharge was effective.

The Code does not indicate what constitutes undue hardship. The predominant test for determining undue hardship is based on *Brunner v. New York State Higher Educ. Services Corp.*, 831 F.2d 395 (2d Cir. 1987), which sets out three standards that must be satisfied to invoke undue hardship: First, the debtor's current income and expenses must be low enough so that if he is required to repay the loan, he will not be able to maintain a minimal standard of living; second, this must not be just a temporary situation, but must be likely to persist over the payment period of the loan; and third, that the debtor must have made a good faith effort to repay the loan. See, for example, *In re Gerhardt*, 348 F.3d 89 (5th Cir. 2003) (there was no undue hardship where the debtor chose to work as a cellist in an orchestra for a low salary, but had the qualifications, ability, and free time to supplement her income); *In re Oyler*, 397 F.3d 282 (6th Cir. 2005) (there was no undue hardship where the debtor chose to work for a low salary as the pastor of a small church, but was qualified for a higher-paying job); *Educational Credit Management Corp. v. Polleys*, 356 F.3d 1302 (10th Cir. 2004) (there was undue hardship where the debtor had debilitating emotional problems that prevented him from taking jobs commensurate with his qualifications); *In re Reynolds*, 425 F.3d 526 (8th Cir. 2005) (there was undue hardship where the debtor, a qualified lawyer, worked in a secretarial job because she could not find employment as an attorney despite diligent efforts, had longstanding serious mental health problems that made it unlikely that she would improve her position, and her fragile mental equilibrium was threatened by the stress of trying to cope with the loan payments); *Krieger v. Educational Credit Management Corp.*, 713 F.3d 882 (7th Cir. 2013) (the court found undue hardship where the debtor, a 53-year-old paralegal, lived with her mother in a rural area, had not been successful in job searches over a 10-year period, and had little prospect of improving her situation).

Some courts find the *Brunner* three-pronged test too restrictive, and prefer a broader evaluation under the totality of the circumstances. Although this test is more wide-ranging and not as predictable, it has the advantage of identifying circumstances that may not be taken into account in the narrower test. See, for example, *In re Dufresne*, 341 B.R. 391 (Bankr. D. Mass. 2006), (the court found hardship where the debtor, after amassing large debt for college and law school tuition, could not pass the bar after multiple attempts and was in a precarious financial situation); *In re Lee*, 352 B.R. 91 (B.A.P. 8th Cir. 2006); *In re Bene*, 474 B.R. 56 (Bankr. W.D.N.Y. 2012) (evolution in the student loan program, including the Income Contingent Repayment Plan, and amendments to §523(a)(8) since *Brenner* was decided call for a more nuanced evaluation of hardship under the totality of the circumstances). (*See also* Example 6.)

Where hardship may not warrant discharge of the entire debt, the court has the power, under its general discretion granted by §105, to discharge part of the debt to the extent necessary to relieve the hardship. See In re *Saxman*, 325 F.3d 1168 (9th Cir. 2003). Even a partial discharge must satisfy the undue hardship test under §523(a)(8): In re *Miller*, 377 F.3d 616 (6th Cir. 2004); In re *Tirch*, 409 F.3d 677 (6th Cir 2005).

(9) Liability for driving under the influence of drugs or alcohol (§523(a)(9)). [A dischargeability determination is not required.] If the debtor incurred liability for death or personal injury, caused by the unlawful operation of a vehicle while under the influence of drugs, alcohol, or another substance, such liability is nondischargeable. This subsection formerly applied only to judgments and consent decrees relating to such liability, but it was amended in 1990 to make it clear that the liability is nondischargeable even if no judgment had been obtained by the time of the petition.

(10) Debts from a prior case in which a discharge was waived or denied (§523(a)(10)). [A dischargeability determination is not required.] Section 523(a)(10) deals with the situation of a debtor who has been bankrupt before and waived the discharge in the prior case or was denied it under any of the grounds in §727(a)(2) through (7). Such a waiver or denial makes all debts in that case permanently nondischargeable. Therefore, if the debtor subsequently seeks bankruptcy relief again, the discharge in the later case does not cover any balance still owing on undischarged debts from the earlier case. Note that §523(a)(10) refers only to §727(a)(2) to (7), so it does not prevent the discharge in a current bankruptcy of debts that survived an earlier case because a discharge was denied under the eight-year rule of §727(a)(8) or the six-year rule of §727(a)(9). Therefore, in the debtor's third or later bankruptcy, debts from the preceding bankruptcy may be discharged if a discharge had been denied in that case solely on the grounds of §727(a)(8) or (9). These surviving debts are treated differently because the denial of the earlier discharge was based on an objective time period, rather than on the debtor's dishonest or obstructive behavior, or on the debtor's consensual waiver of the right to discharge.

Section 523(a)(10) only applies where the earlier discharge was denied in its entirety under §727. It is not applicable to debts that survived an earlier discharge under §523. The treatment of such debts is discussed in section 22.5.5.

(11) Payments under an order of restitution in federal cases (§523(a)(13)). [A dischargeability determination is not required.] The discussion of §523(a)(7), above, noted that *Kelley v. Robinson* found a criminal restitution order to be excluded from the discharge by §523(a)(7) because it could properly be characterized as a penalty, notwithstanding its compensatory aspect. The debt giving rise to the restitution order might also qualify for exclusion under §523(a)(6) as arising from willful and malicious injury. *Kelley* did not entirely clear up the confusion in the treatment of criminal restitution obligations, so Congress added §523(a)(13) in the 1994 Bankruptcy Reform Act in an attempt to clarify that criminal restitution obligations are not dischargeable. However, §523(a)(13) has not been entirely successful in settling this issue because it only covers restitution orders in federal cases. A debt arising from a restitution order under state law is therefore not covered by §523(a)(13) and is dischargeable unless it can be made to fit within the exclusions of §523(a)(6) or (7). In *In re Verola*, 446 F.3d 1206 (11th Cir. 2006), the court did exclude a state court restitution order under §523(a)(7) on the basis that although Congress did not include state court orders in §523(a)(13), there was no indication that it did not intend them to be covered under §523(a)(7).

(12) Matrimonial debts that do not qualify as domestic support obligations (§523(a)(15)). [A dischargeability determination is not required.] The Bankruptcy Reform Act of 1994 added §523(a)(15) to give some protection to matrimonial debts (such as debts arising out of a property settlement on divorce or separation) that do not qualify for exclusion from the discharge as domestic support obligations under §523(a)(5). To be nondischargeable under §523(a)(15), the debt must have been incurred in the course of a divorce or separation or in connection with a separation agreement, divorce decree, or other order of a court or government agency. Prior to 2005, §523(a)(15) did not exclude debts of this kind from the discharge in all cases. Instead, it imposed a balancing test to be used by the court in deciding if the debt should be excluded from the discharge. The court was required to conduct an inquiry into the debtor's ability to pay the debt and to balance the relative hardship and need of the debtor (and his dependents) and the creditor spouse. BAPCPA removed this limitation, making the debt absolutely nondischargeable as a matter of course. Because the evaluation of hardship and need has been eliminated, §523(a)(15) has been removed from the list of sections for which a dischargeability hearing is required under §523(c).

§22.5.5 The Discharge of Nondischargeable Debts in a Subsequent Case

As discussed above, if the debtor was denied a discharge entirely under §727(a)(2) through (7) in a prior bankruptcy, or waived the discharge, the surviving debts are excluded from the discharge in the later bankruptcy by §523(a)(10). Surviving debts that were excluded from a prior discharge under §523 are not covered by §523(a)(10), but are dealt with in §523(b). Provided that the grounds for exclusion no longer apply, §523(b) allows the discharge in a later bankruptcy of three types of debt that were excluded from the discharge in an earlier case: nondischargeable tax debts under §523(a)(1), unscheduled debts under §523(a)(3), and education loans under §528(a)(8).[9] Because these are the only debts included in §523(b), all other debts that were not discharged in the prior case are excluded from the discharge in the later case as well. The basis for the exclusion from the subsequent discharge is that the exclusion in the prior case is res judicata. Once the debt is held nondischargeable, it is always nondischargeable. In re Paine, 283 B.R. 33 (B.A.P. 9th Cir. 2002).

§22.6 THE CH. 11 DISCHARGE

Unlike Ch. 7, the Ch. 11 discharge is available to both individuals and corporate entities. If the debtor is not an individual, §1141(d) brings the discharge into effect upon confirmation of the plan. This used to be true of an individual debtor as well, but BAPCPA added §1141(d)(5), which, in essence, postpones the discharge of an individual Ch. 11 debtor until the completion of all payments under the plan unless the court orders otherwise for cause after notice and a hearing. Section 1141(d)(5) brings the Ch. 11 discharge of an individual more closely in line with the Ch. 13 discharge, which is granted only after consummation of the plan. However, the language of §1141(d)(5) differs from that of §1328(a) in two respects. First, §1141(d)(5) lacks the mandatory language of §1328(a). While §1328(a) says that the court "shall" grant a Ch. 13 discharge on completion of plan payments, §1141(d)(5) says no debts are discharged in an individual Ch. 11 case "until the court grants a discharge" on completion of plan payments. The significance of this difference in language is not clear. It could simply reflect the fact that Ch. 11 gives the debtor and creditors more flexibility to agree on the scope and terms of the discharge and to record this in the plan. Second, §1141(d)(5) contemplates the possibility of an earlier discharge for cause. The section gives no indication of what constitutes cause. In re Sheridan, 391 B.R. 287 (Bankr. E.D.N.C. 2008), provides an example of what a court might accept as cause: The debtor had fully complied with the

---

9. As noted in section 22.5.4, one of the grounds for avoiding nondischargeability of a student loan — the age of the debt — is no longer available in cases commenced after the effective date of the 1998 amendment to the section. Therefore, in such cases, the only basis for changing the grounds of nondischargeability will be hardship that arose since the prior bankruptcy.

plan-confirmation requirements, he had given notice in the disclosure statement of his intent to apply for a discharge on plan confirmation, and there was a strong likelihood that the plan would be successfully consummated.

The Ch. 11 discharge covers all debts that arose before the date of confirmation, including debts deemed under §502(g), (h), and (i) to have arisen prepetition. The discharge of a debt is not dependent on the proof or allowance of the claim or on the holder's acceptance of the plan. The plan itself may contain provisions that expand or reduce the extent of the discharge.

Ch. 11 does not have an equivalent of §727. However, §727 applies in a Ch. 11 case where the debtor is being liquidated under the plan. Section 1141(d)(3) states that confirmation of the plan does not discharge the debtor if the plan provides for the liquidation of all or substantially all of the debtor's estate, the debtor does not engage in business after consummation of the plan, and the debtor would have been denied a discharge under §727(a) if the case had been filed under Ch. 7. The simple point of this provision is that if the debtor is to be liquidated under Ch. 11 and will not remain in business, there is no reason to treat the Ch. 11 discharge differently from that under Ch. 7. Therefore, if the debtor is a corporation, the discharge is precluded by §727(a)(1). If the debtor is an individual, any grounds for the denial of a discharge under any other provision of §727 apply in the Ch. 11 case.

If the debtor is an individual, §1141(d)(2) excludes from the discharge all debts that are nondischargeable under §523, so that the exceptions to the individual debtor's discharge are the same in Chs. 7 and 11 — with one qualification: Under §1141(d) the plan may provide for the discharge of a debt that would otherwise be excluded from the discharge under §523. Of course, a provision of this kind is only feasible where the debtor has enough negotiating leverage to include it in the confirmed plan and the plan satisfies the confirmation standards discussed in Chapter 21. When the Ch. 11 debtor is not an individual, the exclusions from discharge in §523 are not applicable.

Section 1144 permits the court to revoke an order of confirmation, including the grant of the discharge, if the confirmation order was obtained by fraud. Revocation must be requested by a party in interest within 180 days from the entry of the order and can be granted only after notice and a hearing.

§22.7 THE CH. 13 DISCHARGE

§22.7.1 Procedure and Scope

Section 1328(a) requires the court to grant the discharge only after the debtor has completed payments under the plan. (However, an earlier discharge can be granted on the grounds of hardship, as discussed in section 22.7.6.) The Ch. 13 discharge includes all debts provided for by the plan or disallowed under §502. "Provided for" means not that payment must be provided for in the plan, but merely that the debt is dealt with, even if no payment will be made.

§22.7.2 Preconditions to the Grant of the Ch. 13 Discharge

BAPCPA added three provisions to §1328 that impose additional conditions on the grant of a Ch. 13 discharge. First, under §1328(a), to receive the discharge the debtor must certify that he has paid all domestic support obligations that are due at the time of the discharge. The certification must cover all domestic support obligations required to be paid by court or administrative order or by statute as of the date of the certification, including not only current postpetition obligations, but also prepetition obligations to the extent that they are provided for by the plan.

Second, under §1328(g), the debtor is not entitled to the Ch. 13 discharge until he has completed the instructional course on personal financial management required by §111 and approved by the U.S. Trustee. This provision is identical to §727(a)(11), explained in section 22.5.2.

Third, §1328(h) forbids the granting of a Ch. 13 discharge until the court finds, after notice and the opportunity for a hearing, that there is no reasonable cause to believe that §552(q)(1) is applicable, or that there is any proceeding pending in which the debtor may be found guilty of a felony of the kind described in §522(q)(1)(A) or liable for a debt of the kind described in §522(q)(1)(B). This provision is the same as §727(a)(12), discussed in section 22.5.2.[10]

§22.7.3 Exclusions from the Ch. 13 Discharge

As mentioned several times before, when Congress enacted the Code in 1978, it created a number of incentives designed to encourage debtors to choose Ch. 13 over Ch. 7. One of these incentives is a broader discharge

---

10. There is one subtle difference in the wording of these two sections. Section 727(a)(12) states that the court "shall grant the debtor a discharge unless" the court has found reasonable cause to believe that proceedings under §522(q) are applicable and pending. Section §1328(h) says that the court "may not grant a discharge . . . unless" the court has found no reasonable cause to believe that proceedings under §522(q) are applicable and pending. Presumably, the difference in wording is nothing more than an attempt to accommodate the provision to the existing grammatical structure of the sections.

under Ch. 13, which the Code achieves by limiting the applicability of the exclusions from discharge under §523(a) in a Ch. 13 case. Section 1328(a)(2) provides that only the selected exclusions from the discharge specified in the section are applicable in a Ch. 13 case. The idea behind the more generous Ch. 13 discharge is that because a debtor has made the greater effort to pay creditors by committing her disposable income to the Ch. 13 plan, the debtor has likely satisfied a higher percentage of her debt and has earned a less restrictive discharge. The exclusions from discharge that Congress selected to be inapplicable in a Ch. 13 case have always been a bit strange. First, some of them are debts that arose as a result of dishonest or wrongful conduct, which, one would think as a matter of policy should not be dischargeable under any chapter of the Code. Second, many of the selected debts are fairly unusual and are not likely to be owed by most debtors, so the ability to discharge debts of that kind provides no incentive to a large number of debtors.

In the years since 1978, Congress has gradually whittled away at the broader Ch. 13 discharge and has periodically increased the number of §523 exclusions that apply in a Ch. 13 case. In part, the reason for this is that Congress came to realize that some of the §523 exclusions that were inapplicable in Ch. 13 related to debts from which the debtor should never be released. Amendments since 1978, including BAPCPA to a significant extent, have excluded from the Ch. 13 discharge almost all of the debts incurred under wrongful circumstances. Only a small vestigial exclusion remains for debts arising out of willful and malicious injury, as explained below. As a result, the Ch. 13 discharge has become less generous than it used to be. The discharge advantage of Ch. 13 now seems so marginal that it is simply irrelevant to most debtors.

The narrowing of the Ch. 13 discharge seems to accord with the general approach of BAPCPA, which tends to favor pressing debtors into Ch. 13 rather than merely encouraging them to use it. This is particularly evident in the means test of §707(b). Of course, it is important to remember that the means test does not apply to all individual debtors who are eligible for Ch. 13. Section 707(b) provides grounds for dismissing a Ch. 7 case only where the debtor owes primarily consumer debts and the court finds grounds for abuse, either because the debtor's level of disposable income is high enough to give rise to the presumption or because abuse is otherwise established. This means that some debtors still have the relatively unrestricted choice of filing under Ch. 7 or Ch. 13, and in some situations, a debtor may find an advantage in the Ch. 13 discharge.

As discussed in section 20.6, a Ch. 13 debtor must be in good faith both in filing the case and in proposing the plan. Courts have frequently had to consider whether a debtor violates this obligation of good faith by choosing Ch. 13 for the primary purpose of discharging a debt that would be excluded from the discharge under Chs. 7 and 11. Because Congress has provided for a broader discharge in Ch. 13, courts generally adopt the approach that it is not per se bad faith for a debtor to choose Ch. 13 to take advantage of it. However, the debtor may fail the good faith test where the dominant purpose of the Ch. 13 filing is to discharge an otherwise nondischargeable debt, the plan provides no substantial advantage to creditors, and there is no sincere effort to pay to the best of the debtor's ability. (*See* section 20.6 and Example 2 of Chapter 20.) This issue affects fewer cases since the passage of BAPCPA because the opportunity for using Ch. 13 to discharge debts that are otherwise nondischargeable has shrunk dramatically.

Section 1328(a)(2) specifies that the only §523 exclusions from discharge applicable in a Ch. 13 case are those in §523(a)(2), (3), (4), (5), (8), and (9). (Subsections (a)(2), (3), and (4) were added to the list by BAPCPA.) The listed subsections are explained in section 22.5.4. In summary, they cover debts for money, property, or credit obtained by fraud or false pretenses (§523(a)(2)); unscheduled debts (§523(a)(3)); debts for fiduciary fraud, embezzlement, or larceny (§523(a)(4)); domestic support obligations (§523(a)(5)); educational loans (§523(a)(8)); and debts for death or personal injury caused by the debtor while driving under the influence of drugs or alcohol (§523(a)(9)).

The exclusion of priority taxes in §523(a)(1) is not mentioned in §1328(a)(2), but because priority tax claims must be paid in full under the plan unless the holder agrees to different treatment, the discharge of any unpaid balance of the claim does not arise at all or else relates only to the present value enhancement of the claim. (*See* sections 19.6.1 and 20.7.2.)

Neither §523(a)(7) (the exclusion of a noncompensatory fine, penalty, or forfeiture to a governmental unit) nor §523(a)(6) (the exclusion for debts incurred for willful and malicious injury) is listed in §1328(a)(2), so they do not apply in a Ch. 13 case. However, some debts of this kind may qualify for exclusion in a Ch. 13 case under §1328(a)(3) or §1328(a)(4). The exclusions in these sections are narrower than the more general exclusions in §523(a)(6) and (7). If the willful and malicious act was a crime and the debtor was prosecuted and convicted of it, and was fined or ordered to pay restitution as part of his sentence, the fine or restitutionary obligation is excluded from the Ch. 13 discharge by §1328(a)(3).[11] This section is confined to restitution or a criminal fine that is part of the debtor's sentence in a criminal case. It would not be applicable if the creditor had obtained a civil judgment of restitution, or the debtor made a voluntary commitment to

---

11. Section 1328(a)(3) was added to the Code in response to *Pennsylvania Department of Public Welfare v. Davenport*, 495 U.S. 552 (1990), in which the Supreme Court rejected the argument that a criminal restitution order does not qualify as a claim. Because the court characterized the restitution obligation as a claim, there was no barrier to discharging it in a Ch. 13 case under the provisions existing at the time. Congress therefore added §1328(a)(3) to exclude from the Ch. 13 discharge any debt for restitution included in a sentence on the debtor's conviction of a crime.

repay. Section 1328(a)(4), added by BAPCPA, fills part of the gap left by §1328(a)(3). It excludes from the Ch. 13 discharge a debt for restitution or damages awarded against the debtor in a civil action for personal injury or death caused by the debtor's willful and malicious conduct. In short, while the exclusions for the type of wrongful conduct covered by §523(a)(6) and (7) are not fully applicable in a Ch. 13 case, amendments to Ch. 13 have brought the extent of the Ch. 13 discharge a bit closer to that in a Ch. 7 case.

Section 1328 contains two exclusions from the Ch. 13 discharge that relate to particular features of the Ch. 13 process. Section 1328(a)(1) excludes from the discharge any debt provided for by §1322(b)(5). These are long-term debts to be paid beyond the period of the plan (*see* section 20.9). Because the plan contemplates that they will continue to be paid after the consummation of the plan, they necessarily remain enforceable after the discharge.[12] Section 1328(d) excludes from the discharge any debts based on an allowed claim filed under §1305(a)(2) if the trustee's prior approval of the debt was practicable but not obtained. As explained in section 19.2.3, §1305(a)(2) allows a creditor to prove a claim for a post-petition consumer debt incurred by the debtor for household or personal necessities, so that the debt can be handled in the estate. If the debtor obtained the trustee's prior approval or if the prior approval was not practicable, any balance on the debt unpaid in the Ch. 13 distribution is discharged. However, if the trustee's approval could have been obtained and the debtor failed to get it, the debt is excluded from the discharge. (If the creditor knew that trustee approval was practicable but not obtained, the claim is disallowed under §1305(c), so its dischargeability would not be in issue.)

§22.7.4 Discharge in Successive Cases

The grounds for denial of a discharge in §727 are not applicable in a Ch. 13 case, so dishonest, manipulative, or uncooperative debtor conduct is policed under the good faith standard. Sections 727(a)(8) and (9), which bar a discharge in successive bankruptcy filings, are also not applicable in Ch. 13. Before BAPCPA there was no prohibition of a discharge in a subsequent Ch. 13 case filed within a relatively short time of a prior bankruptcy. However, BAPCPA changed that by enacting §1328(f), which precludes the grant of a Ch. 13 discharge if the debtor received a discharge in a prior Ch. 7 or 12 case filed in the four-year period before the petition or in a prior Ch. 13 case filed within the two-year period before the petition.

---

12. Section 1228(a)(1) has an exclusion to the Ch. 12 discharge equivalent to §1328(a)(1).

Note that §1328(f) bars only successive discharges. It does not preclude the debtor from filing a Ch. 13 petition after getting a discharge in Ch. 7 (a so-called "Chapter 20") for the purpose of preventing foreclosure on collateral and forcing a secured creditor into accepting payment by installments. (This strategy is explained in section 20.11.) In *Johnson v. Home State Bank*, 501 U.S. 78 (1991), the U.S. Supreme Court held that there was no statutory bar to "Chapter 20." Therefore, provided that the debtor complied with the general requirement of good faith, he could first file under Ch. 7 to discharge personal liability on debt and then file under Ch. 13 to prevent foreclosure of a mortgage and to force the mortgagee to accept payments in installments. Section 1328(f), enacted after *Johnson* was decided, now precludes a Ch. 13 discharge in a "Chapter 20" situation. However, this limits only successive discharges, not successive filings. Therefore the central holding in *Johnson* has not been overturned. Subject to the requirement of good faith, the debtor may file a Ch. 13 case immediately after having received a Ch. 7 discharge if the purpose is not to obtain a Ch. 13 discharge but to take advantage of the ability to prevent foreclosure and continue paying the secured debt by installments.

§22.7.5 Waiver of Revocation of the Ch. 13 Discharge

Section 1328(a) recognizes a written waiver of discharge, executed by the debtor after the order for relief and approved by the court.

Section 1328(e) permits the court to revoke the discharge on grounds of the debtor's fraud if the applicant for revocation did not know of the fraud until after the discharge was granted. The application for revocation must be made within a year of the discharge and can only be granted after notice and a hearing.

§22.7.6 The Hardship Discharge

As stated earlier, the debtor must normally complete payments under the plan to receive the discharge. However, §1328(b) gives the court the discretion, after notice and a hearing, to grant a hardship discharge to a debtor who has not been able to complete payments under the plan. A hardship discharge may only be granted to the debtor if three conditions are satisfied: The failure to complete payments must result from factors beyond the debtor's control; the distribution actually made to unsecured claims must satisfy the best interests test (i.e., the payments actually made to unsecured creditors under the plan up to the time of discharge must be at least equal to the present value of what unsecured creditors would have received in a Ch. 7 liquidation); and modification of the plan must be impracticable. Because the hardship discharge is given to a debtor who has not consummated the plan, it is not as generous as the normal Ch. 13 discharge and is fully subject to the exclusions in §523(a). In sum, under §1328(c) and (d), the hardship discharge does not extend to secured debts, debts excluded from the plan under §1322(b)(5), postpetition debts for consumer necessities incurred without trustee approval, and all debts excluded from the discharge by §523(a).

§22.8 THE CH. 12 DISCHARGE

The Ch. 12 discharge provisions are modeled on those in Ch. 13, with some variations. Like Ch. 13, the Ch. 12 discharge is normally granted only upon consummation of the plan (§1228(a)). Unlike Ch. 13, Ch. 12 does not provide any restrictions on the exclusions from the discharge in §523(a), which apply fully in a Ch. 12 case. Like the Ch. 13 discharge, the Ch. 12 discharge does not extend to long-term debts paid outside the plan under §1222(b)(5) (a provision almost identical to §1322(b)(5)) or to secured debts to be settled after the plan period under §1222(b)(9). Section 1228(a) allows the debtor to waive the discharge in writing after the order for relief, subject to court approval. BAPCPA added preconditions to the Ch. 12 discharge equivalent to those added to Ch. 13. Section 1228(a), like §1328(a), requires the debtor to certify that he has paid all domestic support obligations due at the time of the discharge. Section 1228(f), like §1328(h), requires the court to satisfy itself that there is no reasonable cause to believe that there is a §522(q) issue in the case. (*See* section 22.7.2.)

Like in Ch. 13, the grounds for denial of discharge in §727 are not applicable in a Ch. 12 case, and policing of debtor conduct must take place under the good faith test for plan confirmation in §1225 or the grounds for dismissal or conversion in §1208. BAPCPA did not amend Ch. 12, as it did Ch. 13, to bar successive Ch. 12 discharges, so unless consecutive filings are abusive, the debtor can obtain a Ch. 12 discharge at any time after a discharge in a prior bankruptcy.

As in Ch. 13, the Ch. 12 discharge can be revoked on grounds of fraud under §1228(d) within a year of discharge. Section 1228(b) provides for a hardship discharge very similar to that in Ch. 13. The grounds for granting the hardship discharge are the same as in Ch. 13, and the discharge is also less generous than normal. Because nondischargeable debts under §523 are excluded from the Ch. 12 discharge in any event, this is not a point of difference in the hardship discharge. However, the hardship discharge does not cover administrative expenses that would otherwise be discharged, and it does not cover secured debts.

Examples

1. Hippocrates Oaf is a successful physician whose hobby was real estate speculation. He embarked upon a large suburban development project, using all his savings as well as borrowed funds. The venture failed, rendering Dr. Oaf insolvent and forcing him into default on his loan. Dr. Oaf plans to seek Ch.7 relief. Dr. Oaf's state of domicile has enacted legislation under §522(b), making nonbankruptcy exemptions applicable in bankruptcy cases. Under the state's exemption law most exemptions are subject to low dollar limits. However, because the state has a strong policy of encouraging its citizens to compose and perform fine music, the state legislature has granted an unlimited exemption in musical instruments.

   Dr. Oaf is tone-deaf and has never owned a musical instrument. In the few weeks before filing his Ch. 7 petition Dr. Oaf sold a number of valuable nonexempt assets, realizing $450,000, which is the market value of the assets sold. He used the $450,000 to buy an antique grand piano. He then filed his Ch. 7 petition. Would or should Dr. Oaf's pre-petition conduct have any impact on his discharge?

2. While employed as a personnel manager, Penny Tentiary padded the company's payroll by adding fictitious names to it. When checks were issued to these nonexistent employees, Penny cashed them and kept the money. She did this for a few months, until her employer discovered her subterfuge, dismissed her, and filed criminal charges. Penny was convicted and was sentenced to a term of imprisonment, suspended on condition that she pay back the stolen funds by specified monthly installments over three years. Under the state's probation statute, Penny was required to make payments to the probation department, which would transmit the funds to the victim of the crime. Penny paid the installments for about six months, and then filed a petition under Ch. 7. She listed the restitution obligation as an unsecured debt. Is the restitution obligation excluded from the Ch. 7 discharge? Would it be excluded from the discharge if she had filed under Ch. 13 instead of Ch. 7?

3. Will Fully owned and operated a retail store as a sole proprietor. He recently filed a Ch. 7 petition. In the months prior to his bankruptcy, Will fell behind in payments due to his suppliers and could no longer buy inventory on credit. To raise cash to buy new inventory, Will sold all his office equipment and furnishings. This property was subject to a valid and perfected security interest in favor of a bank that had financed its purchase. Will realized that the sale was a violation of an express term of the security agreement.

   Will sold the new inventory in the course of business and used its proceeds to pay expenses. This enabled him to operate for a while longer, but his business eventually failed and he filed his Ch. 7 petition. It was only after the filing that the bank discovered that its collateral had been sold and the proceeds dissipated, leaving the bank with an unsecured claim against the estate. (The buyer of the collateral cannot be found, so the bank cannot recover it from him.)

The bank has applied for a determination of nondischargeability under §523(c).

a. Should the debt be excluded from Will's discharge?

b. Would the answer be different if Will had filed under Ch. 13?

4. Comic Kazi has a wonderful sense of humor. He is employed by an auto parts and tire store. One day, as a prank, he threw a lighted firecracker into the store's basement for the purpose of scaring a fellow employee. Because there were gas fumes in the basement, the firecracker set off an explosion that injured the coworker. The coworker sued Comic for damages and obtained a judgment for actual damages of $1,000,000 and punitive damages of $500,000.

Comic filed a petition under Ch. 7. Is the tort judgment dischargeable?

5. Falsus N. Omnibus applied for a credit card from Reliance Bank. He completed a short and simple application form that asked for no information about the applicant's financial affairs. A few weeks later, the card arrived in the mail. Reliance had not checked Falsus's credit. Had it done so, it would have found that he was heavily in debt and had a poor credit record. Upon receiving the card, Falsus immediately went to the mall and bought a home entertainment system, CDs, and DVDs to the full credit limit on the card. Falsus never made any payments to Reliance, which eventually sued him to recover the debt and obtained default judgment against him. Before Reliance could execute on its judgment, Falsus filed a Ch. 7 petition. Six months had elapsed between the purchases and the bankruptcy filing.

Reliance filed an application for a nondischargeability determination on the grounds that Falsus had made a false representation under §523(a)(2)(A). Reliance conceded that Falsus had made no express misrepresentations, but argued that his application and subsequent use of the card constituted an implied representation that he was financially responsible and would pay for purchases charged to the account. Should the debt be excluded from the discharge?

6. Hardy Schipp graduated near the top of his law school class and immediately went to work for a large law firm. Although he earned an excellent salary, he hated the work and found it very unsatisfying. One day he realized that he would never find fulfillment representing rich clients in large commercial transactions. To give his life meaning, he

would have to devote his energies to helping those in desperate need. Hardy therefore resigned from the law firm and went to work for a nonprofit public interest firm that provided legal assistance to poor people. Hardy's earnings dropped to 20 percent of what he had earned at the large law firm, but he did not mind because he was not materialistic and did not need much to live on. The problem was his huge debt for student loans from college and law school. He struggled for about a year to maintain payments on the loans, but it was impossible to survive on what he had left over each month after making those payments. Can Hardy get rid of the loans if he files for bankruptcy?

Explanations

1. Apart from §522(o), which is applicable only to the homestead exemption and therefore not pertinent here,[13] the Code does not forbid debtors from ordering their affairs to take advantage of exemptions in anticipation of filing a petition. In fact, the legislative history of §522 indicates that Congress expected debtors to engage in reasonable prepetition planning to maximize exemptions. (This issue is also discussed in Example 5 of Chapter 13.) However, if a debtor's prepetition planning is abusive or in bad faith, the court has the power to sanction that conduct either by dismissing the case or by denying the debtor a discharge. Because this is a Ch. 7 case, the basis for denying the discharge must be found in §727(a). (Section 523(a) is not applicable because that section applies only where there are grounds for excluding a particular debt from the discharge because of the nature of the debt or the circumstances of its creation.)

Where the debtor has improperly converted nonexempt property into exempt property in anticipation of bankruptcy, the only provision of §727(a) that might be applicable to deny the debtor a discharge is §727(a)(2) — that the debtor transferred property within a year before the petition with the intent to hinder, delay, or defraud creditors. Dr. Oaf's sale of nonexempt assets clearly was a transfer of property within a year of the petition. The issue is whether the disposition had those additional elements of dishonesty that make it fraudulent. This "extrinsic fraud," as it is sometimes called, can take many forms. For example, the debtor may have used new credit to acquire the exempt property, or may have taken steps to conceal the conversion from creditors, or may have sold nonexempt property at sacrifice prices to get rid

---

13. As discussed in section 13.2.3, BAPCPA enacted §522(o), which creates some controls on the conversion of nonexempt assets into a homestead where the state has opted out of federal exemptions and has an unlimited or very generous homestead exemption. However, these controls apply only to the homestead exemption. They are not relevant to the conversion of nonexempt property into some type of exempt property other than a homestead.

of it quickly and complete the conversion before creditors could find out about it. See, for example, In re Reed, 700 F.2d 986 (5th Cir. 1983); In re Smiley, 864 F.2d 562 (7th Cir. 1989); In re Armstrong, 931 F.2d 1233 (8th Cir. 1991). Although extrinsic fraud is usually required for denial of the discharge under §727(a)(2), there is also some case authority that dispenses with the need to establish extrinsic fraud where the conversion is on a great enough scale. For example, in Norwest Bank Nebraska v. Tveten, 848 F.2d 871 (8th Cir. 1988), the court denied a discharge to the debtor, who converted $700,000 worth of nonexempt property into fully exempt insurance and annuity policies. Although there was no evidence of extrinsic fraud, the court considered that the excessive size of the conversion so perverted the Code's fresh start policy that it could not be tolerated.

There is no indication of extrinsic fraud in Dr. Oaf's case, so his prepetition planning is likely effective and will not cause him to be denied a discharge. However, this conclusion is subject to the possibility that the wholesale conversion may go beyond the acceptable to constitute an abuse of the Code, subjecting the debtor to §727(a)(2). Advising a prospective debtor on this kind of prepetition activity requires careful judgment by the debtor's attorney, who must inform the client of his legal rights so that he can make legitimate planning choices, but must not participate in or encourage fraudulent manipulations.

2. Kelley v. Robinson (discussed in section 22.5.4) dealt with issues similar to those presented by these facts and held that a restitution obligation, imposed as a condition of probation in a criminal sentence, is a non-compensatory penalty, excluded from the discharge by §523(a)(7). Penny's restitution obligation arises from the embezzlement of funds, so it could also be excluded under §523(a)(2) or (4). However, from the creditor's perspective, §523(a)(7) is a more advantageous basis for excluding the debt from the discharge because a §523(c) determination of dischargeability is required for §523(a)(2) and (4), but is not required for §523(a)(7).

Had Penny filed under Ch. 13, the creditor would not have been able to exclude the debt from the discharge under §523(a)(7) because it is not one of the provisions of §523 listed in §1328(a)(2). However, §1328(a)(3) provides a partial substitute for §527(a)(7) in a Ch. 13 case, in that it excludes the debt from the Ch. 13 discharge if it is for restitution or a criminal fine included in a sentence on the debtor's conviction of a crime. Although §1328(a)(3) is narrower than §523(a)(7), it does cover Penny's debt and excludes it from the discharge. As an alternative, the creditor could seek the debt's exclusion from the discharge under §523(a)(2) or (4), which were added to the list in §1328(a)(2) by

BAPCPA and are therefore available as a basis for excluding a debt from the Ch. 13 discharge, as they are in a Ch. 7 case.

3. a. Exclusion from the Ch. 7 discharge. Although the willful and malicious injury that excludes a debt from the discharge under §523(a)(6) is often associated with intentional tortious conduct that causes physical injury to property or person, the section's range is broader than that, and can encompass commercial injury. Will's wrongful disposal of collateral is both a breach of contract and a conversion of the secured party's property interest in the collateral. If the disposal is both willful and malicious, it could constitute an injury to the creditor's property as contemplated by §523(a)(6).

   Will's sale of the collateral was a deliberate act. There has clearly been a willful injury to the property interest of the bank. The circumstances strongly indicate that malice was present as well. Will knew that the sale was a breach of the security agreement, and he intended to spend the proceeds, rather than to remit them to the bank. Given his financial circumstances, he must have realized, as a person with some business experience, that he was depriving the bank of its protection against nonpayment at a time when default was a definite possibility. Malice does not require a motive or desire to inflict harm, but is present where the debtor deliberately persists in the injurious conduct, knowing that the consequences are substantially certain to follow. Therefore, even though the bank has lost its security, it may obtain some consolation by having its unsecured debt excepted from the discharge.

   Apart from the possibility of excluding the debt from the discharge under §523, Will's conduct could be bad enough to disqualify him from the Ch. 7 discharge in its entirety under §727. The sale of the collateral may constitute the transfer of property with the intent to hinder, delay, or defraud a creditor as contemplated by §727(a)(2), and his inability to identify the buyer of the collateral could be attributable to a failure to keep and preserve proper records under §727(a)(3).

   b. Exclusion from the discharge if Will had filed under Ch 13. Section 523(a)(6) is not one of the exclusions incorporated into Ch. 13 by §1328(a). Will's debt is therefore dischargeable in Ch. 13 even though he was guilty of willful and malicious injury to the bank's property interest. BAPCPA enacted §1328(a)(4), which deals with debts resulting from willful and malicious injury in a Ch. 13 case but provides for a much narrower exclusion from the discharge than §523(a)(6). Under §1328(a)(4) a debt for willful and malicious injury is nondischargeable in a Ch. 13 case only where the willful and malicious conduct resulted in death or personal injury and a court has awarded restitution or damages in a civil action against the debtor. Section 1328(a)(4) is therefore not applicable on these facts.

4. Unlike Example 3, in which the harm arose out of a commercial transaction, the injury here is caused by a physical tortious act that causes personal injury. Under *Kawaauhau* (discussed in section 22.5.4), both willfulness and malice must be proved, and recklessness is not enough. Comic's act was clearly willful — it was deliberate and intentional. Malice is more difficult to decide. For malice to be present, the creditor does not have to show that the debtor had the motive to injure. It is enough to show that the debtor acted deliberately, realizing that harm was substantially certain. Comic may not have intended to harm his coworker, and his behavior may have been idiotic rather than motivated by the desire to cause injury. However, it is on the dividing line of a subtle distinction. This is shown by the disposition of *In re Hartley*, 869 F.2d 394, *reversed on rehearing*, 874 F.2d 1254 (8th Cir. 1989), on which this Example is based. The bankruptcy court and district court found that throwing a firecracker into a room containing gas fumes was so certain to cause injury that it was malicious. The majority of the court of appeals, with one judge dissenting, found that although the act was reckless, it did not amount to malice. However, in a subsequent en banc hearing, the court of appeals panel was reversed. The conduct was found to be malicious, and the district court judgment was affirmed.

In this case, the coworker's claim has already been adjudicated in state court. If the state court made a finding as to willfulness and malice (which the court likely has done, because it awarded punitive damages), the bankruptcy court may adopt that finding on the principle of collateral estoppel, so that the creditor does not have to prove these elements again in the dischargeability hearing.

The coworker was awarded both compensatory and punitive damages. If the injury is found to have been inflicted willfully and maliciously, the exclusion from discharge should include not only the compensatory damages, but the punitive damages as well. *Cohen v. De La Cruz* (cited in section 22.5.4) found that the grammatical meaning of the language of §523(a)(2) covered punitive damages as well as the original debt. This same reasoning should apply to §523(a)(6) because the structure of its language is even more conducive to this interpretation than the language in §523(a)(2). It excludes from the discharge "any debt . . . for willful and malicious injury."

5. During difficult economic times, credit card issuers may become more cautious in issuing credit cards without checking the applicant's creditworthiness. However, under more exuberant economic conditions, issuers may tend to become less risk averse and less finicky about the

603

fiscal means or responsibility of their customers. Reliance has been careless in vetting its applications, and Falsus has taken advantage of this by incurring debt on the card beyond his ability to pay. Falsus has not made any express fraudulent misrepresentation, so if Reliance seeks to exclude the debt from the discharge under §523(a)(2), it must make the argument indicated in the Example—that by using the card, Falsus made a false representation by conduct that he had the means and intent to pay the debt incurred. Most courts are willing to find an implied misrepresentation under these circumstances. However, Reliance must prove all the elements of fraud on the preponderance of the evidence. Reliance is not aided by the presumption of fraud in §523(a)(2)(C). Although the spending spree apparently involved consumer transactions, it occurred beyond the periods specified in that section.

For the implied representation of ability and intent to repay to qualify as fraudulent, it must have been false and made with intent to deceive. Fraudulent intent to breach a contract in the future is difficult to establish. It is not enough that the debtor knows he has financial trouble or that he does not have a clear idea of how he will pay the debt. He must have intended, when using the card, never to pay the debt. At least where the misrepresentation is implied, rather than express, the test is subjective — based on what the debtor intended—not objective and based on what he should have realized. See In re Mercer, 246 F.3d 391 (5th Cir. 2001); In re Moore, 365 B.R. 589 (Bankr. D. Md. 2007). Fraudulent intent is judged on the totality of the circumstances, and takes into account such factors as the debtor's financial circumstances and prospects at the time that the debt was incurred, and the extent to which the debtor had the capacity to comprehend those circumstances; whether the debtor had been contemplating bankruptcy at that time; whether the charges were for luxuries or necessities; and whether the spending was unusual or frenetic. Falsus's poor credit record and his immediate purchase of luxury goods to the full credit limit of his new card, at a time that he had no realistic prospects of paying the debt, suggest fraudulent intent.

Fraudulent intent is not the only element to be established for exclusion from the discharge under §523(a)(2). The creditor must also show that it was justified in relying on the misrepresentation. While some courts are intolerant of credit card issuers that do not conduct sufficient inquiry into the creditworthiness of prospective customers, other courts are somewhat more sympathetic and weigh the debtor's dishonesty against the creditor's lack of diligence. They hold that as long as the creditor has conducted a reasonable level of investigation and monitoring, it is entitled to assume, in the absence of suspicious indications to the contrary, that the debtor will use the card honestly. See, for example, In re Mercer, 246 F.3d 391 (5th Cir. 2001). However, because Reliance conducted no inquiry into Falsus's creditworthiness before issuing the card to him, even a more sympathetic court is unlikely to find that it had any justification for reliance on the representation.

6. Section 523(a)(8) excludes qualified educational loans from the discharge. This exclusion applies whether the debtor has filed under Ch. 7, Ch. 11 (*see* §1123(b)(2)), or Ch. 13 (*see* §1328(a)(2)). However, §523(a)(8) gives the court the power to discharge the debt if excepting it from the discharge would impose an undue hardship on the debtor or his dependents. The issue is therefore whether Hardy's circumstances constitute undue hardship. The three-part *Brunner* test, described in section 22.5.4, is the predominant test for determining undue hardship, but some courts use a wider-ranging totality of the circumstances test. Under the *Brunner* test, undue hardship is present where the debtor could not maintain a minimal standard of living if he is required to repay the loan, his financial circumstances are not likely to improve, and he has made a good faith effort to repay the loan.

Hardy's circumstances do not demonstrate undue hardship. He does not satisfy the first two prongs of the test because his lower level of earnings, while nobly motivated, is self-imposed, and could be substantially increased. He does not satisfy the third prong either. Although he has made some attempt at repaying the loan, he has apparently made no effort to negotiate an adjustment of payments and contemplates bankruptcy relatively soon after graduating from law school, with the primary purpose of discharging the loan debt. Congress has made it clear that it considers the protection of education loan programs to be of great importance, so a debtor cannot escape liability for repayment merely by electing to earn less than he is able to earn. It is hard to imagine that the totality of the circumstances test would reveal any additional factors that might change the conclusion reached under the *Brunner* test.

Glossary

Abandonment. In relation to estate property, abandonment is the trustee's relinquishment of estate property that is burdensome to the estate or of inconsequential value or benefit to the estate. (§554). In relation to the debtor's homestead, abandonment is the debtor's permanent termination of residence in the property, so that it no longer qualifies for the exemption.

Absolute priority rule. In a Ch. 11 case, the principle that in a cramdown confirmation, no junior class of claims or interests may receive anything of value from the estate unless a more senior nonaccepting class of unsecured claims or interests is paid in full. (§1129(b)(2)(B) and (C))

Abstention. The court's dismissal or suspension of a bankruptcy case, or its refusal to entertain related proceedings, on grounds of fairness or in deference to another court. (§305; 28 U.S.C. §1334(c))

Acceleration. The termination of the debtor's right to pay a debt in installments or at a future maturity date, so that the debt becomes immediately payable. The payment of a debt may be accelerated under an acceleration clause in a contract, upon the happening of a specified event, usually the debtor's default.

Acceptance of a Ch. 11 plan. The determination, by a majority vote of the members of a class of claims or interests, to acquiesce in a proposed Ch. 11 plan. (§1126)

Account, or an account receivable. A right to payment for goods sold or services rendered. (Sometimes abbreviated to "receivable.")

Adequate protection. If the estate retains property in which a person other than the debtor has an interest, that interest is entitled to adequate protection. That is, the value of the interest must be maintained during the period of retention, so that if the interest is ultimately foreclosed, the holder will receive no less than would have been received had the property been surrendered or liquidated immediately. (§§361, 1205)

Administrative expenses. Expenses incurred by the trustee or debtor in possession in the conduct of the estate's affairs or the preservation of its property. If allowed under §503, these expenses are paid as a second priority under §507.

Adversary proceedings.   Litigation in the bankruptcy case that is required by Rule 7001 to take the form of a civil suit, initiated by complaint; a full civil lawsuit within the bankruptcy case. *Compare* Contested matter.

After-acquired collateral.   Property acquired by the debtor that, by contract or operation of law, automatically becomes subject to a lien created in advance of the debtor's acquisition of the property. *See also* Floating lien.

Alias writ.   A second writ of execution, issued after the first writ failed to generate sufficient proceeds to satisfy the judgment.

Allowed claim.   A claim that is accepted as owing by the estate under §502 either because it is not objected to or because the court has upheld it following a hearing on the objection.

Antecedent debt.   A debt due by the debtor that arose before the debtor made a transfer to the creditor in respect of the debt.

Antiassignment provision.   A provision in a contract or in law that prohibits the transfer of rights or the delegation of duties by the original holder of those rights and duties. *See* Assignment.

Artisan's or Repairer's lien.   A common law lien (now codified in many states) that may be asserted in personal property by a person who has repaired or improved it. The lien secures the agreed or reasonable cost of the work performed. At common law, it must be perfected by possession, but a statutory alternative of perfection by filing may be available.

Assignment for the benefit of creditors.   An insolvency procedure under state law under which the debtor makes a voluntary transfer of property in trust to another person (the assignee), with instructions to liquidate the property and to distribute its proceeds to creditors who have elected to participate.

Assignment of contract. Strictly speaking, assignment is the transfer of rights under a contract. The transfer of contractual duties is called "delegation." However, "assignment" is often used to mean the transfer of both rights and duties by one of the parties to a contract. It is used in this sense in §365, which empowers the trustee to assume an executory contract of the debtor and then to realize its value by assigning (i.e., selling) the debtor's package of rights and obligations to a third party. *See* Assumption of contract.

Assumption of contract. The estate's adoption of an executory contract entered into by the debtor prior to bankruptcy, so that the estate is substituted for the debtor as party to the contract. (§365). *Compare* Rejection of contract.

Attachment of a lien. Attachment is the creation of the lien, valid and enforceable as between the lienholder and the debtor. (Once the lien becomes effective against third parties as well, it is said to be "perfected.")

Attachment remedy and lien. The prejudgment remedy of attachment is the sheriff's seizure and retention of property of the defendant pending final resolution of the case. Upon attachment, the creditor obtains an attachment lien on the property that has been seized. This judicial lien secures the plaintiff's claim while the case is pending. If the plaintiff ultimately obtains judgment, the plaintiff has the right to sell the property in execution to satisfy the judgment.

Automatic perfection. The perfection of a lien immediately upon its attachment, without the need for any further action by the lienholder.

Automatic stay. The injunction that arises by operation of law, without the need for a court order, immediately upon the filing of a bankruptcy petition. The stay bars creditors from initiating or continuing with efforts to collect or enforce prepetition secured or unsecured debts, or to enforce prepetition claims against estate property or the debtor's property. (§362)

Avoidance. Avoidance is the overturning of a debt or obligation. In bankruptcy, the trustee has the power under §§544 to 553 to avoid certain prepetition dispositions or obligations of the debtor, as well as certain unauthorized postpetition dispositions of estate property. The debtor has the right under §522(f) to avoid specified interests to the extent that they impair qualified exemptions in property.

Backdating. Upon timely completion of the prescribed act of perfection, some liens are given retrospective effect so that their priority will date from some specified earlier time.

Badge of fraud. Suspicious circumstances leading to the inference that a transfer made by the debtor was motivated by the actual intent to defraud creditors.

BAFJA. The Bankruptcy Amendments and Federal Judgeship Act of 1984, which made several significant amendments to the Code.

Balance sheet test. *See* Insolvency.

Bankruptcy Act. The predecessor to the present Code, which was enacted in 1898 and repealed in 1978.

Bankruptcy Reform Act. The 1978 statute which, with amendments, forms the present Code. (The same name was given to the act that amended the Code in 1994.)

Bankruptcy test. *See* Insolvency.

BAP (Bankruptcy Appellate Panel). A court, consisting of three bankruptcy judges, established in some circuits to hear appeals from bankruptcy courts.

BAPCPA. The Bankruptcy Abuse Prevention and Consumer Protection Act of 2005, which made many significant amendments to the Code.

Best interests test. One of the standards for plan confirmation, which requires that the total amount to be paid on a claim under the plan has a present value at least equal to what the claimant would have received had the estate been liquidated under Ch. 7. The requirement of present value is intended to compensate the claimant for having to await distribution over time instead of receiving immediate payment upon liquidation of the estate. The present value of the distribution is determined by adding interest at the market rate to the face value of the hypothetical Ch. 7 payment. (§§1129(a)(7), 1125(a)(4), and 1325(a)(4))

Bifurcation of claim. *See* Claim bifurcation.

Bona fide purchaser. (Latin: "Good faith.") A person who, in a consensual transaction, acquires rights in property in good faith (*i.e.*, with subjective honesty) for value and without actual or constructive notice that the purchase violates rights in the property held by a person other than the transferor. *Compare* Good faith purchaser.

Business judgment rule. A standard for court approval of the trustee's business decision (such as a decision to assume or reject an executory contract) under which the court declines to interfere with the trustee's decision if it was made in good faith and was a reasonable business judgment.

Cash collateral. Cash or cash equivalent that is subject to an interest (such as a security interest) held by a person other than the estate. (§363(a))

Chapter 20. An unofficial name for the debtor's tactic of filing sequentially under Chs. 7 and 13. A debtor may use this tactic to discharge personal liability on debts in the Ch. 7 case, and thereafter prevent foreclosure of a lien on property (which is not discharged) by providing for payment of it by installments in the Ch. 13 plan.

Claim.   Any secured or unsecured right to payment arising in law or equity. (§101(5))

Claim and delivery.   *See* Replevin.

Claim bifurcation.   The splitting of an undersecured debt into a secured claim to the extent of the collateral's value and an unsecured claim for the deficiency. This division is required by §506.

Class of claims or interests.   Claims or interests that have been placed in the same category for treatment in bankruptcy, either because they fall within one of the statutory priority classifications or because the debtor has properly grouped them together in a plan under Ch. 11, 12, or 13.

Codebtors.   Persons who are liable on the same debt. (Also called "joint debtors," not to be confused with debtors in joint cases.)

Cognovit note.   (Latin: "Acknowledgment.") *See* Confession to judgment.

Collateral.   The property subject to a lien or security interest.

Collective proceedings.   General name for proceedings such as assignments for the benefit of creditors, compositions, and bankruptcy, under which the claims of creditors are dealt with collectively to avoid the disruption and inequality of individual creditor action.

Common law lien.   A lien arising by operation of common law, not dependent on agreement, statute, or judicial process. Common law liens are typically intended to provide security for the agreed or reasonable charges owing to a person who has repaired, improved, or preserved personal property or provided personal services at the owner's request. They must usually be perfected by possession.

Composition.   A contract between a debtor and creditors, under which partial payment is promised and accepted in full settlement of claims. A composition may be combined with an extension — an agreement to extend the time in which to pay off the debt.

Confession to judgment.   The debtor's waiver of the right to contest a collection suit, authorizing the creditor to obtain judgment by consent. A confession during the course of litigation (also called a "stipulation") is enforceable if freely made. However, a confession made before default, particularly one contained in the instrument of debt itself (called a "cognovit note" or "warrant of attorney") is subject to particular scrutiny and is usually unenforceable in a consumer transaction.

Confirmation of a plan.   The confirmation of a plan under Ch. 11, 12, or 13 is the court's determination that the plan meets the requirements of the Code, and that it will form the basis for the treatment of claims, disposition of estate property, and conduct of the estate's affairs.

Confirmation of a sale in execution.   Where real property is sold in execution, state law usually requires that the court approves (confirms) the sale.

Consensual lien.   A lien granted in a contract between the lienholder and the debtor, such as a mortgage or a UCC Article 9 security interest.

Consolidation of cases.   *Procedural consolidation* is the consolidation of two separate petitions filed in relation to the same debtor. *Substantive consolidation* is the combination of the estates of two closely related debtors, so that assets are pooled and creditors of each become creditors of the combined estate. *Compare* Joint administration.

Construction lien.   *See* Mechanic's lien.

Constructive fraud.   Fraud established not by proof of actual dishonest intent but by facts that are, as a matter of legal policy, treated as giving rise to an irrebuttable presumption of fraud.

Constructive notice.   *See* Notice.

Constructive trust.   An equitable remedy under which a person who has acquired property by a wrongful act is deemed to hold the property in trust for the victim of the wrong.

Consumer debt.   A debt incurred by an individual primarily for personal, family, or household purposes. (§101(8))

Contested matter.   A proceeding within the bankruptcy case, initiated by motion or objection rather than by the filing of a complaint. *Compare* Adversary proceedings.

Contingent claim.   A claim in which the debtor's potential liability has been created (usually by contract or wrongful act) but actual liability will only arise upon the happening of a future event that may not occur.

Conversion of case.   A change in the Code chapter governing the case, altering the form of bankruptcy relief sought. For example, a case originally filed under Ch. 13 may be converted into a liquidation under Ch. 7 if the debtor's attempt at debt adjustment fails.

Conversion of nonexempt property. The realization of nonexempt property and the use of the proceeds to acquire exempt property. *See also* Prepetition planning.

Core proceeding. A proceeding in a bankruptcy case that involves the adjudication of rights created by the Code, or concerns issues that, by their nature, could only arise in a bankruptcy case. Because core proceedings involve substantive rights granted under the Code, they may be finally determined by the bankruptcy court itself. *Contrast to* Related proceedings.

Cramdown. The confirmation of a plan despite opposition from some creditors, where the plan satisfies the Code's prerequisites for non-consensual confirmation. (§§1129(b), 1225, and 1325)

Credit bid. The secured creditor bids at the foreclosure auction of its collateral, and if it is successful in buying the property, it sets off the debt against the price that it bid at the auction.

Creditor's bill. An equitable suit available to a creditor for the purpose of locating and recovering executable property that has been concealed or wrongfully transferred by the debtor or for reaching assets that otherwise cannot be executed upon using procedures at law.

Creditors' committee. A committee of creditors appointed by the U.S. Trustee in Ch. 11 cases, and sometimes in Ch. 7 cases, to represent the interests of the creditor body as a whole or, if more than one committee is appropriate, a class of creditors.

Creditors' meeting. The statutory meeting of creditors required in all bankruptcy cases by §341. The meeting must be convened by the U.S. Trustee within a prescribed time following the order for relief. Its primary business is the examination of the debtor.

Cross-collateralization. In the context of postpetition financing, a term in the financing contract under which collateral furnished by the estate to secure the new credit also covers an unsecured or under-secured prepetition claim of the lender.

Cure of default. The payment of arrears or the rectification of any other breach of contractual obligations, so that the party's performance is brought into compliance with the terms of the contract.

Custodian. Any person appointed to take charge of the debtor's property under nonbankruptcy law, such as a receiver or an assignee for the benefit of creditors. (§101(11))

Debt. An obligation to pay money. In §101(12) "debt" is defined as liability on a "claim," which is defined in §101(5) as a right to payment.

Debt adjustment. A case under Ch. 12 or 13.

Debtor. In general, a person liable on a debt. In bankruptcy, the debtor is the person concerning whom the bankruptcy case was filed. (§101(13))

Debtor in possession. The new legal personality acquired by the debtor in a Ch. 11 case, under which the debtor administers the estate and fulfills the role of trustee for most purposes. (§§1101(1) and 1107) (The debtor in a Ch. 12 case is also a debtor in possession, but does not exercise the functions of the trustee beyond the conduct of business operations.)

Debtor's equity. The debtor's unencumbered ownership interest in property.

Default. The debtor's material breach of contract, such as the failure to pay a debt on the due date. Some contracts provide that the insolvency or bankruptcy of the debtor constitutes *ipso facto* default. Such a provision is not enforceable in bankruptcy.

Default judgment. A judgment granted on application of the plaintiff when the defendant has failed to file an answer or other required pleading.

Deficiency. The shortfall that results when a debt is undersecured, that is, when the collateral securing the debt is worth less than the amount owing, so that realization of the collateral does not fully satisfy the debt. *See* Equity cushion; Surplus.

Delegation. *See* Assignment.

Delivery bond. *See* Redelivery bond.

Delivery of writ. The transmission of a writ to the sheriff with instructions to execute it.

Discharge. The debtor's release from liability for the unpaid balance of all debts that are provable in bankruptcy and that are not excluded from discharge under the Code.

Discharging/dissolution bond. A bond posted by the debtor for the purpose of releasing property from attachment. The bond is an undertaking by the debtor, supported by a surety, to pay any judgment ultimately obtained by the creditor. Its effect is to terminate the attachment and restore the property to the debtor. *Compare* Redelivery bond.

Disclosure statement.   The statement required by §1123 to be disseminated by the proponent of a Ch. 11 plan, providing sufficient information on the plan to enable the holders of claims and interests to make an informed judgment on it.

Dismissal.   The court's termination of the bankruptcy case upon voluntary withdrawal by the petitioner or on the motion of a party in interest or the court's own motion.

Disposable income test.   A requirement for plan confirmation that the debtor must commit all his or her disposable income to payments under the plan for a period of three or five years. "Disposable income" is that portion of the debtor's income not reasonably necessary for the maintenance and support of the debtor or a dependent and not necessary for the operation and preservation of any business in which the debtor is engaged. The test is only applied upon objection to confirmation by a competent party.

Distraint/distress.   The seizure of property to secure or satisfy a debt. For example, a landlord's right to seize a tenant's goods on the leased premises to satisfy a claim for unpaid arrear rent.

Distress sale.   A forced sale, such as an execution or foreclosure sale. Because of the circumstances of the sale, the price obtained for the property is usually depressed.

Docket.   A record of proceedings in court or the act of making an entry in such record.

Dormant   judgment. A judgment that has become unenforceable because it has not been executed upon within the prescribed time. It can be revived by application. (*Dormancy* must be distinguished from *expiry* of a judgment: When a judgment reaches the end of its statutory lifespan, it becomes ineffective and cannot be revived.)

"Drop-dead" clause.   A provision in a contract or rehabilitation plan that requires exact compliance with the debtor's obligations and gives the creditor an immediate right of action (for example, to accelerate the debt or to foreclose) in the event of default.

Elegit.   An early common law writ, available as an alternative to *fieri facias*, that enabled a judgment creditor to obtain personal property of the debtor or to receive revenues from portion of the debtor's lands. *Compare Fieri facias.*

Enabling loan. *See* Purchase money security interest.

Encumbrance. A right to or interest in property, such as a lien, which diminishes the extent of the owner's title.

Entity. A general term used in the Code to encompass a wide variety of legal persons, including individuals, corporations, and governmental units. (§101(15))

Equitable lien. A lien recognized under principles of equity in the absence of legal lien rights, in order to do justice between the parties and to provide effective relief to an otherwise unsecured creditor.

Equitable subordination. *See* Subordination.

Equity. In addition to its general meaning of fairness or justice, "equity" denotes the body or rules and principles developed by Courts of Chancery (and now applied by courts of combined legal and equitable jurisdiction) to afford relief where remedies at law are inadequate. The word "equity" is also used to refer to an owner's unencumbered interest in property. *See* Debtor's equity.

Equity cushion. The amount of equity held by the debtor in collateral in excess of the value of the claim of a lienholder and any encumbrances senior to the secured claim. This excess value in the collateral is called an "equity cushion" because it provides a margin of safety for the lienholder to cover any adverse change in the collateral-debt ratio caused by future depreciation of the property or the accumulation of interest or costs.

Equity of redemption. The mortgagor's right to save property from foreclosure by paying the mortgage debt before the foreclosure sale. The equity of redemption arises from principles of equity and applies only in the presale period. It must be distinguished from statutory redemption, which extends beyond the sale date and may be exercised against the purchaser of the property. *See also* Redemption.

Equity receivership. *See* Receiver.

Equity security. A share in a corporation or a limited partner's interest in a partnership. (§101(16))

Equity test. *See* Insolvency.

Estate. In general terms, a person's estate is all the property held by that person. In the bankruptcy context, the estate is the legal entity created by the filing of the petition, which succeeds to the debtor's property rights under §541.

Examiner. A person appointed by the court under §1104(b) to investigate the management or conduct of the debtor in a Ch.11 case.

Exception to discharge. A debt that is excluded from the debtor's discharge on one of the grounds enumerated in §523 or §1328.

Exclusivity period. The period following the filing of a Ch. 11 petition, during which the debtor has the exclusive right to file a plan. (§1121)

Executable property. Property of the debtor that is not exempt or otherwise immune from execution, so that it can be subjected to the claims of creditors.

Execution. The enforcement of a judgment by the seizure and sale of nonexempt property of the debtor.

Execution lien. A judicial lien created in property of the debtor levied upon under a writ of execution.

Executory contract. In general, a contract is executory if it has not been fully performed. Upon the bankruptcy of one of the parties, a contract that qualifies as executory for bankruptcy purposes may be assumed by the estate. In bankruptcy, the most widely used test for deciding if a contract is executory is whether the obligations of both parties are so far unperformed that the failure of either to complete performance would be a material breach. The trustee must elect to reject or assume the executory contract under §365.

Exemption. A right granted by statute to an individual debtor to hold specified property free from the claims of creditors. (§522)

Extension. A contract between a debtor and a creditor or creditors, under which the debtor is allowed an extension of time in which to pay debts. *See also* Composition.

Fair and equitable standard. A Ch. 11 plan can only be confirmed by the cramdown method if classes of claims and interests are treated in a fair and equitable manner. This requires not only fair treatment in the usual sense, but also that the specific requirements of §1129(b) (such as the absolute priority rule) are satisfied.

Family farmer. A debtor (including an individual, spouse, or a family-held corporation or partnership) that is engaged in farming operations and meets the other eligibility requirements for Ch. 12 relief. (§101(18), (19), (20), and (21))

Feasibility standard. The requirement for plan confirmation that the debtor has demonstrated a reasonable prospect of being able to make the payments and meet the rehabilitative goals set out in the plan.

Fieri facias.   Originally, a common law writ commanding the sheriff to seize chattels of the debtor to satisfy a judgment. The term is still used in some jurisdictions as the name for the writ of execution. (Abbreviated as "fi fa.") *Compare Elegit.*

Financing statement.   The document filed in public records to perfect a security interest under UCC Article 9.

First-in-time rule.   The general rule of priority under which an earlier perfected lien or interest in property takes precedence over a later one.

Floating lien.   A security interest that extends to collateral of a specified type acquired by the debtor, or to advances made to the debtor, after the execution of the security agreement, or to both. *See* After-acquired collateral; Future advance.

Foreclosure.   The process whereby a lienholder enforces the lien following the debtor's default and subjects the collateral to satisfaction of the debt. Following seizure, the collateral is normally sold and its proceeds applied to payment of the debt. However, strict foreclosure (forfeiture of the property to the lienholder in full satisfaction of the debt) is permitted as an alternative in the case of some liens.

Foreign judgment.   As used in the Uniform Enforcement of Foreign Judgments Act, "foreign" means judgments of the courts of other states and federal courts, not judgments of the courts of foreign nations.

Fraudulent transfer/conveyance.   A disposition of property by a debtor with the actual or constructive intent to defraud creditors or to delay or hinder their collection efforts.

Fresh start.   The rehabilitation of a debtor through the process of bankruptcy, achieved by the resolution and discharge of prepetition debt.

Future advance.   A loan or credit advanced to the debtor after a security interest has been created, and secured by such preexisting security interest. *See also* Floating lien.

Gap creditor.   A person who extends credit or financing to the debtor during the period between two legally significant events, such as between the attachment and perfection of a security interest or between the filing of an involuntary petition and the order for relief.

Garnishment. A creditor's (garnishor's) levy on property of the debtor in the possession of a third party (garnishee), or on a debt or obligation due by the garnishee to the debtor.

Garnishment lien. A judicial lien that arises in property upon which garnishment has been levied.

Going concern value. The value of a business based on its sale as a continuing operation, rather than on the proceeds that would be realized upon the liquidation of its assets.

Good faith. Honesty, usually measured under a subjective test, and (in the bankruptcy context) compliance with the spirit of the Code.

Good faith purchaser. This term is sometimes used synonymously with bona fide purchaser. However, it is also sometimes used to denote a purchaser who acts honestly, but does not satisfy all of the other elements necessary to qualify as a bona fide purchaser. *Compare* Bona fide purchaser.

Holder of a claim. A creditor of the debtor whose claim is provable in the estate.

Homestead exemption. A exemption granted under state law or §522(d)(1) in an individual debtor's interest in property in which the debtor or a dependent resides.

Hypothetical status of trustee. The legal fictions created by §544, permitting the trustee to exercise avoidance rights that would have been available to a bona fide purchaser of real property, a lien creditor, and an execution creditor, had such persons existed on the date that the bankruptcy petition was filed.

Illiquid. Inability to convert assets into cash. *See* Insolvency.

Impaired class of claims or interests. In a Ch. 11 case, a class is impaired unless the rights of each member are unaltered except for the cure of any default and deceleration of the debt. (§1124)

Improvement in position test. One of the requirements for the avoidance of a transfer under §547 is that the transfer enabled the creditor to improve on the position that it would have occupied without the transfer. Improvement in position occurs where the transfer has enabled the creditor to receive more on its claim than it would have been paid in a hypothetical Ch. 7 distribution in the absence of the transfer.

In *custodia legis*. (Latin: "In the custody of the law.") The retention of property for safekeeping by the sheriff, a receiver, or some other person with legal authority.

Individual. A natural person, as distinct from a corporate entity.

Indubitable equivalent. A broad standard for measuring adequate protection under §361(3). The court must be satisfied that a proposed method of protecting an interest in property will undoubtedly provide the claimant with value equal to the value of the interest. Indubitable equivalence is also used as a standard for determining whether a secured claim has been treated fairly and equitably in a cramdown confirmation. (§1129(b)(2)(A)(iii))

Insider. A person who has such a close relationship with another that he or she has special access to information and opportunities for favorable treatment. Several provisions of the Code treat insiders of the debtor differently from other parties. "Insider" is defined in §101(31) to include relatives of an individual debtor and persons in control of a corporate debtor.

Insolvency. Inability to pay debts, determined by one of two tests: inability to pay debts as they fall due (called the "equity test") or an excess of liabilities over assets (called the "bankruptcy" or "balance sheet" test). (§101(32))

Interim trustee. A trustee appointed under §701 following the order for relief in a Ch. 7 case, to serve until a permanent trustee is appointed or elected at the meeting of creditors.

Involuntary case. A case under Ch. 7 or 11 initiated against the debtor by a creditor or creditors who qualify to seek bankruptcy relief. (§303)

Ipso facto clause/provision. (Latin: "By the fact itself.") A provision in a contract or in nonbankruptcy law under which the insolvency or bankruptcy of the debtor is treated as a default.

Joint administration. The administration of the estates of closely related debtors for the purpose of convenience and the reduction of administrative costs. *Compare* Consolidation of cases.

Joint case. A bankruptcy case in which a single voluntary petition is filed by both spouses, placing both their estates in bankruptcy. Although the estates are administered jointly, their assets and liabilities are not consolidated unless appropriate. (§302)

Joint debtors. *See* Codebtors.

Judgment lien.   A judicial lien arising on all the real property owned by the debtor in the county in which the judgment is docketed or recorded. In some states, a judgment recorded in UCC filing records creates a judgment lien on the debtor's personal property.

Judicial lien.   Any lien arising out of court proceedings. (§101(36))

Knowledge.   *See* Notice.

Leverage.   In negotiations, leverage is bargaining power or the ability to exert pressure on the other party to obtain a desired resolution. "Leverage" also has an alternative meaning that relates to debt. For example, the making of an investment consisting largely of borrowed funds or the use of borrowed funds instead of capital.

Leveraged buyout.   The purchase of stock in a corporation with borrowed funds, financed by the corporation itself or secured by its assets.

Levy.   The sheriff's seizure or taking control of property pursuant to a writ.

Lien.   Used broadly, any charge against or interest in property to secure a creditor's right to payment, so that if the debt is not paid, the creditor may have recourse to the property to satisfy the debt. (*See* §101(32).) "Lien" is sometimes used more narrowly to denote only such interests that arise by operation of law or court order, as distinct from interests created by contract, called "security interests."

Lienholder/lienor.   The holder of a lien. (Note: The person who grants the lien is simply called a debtor; there is no such thing as a "lienee.")

Lien stripping.   A strategy whereby the debtor attempts to peg an undersecured debt or a debt that has become unsecured at the value of the collateral as determined by the bankruptcy court, so that if the collateral appreciates after the bankruptcy case, the lien (which survives the bankruptcy) cannot extend to the increase in equity but is frozen at the bankruptcy valuation. Where the lien is undersecured, the fixing of the amount of the lien at the current value of the collateral is called "strip down." If the lien has become fully unsecured (because it is a junior lien and the senior lien has taken up the full value of the collateral) the fixing of the lien value at zero is called "strip off."

Liquidated claim.   *See* Unliquidated claim.

Liquidating plan.   A Ch. 11 plan that provides for the liquidation of the debtor, rather than its rehabilitation.

Liquidation.   The realization of the debtor's executable assets for the purpose of generating proceeds to be applied to the payment of debts.

Lis pendens.   (Latin: "Pending suit.") The doctrine, deriving from common law, that a person who acquires an interest in realty while litigation is pending concerning title, possession, or other rights to it, is bound by the court's ultimate resolution of the controversy. A party wishing to be protected by the doctrine must file a notice of pendency in the real estate records to give constructive notice of the litigation to any potential transferee.

"Loading up."   Excessive spending or borrowing on a credit card or other line of credit, with the effect of increasing the debt just before filing a bankruptcy petition.

Marshalling of assets.   An equitable doctrine that applies when two creditors are competing for satisfaction of their claims from the same fund and one of them has another fund available for application to its debt. Marshalling requires that creditor resort to the other fund before having recourse to the shared fund.

Materialman's lien.   *See* Mechanic's lien.

Mature claim.   *See* Unmatured claim.

Means test.   A nonstatutory term describing the standard for dismissing a Ch. 7 consumer case on the grounds of abuse where the debtor's disposable income, calculated under the formula set out in §707(b), is deemed sufficient to support payments under a plan of rehabilitation. A version of the means test is also used to measure the debtor's disposable income in a Ch. 13 case.

Mechanic's lien.   A statutory lien on real property available to a person who, at the request of the owner or the owner's agent, has furnished services or labor on credit in connection with the improvement of the property. The supplier of materials used in the construction may assert a similar statutory lien called a "materialman's lien." These traditional names for the liens have been abandoned in some states in favor of the more modern "construction lien."

Meeting of creditors.   *See* Creditors' meeting.

Net result rule.   A traditional but inaccurate name for the exception to the avoidance of transfers under §547(c)(4), which validates an otherwise avoidable transfer to the extent that the creditor-transferee gave new unsecured value to the debtor after receiving the transfer.

New value exception. An exception (or corollary) to the absolute priority rule that enables equity holders to retain their interests in the debtor, even though a senior nonaccepting class has not been paid in full, if the equity holders contribute new capital to the debtor equal to or greater than the value of their interests.

No-asset case. A liquidation case in which there are insufficient assets to allow for a distribution.

Nonbankruptcy law. The term used in the Code to describe the entire body of law prevailing in the jurisdiction, both state and federal, apart from bankruptcy law.

"Noncore proceedings." *See* Related proceedings.

Nondischargeable debt. A debt that is excluded from the discharge under §523 or §1328.

Nonrecourse secured debt. A secured debt for which the debtor has no liability beyond the value of the collateral, so that the debtor cannot be held responsible for any deficiency following foreclosure or surrender of the collateral.

Notice. Information concerning a fact, whether deriving from actual knowledge or imputed as a legal consequence of proper recording or other publicity. Imputed knowledge is called "constructive notice."

Notice and a hearing. When a Code provision states that particular action can only be taken after notice and a hearing, this means that appropriate notice must be given, but a hearing is only required if a party in interest requests it. (§102(2))

Nulla bona return. (Latin: "No goods.") The report returned by the sheriff following an attempt at levy in which no executable property could be found.

Objection. A written response required by the Bankruptcy Rules to challenge certain actions or assertions by another party, such as a claim, a claim of exemption, a proposed plan, or the discharge of a debt.

Order for relief. In an involuntary case, the court's grant of the petition for bankruptcy relief. In a voluntary case, no actual adjudication of bankruptcy is required. The filing of the petition itself constitutes the order for relief.

Party in interest.   Although used frequently in the Code, this term has no general statutory definition. It is described in §1109(b) for Ch. 11 purposes to include the debtor, trustee, creditors, equity security holders, and their committees. Courts usually treat the term as having the same meaning elsewhere in the Code. It is usually mentioned in the context of standing to initiate motions or other proceedings.

Perfection.   The process of making a lien effective against persons other than the debtor, who may subsequently acquire rights in the collateral. Perfection is normally accomplished by an act of publicity such as recording the lien or taking possession of the collateral.

Petition.   The pleading filed to initiate a bankruptcy case.

Plenary jurisdiction.   Full jurisdiction over the subject matter of the case and the parties, as distinguished from the more limited "summary" jurisdiction of the bankruptcy court. These terms were used in connection with bankruptcy jurisdiction prior to 1978, but have become outmoded under the Code and the current jurisdictional provisions of Title 28.

Pluries writ.   A writ of execution issued after the second ("alias") writ. *See* Alias writ.

Preference.   An advantage given by the debtor to a creditor through payment or some other transfer that results in the creditor receiving preferential treatment over other similarly situated creditors. Although such preferential treatment is not normally avoidable outside of bankruptcy, the trustee has the power under §547 to avoid a preferential transfer in the prepetition period if the requirements of §547 are satisfied.

Prejudgment remedy or process.   Provisional and ancillary relief available to the plaintiff during the pendency of a civil case to prevent loss or harm before the case is finally resolved. Most prejudgment remedies aim at the preservation of property that is claimed in the suit or may ultimately be sold in execution to satisfy the judgment.

Prepackaged plan.   A Ch. 11 plan that is wholly or substantially settled by the debtor and creditors before the Ch. 11 petition is filed.

Prepetition planning.   The debtor's reordering of his or her affairs prior to filing a bankruptcy petition to maximize the benefits of bankruptcy. A common form of prepetition planning is the realization of nonexempt property and the use of proceeds to acquire exempt property. *See also* Conversion of exempt property.

Present value.   *See* Best interests test.

Priming lien.   A lien granted to secure postpetition credit under §364(d) with priority over an existing lien in the property.

Priority.   The ranking of liens and other interests in the same property.

Priority claim.   An unsecured claim (or that portion of it) that qualifies for inclusion in one of the categories entitled to precedence in payment under §507.

Proceedings in aid of execution.   *See* Supplementary proceedings.

Proceeds.   Any property or money received in exchange for an asset.

Proof of claim.   A creditor's formal submission of a claim against the estate under §501.

Provisional remedy or process.   *See* Prejudgment remedy or process.

Purchase.   The acquisition of rights in property by voluntary act. "Purchase" is not simply a synonym for "buy," but includes also the consensual acquisition of other rights, such as a security interest. (§§101(43) and 101(54))

Purchase-money security interest (PMSI).   A security interest in property, to the extent that it secures a loan or credit given to the debtor for the express purpose of acquiring the property and actually used by the debtor for that purpose.

Reach-back period.   The period immediately before the filing of a bankruptcy petition within which transfers are vulnerable to avoidance.

Reaffirmation.   The debtor's contractual undertaking, executed in compliance with §524 during the period between the petition and the discharge, to pay an otherwise dischargeable debt.

Receivable.   *See* Account.

Receivership.   A proceeding, originating in equity, under which a person (receiver) is appointed to take control of property and to preserve and administer it as the court directs.

Reclamation.   A seller's limited right to reclaim goods when the buyer was insolvent upon receipt of the goods and the seller was unaware of the insolvency. Reclamation is governed by UCC §2.702 and is given qualified recognition in bankruptcy by §546(c).

Redelivery bond.   A bond posted by the debtor for the purpose of regaining possession of attached property pending final determination of the suit. In the bond, the debtor undertakes to redeliver the property or its value if the creditor ultimately obtains judgment. *Compare* Discharging/dissolution bond. Unlike a discharging bond, a redelivery bond does not release the attachment lien.

Redemption.　The debtor's right to buy back property that has been foreclosed upon or otherwise subjected to realization for the satisfaction of debt. Redemption is available only where recognized by principles of equity or by statute (*e.g.*, execution statutes or §722). In some cases creditors junior to the foreclosing party are also given redemption rights. *See also* Equity of redemption.

Referee.　The original name for a bankruptcy judge under the Bankruptcy Act of 1898.

Rehabilitation.　In a general sense, resolution of the debtor's financial difficulties through bankruptcy, so that the debtor's fiscal viability is restored. More specifically, bankruptcy relief by means of a plan under Ch. 11, 12, or 13 as distinct from liquidation.

Rejection of a contract.　The estate's repudiation of a prepetition executory contract of the debtor, so that the estate acquires no performance rights and obligations under the contract and the other party has a general unsecured claim for damages. *Compare* Assumption.

Related proceedings.　Litigation concerning a matter of nonbankruptcy law, the outcome of which affects the rights, liabilities, or administration of the estate. Because the controversy has an impact on the estate, it falls within the nonexclusive jurisdiction of the district court. In the absence of consent by the parties, related proceedings cannot be finally determined by the bankruptcy court, but must be returned to the district court for final judgment. *Contrast* Core proceeding.

Relation-back.　*See* Backdating.

Remand.　The bankruptcy court's return of a matter to the court from which it was removed.

Removal.　The transfer of related proceedings from another court to the bankruptcy court.

Reorganization.　The rehabilitation of a debtor under Ch. 11. Sometimes this word is used in a more general sense to mean rehabilitation under Ch. 11, 12, or 13.

Replevin.　A possessory action for the recovery of specific tangible personal property that has been wrongfully taken or retained. As a prejudgment remedy, replevin enables a plaintiff to obtain provisional seizure and possession of property which is the subject matter of the underlying suit. (Replevin is called "claim and delivery" in some states.)

Return.   The report submitted by the sheriff that states the action taken on a writ or other process.

Revival of judgment.   The renewal of a judgment that has become dormant because it has not been executed upon during its period of enforceability.

"Ride-through."   An arrangement between the debtor and a secured claimant under which the debtor is permitted to retain the collateral in return for a commitment to maintain payments on the debt as originally contracted. The "ride-through" is an alternative in Ch. 7 cases to the more formal reaffirmation. However, some courts have held that it is no longer available to a debtor because of amendments to various Code provisions by BAPCPA.

Safe harbor.   A provision in a statute that shields a person from liability for breach of a statutory duty, on condition that the person meets minimum standards of good faith compliance. (E.g., under §1125, a person who solicits acceptance or rejection of a plan in compliance with the Code is protected from liability for any violation of securities laws.)

Secured debt/claim.   A debt is secured to the extent that the debtor's personal obligation to pay is reinforced by a lien on property of the debtor, so that if the debtor defaults, the secured creditor may have recourse to the property to satisfy the debt. In bankruptcy, provided that the secured debt is allowed as a claim, it is treated as secured to the extent of the value of the collateral. (§506)

Security agreement.   A contract under which a security interest is created. (§101(50) and (51))

Security interest.   Although this term is sometimes used to denote a lien of any kind, it is usually confined to mean a consensual lien. (§101(51))

Self-help.   The pursuit of a remedy without court proceedings, such as a lienholder's seizure of collateral upon default without court authority. Self-help seizure and foreclosure are permitted only in connection with certain liens and are subject to restrictions even when allowed.

Sequestration.   An equitable remedy, similar to attachment, under which the plaintiff may remove property from the defendant's control pending the final resolution of a case. Sequestration is usually available only when the defendant's property interest is equitable in nature and cannot be reached by attachment.

Setoff.   When two persons are mutually indebted, the two debts may be treated as canceling each other out so that neither need be paid. If one of the debts is smaller than the other, setoff operates to the extent of the smaller debt.

Spendthrift trust.   A trust with restrictions on alienation designed to protect the fund from dissipation by the beneficiary or seizure by the beneficiary's creditors.

Standing trustee.   A person appointed by the U.S. Trustee to serve as trustee for all Ch. 12 and 13 cases filed in a region. (More than one standing trustee may be appointed if the volume of cases is large.)

Statutory lien.   A lien arising by virtue of a statutory provision that confers lien rights on otherwise unsecured creditors in particular types of transactions, under specified circumstances. Statutory liens owe their existence to the rights conferred by statute and are not created by contract or judicial process. (§101(53))

Stay.   *See* Automatic stay.

Straight bankruptcy.   Liquidation under Ch. 7.

Strict foreclosure.   A method of foreclosure under which the lienholder acquires ownership of the collateral in full satisfaction of the debt and is not required to conduct a foreclosure sale. The lienholder is therefore not accountable to the debtor for any value in the collateral in excess of the debt and may not claim any deficiency from the debtor if the collateral is worth less than the debt. Strict foreclosure is available only in connection with some liens, and is subject to restrictions, even where permitted.

Strip down and strip off.   *See* Lien stripping.

Strong-arm clause.   The traditional name given to the trustee's avoidance powers under §544(a) and its predecessor in the Bankruptcy Act.

Subordination.   The demotion of a claim, either by consent of the claimant (consensual subordination) or under principles of equity (equitable subordination). Equitable subordination is appropriate where fairness so requires, typically when the claimant has behaved in a dishonest or inequitable manner to the prejudice of a more junior party or of creditors in general. (§510)

Substantial abuse.   The term used in §707(b) prior to its amendment by BAPCPA as a ground for dismissal. Section 707(b) no longer requires a showing of "substantial" abuse, but provides for dismissal of "abuse."

Summary jurisdiction.   *See* Plenary jurisdiction.

Superpriority.   Special priority classifications given to two types of claim: (1) Priority at the top of the administrative expense category, granted by §507(b) to a claimant where adequate protection was attempted but proved to be insufficient to fully protect its interest; (2) An even more elevated priority position, senior to all administrative expenses (including superpriority claims under §507(b)), granted to a post-petition financer under §364(c) as consideration for the extension of credit to the estate.

Supplementary proceedings.   Statutory proceedings in aid of execution, under which a judgment creditor may seek discovery of executable assets or take other steps to subject the debtor's executable property to the satisfaction of the judgment.

Surplus.   The amount in excess of the debt after collateral or property seized in execution has been realized. *See also* Deficiency; Equity cushion.

Title 11.   The Bankruptcy Code. (11 U.S.C. §§101-1523)

Transfer.   Any disposition of property or an interest in property. In the Code, "transfer" is usually used to describe the debtor's transmission of property rights to some other person, resulting in impoverishment of the estate. (§101(54))

Trustee.   A private person appointed by the U.S. Trustee (or elected in some Ch. 7 cases) who represents, administers, and distributes the bankruptcy estate. (§§321, 322, and 323)

Turnover.   The surrender of estate property to the trustee by any person in possession of it. (§§542 and 543)

UCC.   The Uniform Commercial Code. A uniform code, adopted in all states except Louisiana, covering sales, negotiable instruments, security interests in personal property, and other commercial transactions.

UFCA/UFTA.   The Uniform Fraudulent Conveyance Act of 1918 and its successor, the Uniform Fraudulent Transfer Act of 1984. Uniform Acts, adopted in one version or the other in most states, providing for the avoidance of fraudulent dispositions by a debtor.

Undersecured debt. *See* Deficiency.

Unfair discrimination. Unjustified differentiation in a plan between claims of comparable rank that should be treated equally.

Unimpaired (class of claims or interests). *See* Impaired (class of claims or interests).

Unliquidated claim. A claim on which the debtor's liability has arisen, but the amount of which is uncertain and cannot be calculated arithmetically from known data.

Unmatured claim. A claim for a debt that has come into existence but whose date of payment has not yet fallen due.

U.S. Trustee. A federal official, appointed under 28 U.S.C. §581, who is responsible for the appointment and supervision of bankruptcy trustees and for the general oversight of bankruptcy cases.

Venue. The appropriate federal district for the conduct of the bankruptcy case or related proceedings.

Voluntary case. A bankruptcy case initiated by the debtor.

Wage earner plan. The name for the plan under the predecessor of Ch. 13 in the Bankruptcy Act. The term is obsolete but is still sometimes used to describe a Ch. 13 plan.

Warrant of attorney. A provision in a contract or instrument of debt, appointing the creditor to act as the debtor's agent in confessing to judgment if the debtor should default. *See also* Confession to judgment.

Wildcard provision. A nickname for §522(d)(5) (or an equivalent provision in a state statute) under which the debtor may apply a general exemption to any property selected, up to a prescribed value.

Workout. A negotiated settlement under which the debtor and creditors resolve the debtor's financial difficulties by agreeing to terms of payment. A workout may occur outside of bankruptcy, resulting in a composition and extension, or it may take place in the process of formulating a plan in a bankruptcy case.

Writ. A written order issued pursuant to court authority, requiring the sheriff or some other official to perform an act, such as the levy of execution.

Table of Cases

References are to book sections (denoted by the symbol, §) and to Examples and Explanations, denoted by the letter "E" followed by the chapter number and Example number.

203 La Salle Street Partnership, In re 526 U.S. 434 (1999), §21.7.3(3)(ii)(2)(cc)

A.H. Robbins Co., In re 86 F.3d 364 (4th Cir. 1996), cert. denied, 519 U.S. 993 (1996), §7.2.2(b)(2)

ABC-Nabco, Inc., In re 483 F.3d 470 (7th Cir. 2007), §16.1.4(4)

Adbox, Inc., In re 488 F.3d 836 (9th Cir. 2007), §16.1.2(1)

Adkins, In re 425 F.3d 296 (6th Cir. 2005), §20.10

Adolph, In re 441 B.R. 909 (Bankr. N.D. Ill. 2011), §9.7(3)

Aerobox Composite Structures, In re LLC 373 B.R. 135 (Bankr. D.N.M. 2007), §18.2

AFI Holdings, Inc., In re 530 F.3d 832 (9th Cir. 2008), E-6-5

Ahaza Systems, Inc., In re 482 F.3d 1118 (9th Cir. 2007), §16.1.4(2)

Aiello v. Providian Financial Corp., 239 F.3d 876 (7th Cir. 2001), §10.7.3

Airadigm Communications, Inc., In re 616 F.3d 642 (7th Cir. 2010), §19.7.3

All Blacks B.V. v. Gruntruck, 199 B.R. 970 (W.D. Wash. 1996), E-18-3

Alyucan Interstate Corp., In re 12 B.R. 803 (Bankr. D. Vt. 1981), §11.5.3

Amco Insurance, In re 444 F.3d 690 (5th Cir. 2006), §9.5.3(b)

American Energy Trading, Inc., In re 291 B.R. 159 (Bankr. W.D. Mo. 2003), §15.1.3

Anderson, In re 386 B.R. 315 (Bankr. D. Kan. 2008), §13.2.3

Anderson, In re 397 B.R. 363 (B.A.P. 6th Cir 2008), §8.4.1(c)(3)

Andrews, In re 80 F.3d 906 (4th Cir. 1996), E-12-2(b)

APF Co., In re 264 B.R. 344 (Bankr. D. Del. 2001), §10.7.2

Arbaugh v. Y&H Corp., 546 U.S. 500 (2006), §9.6.2(b)(5)

Archer v. Warner, 538 U.S. 314 (2003), §22.5.4

Arecibo Community Health Care v. Commonwealth of Puerto Rico, 270 F.3d 17 (1st Cir. 2001), §7.9.3

Armstrong, In re 291 F.3d 517 (8th Cir. 2002), §16.1.4(4)

Armstrong, In re 931 F.2d 1233 (8th Cir. 1991), E-22-1

Arnold, In re 869 F.2d 240 (4th Cir. 1989), E-20-3

Associates Commercial Corp. v. Rash, 520 U.S. 953 (1997), §19.6.3(e), §20.7.1(a)(ii)

Atlanticrancher, Inc., In re 279 B.R. 411 (Bankr. D. Mass. 2002), §19.7.3

Atlas Machine and Iron Works v. Bethlehem Steel Corp., 986 F.2d 709 (4th Cir. 1993) §9.6.2(b)(3)(ii)

Augie/Restivo Baking Co., Ltd., In re 860 F.2d 515 (2d Cir. 1988), §9.5.2(b)

Baird, In re 228 B.R. 324 (Bankr. M.D. Fla. 1999), §8.4.2(5)

Baker v. Simpson, 613 F.3d 346 (2d Cir. 2010), §7.2.2(b)(2)

Baker, In re 400 B.R. 136 (D. Del. 2009), §13.8

Baldesssaro, in re 338 B.R. 178 (Bankr. D.N.H. 2006), §10.5.3

Ball v. A.O. Smith Corp., 451 F.3d 66 (2d Cir. 2006), §22.5.4(3)(C)(6)

Bandi, In re 683 F.3d 671 (5th Cir. 2012), §22.5.4(2)

Barbosa v. Soloman, 235 F.3d 31 (1st Cir. 2000), §20.10

Barnhill v. Johnson, 503 U.S. 393 (1992) E-16-1

Bartel, In re 404 B.R. 584 (B.A.P. 1st Cir. 2009), §10.4.3(1)

Beal, In re 347 B.R. 87 (E.D. Wis. 2006), §8.4.1(b)

Bellingham Insurance Agency, Inc., In re 702 F.3d 553 (9th Cir. 2012), §7.3.5(4)

Ben Cooper, Inc., In re 896 F.2d 1394 (2d Cir. 1990), §7.3.5

BFP v. Resolution Trust Corp., 511 U.S. 531 (1994), E-16-7

Blausey v. U.S. Trustee, 552 F.3d 1124 (9th Cir. 2009), §9.8.4(b)

Blehm Land & Cattle Co., In re 859 F.2d 137 (10th Cir. 1988), §11.5.4

Blinder, Robinson & Co., Inc., In re 123 B.R. 900 (Bankr. D. Colo. 1991), §6.8(3)(b)

BNY Capital Funding, LLC, 345 B.R. 549 (E.D. Va. 2006), §18.2

Bock Transportation, Inc., In re 327 B.R. 378 (B.A.P. 8th Cir. 2005), §9.6.2(b)(5)(c)

Booth, In re 858 F.2d 1051 (5th Cir. 1988), §9.8.1

Bowman, In re 253 B.R. 233 (9th Cir. B.A.P. 2000), §11.4.2(b)

Braen, In re 900 F.2d 621 (3d Cir. 1990), §22.5.4(2)(c)(6)

Brashers, In re 216 B.R. 59 (Bankr. N.D. Okla. 1998), §9.8.1

Brentano's, In re 27 B.R. 90 (Bankr. S.D.N.Y. 1983), E-7-1(e)

Brinley, In re 403 F.3d 415 (6th Cir. 2005) cert. denied, 126 S. Ct. 1164 (2006), §13.5.6

Brown, In re 219 B.R. 191 (B.A.P. 6th Cir. 1998), §20.10

Brown, In re 342 B.R. 248 (Bankr. D. Md. 2006), §10.3(3)

Brown, In re 375 B.R. 362 (Bankr. W.D. Mich. 2007), §13.4

Brown, In re 95 B.R. 35 (Bankr. E.D. Va. 1989), §13.7.1(5)

Brunner v. New York State Higher Educ. Services Corp., 831 F.2d 395 (2d Cir. 1987), §22.5.4(2)(c)(8)

Bullock v. BankChampaign, N.A., 133 S.Ct. 1754 (2013), §22.5.4(2)(c)(4)

Burdge, In re 198 B.R. 773 (B.A.P. 9th Cir. 1996), §22.5.4(2)(a)

Burgess, In re 438 F.3d 493 (5th Cir. 2006), §12.2.3

Burnett, In re 635 F.3d 169 (5th Cir. 2011), §22.2

Burress, In re 245 B.R. 871 (Bankr. D. Colo. 2000), §22.5.4(2)(c)(4)

Byrd, In re 357 F.3d 433 (4th Cir. 2004), §9.6.2(b)(3)

Caldwell, In re 895 F.2d 1123 (6th Cir. 1990,) E-20-2(c)

California ex rel Brown v. Villalobos, 453 B.R. 404 (D. Nev. 2011), §10.4.3(2)

Caneva, In re 550 F.2d 755 (9th Cir 2008), E-22-3

Capital One Auto Finance v. Osborne, 515 F.3d 817 (8th Cir. 2008), §20.7.1(b)

Carrere, In re 64 B.R. 156 (Bankr. C.D. Cal. 1986), E-18-3

Carrol, In re 903 F.2d 1266 (9th Cir. 1990), §18.10

Castle Ranch of Ramona, In re 3 B.R. 45 (Bankr. S.D. Cal. 1980), §11.4.2

Catapult Entertainment, Inc., In re 165 F.3d 747 (9th Cir. 1999), §18.8.1

Cavanagh, In re 250 B.R. 107 (B.A.P. 9th Cir. 2000), §20.7.3(b)(4)

Celotex Corp. v. Edwards, 514 U.S. 300 (1995), §7.2.2(b)(2), §7.5.1, E-7-1(e)

Central Virginia Community College v. Katz, 126 S. Ct. 990 (2006), §7.2.2(a), §7.9.4, E-7-3(b)

CFLC, Inc., In re 89 F.3d 673 (9th Cir. 1996), §18.12

Charles, In re 332 B.R. 538 (Bankr. S.D. Tex. 2005), §10.5.3

Charter Oaks Associates, In re 361 F.3d 760 (2d Cir. 2004), §7.9.4

Chateaugay Corp., In re 944 F.2d 997 (2d Cir. 1991), §19.2.5

Citizens Bank of Maryland v. Strumpf, 516 U.S. 16 (1995), §10.4.2

Claremont Acquisition Corp., In re 186 B.R. 977 (C.D. Cal. 1995), §18.12

Cleaver, In re 333 B.R. 430 (Bankr. S.D. Ohio 2005), §8.4.1(c)(iii)

Cleaver, In re 407 B.R. 354 (B.A.P. 8th Cir. 2009), §13.5.5

Cobb, In re 343 B.R. 204 (Bankr. C.D. Ark. 2006), §8.4.1(c)(iii)

Cohen v. De La Cruz, 523 U.S. 213 (1998) §22.5.4(2), §22.5.4(6), E-22-4

Commonwealth Companies, Inc., In re 913 F.2d 518 (8th Cir. 1990), §10.4.3(2)

Concannon, In re 338 B.R. 90 (B.A.P. 9th Cir 2006), §19.6.3(b)

Concrete Pumping Service, Inc., In re 943 F.2d 627 (6th Cir. 1991), §9.6.4(a)

Connolly North America LLC, In re 398 B.R. 564 (Bankr. E.D. Mich. 2008), §16.1.2(5)

Consolidated Freightways Corp. of Delaware, In re 564 F.3d 1161 (9th Cir. 2009), §19.6.4

Corporation de Servicios Medicos Hospitalarios de Fajardo, In re 805 F.2d 440 (1st Cir. 1986), §10.4.3(2)

Crawford, In re 324 F.3d 539 (7th Cir. 2003), §20.7.3(b)(4)(c)

Cullen, In re 329 B.R. 52 (Bankr. N.D. Iowa 2005), §10.7.4

Cushman, In re 217 B.R. 470 (Bankr. E.D. Va. 1998), §20.11

Dant & Russel, Inc., In re 853 F.2d 700 (9th Cir. 1988), §17.2.1

Davenport Communications Ltd., In re 19 Bankr. Ct. Dec. (CCR) 1980 (Bankr. S.D. Iowa 1990), E-6-2

Davis, In re 348 B.R. 449 (Bankr. E.D. Mich. 2006), §20.7.3(b)(1)

Davis, In re 716 F.3d 331 (4th Cir. 2013), §20.8.3, §20.11

Davis, In re 889 F.2d 658 (5th Cir. 1989), §14.5

Dawson, In re 390 F.3d 1139 (9th Cir. 2004), §10.7.3

Dean, In re 537 F.3d 1315 (11th Cir. 2008), §20.7.1

DeFrantz, In re 454 B.R. 108 (B.A.P. 9th Cir. 2011), §8.5

Delta Towers, Ltd., In re 924 F.2d 74 (5th Cir. 1991), E-19-4

Deuel, In re 594 F.3d 1073 (9th Cir. 2010), §15.1.2

Dewsnup v. Timm, 502 U.S. 410 (1992), §19.6.3(b), E-19-1(b), §20.8.3, §20.11

Dilley, In re 339 B.R. 1 (B.A.P. 1st Cir. 2006), §9.6.2(b)(3)

Disney, In re 386 B.R. 292 (Bankr. D. Colo. 2008), §20.10

Dixon, In re 338 B.R. 383 (B.A.P. 8th Cir. 2006), §8.4.1(c)(iii)

DLC, Ltd., In re 295 B.R. 593 (8th Cir. B.A.P. 2003), §15.1.3

Dominic's Restaurant of Dayton, Inc. v. Mantia, 683 F.3d 757 (6th Cir. 2012), §10.4.1(1)

Dorsey, In re 373 B.R. 528 (Bankr. N.D. Ohio 2007), §10.4.3(1)

DSC, Ltd., In re 486 F.3d 940 (6th Cir. 2007), §9.6.2(5)(c)

Dufresne, In re 341 B.R. 391 (Bankr. D. Mass. 2006), §22.5.4(8)

Dufva, In re 388 B.R. 911 (Bankr. W.D. Mo. 2008), §13.2.2

Duke, In re 79 F.3d 43 (7th Cir. 1996), §13.7.1

Dumont, In re 581 F.3d 1104 (9th Cir. 2009), §13.8

Dyer, In re 322 F.3d 1178 (9th Cir. 2003), §7.5.2, §10.7.5

Eads, In re 69 B.R. 730 (Bank. 9th Cir. 1986), E-15-3(b)

Educational Credit Management Corp. v. Polleys, 356 F.3d 1302 (10th Cir. 2004) §22.5.4(b)(8)

Electric Machinery Enterprises, Inc., In re 479 F.3d 791 (11th Cir. 2007) §7.3.5(1)

Ellis v. Consolidated Diesel Electric Corp., 894 F.2d 371 (10th Cir. 1990), §10.7.1

Elmendorf, In re 345 B.R. 486 (Bankr. S.D.N.Y. 2006), §8.4.1(c)(i)

Energy Co-Op, Inc., In re 832 F.2d 997 (7th Cir. 1987), E-16-1

Enloe, In re 373 B.R. 123 (Bankr. D. Colo. 2007), §8.4.1, E-8-4

Entringer Bakeries, Inc., In re 548 F.3d 344 (5th Cir. 2008), §16.1.2(1)

Escobedo, In re 28 F.3d 34 (7th Cir. 1994), §20.3(3)

Estrada, In re 439 B.R. 227 (Bankr. S.D. Fla. 2010), §13.7.1

Euro-American Lodging, In re 365 B.R. 421 (Bankr. S.D. N.Y. 2007), §8.5

Exaeris, Inc., In re 380 B.R. 741 (Bankr. D. Del. 2008), §17.2.2

Exide Technologies, In re 544 F.3d 196 (3d Cir. 2008), §7.3.5

Faberge Restaurant of Florida, In re 222 B.R. 385 (Bankr. E.D. Fla. 1997), §9.6.2(b)(3)

Fabricators, Inc., In re 926 F.2d 1458 (5th Cir. 1991), §19.7.2

Falcon Products, In re 381 B.R. 543 (B.A.P. 8th Cir. 2008), §16.1.2

Farmland Industries, Inc., In re 567 F.3d 1010 (8th Cir. 2009), §7.2.2(b)(2)

Fed-pak Systems, In re 80 F.3d 207 (7th Cir. 1995), §7.2.2(b)(2)

Ferandos, In re 402 F.3d 147 (3d Cir. 2005), §20.8.3

Fidelity Financial Services v. Fink, 522 U.S. 211 (1998), §16.1.3(3), §16.1.4(3), E-16-4

Field v. Mans, 516 U.S. 59 (1995), §22.5.4(2)(a), §22.5.4(2)(c)

Findley, In re 593 F.3d 1048 (9th Cir. 2010), §22.5.4(c)(7)

Fleming Companies, Inc., In re 499 F.3d 300 (3d Cir. 2007), §18.12

Flores, In re 692 F.3d 1021 (9th Cir. 2012), §20.7.3(1)

Foreside Management Co., LLC, In re 402 B.R. 446 (B.A.P. 1st Cir. 2009), §17.3.4

Fox, In re 370 B.R. 639 (Bankr. N.J. 2007), §8.5

Francis, In re 273 B.R. 87 (B.A.P. 6th Cir. 2002), E-20-2(c)

Francisco, In re 390 B.R. 700 (B.A.P. 10th Cir. 2008), §8.4.1(c)(ii)

Frankel, In re 391 B.R. 266 (Bankr. M.D. Pa. 2008), §10.7.2

Frey Mechanical Group, Inc., In re 446 B.R. 208 (Bankr. E.D. Pa. 2011), §16.1.4(2), §16.1.4(4)

Fuger, In re 347 B.R. 94 (Bankr. D. Utah 2006), §20.7.3(1)

FV Steel Wire Co., In re 324 B.R. 701 (Bankr. E.D. Wis. 2005), §10.4.3(2)

Gee, In re 332 B.R. 602 (Bankr. W.D. Mo. 2005), §8.4.1(c)(2)

Gerhardt, In re 348 F.3d 89 (5th Cir. 2003), §22.5.4(7)

Giles, In re 361 B.R. 212 (Bankr. D. Ut. 2007), §8.4.1

Giller, In re 962 F.2d 796 (8th Cir. 1992), §9.5.3(b)

Giorgio, In re 862 F.2d 933 (1st Cir. 1988), §19.7.2

Global Video Communications Corp., In re 19 Bankr. Ct. Dec. (CCR) 1311 (Bankr. M.D. Fla. 1989), E-6-2

Goodman, In re 873 F.2d 598 (2d Cir. 1989), §22.1

G.P. Express Airlines, Inc., In re 200 B.R. 222 (Bankr. D. Neb. 1996), §18.8.1

Granfinanciera, S.A. v. Nordberg, 492 U.S. 33 (1989), §7.3.2, §7.3.5(2), E-7-2(c)

Greene, In re 583 F.3d 614 (9th Cir. 2009), §13.2.3

Gregory, In re 245 B.R. 171 (10th Cir. B.A.P. 2000), E-13-1

Griffin, In re 491 B.R. 602 (Bankr. S.D. Ga. 2013), §22.5.4(7)

Grogan v. Garner, 498 U.S. 279 (1991), §22.5.4(2)

Grossman's, Inc., In re 607 F.3d 114 (3d Cir. 2010), §19.2.5

Gruntz, In re 202 F.3d 1074 (9th Cir. 2000), §10.4.3(1)

Guterl Special Steel Corp., In re 316 B.R. 843 (Bankr. W.D. Pa. 2004), §12.4

HAL, Inc., In re 122 F.3d 851 (9th Cir. 1997), E-16-8

Hall, In re 228 B.R. 483 (Bankr. M.D. Ga. 1998), §22.5.4(2)(b)

Hamilton v. Lanning, 130 S. Ct. 2464 (2010), §20.7.3(b)(2), §20.7.3(b)(3), E-20-1

Hampton, In re 319 B.R. 163 (Bankr. E.D. Ark. 2005), §10.4.1(1)

Hanover National Bank v. Moyses, 186 U.S. 181 (1902), §5.3, §9.8.4(a), §13.2.1

Hart, In re 402 B.R. 78 (Bankr. D. Del. 2009), §13.8

Hartford Underwriters Ins. Co. v. Union Planters Bank, 530 U.S. 1 (2000), §19.6.3(d)

Hartley, In re 869 F.2d 394, E-22-4

Hashemi, In re 104 F.3d 1122 (9th Cir. 1996), §22.5.4(2)(a)

Hechinger Investment Co. of Delaware, Inc., In re 489 F.3d 568 (3d Cir. 2007), §16.1.4

Henderson, In re 235 B.R. 425 (Bankr. C.D. Ill. 1999), §19.6.3(e)

Henderson, In re 364 B.R. 906 (Bankr. N.D. Tex. 2007), §8.4.1(c)(iii), E-8-4

Henry, In re 457 B.R. 402 (Bankr. E.D. Pa. 2011), §19.6.3(e)

Hentges, In re 351 B.R. 758 (Bankr. N.D. Okla. 2006), §9.6.6

Heritage Highgate, Inc., In re 679 F.3d 132 (3d Cir. 2012), §19.6.3

Herrig, In re 217 B.R. 891 (Bankr. N.D. Okla. 1998), §22.5.4(2)(a)

Hess, In re 347 B.R. 489 (Bankr. D. Vt. 2006), §8.4.1(c)(ii)

Higgins v. Vortex Fishing Systems, Inc., 379 F.3d 701 (9th Cir. 2004), §9.6.6(1)

Hines, In re 147 F.3d 1185 (9th Cir. 1998), §6.6.2(d)

HovdeBray Enterprises, In re 483 B.R. 187 (B.A.P. 8th Cir. 2012), §16.1.4

Howard Delivery Service, Inc., In re 547 U.S. 651 (2006), §19.6.4

Hubbard, In re 332 B.R. 285 (Bankr. S.D. Tex. 2005), §8.4.1(c)(iii)

Hunter v. Philpott, 373 F.3d 873 (8th Cir. 2004), §22.5.4(2)(b)(4)

Indian Palms Associates, Ltd., In re 61 F.3d 197 (3d Cir. 1995), E-11-5

Industrial Salvage, Inc., In re 196 B.R. 784 (Bankr. S.D. Ill. 1996), §19.2.1

Institute Pasteur v. Cambridge Biotech Corp., 104 F.3d 489 (1st Cir. 1997), §18.8.1

Table of Cases

Jackson, In re 184 F.3d. 1046 (9th Cir. 1999), §7.9.3

James A. Phillips, Inc., In re 29 B.R. 391 (S.D.N.Y. 1983), E-17-1(c)

James, In re 358 B.R. 816 (Bankr. S.D. Ga. 2007), §10.5.3

Jamo, In re 283 F.3d 392 (1st Cir. 2002), §13.7.1

Jan Weilert RV, Inc., In re 315 F. 3d 1192, as amended, 326 F. 3d 1028 (9th Cir. 2003), §16.1.4(2)

Jendusa-Nicolai v. Larson, 677 F.3d 320 (7th Cir. 2012), §22.5.4

Jercich, In re 238 F.3d 1202 (9th Cir. 2001), §22.5.4(6)

Joelson, In re 427 F.3d 700 (10th Cir. 2005), §22.5.4(2)(a)

John Richards Home Building Co., In re LLC, 312 B.R. 849 (E.D. Mich. 2004), §9.6.6

John Richards Homes Building Co., In re LLC, 475 B.R. 585 (E.D. Mich. 2012), §10.7.5

Johnson v. Home State Bank, 501 U.S. 78 (1991), §20.11

Johnson, In re 386 B.R. 171 (Bankr. W.D. Pa. 2008), §19.6.3(b)

Johnson, In re 397 B.R. 289 (Bankr. M.D.N.C. 2008), §22.5.4

Johnson, In re 501 F.3d 1163 (10th Cir. 2007), §10.7.2

Johnson, In re 611 F.3d 313 (6th Cir. 2010), §16.1.3

Jones, In re 530 F.3d 1284 (10th Cir. 2008), §20.7.1(b)

Jones v. Cain, 804 A.2d 322 (D.C. Cir. 2002), §10.7.1

JTS Corp., In re 617 F.3d 1102 (9th Cir. 2010), §15.1.3

Jump, In re 356 B.R. 789 (B.A.P. 1st Cir. 2006), §10.5.3

Just Brakes Corporate Systems, Inc., In re 108 F.3d 881 (8th Cir. 1997), §10.7.2

Kalter, In re 292 F.3d 1350 (11th Cir. 2002), E-12-1(b)

Kaneb, In re 196 F.3d 265 (1st Cir. 1999), §10.7.2, §10.7.3

Kaplan, In re 331 B.R. 483 (Bankr. S.D. Fla. 2005), §13.2.3

Kawaauhau v. Geiger, 523 U.S. 57 (1998), §22.5.4(6), E-22-4

Keach, In re 243 B.R. 851 (B.A.P. 1st Cir. 2000), §20.6

Kellett, In re 379 B.R. 332 (Bankr. D. Or. 2007), §8.5

Kelley v. Robinson, 479 U.S. 36 (1986), §22.5.4(7), §22.5.4(11), E-22-2

Kelley, In re 841 F.2d 908 (9th Cir. 1988), §9.8.1

Kennedy v. Medicap Pharmacies, Inc., 267 F.3d 493 (6th Cir. 2001), §22.2

Kestell, In re 99 F.3d 146 (4th Cir. 1996), §9.7

Kline, In re 472 B.R. 98 (B.A.P. 10th Cir. 2012), §10.7.1

Kolich, In re 328 F.3d 406 (8th Cir. 2003), §13.5.6

Kosinski, In re 424 B.R. 599 (B.A.P. 1st Cir. 2010), §22.5.4(2)(c)

Kountry Korner Store, In re 221 B.R. 265 (Bankr. N.D. Okla. 1998), §22.5.4(2)(a)

Krieger v. Educational Credit Management Corp., 713 F.3d 882 (7th th Cir. 2013), §22.5.4

Kuehn, In re 563 F.3d 289 (7th Cir. 2009), E-10-6

Kujawa, In re 112 B.R. 968 (Bankr. E.D. Mo. 1990), E-6-2

Kujawa, In re 270 F.3d 578 (8th Cir. 2001), E-6-2

Laher, In re 496 F.3d 279 (3d Cir. 2007), §12.2.2

Lamie v. U.S. Trustee, 540 U.S. 526 (2004), §6.6.1, §6.6

Lancaster, In re 280 B.R. 468 (Bankr. W.D. Mo. 2002), §20.6, E-20-2(c)

Langenkamp v. Culp, 498 U.S. 42 (1990), §7.3.5, §7.4(1), E-7-2(c)

Laracuente v. Chase Manhattan Bank, 891 F.2d 17 (1st Cir. 1989), §22.2

Larson, In re 513 F.3d 325 (1st Cir. 2008), §13.2.3

Layton, In re 480 B.R. 392 (Bankr. M.D. Fla. 2012), §8.5

Leasing Services Corp. v. First Tennessee Bank, 826 F.2d 434 (6th Cir. 1987), §18.11

Lee, In re 352 B.R. 91 (B.A.P. 8th Cir. 2006); Bene, 474 B.R. 56 (Bankr. W.D.N.Y. 2012), §22.5.4(8)

LeMaire, In re 898 F.2d 1346 (8th Cir. 1990), §20.6

Lemco Gypsum, Inc., In re 911 F.2d 1553 (11th Cir. 1990)

Lionel Corp., In re 722 F.2d 1063 (2d Cir. 1983), E-17-2

Littman, In re 370 B.R. 820 (Bankr. D. Idaho 2007)

Lively, In re 717 F.3d 406 (5th Cir. 2013), §21.7.3(b)(ii)(2)(b)(2)

LNC Investments v. First Fidelity Bank, 247 B.R. 38 (S.D.N.Y. 2000), §11.5.5

Lockerby v. Sierra, 535 F.3d 1038 (9th Cir. 2008), §22.5.4(6)

Lockyer v. Mirant Corp. 398 F.3d 1098 (9th Cir. 2005), §10.4.3

Lombardo, In re 370 B.R. 506 (Bankr. E.D.N.Y. 2007), §9.7(3)

Loretto Winery Ltd., In re 898 F.2d 715 (9th Cir. 1990), E-15-4

Lumbar, In re 457 B.R. 748 (B.A.P. 8th Cir. 2011), §16.3.5

Magness, In re 972 F.2d 689 (6th Cir. 1992), §18.12, E-18-4

Maharaj, In re 681 F.3d 558 (4th Cir. 2012), §21.7.3(b)(ii)(2)(bb)

Majewski, In re 310 F.3d 653 (9th Cir. 2002), §22.3

Mansfield, In re 394 B.R. 783 (Bankr. E.D. Pa. 2008), §6.6.2(d)

Maple-Whitworth, Inc., In re 556 F.3d 742 (9th Cir. 2009), §9.6.6(1)

Marchiando, In re 13 F.3d 1111 (7th Cir. 1994), §22.5.4

Mark IV Industries, Inc., In re 459 B.R. 173 (S.D.N.Y. 2011), §19.2.1

Maronde, In re 332 B.R. 593 (Bankr. D. Minn. 2005), §13.2.3

Marrama, In re 549 U.S. 365 (U.S. 2007), §8.5, §9.7(1)

Martin, In re 197 B.R. 120 (Bankr. D. Colo. 1996), §6.6.2

Marvel, In re 372 B.R. 425 (Bankr. N.D. Ind. 2007), §12.2.3

Mayco Plastics, Inc., In re 379 B.R. 691 (Bankr. E.D. Mich. 2008), §19.6.4

Mazzeo, In re 167 F.3d 139 (2d Cir. 1999), §11.4.1

McCabe, In re 280 B.R. 841 (Bankr. N.D. Iowa 2002), §13.2.3

McCannon v. Marston, 679 F.2d 13 (3d Cir. 1982), §15.1.2(3)

McDade, In re 282 B.R. 650 (Bankr. N.D. Ill. 2002), §22.5.4(4)

McGough, In re 467 B.R. 22 (B.A.P. 10th Cir. 2012), §16.3.3

McIver, In re 177 B.R. 366 (Bankr. N.D. Fla. 1995)

McLain, In re 516 F.3d 301 (5th Cir. 2008),

McNabb, In re 326 B.R. 785 (Bankr. D. Ariz. 2005), §13.2.3

McNutt, In re 87 B.R. 84 (9th Cir. B.A.P. 1988), E-13-1

MD Promenade, Inc., In re 51 BCD 22 (Bankr. N.D. Tex. 2009), §10.7.2

Mellors, In re 372 B.R. 763 (Bankr. W.D. Pa. 2007), §20.10

Mendez, In re 367 B.R. 109 (B.A.P. 9th Cir. 2007), §8.4.1(c)(2)

Mendoza, In re 111 F.3d 1264 (5th Cir. 1997), §20.8.1

Mercer, In re 246 F.3d 391 (5th Cir. 2001), E-22-5

Microage Corp., In re 288 B.R. 842 (Bankr. D. Ariz. 2003), §7.9.4

Midlantic National Bank v. New Jersey Department of Environmental Protection, 474 U.S. 494 (1986), §12.4

Milavetz, Gallop & Milavetz, P.A. v. U.S., 559 U.S. 229 (2010), §6.7.1, §6.7.3

Miles, In re 430 F.3d 1083 (9th Cir. 2005), §9.6.6(2)

Miller, In re 377 F.3d 616 (6th Cir. 2004), §22.5.4(8)

Mingueta, In re 338 B.R. 833 (Bankr. C.D. Cal. 2006), §8.4.1(c)(iii)

M.M. Winkler & Associates, In re 239 F.3d 746 (5th Cir. 2001), §22.5.4

Moffett, In re 356 F.3d 518 (4th Cir. 2004), E-12-1(b)

Moore v. Bay, 284 U.S. 4 (1931), §15.1.3, E-15-2

Moore, In re 357 F.3d 1125 (10th Cir. 2004), §22.5.4(6)

Moore, In re 365 B.R. 589 (Bankr. D. Md. 2007), E-22-5

Morehead, In re 249 F.3d 445 (6th Cir. 2001), §16.1.3(2)

Mort Ranta v. Gorman, 2013 WL 3286252 (4th Cir. 2013), §20.7.3(b)(2)

Morton, In re 410 B.R. 556 (B.A.P. 9th Cir. 2009, §13.7.1(6)

Mosier v. Callister, Nebeker, & McCullough, 546 F.3d 1271 (10th Cir. 2008), §12.2.1

Moustafi, In re 371 B.R. 434 (Bankr. D. Ariz. 2007), §13.8

Muhaimin, In re 343 B.R. 159 (Bankr. D. Md. 2006), §11.4.4

Mullarkey, In re 536 F.3d 215 (3d Cir. 2008), §7.2.2(b)(2)

Murrin, In re 477 B.R. 99 (D. Minn. 2012), §9.6.1, §9.6.4(a)

Musicland Holding Corp., In re 462 B.R. 66 (Bankr. S.D.N.Y. 2011), §16.1.4(4)

Mystic Tank Lines Corp., In re 544 F.3d 524 (3d Cir. 2008), §10.4.3(2)

N.L.R.B. v. P.I.E. Nationwide, Inc., 923 F.2d 506, 511-512 (7th Cir. 1991), §10.4.3(2)

Nam, In re 273 F.3d 281 (3d Cir. 2001), §22.5.4(7)

National Eastern Corp., In re 391 B.R. 663 (Bankr. D. Conn. 2008), §7.7.3(1)

New York City Shoes, Inc., In re 880 F.2d 679, 680 (3d Cir. 1989), §16.1.4(4)

Nobelman v. American Savings Bank, 508 U.S. 324 (1993), §20.8.3, E-20-7

Nolan, In re 232 F.3d 528 (6th Cir. 2000), §20.10

Nortel Networks, Inc., In re 669 F.3d 128 (3rd Cir. 2011), §10.4.3(2)

Northern Pipeline Constr. Co. v. Marathon Pipe Line Co., 458 U.S. 50 (1982), §7.3.2, §7.3.3, §7.3.5, §7.6.2, E-7-2

Norwest Bank Nebraska v. Tveten, 848 F.2d 871 (8th Cir. 1988), E-22-1

Norwood, In re 178 B.R. 683 (Bankr. E.D. Pa. 1995), E-20-2(c)

Oberle, In re 2006 WL 3949174 (Bankr. N.D. Cal. 2006), §8.4.1(c)(ii)

Official Committee of Unsecured Creditors for Dornier Aviation (North America) Inc., In re 453 F.3d 225 (4th Cir. 2006), §14.4

Official Committee of Unsecured Creditors of Cybergenics Corp. v. Chinery, 330 F.3d 548 (3d Cir. 2003), §14.4

Ohio v. Kovacs, 469 U.S. 274 (1985), §19.2.1, E-19-3, §22.2

Oldco M Corpn., In re 484 B.R. 598 (Bankr. S.D. N.Y. 2012), §7.3.5(1)

Otero, In re 2010 WL 580033 (2010), §8.4.1(c)(iii)

Owen v. Owen, 500 U.S. 305 (1991), §13.5.6

Owens Corning, In re 419 F.3d 195 (3d Cir. 2005), §9.5.3(b)

Oyler, In re 397 F.3d 282 (6th Cir. 2005), §22.5.4

Pacor, Inc. v. Higgins, 743 F.2d 984, 994 (3d Cir. 1984), §13.5.5, §7.2.2(b)(2)

Padilla, In re 222 F.3d 1184 (9th Cir. 2000), §9.7(3)

Paine, In re 283 B.R. 33 (B.A.P. 9th Cir. 2002), §22.5.5

Parker, In re 334 B.R. 529 (Bankr. D. Mass 2005), E-10-6

Paschal, In re 337 B.R. 274 (Bankr. E.D.N.C. 2006), §10.5.3

Patch, In re 526 F.3d 1176 (8th Cir. 2008), §22.5.4(6)

Patterson v. Shumate, 504 U.S. 753 (1992), §12.2.2

Payless Cashways, Inc., In re 287 B.R. 482 (Bankr. W.D. Mo. 2002), §19.6.3(c)

Payton, In re 481 B.R. 460 (Bankr. N.D. Ill. 2012), §8.4.1(b)

Pegasus Gold Corp., In re 394 F.3d 1189 (9th Cir. 2005), §7.9.3

Penn Terra Ltd. v. Department of Environmental Resources, 733 F.2d 267 (3d Cir. 1984), §10.4.3(2)

Pennsylvania Department of Public Welfare v. Davenport, 495 U.S. 552 (1990), §22.2

Pennsylvania Dept. of Environmental Resources v. Tri-State Clinical Laboratories, Inc., 178 F.3d 685 (3d Cir. 1999), §19.6.4

Perlin v. Hitachi Capital America Corp., 497 F.3d 364 (3d Cir. 2007), §9.7(3)

Pierotti, In re 645 F.3d 277 (5th Cir. 2011), §20.9

Pioneer Ford Sales, Inc., In re 729 F.2d 27 (1st Cir. 1984), §18.12

Piper Aircraft Corp., In re 58 F.3d 1573 (11th Cir. 1995), §19.2.5

Platt, In re 292 B.R. 12 (Bankr. D. Mass. 2003), E-12(1)(e)

Polo Builders, In re 433 B.R. 700 (Bankr. N.D. Ill. 2010), §15.1.2(3), §16.1.2(5)

Pomona Valley Medical Group, Inc., In re 476 F.3d 665 (9th Cir. 2007), §18.5

Pracht, In re 464 B.R. 486 (Bankr. M.D. Ga. 2012), §20.7.3(4)(c)

Price, In re 280 B.R. 499 (9th Cir. B.A.P. 2002), §9.8.1

Probasco, In re 839 F.2d 1352 (9th Cir. 1988), E-15-3(b)

Puetz, In re 370 B.R. 386 (Bankr. D. Kan. 2007), §20.7.3(3)

Quebecor World (USA), In re Inc, 491 B.R. 363 (Bankr. S.D.N.Y. 2013), §16.1.4(2)

Quinlivan, In re 434 F. 3d 314 (5th Cir. 2005),
§22.5.4(2)(a)
QuVis, In re 446 B.R. 490 (Bankr. D. Kan.
2011), §16.1.2(4)

RadLAX Gateway Hotel, LLC v. Amalgamated Bank.
132 S.Ct. 2065 (2012), §21.7.3(b)(i)(2)
Ragos, In re 700F.3d 220 (5th Cir. 2012),
§20.7.3(2)
Rainbow Magazine, In re 77 F.3d 278 (9th Cir.
1996), §7.5.3
Ransom v. F.I.A. Card Services, N.A., 131 S.Ct.
716 (2011), §20.7.3(b)(3)
Rashid, In re 210 F.3d 201 (3d Cir. 2000),
§22.5.4
Ravenswood Apartments, Ltd., In re 338 B.R. 307
(B.A.P. 6th Cir. 2006), E-18-1(a)
Ray, In re 624 F.3d 1124 (9th Cir. 2010),
§7.2.2(b)(2)
Reed, In re 700 F.2d 986 (5th Cir. 1983),
E-22-1
Regional Anesthesia Associates, In re 360 B.R.
466 (Bankr. W.D. Pa. 2007),
§9.6.2(b)(3)
Register, In re 95 B.R. 73 (Bankr. M.D. Tenn.
1989), §18.11
Reider, In re 31 F.3d 1102 (11th Cir. 1994),
§9.5.3(b)
Rembert, In re 141 F.3d 277 (6th Cir. 1998),
§22.5.4(2)(a)
Repine, In re 536 F.3d 512 (5th Cir. 2008),
§10.7.2
Resource Technology Corp., In re 624 F,3d 376
(7th Cir. 2010), §18.12
Reswick, In re 446 B.R. 362 (B.A.P. 9th Cir.
2011), §10.5.3
Reyes, In re 361 B.R. 276 (Bankr. D. Fla. 2007)
aff'd 2007 WL 6082567 (S.D. Fla 2007),
Reynolds, In re 425 F.3d 526 (8th Cir. 2005),
§22.5.4(8)
Richardson, In re 217 B.R. 479 (Bankr. M.D. La.
1998), §8.4.1(b)
Rimell, In re 946 F.2d 1363 (8th Cir. 1991),
§9.6.4(a)
Riodizio, Inc., In re 204 B.R. 417 (Bankr.
S.D.N.Y. 1997), §18.2
Robbins, In re 964 F.2d 342 (4th Cir. 1992),
§11.4.1
Rodriguez, In re 375 B.R. 535 (B.A.P. 9th Cir.
2007), §20.7.1(b)
Rodriguez, In re 629 F.3d 136 (3d Cir. 2010),
§19.2.2

Roedemeier, In re 374 B.R. 264 (Bankr. D. Kan.
2007), §21.7.1(8), §21.7.3(b)(ii)(2)(bb)
*Roman Catholic Archbishop of Portland in Oregon, In
re* 339 B.R. 215 (Bankr. D. Or. 2006),
§19.2.5
Rome v. Braunstein, 19 F.3d 54 (1st Cir. 1994),
E-6-3(a)
Romero, In re 349 B.R. 616 (Bankr. N.D. Cal.
2006), §8.4.1(c)(iii), E-8-4
Rose, In re not reported in B.R., 2008 WL
4205364 (Bankr. E.D. Tenn. 2008),
§19.6.4
Rosson, In re 545 F.3d 764 (9th Cir. 2008),
§9.7(1)
Rountree, In re 478 F.3d 215 (4th Cir. 2007),
§22.5.4(2)(a)
Rucker, In re 454 B.R. 554 (Bankr. M.D. Ga.
2011), §9.8.1
Ryan v. Homecomings Financial Network, 253 F.3d
778 (4th Cir. 2001), §19.6.3(b)

Sabban, In re 600 F.3d 1219 (9th Cir. 2010),
§22.5.4
Samala, In re 295 B.R. 380 (Bankr. D.N.M.
2003), §20.8.3
Sandburg Financial Corp., In re 446 B.R. 793 (S.D.
Tex. 2011),
Sandy Ridge Oil Co., In re 807 F.2d 1332 (7th Cir.
1986), E-15-3(b)
Saxman, In re 325 F.3d 1168 (9th Cir. 2003),
§22.5.4(8)
Saybrook Mfg. Co., Inc., In re 963 F.2d 1490
(11th Cir. 1992), §17.3.3
Scarborough, In re 461 F.3d 406 (3d Cir. 2006),
§20.8.3
Schafer, In re 315 B.R. 765 (Bankr. D. Colo.
2004), §10.4.2
Schaitz, In re 913 F.2d 452 (7th Cir. 1990),
E-20-2(c)
Schifano, In re 378 F.3d 60 (1st Cir. 2004),
§22.5.2(3)
Schulte v. United States, 529 F.3d 343 (6th Cir.
2008), §9.8.4(a)
Schultz, In re 463 B.R. 492 (Bankr. W.D. Mo.
2011), §20.7.3(3)
Schwab v. Reilly, 130 S.Ct. 2652 (2010), §13.4
Schwartz, In re 954 F.2d 569 (9th Cir. 1992),
§10.7.1
Scotia Pacific Co., LLC, In re 508 F.3d 214 (5th
Cir. 2007), §11.4.3
Scott, In re 457 B.R. 740 (Bankr. S.D. Ill. 2011),
§20.7.3

Seelye, In re 243 B.R. 701 (Bankr. N.D. Ill. 2000), §13.7.1

Seven Fields Development Corp., In re 505 F.3d 237 (3d Cir. 2007), §7.7.3(1)

Sharpe, In re 351 B.R. 409 (Bankr. N.D. Tex. 2006), §22.5.4(2)(a), §22.5.4(2)(c)

Shartz, In re 221 B.R. 397 (B.A.P. 6th Cir. 1998), §22.5.4(2)(a)

Shat, In re 424 B.R. 854 (Bankr. D. Nev. 2010), §21.7.3(b)(ii)(2)(bb)

Shaw v. Aurgroup Financial Credit Union, 552 F.3d 447 (6th Cir. 2009) §20.3(3)

Sheridan, In re 391 B.R. 287 (Bankr. E.D.N.C. 2008), §22.6

Sicroff, In re 401 F.3d 1101 (9th Cir. 2005), §22.5.4(6)

Sidebottom, In re 430 F.3d 893 (7th Cir. 2005), §20.11, E-20-2(c)

Sikes v. Global Marine, Inc., 881 F.2d 176 (5th Cir. 1989); In re Siciliano, 13 F.3d 748 (3d Cir. 1994), §10.7.1

Sims, In re 994 F.2d 210 (5th Cir. 1993), §9.6.2(b)(3)(i)

Skye Marketing Corp., In re 11 B.R. 891 (Bankr. E.D.N.Y. 1981), §9.6.2(b)(3)(i)

Smart, In re 214 B.R. 63 (Bankr. D. Conn. 1997), E-20-7(b)

Smiley, In re 864 F.2d 562 (7th Cir. 1989), E-22-1

Smith, In re 395 B.R. 711 (Bankr. D. Kan. 2008), §11.4.4

Smith's Home Furnishings, Inc., In re 265 F.3d 959 (9th Cir. 2001), §16.1.4(4)

Southmark Corp., In re 163 F.3d 925 (5th Cir. 1999), §7.7.3(1)

Spookyworld, Inc., In re 346 F.3d 1 (1st Cir. 2003), §10.7.2

St. Paul Fire & Marine Ins. Co. v. Labuzan, 579 F.3d 533 (5th Cir. 2009), §10.7.2

Stage, In re 321 B.R. 486 (B.A.P. 8th Cir. 2005), §22.5.4(6)

Stanford, In re 373 B.R. 890 (Bankr. E.D. Ark. 2007), §10.5.3

Starlite Houseboats, Inc., In re 470 B.R. 191 (Bankr. D. Kan. 2012), §9.6.6(1)

Stephens Industries, Inc. v. McClung, 789 F.2d 386 (6th Cir. 1986), E-17-2

Stephens, In re 704 F.3d 1279 (10th Cir. 2013), §21.7.3(b)(ii)(2)(bb)

Stern v. Marshall, 131 S.Ct. 2594 (2011), §7.3.5, E-7-2(c), E-7-2(d), §9.6.2(b)(5)

Sternberg v. Johnston, 582 F.3d 1114 (9th Cir. 2009), §10.7.2

Stoney Creek Technologies, LLC, In re 364 B.R. 882 (Bankr. E.D. Pa. 2007), §17.3.2(4)

Stovall, In re 209 B.R. 849 (Bankr. E.D. Va. 1997), §9.8.1

Straightline Investments, Inc., In re 525 F.3d 870 (9th Cir. 2008), §17.2.1

Streets & Beard Farm Partnership, In re 882 F.2d 233 (7th Cir. 1989), E-18-1

Sullivan, In re 680 F.2d 1131 (7th Cir. 1982), cert. denied, 459 U.S. 992 (1983), §13.2.1

Summers, In re 344 B.R. 108 (Bankr. N.D. Ariz. 2006), §13.2.3

Sun Runner Marine, Inc., In re 945 F.2d 1089 (9th Cir. 1991), §18.8.2

Sun Valley Ranches, In re 823 F.2d 1373 (9th Cir. 1987), §11.4.2

Sunahara, In re 326 B.R. 786 (B.A.P. 9th Cir. 2005), §20.10

Sutton, In re 904 F.2d 327 (5th Cir. 1990), §11.4.2(a)

Taggart, In re 249 F.3d 987 (9th Cir. 2001), §22.5.4(7)

Talsma, In re 436 B.R. 908 (Bankr. N.D. Tex. 2010), E-6-1

Tavenner v. Smoot, 257 F.3d 401 (4th Cir. 2001), §16.3.5

Taylor v. Freeland & Kronz, 503 U.S. 638 (1992), §13.4

Taylor, In re 913 F.2d 102 (3d Cir. 1990), E-18-3

Tejal Investment, LLC, In re 2012 WL 6186159 (Bankr. D. Utah 2012), §11.4.4

Tennessee Student Assistance Corp. v. Hood, 541 U.S. 440 (2004), §7.2.2(a)

Terrel, In re 892 F.2d 469 (6th Cir. 1989), E-18-1(a)

The V Companies, In re 292 B.R. 290 (6th Cir. B.A.P. 2003), §14.4

Thomas, In re 291 B.R. 189 (Bankr. M.D. Ala. 2003), §20.10

Thompkins v. Lil' Joe Records, Inc., 476 F.3d 1294 (11th Cir. 2007), §18.4

Thompson, In re 418 F.3d 362 (3d Cir. 2005), §22.5.4(7)

Thompson, In re 686 F.3d 940 (8th the Cir. 2012), §22.5.4(4)

Till v. S.C.S. Credit Corp., 541 U.S. 465 (2004), §20.7.1(a)(2)

639

Table of Cases

Timmerman, In re 379 B.R. 838 (Bankr. N.D. Iowa 2007), §8.4.1(c)(ii)

Tirch, In re 409 F.3d 677 (6th Cir 2005), §22.5.4

Toibb v. Radloff, 501 U.S. 157 (1991), §21.1.2

Torwico Electronics, Inc., In re 8 F.3d 146 (3d Cir. 1993), §19.2.1

Trans World Airlines, Inc., In re 134 F.3d 188 (3d Cir. 1998), §16.1.2

TransTexas Gas Corp., In re 597 F.3d 298 (5th Cir. 2010), §16.3.3

Trantham, In re 304 B.R. 298 (B.A.P. 6th Cir. 2004), §22.5.4

Trejos, In re 374 B.R. 210 (B.A.P. 9th Cir. 2007), §20.7.1

Tribune Co., In re 418 B.R. 116 (Bankr. D. Del. 2009), §7.2.1

Trusted Net Media Holdings, LLC, In re 550 F.3d 1035 (11th Cir. 2008), §9.6.2(b)(5)

U.S. Medical, Inc., In re 531 F.3d 1272 (10th Cir. 2008), §16.1.2(4)

UAL, In re 368 F.3d 720 (7th Cir. 2004), §18.8.2

United Rentals v. Angell, 592 F.3d 525 (4th Cir. 2010), §16.1.2(5)

United Savings Association of Texas v. Timbers of Inwood Forest Associates, 484 U.S. 365 (1988), §11.4.2(b)

United States v. Harchar, 331 B.R. 720 (N.C. Ohio 2005), §10.7.3

United States v. Noland, 517 U.S. 535 (1996), §19.7.2

United States v. Ron Pair Enterprises, 489 U.S. 235 (1989), §19.6.3(c)

United Student Aid Funds, Inc. v. Espinosa, 130 S.Ct. 1367 (2010), §22.5.4(8)

Universal Church v. Geltzer, 463 F.3d 218 (2d Cir. 2006), §16.3.3

Vanguard Diversified, In re 31 B.R. 364 (Bankr. E.D.N.Y. 1983), §17.3.3

Vargas, In re 257 B.R. 157 (Bankr. D.N.J. 2001), §13.7.1(5)

Verola, In re 446 F.3d 1206 (11th Cir. 2006), §22.5.4(7), §22.5.4(11)

Visionaire Corp., In re 290 B.R. 348 (Bankr. E.D. Mo. 2003), §19.6.4

Vivian, In re 150 B.R. 832 (Bankr. S.D. Fla. 1992), §22.3

Waldman v. Stone, 698 F.3d 910 (6th Cir. 2012), §7.3.5(1)

Waldo, In re 417 B.R. 854 (Bankr. E.D. Tenn. 2009), §6.6.2(d)

Walker, In re 381 B.R. 620 (Bankr. M.D. Pa. 2008), §9.8.5

Walls v. Wells Fargo Bank, N.A., 276 F.3d 502 (9th Cir. 2002), §22.3

Ward, In re 857 F.2d 1082 (6th Cir. 1988), §22.5.4

Wells, In re 561 F.3d 633 (6th Cir. 2009), §16.1.2

Welzel, In re 275 F.3d 1308 (11th Cir. 2001), §19.6.3(c)

West Electronics, Inc., In re 852 F.2d 79 (3d Cir. 1988), §18.8.1

Westberry, In re 215 F.3d 589 (6th Cir. 2000), §9.8.1

Westside Community Hospital Inc., In re 112 B.R. 243 (Bankr. N.D. Ill. 1990), §9.6.4

Wicks, In re 215 B.R. 316 (E.D.N.Y. 1997), §10.4.2

Wilbur, In re 344 B.R. 650 (Bankr. D. Utah 2006), §20.7.3(b)(3)

Williams, In re 290 B.R. 83 (Bankr. E.D. Pa. 2003), §12.2.2

Williams, In re 394 B.R. 550 (Bankr. N.D. Colo. 2008), §20.7.3(b)(3)

Williams, In re 435 B.R. 552 (Bankr. N.D. Ill. 2010), §9.7(1)

Wingard, In re 382 B.R. 892 (Bankr. W.D. Pa. 2008), E-10-7

Wisconsin Dept. of Workforce Development v. Ratliff, 390 B.R. 607 (E.D. Wis. 2008), §19.6.4

WitKo, In re 374 F.3d 1040 (11th Cir. 2004), E-12-1

Wolverine Radio Co., In re 930 F.2d 1132 (6th Cir. 1991), §7.3.5

Wood, In re 825 F.2d 90, 97 (5th Cir. 1987), §7.3.5(1)

Zarnel, In re 619 F.3d 156 (2d Cir. 2010), §8.4.1(c)(ii), §9.6.2(b)(5), §10.3(3)

Zell, In re 284 B.R. 569 (Bankr. D. Md. 2002), §19.6.3(e)

Zilog, Inc., In re 450 F.3d 996 (9th Cir. 2006), §19.2.5

Zimmer, In re 313 F.3d 1220 (9th Cir. 2002), §20.8.3

Table of Statutes

References are to book sections (denoted by the symbol, §)and to Examples and Explanations, denoted by the letter "E" followed by the chapter number and Example number.

11 U.S.C.

§101	§5.4.1
§101	§14.2, §16.1.1, E-16-8
§101(3)	§6.7.1
§101(4A)	§6.7.1
§101(5)	§6.5, §16.1.2, §19.2.1, §19.2.2, §E-19-2, E-19-3, §20.7.3, §20.11, §22.2
§101(7A)	§8.4.2
§101(8)	§8.3.2, §9.8.1, E-9-4
§101(9)	§6.4.2, §8.3.1
§101(10)	§6.5, §16.1.2, E-16-8
§101(10A)	§9.8.4, §9.8.6, §E-9-6, §20.7.3, E-20-1,
§101(10B)	§18.4
§101(11)	§9.6.4
§101(12)	§16.1.2, §22.2
§101(12A)	§6.7.1
§101(13)	§8.3.1
§101(13A)	§20.8.3
§101(14)	§6.2.1, §6.6.2, E-6-1, E-6-4, E-6-5
§101(14A)	E-6-1, §13.5.2, §16.1.4, §19.6.4, §21.7.2, §22.5.4
§101(15)	§6.5, §10.3, E-16-8
§101(16)	§6.4.2, §21.4.2
§101(17)	§21.4.2
§101(18)	§8.3.3, §8.4.2, E-18-1
§101(19)	§8.4.2, E-18-1
§101(20)	§8.4.2, §9.6.2
§101(21)	§8.4.2, E-18-1
§101(27)	§7.9.1, E-10-5, E-16-8, §19.6.4
§101(30)	§8.4.2, E-8-3,
§101(31)	E-9-2, §16.1.2, E-21-3
§101(32)	§15.3.2, §16.1.2, §16.3.3, E-16-1
§101(36)	§15.1.2
§101(37)	§19.6.3
§101(39A)	§9.8.4
§101(41)	§8.3.1, §21.1.1
§101(51B)	§11.4.3, E-11-5

§101(51C)	§21.1.1, §21.4.3
§101(51D)	§6.5, §21.1.1
§101(53)	§15.2
§101(54)	§14.1, §16.1.2, E-16-2, E-16-3, E-16-7,
§102	§12.4, §17.1
§102(1)	§11.2
§102(2)	§19.2.4
§104	§8.4.2, §8.6.1, E-8-3, E-9-1, §13.8, §19.6.4
§105	§8.5, §8.6.1, §10.3, §10.4, §10.7.2, §19.7.3, §22.2, §22.5.4
§105(a)	§7.5, §7.5.1, §7.5.2, §7.5.3, §8.5, §9.7, E-9-5, §10.7.5, E-10-1, §13.7.1
§106	§7.9.1
§106(a)	§7.9.1, §7.9.2, §7.9.3, E-7-3, E-7-4
§106(b)	§7.9.1, §7.9.3, E-7-3, E-7-4
§106(c)	§7.9.1, §7.9.4, E-7-4
§108	§10.6
§108(c)	§10.6
§109	§8.4, §8.4.1, §8.4.2, §10.3
§109(a)	§8.4.1
§109(b)	§8.4.2, E-8-1, E-8-3
§109(c)	§8.4.2
§109(d)	§8.4.2, E-8-1, §21.1.2
§109(e)	§8.4.2, E-8-4, E-8-1, E-8-2, §20.1, §20.4
§109(f)	§8.4.2, E-8-1
§109(g)	§8.4.1
§109(g)(1)	§8.4.1
§109(g)(2)	§8.4.1
§109(h)	§8.4.1, E-8-4, §9.3, §10.3, §22.5.2
§109(h)(1)	§8.4.1, E-8-4
§109(h)(2)	§8.4.1, E-8-4
§109(h)(3)	§8.4.1, E-8-4
§109(h)(4)	§8.4.1, E-8-4, §22.5.2
§301	§8.6.1, §9.1
§301(b)	§9.4
§301(i)(1)	§9.6.6

§301(i)(2)	§9.6.6	§362(a)(3)	§10.4.1, §10.4.2, E-10-2
§302	§9.5.1	§362(a)(4)	§10.4.1, E-10-1, E-10-2,
§303	§9.1, §9.6.1, §9.6.2, §9.6.3		E-10-4
§303(a)	§9.6.1, §9.6.2	§362(a)(5)	E-10-2
§303(b)	§9.6.1, §9.6.2, E-9-1, E-9-2	§362(a)(6)	§10.4.1, §10.4.2, E-10-4,
§303(b)(1)	§9.6.2, E-9-1, E-9-2		E-10-6,
§303(b)(2)	§3.9.2, §9.6.2, E-9-1, E-9-2	§362(a)(7)	§10.4.1, §10.4.2
§303(c)	§9.6.1, §9.6.2	§362(a)(8)	§10.4.1
§303(e)	§9.6.3	§362(b)	§10.1, §10.4, §10.4.3,
§303(f)	§9.6.3, §16.4		E-10-3, E-10-4
§303(g)	§6.2.2, §9.6.3	§362(b)(2)	§10.4.3
§303(h)	§9.6.1, §9.6.3, §9.6.4, E-9-3	§362(b)(2)(A)	§10.4.3
§303(h)(1)	§9.6.4, E-9-3	§362(b)(3)	§10.4.3, E-10-4
§303(h)(2)	§9.6.4	§362(b)(4)	§10.4.3, E-10-5
§303(i)	§9.7	§362(c)(1)	§10.5, §10.5.1
§303(i)(1)	§9.6.6	§362(c)(2)	§10.5, §10.5.2
§303(i)(2)	§9.6.6	§362(c)(3)	§10.5, §10.5.3
§303(j)	§9.7	§362(c)(3)(C)(i)	§10.5.3
§305	§7.7.1, §7.7.2, §13.5.5	§362(c)(3)(ii)	§10.5.3
§321	§6.2.1, §6.2.4	§362(c)(4)	§10.5, §10.5.3
§322	§6.2.1	§362(c)(4)(D)	§10.5.3
§324	E-6-4, E-6-5	§362(d)	§10.5, §11.1
§324(a)	§6.2.1	§362(d)(1)	§11.4, §11.4.1, §11.4.2,
§326	§6.2.5		§11.4.3, §11.5, §11.5.1,
§327	§6.6.1, §7.2.2, E-19-5		§11.5.2, E-11-1, E-11-2,
§327(a)	§6.6.1, §6.6.2, E-6-3, E-6-1		E-11-3,
§327(c)	§6.6.1	§362(d)(2)	§11.4, §11.4.2, §11.4.3,
§327(d)	§6.6.1		E-11-1, E-11-2, E-11-3,
§327(e)	§6.6.2		E-11-4, E-11-5,
§328	E-6-3	§362(d)(2)(A)	§11.4.2
§328(b)	§6.6.1	§362(d)(2)(B)	§11.4.2
§328(c)	§6.6.2, E-6-3	§362(d)(3)	§11.4.3
§329	§6.6.1	§362(d)(4)	§11.4.4
§330	§6.6.1, E-6-5	§362(d)(4)(b)	§20.11
§330(a)	§6.6.1	§362(e)	§11.1, §11.2
§330(a)(1)	§6.6.1, §6.6.2	§362(e)(1)	§11.2
§341	§9.9	§362(f)	§11.1, §11.2
§341(c)	§9.9	§362(g)	§11.1, §11.2, §11.4.4
§343	§6.3	§362(h)	§13.8
§348	§8.5, §12.2.3	§362(k)	§10.7.2, §10.7.3, §10.7.5,
§348(a)	§12.2.3		E-10-1
§348(f)	§12.2.3	§362(k)(1)	§10.7.2, E-10-7
§361	§11.5.4, E-11-2, §17.2.3	§365(b)(1)	§10.4.3
§361(1)	§11.5.4	§502	§19.4, §19.5, §19.7.3,
§361(2)	§11.5.4		E-19-5, §22.7.1
§361(3)	§11.5.4, §21.7.2	§502(a)(1)	§19.6.3
§362	§7.5.1, E-7-1, §9.4, §10.1	§502(a)(2)	§19.6.3
§362(a)	§10.1, §10.4, §10.4.1,	§502(b)	§19.4
	§10.4.2, E-10-5, §11.2	§502(b)(1)	§19.4
§362(a)(1)	§10.4.1, E-10-1, E-10-2,	§502(b)(2)	§19.4, §19.5
	E-10-3, E-10-4	§502(b)(6)	§18.4, §19.4
§362(a)(2)	§10.4.1, E-10-1, E-10-2	§502(b)(7)	§18.4, §19.4, E-19-5

§502(c)	§19.3, E-19-2	§522(a)(2)	E-13-3
§502(d)	§12.3, §14.2, §14.5,	§522(a)(5)	E-13-1
	§19.4	§522(a)(6)	E-13-1
§502(e)	§19.4	§522(b)	§13.2.2, §13.5.5,
§502(f)	§19.6.3, E-19-5		E-22-1
§502(g)	§18.4, E-19-5, §21.4.8	§522(b)(3)	§13.2.2, §13.2.3
§502(h)	§19.2.3, §21.4.8	§522(b)(3)(C)	§13.2.2
§502(i)	§21.4.8	§522(c)(2)	E-13-2
§502(j)	§19.4, §20.10	§522(d)	§13.2.1, §13.2.2, §13.2.3,
§503	§6.6.1		§13.3, §13.4, §13.5.5,
§503(b)(3)	§6.6.1		E-13-4
§503(b)(9)	§15.3.2	§522(d)(1)	§13.2.3, E-13-2, E-13-4
§506	§8.6.1, §11.4.2, E-11-4,	§522(d)(2)	E-13-4
	§16.2.2, §19.6.2, §20.7,	§522(d)(3)	E-13-4
	§21.7.4	§522(d)(4)	E-13-6
§506(a)	§19.6.3	§522(d)(5)	E-13-2, E-13-4
§506(a)(1)	§19.6.3, §20.11	§522(d)(6)	§13.5.4, E-13-1, E-13-4
§506(a)(2)	§19.6.3, §19.6.4	§522(f)	§13.1, §13.5.4, §13.5.5,
§506(b)	E-16-2, §19.6.1, §19.6.3		§13.6, E-13-1, E-13-2,
§506(c)	§19.6.1, §19.6.3, E-19-4		E-14-7
§506(d)	§19.4, §19.6.3, E-19-1,	§522(f)(1)(A)	§13.5.1, §13.5.6
	§20.8.3	§522(f)(1)(B)	§13.5.3, §13.5.1, §13.5.6,
§506(d)(2)	§19.4		E-13-1
§507	§8.6.1, §11.5.5, §19.6.1,	§522(f)(2)	§13.5.6
	§19.6.2, §20.7.2, E-21-1	§522(f)(2)(A)	§13.5.6
§507(a)	§19.6.1, §19.6.4, §22.5.4	§522(f)(2)(B)	§13.5.6
§507(a)(1)	E-11-5, §18.4, §19.6.4	§522(f)(3)	§13.5.1
§507(a)(1)(B)	§20.3, §20.7.2	§522(g)	§16.3.5
§507(a)(2)	§11.5.5, §19.6.4, E-19-4,	§522(h)	§14.4
	E-19-5, §21.6.2, §21.7.2,	§522(l)	§13.4
	E-21-1	§522(o)	§13.2.3, E-22-1
§507(a)(3)	§19.6.4, E-19-5, §21.6.2,	§522(p)	§13.2.3
	§21.7.2	§522(q)	§13.2.3, §22.5.2, §22.8
§507(a)(4)	§19.6.4, E-19-5, E-21-1	§522(q)(1)	§22.5.2
§507(a)(5)	§19.6.4	§522(q)(1)(A)	§13.2.3, §22.5.2, §22.7.2
§507(a)(8)	§19.6.4, §21.6.2, §21.7.2,	§522(q)(1)(B)	§13.2.3, §22.5.2, §22.7.2
	E-21-1	§523	§8.6.1, E-10-6, §22.1.2,
§507(a)(8)(B)	E-19-5, E-20-6		§21.4.8, §22.1, §22.5.1,
§507(b)	§11.5.5, E-11-3, E-17-5,		§22.5.4, §22.5.5, §22.6,
	§19.6.2, §19.6.4		§22.7.3, §22.8, E-22-2,
§507(b)(7)	E-19-5		E-22-3
§521	§6.7.2, §9.3, §9.7, §9.8.6	§523(a)	§22.5.4, §22.7.3, §22.7.6,
§521(a)	§9.3, §13.8		§22.8, E-22-1
§521(a)(2)	§13.6, §13.7.2, §13.8	§523(a)(1)	E-19-5, §22.5.4, §22.5.5
§521(a)(3)	§13.6	§523(a)(2)	§22.5.4, §22.5.4, §22.7.3,
§521(a)(4)	§12.3		E-22-2, E-22-4, E-22-5
§521(a)(6)	§13.8	§523(a)(2)(A)	§22.5.4, E-22-5
§521(b)	§9.3	§523(a)(2)(B)	§22.5.4
§521(e)	§9.3	§523(a)(2)(C)	§22.5.4, E-22-5
§522	§13.1, §13.2.1, §13.2.2,	§523(a)(3)	§22.5.4, §22.5.5, §22.7.3
	§13.2.3, §13.5.5, E-13-3,	§523(a)(4)	§22.5.4, §22.7.3, E-22-2
	E-13-5, E-22-1	§523(a)(5)	§22.5.4, §22.7.3

§523(a)(6)	E-19-2, §22.5.4, §22.7.3, E-22-3, E-22-4
§523(a)(7)	§22.5.4, §22.7.3, E-22-2
§523(a)(8)	§22.7.3, E-22-6
§523(a)(9)	§22.5.4, §22.7.3
§523(a)(10)	§22.5.4, §22.5.5
§523(a)(12)	§22.5.4
§523(a)(13)	§22.5.4
§523(a)(14)	§22.5.4
§523(a)(15)	§22.5.4
§523(b)	§22.5.5
§523(c)	§22.5.4, E-22-3, E-22-2
§523(c)(1)	§22.5.4
§524	§8.6.1, §10.6, §13.7.1, §13.7.3, E-13-7, §22.1, §22.3
§524(a)	§22.3
§524(a)(2)	§7.5.1, §10.5.2,
§524(c)	§13.7.1, E-13-7,
§524(d)	§13.7.1, E-13-7, §22.5.1
§524(e)	§22.3
§524(f)	§13.7.1, §22.4
§524(g)	§19.3
§524(k)	§13.7.1
§524(m)	§13.7.1
§525	§22.1
§526	§6.7.2
§§526 to 528	§6.7.1, §6.7.2, §6.7.3
§526(a)	§6.7.2
§526(a)(1)	§6.7.2
§526(a)(2)	§6.7.2, §7.5.1
§526(a)(4)	§6.7.2, §6.7.3
§526(b)	§6.7.2
§526(c)	§6.7.2
§526(d)	§6.7.2
§527	§6.7.2
§528	§6.7.1, §6.7.2, §6.7.3
§528(a)(8)	§22.5.5
§541	§5.5.2, §8.6.1, E-10-1, §11.5.2, §12.1, §12.2.1, §12.2.3, E-12-1, §18.4, §20.1, §20.2, §21.1.2, §21.7.3
§541(a)	§5.5.2, §12.1, §12.2.1, §12.2.2, E-12-2, E-12-1
§541(a)(1)	E-5-1, §12.2.1
§541(a)(5)	E-12-2
§541(a)(6)	§12.2.3, E-12-2, E-17-3
§541(a)(7)	§12.2.3
§541(b)	§12.2.1
§541(c)	§5.5.2, §12.2.2, §17.2.4
§541(c)(1)	E-12-1

§541(c)(2)	§12.2.2, E-12-1
§541(d)	§12.2.1
§542	§12.3, E-12-1, §16.4
§542(a)	§12.3
§542(b)	§10.4.2
§542(c)	§16.4
§543	§12.3
§544	§14.2, §15.1, §15.2, §15.3, E-15-1, E-15-2, E-15-3, §16.1.1, §16.3.1, E-16-3
§544(a)	§15.2, §15.1.3, E-15-1, E-15-3, E-15-4, E-16-3
§544(a)(1)	§15.2, E-15-1, E-15-3, E-15-5
§544(a)(2)	§15.2, E-15-3
§544(a)(3)	§15.2, E-15-3
§544(b)	E-15-2, §15.1.3, E-15-2, E-15-3, §16.3.1, §16.3.4
§544(b)(1)	§15.1.3
§544(b)(2)	§15.1.3, §20.7.3
§545	§14.2, §15.2, §15.3, E-15-4, §16.1.4
§545(1)	§15.2, E-15-5
§545(2)	§15.2, E-15-4
§545(3)	§15.2
§545(4)	§15.2
§546	§10.4.3, §14.2, §15.3, E-15-5, §16.1.3
§546(a)	§14.7, §15.1.3, §15.3, E-15-2
§546(b)	E-10-4, §15.3, E-15-4
§546(b)(1)(A)	E-10-4
§546(b)(2)(A)	E-10-4
§546(c)	§15.3.2, E-15-5
§546(c)(2)	§15.3.2
§547	§7.3.5, E-7-1, §10.4.3, §14.2, E-15-1, §16.1, §16.1.1, §16.1.2, §16.1.3, §16.1.4, §16.2.2, §16.2.3, §16.4, E-16-7
§547(a)(2)	§16.1.4
§547(b)	§16.1.1, §16.1.2, §16.1.4, §16.2.2, E-16-1, E-16-2, E-16-4, E-16-2, E-16-3, E-16-5, E-16-6
§547(b)(1)	§16.1.2
§547(b)(2)	§16.1.2
§547(b)(3)	§16.1.2
§547(b)(4)	§16.1.2
§547(b)(5)	§16.1.2, E-16-1, E-16-2, E-16-4
§547(c)	§16.1.1, §16.1.2, §16.1.4, §16.2.2, E-16-5, E-16-1, E-16-2

§547(c)(1)	§16.1.4, E-16-1, E-16-1, E-16-3, E-16-5
§547(c)(2)	§16.1.4, E-16-1, E-16-5
§547(c)(3)	§16.1.4, E-16-3
§547(c)(4)	§16.1.4, E-16-1, E-16-6
§547(c)(5)	§16.1.4, §16.2.3
§547(c)(6)	§16.1.4
§547(c)(7)	§16.1.4
§547(c)(8)	§16.1.4
§547(c)(9)	§16.1.4
§547(e)	§16.1.3, E-16-3, E-16-4
§547(e)(1)	§16.1.3, E-16-3
§547(e)(1)(B)	E-16-4
§547(e)(2)	E-16-3
§547(e)(3)	§16.1.3, §16.1.4
§547(f)	§16.1.2, E-16-1
§547(g)	§16.1.4
§547(i)	§16.1.2
§548	E-7-2, §13.2.3, §14.2, §15.1.3, E-15-2, §16.1.1, §16.3.1, §16.3.3, §16.3.4, §16.3.5, §16.3.6, E-16-7
§548(a)(1)(A)	§16.3.2
§548(a)(1)(B)	§16.3.3
§548(a)(1)(B)(ii)(I)	§16.3.3
§548(a)(1)(B)(ii)(II)	§16.3.3
§548(a)(1)(B)(ii)(III)	§16.3.3
§548(a)(1)(B)(ii)(IV)	§16.3.3
§548(a)(2)	§16.3.6, §20.7.3
§548(c)	§16.3.4
§548(d)(3)	§16.3.6
§548(d)(4)	§20.7.3
§549	§14.1, §14.2, §16.4
§549(a)	§16.4
§549(a)(2)(A)	§16.4
§549(b)	§16.4
§549(c)	§16.4
§549(d)	§16.4
§550	§14.2, §14.5, §14.7, §16.3.4
§550(a)	§14.5
§550(b)	§14.5
§550(c)	§16.1.2
§550(d)	§14.5
§550(e)	§14.5
§550(f)	§14.7
§551	§14.2, §14.6
§552	§14.2
§552(b)	E-17-3
§552(q)(1)	§22.5.2, §22.7.2
§553	§7.9.4, §10.4.2, §14.2, §16.2, §16.2.2, §16.2.3, E-16-8, E-17-3, §19.6.3
§553(a)(2)	§16.2.3
§553(a)(3)	§16.2.3
§553(b)	§16.2.3
§553(c)	§16.2.3
§554	E-7-1, §12.4
§554(a)	§12.4
§554(b)	§12.4
§554(c)	§12.4
§558	§14.2
§701	§6.2.1, §6.2.2, §8.6.1, §9.4
§703	§8.6.1
§704	§6.2.2, §8.6.1
§706	§8.5, §8.6.1
§706(a)	§8.5
§706(d)	§8.5
§707	§6.3, §8.6.1, §9.7, §9.8.3
§707(a)	§8.4.1, §8.5, §9.7, §9.8.2, §9.8.3, E-9-4, E-9-5
§707(a)(3)	§9.7
§707(a)(8)	§22.5.2
§707(a)(9)	§22.5.2
§707(b)	§8.3.2, §8.4.2 §8.5, E-8-2, E-8-3, §9.1, §9.7, §9.8.1, §9.8.2, §9.8.3, §9.8.4, §9.8.6, E-9-4, E-9-5, E-9-6, §10.5.3, §20.1, §20.5 §20.7.3, §20.11, §21.6.2, §21.6.3, §22.7.3
§707(b)(1)	§9.8.4, §9.8.6, §20.7.3
§707(b)(2)	§9.8.4, §9.8.6, §9.8.7, E-9-6, §20.7.3
§707(b)(2)(A)	§20.7.3, E-20-1
§707(b)(2)(B)	§20.7.3, E-20-1
§707(b)(2)(A)(i)	§9.8.6
§707(b)(2)(A)(ii)	§20.7.3
§707(b)(2)(A)(ii)(1)	§9.8.6
§707(b)(2)(C)	§9.8.6
§707(b)(3)	§9.8.5, §9.8.7
§707(b)(4)	§9.8.8
§707(b)(4)(C)	§9.8.8
§707(b)(5)	§9.8.8
§707(b)(6)	§9.8.4
§707(b)(7)	§9.8.4
§721	§8.6.1, §17.2.1, §17.3.2, E-17, E-19-4, E-19-5
§722	§8.6.1
§726	§8.6.1, §19.5, §19.6.2
§726(a)(5)	§19.5
§726(b)	§19.6.4
§727	§6.3, §13.2.3, §22.1, §22.2, §22.5.1, §22.5.2, §22.5.4, §22.6, §22.7.4, §22.8, E-22-3
§727(a)	§22.5.2, §22.6, E-22-1

§727(a)(1)	§22.5.2, §22.6	§1123(a)(4)	§21.6.2, E-21-4
§727(a)(2)	§22.5.2, §22.5.4, §22.5.5,	§1123(a)(5)	§21.6.2
	E-22-1, E-22-3	§1123(a)(6)	§21.6.2
§727(a)(3)	§22.5.2, §22.5.4, §22.5.5,	§1123(a)(7)	§21.6.2
	E-22-3	§1123(a)(8)	§21.6.2
§727(a)(4)	§22.5.2, §22.5.4, §22.5.5	§1123(b)	§21.6.1, §21.6.3
§727(a)(5)	§22.5.2, §22.5.4, §22.5.5	§1123(b)(2)	E-22-6
§727(a)(6)	§22.5.2, §22.5.3, §22.5.4,	§1123(b)(5)	§21.6.3
	§22.5.5	§1123(a)(5)(D)	§21.2
§727(a)(7)	§22.5.2, §22.5.4, §22.5.5	§1123(a)(8)	§21.1.2
§727(a)(8)	§22.5.2, §22.5.4, §22.7.4	§1125	§8.6.1, §21.4.4, §21.4.7
§727(a)(9)	§22.5.2, §22.5.4, §22.7.4	§1125(a)	§21.5
§727(a)(10)	§22.4, §22.5.2	§1125(a)(1)	§21.4.4
§727(a)(11)	§22.5.2, §22.7.2	§1125(c)	§21.4.4
§727(a)(12)	§22.5.2, §22.7.2	§1125(d)	§21.4.4
§727(b)	§22.2,	§1125(e)	§21.4.4
§727(c)	§22.5.1	§1125(f)	§21.4.4
§727(d)	§22.5.3	§1125(g)	§21.5
§727(e)	§22.5.3	§1126	§8.6.1
§1102	§21.4.2	§1126(b)	§21.5
§1102(a)(3)	§21.4.2	§1126(c)	§21.4.5, E-21-4, E-21-2
§1103	§6.5, §6.6.2, §8.6.1, §21.4.2	§1126(d)	§21.4.5
§1103(b)	§6.6.2	§1126(e)	§21.4.5
§1104	§6.2.4, §8.6.1, §21.4.2	§1126(f)	§21.4.5
§1104(b)	§6.2.1, §6.2.4, §21.4.2	§1126(g)	§21.4.5
§1105	§6.2.4	§1129	§8.6.1, §21.4.6, §21.4.7,
§1106(a)(3)	§20.1		§21.6.1, §21.6.2, §21.7.1
§1106(a)(4)	§20.1	§1129(a)	§21.7.1, §12.7.2, §21.7.3,
§1107(b)	§6.6.1, E-6-1		E-21-2, E-21-3, E-21-4
§1108	§8.6.1, §17.2.1, §17.3.2,	§1129(a)(1)	§21.7.2
	E-17-1(a), E-17-3, §21.4.2	§1129(a)(2)	§21.7.2
§1112	§8.5, §8.6.1, §9.7, §21.4.1,	§1129(a)(3)	§21.7.2
	§21.4.9	§1129(a)(7)	§21.7.2, §21.7.3
§1112(a)	§8.5	§1129(a)(7)(A)	§21.7.2, E-21-1
§1112(b)	§9.7	§1129(a)(7)(B)	§21.7.2
§1112(b)(4)(P)	§21.1.2	§1129(a)(8)	§21.7.1, §21.7.2, §21.7.3,
§1112(e)	§9.7		E-21-3
§1115	§8.6.1, §21.1.2, §21.7.3	§1129(a)(9)	§21.7.2
§1121	§8.6.1, §21.4.3	§1129(a)(9)(A)	§21.6.2, E-21-1
§§1121 through 1129	§21.4.7	§1129(a)(9)(B)	§21.6.2, E-21-1
§1121(a)	§21.4.3, §21.5	§1129(a)(9)(C)	§21.6.2, E-21-1
§1121(e)	§21.4.3	§1129(a)(10)	§21.7.2, E-21-2
§1121(e)(3)	§21.4.6	§1129(a)(11)	§21.7.2
§1122	§8.6.1, §20.7.3, E-20-6,	§1129(a)(14)	§21.1.2, §12.7.2
	§21.4.7, §21.6.2, E-21-2,	§1129(a)(15)	§8.6.1, §21.1.2, §12.7.2
	E-21-1	§1129(b)	§21.7.1, §21.7.2, §21.7.3,
§1122(b)	§21.6.2		E-21-1, E-21-2, E-21-3,
§1123	§8.6.1, §21.4.7, §21.6.1		E-21-4
§1123(a)	§8.4.2, §21.6.1, §21.6.2	§1129(b)(1)	§21.7.3
§1123(a)(1)	§21.6.2	§1129(b)(2)	§21.7.3
§1123(a)(2)	§21.6.2	§1129(b)(2)(A)	§21.7.4, E-21-5
§1123(a)(3)	§21.6.2	§1129(b)(2)(A)(i)	§21.7.3

§1129(b)(2)(A)(ii)	§21.7.3
§1129(b)(2)(A)(iii)	§21.7.3
§1129(b)(2)(B)	E-21-4
§1129(b)(2)(B)(i)	§21.7.3
§1129(b)(2)(B)(ii)	§21.1.2
§1129(b)(2)(C)(i)	§21.7.3
§1129(c)	§21.4.3
§1129(e)	§21.4.3, §21.4.6
§1141	§8.6.1, §21.4.8, §22.1, §22.2
§1141(a)	§21.4.8
§1141(b)	§21.4.8
§1141(c)	§21.4.8
§1141(d)	§21.1.2, §21.4.8, §22.4, §22.6
§1141(d)(1)	§21.4.8, §22.2
§1141(d)(1)(B)	§21.4.8
§1141(d)(2)	§21.1.2, §21.4.8, §22.6
§1141(d)(3)	§21.4.8, §22.6
§1141(d)(5)	§21.1.2, §21.4.8, §22.6, §8.6.1
§1201	§8.6.1
§1202	§6.2.3, §8.6.1
§1203	§8.6.1, §17.2.1, §17.3.2
§1207	§8.6.1, §12.2.3, §12.2.3
§1207(b)	§12.2.3
§1208	§8.5, §8.6.1, §9.7, §22.8
§1208(a)	§8.5
§1208(b)	§9.7
§1222	§8.6.1
§1222(a)	§8.6.1
§1222(b)(5)	§22.8
§1222(b)(9)	§22.8
§1225	§8.6.1, §22.8
§1225(b)	§8.6.1
§1227	§8.6.1, §12.2.3
§1228	§8.6.1
§1301	§20.1
§1302	§6.2.3, §8.6.1, §20.1, §20.4
§1302(a)	§6.2.1
§1302(b)(5)	§20.2
§1302(c)	§8.6.1
§1304	§8.6.1
§1306	§8.6.1, §12.2.3, §20.1, §20.2
§1306(b)	§12.2.3
§1307	§8.5, §8.6.1, §9.7, §20.1, §20.2, §20.6
§1307(a)	§8.5
§1307(b)	§9.7
§1307(c)	§8.5
§1307(c)(9)	§9.7
§1321	§8.6.1, §20.2
§1322	§8.6.1, §20.3, §20.8.1, §20.8.2, §20.10, E-20-3
§1322(a)	§20.3, §20.4, E-20-3
§1322(a)(1)	§20.3
§1322(a)(2)	§20.3, §20.7.2, E-20-1, E-20-6
§1322(a)(3)	§20.3, §20.7.2
§1322(a)(4)	§20.3, §20.7.2
§1322(b)	§20.3, §20.7.2, E-20-3, §21.6.3
§1322(b)(1)	§20.7, §20.7.2, E-20-6
§1322(b)(2)	§20.8.1, §20.8.2, §20.8.3, §20.9, E-20-4, E-20-6, E-20-7
§1322(b)(3)	§20.8.1, §20.8.2, §20.8.3
§1322(b)(5)	§20.8.1, §20.8.3, §20.9, E-20-4, §21.6.3, §22.7.3, §22.7.6, §22.8
§1322(b)(8)	§20.4
§1322(b)(11)	§20.3
§1322(c)(1)	§20.8.3, E-20-4, §20.8.3
§1322(c)(2)	§20.8.3
§1322(d)	§20.5, §20.7.2, §20.10, E-20-1
§1322(d)(1)	E-20-1
§1322(d)(2)	E-20-1
§1325	§8.6.1, §20.3, §20.6, §20.7.3, §20.8.2, §20.11, E-20-1, E-20-3, E-20-1
§1325(a)	§20.3, §20.4, §20.7.1, §20.10, E-20-3, §21.7.2
§1325(a)(1)	§20.3
§1325(a)(2)	§20.3
§1325(a)(3)	§20.3, §20.6, §20.7.3, E-20-2
§1325(a)(4)	§20.3, §20.7.3, E-20-1, E-20-2
§1325(a)(5)	§20.3, §20.7.1, §20.8.2, E-20-1
§1325(a)(5)(A)	§20.7.1
§1325(a)(5)(B)	§20.7.1, E-20-6, §20.7.1
§1325(a)(5)(C)	§20.3, §20.4, E-20-1
§1325(a)(6)	§20.3, §20.6
§1325(a)(7)	§20.3
§1325(a)(8)	§20.7.1
§1325(a)(9)	§20.7.1
§1325(b)	§8.6.1, §20.3, §20.4, §20.7.3, §20.10, E-20-1, E-20-6, §21.1.2, §21.6.2, §21.7.2
§1325(b)(1)(B)	§20.7.3, E-20-2
§1325(b)(2)	§20.7.3, E-20-1, §21.7.2, §21.7.2
§1325(b)(3)	§21.7.2
§1325(b)(2)(A)	§20.7.3
§1325(b)(2)(A)(ii)	§20.7.3
§1325(b)(3)	§20.7.3
§1325(b)(4)	§20.7.3

§1325(b)(4)(A)	E-20-2
§1325(c)	§20.2
§1327	§8.6.1, §12.2.2
§1327(a)	§20.2
§1327(b)	§20.2
§1327(c)	§20.2
§1328	§8.6.1, §20.2, §20.7.1, §20.11, E-20-2, §22.1, §22.2, §22.7.1, §22.7.3
§1328(a)	§21.4.8, §22.4, §22.5.2, §22.6, §22.7.1, §22.7.5, §22.8, E-22-3
§1328(a)(1)	§20.9, §22.7.3
§1328(a)(2)	§22.7.3, E-22-2, E-22-6
§1328(a)(3)	§22.7.3, E-22-2
§1328(a)(4)	§22.7.3, E-22-3
§1328(b)	§22.7.6
§1328(c)	§22.7.6
§1328(d)	§19.2.3, §22.7.3, §22.7.6
§1328(e)	§22.7.5
§1328(f)	§22.7.4
§1328(g)	§22.7.2
§1328(h)	§22.7.2, §22.8

18 U.S.C.

§§151-155	§5.4.2

28 U.S.C.

§151	§7.3.5
§157	§7.3.6
§157(b)	§7.3.5
§157(b)(1)	§7.3.5
§157(b)(2)	§7.3.5
§157(b)(2)(B)	E-7-2
§157(b)(2)(C)	§7.3.5
§157 (b)(2)(F)	§14.5
§157(b)(2)(G)	E-7-2
§157(b)(2)(H)	§7.3.6
§157 (b)(2)(K)	§14.5
§157(c)(1)	§7.3.5, §7.6.1
§157(c)(2)	§7.3.5, §7.6.1
§157(e)	§7.3.6, §7.4
§158	§7.6.1
§158(b)	§7.6.2
§158(b)(5)	§7.6.2
§158(b)(6)	§7.6.2
§§581-589a	§6.3
§581	§5.4.2, §6.3
§586	§6.3
§586(a)(3)(H)	§21.1.

§586(b)	§6.2.3
§586(d)	§6.2.1
§586(e)	§6.2.5
§1334	§5.4.2, §7.1, §7.2.1, §7.2.2, §7.2.3, §7.3, §7.3.5, §7.3.6, §7.7.3, §7.8, E-7-2, §9.2, §9.6.1
§1334(a)	§7.2.2, §7.2.3, E-7-1
§1334(b)	§7.2.2, §7.3.5, §7.7.3, E-7-1
§1334(c)	§7.7.1, §7.7.3, §7.8
§1334(c)(1)	§7.7.3
§1334(c)(2)	§7.7.3
§1334(d)	E-7-1
§1334(e)	§7.2.3
§1334(e)(1)	§7.2.2
§1334(e)(2)	§7.2.2
§§1408 to 1412	§5.4.2
§1408	§5.4.2, §9.2
§1409	§9.2
§1412	§5.4.2, §9.2
§1452	§7.8
§1452(a)	§7.8
§1452(b)	§7.8
§1481	§7.5.2
§2075	§5.4.4

UCC

§101(32)	§16.1.2, §16.3.3, E-16-1
§1-201(23)	§15.3.2
§2.702	§15.3.2, E-15-5
§9.317(2)	§15.1.2, E-15-1

UFTA

§1(12)	§4.2, E-4-1
§1(2)	§4.2, §4.43, E-4-1
§1(3)	§4.2
§1(3)(A)(2)(ii)	§16.3.3
§1(4)	E-4-1
§2(a)	§4.43
§2(b)	§4.43
§3(a)	§4.42
§4(a)(1)	§4.2,
§4(a)(2)	§4.2
§4(a)(2)(i)	§4.4.1, E-4-1, §16.3.2
§4(a)(2)(ii)	§4.4.1
§4(a)(i)	§4.3.1
§4(b)	§4.3.2, §4.5, §16.3.2
§5(a)	§4.4.1
§7	§4.6
§8	§4.6

Index

References are to sections. This index does not include references to the Examples and Explanations However, text sections include references to Examples that deal with topics addressed in the text.

Abandonment of estate property
 effect on stay, 10.5
 grounds and restrictions, 12.4
 prerequisite for redemption, 13.6
Absolute priority rule, 21.1.2, 21.7.3
Abstention, 7.7, 9.6
Abuse. *See* Dismissal of bankruptcy case
Accounts receivable. *See* Collateral
Act of bankruptcy, 5.4, 9.6
Adequate protection
 and adequate assurance of performance, 18.7
 defined, 11.5.2
 in postpetition financing, 17.3
 relief from stay, 11.4.1, 11.5
 shortfall, superpriority of, 11.5.5, 19.6.4
 in use, sale, or lease of property, 17.2.3
Administrative expenses
 adequate protection superpriority, 11.5.5, 19.6.4
 of Chapter 11, 21.6.2, 21.7.2
 following conversion, 19.6.4
 generally, 19.2.3, 19.6.4
 performance under executory contract, 18.4, 18.5
 postpetition credit, 17.3
 preservation of collateral, 19.6.3
 priority, 19.2.3, 19.6.4, 21.6.2
 professional fees, 6.6
 trustee compensation, 6.2
Adverse claim procedure, 3.5
After-acquired property. *See* Secured claim
Alimony and support. *See* Domestic support obligations
Anti-alienation clauses. *See* Nonassignment and forfeiture provisions
Anti-assignment clauses. *See* Nonassignment and forfeiture provisions
Appeals from Bankruptcy Court, 7.6
Appraisal. *See* Valuation
Asset, defined in fraudulent transfer law, 4.4.3

Assignment for benefit of creditors, 3.9.3, 9.6.4, 12.3
Assignment of contract. *See* Executory contracts; Nonassignment and forfeiture provisions
Assumption of contract. *See* Executory contracts; Nonassignment and forfeiture provisions
Attachment of lien, 2.3, 3.4.3
Attachment remedy, 3.3.2, 3.3.3, 3.3.4, 3.3.5, 3.3.6.
Attorney
 conflict of interest and interests adverse to estate, 6.6.2
 debt relief agency, 6.7
 reaffirmation declaration, 13.7.1
 representation of creditors' committee, 6.5
 representation of debtor, 6.6.1, 6.7, 9.3, 13.7
 representation of estate, 6.6.1
Attorney's fees. *See* Costs and attorney's fees
Automatic stay and relief from stay
 actions stayed, 10.4.1
 adequate protection, 11.4.1, 11.5
 burden of proof for relief, 11.4.1, 11.4.2, 11.5.4
 codebtor, 20.1
 contract termination, 18.10
 effect of stay, 10.3, 10.7
 exceptions to stay, 10.4.2, 10.4.3
 forms of relief, 11.3
 grounds for relief, 11.4, 11.5
 in rem relief, 11.4.4
 nature and purpose, 3.8, 10.1, 10.2, 10.3
 procedure for relief, 11.2
 real property collateral, 11.4.4
 relationship to turnover, 12.3
 scope, 10.1, 10.3, 10.4
 serial filings, 10.5.3
 setoff, 10.4.2
 single asset real estate cases, 11.4.3, 21.1.2, 21.4.3

and statute of limitations, 10.6
termination, 10.5, 10.6
and trustee's use, sale, or lease of property,
    17.2
valuation of property in relief proceedings,
    11.4.2
violation, 10.3, 10.7
voluntary dismissal following relief, 8.4.1
Avoidance of transfers and obligations
adversary proceedings, 14.5
backdating rules applicable, 15.3.1
bankruptcy court jurisdiction, 7.4, 14.5
charitable contributions, 15.1.3, 16.3
by debtor in possession, 14.4
by debtor or other parties, 9.3, 13.5, 14.4
effect and enforcement, 14.2, 14.5, 19.4
estate as successor to actual creditor, 14.2,
    15.1.3
estate's succession to debtor's defense, 14.2
fraudulent transfers
    actual fraud, 4.3, 4.5, 16.3.2
    assignment for benefit of creditors as,
        3.9.3
    badges of fraud, 4.3.2, 4.5, 16.3.2
    bankruptcy and state law, 4.1.2, 15.1.3,
        16.3.1
    charitable and religious contributions,
        16.3.6
    constructive fraud, 4.4, 4.5, 16.3.3
    discharge, ground for denial, 22.5.2
    exempt property, 16.3.5
    generally, 4.1, 4.2, 14.8, 16.3
    good faith transferee, 4.6
    insolvency, 4.4.3, 16.3.3
    leveraged buyout, 4.7
    reachback period, 16.3.4
    reasonably equivalent value, 4.4.2, 4.5,
        4.6
    remedy, 4.6
general principles, 14.1, 14.2, 14.3
good faith transferee, 14.5
hypothetical bona fide purchaser and
    creditor status of trustee, 15.1.2, 15.2
jury trial in avoidance suit, 7.4
limitations, 14.1
policy and goals, generally, 14.8, 16.1.1
postpetition transfers, 16.2, 16.4
preferences
    antecedent debt, 16.1.2, 16.1.4
    avoidance requirements, 16.1.2
    delayed perfection, 16.1.4

earmarking doctrine, 16.1.2
exceptions to avoidance, 16.1.4
improvement in position, 16.1.2
insider, 16.1.2
insolvency, 16.1.2
policy basis, 14.8, 16.1.1, 16.1.4
reach-back period, 16.1.2
state law unavoidability, 3.9.3
timing of transfer, 16.1.3
transfer defined, 16.1.2
valuation, 16.1.4
preservation for estate's benefit, 14.6
reachback periods, 14.7, 16.3.4
recovery of avoided property, 14.1
seller's reclamation right, 15.3.2
setoff, 16.2
statute of limitations, 14.2, 14.7
statutory liens, 14.2, 15.2
"strong arm" power defined, 15.1
subordination, 19.7.2

Backdating. *See* Priority
Bad faith. *See* Good faith
Badges of fraud, 4.3.2, 4.5, 16.3.2
Balance sheet test, 3.9.1, 4.4.3, 15.3.2, 16.1.2
Bankruptcy
collective nature, 5.1, 5.5.2
general description, 5.1, 5.4.2, 5.5.2
historical survey, 4.4, 5.5.2
jurisdiction, *see* Bankruptcy jurisdiction
nonbankruptcy law, *see* Nonbankruptcy law
policies, *see* Bankruptcy policies
rules, *see* Bankruptcy rules
state law insolvency remedies compared,
    3.9.1, 3.9.3
statutory sources, 5.4
structure of Bankruptcy Code, 5.4.2
uniformity, 5.2.1, 5.3, 13.2.1
Bankruptcy appeals and Bankruptcy
    Appellate Panel, 7.6
Bankruptcy clause. *See* Nonassignment and
    forfeiture provisions
Bankruptcy court, nature and powers,
    generally, 6.1, 6.3, 7.5, 9.7. *See also*
    Bankruptcy jurisdiction
Bankruptcy jurisdiction
abstention, 7.7
automatic stay, 10.2, 10.7
bankruptcy court, 7.3, 7.4, 7.5, 7.6
constitutionality, 7.3.3, 7.3.6, 7.4, 7.6
contempt, 7.5, 10.7

core proceedings, 7.3.5, 7.4
district court, 7.2.1, 7.2.2, 7.3.5, 7.3.6
history, 7.2.3, 7.3.1, 7.3.2, 7.3.3
injunctions, 7.5
jury trials, 7.4
related (noncore) proceedings, 7.2.2, 7.2.3,
    7.3.1, 7.3.5
removal and remand, 7.7, 7.8
retention of, in Chapter 11 plan, 21.6.1
subject matter, 7.2.2
and venue, 7.7, 9.2
Bankruptcy policies. *See also* Choice of relief
of Chapter 7, 8.2.1
of Chapter 11, 8.2.2, 21.2
of Chapter 12, 8.2.2
of Chapter 13, 8.2.2, 20.1
creditor protection, 5.5.2
debtor relief, 5.5.2
efficient administration, 5.5.2
estate preservation, 5.5.2, 10.2, 14.8, 16.4
evenhanded treatment, 5.5.2, 10.2, 14.8,
    16.1.1, 16.1.4, 17.3.3, 20.7
fresh start, 5.5.2, 10.2, 22.1
policy favoring Chapter 13, 5.5.2, 20.1,
    22.1, 22.7
reconciliation with other policies, 5.5.2,
    18.12
rehabilitation over liquidation, 5.5.2, 20.1,
    21.2, 22.1, 22.7
respect for nonbankruptcy rights, 5.5.2,
    14.8, 15.2, 16.1.1, 16.2
Bankruptcy power of Congress, 3.9.2, 3.9.3,
    5.2.1
Bankruptcy Review Commission. *See* National
    Bankruptcy Review Commission
Bankruptcy rules, generally, 5.4.3
BAP. *See* Bankruptcy appeals and Bankruptcy
    Appellate Panel
Bona fide purchaser, 4.6, 16.4, 17.2.5
Bond
assignee's, 3.9.3
creditor's, prejudgment remedies, 3.3.3,
    3.3.5
discharging, 3.3.3
indemnifying sheriff, 3.3.3
involuntary case, 9.6.3
redelivery, 3.3.3
trustee's, 6.2
Burden of proof
in avoidance of fraudulent transfers, 4.3.2, 4.4
in avoidance of preferences, 16.1.2

in exclusion from discharge, 22.5.4
in postpetition transactions, 17.2.3, 17.3.2
in prejudgment remedies, 3.3.2
in relief from stay application, 11.4.1,
    11.4.2, 11.5.4
Buyer. *See* Purchaser

Cash collateral, 17.2.5
Chandler Act, 5.4.1
Chapter 7 liquidation
conversion of case, 8.5
discharge, *see* Discharge
dismissal, *see* Dismissal of bankruptcy case
debtor's role, 6.4
duration of case, 8.6.1
eligibility for relief, 8.4.2
involuntary petition, 9.6.2
operation and sale of business, 17.2
payment of claims, 19.4
petition and schedules, 9.3
postpetition credit, 17.3.1
reaffirmation, 13.7
redemption, 13.6
retention of collateral under contract, 13.8
successive filings, 8.4.1, 22.5.2, 22.5.5
trustee, *see* Trustee
Chapter 11 reorganization
absolute priority rule, 21.1.2, 21.7.3
best interests test, 19.5, 19.6.1,
    21.7.2-21.7.4
claim classification, 8.6.1, 21.4.5, 21.6.2
competing plans, 21.4.3
confirmation of plan, procedure and effect,
    12.1, 21.4.6, 21.4.8
consummation, 21.4.9
conversion of case, 8.5, 21.4.1
cramdown, 21.7
creditors' committee, 6.2, 21.3, 21.4.2
cure of default, 8.6.1, 21.6.2
debtor in possession's role, 8.6.1, 6.2, 6.4,
    21.4.2
discharge, *see* Discharge
disclosure statement, 21.4.4, 21.5
dismissal, *see* Dismissal of bankruptcy case
disposable income, 21.1.2, 21.7.2
domestic support obligations, 21.1.2
effective date of plan, 21.4.9
election of undersecured creditors, 21.7.4
eligibility for relief, 8.4.2, 21.1.2
equity security holders, 6.4, 21.4.2, 21.4.8,
    21.7.3

examiner, appointment of, 6.2
exclusivity period, 21.4.3
fair and equitable standard, 21.7.3, 21.7.4
feasibility, 11.4.2, 11.5.3, 21.6.2, 21.7.2
good faith, 21.7.2, 21.7.3
home mortgage protection, 21.6.3
impairment of claims or interests, 21.4.8,
    21.6.2, 21.7.2, 21.7.3
individual debtor, 21.1.2, 21.4.7, 21.4.8,
    21.6.2, 21.7.2, 21.7.3
indubitable equivalent standard, 21.7.3
involuntary petition, 8.6.1, 9.6.2, 21.4.1
liquidating plan, 21.2, 21.7.2, 22.6
modification of plan, 21.4.7
negotiation, 21.3, 21.5, 21.6
operation of business, 17.2
payment under plan, 19.4
plan provisions, 21.6, 21.7, 22.6
policy favoring, 5.5.2, 22.1
prepackaged plan, 21.5
present value test, 19.5, 21.7.3
priority claims, 19.6.1, 21.6.2, 21.7.2
proof of claim or interest, 21.4.2
property of the estate, 8.6.1, 21.1.2
revocation of confirmation, 22.6
sale of assets, 17.2, 17.3
single asset real estate case, 11.4.3, 21.1.2,
    21.4.3
small business debtor, 21.1.2, 21.4.2,
    21.4.3, 21.4.4, 21.4.6
statutory origins, 5.4.1
undersecured creditor's election, 21.7.4
unfair discrimination, 21.7.3
vesting of property in debtor, 12.1,
    21.4.8
voting on plan, 8.6.1, 19.3, 21.4.4, 21.4.5,
    21.4.7, 21.7.2
Chapter 12 debt adjustment
conversion of case, 8.5, 12.2.2
debtor in possession, 6.4, 8.6.1
discharge, *see* Discharge
dismissal, *see* Dismissal of bankruptcy case
eligibility for relief, 8.4.2
family farmer defined, 8.3.3, 8.4.2
family fisherman defined, 8.3.3
involuntary petition, 9.6.2
operation of business, 17.2
payment under plan, 8.6.1, 19.4
present value test, 19.5
procedure and plan confirmation
    standards, generally, 20.1

property of the estate, 8.6.1
vesting of property in debtor, 12.1
Chapter 13 debt adjustment
best interests test, 19.5, 19.6.1, 20.3,
    20.7.3
"Chapter 20," 20.11, 22.7.4
claim classification, 8.6.1, 20.3, 20.7.3
codebtor protection, 20.1, 20.7
commitment period, 20.7.3
confirmation of plan, procedure and effect,
    12.1, 20.2
conversion of case, 8.5, 12.2.2, 20.1
court discretion on confirming, 20.3
cramdown, 20.2
cure of default, 8.6.1, 20.3, 20.7, 20.8, 20.9
debtor's role, 6.4, 8.6.1, 20.2, 20.4
discharge, *see* Discharge
dismissal, *see* Dismissal of bankruptcy case
disposable income, 20.3, 20.7.3, 20.10,
    22.1
eligibility for relief, 8.4.2, 20.1, 20.4
feasibility standard, 20.4
good faith standard, 20.3, 20.6, 22.7
home mortgages, 20.8.3
involuntary petition, 8.6.1, 9.6, 20.1
length of plan, 8.6.1, 20.5
liquidation of property, 20.1, 20.4
long-term debt, 20.9, 22.7
modification of claimant's rights, 20.8
modification of plan, 20.2, 20.5, 20.10
operation of business, 17.2, 20.1
payment under plan, 19.4, 20.2, 20.4, 20.9
postpetition consumer debts, 19.2.3, 22.7
present value test, 19.5, 20.3, 20.7
priority claims, 19.6.1, 20.3, 20.7.2, 22.7
procedural outline, 20.2
property of the estate, 8.6.1, 12.1, 12.2.3,
    20.1
regular income requirement, 8.4.2
revocation of confirmation, 20.2
secured claims, 8.6.1, 20.3, 20.7.1, 20.8
strip down, 20.7.1, 20.11
successive filings, 20.11, 22.7
trustee, *see* Trustee
vesting of property in debtor, 12.1, 20.2,
    20.7
"Chapter 20," 20.11, 22.7.4
Charitable and religious contributions, 15.1.3,
    16.3, 20.7.3
Child support claims. *See* Domestic support
    obligations

Choice of relief
    bankruptcy versus state law, 3.9.1
    Chapter 7 versus Chapter 11, 5.4.2, 6.2, 8.2,
        8.6, 10.3, 12.1, 12.2, 13.7, 14.3, 17.1,
        17.2, 17.3, 18.4, 19.4, 19.6.1, 20.1,
        20.8, 22.1, 22.7
    Chapter 7 versus Chapter 13, 5.4.2, 6.2, 8.2,
        8.6, 12.1, 12.2.2, 14.3, 17.2, 19.4,
        19.6.1, 20.1, 20.8, 22.1, 22.7
    Chapter 11 versus Chapter 13, 8.6, 19.4,
        20.2, 21.1, 21.3, 21.4.2, 21.4.3,
        21.4.8, 22.1
    Chapter 12 versus Chapter 7, 6.2, 8.2, 8.6,
        12.1, 12.2.2, 14.3, 17.2, 19.4, 22.1
    Chapter 12 versus Chapters 11 and 13,
        8.3.3, 8.6, 20.1, 22.1, 22.8
    generally, 8.6, 19.6.1, 20.7, 21.4.1
Claim
    administrative expense, *see* Administrative
        expenses
    against property only, 19.2.4
    allowance, 19.4, 19.6.3, 19.6.4
    bifurcation, 19.4, 19.6.3, 20.7, 20.8, 21.7.4
    classified, 20.3, 20.7, 21.4.5, 21.6.2
    consumer debts, postpetition, 19.2.3, 22.7
    contingent, 8.4.2, 9.6, 19.2.2, 19.3
    counting for purpose of
        involuntary petition, 9.6
    creation, 19.2.5
    damages for rejection of executory contract,
        18.4, 19.2.3
    defined in bankruptcy, 6.5, 16.1.2, 19.2, 22.2
    defined in fraudulent transfer law, 4.2
    disallowance following avoidance, 14.5
    distinguished from other rights, 18.4,
        19.2.1, 22.2
    estimation, 19.3
    and executory contract obligation, 18.4
    fair or reasonable contemplation test,
        19.2.5, 19.3
    governmental unit. *See* Sovereign immunity
    impairment, 21.4.8, 21.6.2
    interest and costs, 19.5, 19.6.3
    mass torts, 19.3
    payment, 19.4, 19.6.1, 19.6.4, 20.2, 20.4,
        20.9
    priority, *see* Priority
    proof, 19.2.3, 19.4, 20.2, 21.4.2
    recharacterization, 19.7.3
    secured, *see* Secured claim
    subordination, 19.7.1, 19.7.2
    unliquidated, 19.2.2, 19.3

    unmatured, 19.2.2
    unsecured, *see* unsecured debt
Claim and delivery. *See* Replevin
Codebtor.
    effect of discharge, 22.3
    joint petitioner distinguished, 9.5
    proof of claim, 19.4
    surety, 1.3, 20.1, 20.7
Cognovit, 3.4.1
Collateral. *See* Adequate protection; Automatic
        stay; Deficiency; Equity cushion;
        Secured claim; Unsecured debt;
        Valuation
Collective proceedings defined, 3.9.1, 5.1,
        5.5.2. *See also* Choice of relief
Composition and extension, 3.9.2
Confession to judgment, 3.4.1
Confirmation of execution sale, 3.5
Confirmation of plan. *See* Chapter 11
        reorganization; Chapter 12 debt
        adjustment; Chapter 13 debt
        adjustment
Conflict of interest, 6.2, 6.6
Consolidation of cases or estates, 9.5
Constructive fraud. *See* Avoidance of transfers
        and obligations
Constructive notice. *See* Notice
Consumer debt defined, 8.3.2, 9.7
Contempt of court
    bankruptcy court punishment power, 7.5,
        10.7.5
    civil compensation order as claim, 19.2.1,
        22.3
    civil distinct from criminal, 7.5.2, 22.3
    violation of stay, 10.3, 10.7
Contingent debt or claim. *See* Claim
Contract. *See* Executory contracts
Conversion of case
    administrative expenses, 19.6.4
    damages for rejection of executory contract,
        8.4
    estate property, 12.2.2
    generally, 5.4.2, 8.5, 9.7, 20.1, 21.4.1
Core proceedings. *See* Bankruptcy jurisdiction
Corporate debtor, defined, 8.3.1
Costs and attorney's fees
    as administrative expense, 6.6
    discharge injunction violation, 22.3
    dismissal of involuntary petition,
        9.6.6
    oversecured claims, 19.5
    stay violation, 10.7.2

Index

Counterclaim
    compulsory, 7.9.3, 7.9.4
    jurisdiction, 7.3.5
    jury trial, 7.4.2
    sovereign immunity, 7.9.3
Cramdown. *See* Chapter 11 reorganization;
    Chapter 13 debt adjustment
Credit counseling, 8.4.1, 22.5.2, 22.7.2
Creditor defined, 4.2, 6.5, 16.1.2
Creditors' bill, 3.7, 4.6
Creditors' committee
    appointment and function in Chapter 7, 6.5
    appointment and function in Chapter 11,
        6.2, 6.5, 21.3, 21.4.2
    avoidance power, 14.4
    legal representation, 6.9
Creditors' meeting, 9.9, 20.2
Criminal prosecution and penalties
    dischargeability, 22.2, 22.7
    exclusion from automatic stay, 10.4.3
Cross-collateralization, 17.3.3
Current monthly income. *See* Disposable
    income; Means test
Custodian of debtor's property, 9.6.4, 12.3

Damages
    discharge injunction violation, 22.3
    dismissal of involuntary petition, 9.6.6
    rejection of executory contract, 18.4,
        19.2.3, 19.4, 22.5.1
    stay violation, 10.3, 10.7
Debt. *See also* Claim
    antecedent, 16.1.2
    defined, 16.1.2, 22.2
    disputed, 9.6.2, 9.6.4, 19.2.2
    formation, 1.3
    nonpayment and involuntary petition, 9.6.4
    nonrecourse, 19.2.4, 21.7.4
    postpetition and prepetition, 19.2.3, 22.2,
        22.5.1
    scheduling requirement in bankruptcy, 9.3,
        22.5.4
Debt adjustment. *See* Chapter 12 debt
    adjustment; Chapter 13 debt
    adjustment
Debtor definition and role, generally, 1.1, 6.4,
    8.3, 9.5, 9.7
Debtor in possession, 6.2, 6.4, 6.5, 14.4, 17.1,
    18.1, 21.4.2
Debt relief agency, 6.7
Default judgment. *See* Judgment

Deficiency
    claim bifurcation, 19.4, 19.6.3, 20.7, 20.8
    cross-collateralization, 17.3.3
    defined, 2.5.3
    failure of adequate protection, 11.5.5,
        19.6.4
    following foreclosure, 2.6.2
    lien stripping, 20.8
    nonrecourse claim, 2.6.1, 19.2.4, 21.7.4
Discharge
    under Chapter 7, 8.6.1, 22.5
    under Chapter 11, 8.6.1, 21.4.8, 22.6
    under Chapter 12, 8.6.1, 22.8
    under Chapter 13, 8.6.1, 19.2.3, 20.2, 20.8,
        22.7
    and claim priority, 19.6.4
    codebtor, 22.3
    comparison between Chapters 7, 11, 12,
        and 13, 20.2
    confined to claims, 19.2.1, 22.2
    corporation, 8.2.1, 8.6.1, 21.2, 22.1, 22.6
    denial, 22.5.2, 22.6, 22.7
    dischargeability determination, 22.5.4
    exclusions from the discharge, 19.4, 21.4.8,
        22.5.4, 22.5.5, 22.6, 22.7.3, 22.8
    financial management course, 22.5.2
    and good faith, 22.5.2, 22.5.4, 22.7
    hardship, 22.7, 22.8
    injunction, 10.3, 10.5, 10.6, 10.7, 22.3
    prohibition on discrimination, 22.3
    reaffirmation of discharged debt, *see*
        Reaffirmation
    revocation, 22.5.3, 22.6, 22.7, 22.8
    secured claim, 19.4, 19.6.3, 22.2, 22.3
    sovereign immunity, 7.9.2, 7.9.3
    in state law insolvency proceedings, 3.9.2,
        3.9.3
    successive cases, 20.11, 22.5.2, 22.5.5,
        22.7.4
    waiver, 22.4, 22.5.4, 22.8
    of willful injury, 22.5.4
Disinterested person, 6.2, 6.6
Dismissal of bankruptcy case
    abstention as, 7.7.2
    for abuse, 8.3.2, 8.4.2, 8.5, 9.8
    effect on stay, 10.5
    generally, 9.7, 21.4.1, 21.4.6, 22.1
    involuntary case, 9.6.3, 9.6.6, 9.7
    as limitation on subsequent filing, 8.4.1
    presumption of abuse and means test, 9.8
    voluntary dismissal, 9.7

Disposable income, 8.3.2, 8.4.2, 9.8, 20.7.3, 20.10, 21.1.2, 21.7.2
Disputed debt, 9.6.2, 9.6.4, 19.2.2
Divorce. *See* Domestic support obligations
Docketing. *See* Judgment
Dollar amount adjustments, generally, 5.4.3
Domestic support obligations
   alimony and support, 22.5.4, 22.7
   Chapter 11 case, 21.1.2, 21.7.2
   classification, 13.5.2, 22.5.4
   discharge, 22.5.4
   exemption from avoidance as preference, 16.1.4
   exemption from stay, 10.4.3
   judicial lien for, 13.5.2
   priority, 19.6.4
Domicile of debtor, 9.2, 13.2.2
Due process in prejudgment remedies, 3.3.2

Earmarking doctrine, 16.1.2
Elegit, 3.5
Eleventh Amendment. *See* Sovereign immunity
Eligibility for relief
   Chapter 7 liquidation, 8.4.2
   Chapter 11 reorganization, 8.4.2, 21.1.2
   Chapter 12 debt adjustment, 8.4.2
   Chapter 13 debt adjustment, 8.4.2, 20.1, 20.4
   credit counseling requirement, 8.4.1
   conversion, 8.5
   generally, 8.4.1, 8.4.2
   serial filings, 8.4.1
Employee wage claim priority, 19.6.4
Entity, 6.5
Equitable property and interests of debtor, 3.3.3, 3.7, 12.2.1
Equitable remedies
   bankruptcy court powers, 7.5, 9.7
   as claim, 19.2.1
   creditors' bill, 3.7
   injunction, 3.3.7, 7.5, 10.3, 10.4. *See also* Automatic stay; Discharge
   jury trial, 7.4
   receivership, 3.3.6
   recharacterization of claim, 19.7.3
   sequestration, 3.3.2
   subordination, 19.7.2
Equitable subordination, 19.7.2
Equity cushion
   and adequate protection, 11.5.3
   defined, 2.5.3
   interest and costs chargeable against, 19.5

Equity of debtor in property
   exempt, *see* Exemptions
   generally, 2.6
   nonexempt, estate's rights, 11.4.2, 13.6
   relevance to relief from stay, 11.4.2
Equity security holders, 6.4.2, 21.4.2, 21.4.8, 21.7.3
Equity test. *See* Insolvency
Estate
   consolidation, 9.5
   legal representation, 6.6, 6.9
   operating debtor's business, 6.4, 9.6, 16.4, 17.2, 17.3, 19.6.4, 20.1,
   preservation of, 5.5.2, 10.2, 14.8
   property, *see* Property of the estate
Executable property, 3.2, 3.3.3, 3.5
Execution, 3.2, 3.5, 3.3.3, 3.7
Executory contracts
   applicability of stay, 18.8
   assignment, 18.8, 18.12
   assumption, 18.4, 18.5, 18.6, 18.9
   burdensome test and business judgment test, 18.5
   claim distinguished, 18.4
   cure of default, 18.7, 18.9
   damages for rejection, 18.4, 19.2.3, 19.4, 22.5.1
   defined, 18.2
   financing contracts, 18.8.2
   interim performance, 18.6
   rejection, 18.4, 18.5, 18.11, 19.2.3, 19.4, 22.5.1
   schedule of, 9.3
   termination by nondebtor party, 18.8, 18.9, 18.10
   time for election, 18.5
   transfer restrictions, 18.8, 18.9, 18.12
   vested rights protection, 18.11
Exemptions
   abandonment of exempt property, 12.4
   avoidance of impairing liens, 9.3, 13.5
   claim of, 9.3, 13.4
   domicile governing, 13.2.2
   effect on consensual lien, 9.3, 13.5
   exemption planning, 13.2.3
   generally, 5.3, 5.5.2, 8.3.1, 13.1, 13.3, 20.1
   homestead restrictions, 13.2.3, 22.5.2
   objections, 13.4
   opt out by states, 5.3, 13.2, 13.3, 13.5
   procedure for claiming, 13.4
   reaffirmation, *see* Reaffirmation

redemption, 13.6

state law collection proceedings, 3.2, 3.3.4, 3.4.3, 3.6, 13.1

uniformity, 5.3, 13.2.1

Family farmer. *See* Chapter 12 debt adjustment

Family fisherman. *See* Chapter 12 debt adjustment

Fieri facias, 3.5

Financial management course requirement, 22.5.2

First-in-time rule. *See* Priority

Floating lien. *See* Secured claim

Foreclosure. *See* Secured claim

Foreign judgment, 3.4.4

Forfeiture clauses. *See* Nonassignment and forfeiture provisions

Fraud. *See* Avoidance of transfers and obligations; Discharge; Good faith

Fraudulent transfers. *See* Avoidance of transfers and obligations

Fresh start. *See* Bankruptcy policies; Discharge; Exemptions

Future advances. *See* Secured claim

Gap creditor, 15.1.2

Gap period. *See* Involuntary bankruptcy

Garnishment

of earnings, 3.3.4

lien, 3.3.4, 3.6

postjudgment, 3.6

prejudgment, 3.3.4

Good faith

assignment for benefit of creditors, 3.9.3

composition, 3.9.2

of debtor in Chapter 11, 21.7.2, 21.7.3

of debtor in Chapter 13, 20.3, 20.6

defense to failure to surrender estate property, 12.3, 16.4

discharge, 22.1, 22.5.2, 22.5.4, 22.7

dismissal for bad faith, *see* Dismissal of bankruptcy case

disputing debt, 9.6.4

fraudulent transfer law, 4.3, 4.4, 4.5

general policy of, in bankruptcy, 6.4, 22.1

of plan proponent in Chapter 11, 21.4.4

postpetition lender, 17.3.2

subordination, 19.7.2

totality of circumstances test, 9.8.3, 9.8.5, 20.6

transferee's, in fraudulent transfer law, 4.6

transferee's, on trustee's avoidance power, 14.5

of trustee or debtor in possession in rejecting or assuming executory contract, 18.5

Governmental unit

defined, 7.9.1

fines and penalties not discharged, 22.2, 22.5.4

police and regulatory power excluded from stay, 10.4.1, 10.4.3

sovereign immunity, 7.9

Immunity. *See* Sovereign immunity

Imprisonment for debt, 5.5.2

Individual debtor, defined, 8.3.1, 8.3.2

Injunction, 3.3.7, 7.5, 10.3, 10.4. *See also* Automatic stay; Discharge

Insider, 9.6.2, 9.6.3, 16.1.2, 16.3.3, 21.7.2

Insolvency

balance sheet test, 3.9.1, 4.4.3, 15.3.2, 16.1.2

equity test, 3.9.1, 4.4.3, 9.6.4, 15.3.2, 16.1.2

in fraudulent transfers, 4.4.3, 16.3.3

ground for involuntary petition, 9.6.4

in preferential transfers, 16.1.2

in seller's reclamation right, 15.3.2

Insolvency proceedings. *See* Assignment for benefit of creditors; Choice of relief; Composition and extension

Interest on claims, 11.5.5, 19.5

Interim trustee. *See* Trustee

Inventory. *See* Secured claim

Involuntary bankruptcy

assignment for benefit of creditors as grounds, 3.9.3, 9.6.4

automatic stay, 10.3

chapters in which available, 8.6.1, 9.6.2, 20.1, 21.4.1

dismissal, 9.6, 9.7

gap period, 9.6.3, 16.4, 19.6.4, 21.6.2, 21.7.2

grounds for relief, 9.6.4

historical overview, 5.5.2

order for relief, 9.6.3, 9.6.5

petitioner liability upon dismissal, 9.6.6

procedure, 9.6.3, 19.4, 21.4.1

qualifications for filing, 9.6.2

trustee appointment, 6.2

Ipso facto clauses. *See* Nonassignment and forfeiture provisions

Joint case
   Chapter 13 eligibility, 8.4.2
   combined exemptions, 13.2
   generally, 9.5
Judgment.
   attachment, effect, 3.3.3
   confession to, 3.4.1
   default, 3.4.1
   docketing, 3.4.3
   duration, 3.4.2, 3.5
   lien, *see* Secured claim
   enforcement of, in another state, 3.4.4
   and prejudgment garnishment, 3.3.4
   and replevin, 3.3.5
Jurisdiction. *See* Bankruptcy jurisdiction
Jury trials, 7.4

Knowledge. *See* Notice

Lease.*See* Executory contracts
Leveraged buyout, 4.7
Levy
   in another state, 3.4.4
   of attachment, 3.3.3
   defined, 3.2
   of execution, 3.5
   of garnishment, 3.6
   on intangibles, 3.2.2, 3.5
   nulla bona return, 3.3.3, 3.5, 3.7, 4.2
   on personal property, 3.2.2
   on property assigned for benefit of creditors,
      3.9.3
   on property not owned by debtor, 3.3.3
   on real property, 3.2.2, 3.5
   return, 3.2.2, 3.3.3, 3.5
   sheriff's indemnity, 3.3.3
Liens. *See* Secured claim
Lien stripping, 19.6.3, 20.7, 20.8, 21.6.3
Liquidated debt. *See* Unliquidated debt
Liquidation
   under assignment for benefit of creditors,
      3.9.3
   under Chapter 7, *see* Chapter 7 liquidation
   under Chapter 11, 21.2, 21.7.2, 22.6
Lis *pendens*, 3.3.8

Maintenance. *See* Domestic support obligations
Matrimonial and support claims. *See* Domestic
      support obligations
Means test, 8.3.2, 8.4.2, 8.5, 9.8, 20.7.3,
      21.7.1

Median family income, 9.8.4, 9.8.6, 20.7.3
Modification. *See* Chapter 11 reorganization;
      Chapter 13 debt adjustment

National Bankruptcy Review
   Commission, 1994, 5.3, 5.4.1, 5.4.2,
      6.5, 7.3.4, 7.3.6, 7.6.1, 7.6.2, 8.3.3,
      8.5, 13.2, 13.3, 18.1, 18.2, 18.3, 21.1,
      21.7.3
Negotiable instruments
   as cash collateral, 17.2.5
   check payment as transfer, 16.1.4, 16.4
Nonassignment and forfeiture provisions
   effect on executory contracts, 18.8, 18.9, 18.13
   restricting transfer to estate, 12.2.2
   statutory lien arising on bankruptcy, 15.2
   and use, sale, or lease of estate property,
      17.2.4
Nonbankruptcy law
   abstention from cases involving, 7.7.3
   antiassignment clauses and laws, *see*
      Nonassignment and forfeiture
      provisions
   contract rights determination, 18.8, 18.10,
      18.11, 18.13
   defense to claim, 19.4
   defined, and relationship to bankruptcy law,
      5.2.2, 5.5.2
   effect on bankruptcy exemptions, 5.3, 13.2,
      13.3, 13.5
   impact of, in Chapter 11, 21.3
   jurisdiction to determine rights under, 7.2,
      7.3
   property rights determination, 12.2.1
   removal of cases involving, 7.8
   validity and priority determination of
      secured claims, 19.6.1, 19.6.3
Noncore proceedings. *See* Bankruptcy
      jurisdiction
Notice
   "after notice and a hearing" defined, 11.2,
      12.4, 17.1, 20.2
   of bankruptcy and effect on stay, 10.3
   of bankruptcy by clerk of court, 9.3, 19.4
   of lis *pendens*, 3.3.8
Nulla bona return. *See* Levy

Operating debtor's business. *See* Estate
Order for relief, 9.4. *See also* Involuntary
      bankruptcy; Voluntary bankruptcy
Ordinary course of business, 16.4.1, 17.2.2

Index

Pension plans, as property of estate, 12.2.2

Perfection. *See* Secured claim

Petition. *See* Involuntary bankruptcy; Voluntary bankruptcy

Plan. *See* Chapter 11 reorganization; Chapter 12 debt adjustment; Chapter 13 debt adjustment

Police and regulatory powers. *See* Governmental unit

Postpetition transfers. *See* Avoidance of transfers and obligations

Preferences. *See* Avoidance of transfers and obligations

Prejudgment remedies, generally, 3.3. *See also specific remedies*

Presumption of abuse. *See* Dismissal of bankruptcy case; Means test

Presumptions. *See* Burden of proof

Priority
  adequate protection shortfall, 11.5.5, 19.6.4
  administrative expenses, *see* Administrative expenses
  assignee for benefit of creditors, 3.9.3
  avoided lien, trustee's succession, 14.6
  backdating, 3.5, 15.3.1, 16.1.3, 16.1.4
  bankruptcy distribution, generally, 19.6.2, 19.6.4
  Chapter 11 case, 21.6.2, 21.7.2
  Chapter 13 case, 20.3, 20.7, 22.7
  competing interests in property, 2.5.2
  competing judicial liens, 3.5
  deficiency, 19.6.3
  execution lien, 3.5
  first-in-time rule, 2.7.2-2.7.4
  generally, 2.7.1-2.7.3, 19.6.2
  impact of bankruptcy discharge, 19.6.4, 22.5.4
  judgment lien, 3.4.3
  lien foreclosure, 2.6.1
  order of ranking, 19.6
  postpetition credit, 17.3, 19.6.4
  recharacterization, 19.7.3
  secured claims, *see* Secured Claims
  subordination, 19.7.1, 19.7.2
  superpriority, 11.5.5, 17.3, 19.6.4
  unmatured interest, 19.5

Property of the debtor. *See* Abandonment of estate property; Automatic stay; Assignment for benefit of creditors; Equitable property and interests of debtor; Executable property; Exemptions; Discharge; Levy; Property of the estate

Property of the estate
  abandonment, *see* Abandonment of estate property
  automatic stay, 10.4.1, 10.5.1
  Chapter 7 estate, 8.6.1, 12.2
  Chapter 11 estate, 8.6.1, 12.2.3, 21.1.2
  Chapter 13 estate, 8.6.1, 12.1, 12.2.3, 20.1
  collateral for postpetition credit, 17.3
  exclusions, 12.2.1
  inclusions, 11.5.2, 12.1, 12.2.1, 14.1, 14.6, 18.4, 18.10, 20.1, 20.2, 21.1.2
  jurisdiction over, 7.2.2
  nonbakruptcy transfer restrictions, 12.2.2, 17.2.4, 18.8, 18.9
  postpetition acquisition, 12.2.3, 14.1, 14.6, 20.1, 20.2, 21.1.2
  postpetition transfer, 16.4
  proceeds, 12.2.2
  state law determination of property, 12.2.1
  turnover, 12.3, 16.4
  use, sale, or lease, 17.2
  vesting in debtor, 12.1, 20.2, 20.7, 21.4.8

Property settlement claims. *See* Domestic support obligations

Provisional remedies, generally, 3.3. *See also specific remedies*

Public rights doctrine, 7.3.2

Punitive damages, violation of stay, 10.3, 10.7.4

Purchase money security interest. *See* Secured claim

Purchaser
  bona fide, 4.6, 16.4, 17.2.5
  at execution sale, 3.5
  rights against lienholder, 2.7.4
  rights under executory contract, 18.11

Reaffirmation
  alternatives to, 13.6, 13.8
  and Chapter 13, compared, 13.7, 20.8
  requirements and effect, 13.7, 22.4
  "ride through" distinguished, 13.8
  statement of intent, 9.3, 13.7

Reasonably equivalent value. *See* Fraudulent transfers

Receivership
  generally, 3.3.6
  as grounds for involuntary bankruptcy, 9.6.4
  turnover on bankruptcy, 12.3

Recharacterization of claim, 19.7.3
Reclamation rights of seller, 15.3.2
Recording. *See* Secured claim
Redemption
    comparison to Chapter 13, 13.6, 20.8
    comparison to reaffirmation, 13.7
    equity of, 3.5
    requirements and effect, 13.6
    "ride through" distinguished, 13.8
    statement of intent, 9.3, 13.6
    statutory, 3.5
Rehabilitation. *See* Discharge
Related proceedings. *See* Abstention;
        Bankruptcy jurisdiction;
        Nonbankruptcy law; Removal and
        remand
Relief from stay. *See* Automatic stay
Removal and remand, 7.8
Reorganization. *See* Chapter 11 reorganization
Replevin, 3.3.5
Return. *See* Levy
"Ride-through," 13.8

Salary and wage claim priority, 19.6.4
Sale
    of estate property, 16.4, 17.2
    as executory contract, 18.11
    seller's reclamation right, 15.3.2
Sanctions for improper conduct, 7.5.3
Schedules. *See* Involuntary bankruptcy;
        Voluntary bankruptcy
Secured claim
    adequate protection, *see* Adequate protection
    artisan's lien, 2.4.3, 2.4.4, 2.7.3
    assignment subject to, 3.9.3
    attachment lien, 3.2, 3.3.3
    attachment of, 2.3, 2.7.5, 3.4.3, 13.5.2
    automatic stay, *see* Automatic stay
    avoidance by debtor in bankruptcy, 9.3,
        13.5
    avoidance by trustee, *see* Avoidance of
        transfers and obligations
    backdating, 3.5, 15.3.1, 16.1.3, 16.1.4
    bankruptcy treatment, generally, 6.5,
        11.5.2, 13.5, 13.6, 19.6.1, 19.6.3
    Chapter 11 treatment, 21.7.3, 21.7.4
    Chapter 13 treatment, 20.3, 20.7.1, 20.8
    collateral
        abandonment of, 12.4
        accounts, 16.1.4
        after-acquired, 2.2.4, 14.2, 16.1.4
        cash, 17.2.5
        cost of preservation, 19.6.3
        cross-collateralization, 17.3.3
        defined, 2.1.2, 2.2
        inventory, 2.7.4, 16.1.4
        postpetition credit, use to secure, 17.3
        proceeds, 17.2.5
        redemption, 13.6, 13.7
        retention under contract in Chapter 7,
            13.8
        seizure by replevin, 3.3.5
        surrender of, 20.7.1
        valuation, 19.4, 19.6.3, 20.7, 20.8,
            21.7.4
    common law liens, 2.4.4
    consensual lien defined, 2.4.1
    costs and interest, 16.2, 19.5, 19.6.3
    defined, 2.1.1, 2.1.2, 19.6.3
    disallowance, 19.6.3
    discharge of personal liability, 19.2.4, 19.4,
        19.6.3, 22.3
    effective date, 2.7.5
    equitable, 2.4.5
    execution lien, 3.2, 3.3.3, 3.5
    exemptions, effect, 9.3, 13.5
    floating lien, 2.2, 14.2, 16.1.4
    foreclosure, 2.6
    fraudulent transfer ineffective, 4.1, 4.2
    future advances, 2.2.3, 16.1.4
    garnishment lien, 3.3.4, 3.6
    grant as fraudulent transfer, 4.7
    grant as preference, 16.1.2
    involuntary petition disqualification,
        9.6.2
    judgment lien, 3.4.3, 4.6, 9.3, 13.5
    judicial lien, 2.4.2, 3.2, 9.3, 13.5, 15.1.2
    landlord's lien, 2.4.3, 2.4.4, 15.2
    lis pendens, 3.3.8
    mechanic's or construction lien, 2.2.2,
        2.4.3, 19.2.4
    payment for redemption, 13.6
    perfection, 2.3, 2.7.5, 3.4.3, 14.8, 15.1.2,
        16.1.4
    postpetition financing, 17.3
    priority, *see* Priority
    proof of claim, 19.4, 19.6.3
    protection in proposed use, sale, or lease,
        17.2.3
    purchase money, 2.2.5, 16.1.4
    reaffirmation, 13.7.1, 13.7.2
    repairers or artisan's lien, 2.4.3, 2.4.4, 2.7.3

replevin remedy, 3.3.5
"ride-through," 13.8
secret lien, 14.8
setoff as, 16.2, 19.6.3
statutory lien, 2.4.2, 2.4.3, 2.4.5, 2.7, 15.2,
    15.3.2, 16.1.4
strip down and strip off, 19.6.3, 20.7, 20.8,
    20.11, 21.6.3
subordination, 19.7
transferee's lien in avoidance suits, 4.6,
    14.5
Sequestration, 3.3.3
Serial flings. See Automatic stay; "Chapter 20";
    Discharge; Eligibility
Setoff
    automatic stay, 10.4.2
    generally, 16.2.1, 16.2.2, 19.6.3
    governmental claims, 7.9.4
    limitations and avoidance, 16.2.3
Single asset real estate cases, 11.4.3, 21.1.2,
    21.4.3
Small business reorganization. See Chapter 11
    reorganization
Sovereign immunity
    abrogation, 7.9.2
    general principles, 7.9.1
    setoff, 7.9.4
    waiver, 7.9.3
Spendthrift trust, 12.2.2
Spouses, defined, 9.5.1
Statute of limitations
    avoidance proceedings, 14.7
    effect of stay, 10.6
Statutory redemption. See Redemption
Stay. See Automatic stay
Strict foreclosure. See Foreclosure, generally
Strip down and strip off. See Lien stripping
"Strong arm" power. See Avoidance of transfers
    and obligations
Subordination, 19.7
Substantial abuse. See Dismissal of bankruptcy
    case
Superpriority. See Priority
Supplementary proceedings. See Execution
Support claims. See Domestic support
    obligations
Suretyship. See Codebtor
Surplus. See Equity cushion
Surrender of property. See Turnover of estate
    property
Suspension of bankruptcy case, 7.7.2

Tax claim priority and nondischargeability,
    19.6.4, 21.6.2, 22.5.4
Tithes, 15.1.3, 16.3, 20.7.1
Totality of circumstances test. See Good faith
Transfer of case, 9.2
Transfer of property. See Avoidance of transfers
    and obligations; Fraudulent transfers;
    Preferences
Trust, as property of estate, 12.2.2
Trustee
    appointment and qualifications, 6.2.1
    avoidance power, see Avoidance of transfers
        and obligations
    bond, 6.2.1
    in Chapter 7 cases, 6.2.2
    in Chapter 11 cases, 6.2.4
    in Chapters 12 and 13 cases, 6.2.3, 20.1,
        20.2, 20.4
    compensation, 6.2.5, 6.6
    debtor in possession as, 6.2.3, 6.2.4, 6.4,
        6.5, 14.4, 17.1, 18.1, 21.4.2
    election, 6.2
    generally, 6.2
    good faith, 18.5
    as hypothetical bona fide purchaser, 15.1.2,
        15.2
    as hypothetical execution creditor, 15.1.2
    as hypothetical lienholder, 15.1.2
    interim trustee, 6.2, 9.4, 9.6.3
    objection to discharge, 22.5.2, 22.5.3
    qualifications, 6.2
    relationship with creditors, 6.5
    standing trustee, 6.2, 20.1
Turnover of estate property, 12.3, 14.5, 14.7, 16.4,

Uniformity of bankruptcy law, 5.2.1, 5.3,
    13.2.1
United States Trustee
    and bankruptcy court, 6.3
    creditors' committee, appointment, 7.6.5,
        6.5, 11.6.2, 21.4.2
    creditors' meeting, duties of, 9.9
    equity security holders'
        committee, appointment, 21.4.2
    functions and duties, 6.3
    objection to discharge, 22.5.2, 22.5.3
    power to seek dismissal of case, 9.7
    service as case trustee, 6.2
    and trustees, 6.2, 6.3
Unliquidated debt, 19.2.2, 19.3
Unmatured debt as claim, 19.2.2

Unsecured debt. *See also* Claim; Debt
  cross-collateralization, 17.3.3
  enforcement under state law, 1.4
  impact of postpetition credit, 17.3.1
  impact of sale of estate property, 17.2.3
  incurred by estate, 17.3
  reaffirmation, 13.7.1, 13.7.3

Valuation
  in avoidance proceedings, 16.1.2, 16.1.4
  of collateral, 2.5.3, 19.6.3, 21.7.4
  to determine insolvency, 16.1.2
  in execution sale, 3.5
  in fraudulent transfer law, 4.4.2, 4.4.3, 4.6
  in redemption, 13.6
  in relief from stay, 11.4.2
Voluntary bankruptcy
  debtor's attorney's role, 9.3

  dismissal's effect, 8.4.1
  grounds not required for relief, 8.4.1
  joint petition, 9.5
  order for relief, 9.4
  petition and schedules, 9.3, 13.4, 13.6,
    19.4, 21.4.1
  trustee appointment, 6.2

Warrant of attorney, 3.4.1
Workout, defined, 3.9.2. *See also* Chapter 11
    reorganization; Composition and
    extension
Writ
  attachment, 3.3.3
  execution, 3.5
  garnishment, 3.3.4, 3.6
  levy, *see* Levy
  replevin, 3.3.5